FUNDAMENTAL
THEOLOGY

FUNDAMENTAL THEOLOGY

Fernando Ocáriz & Arturo Blanco

Midwest Theological Forum
Woodridge, Illinois

Published in the United States of America by

Midwest Theological Forum
1420 Davey Road   Woodridge, Illinois 60517
Telephone: (630) 739-9750   Fax: (630) 739-9758
E-mail: *mail@mwtf.org*   www.theologicalforum.org

FUNDAMENTAL THEOLOGY
Original title: *Teología Fundamental*
Second Revised and Actualized Edition
Copyright © 1998, 2008 Fernando Ocáriz & Arturo Blanco
Copyright © 1998, 2008 Ediciones Palabra S.A. – Madrid (Spain)

This English edition copyright © 2009 Rev. James Socias

General Editor: Rev. James Socias
Editor-in-Chief: Mr. Jeffrey Cole
Design and Production: Kimberly Chojnicki, Cristina Martinez

In accordance with c. 827, permission to publish is granted on April 2, 2009 by the Very Reverend John F. Canary, Vicar General of the Archdiocese of Chicago. Permission to publish is an official declaration of ecclesiastical authority that the material is free from doctrinal and moral error. No implication is contained therein that those who have granted it agree with the content, opinions, or statements expressed in the work; nor do they assume any legal responsibility associated with publication.

Library of Congress Cataloging-in-Publication Data
Ocáriz Braña, Fernando.
  [Teología fundamental. English]
  Fundamental theology / Fernando Ocáriz & Arturo Blanco.
    p. cm.
  Includes bibliographical references and index.
  ISBN 978-1-890177-24-9 (hardcover : alk. paper) 1. Catholic Church--Doctrines. I. Blanco, A. (Arturo) II. Title.
  BX1751.3.O2313 2009
  230'.2--dc22

                    2009020719

ISBN 978-1-890177-24-9   *Printed in the United States of America*

CONTENTS

PART ONE
FUNDAMENTAL DOGMATICS

PART TWO
FUNDAMENTALS OF APOLOGETICS

CHAPTER 12
Credibility of Jesus of Nazareth as the Messiah, Son of God

CHAPTER 13

The Credibility of the Church and
her Testimony about Jesus of Nazareth

BIBLICAL ABBREVIATIONS

Old Testament

Gen	Genesis	**Tb**	Tobit	**Ez**	Ezekiel
Ex	Exodus	**Jdt**	Judith	**Dn**	Daniel
Lv	Leviticus	**Est**	Esther	**Hos**	Hosea
Nm	Numbers	**1 Mc**	1 Maccabees	**Jl**	Joel
Dt	Deuteronomy	**2 Mc**	2 Maccabees	**Am**	Amos
Jos	Joshua	**Jb**	Job	**Ob**	Obadiah
Jgs	Judges	**Ps(s)**	Psalms	**Jon**	Jonah
Ru	Ruth	**Prv**	Proverbs	**Mi**	Micah
1 Sm	1 Samuel	**Eccl**	Ecclesiastes	**Na**	Nahum
2 Sm	2 Samuel	**Sg**	Song of Solomon	**Hab**	Habakkuk
1 Kgs	1 Kings	**Wis**	Wisdom	**Zep**	Zephaniah
2 Kgs	2 Kings	**Sir**	Sirach	**Hg**	Haggai
1 Chr	1 Chronicles	**Is**	Isaiah	**Zec**	Zechariah
2 Chr	2 Chronicles	**Jer**	Jeremiah	**Mal**	Malachi
Ezr	Ezra	**Lam**	Lamentations		
Neh	Nehemiah	**Bar**	Baruch		

New Testament

Mt	Matthew	**Eph**	Ephesians	**Heb**	Hebrews
Mk	Mark	**Phil**	Philippians	**Jas**	James
Lk	Luke	**Col**	Colossians	**1 Pt**	1 Peter
Jn	John	**1 Thes**	1 Thessalonians	**2 Pt**	2 Peter
Acts	Acts of the Apostles	**2 Thes**	2 Thessalonians	**1 Jn**	1 John
Rom	Romans	**1 Tm**	1 Timothy	**2 Jn**	2 John
1 Cor	1 Corinthians	**2 Tm**	2 Timothy	**3 Jn**	3 John
2 Cor	2 Corinthians	**Ti**	Titus	**Jud**	Jude
Gal	Galatians	**Phlm**	Philemon	**Rv**	Revelation

PROLOGUE

With the title *Fundamental Theology* we are pleased to present this revised edition of *Revelation, Faith, and Credibility* which was first published in 1998. This revision results from the introduction of certain changes to the original which, while still following its basic design, are intended to present even more clearly the nature of this inquiry as part of a broadening collection of manuals of theology.

This revised edition incorporates minor improvements to the original text and takes advantage of the practical experiences of those who have used *Revelation, Faith, and Credibility*. Additionally, it seeks to clarify certain points for better understanding while omitting those parts which were not essential for the subject, but are better left for more specialized studies.

Fundamental Theology also utilizes those documents relevant to the subject which have been issued by the Magisterium since the original publication of *Revelation, Faith, and Credibility*. In this regard, *Fundamental Theology* presents the reader with the latest and most up-to-date teachings of the Church. Included in this edition are John Paul II's encyclical *Fides et ratio*, which examines the diverse aspects in the relationship between faith and reason; *Dominus Iesus*, which presents the declaration by the Congregation for the Doctrine of the Faith regarding Christian and non-Christian religions; and the recent book of Pope Benedict XVI, *Jesus of Nazareth*, which examines the identity between the Jesus of history and the Christ of Faith.

In presenting this book we renew our desire that it will be useful for students of theology and for all those who are interested in studying the fundamentals of the Catholic Faith. Furthermore, it is our hope that it will lead the reader to a profound Christian awareness that cooperates with the grace of God in sustaining the Faith, lends reason to our hope, and helps others to receive this great gift of knowing and loving Christ, discovering that "everything Christ did has a transcendental value, showing us the nature of God" (cf. St. Josemaría Escrivá, *Christ is Passing By*, 109).

FOREWORD

Fundamental Theology is a relatively recent discipline. In general, its object and method are concerned with the theology of the "fundamentals."

Fundamental Theology, as a proper discipline, distinct from other branches of theology, especially distinct from Apologetics, came into being in the nineteenth century. It was a response to the need to give new direction to the defense of the Faith. Classical apologetics, the previous defense of the faith, rarely took Revelation into account.

If we accept that *Fundamental Theology* sets forth, expanding on and redefining the heritage of the discipline born in the sixteenth century called "Apologetics," the history of Fundamental Theology would take us back to the first Apologists at the very dawn of Christian theological discourse in second century.

The first writers to use the expression Fundamental Theology were L. Guzmics, 1828, F. Brenner, 1837, and A. Knoll, 1852. But the first to develop Fundamental Theology in the modern sense of the term was, J.N. Ehrlich, sometime between 1859 and 1864.[1]

What characterized the newly formed discipline was the theory of Revelation in its historic-salvific aspect with explicit references to Christ. Christ is rightly considered the center and key of Revelation, of faith, and of credibility. Thus, when studying these three matters, it linked more or less explicitly and effectively, the dogmatic and apologetic considerations. This meant considering Revelation as both a mystery and an event, faith as supernatural knowledge with a human and historical basis, and credibility as something intimately related to these realities.

The new discipline sets forth the themes which form the basis of classical apologetics, but adds others. The principal difference is not to have an exclusively apologetic treatment of the major themes, that is religion, Revelation, faith, Church, miracles, Resurrection, etc., but to consider them according to their nature as a mystery.

From the very beginning this new discipline was established as a foundation for the entire subject of theology, and has remained so today, in spite of the innumerable changes of focus and other developments that have taken place especially in the second half of the twentieth century. These developments include many aspects, namely the traditional, anthropological, historical-salvific, hermeneutic, analytic, linguistic, logical, theoretical-scientific. For example, E. Biser defines his fundamental theology as hermeneutic FT, P. Knauer as ecumenical FT, A. Darlap as historical-salvific FT, that of H. Fries is considered theological-transcendental FT, etc.[2] These various differences show that there is an unavoidable thematic nucleus that depends on Revelation, its knowledge and acceptance; that is, it depends on faith and credibility.

In this book, this discipline is understood as *theology of the fundamentals of theology*, considering the term "fundamental" as that upon which something rests and is supported. It is also the principle and source of the reality that it sustains and develops. Studying the fundamentals involves describing and analyzing them, and also showing their solidity and capacity for basing and sustaining what is built on them.

In these pages, we will develop Fundamental Theology *as a study of Revelation and faith*. All Christian discourse on God is based on and is nourished by these two realities. Saying this is not tautological, Fundamental Theology is *also the study of the credibility of historical Revelation*, thus it includes Apologetics, understood as the science of the credibility of the revealed Word.

We could say that this discipline is the theological study of the first words of the Creed, i.e., "I believe" or "We believe" and the final word of the Creed i.e., "Amen." "Amen" is a Hebrew word which means the same as the Greek word *pistis* i.e., faith. "Amen," in Greek can also mean certainty. Thus, the Creed is between two words that in essence mean the same thing and that refer both *to a content* (what is between both words), and also *to someone* from whom news or content is received. Thus, it is clear that we are considering both Revelation from God and divine faith. For this reason "fundamental theology" is the discipline "whose object is the fact of Christian revelation and its transmission in the Church."[3] It is also clear in what sense we say that the theological study of the Revelation and of the Faith is a fundamental treatise: it is concerned with the very fundamentals of all other theological treatises.

Revelation and faith are two essentially connected realities. To understand faith is related to the understanding of Revelation. To understand credibility is also related to the understanding of Revelation and faith. Credibility prepares the way to the answers that faith gives, and finds in historical Revelation the fundamental arguments for it. We find the interconnection between these three concepts in the documents that the last two ecumenical councils have dedicated to these matters, namely the dogmatic Constitution *Dei Filius* on Catholic faith (April 24, 1870) and the Dogmatic Constitution *Dei Verbum* on Divine Revelation (November 18, 1965).[4] The Encyclical *Fides et ratio* also deals with them.

In this discipline, Christian theology undertakes the indispensable task of supporting everything it says. When it considers the relation between God and man, it establishes the bases for going into depth about what God is, wants, and does, and also to better recognize what man is and what he is called to be, according to the divine design. This study is centered on the contemplation of Christ, who is the fulfillment of the Divine Revelation to men, to whom man must unite through faith. "Christ, the final Adam, by the revelation of the mystery of the Father and His love, fully reveals man to man himself and makes his supreme calling clear."[5]

The study of the structure and the realization in history of the salvific relation between God and man gives this discipline a theological dimension, a Christocentric dimension, and an anthropological dimension. All three are necessary and each sheds light on the other. "The particular content of your theological discipline," said John Paul II, addressing a group of specialists in Fundamental Theology, "is the revelation of God to humanity. That is also the great and true center of our faith: God who reveals His mystery of love and, while He fills with light the mind of him who receives Him, it dazzles him to the point that it makes his understanding partial and necessarily incomplete. The revelation opens the way for us to profoundly understand the same mystery of man."[6]

Fundamental Theology studies the dialogue between God and man. This is a dialogue of salvation that develops in the world throughout history, when God sends his Word and his Gift, and man responds by accepting in faith the Word of God moved by his Love. Salvation comes in the form of a dialogue, and this discipline uncovers and analyzes the structure of this dialogue. The dialogue of Revelation and faith between God and man is at the basis of all Christian theological reflection. "Revelation, that is, the supernatural relationship established with humanity on the initiative of God Himself, can be represented in a dialogue in which the Word of God is expressed in the Incarnation and, therefore, in the Gospel. The paternal, holy colloquy, interrupted between God and man because of Original Sin, has been wonderfully resumed in the course of history. The history of Salvation precisely narrates this long and varied dialogue that arises from God, and is woven with man in an admirable and multiple conversation."[7]

The study of Revelation and of faith can be carried out in two very different ways, either dogmatically or as Apologetics. The distinction lies in the starting point of the reflection. It can start from the Revelation accepted through faith, and in this case it is a *dogmatic study*; or it can start from what reason—without necessarily invoking faith—can discover in the world, in man, and in history, and in this case it is an *apologetic study* that aims to show the credibility of the Revelation of God in Christ.[8]

This is the reason for the division of this book into two parts. First, *Fundamental Dogmatics*, where, in accordance to the methodology of a dogmatic science, we discuss the historical Revelation of God and of his transmission of theological faith in the Church, and through the Church. These are the fundamentals of Dogmatic Theology. Second, *Fundamentals of Apologetics*, where, leaving aside those aspects of the science of credibility that depend on its historical contextualization, we discuss the fundamental structure of the credibility of the Word Incarnate, and the fundamental elements that manifest it in men in any period in the history of the Church.[9]

Obviously, in the second part, we have to respect the methodology of Apologetics, which, among other things, takes into account the position of the interlocutor, who supposedly has not yet come to the Christian faith or, at least, has not fully reached it. For this reason, in the second part of the book, texts of Scripture, Tradition, and the Magisterium will be used not according to the value and authority that Christian faith gives them, but according to the historical and social value that they possess in themselves, but which will be critically controlled to satisfy the demands of this aspect of science.[10] This way of proceeding does not take away any theological value from the study. And even though the study is not based on the authority of the Revelation, Christian apologetics still proceeds with the light of faith, which helps it find reasons and arguments which are understandable to those who do not have faith, and are helpful to show that the Christian option is highly reasonable and human.[11]

God has revealed himself to men. But he gives himself within a mystery according to a system that is also mysterious, that reaches out to man in this life and explains it. Thus, Revelation brings with it motives to attract man's attention. It helps his intelligence and his freedom to follow Christ as the Way, the Truth, and the Life (cf. Jn 14: 6). Thus, *Fundamental Theology is made up of both the dogmatic consideration and the apologetic perspective, which are intertwined, and mutually shed light.*[12]

PART ONE

FUNDAMENTAL
DOGMATICS

INTRODUCTION

As already mentioned, the first part of the book will deal with both Divine Revelation and its transmission in and by the Church (chapters 1–5) and of supernatural faith, which is man's response to the Revelation of God (chapters 6–9).

Revelation

The Incarnate Word is thus the fulfillment of the yearning present in all the religions of mankind: This fulfillment is brought about by God himself and transcends all human expectations. It is the mystery of grace.

> In Christ, religion is no longer a "blind search for God" (cf. Acts 17: 27) but the *response of faith* to God, who reveals himself. It is a response in which man speaks to God as his Creator and Father, a response made possible by that one Man who is also the consubstantial Word in whom God speaks to each individual person and by whom each individual person is enabled to respond to God. What is more, in this Man all creation responds to God. Jesus Christ is the new beginning of everything. In him all things come into their own; they are taken up and given back to the Creator from whom they first came.[1]

The communication of God with mankind begins with the gift of life; it is perfected in grace and consummated in glory, which are granted by God to his children in Christ through the Holy Spirit. "The economy of the Old Testament," according to Vatican Council II, "was deliberately so orientated that it should prepare for and declare in prophesy the coming of Christ, redeemer of all men, and of the messianic kingdom (cf. Lk 24: 44; Jn 5: 39; 1 Pt 1: 10), and should indicate it by means of different types (cf. 1 Cor 10: 11)."[2] Therefore, every manifestation of God by means of figures and words in history is centered around Christ, "who is himself both the mediator and the sum total of revelation."[3]

The Christian religion is not a body of doctrines arising from the human search for God. The Christian religion is God himself, who has revealed himself to humanity and seeks out individuals so as to make them participants in the divine life of Christ. God has made himself known to mankind in the work of creation and established a dialogue with humanity from the very beginning. He continued this conversation since the original fall, and he extends it down through the ages, first with the people of Israel in the Old Testament (chapter 1), manifesting and communicating himself in ways that reach their fullness in Christ (chapter 2).

One of the fundamental aspects of the relationship between revelation itself and the people of God—Israel in the Old Testament and the Church in the New Testament—is the transmission of revelation, the work of the people of God. Hence, we begin our study of the transmission of revelation with an analysis of the relationship between revelation and Church, and we continue it with the consideration of the specific channels of transmission (Sacred Scripture, Tradition, and the Magisterium). By divine wish, these are the intimately related channels for complete and faithful communication of the word of God; they are different but inseparable (chapter 3).[4]

Our theological reflection on revelation begins from this very important point: Christianity is essentially an interpersonal relationship between man and God based on divine communication through history. Christianity is a historical religion. From the very beginning, its roots are in actual historical events.[5] Revelation is intrinsically linked to the salvation of mankind because God speaks with humanity to establish a covenant and communion that, together, will bring about mankind's eternal happiness and perfection. The history of revelation is, therefore, the history of salvation, because it is directed toward the fullness shown and granted in Christ, God and man united in one person (chapter 4).

This study of the transmission of revelation to the Church and by the Church is completed with a detailed analysis of the relationship between Sacred Scripture and Tradition. It is of the utmost importance to understand the unity of the two in the constitution of the deposit of faith (chapter 5).

Faith

"By his Revelation, then, 'the invisible God (cf. Col 1: 15; 1 Tm 1: 17), from the fullness of his love, addresses men as his friends (cf. Ex 33: 11; Jn 15: 14–15), and moves among them (cf. Bar 3: 38), in order to invite and receive them into his own company.'"[6] The proper response to this invitation is faith. By faith, one entirely submits his or her intelligence and will to God. With all his being, the individual consents to the God who reveals himself.[7] Sacred Scripture calls this response of man to God the "obedience of faith" (cf. Rom 1: 5; 16: 26).[8] Christian faith is a great and admirable reality.

The relationship between God and humanity is a living relationship: it is all-embracing and transforming. Man unites to God the Father through his Incarnate Word when he lets himself be moved by the grace the Holy Spirit gives him (cf. Lk 1: 35, 38, 45; Jn 1: 9–14; Eph 3: 17; 1 Thes 2: 13). The fulcrum of this faith is one's adherence to the word of God. That is why, without losing any of the breadth of its entirety, it is strongly marked by its purely intellectual nature, as a formal acceptance of the word of truth.

Christian faith is a mystery in itself because it refers immediately and intrinsically to the divine Word. It is a supernatural reality that can never be exhaustively explained due to the nature of revelation itself. It is, moreover, a complex reality that allows for various considerations: its object, subject, motivation, purpose and necessity, act, origin and genesis, and development. The mysterious nature of faith can especially be seen in some of its aspects that appear particularly obscure from a purely rational perspective. For example, faith is a free act, and, at the same time it is carried out under the influence of grace, simultaneously involving intelligence and will. It is an intellectual apprehension;

and at the same time it is a gift of the whole person, an individual act that has a communal dimension, both theoretical and practical.

We will analyze the issues relating to faith while taking into consideration these difficulties. Chapter 6 examines what the Bible says about faith and its object, God. In chapter 7, we will consider the structure of faith—a human response to God, a response that becomes true in an act in which grace, intelligence, and will participate. In chapter 8, we analyze the subject of the response of faith, that is, the person and the Christian community. Chapter 9 looks at faith as a dynamic principle of human conduct, both individual and communal, as the origin of definite and specific works that accompany and manifest faith.

Nevertheless, before starting the detailed exposition of these issues, it seems only proper to give a brief summary of the history of the way theology has dealt with revelation and faith.[9]

Introduction to the Notion of Revelation and Its Theological Development

Underlying all the Church's thinking is the awareness that she is the bearer of a message which has its origin in God himself (cf. 2 Cor 4: 1–2). The knowledge which the Church offers to man has its origin not in any speculation of her own, however sublime, but in the Word of God which she has received in faith (cf. 1 Th 2: 13). At the origin of our life of faith there is an encounter, unique in kind, which discloses a mystery hidden for long ages (cf. 1 Cor 2: 7; Rom 16: 25–26) but which is now revealed.[10]

Revelation, in all its extension as an action of God speaking to humanity, has always been present in theological reflection. A similar statement can be made about faith, in which man receives the divine Word.

Still, revelation itself has not been the subject of specialized study until relatively recently, when different streams of critical and rationalist thought came to question the communication between God and humanity. The rationalists questioned the very possibility of a relationship between God and humans beyond the mere generic reverence to a distant and unknown Creator.

While medieval theologians were interested in prophetic revelation, which certainly is an important issue, they did not examine the general notion of the Revelation of God to mankind. In the period immediately after the Council of Trent (1545–1563), theologians centered their attention on the transmission of revelation, a question that makes no sense to the synthesis of a complete theory of revelation.

During the eighteenth century Enlightenment, many of the most influential thinkers radically separated faith and reason, thus impairing any understanding of an intimate and personal relationship between God and mankind. It became absolutely necessary for theologians and Christian thinkers to show that tenets separating faith and reason were unfounded and inconsistent with human nature. This has not been an easy undertaking; theologians have not found a swift response to these challenges. The study of revelation has developed slowly, following a path that has reached some important goals and promises a bright future.

The First Stage of the Elaboration of the Theological Concept of Revelation: From the Council of Trent (1545–1563) to Vatican I (1869–1870)

The first attempts were characterized by looking at revelation as God talking to man, teaching him what he did not and could not know because it was a mystery to him, and proving with words and signs the existence of realities and beings that are completely out of human reach. This attempt qualifies as a theological reading because the perspective is "from God" as Beginning, as he who enlightens and teaches. A key element of this approach is the distinction between immediate revelation (an enlightening of the spirit to knowledge of truth), which is a direct relationship between God and man, and mediate revelation (the proposition of divine truth through a tradition that guarantees the truth of the proposition by the signs that support its mission).

A pervasive use of philosophy and the neglect of other sciences (such as psychology, philology, and history) characterized the cultural context of this period. Writers were excessively intellectual, sometimes rigidly logical, with few biblical and patristic references in their works. The authors of this period often prided themselves on being literal follow-ers of the great medieval writers, from whom, regrettably, they often did not inherit either scriptural breadth or extensive intellectual prep-aration. Given this situation, the concept of revelation proposed in this first stage (which was initiated in the seventeenth century, consolidat-ed in the eighteenth century, and survived until the twentieth century) appears simplistic.

One should not conclude from these limitations that the attempts of these writers were fruitless. In fact, those theological efforts—as a first approach to the issue, an approximation and a sizing up—contributed in good measure to the defense of Christian doctrine about God and his communication with humanity. The skeptical and rationalist criti-cism of those centuries has since been transformed into radical forms of agnosticism and Deism. Sometimes, it has reared its head in oppos-ing forms of fideism and traditionalism; occasionally it adopts forms such as semi-rationalism or atheism.

So, one ought to keep in mind this historical and philosophical context in order to adequately appreciate the first stage of the study of the no-tion of revelation. It established the *specificity of Christian revelation*, showing, with logically accessible arguments, its supernatural nature, its origin, contents, finality, and consequently, its *absolute necessity for salvation*. Revelation cannot be replaced by any human expression of philosophy, science or culture.

Vatican Council I definitively verified this:

> It is indeed thanks to this divine revelation, that those matters concerning God which are not of themselves beyond the scope of human reason, can, even in the present state of the human race, be known by everyone without difficulty, with firm certitude and with no intermingling of error.[11] It is not because of this that one must hold revelation to be absolutely necessary; the reason

is that God directed human beings to a supernatural end, that is a sharing in the good things of God that utterly surpasses the understanding of the human mind.[12]

The Council ratified this teaching with two canons, condemning whoever says either "that it is useless or impossible that man be instructed by Divine Revelation about God and about cult,"[13] or that "man cannot be elevated by God to a knowledge and perfection that surpass human nature, but that by himself can and must, through a constant progress, possess the good and truth."[14]

The Second Stage of the Elaboration of the Theological Concept of Revelation: From Vatican I (1869–1870) to Vatican II (1962–1965)

A second attempt, initiated in the nineteenth century by theologians from Tubinga (such as J.S. von Drey) addressed the concept of revelation from a new perspective and took as a point of departure the salvific-historical character of revelation and its undeniable Christological center, since the Incarnate Word is clearly the fullness of divine communication with mankind. The issues of the possibility, convenience, and necessity of revelation, which had previously been the center of attention, were relegated to a secondary status. Since the beginning of the twentieth century, this notion of revelation has been a key concept in theology. This notion was later developed on the teachings of the Bible and the Church Fathers.

The twentieth century was characterized by the consolidation of the new sciences—specifically that of psychology, the various approaches of history, sociology, philology, hermeneutics, anthropology, and comparative religion. In philosophy, Enlightenment ideology and idealism remained the dominant schools of thought, but were qualified by the appearance of new philosophical perspectives that, even as they remained in the basic framework of Kantian epistemology, sought to overcome its inherent limitations. Examples of such philosophies are, first, the existentialism of Kierkegaard, followed by that of Heidegger and Sartre, as well as the hermeneutics of Gadamer and Ricoeur, structuralism, and others.

In the development of the concept of revelation in the twentieth century, three great schools or groups of thought, can be distinguished, although they do not always oppose one another.

The first group is represented by A. Gardeil, J. V. Bainvel, R. Garrigou-Lagrange, H. Dieckmann, C. Pesch, L. Lercher, S. Tromp, and J. Brinktrine.[15] These theologians basically followed the theoretical position of the previous stage, though they made some advances and developments.[16]

The second group is made up of those Catholic and Protestant theologians who look for a notion of revelation that is founded in the Bible and enriched by the Fathers of the Church. These authors reach a concept of revelation as history, as event, the intervention of God in history. Moreover, they see revelation as a personal disclosure of God. It is God himself who communicates with mankind, who opens his intimacy by giving man access to it. Revelation itself remains a mystery. These authors stress that it is God who both reveals and is revealed. God is revealed not merely in a divine heritage (as some members of the first group tended to claim) but in Christ and by Christ, who is the Incarnate Word. A few theologians of the second group are R. Guardini, J. Mouroux, G. Söhngen, L. Charlier, J. Danielou, M.D. Chenu, R. Aubert, H. Bouillard, and H. de Lubac.[17]

In the same group we might also include many biblical scholars who have approached the issue in their writings or the Bible. These writers include J. Dupont, C. Spicq, J. Coppens, H. Schlier, R.E. Brown, C.H. Dodd, R. Schnackenburg, H. Schulte, G. Kittel, G. Friedrich, A. Oepke, A. Althaus, H. Strathmann, and K.H. Rengstorff.[18] These studies elucidate the progressive nature of revelation: its pedagogic dimension, the permanent and intrinsic relationship between revelation and history, the different modes and expressions of revelation, its personal nature as dialogue, its relation to the Church, and above all, its focus on Christ.

Those theologians who have identified revelation as the notion that can express and summarize the relationship of God with man, covering and enlightening all other theological issues, comprise the third group. This position, obviously, assumes the previous ones and extends their scope. Some, perhaps even many, of the authors mentioned in the preceding paragraphs might be included in this group. Undoubtedly, the following authors are particularly clear examples of this group and agree on this position in spite of their other divergences: K. Barth, R. Bultmann, K. Rahner, H.U. von Balthasar, and W. Pannenberg. These authors all stress the centrality of the relationship between God and man (in all its variations: faith-reason, nature-grace, transcendence-immanence, eternity-time, word-history, etc.). They also attempt to clarify the relationship between Christianity and modern society (with all its variations: church-world, Christianity-culture, tradition-eschatology, dogma-interpretation).

In the Dogmatic Constitution on Divine Revelation, Vatican Council II has taken into account the principal contributions of the preceding theology.[19]

A characteristic of this document is the presentation of revelation centered *on Christ* and starting from the *Trinity*, according to an economy that is *historic-salvific*. "Thus, the profound truth about God and the salvation of man through this revelation becomes clear to us in Christ, who is at the same time the mediator and the fullness of the complete revelation."[20]

We should also say, on the other hand, that Vatican Council II did not adopt approaches such as the Barth's or Bultmann's fideism, nor does it fully identify revelation and history, as Pannenberg seeks to do. Nor does it accept the general design on the Revelation developed by Rahner, nor does it esthetically express man's approach to God, as von Balthasar suggests.[21]

However, the Council teaches that "this plan of revelation is carried out through the events and words intrinsically connected to each other, in such a way that the events brought on by God in the history of salvation manifest and reinforce the doctrine and the realities expressed by the words, and in turn, the words make known the acts and elucidate the mystery that they contain."[22] And it also says that Christ, "with all his presence and manifestation, with words and with deeds, with signs and miracles, but mainly with his death and glorious resurrection from among the dead, and lastly sending to Spirit of truth, concludes the revelation completing it and he confirms it with his divine testimony": and it concludes: "the Christian economy… will never disappear and we no longer have to wait for any other public revelation before the glorious manifestation of our Lord Jesus Christ."[23] Throughout the following chapters, we will study in detail the teaching of Vatican II on divine revelation.

CHAPTER 1

REVELATION
IN THE OLD TESTAMENT

The divine plan of salvation begins with Creation: God created the world from nothing, brought creatures into being, and gave each one of them unique characteristics. In this chapter, we will study how God reveals himself via creation and how, on the basis of this first manifestation, he communicates with mankind by means of his intervention in history.

I. Revelation and the Word of God

In the Old Testament, there is no specific term or concept that corresponds to revelation. Yet, there are several ways employed to make reference to God's intervention in human history. Among them, the term that most clearly represents a revelation of God to man is, the *divine speech*, that is, the word of Yahweh.[1]

Word in the Hebrew language is *debar*, or *dabar*. Its origins are uncertain; its corresponding verbal root could indicate the idea of "being behind of" and "push," or "to express what is inside" and so would mean "to talk" (and think), as well as "to produce."[2]

The word *debar* in the Old Testament has a broader meaning than our term *word*. Sometimes it means a locution that expresses an idea, a thought. At other times, it means either the thing to which that locution refers or to an action or an event. For instance, *dibre Selomo* (cf. 1 Kgs 11: 41) does not mean "the words of Solomon" but "the acts or works of Solomon."

The word has, therefore, its own efficacy, not only to signify—i.e., to make known, etc. (*noetic value*)—but sometimes it also has power to carry out what it means (*dynamic power*). Examples of this double dimension of the word in the Old Testament are the blessings and curses, which, once they have been pronounced, have a sort of efficacy of their own. They cannot be retracted (cf. Gen 27: 33–35; Jos 6: 26 related to 1 Kgs 16: 34).[3]

In the Greek translation of the Septuagint, *debar* is sometimes translated as *logos* and sometimes as *rhéma*. The first principally means the noetic value; the second, the dynamic value of the word because, besides meaning "word," *rhéma* means "thing." The original Greek text of the New Testament uses both *logos* and *rhéma* to express the Hebrew idea of *debar*. On the other hand, the Latin text of the Vulgate occasionally translates *rhéma* as *res*, "thing" (cf. Gen 18: 14), and at other times it is translated as *verbum*, "word" (cf. Lk 1: 37).

This double dimension of *word* is eminently shown in the Old Testament, when it deals with the Word of God (*Debar Yahvé*, translated to Greek as *ho logos tou Theou* or *tó rhema tou Theou*). So, we read in Isaiah 55: 10–11, "For as the rain and the snow come down from heaven, and return not thither but water the earth, making it bring forth and sprout, giving seed to the sower and bread to the eater, so shall my word be that goes forth from my mouth; it shall not return to me empty, but it shall accomplish that which I purpose, and prosper in the thing for which I sent it."

The Word of God is revealing; it communicates knowledge to men. It is also effective, which is to say, the Word of God influences human history. It is the cause of concrete events, conducting history and, moreover, it carries out the history of Israel as the people of God.

Divine Revelation is united to the Word of God in the Old Testament in such manner as to make the rest of the divine manifestations (theophanies, dreams, etc.) ways of transmitting the Word.[4]

For example, in the theophany of Mambré revelation (cf. Gen 18: 1ff.), the divine manifestation is not exactly in the human appearance under which God appeared, but in the words God speaks to Abraham. In any event, it is true that revelation is also actualized through *actions* or *events* that are inseparable from the Word. Later, we will examine the relationship between the Word and event.

In the Old Testament, the Word of God enjoys three principal forms:

1. The Word of creation, which constitutes natural or cosmic revelation
2. The Word of the covenant (promise and law)
3. The prophetic Word

These last two forms of the Word constitute supernatural, or historical, revelation.

Nevertheless, the Word of God in the history of the Old Testament can be studied with other divisions if contents are considered more important than form. For instance, distinctions could be made among *Word of announcement*, *Word of teaching*, and *Word of cult.*[5]

The Word of God in all its forms is directed to man to cause a response: this *dimension of dialogue* is essential for every truthful word.[6] Thus, the *response of man to the divine Word* helps us understand the sense and finality of what God wants to communicate. This is so even when the response is not the one that God wished. (In this case, the response is interpreted in the light of God's judgment.)

The response of man to the Word of God in the Old Testament is an interior fundamental reality: faith (or incredulity), which tends to express itself through words and actions. Human words responding to the Word of God principally take two forms: words of praise and words of complaint, which can have other variants (gratitude, worship, repentance, etc.). Human actions in response to the Word of God are found in *obedience* (or disobedience) in ordinary life and cult.[7]

Human responses to the Word of God have value in revelation insofar as they aid in understanding the sense and finality of the Word.

Apparently, God wished to have Sacred Scripture record not only his words and actions in history, but also the way in which people responded them. This explains why accounts of numerous words and actions of men have been transformed into the Word of God. "Sacred Scripture is the speech of God as it is put down in writing under the breath of the Holy Spirit."[8]

Fundamentally, "the Word of God in the Old Testament directs and inspires a history that begins with the Word of God in Creation and ends with the Word made flesh."[9]

II. The Creative Word: Natural or Cosmic Revelation

"And God said, 'Let there be light'; and there was light" (Gen 1: 3); "And God said, 'Let the waters under the heavens be gathered together into one place, and let the dry land appear.' And it was so" (Gen 1: 9). From the very first page of the Bible, we find the eminently dynamic and efficacious power of the Word of God, and its power as the creating Word found in subsequent biblical texts. For example, Psalm 33 states, "By the word of the LORD the heavens were made, and all their host by the breath of his mouth.... For he spoke, and it came to be; he commanded, and it stood forth" (Ps 33: 6, 9).

Creation is something *said by God* and, therefore, is revelation.[10] The very things of this world can be considered words of God directed to mankind: "Day to day pours forth speech, and night to night declares knowledge. There is no speech, nor are there words; their voice is not heard; yet their voice goes out through all the earth, and their words to the end of the world. In them he has set a tent for the sun, which comes forth like a bridegroom leaving his chamber, and like a strong man runs its course with joy" (Ps 19: 2–5).

Both the Book of Wisdom and St. Paul (cf. Rom 1: 18–23) teach us that the created world constitutes a *natural or cosmic revelation*. "The marvelous 'book of nature,' which, when read with the proper tools of human reason, can lead to knowledge of the Creator."[11] his revelation is not a word explicitly directed in a personal manner to man as is historical revelation. However, it allows man to know the existence, the majesty, the power of God through his works. It gives man the opportunity to respond by praising this God, who speaks in creatures and through creatures.

The Word of Creation has a special importance in the *creation of man*. "Then God said, 'Let us make man in our image, after our likeness'" (Gen 1: 26). In cosmic revelation, man is the *word* that reveals God. The human mind is capable of discovering God, not only through created material reality, but also through his own spirituality, by the testimony of his own conscience (cf. Rom 2: 14ff.).

Cosmic revelation is not imposed on man. Man should come to recognize the world as the Word of God. He should recognize God *per ea quae facta sunt*, through analogy (a term that appears in the original Greek of the Book of Wisdom [cf. Wis 13: 5], which means proportion, likeness, and concordance).

In practice, this recognition may be found throughout human history in the various *religious phenomena* of distinct cultures. Often, these phenomena have been full of imperfection, even to the point of denying a personal God who is distinct from the world. Indeed, it can be said, "if polytheism represents the error of popular cosmic religion, pantheism is the metaphysical temptation."[12] Another type of natural religion's deviations from truth may be found in the diverse manifestations of *dualism*. All of this is a clear historical indication that creation calls to mankind as Word of God, as Divine Revelation. The origin of these errors is, as we know from supernatural revelation, Original Sin. This is why supernatural or historical revelation was necessary: so that everyone might reach the knowledge of God with relative ease, with confidence, and without error.[13]

The faith of the Church has always insisted that between God and us, between his eternal Creator Spirit and our created reason there exists a real analogy, in which—as the Fourth Lateran Council in 1215 stated—unlikeness remains infinitely greater than likeness, yet not to the point of abolishing analogy and its language. God does not become more divine when we push him away from us in a sheer, impenetrable voluntarism;

rather, the truly divine God is the God who has revealed himself as *logos* and, as *logos*, has acted and continues to act lovingly on our behalf.[14]

Vatican I proclaimed that it is *possible* for fallen man to know of the living and true God with certitude by the strength of reason and knowledge of the *created world*.[15] This capacity is of critical importance—whether or not people make use of it—because if man were not capable of knowing God by his own nature, then he would not be capable of recognizing a supernatural revelation of God. If man were not capable of naturally knowing God, supernatural revelation would be unintelligible to him.

It is interesting to consider momentarily the Protestant position about this issue, which has been formulated in various directions. It may be generalized that the intellectual tradition of the Protestant Reformation has habitually denied the possibility of natural theology. Protestant theologians tend to posit a fideism based on the fiduciary character of faith. Among Protestant theologians of the twentieth century, the one with, perhaps, the most interesting position about this issue has been Karl Barth. In the development of his thinking, one may observe how influential is his stance that God cannot be known through the strength of the human intellect alone.

God can be known only through the revelation of himself to Israel and in Jesus Christ, as recorded in the Bible. Barth affirms that God is "the absolutely other," unreachable for man, not deducible from the world and anthropology. According to Barth, the *analogia entis* ought to be rejected because it is opposed to the biblical message. Rather, what should be accepted is the *analogia fidei*.

Following the epoch of his *dialectic theology* (1931), Barth sought to explain how it was possible for human words to express the mystery of God using a special notion he developed called *analogia fidei*. This notion proposes that God, in revelation, gives words the capacity to let us know that something is his. This is so because our words, Barth wrote, are really more his than ours and, therefore, in and of themselves are more apt to signify God than the world.[16] It is crucial to understand why Barth's theory is totally insufficient. If man were not naturally capable of knowing God, then he would not be capable of recognizing supernatural revelation as the Word of God (what Barth calls *analogia fidei*). This was already made clear—in a direct challenge to Barth—by another Protestant theologian, the Swiss thinker Emil Brunner, who tried to make Barth understand the defect present in his *analogia fidei* unaccompanied by *analogia entis*.[17]

This painstaking discourse within Protestant thinking serves to underline the *theological* and philosophical importance of the possibility of natural knowledge of God as taught by the First Vatican Council. In this respect, it is useful to underline the importance for theologians to always recall the *analogical nature of our reasoning about God*. It cannot be maintained that there is a similitude between creatures and God without assuring, at the same time, that there is an even bigger difference between them.[18]

It is worth keeping in mind that our knowledge of God is *dialectic* in nature. It is constituted by those three paths—*affirmatinionis, negationis*, and *eminentiae*—which St. Thomas Aquinas developed in a masterly fashion using the metaphysical notion of participation, taking the Pseudo-Dionisian position as his starting point.[19]

Today as always, the created world is the word of God directed to mankind. Yet, in many environments—for different and well-known reasons—it seems more difficult than ever for man to recognize the Word of God in created things. This is why the historical revelation has become even more necessary.

III. Supernatural or Historical Revelation

God has manifested himself to mankind through creation since the dawn of time. Additionally, he has always sought to establish a relationship with man that was above the natural order or simply Creator-creature. He has wanted man to be his friend. This is the story of revelation. The Second Vatican Council summarizes the long periods of history before the coming of Christ, saying:

> God, who creates and conserves all things by his Word
> (cf. Jn 1: 3), provides men with constant evidence of himself in

created realities (cf. Rom 1: 19–20). And furthermore, wishing to open up the way to heavenly salvation, he manifested himself to our first parents from the very beginning. After the fall, he buoyed them up with the hope of salvation, by promising redemption (cf. Gen 3: 15); and he has never ceased to take care of the human race. For he wishes to give eternal life to all those who seek salvation by patience in well-doing (cf. Rom 2: 6–7). In his own time God called Abraham, and made him into a great nation (cf. Gen 12: 2). After the era of the patriarchs, he taught this nation, by Moses and the prophets, to recognize him as the only living and true God, as a provident Father and just judge. He taught them, too, to look for the promised Savior. And so, throughout the ages, he prepared the way for the Gospel.[20]

A. Primitive Revelation

The history of the origin of the world and mankind has been recorded, through divine inspiration, in the first chapters of the Book of Genesis. With its distinctive literary style, those stories give us a profound sense of the primordial happenings in salvation history. First, we need to note how the two narrations of the creation of man (cf. Gen 1: 26–29; 2: 7–24) specially emphasize the dignity of man, who is created *in the image and likeness of God*, as well as noting the particular familiarity that man had with his Creator from the beginning. That primitive state of man is expressed most clearly when contrasted with the state of our progenitors after Original Sin. When man rebelled against God, he lost his intimacy with God and was subject to suffering and death (cf. Gen 3: 1–24).

We will not spend more time on these important issues because they pertain to other theological realms of study. We will, however, point out the existence of a *Divine Revelation* from the beginning of mankind, which is different and beyond the testimony that God offers of himself through creatures. This revelation is, therefore, supernatural; it establishes a friendship between God and man above and beyond the relationship of Creator-creature.

Man was created in a state of sanctity and justice. As a result of Original Sin, man lost supernatural grace and his friendship and intimacy with God. The deprivation of supernatural grace, accompanied by sufferings, the weakening of the natural capacities to know the truth and to do the good, and the subjection to death, has been handed down to every person as part of our human nature.[21]

With the promise of redemption, God assured our forefathers of the hope of salvation after the fall.[22] This promise of redemption is narrated in Genesis 3: 15 (that is why this verse is called the *Proto-gospel*) as an announcement of the future victory of the woman's descendants over the devil (the serpent), who was the tempter.[23]

In primitive revelation to man, God manifested not only his creative power, but particularly his love of man himself, who was offered a participation in divine intimacy: the beatific communion with him. Man, for his part, had to respect divine precepts (as summarized in the Genesis narration in the prohibition to eat the fruit of the tree). Man had to trust God and, consequently, obey him. This prohibition was certainly a test for man but not in the sense that God demanded compensation for his gifts. The essence of the test was, on the one hand, to reveal God's respect for human freedom. On the other hand, God wanted to manifest the divine love, which is the sole origin of his gifts. His is a love that wishes to make it possible for man, with his freedom and love of God, to deserve such gifts. This "is the delicate and most intimate point of the relationship God wishes to establish with man: his having a basic respect for man's freedom, while simultaneously encouraging loyalty and obedience rooted in love."[24]

Even after man's infidelity, it is manifested—through the promise of Redemption—that the love of God for man is a *faithful love*. This fidelity of God is manifested constantly in history via the Divine Revelation.

B. The Word of the Covenant

The origin of the Hebrew term *berith* (covenant) is uncertain. It could derive from either *biritu* (chain) or *birit* (between), because a covenant is a kind of union between two persons. According to the most frequent use of the term in the Old Testament, *berith* signifies a perpetual agreement contracted between two persons before God, generally through a sacrifice offered to him, which entails bilateral rights and duties.[25]

Although an agreement of this nature normally presupposes a certain equality between parties, a covenant can be made between a stronger and weaker party. Moreover, in the Old Testament the term *berith* does not always mean a covenant or formal agreement; it can also mean a simple solemn promise similar to an oath. This was the case, for example, of the *berith* made by Zedechiah with the people (cf. Jer 34: 8), a promise to proclaim the freedom of slaves.

The corresponding Greek terms are *synthéké* and *diathéké*. The first almost exclusively denotes the idea of agreement or covenant, whereas the second—used by St. Paul—also can mean "testament." That is why the Latin text refers in some cases to the covenant as *testamentum* instead of the habitual *foedus* and *pactum*.

Covenant was a common figure among mankind, and God himself established a series of pacts with men: his covenant with Noah after the flood (cf. Gen 9: 9–10) and, particularly, his covenant with Abraham (cf. Gen 9: 15–17). In the latter covenant—that is the covenant par excellence—God took the initiative. It was God who *promised* to give Abraham many descendants and make them a great people, to give him a new land—the *Promised Land*—and, lastly, to make all nations blessed by God because of this nation. This is the announcement and promise of the universal salvation of mankind. From Abraham, *God demanded* monotheism and the compliance of Abraham's will. He asked for faith, especially in its dimension of trust and obedience. Abraham's faith allowed him to pass the great *test* constituted by the divine demand to sacrifice his own son Isaac (cf. Gen 22: 1–18). As a sign of the covenant, circumcision was established. (That is why it is a prophetic figure of the future Christian baptism.)

The covenant was later renewed with Isaac (cf. Gen 26: 2–5) and then with Jacob (cf. Gen 28: 12ff.; 35: 9–12). Still, it reached its most complete expression with Moses as found in Exodus 6: 2–8 and precisely formulated in Exodus 19–23.[26]

With Moses, God fulfilled the promise he made to Abraham to create a great people from his descendants. God liberated the Hebrews from slavery in Egypt and, after the Exodus, God fulfilled his promise to give them their Promised Land. Another key aspect of God's covenant with Moses and the people of Israel is *the law*. God expects his people to obey its precepts. The *Decalogue* (the ten words: Ex 34: 28; the words of the covenant: Ex 20: 1–17) and other legal dispositions make up "the law of Moses," of which St. Paul teaches "the law was our custodian until Christ came" (Gal 3: 24). Naturally, the body of laws was revealed to the Hebrew people gradually though time. There is a significant difference between the importance of the commandments (Decalogue) and the rest of the legal prescriptions. However, it is not necessary to stop and focus on these issues now.

The fact that God imposes a law on the people of the covenant does not diminish the character of a free gift of the covenant. As a matter of fact, the law is also a gift from God; it is how he shows his chosen people the way to complete fulfillment and happiness.[27] The Word of the law is a word of instruction. The term *torah* is used occasionally in this sense in the Old Testament (cf. Prv 1: 8). The law is, therefore, a light and not a weight: "Smoke went up from his nostrils, and devouring fire from his mouth; glowing coals flamed forth from him. He bowed the heavens, and came down; thick darkness was under his feet" (Ps 18: 8–9).

Thus, the Word of the covenant (promise and law) reveals God's truth and fidelity, his justice and love.[28] This Word is the essence of the historical revelation in the Old Testament and, in general, of the prophetic Word. Some exegetes claim that the essential theme of the covenant for a long time after Moses was the liberation or salvation from the Egyptian yoke, the event that signaled the birth of Israel as a free nation.[29] In any event, the covenant stands as the essence of the Word in the Old Testament because the liberation from Egypt was the fulfillment of one of the promises made by God to Abraham. Nevertheless, it is possible that people considered *berith* more a solemn promise than a covenant, and only later, especially due to the prophets, did it come to be considered a covenant in the strict sense of the term.

C. The Prophetic Word

The revelation on Mount Sinai is the essence of the religion of Israel. However, the faithful conservation and transmission of this Word in later centuries was in great measure carried out by means of the *prophetic Word*. This was not a mere human transmission, a simple presentation of the Word expressed by God in the covenant but, rather, *new Words of God*. God chose *prophets* and enlightened them with his Word. Consequently, the prophetic Word possesses its own power and efficacy because it is the Word of God in itself, not only human words that recall the Word of the covenant.

Prophet (in Hebrew *nabi*) originally meant "the one who has been called," but in the concrete usage of the Old Testament it means "he who speaks in the name of another." For example, God calls Aaron the *nabi* of Moses (cf. Ex 7: 1). Subsequently, the term *nabi* was reserved (in Greek *prophétes*, an interpreter of oracles) to those chosen by God to speak to the people in his name.[30]

From the beginning of the history of the people of Israel, the prophetic Word existed in great variety and richness. Abraham and Moses, for example, may be considered true prophets. Indeed, Deuteronomy states, "And there has not arisen a prophet since in Israel like Moses, whom the LORD knew face to face" (Dt 34: 10). Although the chain of *prophetic writers* began with Amos (750 BC) there were great prophets before him such as Samuel, Nathan, Elijah and Elisha.

The prophetic Word is *intimately united to history*. Sometimes, it is an interpretation or remembrance of past times. On other occasions, the Word represents the present (for instance, the vocation of Saul and David revealed through the prophet Samuel [cf. 1 Sm 9: 27; 10: 1; 16: 12–13]). The prophetic Word can also announce the future (historical as well as apocalyptic).

Future prophecies are of two types: *punishment prophecies*, normally a reproach from God for the sins of the people (cf. Is 5: 2–30) and *salvation prophecies* (cf. Jer 31: 31–34). The announcement of future salvation is the essential element of the prophetic Word. It is in this context that the past interventions of God in favor of his people are remembered. Confidence in the prophetic Word is based on God's fidelity to his promises.[31]

Alongside the prophecies of salvation are the prophecies of punishment. This is because God always has man's salvation in mind when he administers his punishments. Here we may recall, for example, the prophecy of punishment made by Jonah to Nineveh: "Jonah began to go into the city, going a day's journey. And he cried, 'Yet forty days, and Nineveh shall be overthrown!'" (Jon 3: 4). After the repentance and penance of the Ninevites, we learn, "When God saw what they did, how they turned from their evil way, God repented of the evil which he had said he would do to them; and he did not do it" (Jon 3: 10).

In its diverse manifestations, the prophetic Word is specifically the *Word communicated by God to the prophet*. God communicates an idea, image, or interior light to the prophet who then interprets it. God may also give a prophet the ability to interpret a historical event, the dream of another person, etc.[32] In most cases, the prophets are conscious of the fact that they speak in the name of the Lord. Yet, this awareness is not essential for a true prophecy.[33]

Among the prophecies of the Old Testament, the explicitly *messianic ones* are most important. Some of them announce a new covenant that will be eternal and definitive. Thus, God spoke through Isaiah: "Incline your ear, and come to me; hear, that your soul may live; and I will make with you an everlasting covenant, my steadfast, sure love for David" (Is 55: 3); "For I the LORD love justice, I hate robbery and wrong; I will faithfully give them their recompense, and I will make an everlasting covenant with them" (Is 61: 8). Even clearer in this sense is Jeremiah:

> "Behold, the days are coming, says the LORD, when I will make a new covenant with the house of Israel and the house of Judah,

not like the covenant which I made with their fathers when I took them by the hand to bring them out of the land of Egypt, my covenant which they broke, though I was their husband, says the LORD. But this is the covenant which I will make with the house of Israel after those days, says the LORD: I will put my law within them, and I will write it upon their hearts...for I will forgive their iniquity, and I will remember their sin no more." (Jer 31: 31–34)

The prophetic Word recalls the old covenant so as to emphasize God's fidelity. This is a prelude to the new covenant that will be a *reality of salvation* (bringing forgiveness of sins).

The new covenant is announced as a new and more immediate divine presence among mankind. Thus, God says through Ezekiel, "I will make a covenant of peace with them; it shall be an everlasting covenant with them; and I will bless them and multiply them, and will set my sanctuary in the midst of them for evermore. My dwelling place shall be with them; and I will be their God, and they shall be my people" (Ez 37: 26–27). These words reach their highest fulfillment in the Incarnation, as St. John later wrote: *kai ho logos sarx egheneto kai eskénosen en hémin* ("And the Word became flesh and dwelt among us") (Jn 1: 14). The expression used by St. John indicates a dwelling of God among men that is by nature definitive. The verb *skenoó* means "to put up the tents" and is a literal translation of the Hebrew *schekan*, deriving from the *schekina*, the presence of God in the camp of Israel in the desert.[34]

In supernatural revelation, the Word of God is intimately involved with history and salvation. Later, we will give particular attention to the relationship between revelation, history, and the salvation of humanity. But before this, it behooves us to analyze the mystery of Christ inasmuch as he is the plenitude of revelation, cosmic as well as historical.

CHAPTER 2

CHRIST, FULLNESS OF THE REVELATION OF GOD

After God had spoken many times and in various ways through the prophets, "in these last days he has spoken to us by a Son" (Heb 1: 2). For he sent his Son, the eternal Word who enlightens all men, to dwell among men and to tell them about the inner life of God. Hence, Jesus Christ... "utters the words of God" (Jn 3: 34), and accomplishes the saving work that the Father gave him to do (cf. Jn 5: 36; 17: 4). As a result, he himself—to see whom is to see the Father (cf. Jn 14: 9)—completed and perfected revelation and confirmed it with divine guarantees. He did this by the total fact of his presence and self-manifestation—by words and works, signs and miracles, but above all by his death and glorious Resurrection from the dead, and finally by sending the Spirit of Truth. He revealed that God was with us, to deliver us from the darkness of sin and death, and to raise us up to eternal life.[1]

In this way, Vatican II describes the various issues raised by affirming that Christ is the plenitude of revelation, while it stresses the intimate and essential relationship between revelation and salvation. Let us carefully read the initial text of the Letter to Hebrews briefly cited in the above text.

In many and various ways God spoke of old to our fathers by the prophets; but in these last days he has spoken to us by a Son,

whom he appointed the heir of all things, through whom also
he created the world. He reflects the glory of God and bears the
very stamp of his nature, upholding the universe by his word
of power. When he had made purification for sins, he sat down
at the right hand of the Majesty on high, having become as
much superior to angels as the name he has obtained is more
excellent than theirs. (Heb 1: 1–4)

These initial verses in St. Paul's Letter to the Hebrews summarize the
history of salvation. They are a clear expression of the *plenitude* that
revelation, united intimately to salvation itself, has in Christ, eternal
Word of God, Son of God made man. Hebrews presents Jesus as the
culmination of historical revelation and of history itself. The reference
to the work of creation leads us to consider the mystery of Christ as the
plenitude of the cosmic revelation.

The mystery of Christ, as Son of God made Man, shows a new
and very particular event about the divine manifestations of
the past.... It is a unique and absolute fact that sets itself apart
from what had been revealed before and situates itself as the
beginning of a completely new and unprecedented relation
of filial communion of man with God.... Therefore, while we
consider Christ as the conclusion and plenitude of revelation, we
have to avoid the error of considering him in the same existential
line as the Old Testament. We have to consider Christ for what
he really is, as an absolutely new event, without diminishing the
preparatory purpose of the old.[2]

I.   Christ, Fullness of the Creative Word

The affirmation, "Christ is the plenitude of the creative Word," has a
rich and diverse meaning. It signifies that Christ possesses perfect humanity because it is the humanity of God, and God is perfect. In the
glorious Christ, therefore, all created things are destined to attain to
the new heaven and the new earth.

All things have been created because of Christ. He is heir to all things, and not only because he is and always will be the universal Lord. All created things—all in their own way—are destined to constitute a certain glorious unity with Christ at the end of history in such way that "God may be everything to every one" (1 Cor 15: 28).

Nature does not require grace. The "new creation" is not the result of the development or evolution of the first creation. Yet, according to the plan of God, the first creation is destined from the beginning to become the second and definitive one.

A. Creation Has Been Made in View of Christ

In the aforementioned text (Heb 1: 1–4), St. Paul speaks of a double dimension between created things and Christ: God "has made the world through his Son," and he "has named Christ heir of all things." The first aspect of this relationship refers, obviously, to Christ as God (the eternal Word before the Incarnation). The second refers, undoubtedly, to Christ as the Incarnate Word. In fact, it is only as man that Christ is "heir of all things" (*kleronomon pantón*), since it is only as a man that Christ "has inherited" (*kekléronomekén*) that excellent name which is referred to in Hebrews 1: 4: This name is *Kyrios* (the Lord) (cf. Phil 2: 9).

Considering the first aspect, we learn the following: *God carried out creation "by means of his Son."* St. John writes, "In the beginning was the Word, and the Word was with God, and the Word was God. He was in the beginning with God; all things were made through him, and without him was made nothing that was made" (Jn 1: 1–3).

The work of creation is common to the three divine Persons. Thus, the expression "through him (the Word)" cannot be understood in an instrumental sense. In order to comprehend the meaning of the above passage, we must take into account the following words of St. Paul: "He is the image of the invisible God, the first-born of all creation; for in him all things were created, in heaven and on earth.... He is before all things, and in him all things hold together" (Col 1: 15–16a, 17).[3]

Although this creative power belongs to the entire Trinity, we must affirm that a special relationship exists between created things and the Logos. Thus, St. Thomas Aquinas writes, "The Son, from the very fact that he is the Word which perfectly expresses the Father, expresses all of creation."[4] Elsewhere (and more concisely), he states that the Word is the "efficient cause of the things that God creates."[5]

Logos is the eternal Word of God. But in some way, it is also the Word manifested to creatures. In any event, creatures have this special relationship with the Logos inasmuch as *this relationship manifests the divine nature*. Consequently, this relationship does not give man the possibility of a natural knowledge of the Trinity by means of creatures. This relationship of creatures with the divine Logos has the same root as the *logic* of the world[6]: of its truth, its intelligibility, and, therefore, its being the starting point of man's natural knowledge of God. In this vein, certain Church Fathers wrote about the presence of the Word in the world before the Incarnation (particularly St. Justin and St. Irenaeus).[7]

It is clear that St. John, in the expression *di'autou* (Jn 1: 2), referred to the Word in its eternal pre-existence before the Incarnation. St. Paul also referred to Christ as the God-Man (*en autó*: Col 1: 16–17) in his divinity. However, St. Paul emphasized Christ as God acting in the creation and conservation of the world.

Let us now consider another aspect of the relationship between Christ and the whole of creation, one taken from the beginning of the Letter to the Hebrews: *Christ has inherited everything.* Christ has been ordained Lord of all creation. Nevertheless, we must point out another important facet of this issue indicated by St. Paul in the Letter to the Colossians: "All things were created through him and for him [*ta panta di'autou kai eis autom ektistai*]" (Col 1: 16). In the Vulgate, the translation is *omnia per ipsum et in ipso creata sunt*. In the Neo-Vulgate this passage is translated in a more precise manner: *omnia per ipsum et in ipsum creata sunt*, expressing in this way the dynamic sense of finality that in Greek the *ein* has with the accusative, which corresponds in Latin with the *in* of the accusative.

Therefore, in this text (Col 1: 16b), St. Paul—in addition to reaffirming that creation was carried out through the Word (*di'autou*)—affirmed that creation was carried out *because of Christ*. In the exegesis, the interpretations are not unanimous as to whether the Apostle was talking about Christ just in his divinity, in his divinity and humanity, or in his being God-Man. The most commonly held and best grounded opinion is that the expression *eis autum* refers to Christ as God made Man, because St. Paul says soon thereafter, "He is the head of the body, the church; he is the beginning, the first-born from the dead, that in everything he might be pre-eminent" (Col 1: 18). This passage, evidently, does not refer to Christ only in his divinity, but in his mystery of God-Man.[8]

Consequently, we can state that the *cosmic revelation—creation—was carried out in preparation for the Incarnation of the personal Word of God: in preparation for the coming of Christ.*

There is no necessary connection between creation and Incarnation, but God apparently wished and foresaw such a relationship "before creation." "Before creation," the free divine plan included all human history: creation, sin, and redeeming Incarnation with or without the fall of man.[9]

B. The Humanity of Christ, Fullness of Creation

Christ, in his humanity, is the plenitude of the Word of creation; He is the plenitude of creation. The Word of creation reveals God in man, because man was created "in our image, after our likeness" (Gen 1: 26). Christ is the *perfect man, the new Adam*. He is not made to the likeness of the first Adam because Adam was the one who was "a type of the one who was to come" (Rom 5: 14), the Lord Christ.[10]

> He who is the "image of the invisible God" (Col 1: 15), is himself the perfect man who has restored in the children of Adam that likeness to God that had been disfigured since the first sin. Human nature, by the very fact that it was assumed in him, not absorbed, has also been raised in us to incomparable dignity.[11]

The humanity of Jesus is the supreme expression of the word of creation. Christ reveals his perfect humanity to man, and, in addition, he shows mankind the unity of his divine Person, *the same eternal Word of God* made visible in flesh. In other words, his human nature is *the humanity of God*, and, therefore, it is *"a way of being* of God: the way of being not divine that the Son of God has taken for himself."[12] The fact that the humanity of Christ is true (not divine) humanity does not diminish its character as a *way of being of God* and, therefore, a manifestation of God. Here we may draw the analogy of a musical instrument that has a distinct nature from the one who plays it. "Everything Christ did has a transcendental value. It shows us the nature of God."[13] The Lord himself asserted with great clarity, "He who has seen me has seen the Father" (Jn 14: 9).

In this way St. John, inspired by God, was able to say about Christ, "And the Word became flesh and dwelt among us, full of grace and truth; we have beheld his glory, glory as of the only Son from the Father" (Jn 1: 14). The term *glory* (*doxa* in Greek, *kabod* in Hebrew) means the divine being as he manifests himself to men.[14]

St. John also wrote, "That which was from the beginning, which we have heard, which we have seen with our eyes, which we have looked upon and touched with our hands, concerning the word of life…we proclaim also to you" (1 Jn 1: 1, 3). There have been several interpretations of this text claiming that the phrase "the word of life" might not refer to the divine Person of the Word. Yet, it would seem most logical for St. John to use the term *logos* to refer to Christ in a personal sense rather than to use the term logos for some other purpose.[15]

C. The New Creation in Christ

Christ, whose humanity is "full of grace and truth" (Jn 1: 14), is also revelation because he is the divine Word that means and carries out supernatural salvation, which is a *new creation* (cf. Gal 6: 15; 2 Cor 5: 17).

Above all, Christ, who has risen and is seated at the right hand of the Father, is the plenitude of the Word of creation, "For in him the whole fullness of deity dwells bodily [*en autó katoikei pan to pléróma tés theotétos sómatikós*]" (Col 2: 9). This text, although directly understood as an affirmation of the Incarnation (the personal union of divinity and humanity in Jesus), refers particularly to the complete glorification (deification) of the most holy humanity of Christ after his Resurrection and Ascension.[16] Moreover, the glorification of the body of Christ, which we consider a proper and authentic—although mysterious—*deification of matter*, may be due to an ontologically prior spiritualization of matter (cf. 1 Cor 15: 44): a new manner of uniting body and soul that confers quasi-spiritual properties upon the body and that, in addition, implies that the resurrected Christ is *immortal* in the strict sense of the word (cf. Rom 6: 9; 1 Cor 15: 23).[17]

This plenitude of the Word of creation that manifests itself in the totally glorified holy humanity of Jesus will produce *the new heaven and the new earth* at the end of history (cf. Rom 8: 19–23; 2 Pt 3: 13; Rv 21: 1). Visible creation *will be called forth anew*, because of the divine plan "to unite all things in him [*anakephalaiósasthai ta panta en tó Christó*]" (Eph 1: 10). Thus, the glorious Church will be "the fullness of him who fills all in all" (Eph 1: 23) because the glorious Christ will fill all things (cf. Eph 4: 10) and because these participate in his plenitude (cf. Col 2: 9).

The exegesis of this *anakephalaiósis* or *recapitulation* of everything in Christ has had a long and rich history. The etymology seems clear: It comes from *ana* (as a verb prefix means "again," or "re-" in addition to meaning "upward," or "backward"; and from *kephalaion* ("chapter" or "summit"). Nevertheless, the precise meaning of the term *anakephalaiósasthai* in the text of Ephesians 1: 10 is not entirely clear. In any case, the translation of the Neo-Vulgate is preferable to that of the Vulgate (*recapitulare omnia in Christo*). St. Paul uses this term on another occasion to indicate that all of the law is *recapitulated* (*anakephalaioutai*) in the double precept of charity (cf. Rom 13: 9).

Among the Greek Fathers, St. Irenaeus stressed the importance of Ephesians 1: 10, considering the recapitulation of all things in Christ as finality of the *parousia* together with the resurrection of humanity

and the universal judgment.[18] Further, the exegesis of St. John Chrysostom, St. Theodoret of Cyrrhus and St. John Damascene are particularly important on this topic.

St. John Chrysostom indicates two meanings of the term
anakephalaiósis. The first and more direct is "recapitulation," understood as a brief summary of all that has been previously said (taking
into consideration that the term derives from *kephalaion*). In this sense,
Ephesians 1: 10 means that everything that God had previously made
for the salvation of the world is contained in Christ.[19] Then, Chrysostom immediately adds that *anakephalaiósis* has another meaning: "to
assign a head again" or "to reinstate as head" (based on the term deriving from *kephalé*). That is why, according to him, in Ephesians 1: 10,
St. Paul also speaks of placing Christ as head of all terrestrial and celestial creatures.[20] In this context it may be deduced that the terrestrial
and celestial beings to whom St. Paul refers are angels and men, but
one cannot exclude the fact that he attributes to *anakephalaiósis* a more
universal sense that really comprehends all that has been created.

St. Theodoret of Cyrrhus was the one who most explicitly interpreted
anakephalaiósis in a cosmic universal sense. According to him, at the
end of history everyone will be gathered under Christ, who will be the
head not only of angels and men but also of the entire universe, which
will be transformed and become incorruptible. In that sense, Theodoret interprets Ephesians 1: 10 together with Romans 8: 19–22: "The
whole creation has been groaning in travail until now."[21]

St. John Damascene took a third exegetical position, seeing *anakephalaiósis* as "restoration." He interpreted St. Paul as teaching in Ephesians 1: 10 that at the end of history Christ will restore angels and men
to a primitive state of happiness and sanctity (not in the sense of *apo-
katastasis pantón* suggested by Origen, but in the sense of canceling
the mourning that exists even in heaven—among angels—through the
complete salvation of just men).[22]

This interpretation of Damacene's was very common among the Latin
Fathers, mainly because in the versions of Scripture they possessed,
anakephalaiósasthai had been translated as *to restore* or *to establish*.

For instance, St. Augustine wrote about the "restoration" of men and angels (in the sense that the number of fallen angels will be restored through the men that will be saved).[23] St. Jerome, among the Latin Fathers, interpreted this passage according to the sense of the Greek text and translated *anakephalaiósasthai* as *to recapitulate* (as Tertullian had already done), thereby giving the same explanation as St. John Chrysostom.[24]

The medieval exegetes principally depended on the Latin Fathers for the translation of Ephesians 1: 10, where they found *to restore* or also *to establish*. Thus, their possible interpretations were limited. St. Thomas Aquinas felt that the text, when it says *instaurare omnia in Christo*, refers not only to angels and men but to the whole cosmos as well. The final destiny of the universe depends on the destiny of man because everything that was created is according to man.[25]

In his commentary on Romans 8: 19, St. Thomas Aquinas referred to Revelation 21: 1 and wrote of a cosmic recapitulation of creation. The eschatological glorification will encompass not only the human body but also the whole cosmos.[26] Thus, the whole creation will truly constitute a certain glorious unity with angels and men in Christ and under Christ.

Contemporary exegesis offers different directions of interpretation in this area that can be considered complementary and that coincide substantially with some already posited by the Church Fathers.[27]

In summary, we can say:

> *"To restore all things in Christ"* should be interpreted in the sense that God (the Father) gives all things, celestial and terrestrial, the whole creation, to one sole head, who is Jesus Christ. Christ, therefore, is head of the Church (cf. Eph 1: 22), which is *his body and his plenitude* (cf. Eph 1: 23). In other words, Christ is head of the universe, but especially of the Church. The whole universe is placed under Christ, is unified in him and elevated in him.[28]

This "elevation" of the whole creation into the "glorious Christ" entails a supernatural transformation of the entire cosmos into a "new creation." The transformation will be the plenitude of the creating Word (also as revelation) because it will constitute an "adjustment" of the visible world to the senses of the resurrected man. This is what St. Thomas boldly and deeply explained as the *lumen gloriae*.[29]

Of course, this "new creation in Christ," as the plenitude of the creating Word, will be carried out fully only at the end of history. Still, it has already been partially accomplished in the humanity of Jesus Christ. Therefore, the definitive state of the "new creation" will not be something completely new. The *recapitulation* of everything in the glorious Christ (cf. Eph 1: 10) will complete what the Incarnation started: "The 'firstborn of all creation' (Col 1: 15) becoming incarnate in the individual humanity of Christ, unites himself in someway with the entire reality of man, which is also 'flesh' (cf., i.e., Gen 9: 11; Dt 5: 26; Jb 34: 15; Is 40: 6; 52: 10; Ps 145: 21; Lk 3: 6; 1 Pt 1: 24)—and in this reality with all 'flesh,' with the whole of creation."[30]

Between creation and the "new creation," there is discontinuity because the "new creation" is not the consequence of an immanent evolution. There is also a certain continuity because the first creation is not to be destroyed, but transformed (cf. Rom 8: 19–22; 2 Pt 3: 7–13).

II. Christ, Fullness of the Word of the Covenant

In the covenant, God established a relationship with mankind: a union that, naturally, did not diminish in any way God's transcendence over man. In Christ we see a definitive and perfect covenant carried out: he is, really, true God and true man in a personal unity (cf. Jer 31: 31–34; 1 Cor 11: 25). In him, the divine nature and human nature are united in the most intimate and definitive way imaginable while simultaneously remaining distinct.[31]

Moreover, the covenant was a relationship based in love that is presented in the Old Testament as *adoption*—Israel is adopted as God's son (cf. Ex 4: 22; Hos 11: 1)—and as the *marriage union* (cf. Is 54: 5–8; Ez 16). In this manner, the promised Incarnation is treated as the fulfillment of the covenant. In fact, it is in Christ that mankind acquires the plenitude of divine sonship because in him there is no simple adoption.[32] The comparison between the covenant of God and the people of Israel via the marital union reaches its fullness in Christ because he is the Spouse of the Church (cf. Eph 5: 25–27: 32).

Consequently, Christ carries out the fullness of the covenant. In him the meaning of revelation regarding the covenant reaches its plenitude. In fact, the old covenant was mainly a revelation, in human history, of the truth and fidelity, justice, and love of God. It is in Christ that the perfect manifestation of God to mankind takes place, of his perfect fidelity to his promises, of his supreme justice united with mercy, as demonstrated, above all, in the sacrifice of the cross.[33]

Naturally, just as the Old Testament reveals, in addition to the love and the faithfulness of God, many other things about God and man[34], so in Christ is the supreme fulfillment of the divine revelation realized in all its multiform content, especially about God in his Trinity of Persons, and about man. In fact, Christ is the "fullness because he expresses the mystery of the Father and works with the power of the Spirit."[35] "Christ, who is the new Adam, by revealing the mystery of the Father and of His love, fully reveals man to man, and manifests to him his highest vocation."[36]

The covenant had, as its essential elements, the *Promise and the Law*. Let us now consider how in Christ the Promise, is completely fulfilled, and how in him the Law reaches its perfection, becoming a perfect law of liberty.

In Christ, *the Promise reaches its complete fulfillment.* Among the promises made to Abraham by God, those that referred to the descendants of Abraham, their establishment as a great people—through liberation from the Egyptian yoke—and that of giving his people the promised land, had already been fulfilled in the history prior to Christ. But only with the Incarnation is the Promise completely fulfilled with respect to universal salvation, that is, only through Christ and in Christ is the word given by God to Abraham fulfilled: "And by your descendants shall all the nations of the earth bless themselves" (Gen 22: 18; cf. Gal 3: 16, 26–29).

Through the Incarnation, the Law also reaches its perfection and fullness.

> Christ instituted this new covenant, namely the new covenant in his blood (cf. 1 Cor 11: 25); he called a race made up of Jews and Gentiles that would be one, not according to the flesh, but in the Spirit, and this race would be the new people of God. For those who believe in Christ, who are reborn, not from a corruptible seed, but from an incorruptible one through the word of the living God (cf. 1 Pt 1: 23), not from flesh, but from water and the Holy Spirit (cf. Jn 3: 5–6), are finally established as "a chosen race, a royal priesthood, a holy nation," who in times past were "no people" but now are "God's people" (1 Pt 2: 9–10).[37]

Christ, therefore, is the perfect covenant in himself, and in him all of the promises are completely fulfilled: the new people of God is constituted; it is universal in nature, and it is freed from the slavery of sin by the new Passover to be sons of God (cf. Rom 8: 21). By means of the Incarnation, the *law also reaches its perfection and fullness*. The issue of the relationship between the old law and the new law is presented in several books of the New Testament in ways that though articulate, sometimes do not lend themselves to easy interpretation.[38]

The purpose of the law is to teach and encourage men to lead just lives. Consequently, the law of the Old Testament itself could not justify men; it could only present and promise justice. According to the words of the Apostle: "For God has done what the law, weakened by the flesh, could not do: sending his own Son in the likeness of sinful flesh and for sin, he condemned sin in the flesh, in order that the just requirement of the law might be fulfilled in us" (Rom 8: 3–4).[39] The new law does not merely teach what is just and unjust. It also carries an *inner grace* that gives one strength to *act in justice*: "The New Law is the grace of the Holy Spirit, that is given to the faithful."[40] In this sense we can understand the aforementioned text of Jeremiah (cf. Jer 31: 31–34), in which is announced, as characteristic of the times of the future covenant, *a law carved by God in the hearts of men*. In its concrete moral precepts, Christ carried out the old law to its fulfillment and plenitude, especially by his teaching. For it was Christ who explained the true sense of its precepts (for instance, extending them to the intentions of men's hearts [cf. Mt 5: 20]). It was Christ who directed their accomplishment toward the perfect way (for example, in relation to oaths [cf. Mt 5: 33]).[41]

Another important aspect of this issue is that the law of Christ is *the perfect law of freedom* (*ho nomos teleios tes eleutherias*) (cf. Jas 1: 25). St. Paul even went so far as to write, "For freedom Christ has set us free; stand fast therefore, and do not submit again to a yoke of slavery" (Gal 5: 1). Because of the context, it is obvious that St. Paul makes a distinction between the old law, understood as the law of slavery, and the new one, understood as the law of freedom. The reason he drew this distinction is this: the new law is essentially *the law of grace and charity* (cf. Gal 5: 4–14). In the same way, St. Paul presents the distinction between the old law, which is *letter* (cf. Rom 7: 6), and the law of Christ, which is a law of the spirit (cf. Rom 8: 2). To the Gentiles, the Apostle emphasized the connection between spirit and liberty: "Where the Spirit of the Lord is, there is freedom" (2 Cor 3: 17). In this text, "Spirit" does not seem to refer to the Person of the Holy Spirit, but to the "spirit of Christ," understood as the inner world of the grace of Christ in the spirit of redeemed man.[42]

The "law of Christ is freedom"—that is the paradox of Paul's message in the Letter to the Galatians. This freedom has content, then, it has direction, and it therefore contradicts what only apparently liberates man, but in truth makes him a slave. The "Torah of the Messiah" is totally new and different—but it is precisely by being such that it fulfills the Torah of Moses.[43]

The relationship between grace, charity, and liberty that allows the new law to be a "perfect law of freedom" is skillfully expressed by St. Augustine in his famous words "Love and do whatever you wish,"[44] and "There is no chain that coerces because freedom belongs to love."[45] Similarly, St. Thomas Aquinas wrote, "Insofar as a man has more charity, he has more freedom."[46]

Complete freedom is dependent on charity (*libertas est caritatis*) because freedom is a person's capacity to love the good itself. It involves a person's ability to choose correctly among different goods, without any coercion of the will. It is in this arena that the love of God reaches its complete fulfillment. As we know, the spirit of charity should inform the life of Christians in such a way that they do everything out of love. It is not possible to love without freedom.[47] In other words, the new law is a law of perfect freedom, not just because it commands us *to love*—the old law also commanded the same—but, primarily, because it gives us the strength (*charity*) to love.[48]

III. Christ, Fullness of the Prophetic Word

Inasmuch as the prophetic Word is the Word of God in human form, it is, in itself and forever, a preparation for the Incarnation of the eternal Word. But in the Old Testament, the prophetic Word is also and principally the preparation of the Incarnation of God, because when it announces salvation it announces Christ implicitly and, oftentimes, explicitly. Such is the case, for example, in the *messianic prophecies*.

Christ is the plenitude of the prophetic Word because he himself is the *perfect Prophet*, not only because in him prophecies are fulfilled. Above all, he is the *Master*. In fact, the Old Testament announced that the Messiah would be a great prophet. For instance, God said to Moses, "I will raise up for them a prophet like you from among their brethren; and I will put my words in his mouth, and he shall speak to them all that I command him" (Dt 18: 18). Through Isaiah, God announced the Messiah with these words: "Behold, I made him a witness to the peoples, a leader and commander for the peoples" (Is 55: 4). The contemporaries of Jesus expected a Messiah who was also "the Prophet," although not everybody clearly saw the identification between "the Prophet" and "the Messiah" (cf. Jn 1: 21–25).

Undoubtedly, Jesus was sent by the Father as a *prophet* to convey the divine word to humanity. He taught with divine authority. The Father himself, in fact, commanded all to listen to Jesus' words (cf. Mt 17: 5). Christ declared the plenitude of his teaching about God, assuring the exclusive relationship of complete knowledge between him and the Father. "All things have been delivered to me by my Father; and no one knows the Son except the Father, and no one knows the Father except the Son and any one to whom the Son chooses to reveal him" (Mt 11: 27).

However, Jesus is more than a prophet. He is the *Master* (*Rabbi, didaskalos*) who teaches with his own authority, because he is Man and God in a personal unity (cf. Mt 7: 29; Jn 13: 13). This authority, shown by Christ when he teaches, is strongly expressed in the words "I say to you" (cf. Mt 5: 22, 28, 39; Jn 8: 51).[49] That is why *in Christo Deus docet immediate*[50]; Christ's words are the *human words of God*.

Another aspect of Christ's prophetic function that manifests its plenitude is the following: Jesus is concurrently the One that teaches (Master) and the Truth that is taught. *He is the Truth* (cf. Jn 14: 6). Therefore, since he is the *Mediator* regarding the Truth (Master and Prophet), his mediation is perfect (being the fullness of prophetic mediation). This is true because it is the *most immediate possible mediation*: "In the mediator Christ we immediately find God."[51]

Finally, we ought to remember that Christ reveals not only with his human words, but also in himself with all his works: *gestis verbisque*.[52] Therefore, as we have already noted, simply to see Christ is to see the Father (cf. Jn 14: 9).

IV. The Fullness of Revelation and the Fullness of Time

Christ is the plenitude of revelation "because after him and above him there is no more to tell, because in him God has revealed himself."[53] Therefore, there will not be another revelation of God after Christ; the *new covenant is definitive*. "The Christian economy, therefore, since it is the new and definitive covenant, will never pass away; and no new public revelation is to be expected before the glorious manifestation of our Lord, Jesus Christ (cf. 1 Tm 6: 14; Ti 2: 13)."[54] The historical nature of revelation requires that the fullness of revelation entail a plenitude of history, in other words, *a plenitude of times*.

In the New Testament, two of the terms used that relate to temporality are particularly relevant to the matter under consideration. The first is *kronos* (similar to the Hebrew *eth*), which points to *time* generically without a special meaning, what we could call *quantitative time*, or simple duration. Secondly, we have *kairos* (similar to the Hebrew *zemán*), which means "opportune time," or "propitious occasion." This is what we could call *qualitative time*.[55] Naturally, we are not talking about two "types" of time, but two ways of considering time. For instance, in St. Paul's writings, *kronoi* are generally periods of time between two *kairoi*. *Kairoi* are understood as the moments when God intervenes in history in a special way. Therefore, considering time in a "quantitative" or "qualitative" way, Christ determines the "fullness of time," the fullness of history.

When Christ began his public life he said, "The time is fulfilled [*peplérotai ho kairos*]" (Mk 1: 15). Because *kairos* means "qualitative time" (*opportune* time), we can understand this text and others accordingly (i.e., Eph 1: 10), not merely in a strictly literal sense (i.e., the opportune moment has come for the beginning of the public presentation of Christ). We can also understand these writings in the sense that with the Incarnation, qualitative time has reached its plenitude (*peplérotai*). The different *kairoi*, or concrete moments of the special intervention of God in history, have been completely fulfilled.[56]

Accordingly, the Incarnation stands as the *central point of history* in the precise sense that it determines a *qualitative* line of demarcation between "the new" and "the old." In Christ, all human history acquires its *center*: the past is oriented and has meaning in him, and the future after Christ draws its meaning and value with regard to him.[57] *Christ is the center of history* because in him the Incarnation of divine eternity in human time has been carried out, conferring to time a transcendental quality: the foundation of the past and the future. Christ is "the Alpha and the Omega, the beginning and the end" (Rv 21: 6). In other words, the coming of Christ represents the fullness of time because this event determines the center of history in a qualitative sense.

Christ's fulfillment of history has another meaning. We have shown that he determines the "plenitude of quantitative time." In fact, "the time had fully come" (Gal 4: 4). Although the literal sense seems to indicate that the period of time or duration that the Father established for the preparation of the Incarnation has reached its end,[58] we can also say that the "plenitude of quantitative time" means the fulfillment of time that has reached its end. Then, in what sense should we say that the Incarnation is the end of time (the end of history)?

Christ's fulfillment of chronological history (quantitative time) obviously does not mean that history ended twenty centuries ago. Rather, it means that *every historical moment after the Incarnation sees Christ as the present, not the past*. In fact, "Jesus Christ is the same yesterday and today and for ever" (Heb 13: 8). *This contemporaneity* of Christ with every historical time after the Incarnation is not only that of Christ in his glorious state because he lives forever, but also the contemporaneity of the mysteries of his life, Death, and glorification truly present in the mysterious (sacramental) life of the Church.

It might seem, therefore, that *the time of the Church*, considered as the end of history, would have to remain undefined forever. However, in reality we know that history will have "another end." This will be the end of time when the Lord will come again in the *Parousía*, and it will represent an undeniable novelty for the whole creation. But, this eschatological novelty will not be an essentially new one.

In the explanation and spreading of this interpretation of history, Christ is the *center and the end* in the previously mentioned sense (a center that has a conclusive character but is not yet at its end). Oscar Cullmann has made an important contribution to our understanding of these issues, particularly by means of his *Christus und die Zeit* (1946) and *Heil als Geschichte* (1964).

Cullmann viewed the historical centrality of Christ as a key moment of movement in a series of *progressive reductions*: creation-mankind-people of Israel-remainder of Israel-Christ-Apostles-Church-mankind-creation.[59]

Cullmann illustrated the ultimately conclusive character of this series of terms by means of an apt analogy, saying:

> In a war, the decisive battle could be held in the course of one of the first stages of the campaign, nevertheless, hostilities go for a long time yet.... This is exactly the situation in which we find

the believer *vis-à-vis* the New Testament. Revelation proclaims the fact that Christ has won the battle of universal salvation by means of his death on the cross, followed by his glorious Resurrection. The believer, therefore, has a certitude of faith that allows him to enjoy the results of this victory, to in some fashion participate in the sovereignty of God over time.[60]

Cullmann's work acts as a vigorous challenge to the Bultmannian thesis, for Cullmann emphasized the essential importance of historical facts in revelation and salvation. Cullmann and Bultmann disagree as to whether or not one can reduce salvific-historical events to myths. Some Protestant errors prevent Cullmann from being clear on this question. For example, in the above quoted text, one can observe a certain reduction of revelation to a simple event with some forgetfulness of the noetic essential dimension of the Word of God.

CHAPTER 3

REVELATION AND THE CHURCH

Having studied how God communicates with men through his incarnate Word, we shall now see how divine revelation is preserved and transmitted through time. Christ has entrusted this mission to the Church: "Go therefore and make disciples of all nations, baptizing them in the name of the Father and of the Son and of the Holy Spirit, teaching them to observe all that I have commanded you; and lo, I am with you always, to the close of the age" (Mt 28: 19–20). This teaching mission implies a special authority and assistance given to the Church.

I. The Transmission of Revelation in the Church and by the Church

A causal relationship exists between revelation and the Church. On the one hand, the Church is engendered by the Word of God; on the other hand, even though the Church does not "produce" revelation, she manifests it to people of all times. She guards and interprets revelation with authority from Christ. Before studying this inter-relationship, we need to consider the event that essentially predetermines it: Revelation ended with the death of the apostles.

A. Revelation Ended with the Apostles

From the fundamental reality that Christ is the plenitude of revelation, it logically follows—as was previously mentioned—that "the Christian economy, it is the new and definitive covenant, which will never pass away; and no new public revelation is to be expected before the glorious manifestation of our Lord, Jesus Christ (cf. 1 Tm 6: 14; Ti 2: 13)."[1]

Revelation has come to us through the testimony of the apostles, to whom Christ transmitted the mission of announcing the Gospel to all nations (cf. Mt 28: 19–20).

Nevertheless, the apostles did not receive the plenitude of this revelation before the Ascension of Jesus. In fact, the Lord told them, "I have yet many things to say to you, but you cannot bear them now. When the Spirit of truth comes, he will guide you into all the truth; for he will not speak on his own authority, but whatever he hears he will speak, and he will declare to you the things that are to come. He will glorify me, for he will take what is mine and declare it to you" (Jn 16: 12–14). Therefore, following the Ascension, revelation continued until the death of the apostles without compromising the truth that Christ is the plenitude of revelation.

The Holy Spirit's special assistance to the apostles—assistance that we can call "constitutive" of revelation—is a characteristic that is proper and exclusive to the *apostolic times*. In fact, it has been understood thus since the beginning of the Church: "The apostles, in handing on what they themselves had received, warn the faithful to maintain the traditions that they had learned either by word of mouth or by letter (cf. 2 Thes 2: 15); and warned them to fight hard for the faith that had been handed on to them once and for all (cf. Jud 3)."[2] This text clearly says *hapax paradotheisé*, the Latin translation of which is not only *semel traditae* (delivered at only one time) but *semel pro semper traditae* (delivered once and forever).[3]

The fact that there is no other revelation after the apostles leads St. Paul, inspired by God, to speak about the contents of revelation as a *deposit* (*parathéké*) (cf. 1 Tm 6: 20; 2 Tm 1: 14). It is as something delivered to someone in order to preserve and guard it.[4]

During patristic times there was no shortage of voices promoting the existence of new "revelations" that needed to be added to the apostolic tradition; voices that the Fathers fought firmly against, especially St. Irenaeus.[5] The comment of St. Vincent of Lerins about the text of 1 Timothy 6: 20 is well known. He emphasizes that we have received the *depositum* through public transmission. We are not its authors but its guardians.[6]

Moreover, the universal Magisterium of the Church has stated on several occasions that there is no public revelation other than that transmitted by the apostles.[7] In this regard, we would do well to remember, the condemnation in the decree *Lamentabili* of the modernist thesis that claims that revelation was not completed with the apostles.[8]

B. The Church: Summoned and Engendered by the Word of God

The Church primarily originates in God the Father, who sent his Son to the world to be the Redeemer of men and head of the Church, whose members are incorporated into him through the work of the Holy Spirit. According to the well-known words of St. Cyprian, we say that the Church of God, the Church of Christ, is "a people united by the unity of the Father, of the Son and of the Holy Spirit" (*de unitate Patris et Filii et Spiritus Sancti plebs adunata*).[9]

This divine action of the foundation of the Church has been carried out in Christ and through Christ. We will not discuss here arguments concerning Christ's will to found the Church.[10] Nevertheless, it is interesting to remember that during Jesus' life, there is neither a time nor a concrete and determined act that can be considered the moment of the foundation of the Church. From a radical point of view, we might say that the Church, as a mystery, was born at the moment of the Incarnation. Yet, we can state that in its visible reality as the new people of God, Jesus gradually founded the Church until the arrival of the Holy Spirit in Pentecost.

> For the Lord Jesus inaugurated his Church by preaching the Good News, that is, the coming of the kingdom of God, promised over the ages in the scriptures: "The time is fulfilled, and the kingdom of God is at hand" (Mk 1: 15; cf. Mt 4: 17). This kingdom shone out before men in the word, in the works and in the presence of Christ.... When Jesus, having died on the cross for men, rose again from the dead, he was seen to be constituted as Lord, the Christ, and as Priest for ever (cf. Acts 2: 36; Heb 5: 6; 7: 17–21), and he poured out on his disciples the Spirit promised by the Father (cf. Acts 2: 33).[11]

In this way, the process of the foundation of the Church coincides with the fulfillment of the plenitude of revelation. The Church is summoned and engendered by the words and human actions of Christ—these are words and human actions of God:

> The word of Christ that initiates the apostles into the secrets of the Father founds the Church, giving her also the three powers of preaching, sanctifying and governing. The word of Christ conferred upon the apostles the mission of inviting men to faith and of incorporating them by means of Baptism into the society of the Father and the Son in one and the same Spirit.... In a certain way, we can, therefore, state that the Word summons and engenders the Church.[12]

The causal relationship between the Word and the Church is reflected in the name *ekklésia*, derived from *ekkalein* (to summon). It is also shown through the names used to name Christians in the New Testament, such as *kletoi* ("called," 1 Cor 1: 24; Rom 1: 6–7; Rv 17: 14) and *ekklektoi* ("the chosen," cf. Rom 8: 33; Col 3: 12; 2 Tm 2: 10).

This announcement and the generation of the Church by the Word is a constant reality. It belongs to the initial implantation carried out immediately by Christ. This is seen with utmost clarity, for instance, in the birth of the different local churches in apostolic times (cf., i.e., Acts 2: 41–42; 8: 12–14; 2 Cor 3: 3; Eph 1: 13). The expansion of the

Church coincides with the spreading of the Word: "The word of God grew and multiplied" (Acts 12: 24); "the word of the Lord spread throughout all the region" (Acts 13: 49).[13]

When we say that the Church is summoned and engendered by the Word of God, it is obvious that we are using the expression "Word of God" in its fullest sense: not just to express its noetic contents, but also to express it as being an efficacious force for transforming reality. It is not, therefore, the simple "exterior preaching" of the gospel that generates the Church, but this preaching combined with the interior action of the Holy Spirit, which leads to faith and to the sacraments of faith (cf. Mt 28: 19–20; Mk 16: 15–16; Acts 2: 38; Rom 10: 14ff.).[14]

C. The Church Presents the Word of God to Men

"God graciously arranged that the things he had once revealed for the salvation of all peoples should remain in their entirety, throughout the ages, and be transmitted to all generations."[15] This transmission of Divine Revelation is accomplished in the Church by means of Sacred Tradition and Sacred Scripture.

1. Tradition and Scripture

The apostolic preaching, which is expressed in a special way in the inspired books, was to be preserved by an unending succession of preachers until the end of time. Therefore the Apostles, handing on what they themselves had received, warn the faithful to hold fast to the traditions which they have learned either by word of mouth or by letter (see 2 Thes 2: 15), and to fight in defense of the faith handed on once and for all (see Jud 3) (First Vatican Council, Dogmatic Constitution on the Catholic Faith, Chap. 3, "On Faith:" Denzinger 1789 (3008)). Now what was handed on by the Apostles includes everything which contributes toward the holiness of life and increase in faith of the peoples of God; and so the Church, in her teaching, life and worship, perpetuates and hands on to all generations all that she herself is, all that she believes.[16]

This transmission, or *tradition* (*paradosis*), of revelation has, therefore, as its object (*obiectum traditum*) the entire reality of Christianity. The gospel is understood not only as an announcement or word, but as saving force according to St. Paul's assertion: The gospel is the force of God (*dynamis theou*) to save all believers (cf. Rom 1: 16).

The whole Church is the subject of Tradition (*subiectum tradens*) accomplished (*actus tradendi*) by the whole life of the Church, which we can, therefore, summarize in *Traditio evangelii*, which has as its constitutive dimensions the preaching of the Word and sacramental celebration.[17]

The term *Tradition* (*Paradosis*), aside from the wide sense of *transmission*—which corresponds to its etymological meaning—has a restricted sense in theology: It is the *oral transmission* of revelation made by the apostles and continued in many ways (including writing) from generation to generation in the Church. This apostolic preaching was put into writing, with the inspiration of the Holy Spirit, in the books of the New Testament.[18] In other words, Divine Revelation, transmitted by the apostles, comes to us by means of Sacred Scripture and Sacred Tradition (understood in a strict sense).[19]

Unquestionably, "the Sacred Scriptures are the preeminent documents of apostolic preaching. Due to the cause and virtue of divine inspiration, they have a 'special title' of quality, unique in its gender, which confers to the sacred books a privileged and irreplaceable function in the transmission of revelation."[20] In fact, the inspired books are the Word of God themselves, not merely human writings narrating the apostolic preaching (as in the case of the post-apostolic texts). "Everything asserted by the inspired authors or sacred writers must be held to be asserted by the Holy Spirit."[21]

Therefore, the temporal priority of Tradition above Sacred Scripture does not exclude the latter's preeminence in the above sense. Additionally, the existence of Scripture does not exclude the need for Tradition, not only for the purpose of knowing which books are inspired by God, but also for the transmission of the whole Divine Revelation. In this sense, we speak about *Traditio interpretativa* when Tradition transmits something that is already contained in the Bible. If it is explicitly stated in Scripture, the interpretative Tradition is named *Traditio declarativa*; if it is only implicitly contained, then we speak about *Traditio inhaesiva*. Tradition is considered *constitutive* when it transmits what is in no way contained in the inspired books.[22] In reality, the existence or nonexistence of revealed truths that are not stated in Scripture is a question that is open to many theological opinions. In any case, Sacred Scripture and Sacred Tradition are so intimately and essentially linked that by studying their reciprocal relationship, one can reach a complete knowledge of Scripture and Tradition.

An essential characteristic of Tradition is that it is a *living* reality. In fact, as explained by the Second Vatican Council:

> The Tradition that comes from the apostles makes progress in the Church, with the help of the Holy Spirit. There is a growth in insight into the realities and words that are being passed on. This comes about in various ways. It comes through the contemplation and study of believers who ponder these things in their hearts (cf. Lk 2: 19, 51). It comes from the intimate sense of spiritual realities that they experience. And it comes from the preaching of those who have received, along with their right of succession in the episcopate, the sure charism of truth. Thus, as the centuries go by, the Church is always advancing toward the plenitude of divine truth, until eventually the words of God are fulfilled in her.[23]

Tradition, therefore, is not a simple repetition; it is something that "advances" (*proficit*). Although Revelation has ended, the interpretation that gives it its meaning has not been closed: "'Revelation' has finished, but not its binding interpretation."[24]

We have before us, therefore, authentic intellectual *progress*, but the progress is in the understanding of the *depositum* because what progresses is "the Tradition of apostolic origin;" "Nothing can exist that does not derive from the apostles. Nothing should be taken away from what they have handed on."[25]

Therefore, revelation, completed and concluded with the deaths of the apostles, comes to people of all times, not as a simple remembrance of the past, but as a living and operative reality as Christ lives and operates in his Church: "Lo, I am with you always, to the close of the age" (Mt 28: 20).

For every person, Revelation is the Word of God that communicates knowledge and salvation. So it is today; Revelation is for everyone a *personal encounter* with the God who saves. This encounter takes place *in the Church* because it is the Church, and not individuals as such, to whom Christ has entrusted the Word of God: "The doctrine of the faith which God has revealed is put forward…as a divine deposit committed to the spouse of Christ."[26] "Sacred Tradition and Sacred Scripture make up a single sacred deposit of the Word of God, which is entrusted to the Church."[27]

Tradition is, in this sense, the whole life of the Church. Obviously, not every manifestation of this life or every doctrine that may be found in the Church's past belongs to Tradition. This means that not everything that is said or done (and has been said or done) in Christian communities is of apostolic origin and therefore, binding for the Church herself. The Church has *criteria of Tradition*. The fundamental criteria were summarized by St. Vincent of Lerins in the fifth century: universality, antiquity, and unanimity.[28]

One may determine whether or not a doctrine fulfills these characteristics in the *Magisterium of the Church*, the teachings of the *Fathers of the Church*, the *liturgy*, and the *common opinion of the faithful*.[29]

Ecclesiastical writers are named *Fathers of the Church* by meeting these characteristics: orthodox doctrine, holiness, antiquity, and approval of the Church.[30] The teachings of the Fathers constitute a privileged testimony of Tradition because of their antiquity and proximity to the apostolic times. In the words of the Second Vatican Council, "the sayings of the Holy Fathers are a witness to the life-giving presence of this Tradition."[31]

Naturally, not all statements of the Fathers on matters of faith are expressions of apostolic Tradition. In order to recognize them as such, these statements need to have the moral unanimity of the other Fathers. Such moral unanimity can also be recognized based on the concordance of a small number of the Fathers if they had much authority and influence in the Church. In some cases, even the testimony of one Father may constitute a sure criterion of Tradition if he exercised a significant role in developing that issue. For instance, this is the case of St. Anastasius with regard to the doctrine of the Trinity, and St. Cyril of Alexandria with regard to Christological matters.[32] Finally, recalling that the primary and fundamental function of Tradition is the interpretation of Sacred Scripture, the Church considers as infallible the unanimous *consensus Patrum* in their interpretation of biblical texts.[33]

2. Tradition and the Magisterium

The totality of the Church, which has received the deposit of revelation, lives from it and transmits it from the beginning. Nevertheless, the apostles, who had a particular and more intense knowledge of the mystery of Christ (cf. Mt 13: 11; 16: 18; Mk 9: 31) received from the Lord the special mission of preaching the gospel: "All authority in heaven and on earth has been given to me. Go therefore and make disciples of all nations" (Mt 28: 18–19).

In addition to the permanent assistance of the Lord in the exercise of their mission, the apostles also received the help of the Holy Spirit (cf. Jn 14: 15–17; 15: 26; 16: 13). Further, among the apostles, Peter received the special mission of *confirming his brothers* (cf. Lk 22: 32).[34]

The apostles faithfully carried out their teaching function (*magisterium*) (cf. Acts 2: 32; 5: 14) with an *authority recognized* from the start in the primitive community of disciples, who "devoted themselves to the apostles' teaching" (Acts 2: 42).

This mission was later transmitted by the apostles to their successors (cf. Acts 20: 25–27; 2 Tm 4: 6; Ti 1: 5). Thus, the Second Vatican Council explained: "That divine mission, entrusted by Christ to the apostles, will last until the end of the world (cf. Mt 28: 20), since the Gospel they are to teach is for all time the source of all life for the Church. And for this reason the apostles, appointed as rulers in this society, took care to appoint successors."[35] The episcopal order, which is constituted by the bishops (the successors of the apostles), carries out this apostolic succession. The bishops are *subject* within the magisterial function of the Church, which is carried out in communion with the successor of Peter, the Roman pontiff.[36]

Even though all members of the Church have the mission to transmit the gospel, *authenticity* is a fundamental and exclusive characteristic of the episcopal Magisterium: "But the task of giving an authentic interpretation of the Word of God, whether in its written form or in the form of Tradition, has been entrusted to the living teaching office of the Church alone."[37]

The exclusive teaching authority of the Church in the *authentic* interpretation of the Word of God does not mean that others cannot interpret revelation in an "authentic way," if we understand authentic as "genuine," "according to the truth." It is obvious, for instance, that theologians have carried out and may carry out valuable and genuine interpretation of Sacred Scripture and Tradition. Actually, the *authenticity* that is exclusive and proper to the Magisterium lies in the Magisterium's function of interpreting revelation according to *authority*. It means that "the authentic Magisterium has authority," but not the simple authority of one who "possesses a science" ("scientific authority") but the same *authority of Christ*.[38] This authority, therefore, obliges the faithful in all conscience.[39] The Second Vatican Council is quite clear on this question: The bishops are *doctores authentici seu auctoritate Christi praediti* (authentic teachers, or rather, teachers endowed with the authority of Christ).[40]

The *authority* with which the Magisterium transmits and interprets the Word of God does not in any way imply that the Magisterium of the Church substitutes for the source of Revelation (God himself still speaking to men through Sacred Scripture and Tradition) as several contemporary Protestant authors have claimed.[41] The Second Vatican Council taught: "This Magisterium is not superior to the Word of God, but is its servant. It teaches only what has been handed on to it.

At the divine command and with the help of the Holy Spirit, it listens to this devotedly, guards it with dedication and expounds it faithfully."[42]

As has been mentioned before, the subjects of the Magisterium—the bishops—receive a *participation* in the same authority of Christ in the sacrament of holy orders, through which apostolic succession is carried out. Its authority is, therefore, of a sacramental-charismatic nature, not a scientific-human one, and its exercise depends upon the assistance of the Holy Spirit. Through episcopal orders, in fact, bishops receive their *carisma veritatis*.[43] Due to the divine nature of magisterial authority, the Church teaches that the Magisterium of the Church is infallible when it is fully exercised with an *infallibility* that participates in divine infallibility.

The proper *object* of the Magisterium is, therefore, the transmitted or written Word of God. This object is traditionally described in several ways pertaining to the contents that can be summarized in the following expression of patristic origin: *res fidei et morum*, matters of faith and morals.[44]

The authority of the Magisterium in the exposition and interpretation of the contents of the Word of God—that is, of revealed truths—also holds regarding other truths that, although they have not been explicitly revealed, are necessary in order to teach and defend revealed truth. It is the Church's duty to indicate the elements in a philosophical system which are incompatible with her own Faith. In fact, many philosophical opinions—concerning God, the human being, human freedom and ethical behaviour—engage the Church directly, because they touch on the revealed truth of which she is the guardian.[45] Thus, a distinction is drawn between *primary objects* of the Magisterium, which are *formally* revealed truths (explicitly or implicitly), and *secondary objects*, which are truths that are not contained in Revelation but are necessary to duly expose and defend the deposit of revelation. Some authors call these issues *virtually* revealed truths.[46]

The *modalities of exercise* of the Magisterium are manifold, but they can be summarized into two principal orders: the *ordinary Magisterium*, which is the individual teaching of each bishop, and the *solemn*

Magisterium, which is made up of the councils or the pope when he teaches *ex cathedra*.

The clear significance of this is that the magisterium is an integral part of the Church's Tradition; and, at the same time, the authentic means of interpreting this Tradition.

Tradition is the transmission not only of doctrine, but also of the whole reality of the Church. Consider again the words of the Second Vatican Council: "The Church, in her doctrine, life, and worship, perpetuates and transmits to every generation all that she herself is, all that she believes."[47] Thus, we must understand that the apostolic succession, from the apostles to the bishops and from St. Peter to the bishop of Rome, is a succession that obeys the will of Christ in his founding of the Church.[48] This is the sacramental form of Tradition and its unifying presence.[49]

Consequently, in the transmission of divine revelation, we find three intimately related realities: "Sacred tradition, Sacred Scripture and the teaching authority of the Church, in accord with God's most wise design, are so linked and joined together that one cannot stand without the others, and that all together and each in its own way under the action of the one Holy Spirit contribute effectively to the salvation of souls."[50]

D. The Apostolic Church and the Post-Apostolic Church

In the apostles' mission, there was an element that *could not be transmitted*. This element was the constitution of the *depositum* by the special assistance of the Holy Spirit that Christ promised to them. In that sense, regarding the revelation-Church relationship, there is a certain *discontinuity* between apostolic and post-apostolic time, between the apostolic and post-apostolic Church.

Protestant theology has argued that this discontinuity could justify the negation of the principle of Tradition in the post-apostolic Church. Consequently, a distinction has been drawn between the apostolic

Tradition, which we can reach only by Scripture, and the post-apostolic Tradition, which would be, therefore, a non-binding tradition.[51]

O. Cullmann advocated this Protestant theory of the discontinuity between the apostolic and the post-apostolic Church (between "the apostles' Church" and "the bishops' Church"). He claims that the discontinuity arises from the fact that the principle of Tradition, which the apostolic Church had been living, lost its validity with the birth of Scripture. According to Cullmann, the proof of this argument lies in the organization of the *biblical canon* by the same Church in the second century. "Upon establishing the *principle* of a canon, the Church has recognized that *from that moment on* tradition was not a criterion of truth anymore."[52]

History tells a different story. When the Church established the biblical canon, she did not find it expedient to expunge the principle of Tradition from her life. As a matter of fact, Tradition was one of her most valuable resources when recourse to Sacred Scripture did not seem sufficient to teach the full deposit of revelation.

Further, the recognition of the authority of the writings of the New Testament cannot be reduced to a special moment; rather, it is the product of the process of the transmission of the Church's living Tradition. This process does not pertain solely to the second century. In reality, from her earliest days (even during the lives of the apostles), the Church recognized an absolute authority in some writings that were considered "apostolic."[53]

The Church's fidelity to the apostolic faith ensures that the Church of all times is the *same* Church of Christ and the apostles. This fidelity, with the help of the Holy Spirit, is guaranteed by Scripture and, in an inseparable way, by Tradition (with the Magisterium as an interpreter of Tradition itself). Hence, the discontinuity between the apostolic and post-apostolic Church is not a total discontinuity. It is more a continuity than a discontinuity; *the apostolic and post-apostolic Church are the same*: the Church of Christ. They impart the same Revelation, the same Word of God that the apostles faithfully received from Christ and the Holy Spirit through a special charism (*inspiration*). The same Word resounds in the Church of all times due not only to Scripture, but also and inseparably to Tradition and the Magisterium.

Finally, it is interesting to observe that "the insistence about continuity, characterizing the Catholic vision about the transmission of revelation and the discontinuity, which is the basis of the Protestant position, belies a different way of reading the reality of salvation and its position in human history."[54]

In fact, the Catholic Faith recognizes that the Church is not only a "saved" but also a "saving" reality. The Church is not merely a "congregation" of those "saved directly by God." She is not merely an "occasion" for God to save man (with a salvation, moreover, that is only extrinsic) as Protestant thought tends to argue. The Church is "in Christ, is in the nature of sacrament—a sign and instrument, that is, of communion with God and of unity among all men."[55] In conclusion, "it is necessary to get used to the recognition of the Church as Christ himself. In fact, it is Christ who lives in his Church, who teaches through her, who governs and communicates sanctity."[56]

The fundamental reason to support the contradistinction (and not only the distinction) between Scripture and Tradition, between the gospel and the Church, between the apostolic and the post-apostolic Church, is the Protestant theologians' lack of knowledge of the *sacramentality* of the economy of salvation.

II. The Infallibility of the Church and Her Infallible Magisterium

Having recognized the Magisterium of the Church as an integrating element and interpretative authority of Tradition (at the same time inseparable from Scripture), we can examine the infallibility of the Magisterium as an aspect of the Church's general infallibility.

A. The Infallibility of the Church
"In credendo" and "In docendo"

> Advancing through trials and tribulations, the Church is strengthened by God's grace, promised to her by the Lord so that she may not waver from perfect fidelity, but remain the worthy bride of the Lord, ceaselessly renewing herself through the action of the Holy Spirit until, through the cross, she may attain to that light which knows no setting.[57]

This *perfect nature of the Church* promised by Christ after St. Peter's confession (cf. Mt 16: 16) means that the Church will always be what she already is. Christ promises continuity in her being and essence. This perfection includes, as an essential element, *perfect fidelity to the apostolic faith* guaranteed by the permanent assistance of the Holy Spirit, who is "the Spirit of truth" (Jn 14: 17; cf. Jn 14: 26). God, in fact, stipulated in his immense goodness that what had been revealed for the salvation of all people would remain thus constituted forever.[58]

The permanent integrity of revelation that is guaranteed by the assistance of the Holy Spirit refers to revelation inasmuch as it has been accepted and received by the Church through faith. Therefore, in the words of St. Thomas Aquinas, "it is impossible that the judgment of the universal Church may be mistaken regarding faith."[59]

The Church is infallible when *believing and professing faith*: "God himself, therefore, who is absolutely infallible, has wished to grant his new people, that the Church is, of a participated infallibility, circumscribed by the things referring to faith and morals."[60] This not only refers to a "fundamental" permanency in truth, which might be compatible with occasional errors, but to true and proper infallibility.[61] Certainly, each Christian can err in matters of faith, but the Church, as such, cannot err.[62]

In contrast to our universal experience of human fallibility, the idea of infallibility presents itself as something super-human—and it certainly is. Nevertheless, intelligence is infallible *per se in itself* because it is by nature attracted only to the truth,[63] and it is fallible *per accidens* (on occasion), especially when free will unduly influences the intellect.[64] Therefore, infallibility is not just a gift from the Omnipotent; it is also consistent with our created nature.

In addition to the infallibility of the Church *in credendo*, belonging to the faithful as a whole, we know that the Magisterium is infallible *in docendo*:

> Although the bishops, taken individually, do not enjoy the privilege of infallibility, they do, however, proclaim infallibly the doctrine of Christ on the following conditions: namely, when, even though dispersed throughout the world but preserving for all that amongst themselves and with Peter's successor the bond of communion, in their authoritative teaching concerning matters of faith and morals, they are in agreement that a particular teaching is to be held definitively and absolutely. This is still more clearly the case when, assembled in an ecumenical council, they are, for the universal Church, teachers of and judges in matters of faith and morals, whose decisions must be adhered to with the loyal and obedient assent of faith....
>
> The Roman Pontiff, head of the college of bishops, enjoys this infallibility in virtue of his office, when, as supreme pastor and teacher of all the faithful—who confirms his brethren in the faith (cf. Lk 22: 32)—he proclaims in an absolute decision a doctrine pertaining to faith or morals.[65]

In summary, there are *three manifestations of magisterial infallibility*: definitions of ecumenical councils, definitions of the Roman pontiff *ex cathedra*, and the teachings of the universal ordinary Magisterium.

This last manifestation or expression of the infallible Magisterium, although not solemn, is the most important in the sense that it is the most frequent, in that, it comprises the greatest part of the doctrine of the Church. In the words of John Paul II, "The universal ordinary Magisterium can truly be considered as a usual expression of the infallibility of the Church."[66]

The infallibility that God has given his Church is a *participated* infallibility,[67] that is to say, it has been *received* (from God) and it is *partial*. The partial character shows mainly in the limitation of the infallibility (referring only to faith and morals) and in the way that it is received (not by each member of the Church, but by the Church as a whole and by her Magisterium, but only under particular conditions).

B. The *"Sensus Fidei"* of the People of God and the Magisterium

> The whole body of the faithful who have an anointing that comes from the holy one (cf. 1 Jn 2: 20, 27) cannot err in matters of belief. This characteristic is shown in the supernatural appreciation of the faith (*sensus fidei*) of the whole people, when, "from the bishops to the last of the faithful" they manifest a universal consent in matters of faith and morals. By this appreciation of the faith, aroused and sustained by the Spirit of truth, the People of God, guided by the sacred teaching authority (*magisterium*), and obeying it, receives not the mere word of men, but truly the word of God (cf. 1 Thes 2: 13), the faith once for all delivered to the saints (cf. Jud 3). The People unfailingly adheres to this faith, penetrates it more deeply with right judgment, and applies it more fully in daily life.[68]

Neither Patristic nor Scholastic theology uses the expression *sensus fidei*.[69] Nevertheless, the reality that this expression signifies has always been understood and defended by the Church. Among the Fathers, St. Augustine is perhaps the one who resorted most frequently to the faith of Christian people to test some truths of faith.[70] At the beginning of some sessions of the Council of Trent (1545–1563), certain conciliar Fathers appealed to the faith of the Church.[71] Lastly, to quote another example, Pope Bl. Pius IX and Pius XII both made explicit references to the faith of the people of God as part of their respective arguments in the definitions of the dogmas of the Immaculate Conception and of the Assumption of the Virgin Mary.[72]

With the expression *sense of faith,* we are not just dealing with the capacity of the believer to believe in what is presented by the Church as truths of faith. We are also dealing with the believer's ability to discern—as if by instinct—what coincides with one's faith and what does not. We are also concerned with the ease of a believer growing in understanding of deeper consequences of truths taught by the Magisterium, not by the way of theological reasoning, but, spontaneously, by a sort of co-natural knowledge.[73] The virtue of faith (*habitus fidei*) produces a *co-natural manner* of the human spirit with revealed mysteries and makes it possible for supernatural truth to *attract* the intellect.[74]

Consequently, we can say that no new supernatural gift has been discovered with the expression *sensus fidei*. Rather, it merely identifies another way that the believer understands the already believed revealed truth thanks to the virtue of faith and the gifts of the Holy Spirit.[75]

In the aforementioned text of *Lumen gentium, the infallibility of the whole people of God* was assured; the entirety of the faithful *in credendo falli nequit* (cannot be deceived in their belief). This impossibility of error when believing is attributed to the *sensus fidei*. Similarly, the Council explicitly taught that the Holy Spirit is the direct cause of such infallibility; therefore, this is not a simple consequence of the infallibility of the Magisterium.

The distinction between the people of God and the Magisterium as two aspects of the infallibility of the Church is not a distinction between two completely different parties, because the subjects of the Magisterium (the bishops) are also part of the people of God.[76] On the other hand, the group of this people is infallible not only because a part of it (the group of bishops and the pope alone) has the charism of infallibility *in docendo* but because everyone (the pope, the bishops, and the rest of the faithful) has the supernatural *sensus fidei.*

At the same time we have to add, as the Second Vatican Council also affirmed, that the faith of the people of God is arrived at "under the guidance of the Magisterium" (*sub ductu magisterii*). Hence, the distinction between the people of God and the Magisterium as subjects

of the infallibility of the Church does not render them completely independent of each other.

Another important concept, shown in *Lumen gentium*, is the distinction between *sensus fidei* and *consensus fidelium*. The infallibility of the
sense of faith is manifested when belief that a truth belongs to faith is
verified (that is, moral unanimity of the faithful).

Therefore—although the terminology has not always been uniform—
we ought to say that *sensus fidei*, understood as characteristic of the
ordinary faithful, is in itself infallible, as infallible as faith itself.[77] Still,
individual members of the faithful can make mistakes, to the extent
that *per accidens* their *sensus fidei* can be obstructed, mainly by a defect
of the will.[78] In contrast, when a true *consensus fidelium* exists, we are
undoubtedly witnessing an authentic manifestation of the *sensus fidei*
inspired by the Holy Spirit.

In the case of truths taught infallibly by the Magisterium, the infallibility of the *sensus fidei* of the people of God means that assent must be
given by the faithful to these truths.[79]

The infallibility of the *sensus fidei* manifested by *consensus fidelium*
also exists when considering truths not yet proclaimed infallibly by
the Magisterium. According to the Second Vatican Council, the people
of God in its entirety simply cannot err when believing in such a manner. In this case, *consensus fidelium* is a true criterion of truth because
it is *criterium divinae Traditionis*.[80] In this case, the relationship of this
consensus to the Magisterium is clear: When the sacred Magisterium
is the only authentic and infallible interpreter of Tradition,[81] only this
Magisterium can infallibly judge if the *consensus fidelium* authentically exists, that is to say, if a moral unanimity in the Church regarding certain truths exists. However, *consensus fidelium* as an expression
of the infallibility of the *sensus fidei* inspired by the Spirit of truth is
also accomplished in this case *sub ductu magisterii*. Here, the *sensus fidei* receives the Magisterium's teachings as the Word of God, deepens
awareness of them, and applies them to life with more plenitude.[82]

Clearly, there is a unique infallibility in the Church, which all members participate in an organic and differentiated way. Each person acts

according to his own ecclesiastical role. Together, the members constitute an *organic* infallibility, as organic as the Church herself.[83]

C. Extension of the Infallibility of the Church

The matters that fall under the jurisdiction of the Magisterium's infallibility are identical to the matters that fall under the jurisdiction of Magisterium properly considered, the authentic Magisterium.[84]

In fact, there is no reason to attribute a different jurisdiction than that of the infallible Magisterium to matters considered by the non-infallible authentic Magisterium. A diversity of the jurisdiction of infallibility is never asserted either in Revelation or by the Magisterium. Moreover, the distinction between the simply authentic (non-infallible) Magisterium and the infallible Magisterium has never been dependent on the object of the teachings, only on the subjects and the way these teachings have been imparted.

Interestingly enough, the discussions that took place during the First Vatican Council about papal infallibility did not define its limits. On the contrary, the Council proclaimed the formula *doctrina de fide vel moribus* (doctrine regarding faith or morals), a terminology that had long been used to describe, in general, the issues dealt with by the Magisterium.[85] Moreover, the First Vatican Council proclaimed a definition of infallibility,[86] stating that the Magisterium can infallibly teach the truths "contained in the deposit of expressed faith or implicitly or by essential and necessary connection."[87]

Looking at the texts of Vatican II, it is very significant that the Council, in its constitution *Dei Verbum*, describes the jurisdiction of the authentic Magisterium with words equivalent to those used in the constitution *Lumen gentium* to describe the jurisdiction of infallibility. Both texts assert that the jurisdiction is the revealed (transmitted) truth and all that is necessary for the holy guarding and faithful transmission of these truths.[88]

In fact, *Lumen gentium* asserts, "This infallibility with which the Divine Redeemer willed His Church to be endowed in defining doctrine of faith and morals, extends as far as the deposit of Revelation extends, which must be religiously guarded and faithfully expounded."[89] The Theological Commission of the Council provided an official explanation of this text, declaring that the jurisdiction of matters of infallibility extends to the revealed deposit and to what is necessary to properly guard and transmit this deposit.[90]

Therefore, it is a *truth of faith* that the Magisterium of the Church can infallibly teach the truths contained in Revelation. Further, it pertains to *Catholic doctrine* that this possible infallibility extends also to non-revealed truths when their teaching is necessary to expound and defend the revealed truth in an adequate manner.[91]

This authentic interpretation of the text of *Lumen gentium* regarding the possible jurisdiction of the infallible Magisterium is obviously and *a fortiori* applicable to the text of *Dei Verbum* regarding the possible object of the authentic Magisterium.

Additionally, we cannot fail to take into account that the Magisterium is authentic when it teaches *with the authority of Christ*.[92] This authority is precisely the basis of infallibility—conferred by the sacrament of holy orders, subject to the assistance of the Holy Spirit, and exercised in the hierarchical communion.[93] This authority can be exercised on different levels depending on the matter at hand and the modalities of the Magisterium, but not on the issue being taught (naturally, whenever it relates to faith and morals).

In recent years, there has been some confusion about this important issue. For instance, many people have come to believe that particular or specific norms of natural morals are not a possible object of the infallible Magisterium, despite the fact that they are a possible object of the authentic Magisterium.[94] Based on the above discussion of infallibility, it is clear that such a generalized opinion ought to be discarded. In fact, if the Church has the authority to teach (with binding authority for the faithful) about a specific issue, then she can also teach infallibly about it. Of course, she does not always exercise this power. As we have seen, the

Magisterium is capable of studying and deepening the truth, although the conditions for the Magisterium to exercise to the highest degree the authority received from Christ do not always exist.[95]

III. Immutability and Development of Dogmas

The Greek word *dogma* can mean opinion, doctrine, decree, or legal prescription. For instance, in the New Testament, we find this word used to name a decree issued by Caesar Augustus (cf. Lk 2: 1), the decisions (plural, *dogmata*) of the apostles in the Council of Jerusalem (cf. Acts 16: 4), and the prescriptions of Mosaic law (cf. Eph 2: 15). In Christian language, the word *dogma* was, for a long time, also used in a wider sense to indicate the doctrine of the Church in general. It seems that Melchor Cano, in his work *De locis theologicis* (AD 1563) was the first to employ the word *dogma* in a more restricted sense: to designate a truth revealed by God and defined as such by the Church. A definition of *dogma* in this sense is found in P.N. Chrismann's work *Regula Fidei et collectio dogmatum credendorum in* (AD 1792).[96]

A. Dogma and its Immutability

The Magisterium of the Church, particularly from the First Vatican Council forward, has used this restricted sense of the word *dogma*: "All those things are to be believed which are contained in the word of God as found in Scripture and tradition, and which are proposed by the Church as matters to be believed as divinely revealed, whether by her solemn judgment or in her ordinary and universal magisterium."[97]

Thus, a *dogma* is a revealed truth infallibly taught by the Church. An infallibly taught truth that is not part of revelation is not called dogma. Taking into consideration that, in practice, when the existence of the universality of the ordinary Magisterium in referring to a specific truth cannot be absolutely clear, the category *dogma* is usually reserved to revealed truths and infallible dogmatic definitions of popes or ecumenical councils.

The fact that the technical use of the word *dogma* is of recent origin in the history of the Church does not mean that the reality it designates is of recent origin. Since apostolic times, the Church has been conscious of definitive and binding doctrinal teachings of faith such as the primitive creeds and the doctrinal canons of the first ecumenical councils.[98]

The notion of dogma is of *divine character*. Dogma, in its specific literal formulation, comes from the Church (pope, council, etc.), but as truth, it comes from revelation and, therefore, directly from God. This assertion, so obvious for one who understands revelation, is nevertheless, more problematic for someone who has a mistaken notion of revelation. This was the case, for instance, at the beginning of the twentieth century when authors called *modernists*, beginning from an immanent concept of revelation, reduced this understanding to a merely human religious experience. They considered dogmas of the Church expressions of human interpretation of religious phenomena. Pope St. Pius X condemned their teachings in the decree *Lamentabili*.[99]

The very notion of dogma implies the *content of truth*, that is, the expression of a true intellectual knowledge. Modernism denied this essential characteristic of dogma, particularly in E. Le Roy's *practical notion* of dogma. Dogmas, according to Le Roy, are not expressions of faith as intellectual knowledge of realities independent from man, but only expressions of practical norms of human behavior derived from religious experience. For instance, according to him, the value of the Christological dogma is only that it indicates that Christians must be related to Christ as with an incarnate divine Person. The value of the eucharistic dogma lies in the faithful's relationship with Christ as really present in this sacrament.[100] According to this concept, dogmas have binding force for the intellect only in a negative way, inasmuch as they compel one to refuse a speculative elaboration of dogmas that are incompatible with the *practical norm*.[101] The Church, however, has condemned this *practical-oriented* conception of dogmas.[102]

The bond between the teaching on dogma and the teaching on infallibility is so essential that when infallibility is denied, the correct understanding of the truth-affirming value of dogma is also affected.[103]

In the face of recent errors about issues, the Congregation for the Doctrine of the Faith, with Paul VI's approval, declared:

> The very sense of dogmatic formulas remains in the Church, truthful and coherent in itself, even when this sense is clarified and more completely understood. Therefore, the faithful should reject the opinion that, firstly, maintains that dogmatic formulas (or some of them) cannot signify the truth in a specific way, but only in its changing approaches, that they are, in a certain way, deformations and modifications of them. The faithful should not believe that said formulas manifest the truth only in an imprecise way, which (the truth) has to still be realized. He who embraces such an opinion cannot escape from dogmatic relativism and will undermine the concept of the infallibility of the Church, a truth that has to be taught and maintained in a specific way.[104]

From the content of the truth of dogmas and the definitive (infallible) character of magisterial acts by which dogmas have been proposed, the *immutability* of dogmas follows logically. So taught the First Vatican Council, saying, "Hence, too, that meaning of the sacred dogmas is ever to be maintained which has once been declared by holy mother Church, and there must never be any abandonment of this sense under the pretext or in the name of a more profound understanding."[105]

Nevertheless, inasmuch as the divine truth, because of its transcendent nature, surpasses all human comprehension and expression, the immutability of dogmas does not mean that the Church cannot reach a deeper comprehension of the corresponding truths. In other words, a dogma can be formulated through time in a more complete or clearer way.

Still, this development in the knowledge and formulation of dogmas does not imply a change in their basic meanings. The First Vatican Council made special note of this, employing the famous quotation from St. Vincent of Lerins.[106] Therefore, even when the Church reaches a more complete or clearer knowledge and formulation of a specific dogma, the preceding formulation has been and will always be true. Hence, "we have to say that dogmatic *formulas* of the Magisterium of the Church have adequately communicated the revealed truth from the beginning, and they are still adequate to communicate the truth to those who properly interpret them."[107]

B. Dogmatic Development in the Church

The existence of dogmatic development is a well-established fact in modern Church history. There are more dogmas in the Church than there were in past centuries. For examples we need only think about the dogmas of the Immaculate Conception and the Assumption of the Blessed Virgin Mary, defined by Pope Bl. Pius IX in 1854 and Pius XII in 1950, respectively. It is not only important to know that a specific dogma can become known and formulated in a better way by the Church; it is also significant that the group of dogmas is growing. The Church defines *new dogmas* with the passing of time.

We must mention the fact that divine origin is included in the very notion of dogma. New dogmas are not invented by the Church; they are necessarily truths revealed by God. Therefore, the dogmatic development is precisely the *development* of a reality (*deposit of faith, contents of revelation*), not the addition of new elements to this reality. In other words, new dogmas are truths contained in Revelation that the Church has not yet infallibly proposed as revealed.

Such dogmatic development can be seen in the dogmatic definition of a truth—that was always known as revealed and up to a given time was peacefully accepted within the Church—made to condemn error. Even this definition is simplistic. As history has shown repeatedly, dogmatic development is mainly due to the Church's progress in the knowledge of the contents of Revelation. This is easily understood if one remembers that the Tradition of the Church (of which the Magisterium is both a member and an interpretative institution with authority) is a living reality, growing and progressing. Tradition is not simply a repetitive transmission.

Naturally, the main factors of the development of dogmas also determine the progress of the living tradition of the Church, which the Second Vatican Council summarized as follows:

> This tradition which comes from the Apostles develop in the Church with the help of the Holy Spirit.[108] For there is a growth in the understanding of the realities and the words which have been handed down. This happens through the contemplation and study made by believers, who treasure these things in their hearts (see Lk 2: 19, 51) through a penetrating understanding of the spiritual realities which they experience, and through the preaching of those who have received through Episcopal succession the sure gift of truth. For as the centuries succeed one another, the Church constantly moves forward toward the fullness of divine truth until the words of God reach their complete fulfillment in her.[109]

In summary, there are three key factors in doctrinal development: contemplation and study of revealed truth (theological work obviously included), the *sensus fidei* of the people of God, and the preaching of shepherds of the Church with their peculiar *carisma veritatis* of sacramental origin.[110]

In different ways, theologians seek to deepen the understanding of the interrelationship of these factors and how they affect dogmatic development. They work to elaborate universal explanations of the issue. Among the theologians most distinguished by their explanations, Ven. John Henry Cardinal Newman[111] and Marín-Sola[112] particularly stand out.

Considering the nature of the factors of dogmatic development, a new dogma—even though it is a revealed truth—does not need to be deduced from Sacred Scripture or from previous dogmas through logical reasoning. In other words, dogmatic development, as the development of the Tradition upon which it is based, is not a purely rational process but wholly pertains to the sphere of faith and has the Holy Spirit as its primary activating principle.

C. Historicity and Permanent Value of Dogmatic Formulas

Dogmatic formulas, as linguistic formulas used by the Church to express dogmas, constitute a singularly important encounter between the faith of the Church and human language and culture.[113]

Any dogmatic formula is always valid in itself. "It must be stated that the dogmatic formulas of the Church's Magisterium were from the beginning suitable for communicating revealed truth, and that as they are they remain forever suitable for communicating this truth to those who interpret them correctly."[114]

This assertion of the enduring validity of dogmatic formulas is consistent with natural capacities. It assumes the capacity of human language to express objective truth. It also assumes that concepts and language are formed in the context of a natural human capacity to reach the truth, and not in the context of any particular philosophical system.

This is a complex theme to ponder, since one must examine the meaning which words assume in different times and cultures. Nonetheless, the history of thought shows that across the range of cultures and their development, certain basic concepts retain their universal epistemological, value and thus retain the truth of the propositions in which they are expressed.[115]

Furthermore, the teachings of the Church about the enduring validity of dogmatic formulas are fully consistent with cognitive realism, the reality of analogy, and the infallibility of the Church.[116]

In any event, the Church faces the challenge of communicating her dogmatic formulas through diverse and changing cultures and languages, although these formulas remain valid and immutable. As Pope Bl. John XXIII stated, "one thing is the same deposit of faith, that is, the truths contained in our doctrine, and another thing is the way they are stated, always preserving the same sense and the same meaning."[117]

At the opening of the Second Vatican Council, John XXIII referred to the perfectibility of the formulas that express faith and to the program of the Council regarding the exposition of doctrine in the most efficacious *pastoral* way.

This topic was taken up by the pastoral constitution *Gaudium et spes*, referring to the exposition of theologians, who were invited "to seek out more efficient ways...of presenting their teaching to modern man: for the deposit and the truths of the faith are one thing, the manner of expressing them is quite another."[118] Vatican II also confirmed the perfectibility of dogmatic formulas in its decree on ecumenism.[119]

Dogmatic formulas can be perfected as the Church comes to a more complete understanding of them, as was previously stated. This evolution of understanding refers to the dogmas themselves as well as to their development via the diversity and changes of human language. Consequently, we can see that dogmatic formulas have their own historicity and perfectibility.

The oldest dogmatic formulas are the *symbols of faith*, or *creeds*. These formulas were initially baptismal formulas, phrased as questions and answers ("Do you believe in God the Father...?"—"I believe..."). This primitive way of professing the faith has its origin in the word *symbol*, which is a more complete profession of the faith that is not in an interrogative form. As a matter of fact, *symbolon* derives from the verb *symballo*, meaning that it joins the two parts of a sign of mutual recognition between two persons. The symbol of faith (or creed) as questions and answers, therefore, constitutes a sign of recognition between believers. As a result, such symbols are essentially *ecclesiastical*, not just in their meaning but in their linguistic expression as well. Furthermore, symbols do not merely *manifest* a unity of faith; in some way they *produce* faith, as the expression "faith comes from what is heard [*fides ex auditu*]" (Rom 10: 17). These foundational dogmatic guidelines also apply to subsequent dogmatic formulas. This highlights the fact that the possible perfecting of formulas of faith is not—and cannot be—a private matter, but the *Church's task*.

At the same time, we must stress that perfecting formulas of the Faith is not a matter of adapting the presentation of the Christian message to any language. We cannot say, for example, that simply because in primitive and medieval Christendom the gospel was presented in the milieu of Greek culture and philosophy, that today the gospel must be presented in the milieu and language proper to modern culture and philosophy. From a historical standpoint, we should recognize that if this had been the ecclesiastical criterion of primitive Christian preaching, the Church would have assumed Nestorianism (more "translatable" to Greek philosophy than the dogma of Ephesus). Even earlier (in the second century) the Church would have communicated its dogmas via Gnostic thought.[120]

Without a doubt, many words used in dogmatic formulas come from the sphere of philosophy. As then Cardinal Ratzinger explained:

> After a long history of disputes between faith and philosophy, and after going beyond their prehistory and departing from it, they became specific expressions of what faith, questioned by human thought, can say about itself.... Therefore, these words are not merely Platonic, Aristotelian, or that of any other philosophy. They have become a part of the history of the proper language of faith that certainly must go on and indeed does go on. But we can say with certitude that this relationship will not be saved if the relationship with the past is severed.[121]

In this regard, Pius XII asserted that there are terms used by the Magisterium of the Church in the proposition of dogmas that cannot be abandoned without great damage to the faith.[122] Paul VI, building on the assertion of Pius XII, wrote, "These formulas, like the others which the Church uses to propose the dogmas of faith, express concepts which are not tied to a certain form of human culture, nor to a specific phase of human culture, nor to one or other theological school. No, these formulas present that part of reality which necessary and universal experience permits the human mind to grasp and to manifest with apt and exact terms taken either from common or polished language. For this reason, these formulas are adapted to men of all times and all places."[123]

Cognitive realism, therefore, requires the objectivity of faith and the permanent validity of dogmatic formulas as a starting point. It assumes an effort on the part of the believer to discern the *value of truth* found in cultures, languages and philosophies. Consequently, it is not possible to *translate* the Gospel either into a Hegelian language or into a Marxist one. If a certain culture lacks or misunderstands, for example, the concepts of *nature* or *person*, that culture needs to be enriched with these concepts. These concepts are necessary—because they answer to the truth of reality—to introduce the highest Christian mysteries—the Trinity and the Incarnation.

> It is certainly no problem whatsoever for the Church to consider that it is her duty, also taking into account the new ways of men's thinking, not to omit any effort so that these mysteries are more deeply understood through the contemplation of faith and the study of her theologians. Her mysteries need to be better explained and properly formulated over the course of time. Nevertheless, while the necessary investigation task is being carried out, it is important to be attentive so that those arcane mysteries should never be understood in a different way from the way the Church has understood and continues to understand them.[124]

In other words, we must keep in mind that the essence of Christian preaching is not the *adaptation* of the Gospel to cultures. Rather, it is the living transmission of the truth that saves, of the truth that purifies and infuses cultures with Christian values, of the truth that conveys a conceptual and linguistic enrichment wherever it is imparted.

D. The Interpretation of Dogmatic Formulas

> The transmission of Divine Revelation by the Church encounters difficulties of various kinds. These arise from the fact that the hidden mysteries of God "by their nature so far transcend the human intellect that even if they are revealed to us and accepted by faith, they remain concealed by the veil of faith itself and are as it were wrapped in darkness."[125] Difficulties arise also from the historical condition that affects the expression of

Revelation. With regard to this historical condition, it must first be observed that the meaning of the pronouncements of faith depends partly upon the expressive power of the language used at a certain point in time and in particular circumstances. Moreover, it sometimes happens that some dogmatic truth is first expressed incompletely (but not falsely), and at a later date, when considered in a broader context of faith or human knowledge, it receives a fuller and more perfect expression. In addition, when the Church makes new pronouncements she intends to confirm or clarify what is in some way contained in Sacred Scripture or in previous expressions of Tradition; but at the same time she usually has the intention of solving certain questions or removing certain errors. All these things have to be taken into account in order that these pronouncements may be properly interpreted. Finally, even though the truths which the Church intends to teach through her dogmatic formulas are distinct from the changeable conceptions of a given epoch and can be expressed without them, nevertheless it can sometimes happen that these truths may be enunciated by the Sacred Magisterium in terms that bear traces of such conceptions.[126]

It is not that these formulas, which go beyond the human intellect, will always be *perfectible* even though they are always valid in themselves. The issue is that they need to be correctly *interpreted*. The interpretation can be *authentic* (accomplished by the Magisterium itself), or simply *theological* (when it is theologians' work). As a matter of fact, the deepening in the truth taught by the Magisterium is one of the functions of theology and always entails, to a certain extent, the work of interpretation.

Among the criteria for the interpretation—*hermeneutic criteria*—of dogmatic formulas and, in general, of the teachings of the ecclesiastic Magisterium, we find the crucial need to consider each specific formula or specific teaching in its own context. There must be, first of all, a consideration of its place in the general context of all revealed truth (*analogia fidei*), then in its historical-doctrinal context. Many of the interventions of the solemn as well as the ordinary Magisterium have been intimately related to this context because the Church has been acting to confront errors in doctrinal analyses of specific historical moments. As the aforementioned *Mysterium Ecclesiae* shows, the conditioning of a specific culture affects the Church's expression of it to a certain extent.

Overall, the major or minor binding of Magisterial teachings to their historical-doctrinal and cultural context does not mean that such teachings are valuable only in a limited context. However, it is evident that the knowledge of the relevant historical context is useful—and sometimes necessary—in order to perceive the true meaning and scope of the proposed teaching.

The importance of this hermeneutic criterion is primarily observed in cases, not rare in the history of the Church, where it is found that if a magisterial text is taken literally and out of context it seems to oppose other teachings of the Magisterium in another epoch. This has happened particularly when there has been a *change in terminology used to indicate the same truth* or a *change in meaning of the terms*.

As an example of the second case, the Church's condemnation of the assertion that the Son is *consubstantial* to the Father stands out. According to the testimony of some of the Fathers such as St. Basil the Great, the Synod of Antioch issued this condemnation in AD 264.[127]

Not long afterwards, the Council of Nicea, in AD 325, apparently defined the opposite meaning in its creed: the Son is *consubstantial* with the Father.[128] It would seem that the Council of Nicea proclaimed exactly the opposite of the Synod of Antioch. But, if we consider the change that had taken place in the realm of doctrinal development, it is clear that the two teachings are identical in content and meaning. The Synod of Antioch condemned the term *consubstantial* as Paul of Samosata used it. Samosata used the term *consubstantiality* to mean that there was no real distinction between the two divine Persons of the Father and the Son. The historical-doctrinal situation, however, changed significantly over the next sixty years. The Church in the Council of Nicea was facing the grave Arian crisis. Under these circumstances, she hoped to use the term of *consubstantiality* of the Father and the Son to better define the true divinity of the Son as a person distinct from the Father.

At times we may find that when the terminology changes in meaning, the change reflects doctrinal development. This can pose a serious problem in determining the correct understanding of terms and texts. This has been the case, for instance, in the teachings of the Second Vatican Council about *religious freedom*. Prior to this Council, we can find many assertions about Church-state relations, made by the Magisterium and frequently repeated by the Roman pontiffs, that would seem to contradict the teachings of Vatican II and the contemporary Church on this issue. Yet, it is important to recall that this is not an easy question. We need to take a closer and deeper look at the relevant historical-doctrinal context of the various magisterial statements. Such a study shows that there is no contradiction, but, rather, doctrinal development.[129]

CHAPTER 4

THEOLOGICAL REFLECTION ON REVELATION

From all that we have studied to this point, it should be clear that there exists an intimate relationship between revelation, history, and salvation. In addition, these three realities find their utmost unity and fullness in Christ. We will now deal with some of the main aspects of this unity. Still, before we do, we should take a moment to reflect upon the notion of revelation and the nature of man's involvement in it.

I.   Revelation as the Communication of God in the Word

Relative to the historical development of Revelation and to the various terms used by Sacred Scripture to indicate revelation,[1] we have learned that *God gives the Word to men*. God becomes involved in human history as an efficacious Word. It is he who has a deep and transforming influence in the history of salvation.

A. The Essence and Characteristics of Historical Revelation

In the dogmatic constitution *Dei Filius* of Vatican I, we read that God wished "to reveal himself and the eternal laws of his will to the human race"[2] in a supernatural way. In Vatican Council II we find a similar assertion: "It pleased God, in his goodness and wisdom, to reveal himself and to make known the mystery of his will (cf. Eph 1: 9)."[3] The

Second Vatican Council, out of respect for the First Vatican Council, preferred the word *decree* over *mystery* (*sacramentum*) because the former sounded more biblical. In these magisterial assertions, *to reveal* is used with its direct meaning, which is "to disclose" or "to let what was secret and hidden before be known." The *object of this revelation* is God himself and the mystery of his will.

How was this revelation accomplished? We know the answer to this very well: through the *Word of God*. In fact, the text of *Dei Verbum* elaborates, saying, "By this revelation, then, the invisible God (cf. Col 1: 15; 1 Tm 1: 17), from the fullness of his love, addresses men as his friends (cf. Ex 33: 11; Jn 15: 14–15), and moves among them (cf. Bar 3: 37)."[4] Consequently, revelation is not an impersonal communication of truth but a *dialogue* or, at least, an invitation to a dialogue. It is a direct communication from God to people. Revelation has a precise *finality*: the supernatural salvation of mankind, the communion of life with the divine Trinity though grace and, then, glory. Therefore, revelation has been carried out "to invite and receive them into his [God's] own company."[5]

Consequently, revelation is not only a *self-manifestation* (*Selbst-Erschliessung*) of God to people as an object of knowledge; it is also a *self-communication* (*Selbst-Mitteilung*) of God himself that allows his people to share in the divine life. We have, therefore, a "theoretical-communicative-participative concept" of revelation.[6] Thus, revelation is made up of events and words (*gestis verbisque*)[7]: the *Word of God*, as we know, has a noetic and dynamic value. It lets the truth be known, and it saves. Further, the same noetic contents of the divine Word serve as a reality of salvation, because it *frees from error and ignorance*. Moreover, "this is eternal life, that they know thee the only true God, and Jesus Christ whom thou hast sent" (Jn 17: 3). In that critical text, "to know the only true God and Jesus Christ" has a wide meaning. It suggests the vital union between God and Christ, a personal union of knowledge and love that makes up the divine life. God's word is not reducible, to a noetic level, although it certainly includes it.[8]

Thus, saying that revelation is a *self-communication* of God to man emphasizes the salvific dimension of revelation. Nevertheless, there are other gifts from God to man that are not properly Revelation (i.e., the sacraments). Therefore, it is useful to define revelation as self-communication of God *in the Word*, which further stresses the noetic dimension, stressing that auto-communication is at the same time auto-manifestation. This definition better coincides with the more biblical and traditional *Word of God to men*, and the *locutio Dei ad homines*,[9] thereby understanding God's "speaking" in all of his plenitude.

Speaking is not a simple impersonal communication of concepts or truths. As has been previously indicated, speaking by itself tends to establish a personal relationship, a true dialogue. Still, when considering Revelation as the Word of God delivered to man, some of its essential characteristics ought to be emphasized.

First of all, speaking is a *free* activity, and it is not a necessarily *self-communication*. As a result, defining revelation as auto-communication of God in the Word, or as *locutio Dei ad homines*, stresses that the activity is *free*. It is the result of divine freedom, of God's love for mankind. Sacred Scripture continually emphasizes this reality, especially via the notion of *divine election*: God chose Abraham, Moses, and the prophets. He personally chose the moments of time for his intervention in history.[10]

Referring to the *freedom of the response* that one gives to the Word of God is a good way to get at revelation as *Word* or *locutio*. As Paul VI wrote:

> The dialogue of salvation did not physically compel anyone to embrace it. It was a formidable requirement of love. It was a tremendous responsibility for those who received it, but it left them free to embrace or refuse it, even adapting the measure (cf. Mt 12: 38) and the proving force of miracles (cf. Mt 13: 13) to the demands and spiritual dispositions of the listeners. Consequently, God has made man's free consent to divine revelation in some fashion easier, without taking away the merit of said consent.[11]

Another essential characteristic of Divine Revelation is not necessarily included either in the notions of *self-communication or locution*. Revelation serves as a *Word of testimony*.

Testimony is a particular sort of word; it is not just words communicating a concept. It demands a consent of faith from the one who receives the message based on the authority (scientific moral) of the one who gives the word.

Historical revelation has been manifested to us as God's testimony about himself. In and of itself, the Word of God is testimony, and, as a matter of fact, it could not fail to be testimony. God has chosen to reveal himself to certain chosen persons so that they, in turn, might give testimony to the truth to all men. In fact, inasmuch as this revelation is supernatural, man cannot embrace it except with the consent of faith. (Only in heavenly glory will the immediate vision of God take the place of supernatural faith.)

Divine testimony, moreover, has a property that human testimonies do not have. It is not only external, but also internal. It enters into each person who receives it. In other words, Divine Revelation has also an inner dimension: the gift of faith.

B. Revelation and Revealed Truth

Any word or dialogue has its own *content*. Even in ordinary conversation, the content is essential because, through it, what has to be said is manifested. The content determines the importance of the conversation. At the very least, the content affects the will of the parties to be in communication:

> This economy of revelation is realized by deeds and words, which are intrinsically bound up with each other. As a result, the works performed by God in the history of salvation show forth and bear out the doctrine and realities signified by the words; the words, for their part, proclaim the works, and bring to light the mystery they contain. The most intimate truth that this revelation gives us about God and the salvation of man shines forth in Christ, who is himself both the mediator and the sum total of revelation.[12]

It is not enough, then, to say that revelation is *locutio Dei ad homines*, understanding this to mean that God gives "information" to man so that he might *know* certain truths. Yet, it would be equally wrong to deny or refuse to consider that revelation is the *communication of truth* from God to man. As we have already seen, the creative Word gives humanity a true, albeit imperfect, knowledge of God. For its part, historical revelation, especially in its plenitude in Christ, is essentially inseparable from the idea of *truth* as it is manifested with particular clarity in the Gospel of St. John (cf. Jn 1: 14; 4: 23; 8: 31–32; 8: 40–47; 14: 6; 15: 1; 16: 13; 17: 17–19; 18: 37).[13]

The biblical concept of truth has a broad meaning. In the Old Testament, *emeth* can mean fidelity, norm or law, or truth (in the sense of adequacy between word and reality). In the New Testament, *alétheiea* does not share the restricted sense of the Greek culture or the Latin *veritas*, but shares the breadth of the Hebrew *emeth*. This last term allows for a multiple use of the term, which includes truth understood as *object of knowledge* offered by the Word of God to man.[14]

For example, Jesus says, "If you continue in my word, you are truly my disciples, and you will know the truth, and the truth will make you free"(Jn 8: 31–32). The purely intellectual sphere is not excluded by the sense of his words but included in it. It presents the truth (*alétheia*) as object of knowledge (*gnósesthe*, future tense of *ginóskó* that, in St. John's writings, has a wide meaning, including intellectual knowledge).

The same thing happens in many other passages where the *doctrine or teaching* (*didaché*) of Jesus is clearly understood as a series of truths taught by him to his disciples so that they would faithfully keep and transmit them (cf. Jn 7: 16–17; Acts 5: 28; Rom 6: 17; 1 Tm 4: 6; 2 Tm 4: 3; Ti 2: 7; 2 Jn 9). Moreover, the Fathers and the Magisterium of the Church unanimously affirmed this doctrinal content of historical revelation from the beginning (as the first creeds demonstrate).

After these considerations of the notion of Revelation, we certainly cannot accept the frequent accusation of Protestant theologians about the Catholic concept of revelation. They often mistakenly assert that the Catholic position claims that Revelation is a simple and impersonal communication of truths to believe without any reference to history or salvation. Take, for example, the argument of P. Althaus. More than half a century after Vatican I had asserted that in revelation, God reveals *himself*, Althus wrote, "Depersonalization of the concept of revelation (in Roman Catholic theology) is shown in the fact that it never mentions that God revealed himself."[15] This type of criticism has generally been directed toward some apologetic treatises that overemphasized the intellectual aspect of revelation while disregarding the salvific-historical aspects. On the other hand, this apologetic orientation, while never denying the historical-salvific character of revelation, stressed the intellectual aspect precisely as a reaction to Protestant thought, liberal as well as dialectic or existential. Such Protestant thinking removed the noetic contents from the Word of God, reducing the sense of revelation to the salvation event. In fact, from Luther to Bultmann's *existential theology*, a progressive emptiness of the intellectual contents of revelation—and consequently, of faith itself—has evolved. Thus, through a process of *demystification*, some of these thinkers have lately come to assert that nothing is revealed to man in the New Testament except man himself:

> Therefore, what has been revealed to us? On the one hand, *absolutely nothing*, inasmuch as the question about revelation puts the problem about doctrines, to which perhaps no man could ever have had access, about mysteries that once revealed would be known forever. On the other hand, everything, inasmuch as man's eyes are opened to himself and to the extent that man can understand himself.[16]

Revelation, according to Bultmann, "is not a process taking place out of us and that later we get to hear about, but an event taking place in ourselves that immediately affects us."[17] It teaches nothing that was not already known by us.

According to Bultmann, the Gospel, the Bible, the life of Jesus, or the doctrine of St. Paul have only an orientative value, of induction and questioning, and only in this way are they words of God and revelation. Any attempt to theoretically or practically attribute to the Bible and the Gospel a prescriptive value that attempts to regulate the existence of man would be a distortion of its sense. At the root of his conclusions is the completely unfounded prejudice that negates the possibility of the supernatural.

C. Human Mediation in Revelation

According to St. Thomas Aquinas, there is an evident human mediation, or involvement, in the prophetic charisma of the historical revelation of the Old Testament (the Word of the covenant and the prophetic Word). God speaks to men through human words, not necessarily exterior sounds, but as signs that may be only inner in character.[18]

In the plenitude of revelation, there is another kind of human mediation. Christ is the eternal Word of God made flesh (cf. Jn 1: 14): "God, when wishing to manifest himself to men, covers with flesh, in time, his Word conceived from eternity."[19] There is, therefore, human mediation. Christ is, in his humanity, the perfect *mediator* between God and mankind (cf. 1 Tm 2: 5). In his human nature, he is the first and primordial recipient of the plenitude of revelation; however, in contrast to the prophets, he is revelation: *mediator simul et plenitudo totius revelationis*.[20]

The question of human mediation of the divine Word brings with it the issue of the very possibility of historical Revelation. Specifically, allowing for divine transcendence, how is it possible that God speaks with human words without turning his speech into a merely human and imperfect communication, and thereby limiting the transmission of his divine mystery?

With this question, we are not trying to look for *a priori* conditions of possibility for revelation. We start from historical revelation as it has been accomplished and ask how human words can serve as vehicles of the mystery of divine intimacy.

First, it is possible for man to recognize that God speaks to him in supernatural revelation. This possibility, as we have already pointed out regarding cosmic revelation, is based on man's natural capacity to know God in an analogical way through created things (*per ea quae facta sunt*).

Subsequently, it is possible for human words to analogically express divine intimacy, which is due also to the real analogy between the world and God (an analogy that in man reaches the level of the image). As St. Thomas explains, human concepts, in spite of coming from the knowledge of creatures, can truly—albeit imperfectly—come to signify the transcendent reality of God. This is because every concept and word that relates to perfection *according to its meaning* is primarily applied to God, for all perfection comes from him even though it is first applied to creatures *according to their way of meaning*.[21]

Consequently, taking into consideration historical revelation in its plenitude in Christ, with R. Latourelle we come to the conclusion that:

> Christ was able to use all the resources of the created universe to provide us with the knowledge of God and his divine life. This is because the creating word preceded and provides foundation to the revealing word, and because one and the other have as beginning the same inner Word of God. The revelation of Christ assumes the truth of the analogy.[22]

Moreover, people possess the potential to both *listen to* revelation as self-manifestation of God and *receive* revelation as self-communication of God himself, because people can be elevated to a supernatural order through grace. This is called the obeisant potency (*potentia oboedientialis*) regarding the participation in the intimate life of God.[23]

This capacity of man to *receive God himself in his Word* (and not merely to listen to the Word) stems from the fact that man is made in the image of God. "The soul, by nature, is capable of grace; by the same fact of having been created in the image of God, it is capable of God through grace."[24] Certainly man could *listen* to revelation without grace, but he could not *receive* it. This is because revelation is not only self-manifestation but also self-communication of God. That is why Karl Rahner's argument of *potentia oboedientialis* of receiving revelation as different from *potentia oboedientialis* to receive grace is difficult to accept.[25]

Man is capable of listening to revelation because he has an obeisant potency regarding grace (as opposed to man having an obeisant potency to listen to revelation). This potency enables him to receive the self-communication of God himself, that is to say, revelation in all of its fullness. Therefore, Rahner's notion of an obeisant potency before revelation, different from the obeisant potency before grace, is both superfluous and insufficient. Rahner thus weakens his own argument, in which he maintains, "Philosophy is as ontology of an obeisant potency before revelation."[26] Rahner himself recognizes the problem of making such a distinction between these two potencies, and he asserts that in the final analysis they cannot actually be distinguished.[27] Consequently, we face an even greater problem within Rahner's thinking, which relates to our understanding of the nexus between the natural and the supernatural[28] that is manifested in the ambiguity of its approach in regard to ordinary Christians.[29]

II. Revelation and History

God's Revelation is therefore immersed in time and history. Jesus Christ took flesh in the "fullness of time" (cf. Gal 4: 4); and two thousand years later, I feel bound to restate forcefully that "in Christianity time has a fundamental importance."[30] It is within time that the whole work of creation and salvation comes to light; and it emerges clearly that, with the Incarnation of the Son of God, our life is even now a foretaste of the fulfilment of time which is to come (cf. Heb 1: 2). The truth about himself and his life which God has entrusted to humanity is immersed therefore in time and history; as it was declared once and for all in the mystery of Jesus of Nazareth.[31]

The relationship between revelation and history can be established by pointing out how revelation has affected history, why there is a history of revelation. It can also be asserted that revelation has been accomplished, as we have seen, *through history*, that is to say, history itself is revelation. Nevertheless, this last assertion calls for precision: History is revelation, not as a simple event (although it may be due to an extraordinary divine intervention), but as an event accompanied by the word that explains the meaning of the event.

As *Dei Verbum* asserts, there exists a mutual dependence between words and historical events (*verba et gesta*) in the sense that the works accomplished by God in history manifest and reinforce the doctrine and the realities meant by those same words. Words proclaim works and enlighten the mystery contained in them. This connection between word and event is particularly evident in the New Testament. Consider, for instance, the healing of the paralyzed man as an event that shows the truth of Christ's Word according to which the Son of Man has the power to forgive sins (cf. Mt 9: 6–7). Another example lies in the words of Christ considered in their entirety followed by those of the apostles. Knowledge of this testimony is indispensable for any understanding of the salvific dimension of the events of the life, Death and Resurrection of Jesus.

Yet, we need to keep in mind that "this intimate and living union of works and words" is "a union of nature, not always of time. Sometimes, work and word coincide...on other occasions the event precedes the word... and at other times, the word precedes the event."[32]

W. Pannenberg's opinion about the identity between revelation and history, as developed in his work (jointly with R. Rendtorff, U. Wilckens, and T. Rendtorff) *Offenbarung als Geschichte* (1961) relates to this matter. Pannenberg was the main thinker of the so-called *Circle of Heidelberg* and was one of Bultmann's disciples. He departed from the existential line to forcefully reassert the validity and priority of the historical element in revelation and salvation. Even so, Pannenberg undervalues the doctrinal dimension of revelation (as is more or less characteristic of Protestant theology). He also emphasizes the identification between revelation and historical event, asserting that *history is a progressive revelation of the absolute*. He understands this in a Hegelian sense, and, therefore, identifies history and reality as the same thing.[33]

Such identification "reality = history = revelation" represents a complete and explicit denial of the revealing value of the Word. It is united with the claim that events—interventions of God in history—are parts of a process that achieves its value only when the process is completed. Therefore, according to Pannenberg, revelation is properly accomplished only at the end of history.[34]

This Hegelian conception of revelation completely and explicitly denies every difference between the natural and the supernatural. It denies any permanent value in the biblical expression of revelation.[35] Moreover, it entails a "historification" of God himself that entraps God in the circumstances of human development. It denies divine transcendence, since the dialectical arguments of Pannenberg assert the "Hegelian God," but certainly not the true God.[36]

Certain authors of *liberation theology* also fall into the error of proposing a more or less explicitly Hegelian relationship between revelation and history as a foundation for importing some Marxist elements into their theological arguments.[37] All of this reminds us how important it is to safeguard the proper relationship between word and event. Otherwise, we endanger any effort to develop a valid theology of revelation.

Naturally, when we speak about the relationship between revelation and history, we cannot forget that the plenitude of revelation is also the plenitude of history (its center and final end). The historical character of revelation is manifested in its *progressive* nature and in its being *finalized* (to Christ). These are two determining characteristics of the linear conception (Jewish and Christian) of history, in contradistinction to the cyclical conception (Greek).

The historical character of revelation—and of salvation—is also manifested in that the history of revelation is authentic human history. It is a history of *freedom*: of divine and human freedom. The Word of God is embraced in human history and is fully integrated within it, precisely through freedom helped by the grace of faith. Without freedom, in fact, there is no true history.[38]

We should also address the *perennial validity* of historical revelation. How is it possible that historical revelation is neither essentially conditioned nor deformed by the historical development of cultures, by human thinking, or by language? The answer is simple: Revelation is, in fact, historical, but its historicity is not a simple human reality. It is guided by God. God, in fact, speaks, chooses Israel, and chooses the prophets. God himself becomes man in Christ, taking revelation to its plenitude. God always protects the transmission of revelation through the assistance of the Holy Spirit within the Church.[39]

III. Revelation and Salvation

Dei Verbum presents the relationship between revelation and salvation with regard to the idea of *finality*. God has revealed himself to people *to invite and admit them to communion with him*. This communion with God is precisely the salvation of mankind. That is why the Council teaches that revelation has been accomplished "in the history of salvation." This means that the history of revelation and the history of salvation coincide in the sense that revelation is an integral part of the work of salvation.

Although revelation is finalized for the salvation of man, this does not mean that either in the world or in history there is some last end other than the glory of God, because man glorifies God by his free acceptance of revelation and salvation. Thus, the *finality of Revelation is the salvation of man for the glory of God* (cf. Eph 1: 3–6, 12, 14).

Nevertheless, the relationship between revelation and salvation is not a simple means / ends relationship. Revelation is not only a means of salvation but is, in and of itself, *the content of salvation*. This relationship of revelation to salvation is founded, as we have said several times, in the fact that revelation is the *Word of God*. It does not only signify (announce); it also accomplishes what it signifies. "The word of God is living and active, sharper that any two-edged sword" (Heb 4: 12).

The salvific essence of historical revelation is clearly manifested in the manner of its accomplishment in the Old and, particularly, the New Testaments. Many passages of the New Testament demonstrate this reality. One good example is the relationship (almost of identity) between *light* and *life* (cf. Jn 1: 4; 9: 5; 12: 35–36),[40] *truth* and *life* (cf. Jn 14: 6); *light* and *salvation* (cf. Mt 4: 16; 5: 14; Lk 1: 79; 8: 16), and *truth* and *salvation* (cf. 1 Tm 4: 3; 6: 5; 2 Tm 2: 18; 3: 8; 4: 4; Ti 1: 14).

A direct reference to the *Word of God* may be found in the words of our Lord, "Blessed rather are those who hear the word of God and keep it [*makarioi oi akouontes ton logon tou Theou kai phylassontes*]" (Lk 11: 28). *Akouontes* includes not only those who passively listen, but also those who receive and accept the word. *Phylassontes* means not only those who put in practice the received teaching, but those who "guard" or "preserve in themselves" the received word. (In fact, *phylassó* means, among other things, "to put in practice," "to observe," "to accomplish," as well as "to guard or preserve.") *Makarioi* are happy and joyful, and therefore saved because "they have in themselves" the Word of God.

In concluding these brief biblical references, we would do well to recall the affirmation of St. Peter directed to Christ: "You have the words of eternal life [*rhémata zóés aióniou écheis*]" (Jn 6: 68). The words (*rhemata*) properly correspond to the Hebrew *debarin*. It means words that both announce eternal life (salvation) and accomplish it.[41] Thus, revelation is reality of salvation in itself because it is not just a message; it is also a transforming force. Receiving revelation is a matter of not only "hearing" the word of God, but of really "listening to it," receiving it, guarding it *through faith*—a faith that is the foundation and root of all justification.[42]

So, St. Paul writes to the Romans that the gospel (good news, message)"is the power of God [*dynamis Theou*] for salvation to every one who has faith" (Rom 1: 16). In fact, revelation as the salvation of the individual is revelation that has been accepted, that is, faith that is not only an answer of man to revelation but also, and primarily, a gift from God.[43] It is interesting to note, regarding this Pauline consideration of the gospel as *dynamis Theou*, that the same St. Paul applies that expression to Christ (cf. 1 Cor 1: 24), who is not only the mediator of salvation (the way) but he himself *is* salvation (truth and life) (cf. Jn 14: 6). Similarly, revelation is not only the means of salvation; it is salvation.

IV. Revelation, the Church, and the Vocation to Sanctity

Man's vocation to sanctity pertains to the very essence of divine revelation in history: "the invisible God, from the fullness of his love, addresses men as his friends, and moves among them, in order to invite and receive them into his own company."[44] This vocation to holiness is the highest justification of the dignity of man.[45] It is the expression of the universal salvific will: God "desires all men to be saved and to come to the knowledge of the truth" (1 Tm 2: 4). In the language of the New Testament, "to come to the knowledge of the truth" (*eis epignósin alétheias*) means, in fact, to reach a personal union of knowledge and love with that Truth that is the Way and Life with Christ (cf. Jn 14: 6) and, in him, with the Father and the Holy Spirit.

This communion with the Trinity is *sanctity*. It is the created person's participation in the sanctity of God.[46] Regardless of the semantic difference, there is a basic relationship between salvation and sanctity. The universal salvific will is expressed in the universal vocation to sanctity: "this is the will of God, your sanctification" (1 Thes 4: 3).

Vocation presupposes *election*: God has *chosen* us in Christ, "before the foundation of the world, that we should be holy and blameless before him" (Eph 1: 4). Therefore, we can say, "Jesus Christ, the Chosen One *par excellence*, takes to himself every divine election, so that Christians will be men and women *in* Christ."[47] The universal vocation to sanctity is a *Christian vocation*.[48]

Sanctity (communion with God) is the plenitude of identification with Christ, the only Son of the Father, and, therefore, the plenitude of divine *filiation*.[49] Total identification with Christ is inseparable from the perfection of charity because charity is "a certain participation of the infinite love that the Holy Spirit is,"[50] and because people are "regenerated as children in the Son"[51] by the Holy Spirit. Consequently, in the operative order of virtues, charity is the *plenitude of the law* (cf. Rom 13: 10; 1 Cor 13: 1–13).

The vocation to sanctity is, consequently, universal, and this call, according to the divine plan, reaches every person through the mediation of the Church. She is not only the recipient of the election-vocation prefigured by the vocation of Israel, but she inseparably receives the mission to make this vocation present to men with the efficacy proper to the Word of God. The Church does not just call individuals to sanctity; she also makes them saints. The Church is the summoning (*ekklésia*) of the saints. Baptism itself is an effective vocation to sanctity.

By means of this sacrament, men are "called through water" (*aqua vocatos*)[52] to communion with the Father, the Son, and the Holy Spirit. They are thus introduced to that communion of sanctity: They have really been "made sons of God in the baptism of faith and partakers of the divine nature, and so are truly sanctified."[53] By its very nature, the vocation to sanctity is a *vocation to apostolate*.[54] It is a calling to announce, actualize, and spread the mystery of communion of the Church. It is a vocation to gather everyone and everything in Christ.[55]

For centuries, Christians have not clearly understood the doctrine of the universal vocation to sanctity.[56] The subjective dimension of the universality of this vocation—we are all called to holiness—is present in the writings and preaching of saints and spiritual authors of all times. Several examples are St. Augustine, St. Thomas Aquinas, St. Francis de Sales and St. Therese of Lisieux, among others.[57] However, this universality has historically been understood in a rather weak sense. Generally, it was thought that, while it was possible and desirable for ordinary people to struggle for sanctity, such an attitude and activity would be rather exceptional.

The objective dimension of the universal call to holiness has been even more neglected recently. By this, we mean that most Christians are to find their calling to sanctity not in special activities added to their ordinary lives, but *in* and *through* their ordinary lives, as St. Josemaría Escrivá tirelessly preached, starting in 1928. "Sanctity is not something for privileged ones, but all the ways on earth can be divine, all states, all professions, all honorable tasks."[58]

Following Vatican II,[59] this doctrine has become more popular. Nevertheless, many Christians continue to hold onto the notion that the vocation to sanctity is something within the reach of only a few Church members by means of extraordinary activities.

> The word *saint* in the course of times and even today has suffered a dangerous restriction. We think about saints as statues venerated on altars, as "super-Christians" who perform miracles; people with heroic virtues. We thus convince ourselves that sanctity is something reserved for a few chosen persons, among whom

we cannot hope to be counted. We leave sanctity for those few unknown people. We thereby accept ourselves just as we are. Josemaría Escrivá has shaken people from this spiritual apathy. He has reminded us that sanctity is for all the baptized. It is not something strange but a usual and normal reality. Sanctity does not consist of battles of unbelievable heroism. It has thousands of expressions, and can be accomplished in any state and condition.[60]

Accordingly, sanctity that expresses itself in the perfection of charity is not ordinarily linked to more or less extraordinary activities added to daily life. Charity can and must form all actions, even those apparently most trivial, and in them and through them, the human person lives and grows in communion with God. As St. Paul wrote, "Every one should remain in the state in which he was called" (1 Cor 7: 20). In most cases, the Christian vocation to sanctity does not require the baptized to change their condition in the world. Moreover, by the mere fact that the Church asks each person to remain in his or her place, we can see that she blesses the ordinary life as a place and means to reach the finality of the Christian vocation: sanctity.[61]

The divine call to holiness, therefore, in its *objective* universality, is not merely a calling to personal sanctification and the collaboration in the sanctity of other people. It is a vocation to free creation from disorder, to sanctify the world: "Christians, working in the world, have to reconcile all things in God, placing Christ at the top of all human endeavors."[62]

The whole Church and every one of its members share in this mission of the sanctification of the world. In summary, the mission of the laity is to sanctify the world *from within* their worldly activities and temporal structures.[63]

This positive Christian perspective on the world is inseparably linked to the recognition of the primacy of Christ's grace in the economy of the redeeming Incarnation: "Apart from me you can do nothing" (Jn 15: 5). In this vein, it is useful to remember St. Mark's brief description of the calling of the apostles, who were chosen by our Lord so they could "be with him, and to be sent out to preach and have authority to cast out demons" (Mk 3: 14–15). *To be with Christ* is the starting point and indispensable condition for the full efficacy of both the apostles and all Christians. We are all called to actively participate in the apostolic mission to spread the gospel and to free the world from Satan's grasp.

Being with Christ has its fullest expression in the Eucharist, where our Lord gives us his Body and transforms us into his one Body.[64] By this means, we capture the radical centrality of the Eucharist in Christian life. The Eucharistic sacrifice is "the center and the source of a Christian's spiritual life."[65] The Church fulfills and manifests herself in her most essential manner through her Eucharistic root.[66] The Eucharist is nothing more and nothing less than *the wellspring of Christian life* and, therefore, the sign and instrument for the salvation of the world.[67]

CHAPTER 5

THE RELATIONSHIP BETWEEN SCRIPTURE AND TRADITION

The relationship between the Bible and Tradition has always been of great importance in theology and in the life of the Church. Believers have sometimes failed to properly understand this relationship in crucial moments of Church history, such as the Protestant Reformation. Generally, this failure has negatively effected the development of theological methods.

I. Biblical Testimony

Sacred Scripture, in both the Old and New Testaments, offers numerous indications of the proper relationship between Scripture and Tradition.

First, it is clear that *oral Tradition preceded the written record of Revelation in both Testaments*. Take, for example, the plain fact that in the New Testament, Jesus Christ did not write anything, instead communicating his message through his deeds and words. The apostles, for their part, transmitted the Christian message by preaching and building the Church before doing so in writing. Moreover, not all the apostles left written testimonies.

Scripture indicates another very important aspect of the above-mentioned relationship between Scripture and Tradition: *The writing of revelation did not replace oral tradition.*

In fact, the origin, final work, and contents of each of the writings of the New Testament show its *partial* character as a reporting of all apostolic preaching. For instance, the synoptic Gospels, in spite of the similarity of their contents, clearly diverge in many significant aspects. For example, Mark does not mention the Sermon on the Mount, the promise of primacy to St. Peter, or the account of Jesus' childhood. The differences between the synoptic Gospels and the Gospel of St. John are also evident. St. John stresses, moreover, that many aspects of the life of Jesus have not been written (cf. Jn 20: 30; 21: 25). It is erroneous to argue against the partial nature of the written Gospels by claiming that the *body* of the four Gospels contains all the apostolic preaching about the life and teachings of Christ. Even if that were so, it is clear that, for at least the first century, no Christian community had possession of the four Gospels.[1] This *incompleteness* is even more evident when considering the epistles of the New Testament, which were written with a specific purpose and content.

This is not to say that the body of Sacred Scripture does not contain the totality of Revelation. What is clear, however, is that *in apostolic times*, people were not as attentive to the written word as we are today. Written testimony was not meant to substitute for the oral preaching of Christ's message.[2]

There are, moreover, some particular texts, mainly in the Pauline epistles, that explicitly state that the written tradition could not replace the oral, personal one. "Stand firm and hold to the traditions which you were taught by us, either by word of mouth or by letter" (2 Thes 2: 15). Note how the Apostle gave "traditions" the same importance whether referring to his oral or written teachings.[3] In fact, *tradition* (*paradosis*) is carried out both *dia logou* (through the spoken word) and *di'epistolés* (through the written word). These realities are reciprocally related because they are both based on the same root word: *krateite* (from *krateó*, meaning "to keep with force").[4]

Another relevant Pauline text states, "Follow the pattern of the sound words which you have heard from me, in the faith and love which are in Christ Jesus" (2 Tm 1: 13; cf. 1 Tm 1: 14). The word *hypotyposis* indicates not so much a totally finished piece, but a "working norm or model" that needs to be developed. In this sense, the words of 2 Timothy 1: 13 can be considered indicative of the living character of Tradition: to "guard the truth that has been entrusted to you by the Holy Spirit" (2 Tm 1: 14). It is a form of preservation that is also developing.[5] Consequently, it cannot replace Scripture.

Sacred Scripture provides us with yet another perspective on the relationship between the sacred writings and Tradition during the days of the apostles. This perspective relates to the role Tradition plays in the interpretation of Scripture. For this, we must remember the following statement of St. Peter: "First of all you must understand this, that no prophecy of scripture is a matter of one's own interpretation" (2 Pt 1: 20). This text refers to the Old Testament prophecies, which are comparable to Paul's letter (cf. 2 Pt 3: 16). Therefore, the assertion is also valid concerning New Testament writings.[6] The interpretation of Scriptures is necessary because Scripture contains aspects that are "hard to understand" (2 Pt 3: 16), and this interpretation is not a private matter for the faithful. Consequently, even though St. Peter does not say it in an explicit manner, the interpretation of Scripture clearly has to be done in accord with apostolic Tradition.[7] To arrive at the correct comprehension of Scripture, we must work in conjunction with Tradition. This rule applies to both apostolic and post-apostolic times. In this way, Scripture remains immutable in content, and the Deposit of Faith can be handed down throughout time without corruption.

Regarding the relationship between Scripture and Tradition as to material contents, that is to say, whether one may find revealed truths in Tradition that are not contained in Scripture, biblical testimony does not offer a decisive answer. We cannot even find a definitive answer to this question in the letters of St. Paul, and they are the primary doctrinal source of the New Testament.[8]

II. Reflection of Christian Authors

As we said before, the relationship between Scripture and Tradition has attracted the attention of Christian authors since the beginning of the Church. They have worked to achieve greater precision in understanding this issue. In this section, we will analyze the most important aspects of this progressive understanding.

A. Scripture and Tradition according to the Fathers of the Church

The Fathers of the Church and early apologists had a broad idea of Tradition, even though the terms *paradosis* and *paradidómi* are infrequently used. "Tradition," in their writings, means the transmission of the gospel (understood in a wide sense as the passing on of the Christian doctrine and way of life). Thus, the object of this transmission is the apostles' teaching without any distinction between oral and written teaching. As an important aspect, it includes the specifically *Christian* interpretation of the Old Testament.[9]

Beginning at the end of the second century and continuing in the third, the distinction between Sacred Scripture and Tradition became clearer and more frequently noted due to the growing diffusion of the Scriptures of the New Testament and the corresponding recognition of their status as inspired books. Tradition was no longer understood only in a wide sense (including written transmission) but also in a restricted sense of *oral* transmission. In this period, the work of St. Irenaeus of Lyons particularly stands out.[10]

St. Irenaeus sometimes considered Tradition in a wide sense, identifying it with oral and written apostolic preaching.[11] The Church, through apostolic succession, faithfully guards this Tradition.[12] It is, then, a tradition that is public and shown forth as opposed to the reputed hidden tradition of private teachers held by the Gnostics. Nevertheless, St. Irenaeus, confronting the incorrect use that the heretics make of Sacred Scripture, also insisted on the restrictive sense of Tradition as *unwritten Tradition*, the content of which is particularly the *interpretation of Scripture*.[13] Consequently, Scripture cannot be correctly read or interpreted outside the Church.[14] St. Irenaeus vehemently insisted on the historical fact of apostolic succession—precisely in opposition to the private and hidden false "tradition" of the Gnostics. He also asserted that the assistance of the Holy Spirit is essential to the faithful care of God's communication to mankind.[15]

The other Fathers and writers of the third century, although with different nuances and sometimes lacking his clarity, concurred with St. Irenaeus that only by means of the Church and through the apostolic Tradition which she guards can Sacred Scripture be correctly interpreted. The Scriptures, moreover, have been received by the Church, and are recognized as *canonical* through this Tradition.[16] Tertullian (before becoming a Montanist) was particularly clear in these points. His work, *De praescriptione haereticorum*, can be considered the first book in Church history dedicated explicitly to the issue of Tradition.[17]

These fundamental aspects of Tradition—particularly those connected to the relationship between Tradition and apostolic succession and the necessity of Tradition for the faithful interpretation of Scripture—were completely accepted by the Fathers in the following centuries. Moreover, from the fourth century on, the distinction between Scripture and Tradition (understood as oral Tradition) grew clearer. The writings of the Fathers began to be read as the testimony of Tradition. Criteria were elaborated to distinguish what belongs to Tradition in the early writings (consider, for instance, St. Augustine's writings). The *living* character of Tradition, thus, became more explicit in the sense of dogmatic development (for instance in the *Commonitorium* of St. Vincent of Lerins).[18]

When considering the material *sufficiency* or *insufficiency* of Scripture to transmit all Revelation, there are many patristic texts that seem to assert the total *sufficiency* of Scripture as a means of transmission of the whole of revelation. For instance, St. Augustine wrote that Scripture contains everything regarding faith and morals.[19] Then again, St. Augustine stated unequivocally that there was a sufficiency in Scripture inasmuch as it is received and interpreted by the Church in accordance with Tradition. The same thing holds true regarding similar assertions of Tertullian and other Fathers (i.e., St. Anastasius, St. John Chrysostom, St. Cyril of Jerusalem, and St. Cyril of Alexandria).[20]

There were many statements about these issues dating particularly from the fourth century, such as those we have already studied
in Tertullian and St. Clement of Alexandria. These statements dealt
both with "unwritten traditions," and explicitly with aspects contained in Tradition that are not contained in Sacred Scripture. A text
of St. Basil the Great is particularly famous for this. In fact, it was later
quoted by the Council of Trent when it defined that some truths of
Church doctrine are contained in Scripture and others have reached
us by means of apostolic Tradition.[21] Similar assertions are found in
St. John Chrysostom, St. Augustine, St. Vincent of Lerins and St. John
Damascene.[22]

So, it is unquestionable that not all apostolic Tradition has been written, not only because the interpretation of Scripture has been orally
transmitted, but also because "part of the contents" of apostolic Tradition is not found in Sacred Scripture. Which part? For a *patristic answer*
to this question, we need to consider primarily the Fathers' assertions
in which they stated *which matters are not contained in Scripture and are
therefore attributable* to apostolic Tradition.

We find that the matters are nearly always disciplinary and cultural. They
concern the celebration of Sunday and Easter, some ritual elements of
Baptism and the Eucharist, norms about fasting, blessing of water and
oil, etc. Still, there are some aspects of greater doctrinal content. For
instance, they might involve issues regarding the baptism of children,
the validity of baptisms conferred by heretics, worship owed to the
Holy Spirit, prayers for the dead, or the cult of images.[23] It may easily
be seen that those aspects with a dogmatic content—or with dogmatic
implications—have a biblical foundation. Other aspects, even when it
is stressed that they have an apostolic origin, are disciplinary and liturgical questions. Many of these questions have lost force or were never
universal in the first place.

From all of this, we could deduce a distinction between *Tradition*, the
correct interpretation of Scripture, and non-binding liturgical and disciplinary *traditions*. However, that distinction—so understood—would
be superficial. In any case, there is no doubt that, for the Fathers, Scripture without the Church is nothing. Similarly, the Church is nothing
without Scripture.[24]

B. Theology Prior to the Council of Trent

It is difficult to summarize the different ways that theologians have understood the relationship between Tradition and Scripture over time.[25]

In general, Scholasticism holds that the whole of Revelation is contained in Scripture and *non omnia scripta sunt* (not everything was recorded in writing). Although the Scholastics infrequently use the term *Traditio*, they do affirm that Scripture has to be read and interpreted by the Church according to Tradition, incarnate in *auctoritates* (texts from the Fathers and the councils).[26] Consequently, these authorities are not ordinarily thought of as a *source* of revelation apart from Scripture. The *non omnia scripta sunt* is present specifically in reference to liturgical and disciplinary traditions but sometimes also in reference to aspects of indubitable dogmatic relevance, as in, for instance, the essence of certain sacraments.

On this subject, the thought of St. Thomas Aquinas is of particular interest. In his works, it is possible to identify mainly three types of texts, that could seem, at first glance, difficult to consolidate according to just one overall conception of the relations between Tradition and Scripture. On the other hand, they are not texts that appertain to three different periods of time and that, therefore, indicate an evolution of thought. Therefore, we must conclude that the three types of texts indicate three aspects of just one conception.[27]

The first aspect is that only canonical Scripture can give guidance in faith.[28] For example, speaking about the motive for the Incarnation, St. Thomas firmly asserted that we can know realities depending on divine freedom only in the measure that they appear in Sacred Scripture.[29]

In the second series of texts, St. Thomas Aquinas referred to the union of Scripture and Tradition when he asserted that the object of faith is manifested to us in Scripture and the Church's doctrine.[30] Nevertheless, Scripture and Church are not a double "place" where one may find revelation. St. Thomas immediately explained that the truth of faith is proposed to us "in Scriptures, rightly understood according to the Church's doctrine."[31] Aquinas frequently asserted that this *doctrina Ecclesiae* is binding for faith because it exists in the truth contained in Sacred Scripture interpreted with the help of the Holy Spirit.[32] In this context, the principle of Tradition appears more implicitly than explicitly, particularly with reference to the organ of authentic interpretation of this Tradition, namely, the Magisterium of the Church. St. Thomas recognized the authority of the Fathers; he saw their consensus in the interpretation of the Scriptures as an expression of the apostolic Tradition.[33]

From the two groups of texts considered until now, we might conclude that St. Thomas thought Revelation was completely contained in Sacred Scripture inasmuch as it is received by the Church and interpreted according to Tradition, the organ of authentic interpretation which is the Magisterium. If so, his is a fully traditional concept; however, all of this must be integrated with what St. Thomas pointed out in a third series of texts, which also contain his reflections on the Patristics.

As a matter of fact, there are texts in which St. Thomas wrote about *unwritten traditions*, in which he made reference not only to liturgical and disciplinary issues, but also to aspects regarding faith, and therefore, revelation. Commenting, in a general way, on the passage of 2 Thessalonians 2: 15, he asserted that there are many unwritten aspects in the Church that have been taught by the apostles, and, consequently, form part of the Church's patrimony that needs to be maintained.[34] These unwritten aspects, although they pertain to faith, do not belong to aspects necessary for salvation or for the structure of the Church.[35] For instance, they include some aspects of the essence of sacraments (not only liturgical rites).[36] Thomas made the connection between the two quoted texts as a continuation of the first one, when he asserted that not everything pertaining to the essence of confirmation and the anointing of the sick may be found specifically supported by Scripture. These two sacraments are not necessary either for salvation or for the structure of the Church.[37] For another example, Thomas posited the truth of the Assumption of the Virgin on one occasion as *Scriptura non tradit*,[38] but on another occasion, he realized that this truth was pre-announced, at least in a metaphorical sense, in Song of Solomon 6: 10 and Psalm 132: 8.[39] Regarding the perpetual virginity of

Mary, Thomas argued that it can be deduced from Scripture. He held the same position regarding the descent of Christ into hell. According to Thomas, it does not seem that more truths are understood if we consider Tradition without reference to Scripture.[40]

From all that we have seen, we can conclude that for St. Thomas, everything that is necessary for salvation and the right structure of the Church is contained in Scripture, and Tradition is necessary, above all, to correctly interpret Scripture. Tradition also transmits some unwritten oral revealed truths. Still, these truths are not absolutely necessary either for salvation or the structure the Church.

Patristic and Scholastic conceptions endured through the fourteenth and fifteenth centuries, but theologians developed radical positions about the aforementioned argument with the passing of time. On the one hand, certain theologians began to argue that, at least as a matter of fact and due to the development of canon law, the rule of faith is that of the Church. On the other hand, Henry of Ghent asserted the possibility of a distinction between Church and Scripture that implied a certain subordination of the Church to Scripture. Here we find a germ of the Protestant Reformation that subsequently came to fruition when Wycliff explicitly defended the idea of a distinction between Scripture and the old Church and Scripture and the present Church.

In summary, immediately before the Council of Trent there were three primary conceptions of the relationship between Tradition and Scripture:

1. All revealed truths are contained in Scripture, at least in their foundations; Tradition is essentially the interpretation of Scripture.

2. Besides Scripture, there are unwritten traditions having the same authority as Scripture.

3. Revelation is only in Scripture (*sola Scriptura*, understood in the Protestant sense).

This last conception does not accept the principle of Tradition. Remember that the principle of *sola Scriptura* is fundamental to all

Protestant thought. While there are some discrepancies among authors, in efforts to justify the principle of *sola Scriptura*, as well as for
the place assigned to it in the body of doctrine, it is always an essential principle. It is intimately linked to another principle of the Reformation, *sola fides*. Just as only God saves, without taking into account
men's works, so revelation is only in the Bible, the Word of God, without taking into account men's works (in this case, Tradition and the
Magisterium of the Church). Scripture, according to this principle, is to
be interpreted by itself. "Free examination" is not conceived as pure
subjectivism or relativism, although the history of Protestantism demonstrates that it leads to these philosophies. "Free examination" is,
rather, thought of as an assertion of the clarity of the Word of God. This
Word becomes crystal clear, not by means of the corrupt human mind,
but by the work of the Holy Spirit in each one of the faithful (who has
fiduciary faith). In other words, the principle of *sola Scriptura* stresses
not only the *material sufficiency* but also the *formal sufficiency* of Sacred
Scripture.[41]

C. The Council of Trent and Post-Tridentine Theology

The decree *Sacrosancta*, enacted on April 8, 1546 in the fourth session
of the Council of Trent, begins by stating that the main purpose of the
Council is the conservation of the purity of the gospel through the elim-
ination of errors.[42] These errors had to do with Protestant teachings.

In this decree, the Council asserted that the gospel is the one promised
by the prophets and enacted by Christ, which reaches us through the
books of the Old and New Testament as well as by unwritten traditions. The Church receives both Scripture and Tradition with the same
piety and reverence.[43]

It is interesting to note that the decree applies the notion of *source* (of
all truths of salvation and moral discipline) neither to Scripture nor
traditions but to the gospel understood in a broad sense: the teaching of Christ and the apostles. Scripture (Old and New Testaments)
and unwritten traditions are the *means through which* the gospel
is transmitted. The relationship between Scripture and unwritten

traditions is asserted to be that both are means, channels, or ways of the transmission of the gospel.

Nevertheless, the Council does not indicate what relationship exists between Scripture and Tradition from the standpoint of material content. In other words, the Council does not state if the whole gospel is transmitted by each of those means or if Scripture and Tradition each contain part of revelation.[44] In any case, there is no doubt that the primary intention of the Council was to reaffirm—against the Lutheran principle of *sola Scriptura*—the existence and necessity of Tradition. Because of its divine and apostolic origin, Tradition is received in the Church with "the same" piety and worship as Sacred Scripture.[45]

Theologians contemporary with and following the Council of Trent up to the eighteenth century focused on responding to the Protestant controversy. Regarding our special area of interest, Pérez de Ayala y Cano in the sixteenth century, St. Robert Bellarmine, and J.B. Bossuet in the seventeenth century, and C.R. Billuart in the eighteenth century are particularly relevant.[46] Post-Tridentine theologians developed an interpretation of Trent that treated Scripture and Tradition as *two* materially different *sources* of revelation.[47] Nevertheless, others have refuted that idea.[48]

In any case, Post-Tridentine theology generally asserted the formal and material *insufficiency* of Scripture. It is *formal*, because the Bible has to be interpreted according to Tradition. It is *material* because there are things universally received in the Church that are not contained in Scripture but that have been transmitted by the Tradition of the apostles. Nevertheless, some authors of this period—for instance, Martín Pérez de Ayala—clearly asserted that Scripture and Tradition were not two independent sources because Tradition transmits the contents of Scripture jointly with some unwritten "traditions." Clearly, not all traditions have the same value, but there are some of apostolic-divine origin concerning truths pertaining to the faith.[49]

In conclusion, we can say that, regarding the relationship between Scripture and Tradition, we find a substantially traditional theological conception, following Patristic and Scholastic thought, but with more or less diverse accents, systematization, and arguments. In any case, there was great interest in determining and valuing unwritten traditions in this period. Moreover, there was a tendency to give particular importance to the Magisterium of the Church to the point that it seemed to be completely identified with Tradition.[50]

A famous theological renewal was carried out in the nineteenth century, mainly by the School of Tubingen (led by J.A. Möhler), the Roman School (J.B. Franzelin was the major representative), and two other great personages: J.H. Newman and M.J. Scheeben.[51]

In *Die Einheit in der Kirche*, published in 1825 when he was only twenty-nine years old, Möhler forcefully stressed the "pneumatic dimension" of the Church, and, therefore, of Tradition, which is "the living gospel,"[52] without diminishing the hierarchical and institutional dimension of the Church. Nevertheless, there are still vague points in his argument. He had been influenced to a certain extent by Schleiermacher's religious subjectivism.[53]

Möhler's position on the relationship between Scripture and Tradition can be considered traditional, in keeping with the Patristics and the Scholastics. Nevertheless, even as he stressed the unity of the Church as unity in the Holy Spirit, Möhler insisted on the *unity between Scripture and Tradition* and in the nature of *a living Tradition*.

> Tradition is the expression of the Holy Spirit that encourages the community of the faithful. It crosses all times, survives at every moment, and takes bodily form continually.... Scripture is the expression of the Holy Spirit that has first taken bodily form, at the beginning of Christianity, by the particular grace granted to the apostles. That is why he is the first member of written Tradition.... The question as to whether Tradition and Scripture are coordinated or subordinated cannot even be set out, because it is based upon false premises. There is no contrast between one and the other. All of this reasoning is founded upon the idea that Tradition and Scripture run alongside each other as two parallel lines. But in reality it is not that way, and this has been demonstrated throughout history. Tradition and Scripture have

diverged between each other, traveling through the centuries one inside the other, living in intimate unity. And because in the Church Scripture has never been read without the influence of ecclesiastical education, we cannot think that in the second and third centuries there was this kind of education—namely, an ecclesiastical faith—without the influence of Scripture.[54]

Consequently, as Möhler frequently repeats in his anti-Protestant argument stating that the Church is not founded upon the Scriptures:

> The Christian Church is not based on Scripture. Christianity was lived in the soul of the Lord—and in the souls of his apostles full of the Holy Spirit—before becoming concept, discourse and letter. That is why we assert: before the letter, the spirit, he who has the invigorating spirit will without a doubt understand the letter, that is, its expression.... Outside of the Church, Sacred Scripture cannot be understood. The reason is this: where the Spirit is, there also the Church is. Where the Church is, there also the spirit is.... Only the Church can explain the Bible.[55]

Similarly, he states, "Tradition is the word of the divine Spirit, carried down throughout the centuries. That is why Tradition, as well as Scripture, are so badly understood outside of the Church."[56]

Therefore, according to Möhler, Tradition is the life of the Church inspired by the Holy Spirit inasmuch as that same life is also the transmission of the gospel (understood in its widest sense: as the whole reality of Christianity). Thus, Tradition is not simply the transmission of the *depositum*. It includes the progress and doctrinal development in the Church. The Bible is the first written expression (written by divine inspiration) of Tradition. Tradition explains the sense of Scripture and is, for its part, fed by Scripture. The soul of all this living transmission of the gospel is the Holy Spirit. If we begin from this understanding, we see that asking if Tradition contains truths not contained in Scripture is meaningless; Tradition and Scripture are inseparable realities.[57]

J.B. Cardinal Franzelin is the first representative of the Roman School initiated in the Roman College by Perrone in 1824. In *Tractatus de divina Traditione et Scriptura*, Franzelin made an important effort to clarify these issues. His theological conception is best characterized, perhaps, by his insistence upon the role of the Magisterium of the Church—as a principal part of active Tradition, as a functioning element in the discernment and preservation of authentic traditions.

Besides exposing the formal insufficiency of Scripture,[58] Franzelin asserts that an a *priori* answer—taking into consideration the nature of revelation, Scripture and Tradition—cannot be given to the question of whether there are revealed truths that are not contained in Scripture. He argues that this question depends on divine freedom. Therefore, a historical investigation is necessary to find out if such truths exist or not. He answers in the affirmative: there is *dogmata non scripta*.[59] As examples, he quotes following the teaching of the Church Fathers, the authorization of the canon of inspired books, the baptism of children, and the validity of baptism conferred by heretics. Nevertheless, immediately after giving those examples, Franzelin insists that the truly important point in his argument with the Protestant theologians is not this question, but the formal principle of Tradition.[60]

D. The Theology of the Twentieth Century and Vatican Council II

The definition of the dogma of the Assumption of Mary in 1950 was the occasion for a renewal of studies concerning the relationship between Scripture and Tradition. The main question raised by this definition was whether revealed truth is contained only in unwritten Tradition—and if there is a constitutive dogmatic Tradition for it—or whether the Assumption is revealed in some way in Scripture.[61]

In 1956, J.R. Geiselmann published an article in which he posited the *material sufficiency of Scripture*, presenting it as a faithful interpretation of the Council of Trent.[62] Even though this thesis had some precedents,[63] it contradicted traditional and common doctrine. The publication of Geiselmann's thesis gave birth to many studies and a vibrant controversy that lasted until Vatican Council II. Theologians took various positions on the question that can be summarized in three basic groups.

First, H. Lennerz proposed the thesis of the *material insufficiency of Scripture* in a polemic against Geiselmann.[64] In addition to the formal distinction between Scripture and Tradition, Lennerz asserted the material distinction between Scripture and *unwritten traditions* affirmed by the Council of Trent. In this sense, Scripture and traditions (not Tradition) "exclude each other: something is either written or it is not written."[65] This is self-evident. Nevertheless, these unwritten traditions, which certainly are not contained in Scripture, either have some truths of faith or specify only cultural and disciplinary aspects. Lennerz and many others in those years and before argued that there are also truths of faith transmitted by unwritten traditions. The Council of Trent's decree *Sacrosancta* does not limit the contents of such traditions to cultural and disciplinary aspects. The supporters of this position interpreted the teaching of Vatican I in the same way. They literally included the Tridentine teaching.[66]

Geiselmann's thesis of the *material sufficiency of Scripture,* the second thesis, obviously cannot be identified with the Protestant principle of *sola Scriptura* because it asserts the *material* sufficiency of Scripture while recognizing its *formal* insufficiency. Moreover, his thesis admits the existence of a *constitutive tradition* related to *morals* and *customs* of the Church. According to this argument, Tradition, regarding the contents of faith, is only explanatory and interpretative.[67] Geiselmann defended his thesis with a historical analysis of the writings of St. Irenaeus and St. Vincent of Lerins.[68]

The third theory was best put forward by J. Beumer. It can be considered an attempt to find middle ground between the two previous theories. Beumer called his proposal "the Theory of the Relative Sufficiency of Scripture." He insists heavily on the union of Scripture and Tradition and on their interdependence, drawing inspiration from Möhler and Scheeben. The substance of his thesis can be summarized as follows: *All* revealed truths are *formally* contained in Tradition (explicitly or implicitly) and *all are substantially* contained in Sacred Scripture in the sense that all have their *foundation* in Scripture although not all can be deduced from Scripture.[69]

This theological environment greatly influenced the deliberations of Vatican II that preceded the approval and promulgation of the dogmatic constitution *Dei Verbum*.[70]

The Council described the relationship between Scripture and Tradition first as *unity*: "Sacred Tradition and Sacred Scripture, then, are bound closely together, and communicate one with the other. For both of them, flowing out from the same divine well-spring, come together in some fashion to form one thing, and move toward the same goal."[71] Their unity arises from their common divine origin, their interdependence that in a certain way constitutes them in one reality, and their common purpose of transmitting Divine Revelation. Scripture and Tradition are not two complementary deposits. They constitute one deposit of revelation.

There is unity, but there is also *distinction*: Scripture is by itself *locutio Dei* (pronouncement of God) not just in content but also in its expression. Yet, we must always remember that Tradition is human word, although it transmits faithfully and completely thanks to the assistance of the Holy Spirit, the Word of God as directed to the apostles by Christ. Therefore, it is not only a question of distinguishing what is written from what is not. The Council reaffirmed what the Church has always taught: that Scripture alone is not enough for the Church to possess the totality of what God has revealed to mankind.[72]

From the text and the history of its elaboration, it is evident that *Dei Verbum* left open the issue of the relationship between Scripture and Tradition from the standpoint of their material contents. Nevertheless, we could assert that the Council did not see this question as the most important point. The Church has never considered Scripture without reference to Tradition or Tradition without reference to Scripture, because Tradition itself is continually referring to Scripture. This document teaches, "It is clear, therefore, that, in the supremely wise arrangement of God, sacred Tradition, sacred Scripture and the Magisterium of the Church are so connected and associated that one of them cannot stand without the others."[73]

Finally, the Council taught that because of all this, Scripture and Tradition have to be received with the same veneration and piety, as the Council of Trent had previously taught. "Both Scripture and Tradition must be accepted and honored with equal feelings of devotion and reverence."[74] This obviously does not mean that we should ignore the aforementioned distinction (Sacred Scripture is inspired, whereas none of the particular expressions of the unwritten Tradition are so informed).[75]

III. Conclusion

From all that has been said up to this point, we can draw some conclusions about three aspects: the unity and distinction between Scripture and Tradition, the interdependence between them and their relation in regard to material content.[76]

A. Unity and Distinction

The unity between Scripture and Tradition is based on *their common origin* in God. God is the primary author of Scripture by means of inspiration. Also, it is God who established the principle of Tradition through entrusting the task of preaching the gospel with the Holy Spirit's assistance to the apostles (and thereafter to the Church of all times, although in different ways).

Moreover, the unity between Scripture and Tradition lies in their *common finality*, which is the transmission of the Word of God, of the gospel understood in a wide sense, namely, of all the reality of Christianity for the glory of God and the salvation of mankind.

There is, moreover, a third root of unity between the Bible and Tradition, which is intimately related to their common finality, and that is their *common content*. In fact, both Scripture and Tradition transmit the same reality: the gospel. About this there is no doubt. Nevertheless, as we well know, there are different answers to the question of whether Tradition contains truths that are not present in Scripture. In order to reach a conclusion on this, we need to summarize some fundamental information about other aspects of their relationship.

The *distinction or difference* between Sacred Scripture and Sacred Tradition is obviously important since it relates to the *way or manner* of transmission of the gospel (written and oral). Nevertheless, this aspect—considered in its simple materiality—does not reflect the essence of the difference because, among other things, oral tradition is often written down.

The main aspect of the difference is structural. The structure of the Bible is the one of written text, and therefore, fixed and definitive in itself. The structure of Tradition is one of a living reality in the sense that growth and development pertain to its essence. This growth does not arise from the addition of novelties to the original deposit (because then it would be neither tradition nor transmission). Rather, it is the deepening or growth in the intelligence of the deposit, by the explicitness of what was in the original deposit if only in an implicit manner.[77]

Another aspect of the difference, also "structural," is this: Scripture, by itself, is the *Word of God* (by inspiration), whereas Tradition is the *human word* that reminds and explains divine teaching with the Holy Spirit's assistance. The Holy Spirit prevents errors in the body of Tradition (although not in each one of its individual expressions) and in some specific acts (dogmatic definitions of the Church).

B. Interdependence

The interdependence between Scripture and Tradition is, somehow, the aspect that precisely determines the scope of unity and difference. We can find a reciprocal dependence between Scripture and Tradition in their formation, recognition and function in the life of the Church.

As a matter of fact, it is evident that Scripture depends on previous oral tradition for its *formation*. Still, something is also very clear: as the inspired books were being written, the oral preaching was correctly maintained in the written texts.

Moreover, Scripture and Tradition need each other for *recognition*. It is particularly clear that Scripture is recognized as such (as inspired) thanks to Tradition.[78] Further, Scripture needs this recognition, as it pertains to apostolic Tradition, as something received from the past. That is because this recognition is the only immediate testimony of apostolic preaching. Obviously, this does not mean that the contents of Scripture can be thought of as coming only from the apostles. It means that anything that contradicts Scripture cannot be part of the true apostolic tradition, despite any other attribute that may be presented or adduced (i.e., antiquity).

Lastly, the interdependence between Scripture and Tradition regarding their *function in the life of the Church* derives from the historically proven fact that Tradition interprets Scripture. Tradition depends on Scripture for its primary function (without Scripture, there is no interpretation). Also, without Tradition "there is no Scripture": the letter exists, but it is dead. As St. Hilary of Poitiers wrote, "Scripture is meant to be understood, not merely read."[79] The true intelligence of Scripture is not limited to what could come from literary or philological analysis. It includes—and this is the essential point—a superior intelligence. It includes, above all, the Holy Spirit's active assistance to the Church, assistance from *analogia fidei*, and help from the Christological reading of the Old Testament, which is carried out considering the unity between both Testaments. In this sense, the interpretation of the Bible by Tradition does not consist only or mainly in the transmission of interpretation of specific texts accomplished orally by the apostles. It also consists in the application, through the history of the Church, of the *method of interpreting the Bible* used and taught by Christ and the apostles.[80]

C. Relationship with Regards to Material Content

Now we can renew our analysis of whether or not Tradition contains something that is not contained in Scripture. The first answer is a consequence of all that has already been said: Tradition contains many *unwritten* things, *but they are "contained"* in Scripture.

We are dealing here with semantics. In Tradition, we find truths—solemnly defined by the Magisterium of the Church—that are neither explicitly nor implicitly found in Scripture (if we understand "implicitly" in its most restricted sense). Although these truths are not to be found in Scripture by the merely human means of hermeneutics (philological, historical, etc.), they are, nevertheless, *contained in Scripture as interpreted* by Tradition. For example, consider the question of the *post-partum* virginity of the Blessed Virgin Mary. The Bible does not explicitly assert it. It cannot be deduced with absolute certainty by means of human reasoning from other explicit biblical texts. Nevertheless, this truth is contained in *Scripture as interpreted by Tradition* by means of the principle of the Christological reading of the Old Testament (especially the prophecy in Ez 44: 1–2) and with the assistance of the Holy Spirit. In this same sense, it is clear that there are also other unwritten truths that are contained in Scripture and interpreted by Tradition.

There is no doubt that there are *specific unwritten apostolic traditions* referring to cult and ecclesiastical discipline that carry doctrinal implications (for instance, the baptism of children, the validity of baptism conferred by heretics). In any event, the doctrinal implications of those traditions, as was first pointed out by the Fathers and then by theologians, can be considered "contained in interpreted Scripture," even when they are not written.

Nonetheless, we must not exclude *a priori* the possibility of the existence of truths of faith that are not contained in Scripture, because we cannot arbitrarily limit the parameters of divine communication to humanity. As we have seen, this is a matter of fact, not of possibility. Should a specific truth of faith not be found at all in the Bible, we must say that the corresponding *constitutive* tradition backing up this truth exists in a strong sense. Until now, it does not seem that any truth of faith without foundation in Scriptures has been found, and it is very difficult for such a truth to exist because of the union between truths. Let us recall, for instance, that the solemn Magisterium of the Church, upon defining the dogmas of the infallibility of the Roman pontiff and of the Assumption of the Virgin, had based these declarations solely on Scripture and not on Tradition.[81] Although these truths are not to be found in the Bible, either explicitly or implicitly in a strict sense, we can consider them "contained in Scripture as interpreted by Tradition."

Lastly, we can point out that the study of the interdependence between Scripture and Tradition helps us to better understand the scope of the unity between them. Vatican II rigorously affirmed this unity when the Council Fathers taught that Scripture and Tradition (as well as the Magisterium as the authentic interpreter) "cannot stand without the others."[82] This reality constitutes a fundamental principle for any theological study.

CHAPTER 6

FAITH IN GOD
ACCORDING TO THE BIBLE

Biblical teaching presents supernatural faith as the *utmost adherence to the Word of God*. To believe in God is to *receive the Word of the Father through the action of the Holy Spirit* (cf. Lk 1: 35; 38: 45).[1] It is to receive his Word in such a way that it presides over and enlightens one's life and thought (cf. Jn 1: 9–14; Eph 3: 17).[2]

According to biblical teaching, belief is adherence to the divine word inasmuch as the word *word* is understood as the principle of knowledge and spiritual life and inasmuch as the word *divine* is the norm, the primary and absolute criterion of all knowledge and spiritual dynamisms (cf. 1 Thes 2: 13; 2 Cor 5: 20; Phil 2: 13; Heb 11: 1–40; 1 Pt 1: 23; Jas 1: 18; 1 Jn 5: 9–11).[3]

I.   The Faith of Abraham

The Letter to the Hebrews, in its great eulogy of the faith of Israel's ancestors, lays special emphasis on Abraham's faith: "By faith Abraham obeyed when he was called to go out to a place which he was to receive as an inheritance; and he went out, not knowing where he was to go" (Heb 11: 8; cf. Gen 12: 1–4). By faith, he lived as a stranger and pilgrim in the promised land (cf. Gen 23: 4). By faith, Sarah was given to conceive the son of the promise. And by faith Abraham offered his only son in sacrifice (cf. Heb 11: 17).

Abraham thus fulfils the definition of faith in Hebrews 11: 1: "Faith is the assurance of things hoped for, the conviction of things not seen" (Heb 11: 1): "Abraham believed God, and it was reckoned to him as righteousness" (Rom 4: 3; cf. Gen 15: 6). Because he was "strong in his faith," Abraham became the "father of all who believe" (cf. Rom 4: 11; Gen 15: 15).[4]

The exemplary value of the faith of Abraham was manifested during his life by actions of fear, reverence, worship, obedience, and hope. This faith can be summarized in three fundamental, connected features: obedience, trust, and fidelity, which have Abraham's knowledge of God as omnipotent, trustworthy and loyal as their common root.[5]

A. Faith as Obedience to God

Abraham's obedience particularly manifested his faith in God. The act of obedience presupposes listening, as is indicated by the Greek word *hypakóe* and the Latin *audire/obaudire*. In biblical language, listening connotes the active attitude of a person or a people before God, who reveals himself in the word, the command, or the announcement (cf. Ex 33: 11; Dt 5: 1; 6: 4; 9: 1; 1 Sm 3: 9; Is 8: 9).[6] The obedience of faith is the response to the invitation of God, who calls man to walk with him, to live in intimate friendship with him.

Abraham's obedience to divine commands goes beyond the level of moral virtue and discipline. It becomes an expression of theological faith, precisely because there is a voluntary and exceptional acceptance of the word of God in the essence of the accomplishment of God's orders. It stays voluntary because Abraham remained free to accept or reject such a word, exceptional because he recognized the absolute character of the divine word and placed it above the rest of the words and ideas he knew.

St. Paul used the expression "obedience of faith" (Rom 1: 5; 16: 26), as does St. Peter who calls Christians "obedient children" (1 Pt 1: 14). "To obey (from the Latin *ob-audire*, to "hear or listen to") in faith is to submit freely to the word that has been heard, because its truth is guaranteed by God, who is truth itself. Abraham is the model of such obedience offered us by Sacred Scripture. The Virgin Mary is its most perfect embodiment."[7]

B. Faith as Confidence and Abandonment in God's Hands

Abraham acted on faith; he acted upon a *lack of evidence*. He headed toward an unknown land. He expected a child against all human expectations. He prepared to sacrifice his only son without knowing how the divine promise of giving him numerous descendants would be fulfilled thereafter.

Faith always implies a certain obscurity. It requires living in mystery. When we act in faith, we can never expect a complete explanation or a perfect comprehension of what we believe. When our faith is transformed into the heavenly vision, then it will cease to be faith (cf. Mt 13: 11; Lk 8: 10; Jn 20: 8, 29; 1 Jn 3: 1–2; 1 Cor 13: 8–13; 2 Cor 5: 7; Rom 11: 25–26; Eph 3: 4; 6: 19).

Faith means believing in what we do not see (*fides est de non visis*).[8] "The beginning of a saintly life, that merits eternal life, is a well-grounded faith. In this kind of faith we believe but do not see. The prize for such a faith is that we might see what we believe."[9] The Magisterium of the Church teaches that the object of faith is indeed dark and mysterious. "There are proposed for our belief mysteries hidden in God."[10] We "believe to be true what he has revealed, not because we perceive its intrinsic truth by the natural light of reason, but because of the authority of God himself, who makes the revelation."[11]

Therefore, theological faith properly consists of accepting as true certain things that human reason cannot comprehend and supporting oneself solely upon divine testimony (cf. 1 Jn 5: 1–12). Thus, the attitude of the person who believes in God is contrary to that of the rationalist, who accepts as real and true only what he is able to understand and satisfactorily explain within human parameters.

Faith's *lack of evidence* is overcome by the believer's confidence of in he who speaks. *To believe supernaturally means to be sure of the Word of God* (cf. Ps 19: 8; 1 Kgs 8: 26; Is 49: 7). It means that we should base our own existence and future on the divine word, acting according to the calling of God and his command (cf. Heb 11: 13–16; 2 Cor 5: 1, 6–9).

We should, however, clarify a few points. *Faith and trust are not the same.* Faith has a fiduciary element of decisive significance, but it is not just that. A deeper and more radical aspect of faith is that it is supernatural knowledge of God. Luther did not sufficiently consider this important concept. He interpreted *fides* as *fiducia*, and he referenced it only to one's own salvation: He identified faith with the inner and secure feeling of attaining eternal salvation through God's merciful concession, because of God's grace in Christ.[12]

According to the Protestant Reformers, therefore, the faith that saves is constituted of three elements. There is, first, an intellectual element (the news of divine revelation, of salvation offered to us in Christ). Secondly, there is an affective element (a feeling that inclines us to accept the news of God's power and mercy). Third, there is a fiduciary element (Faith of the promise, or fiduciary faith, whereby one trusts that sins will be forgiven because of Christ's promises).

They consider conversion, hope, and love insufficient causes of justification. Faith alone is the cause.

In response, the Council of Trent condemned anyone who claimed "that faith that justifies is nothing but confidence in mercy itself, which will forgive our sins because of Christ; or that we are justified, only because of that confidence."[13]

C. Faith as Fidelity to God

Abraham's faith was manifested by means of its strength, stability, and perseverance in following God's instructions, especially in Abraham's heroism at the moment of the test.

Faith is an aspect of the covenant with God. It required fidelity because, for his part, God is true to his promises:

> Therefore do not throw away your confidence, which has a great reward. For you have need of endurance, so that you may do the will of God and receive what is promised. For yet a little while, and the coming one shall come and shall not tarry; but my righteous one shall live by faith, and if he shrinks back, my soul has no pleasure in him. But we are not of those who shrink back and are destroyed, but of those who have faith and keep their souls. (Heb 10: 35–39; cf. Is 26: 20; Hab 2: 4)

Divine plans always take into account moments of trial and recuperation. For example, Abraham had to submit to a terrible test. God commanded him to sacrifice his son, the one born according to the promise. It was a command that greatly tested his faith. We might think the divine command was irrational—as Hebrews 11: 18 points out—because Abraham was asked to sacrifice someone, the one from whom many descendants were to be born, and to sacrifice him in his very youth. According to St. John Chrysostom, the divine command to sacrifice Isaac was directly opposed to God's promise concerning Isaac and the descendants he would bring forth to Abraham.[14] This test challenged Abraham's faith, because he had to overcome the temptation to place his understanding above the divine command; to prefer his judgment to the divine judgment. This would have been a serious breach of faith because, up until this time, Abraham had always given absolute priority to the divine word (cf. Gen 12: 1–4; 17: 15–21; 18: 9–15; 21: 1–3; Heb 11: 8–12).

However, as we well know, Abraham remained true through this difficult test. He submitted his own will and intelligence in absolute trust to the divine plan.

II. Supernatural Faith: Participation in God's Self-knowledge

A. The Intellectual Dimension of Biblical Faith

Returning to our previous line of argument, we can inquire how Abraham was able to overcome such a dramatic test of his faith. In order to answer this question properly, we must grasp the power of Abraham's faith, keeping in mind what the Letter to the Hebrews says about him. "He considered that God was able to raise men even from the dead" (Heb 11: 19).

Abraham remained faithful because he knew that God is almighty. He who had given Isaac life, letting him be born from a dead womb and an old man, could just as easily bring him back to life. Abraham was confident that God could do what seems impossible to men (cf. Gen 18: 13–14; Lk 1: 37; Rom 4: 18).

Moreover, the authority of Hebrews 11: 19 allows us to say that *Abraham was faithful because he knew that God would be true to his covenant.* This thought of resurrection expresses his certainty in the fulfillment of the divine promises, even though he had no idea where his descendants might come from after sacrificing Isaac.

The foundation of Abraham's obedient, trusting, and faithful response to divine commands and words is found in his knowledge of God's omnipotence, mercy, and faithfulness. We can conclude, then, that Abraham's faith consisted in that knowledge of God.

This conclusion is confirmed by the biblical presentation of faith, even on a terminological level. In fact, in the Old Testament, the main root referring to faith is *'mn*, which appears fifty-two times in *hifil* form (*he'min*). It means stability, the security born from being supported by someone. This root directs us primarily to the idea of confidence and abandonment.[15] To believe is to trust God as Abraham (cf. Gen 15: 6) and Moses (cf. Ex 4: 31; 14: 31) did and as other people in danger have done (cf. Is 7: 9; 8: 13; 28: 16).

The word 'emun (cf. Dt 32: 20) has the richest meaning of these terms because it recognizes that there is only one God (cf. Dt 5: 7), that his love is exclusive and worthy of all our trust (cf. Dt 6: 5), and that his precepts deserve our full obedience (cf. Dt 7: 12).

The very frequently used term 'emet adds the nuance of sincerity of heart. It leaves open—more than any other term derived from 'mn—the meaning of truth (cf. Ps 26: 3), credibility of persons and commands (cf. Neh 7: 2; 9: 13), and stability (cf. Is 16: 5; 2 Sm 7: 6).

There are other terms that refer to faith. Batah (to trust) is common in prayers and hymns (cf. Ps 13: 6; 25: 2; 26: 1). Hasah (to take refuge) refers to the search for protection for an individual (cf. Ps 64: 10; Is 57: 13) or a community (cf. Ps 2: 12; 5: 12; 17: 7; 18: 30). Hakah, jahal, and qawah (to expect, to await) refer to a desired intervention from the God who saves.

All of these meanings may be grouped together into a more general one, he'emin. This term stresses the relationship between trustworthiness and the truth. Amen is a participating form. It indicates that everything that comes forth from of the mouth of God deserves our trust; it is true and worthy of being believed. It is safe for us and can be taken as a guide and rule of conduct to correctly direct our lives.[16]

Without a doubt, Old Testament terminology describes faith fundamentally as knowledge or recognition of Yahweh and his salvific power revealed in history. This testimony makes it possible for us to trust his promises and obey his commands.[17]

This biblical vision of belief in God does not change when the plenitude of times comes. Instead, it is reasserted and confirmed, although with a very important revision.

In the New Testament we find that the terminology of the Old Testament undergoes a change. A unique yet common word arises: pisteuo / pistis (to believe, to have faith).[18] It is presented as a continuation of several terms of the Old Testament, from which the New Testament collects the significant heritage, referring them to Christ. The novelty is precisely in this radical reference of faith to Christ, which invites everyone to conversion. It consists not only in refraining from actions against divine law, but of directing ourselves to God in a new way: to God as he reveals and communicates with men in the person of Jesus of Nazareth.[19]

The intellectual aspect of faith is by no means lost in the New Testament. It is expressed in many ways now related to Christ. For instance, St. Paul uses the verbs *to know* (*ghinoskein*) and *to believe*: "For we walk by faith" (2 Cor 5: 7) equals "For now we see in a mirror dimly" (1 Cor 13: 12). "The life I now live in the flesh I live by faith in the Son of God" (Gal 2: 20) is the same as "to know the love of Christ" (Eph 3: 19). For St. John, "I believe that you are the Christ, the Son of God" (Jn 11: 27) is synonymous to "know that this is the Christ" (Jn 7: 26; cf. 8: 24, 28; 14: 2, 20). In St. John's texts, "to believe" and "to know" are intimately related (cf. Jn 6: 69; 8: 31–32; 10: 38; 17: 8; 14: 12; 1 Jn 4: 16) although "belief" presupposes "knowledge," not vice versa (cf. 1 Jn 2: 4, 6).[20]

B. Faith and Truth according to the Bible: The Object of Supernatural Faith

In the Bible, the truth is presented with great richness of nuances and perspectives. It always maintains, as in other cultures, a special relationship with intelligence. In its more precise sense, it signifies coherence, proportion, correspondence, and fidelity. It is the *nexus* between promises and their fulfillment, between thoughts and the words expressing them, between intentions and gestures, between concepts and things.

God's truth is identified with his fidelity when he enters into contact with human beings. He establishes a covenant with man and promises him salvation. God is faithful and trustworthy; he is truth itself. Isaiah twice presents the same formula, which can be translated as "God is faithful" or "God is truth" (cf. Is 59: 14, 15; 65: 16; Ps 45: 4; 30: 9).

Based on what we have just discussed, we may assert that the object of supernatural faith (what is known) is divine truth. Further, the motive of supernatural faith (what supports the believer in his own difficulty of supernatural belief) is also divine truth. *The truth that is God appears at the same time as the reality to be believed in and as the motive to believe.*

We said that Abraham overcame the test because he was sure of the divine omnipotence and fidelity. We now add that it was precisely that firm and secure knowledge that enabled him to be faithful and allowed the omnipotence of God to be manifested in his life. Consequently, it can be asserted that, in a certain way, he imitated and participated in the divine fidelity and omnipotence by means of his faith. The Bible, in fact, highlights the fact that, with faith, man participates in the workings of God. It happened thus with Moses (cf. Ex 17: 12; Nm 12: 7) and David (cf. 1 Sm 22: 14; 2 Sm 7: 16). In contrast, one is unstable without faith. He has no weight. He is empty and passes through life without leaving a trace. He becomes like the idols that he worships, which are nothing but vanity, appearance, and deceit (cf. Is 7: 9; 19: 1, 3; Ez 30: 13; Hab 2: 4, 19; Ps 96: 5; 97: 7; Bar 6).[21] From this perspective, we may conclude that *with faith, man participates in the truth that is God.*

The New Testament enlightens the connection between faith and truth that was shown earlier through the Old Testament. We may, therefore, assert that faith is that which puts man beside God, beside the light. Faith takes man out of darkness and sets him apart from evil (cf. Col 1: 12–13; 1 Pt 2: 9). *Supernatural faith puts man in truth and puts truth in man.*[22] The believer reaches a point where he excludes lies and errors because faith heals the will—upon which deceit depends—and enlightens the intelligence—freeing it from mistakes (cf. 1 Jn 2: 27; 3: 9).[23]

When we read Hebrews 11: 1; 1 Corinthians 13: 12; and 1 John 3: 2 together according to this interpretation,[24] we discover that a person, through supernatural faith, not only knows God, but also participates in the same knowledge that God has of himself and of all things in himself. *With supernatural faith, man knows what God and only God knows, and he knows it precisely as God knows it: with his Word.* "Faith as a specific supernatural virtue infused into the human spirit makes us sharers in knowledge of God as a response to his revealed word."[25]

Because the object of faith is what God himself knows as he knows it, it can be stated with the formula used by St. Thomas: *The object char-*

acteristic of supernatural faith is the first truth.[26] We may also say faith is "as a mark or seal of the first truth on the soul" (*est quasi sigillatio Veritatis Primae in anima*).[27] In fact, according to the notion of truth we have delineated before, the expression "first truth" indicates the first correspondence between the first intellect and the first reality. That is, it indicates what God (the first intelligence) primarily knows about himself (the first being), thereby precisely indicating the knowledge God has of himself.

In fact, when God reveals himself to mankind, man responds with faith, accepts his Word and knows with it and because of it. One knows the Father, the Word, and the Holy Spirit. One knows what God has decreed in order to communicate it to creatures. Christian theological tradition summarizes what is properly believed in supernatural faith in two words: the Trinity and the Incarnation.[28] St. Thomas, for instance, brought together all contents of Christian truth in the doctrine of the One and Trinitarian God and man's participation in the life of God through Christ thanks to the Holy Spirit.[29]

It is understood that "the mark of the first truth" is an exclusive effect of that truth. It is "the work of God" (Jn 6: 29); only he can cause it to happen. Faith is a divine gift (cf. Eph 2: 8–9; Mt 16: 16–17). "Faith in itself, even though it may not work through charity, is a gift of God, and its operation is a work belonging to the order of salvation, in that a person yields true obedience to God himself when he accepts and collaborates with his grace which he could have rejected."[30]

Man can do great things with his studies and investigations, with his cultural, scientific, and technological progress. Still, all of these accomplishments remain within the human sphere of things. They cannot attain to those dimensions proper to God. Unaided human reason cannot acquire God's knowledge of himself. People can take in only what God grants them. In other words, man cannot give himself supernatural faith. He can embrace it, and for this, there is no need for great intellectual effort. One needs only to have simplicity and humility of heart (cf. Mt 11: 25–27; 1 Cor 1: 19–31). On the other hand, one can refuse this gift or even lose it after having accepted it (cf. Mk 16: 16; Heb 6: 4–6; 10: 26–31; 2 Pt 2: 20–22).

In the next chapter we will deal with faith as gift and the confluence of freedom and grace in the act of faith.

III. Wisdom and Biblical Faith

The Church has always taught, based on biblical texts, that *faith is knowledge.* The Church shows a clear consciousness that by asserting the belief that faith has intellectual substance, it becomes possible to study its various characteristics in a complete manner.[31] On the other hand, these characteristics immediately appear to be in conflict both with one another and with other dimensions of man when—in keeping with Kantian epistemology—faith is presented as a feeling, as a form of trust of exclusively practical or moral value. This schema systematically denies the intellectual substance of faith. It confines faith solely to the will or affections.[32]

Still, the supernatural faith is not purely speculative or theoretical knowledge. It is always affective and loving knowledge. It is the act of a devoted and loving intelligence precisely because it is the intellectual aspect of the covenant: It is the knowledge involved in a friendship between the one who knows and the known one. This love lasts because it is a participation in God's knowledge of himself. Therefore, supernatural faith is radically distinguished from pagan *gnosis*, which is a knowledge directed to dominating the world and others, the affirmation of the ego and of our own life, and is never directed to service as the gift of God to others.[33] All of these ideas lead us to consider supernatural faith as wisdom.[34]

The knowledge of supernatural faith belongs to the type of knowledge that is somehow linked to wisdom. In Latin, "wisdom" suggests the pleasing character of knowing (*sapientia est quasi sapida scientia*); wisdom is a type of pleasing knowledge. In the Septuagint, the Greek term *sophia*, derived from the Hebrew root *hkm*, relates wisdom to knowledge, intelligence, education, and the fear of God.[35]

According to the Old Testament, the wisdom that one must acquire through his own effort and with the help of teachers is a deep and penetrating comprehension of reality. This comprehension will let him "know how to act," "know how to live," and enable him to judge and advise. Wisdom is highly praised in the Bible because it involves the contemplation of the highest things. It judges everything according to definitive reasons and criteria.[36]

In any event, according to the Bible, the highest and truest wisdom is a gift from God. It comes from him; only those who fear the Lord and keep his commandments can receive it (cf. Wis 1: 1–5; 7: 7). It is not mere theoretical knowledge. Wisdom is also practical, affective, and pious knowledge (cf. Wis 8: 5–18). In conclusion, *wisdom in man consists in knowing God and living according to his Word and his Law* (cf. Prv 1: 7–10; 2: 1–13; 3: 1–20). Wisdom's religious character comes from the fact that wisdom and strength dwell in God. Insight and prudence belong to him (cf. Jb 12: 13). Wisdom is the image of God's greatness and a reflection of his light (cf. Wis 7: 26).[37]

The apostles stress this character of the knowledge of faith. For instance, St. Paul frequently uses the term *gnosis* or *sophia* to indicate the deep and living knowledge of salvation (cf. Rom 15: 14; 1 Cor 1: 5; 2: 6–16; 2 Cor 2: 14; 4: 6; 8: 7; 10: 5; Phil 3: 8; Col 2: 3; 3: 10) and God's will (cf. Rom 2: 20). He does so in spite of the pretensions of Greek culture and philosophy, which were ignorant of much about God and salvation (cf. 1 Cor 1–2; Rom 1–2). The gift of the spirit lets us deepen our sharing in the revealed word (cf. 1 Cor 12: 8; 13: 2). It is a gift superior to spoken languages (cf. 1 Cor 2: 6–7; 14: 6).

In the New Testament, one obtains true wisdom of humanity in relation to Christ. This wisdom consists in believing in Jesus, who is eternal wisdom, the image of the invisible God, the brightness of his glory (cf. Col 1: 15; Heb 1: 3) who became flesh and lived on earth, who died and rose in glory (cf. 1 Cor 1: 22–25; 2: 8). Only those enlightened from on high can understand these things. True wisdom demands that one take in grace and be docile to the action of the Holy Spirit (cf. 1 Cor 2: 13–16).[38]

These apostolic teachings were widely echoed in the early Fathers and in the great Doctors of the Church. They were interested in showing the faithful the greatness of the received gift. St. Thomas, for instance, wrote:

> In everyday life, the prudent man is called wise who directs every human action to its proper end. Therefore, he who contemplates the supreme cause of the universe, which is God, is a wise man par excellence. So, as St. Augustine says, wisdom is the knowledge of divine things. As sacred doctrine deals with God…not only what from him is recognizable through creatures…but it extends to what only he knows and what has been communicated by revelation, such a doctrine must be considered as the minimum expression of wisdom.[39]

In the Greek world, as in Kantian epistemology, the faith was not appreciated like knowledge. Perfection of knowledge, according to the Greeks, cannot reside in accepting another's word. *From the standpoint of the manner of knowing*, that insight is indisputable, as St. Thomas admits. However, if things are *considered from the standpoint of what is known*, it can happen that another's word may be richer and more enlightening than one's own words. "Under the same conditions, seeing is better than listening; but if he through whom something is known is quite above what one is capable to see by oneself, in that case listening is better than seeing."[40] Faith is participation in the knowledge of someone who knows. Divine faith participates in the proper and exclusive knowledge of God.

With his characteristic daring and precision, St. Thomas Aquinas affirmed that the faithful Christian knows more about God and his plans than the best pagan philosophers, even if the Christian is uneducated and ignorant in many human issues.[41] In fact, faith gives Christians a new dimension in contemplating the world and its history.[42] The light of faith allows Christians to look at people and things from a higher and more penetrating perspective. It enables the believer to discover transcendent links that tie him to others, to understand the sense of pain and death, the value of life and work, to distinguish the important from the irrelevant. Christians with faith discover that God is a Father. He is not a distant and irascible being who waits for the occasion to implacably judge. He is a being full of love and tender affection toward his creatures (cf. Prv 8: 31). Nothing escapes his providence. He disposes all for the good of those who love him (cf. Rom 8: 12–39). "How beautiful is our Catholic faith! It provides a solution for all our anxieties; it gives peace to the mind and fills the heart with hope."[43]

CHAPTER 7

THEOLOGICAL REFLECTION ABOUT BIBLICAL FAITH

Man needs to correspond to the historical (supernatural) revelation that comes from God. However, faith is not only the human response to divine revelation; it is also a gift from God. In this sense, we can talk about faith as "interior revelation" or as "an interior gift of revelation."

I.   Faith as an Interior Gift of Revelation

Vatican Council I offered this definition:

> We are obliged to yield to God the revealer full submission of intellect and will by faith. This faith, which is the beginning of human salvation, the Catholic Church professes to be a supernatural virtue, by means of which, with the grace of God inspiring and assisting us, we believe to be true what he has revealed, not because we perceive its intrinsic truth by the natural light of reason, but because of the authority of God himself, who makes the revelation and can neither deceive nor be deceived.[1]

This quotation clearly expresses the two aspects of faith to which we have already referred. In fact, faith is the human response to revelation because it is a voluntary acceptance of revelation. It is also God's gift because, as habitual reality (virtue), it is supernatural and, as an act, it is accomplished *Dei aspirante et adiuvante gratia* (by the inspiration and the assistance of the grace of God).

In its own presentation concerning faith, Vatican II also highlighted these two aspects.

> "The obedience of faith" (Rom 16: 26; cf. Rom 1: 5; 2 Cor 10: 5–6) must be given to God as he reveals himself. By faith man freely commits his entire self to God, making "the full submission of his intellect and will to God who reveals," and willingly assenting to the revelation given by him. Before this faith can be exercised, man must have the grace of God to move and assist him; he must have the interior helps of the Holy Spirit, who moves the heart and converts it to God, who opens the eyes of the mind and "makes it easy for all to accept and believe the truth."[2]

The Council Fathers taught us that faith—inasmuch as it is an interior gift of revelation—is, in reference to the "heart" and "mind" of man, a *conversion of the will and an enlightenment of the intelligence*. Regarding faith as a response of man, they stress its character as *personal donation to God*.

A. Indications in the New Testament

In the New Testament we find many passages that indicate this aspect of faith as an interior gift of God to man. Here, we can recall particularly those passages referring to the gift of faith in which the idea of revelation is explicitly mentioned.

"I thank thee, Father, Lord of heaven and earth, that thou hast hidden these things from the wise and understanding and revealed them [*apekalypsas*] to babes" (Mt 11: 25). Contextual evidence shows this "revelation" made to the little ones is not the public revelation directed, in fact, to everyone (including wise and prudent men). It is the acceptance of public revelation. It is clear, then, that this acceptance of the Word of God—faith—is, in itself, the Father's gift.

A similar text is found in Jesus' response to the confession of St. Peter at Caesarea Phillippi. "Blessed are you, Simon Bar-Jona! For flesh and blood has not revealed this [*apekalypsen*] to you, but my Father who is in heaven" (Mt 16: 17). This is not a new public revelation received only by Peter, but of faith recognized as a private, or interior, revelation.[3]

In other texts, particularly those of St. John dealing with the testimony (*martyria*) given by God for the word and mission of Christ, such testimony can be understood as the interior gift of faith. They testify to the messianism and the divinity of Jesus (cf. Jn 5: 37; 1 Jn 5: 6; 5: 10).

The expressions "interior revelation" and "interior testimony" generally present faith as a gift of God. However, the New Testament has other ways of expressing this reality that more precisely indicate the nature of this gift of God. They are called *attraction* and *enlightenment*.

For example, we can remember Christ's words, "No one can come to me unless the Father who sent me draws him" (Jn 6: 44). The *attraction* carried out by the Father is clearly related to faith, because in the next verse Jesus says, "Every one who has heard and learned from the Father comes to me" (Jn 6: 45; cf. 65).

Regarding faith as enlightenment, we can examine, for example, St. Paul's words, "It is the God that said, 'Let light shine out of darkness,' who has shone (*elampsen*) in our hearts to give the light of the knowledge (*pros phótismon tés gnóseós*) of the glory of God in the face of Christ" (2 Cor 4: 6; cf. Eph 1: 18). The Apostle refers to the knowledge of Christ's divinity ("the glory of God in the face of Christ") and asserts that this knowledge is the effect of an interior enlightenment accomplished by God in man ("in our hearts"). Faith is, then, *enlightenment* of the heart (in this case, "heart" means the center of thought and knowledge).[4]

B. Theological Reflection

We can now explain the nature of this attraction and enlightenment and why this gift of God is necessary so man can receive into himself—believe—the Word of God.

St. Thomas Aquinas taught, "He who believes has good motives to believe. In fact, he is induced by the authority of divine doctrine, confirmed by miracles, and particularly by the internal inspiration of God that invites man to believe."[5] Man is induced to believe not only from the outside, but also by an interior instinct with which God invites him to believe. In another work, St. Thomas asserted that this instinct comes from the mind: "There is another interior call, that is not but a certain instinct of the soul, through which man's heart is encouraged by God to assent to things belonging to faith or virtue."[6]

In other texts, St. Thomas wrote of faith as an interior inclination: "The habit of faith inclines the soul to accept things suitable to the true faith and not to others."[7]

This instinct is the natural tendency of faculties toward their proper objects—these objects "attract" the faculties. We know that the intellect has a natural tendency (instinct) to know the truth. Why, then, does God need to give us another instinct necessary to know revealed truths? The answer can be only this: Because supernatural faith, precisely because it is super-natural, is not manifested to the intelligence through evidence. Therefore, it does not attract the intelligence. In other words, in order for supernatural truth to *attract* the human intellect, it must be made *connatural* to this truth.

At this point, it is necessary to ask why a truly human faith—founded only upon the credibility of a witness without the need for any recourse to the truth other than the natural one—is possible. With human faith, in fact, the truth is not manifested with evidence as truth; nevertheless, the witness who asserts it is believed. This is possible because the intellect, besides seeing the credibility of the witness, sees the proper connaturality with the *natural* truth proposed to it. The intellect has a simple, natural instinct toward truth. It can see the credibility of the witness, and, therefore, the credibility of his testimony. However, it cannot perceive a proper connaturality with that testimony if it has supernatural content (because such connaturality does not exist).

Therefore, to accept supernatural revelation, exterior testimony is not enough. God must make the human mind connatural with the supernatural through an elevation. *Habitus fidei* (habit of faith) is precisely that.[8] The interior gift of revelation is then understood—faith as "interior revelation"—as both *attraction* and *enlightenment*. These notions converge in that of the *instinct*.

As we may recall, in the New Testament this gift of God was termed enlightenment. The Fathers, particularly St. Augustine, used this term many times.[9] The Second Council of Orange asserted, with Augustinian terminology, that it is not possible to believe "without the enlightenment and inspiration of the Holy Spirit" (*absque illuminatione et inspiratione Spiritus Sancti*).[10]

In an exaggerated Augustinian-neoplatonic context, this "enlightenment" was considered the whole substance of divine revelation, thereby reducing public revelation to the recollection of truths previously received and known through "interior revelation" ("enlightenment"). This was, for example, the theory of William of Auxerre in his *Summa Aurea*, which had some influence on post-Scholastics and St. Thomas Aquinas, although he did not fall into the "enlightenment" exaggeration.[11]

St. Thomas frequently wrote about the infused habit of faith as *lumen fidei* or *lumen infusum*. Accordingly, he asserted, for instance, that "infused light, the habit of faith, manifests the articles [of faith], as the light of the agent intellect manifests principles naturally known."[12] It is necessary to understand this and other similar texts from the position of William of Auxerre. St. Thomas clearly pointed out, "as first common principles of natural law are themselves manifested to those who have the use of reason, and do not need to be enacted; so, to believe in God is by itself manifested [*primum et per se notum*] to those who have faith."[13] This means that through the enlightenment of faith (the virtue of faith), the believer knows that he believes God. St. Thomas also says it more clearly: "The faithful know [the things of faith] not because of a sort of demonstration, but because, as we said, they see with the light of faith that they have to be believed."[14] Then, *habitus fidei* (or *lumen fidei*) does not communicate the contents of revelation by itself, but makes the human mind connatural with revealed truth, showing not so much the credibility of the truth, but that it is believable (the fact that truth should be believed).

Thus, there is no real distinction between attraction and enlightenment save the distinction of reason. In fact, to the concept of instinct (suggesting attraction) enlightenment adds the idea of a certain luminosity, which is quite pertinent because in the attraction of the mind to revealed truths there is "news" of its "believability."

From all that we have heretofore argued, we may state *that there is a relationship between public and interior revelation.* Primarily, it is clear that there are not "two types of revelation" but two consecutive moments of the entire revelation (entire in the sense that it was effectively received—assimilated—by man himself).

Moreover, exterior revelation definitely exercises a certain primacy over interior revelation regarding the contents of faith. Still, interior revelation is important for human acceptance of the contents of faith because attraction (or enlightenment) "predisposes" man to receive in himself the revealed truth.

These two moments—the exterior and the interior—can happen separately. In fact, the gospel's announcement can be "heard" but not accepted. The reverse situation, interior revelation without exterior revelation, also occurs. This happens when those who have not heard the gospel have grace, and, therefore, the *habitus fidei,* which is inseparable from grace. This habit makes men connatural and predisposes them to receive exterior revelation when it comes.

Two conditions can cause problems when dealing with our need for interior revelation to believe in exterior revelation. First, there are those who believe in various theories or propositions that are false and unnatural: How is this possible? Do they have a "connaturality" toward the supernatural (or at least, toward the preternatural) in their intelligence? Since it certainly does not come from God, from where does this "connaturality" come? Secondly, there is the case of those who believe authentic supernatural truths who have a faith without formation (i.e., formal heretics. For material heretics this problem does not exist because they have faith, even faith formed by charity, if they are in God's grace).

The answer to these questions is simple. He who believes falsehood can believe falsely—and does so—without any divine attraction and without any true "connaturality" toward that falsehood. His believing is precisely "against nature" because it is a simple human faith not supported by a sufficiently credible witness. In the case of formal heretics, St. Thomas wrote, "He accepts the other articles (without discrepancy with the faith of the Church). He does so not in the same way that the faithful do, that is, by adherence to the First Truth, for which he needs the help of the habit of faith, but he maintains those things of faith by his own will and judgment."[15]

Consequently, we can say that to believe a truth (or falsehood) about questions that are above natural human capacities, human faith or opinion would be enough. In that case, however, belief would no longer mean to receive in oneself the Word of God that saves. It would do well to here remember, as the apostle St. James wrote, "Even the demons believe—and shudder" (Jas 2: 19).[16]

II. Faith as Man's Response to Revelation: The Act of Faith

If *habitus fidei* or *lumen fidei*—interior revelation—is the gift of God that makes man's mind connatural with—attracted to—supernatural truth, then, the act of faith, the act of believing, is *man's response to revelation*. It is the acceptance of exterior revelation made possible by interior revelation.

This acceptance is not a simple intellectual act, because even when the intellect is made connatural with supernatural truth, acceptance is not imposed on the intellect using evidence. Hence, the act of faith is necessarily a free act of the will. Using St. Augustine's famous words, we can say that to believe is to think by assenting (*credere est cum assensione cogitare*).[17] Alternatively we might choose to employ the argument of Peter of Poitiers: Believing is a movement that comes from faith and freedom (*credere enim motus est proveniens ex fide et libero arbitrio*). In this formulation, faith points out the grace of faith, the interior gift of revelation.[18] Finally, as St. Thomas wrote, "we consent with the will to things of faith, not by necessity of reason, since they are above reason."[19]

A. Intelligence and the Will in the Act of Faith

Interestingly enough, the will moves the intelligence, and this is not against the nature of the human spirit. In the field of the spirit's natural activity, there is a relationship of mutual dependency between intellect and will.

As St. Thomas explained:

> If we consider the movements of the soul's potencies from the object that specifies the act, the first beginning of movement pertains to the intellect. Consequently, the understood good moves the will itself, too. If, on the contrary, we consider the movement of the soul's potencies from the action as such, then the beginning of the movement corresponds to the will. In fact, to the potency always corresponds the principal end, which moves the potency to act. This potency is responsible for what is the means for the end, as the military official moves the one who manufactures the reins for the horses. In this way, the will moves itself and all of the other potencies. I understand because I want. In a similar manner I use the rest of my potencies and habits, because I want.[20]

In the case of the act of faith—including human faith—this *intellego quia volo* (I believe because I wish to) carries more weight than the case where the object is presented to the intellect through evidence (mediate or immediate). Nevertheless, this is not something strange to the dynamic proper to the human spirit.

Nonetheless, there are in the life of a human being many more truths which are simply believed than truths which are acquired by way of personal verification. Who, for instance, could assess critically the countless scientific findings upon which modern life is based? Who could personally examine the flow of information which comes day after day from all parts of the world and which is generally accepted as true? Who in the end could forge anew the paths of experience and thought which have yielded the treasures of human wisdom and religion? This means that the human being—the one who seeks the truth—is also *the one who lives by belief.*[21]

Belief is not something exclusively religious. It belongs to the daily life of men and women. We speak about human and divine faith to distinguish two analogous realities that have certain resemblance and profound supernatural differences.

One aspect of their commonality is that *knowledge is a way to know with certainty*—because faith is not an opinion—*non-evident* realities with our own intellect. It acts as a *singular collaboration of will and intelligence.* Biblical indications of the noetic dimension of faith in God are in harmony with the noetic value found in human faith, which also involves the knowledge and certainty of what is not seen. Human faith is a necessary way to know many realities that would otherwise be unattainable by our own experience or personal reasoning.

It is an obvious fact that faith and trust among people are *essential* for family, personal, and social life.[22]

On the other hand, both consist in *accepting the testimony of another about something.*[23] Thus, it is for human faith taken considered with a more general meaning, and so it is for divine faith:

> If we receive the testimony of men, the testimony of God is greater; for this is the testimony of God that he has borne witness to his Son. He who believes in the Son of God has the testimony in himself. He who does not believe God has made him a liar, because he has not believed in the testimony that God has borne to his Son. And this is the testimony, that God gave us eternal life, and this life is in his Son (1 Jn 5: 9–11).

The profound differences are evident: in the testimonies that are believed; in the order of truths that by Faith are known; in the greater difference which the degree of personal faith entails; and in the effort of adhesion to that which is believed.

B. Grace and Freedom in the Act of Faith

In the act of supernatural faith, it is necessary for the will to be helped by an actual grace (by a divine motion) in order for the will to move the intelligence to assert. We should remember that the Second Council of Orange declared this doctrine—that man cannot believe *absque illuminatione et inspiratione Spiritus Sancti* (without the illumination and inspiration of the Holy Spirit).[24] This teaching was reaffirmed by both Vatican Councils.[25] "In faith, the human intellect and will cooperate with divine grace: 'Believing is an act of the intellect assenting to the divine truth by command of the will moved by God through grace.'"[26]

The reason that people need actual grace for the act of faith ("inspiration of the Holy Spirit") in addition to *habitus fidei* ("enlightenment") cannot be other than the transcendence of the supernatural over the natural human capacities. As St. Thomas taught, "In order to assent to the truth of faith, man is elevated above his own nature, and therefore it is necessary that there is in him a supernatural principle that moves him from the inside, and that principle is God. Therefore, faith, regarding the act of assent, which is its principal act, comes from God, who from the inside moves man by grace."[27] Here, St. Thomas refers to the actual grace that moves the will to assent, not habitual faith. This is made clear when he later writes, "The act of believing certainly depends on the will of the one who believes. But it is necessary that the grace of God prepares man's will so that it may be elevated to things above its nature."[28]

Vatican I and Vatican II clearly taught that the act of faith is *plenum revelanti Deo intellectus et voluntatis obsequium* (a full obedience of the intellect and will to the God of revelation).[29] Thus, the whole person— by way of the two specifically human faculties—responds to the Word of God with a holistic attitude of adherence, not only to the noetic contents of the divine Word, but also to God himself. In fact, *obsequium intellectus et voluntatis* is made to God himself: *revelanti Deo*.[30] Therefore, the act of faith is a personal encounter between the person and God, an encounter that comes from and is made possible by the free divine initiative (cf. Is 65: 1; 1 Jn 4: 10).

This encounter of faith draws man toward a *total option* that envelops his whole life, in the intellectual as well as in its affective and effective dimensions. This is because faith as response is, before anything else, trust in God's love for humanity: "So we know (*egnokamen*) and believe (*peristeukamen*) the love (*agapén*) God has for us" (1 Jn 4: 16). Hence, faith as response entails love and benevolence (*agapé*) rendered to God. Faith acts by charity: "faith working through love [*pistis de' agapés energoumené*]" (Gal 5: 6).[31]

The act of faith is, then, a personal and free human response to the offering that God makes in revelation. Nevertheless, while the offering is free and not obligatory, God is owed a free response. The act of faith in its voluntary and free dimension, is—as we have seen—an *act of obedience*: "Through [Christ] we have received grace and apostleship to bring about the obedience of faith (*eis hupakoén pisteós*) for the sake of his name among all the nations" (Rom 1: 5; cf. Rom 16: 26; Acts 6: 7).[32] This obedience (*hupakoé*) refers to faith in an objective sense (revealed message). However, the act of faith is, in itself, obedience: From listening (*akoé*) we pass to obedience (*hupakoé*).[33]

The act of faith entails an act of obedience, *but this obedience to God does not abridge human freedom.* Quite to the contrary, *it is the act of the greatest freedom*, because "freedom finds its true meaning when it is put to the service of the truth that redeems, when it is spent in seeking God's infinite Love, which liberates us from all forms of slavery."[34] The act of faith is the radical and fundamental exercise of freedom toward the truth that saves. It is also the truth of the infinite love of God for each one of us.

C. The Certitude of Faith

Certitude can be based either on evidence (mediate or immediate) or on fully credible testimony. We can find absolute certitude only on the basis of absolute (or divine) testimony. This is the case of divine faith.[35]

So, the response of faith to revelation has absolute certitude, as the Hebrew root *aman* shows, which has passed to the Greek language as *amén.* As such, we have already seen that Abraham's faith was solid, steady and firm.[36]

Nevertheless, there is an undeniable experience for all believers. Doubt is possible, even for the one who has faith. Here we are not talking about a voluntary doubt, the free suspension of assent. We are talking about doubt that is uninvited by the believer. How is the temptation of doubt possible, if by definition faith is certitude?

The answer to this question lies in the fact that even though the certain root of faith is founded upon God's authority, this authority, as the object of faith, is not evident to the believer. In other words, *faith creates its own foundation.* Thus, in spite of motives for belief and, specifically, of *lumen fidei* itself, which may serve to make the mind connatural with supernatural faith, the act of faith, while being reasonable, remains, as Newman always called it, "a surrender of reason."

Consequently, the believer's mind can be induced—by his own will to voluntary doubt or by external agents in temptations against faith—to consider his faith in relation to his own intelligence. In this way, man experiences the lack of evidence of the believed truth. Involuntary doubt, according to this process, is in reality an experience of the supernaturality of faith. In this sense, the brief response of St. Thomas about the doubt of the faithful can be understood: "That doubt does not come from the cause of faith, but only from us, inasmuch as we cannot reach with the intellect alone, the matters of faith."[37]

III. The Theological, Christological, and Ecclesiastical Character of Faith in the New Testament

In the previous chapter, we learned that the object of biblical faith is God as first truth and Christ as incarnate Word. We can now specify that, in history, this object develops in three directions: toward God, toward Christ, and toward the Church. The response of faith, when it is completely explicit, is always theological, Christological, and ecclesiastical. In addition, in each of these directions it is possible to recognize three aspects.

A. Theological Character of Faith

The act of faith, *credere*, has a triple aspect related to God, which St. Augustine pointed out in his renowned formula: *Credere Deo, credere Deum, credere in Deum* (to believe God, to believe that there is a God, to believe in God).[38] *Credere Deo* expresses the fact that, in the act of faith, God himself is the formal object in the sense of *formal motive* by which man believes. Man believes *God*. Man considers what he believes as true because he believes that God gives trustworthy testimony.

Credere Deum means that God is, above all, the known reality when believing. In a way he is the "material object" of faith; God is the first thing believed. In the most basic terms, he is the accepted truth.

Credere in Deum refers to the faith act, inasmuch as God is also his final cause. When man believes, he approaches God as his Savior. He moves toward him as his final end. This is the aspect of personal donation.

We are not, therefore, discussing three distinct acts but one sole act with a triple relation to its object: i.e., three aspects of the same act of faith. Of the three, the most specific is the first one: *credere Deo*.[39] The other two, in fact, derive from the first one (not provisionally but according to the order of nature). Because we believe God, we know God and we effectively direct ourselves toward him.[40]

It is useful to emphasize here that the act of faith, while including an aspect of voluntary adherence to God as an end (*credere in Deum*), is not an act of charity. As St. Thomas explained, "The will to believe is not an act of charity or hope, but a certain desire of the promised good."[41] In other words, "faith does not assume a will that already loves, but a will that has the intention to love."[42] That is precisely why a true act of faith without charity is theoretically possible (this would be a formless faith).

B. Christological Character of Faith

Faith is theological in its formal motive (*credere Deo*), in its material object (*credere Deum*) and in its final motive or cause (*credere in Deum*). Certainly, as a consequence of human mediation in divine revelation, there is also a human mediation in faith. Still, we believe not only in truths referring to God, but also in truths relative to the world and humanity. In contrast, *concerning the final cause, faith is always directly theological.*

The plenitude of revelation in Christ is further manifested by the fact that the response to this total revelation is not only *credere Christo* and *credere Christum*; it is also *credere in Christum.*

In fact, the New Testament says many times that Jesus demands faith in him and in his teachings. Yet, in contrast to the prophets, he presents himself as the finality of faith. He asks that the faith due solely to God be rendered to him.[43] Among the many verses clearly indicating this, we can remember the following words of Christ to his apostles: "Believe in God, believe also in me [*pisteuete eis ton Theon, kai eis eme pisteuete*]" (Jn 14: 1). *Pisteuete* can mean "you believe" in the indicative sense ("you have faith;" in Latin, *creditis*) or in the imperative sense ("have faith, believe;" in Latin, *credite*). Hence, the Vulgate version is translated: *creditis in Deum, et in me credite*, which is the most plausible reading according to the context.[44]

Consequently, Christ equates faith in God and faith in himself and thereby asserts his own divinity.[45]

We should read these passages with some caution because there is a parallelism in the original Greek text of John 14: 1 between *credere in* (in Greek, *eis*) *Deum and credere in* (in Greek, *eis*) *me* (*Christum*). Here, we do not see an explicit indication of the final aspect of faith (*credere in Deum* as different from *credere Deo* and *de credere Deum*). This distinction of grammatical formulation is not Greek but Latin (as we have said, drawing on St. Augustine). In fact, in primitive oriental creeds the expressions *pisteuomen eis Theon...eis Kyrion Iesoun Christon...eis Pneuma aghion* are found, but others are found, such as *eis sarkos anastasin.*[46] In this last phrase the grammatical construction clearly does not indicate the final aspect of faith, although the accusative preceded by the preposition *eis* does have a dynamic meaning.

Faith in Christ has a central position in the letters of St. Paul. The expression *pistis en Christó Iesou* appears (cf. Gal 3: 26; 5: 6; Col 1: 4; Eph 1: 15). Also *pistis eis Christon* (cf. Col 2: 5) appears, or else *eis Christon Iesoun episteusamen* (cf. Gal 2: 16; Phil 1: 29). Faith, or believing, in Christ can mean, depending on the context, *credere Christum* as well as *credere Christo,* or even that faith is accomplished in Christian existence, that is, "to exist *in Christo.*"[47] On the other hand, faith or believing *eis* Christ, because of the dynamic sense of Greek construction, seems to indicate faith directed toward personal union with Christ (*credere in Christum*).[48]

In St. Paul's writings, we also find the expression *faith of Christ: pistis Christou* (cf. Rom 3: 22, 26; Gal 2: 16, 20; 3: 22; Eph 3: 12; Phil 3: 9). Some authors have understood this expression to assert that Jesus had faith. However, according to exegesis, there should be no doubt as to the intended meaning: The "faith of Christ" means "the faith that the faithful have in Christ."[49]

In conclusion, faith in Christ is not like faith in the prophets, even though it has the same properties of faith in God. This is true not only because Christ is God but also because he is God made man. Christian faith is *both theological and Christological: in Cristo.* We participate in the intimate life of the Holy Trinity as adopted children, and this admirable mystery is fulfilled by faith in Christ. According to St. Paul, "In Christ Jesus you are all sons of God, through faith" (Gal 3: 26).

C. Ecclesiastical Character of Faith

The ecclesiastical character of faith could also be expressed according to the three established aspects of the theological and Christological character. However, it would be an improper or rather analogical way to express this reality. In any event, it would require clear explanations of important differences.

We can say that faith is *credere Ecclesiae* (to believe the Church) because, as we have seen, the Church preserves and transmits the Word of God. She offers revelation to the faithful.

Faith is also *credere Ecclesiam* (to believe that there is a Church) because faith is the object of the belief as it is in itself a mysterious and supernatural reality.

Now the fact that faith is *credere in Ecclesiam* (to believe in the Church) can be said *only in a specific way*: inasmuch as, through faith, the individual person is incorporated into the body of Christ, joins him, and, in so doing, joins with the other faithful (cf. Acts 2: 41, 47; 4: 32). Within the Church, the believer joins Christ and, in Christ, God. In this context, St. Cyprian's well-known phrase is quite appropriate, "No one can have God as his Father who does not have the Church as his Mother."[50]

CHAPTER 8

THE COMMUNAL AND PERSONAL DIMENSIONS OF THE FAITH

The response of faith to revelation is an act of the person. At the same time, this response possesses a communal dimension: It is the faith of the Church.

God himself has invited humanity to be in communion with him not only as individuals, but also a human community. Both the Old and New Testaments manifest this desire of God.

> At all times and in every race, anyone who fears God and does what is right has been acceptable to him (cf. Acts 10: 35). He has, however, willed to make men holy and save them, not as individuals without any bond or link between them, but rather to make them into a people who might acknowledge him and serve him in holiness. He therefore chose the Israelite race to be his own people and established a covenant with it. He gradually instructed this people—in its history manifesting both himself and the decree of his will—and made it holy unto himself. All these things, however, happened as a preparation and figure of that new and perfect covenant which was to be ratified in Christ.... He called a race made up of Jews and Gentiles that would be one, not according to the flesh, but in the Spirit, and this race would be the new people of God.[1]

The existence of the two dimensions—individual and communal—is a manifestation of the supernatural character of Christian faith that distinguishes and elevates it above human faith.

I.   Faith and Person

All human knowledge has a personal character. It is oriented to the person because it is not the *intelligence* that knows, but *the person* with his intelligence and will, with his past and his present culture, with his specific circumstances and way of seeing things.[2]

In the preceding chapters, we saw that the response of supernatural faith produces a strong interpersonal encounter between God and man. The act of supernatural faith is presented as a personal donation of the believer to the God who personally reveals himself and invites people to personal intimacy with him. In this section and the next, we will try to deepen our understanding of these concepts in what is proper and exclusive to supernatural faith.

A. The Absolute Characteristic of the Personal Adherence of Those Who Believe with Supernatural Faith

The *complete and voluntary submission of our own intelligence to the divine intelligence*, accepting in an absolute manner God's inviting and announcing word, is specific to supernatural faith. "This is genuine faith: an absolute adherence to things that are not seen."[3]

The example of Abraham's faith demonstrates this to us. *His faith remains a paradigm for all believers, precisely because he always gave absolute priority, in theory and practice, to the word of God.* It is paradigmatic because of the radical mortification of our own thinking before divine thinking—of the total submission of any personal plan (including religious) in view of how it may conform to the divine plan. This dimension of faith was highlighted centuries later by Isaiah, and proclaimed by St. Paul (cf. 1 Cor 1: 18–25).

We have seen that in human and in supernatural faith the intervention of the will is necessary because the *object is not evident to the intelligence,* and in supernatural faith the help of grace is necessary. This is because the object is *transcendent.* Moreover, we know that the adherence to the object must be absolute because its object is *absolute* itself. (Faith is participation in the knowledge that God has of himself.)

Supernatural faith properly consists in believing that the accepted truth is divine (absolutely true). This recognition is necessarily accompanied by absolute (total and complete) adherence to the person by whose testimony truth is accepted. That absolute value lies, additionally, in the absolute characteristic recognized in the person in whom we believe. In fact, supernatural faith is to believe that it is God who speaks to us, even though he does so through a mediator. We believe what God says because we believe it is God who says so: Faith is *credere Deum* because it is *credere Deo.*

> Faith is first of all a personal adherence of man to God. At the same time, and inseparably, it is a free assent to the whole truth that God has revealed. As personal adherence to God and assent to his truth, Christian faith differs from our faith in any human person. It is right and just to entrust oneself wholly to God and to believe absolutely what he says. It would be futile and false to place such faith in a creature (cf. Jer 17: 5–6; Ps 40: 5; 146: 3–4).[4]

Thus, it is understood that what is exclusive to divine faith precisely consists in its complete, absolute and total adherence to one person. Supernatural faith asks for a complete and absolute donation of man to God; it is the response to a divine call to live and think about everything according to God's Word and his love. In other words, the absolute character of adherence of faith implies two things: that everything said by the person believed is accepted and the person who believes adheres with his whole being to the one in whom he believes.

All knowledge is personal, but in the knowledge of God, this is true to a particularly deep and total degree. In the knowledge of God, one must not only act as a person and move as an intelligent and free individual, but must commit his deepest personal being.[5] To know God is to find him, to be conscious that one is seen and known by him. It means starting a personal relationship with him, beginning to live in a new way, allowing oneself to be transformed into a new creature, and maturing as a person.

Therefore, to what has been said, we can add that all knowledge of God is also personal from the point of view of what is acquired by the individual. In fact, the response to supernatural faith involves the individual in all his dimensions: intellectual and volitional, corporal and spiritual, sensitive and affective, individual and social. It affects his present, but also his past and his future. Man does not meet God as a neutral observer; he finds him when he is aware that God questions him.[6]

B. Personal Character of the Believed Truth in Supernatural Faith

From the standpoint of its object, all knowledge of God is personal because God is the supreme personal being. The personal character of an object makes it mysterious to the intelligence. In fact, even when someone knows some aspects of a person with certainty, he cannot totally encompass him and be sure that he completely understands him. Before God, one in essence and three in persons, man necessarily stays fundamentally ignorant of what God is. Man can know God only in an imperfect and analogical manner.[7]

Thus, it is necessary to avoid the error of depersonalizing the truth, of reducing it to empirical information.[8] In the Old Testament, truth in its absolute value and being belongs exclusively to God. It is his patrimony because humans are not truthful and they do not perfectly know the world. Men do not know what man is. God is the truth and men are in the truth and possess it insofar as they believe in God, one and unique. In the New Testament, the theological character of truth is added to the Christological one: Jesus is the truth (cf. Jn 14: 6).[9]

The characteristics of faith that were reserved to God in the Old Testament are now applied to Christ. To him belong absolute obedience, trust, and fidelity. He is the Word that has created all things and knows everything (cf. Jn 1: 14–18; 21: 17). He is the only Savior, the one whom we can definitely trust because he has the words of eternal life (cf. Mt 16: 16–18; Jn 6: 67–69). To him we must be faithful because he is Lord and God (cf. Jn 20: 27–29).

This discussion allows us to understand to what extent the object of divine faith is personal. It is not just to believe in somebody, to believe something about someone, or to believe the word of somebody; it is to believe someone. The testimony of God is received through faith, but this "does not simply consist of accepting a proposition, but to receive a person who brings with him eternal life (cf. Jn 1: 4)."[10] Christian faith means accepting God's Word, knowing that this Word is a Person, *someone in God* equal to God (cf. Jn 1: 1).

The New Testament gives an excellent summary of our Christian faith: "For I decided to know nothing among you except Jesus Christ and him crucified" (1 Cor 2: 2).

The writers of the synoptic Gospels, for example, present Jesus' life as the proclamation and establishment of the reign of God, as the definitive fulfillment of the promise of salvation given to the Jewish people. These writers stress faith as the basic condition for entering the reign of God and being saved (cf. Mt 13: 11–17; Mk 16: 16; Lk 1: 45; 6: 49; 7: 36–50). Belief is the recognition that Jesus is the promised Messiah sent by God, that he is the Son of God (cf. Mt 15: 21–28; 16: 13–20).[11] St. Paul used the term *pistis* to signify *the knowledge and acceptance of the Pascal mission* (cf. Rom 10: 9, 14). Sts. Peter and James concurred in this recognition of the person of Christ (cf. Rom 1: 17; Gal 2: 16; Eph 2: 8; Phil 3: 9). According to St. John, *to believe is to accept the person and mission of the Son*. It is to know that Jesus is the incarnate Word who has come to save all mankind.[12]

The Christian faith is, therefore, an encounter with the Word that is a Person. We are dealing here with a strictly supernatural faith because there is no created Word that is at one and the same time a Person. "The chief difference lies in the fact that the content of the testimony and the person giving the testimony are identical. One cannot find another case like this in the world."[13]

The paths revealed in history which lead a person to God are diverse encounters which may appear insignificant to some but they have incalculable value for others. As will be seen in the second part of this book, these encounters are verified by means of *experiences, signs, and testimonies*. These are the normal means that lead to interpersonal knowledge. People encounter the God of history via these same routes.

Believers come to know their faith in the exercise of the will and sentiments, and, above all, it is an encounter with grace. According to Sacred Scripture, one's experience with God takes place in the center of the person.[14] This reality is reflected in the language of faith, which necessarily uses images, symbols, parables, and other forms of analogy (cf. Mt 13: 10–17).

C. The Radical Transformation of the Believer

Human faith, like supernatural faith, influences a person in the human sphere. Because of one's faith, a person might undertake a business, risk, a long trip, or establish a family. Still, human faith does not alter the human condition; it only affects its relationships. Alternatively, in supernatural faith the believer participates in a radical transformation, as can be seen in St. Paul's Letter to the Galatians.

The Galatians allowed themselves to be tricked by the Judaizers, who said that it was necessary for them to observe the prescriptions of Mosaic law. According to that theory, they did not give sufficient value to faith in Christ. The Apostle taught them that this idea was erroneous:

> O foolish Galatians! Who has bewitched you, before whose eyes Jesus Christ was publicly portrayed as crucified? Let me ask you only this: Did you receive the Spirit by works of the law, or by hearing with faith?… Does he who supplies the Spirit to you and works miracles among you do so by works of the law, or by hearing with faith? (Gal 3: 1–2, 5)

St. Paul argues that the effect of believing in the gospel is radically different from the effect of the observance (also faith) of Mosaic law. The latter does not go as far as the former. Note that the line of argument begins with the more visible and exterior effects—miracles, manifestations of the Holy Spirit; charisma and gifts of diverse types—then passes to the more interior and deeper effect, which is imperceptible and therefore achievable only by faith. "It is men of faith who are the sons of Abraham.... Christ redeemed us from the curse of the law...that in Christ Jesus the blessing of Abraham might come upon the Gentiles, that we might receive the promise of the Spirit through faith" (Gal 3: 7, 13,14). The wondrous thing that the Holy Spirit brings is faith in Christ. He is poured into the heart of the believer and makes him cry out "Abba, Father" (Gal 4: 6). He makes the believer into a Child of God.

In summary, St. Paul taught that "in Christ Jesus you are all sons of God, through faith" (Gal 3: 26). The Pauline teaching states that works do not change or justify man. Consequently, human faith alone does not transform man from inside, either. Only faith in Christ the Son of God and Lord gives mankind new and eternal life and makes them God's children. Faith makes man a "new creature" (Gal 6: 15).[15] Many other New Testament texts support this teaching of St. Paul.

By believing in the Son of God made man, one becomes God's child by participation (cf. 1 Jn 3: 1–2). Just as in God being and knowing are identified, participation—by faith—in the knowledge of God means the faithful enter into a new order of being. The transforming power of faith does not truly reach its effect if man does not fulfill the works accompanying it. It does not lead people to maturity of faith if they do not act through charity (cf. Gal 5: 6).[16] The works of faith, mainly charity, are the manifestation of real belief in God, who reveals himself. They express the deep transformation of the believer. God in turn communicates himself to humanity.[17] That is the most important point in St. Paul's teaching to the Galatians. The works accomplished by people when they believed—the fruit of the Holy Spirit's action in them—offered a sample of the truth and the supernatural quality of their faith.

Supernatural faith is "going toward God." To believe means to start to develop an extremely intimate, absolutely radical relationship with

God. This relationship affects the whole existence of the person: his way of living, thinking, wanting, and being on earth.

The knowledge of God is not only personal; it is also personalized. In fact, the immanent act—the intellectual and volitional act—forms and shapes the person because in that act the person is not only the cause but also the finality of his acting.[18] So, if all knowledge supposes a certain enrichment of man, when the object of knowledge is a person, the enrichment is particularly appropriate and convenient because it helps the knower develop within the environment and level that corresponds to him: that of interpersonal relationships.

Therefore, it is clear that the knowledge of God always implies a personal relationship with him. This knowledge directs man to his personal maturity more than any other.[19]

The process of personal growth is intimately shaped, like theological growth, according to faith, hope, and charity—as a process of progressive conformation with Christ. So did St. Paul teach on several occasions, "So then you are no longer strangers and sojourners, but you are fellow citizens with the saints and members of the household of God, built upon the foundation of the apostles and prophets, Christ Jesus himself being the cornerstone, in whom the whole structure is joined together and grows into a holy temple in the Lord; in whom you also are built into it for a dwelling place of God in the Spirit" (Eph 2: 19–22). Again, from another perspective, St. Paul says, "And we all, with unveiled face, beholding the glory of the Lord, are being changed into his likeness from one degree of glory to another; for this comes from the Lord who is the Spirit" (2 Cor 3: 18).[20]

To grow in the faith, then, is to increasingly discover God in the world and in the Church, in himself and in others, in history and in Christ. It is to grow in knowledge of Christ and in one's relationship with him. This is possible through signs and gestures, words and encounters that put one into personal contact with God. This is accomplished according to the means set down by divine will. These means find their most efficacious expression in the gift of God's Word and of his love.[21]

II. Faith and the Communion of Persons

The supernatural faith implies a radical and living communion with other people, it always possesses a social dimension.

A. The Collective Response of Supernatural Faith in the Old Testament: Israel as a Nation of Believers

In Abraham's time, faith did not refer merely to a person or a family group, but to a whole nation in the person of their progenitor. By the time of Moses, this social aspect was clearly manifested. It is then that a nation, Israel, professes its faith in God as revealed in history.

The Exodus from Egypt is the step from slavery to freedom. This liberation is, fundamentally, a sign of the liberation from sin and eternal death. Still, it also includes other meanings. The exodus from oppression is the step from social disorganization to social order with laws and institutions known and accepted by everyone. It is an exodus from individuality to communion. It is liberation from the egotism that isolates persons and makes them strangers among themselves. It is a step toward taking an interest in others.[22]

God himself takes the initiative to free the Hebrews. He takes the necessary steps to bring the nation together and to give them a collective being. He establishes a covenant with them. When Yahweh dialogues with the nation as on Sinai, his interlocutor is the community, not Moses, even though Moses serves as mediator. The covenant of Sinai is not between Yahweh and Moses but between Yahweh and Israel.

The Exodus and the covenant on Mount Sinai open the door for the collective human response to the God who reveals himself. From that moment on, God explicitly asks for a faith response that comes not only from individual persons, but from the whole community of the entire chosen nation as well. The response of faith of individual persons is simply not sufficient to please God. He is anxious to receive a communal response as well.

The collective or communal character of the response of faith is proper to the vision of the Old Testament. Faith is the bond between the Israelites and Yahweh. Consequently, faith is expressed and is eternally and communally lived mainly through obedience to the law of Sinai. It finds its fulcrum in the confession and worship of the one true God and in the refusal of any form of idolatry and polytheism. Faith is a social and public reality that joins the believer with God. Furthermore, faith shapes Israel as a nation.

As is obvious, the communal aspect does not substitute in any way for the personal dimension of the belief response. Indeed, this aspect acts to defend and develop this dimension. It makes it richer, more certain, and safer. The union of these two aspects was an important object of the prophets' preaching.

The prophets constantly reminded the nation as a whole and each person that they must be faithful to the covenant and persevere in the attitudes of faith and surrender. They insisted upon the importance of the individual's response, denouncing the tendency of some to hide in the anonymity of the group or in external rituals (cf. Is 1: 11, 16–17; Am 5: 21–25; Ez 18: 2–31). They demonstrated that God's demands are sublime and that the covenant introduces us to an inestimable relationship of friendship with God. They present faith as a response of love comparable to the response of a loving and faithful wife.[23] Hosea highlights this. "And I will betroth you to me for ever; I will betroth you to me in righteousness and in justice, in steadfast love, and in mercy. I will betroth you to me in faithfulness; and you shall know the LORD" (Hos 2: 19–20). As it may be deduced from the text, the relation of love refers to both the individual and collective response and professes that faith is not a formal and external adherence, but a profound and intimate act of communion with God.

The history of the prophets demonstrates that an individual response and the collective are inseparable. The faith of an individual is a response that takes place within a group. The faith of the community is united by the response of individual, or singular persons, who have been inspired by certain particularly generous responses (the judges, prophets, and heroines). Individuals, for their part, have learned to believe within the community. They have known Yahweh through others. By means of the community they have known the promise, the law and the covenant.[24]

B. The Communal Response to God in the New Testament: The Church as Subject of Faith

Christ reveals himself in history, and he seeks a response of faith from mankind. He does so in the singular order with Mary, and he does so in the collective order with the Church. We will consider Mary's response in the next chapter. We will now study the historical subject of a response of total and perfect faith. The response of each individual must be inserted in the collective response in order to perfect and complete it.[25]

The Church is a unique subject in the supernatural order of faith and of grace;[26] a community of believers. Faith unites her members, incorporates them into her, and maintains them in her (cf. Acts 2: 41). *Ecclesia per fidem unitur* (the Church is united through faith).[27] Faith is the shared element for all of the members of the Church. "We are one, because we believe."[28] The Church is a community of believers inasmuch as her existence and structure depend upon faith. The Church's essential elements (such as doctrine, cult, hierarchy, laws, and morals) are contained in Revelation, and are known and accepted by faith. They are not a human fabrication.

The Church is presented as a unique subject—regarding faith in Christ—because her response of faith is one and unique. Throughout history and throughout the earth, her profession of faith has remained substantially and invariably the same.[29] "The Church, even though it is spread in the entire world to the remotest place, as she has received faith from the apostles and successors…believes in only one manner as if she had only one heart and one soul. She preaches the truth of faith, teaches and transmits it with a unanimous voice as if she had only one mouth."[30]

The Church acts and presents herself as only one subject because she is the transmitter of the one response of faith.[31] Here, we could paraphrase some of St. Paul's well-known words. He shows that the Church is only one body because it is fed by only one bread (cf. 1 Cor 10: 17; cf. 1 Cor 12: 13; cf. Eph 4: 3–6). The unique and permanent response of faith that the Church has rendered to Christ and the Trinity through-out the centuries demonstrates that she is the sole subject of faith.[32]

The cause and root of the Church's existence as a sole and unique sub-ject of faith is exclusively due to the action of the Holy Spirit. It can-not be attributed to ecclesiastical structure, the action of pastors, or the harmony looked for by the faithful. Structures and expressions of human action in that sense are only secondary causes moved by the Spirit, which is the first cause. "All these are inspired by one and the same Spirit" (1 Cor 12: 11). Using the Pauline analogy upon which we commented before, we could add that this works just as the unity of the body (the Church) is the work of the Paraclete. By the same reason, the unity of the response of faith is carried out by the Spirit of truth promised by Christ (cf. Jn 14: 16–17; 15: 16–27; 16: 14; 1 Cor 12: 3).

"When the work which the Father gave the Son to do on earth (cf. Jn 17: 4) was accomplished, the Holy Spirit was sent on the day of Pentecost in order that he might continually sanctify the Church."[33] The total and permanent donation of the Spirit serves to explain the completely faithful and obedient response of the Church, overcoming every test and difficulty. Vatican II compared the Church to the Mother of God in this way: "She herself is a virgin, who keeps in its entirety and purity the faith she pledged to her spouse. Imitating the mother of her Lord, and by the power of the Holy Spirit, she keeps intact faith, firm hope and sincere charity."[34]

This plenitude of the response of faith of the Church is shown with a perfection that has several manifestations. She cannot make mis-takes regarding faith—she is infallible, "the pillar and bulwark of the truth" (1 Tm 3: 15).[35] She has never been unfaithful throughout history (cf. Mt 16: 18–19); her faith is always united to love (cf. Jn 14: 16).[36] Her response of faith remains unaltered down through the centuries, al-though her comprehension and intelligence of what has been revealed can grow.[37]

C. Ecclesiality: The Response of Christian Faith

The indefectible perfection of the faith is the exclusive patrimony of the Church, in the sense that no other community responds with a total and perfect faith that has the guarantee of plenitude and indefectibility.[38] In addition, no one can accomplish a total and perfect act of faith that is not in communion with the Church.[39]

> No one comprehends the thoughts of God except the "Spirit of God" (1 Cor 2: 11). Now God's Spirit, who reveals God, makes known to us Christ, his Word, his living Utterance, but the Spirit does not speak of himself. The Spirit who "has spoken through the prophets" makes us hear the Father's Word, but we do not hear the Spirit himself. We know him only in the movement by which he reveals the Word to us and disposes us to welcome him in faith. The Spirit of truth who "unveils" Christ to us "will not speak on his own" (Jn 16: 13). Such properly divine self-effacement explains why "the world cannot receive [him], because it neither sees him nor knows him," while those who believe in Christ know the Spirit because he dwells with them (Jn 14: 17). The Church, a communion living in the faith of the apostles which she transmits, is the place where we know the Holy Spirit.[40]

It is understood that only the Church can explicitly state an act of faith in God, One and Triune.[41] The single individual can make only an explicitly trinitarian act of faith thanks to the Church.[42]

The necessity of the Church basis of the faith response of each person can be treated in the double-aspect of the historical-social and theological.

Historically and socially speaking, it can be proved that each person's faith, when explicitly Christian, depends upon the faith of the ecclesiastical community.

> Faith is a personal act—the free response of the human person to the initiative of God who reveals himself. But faith is not an isolated act. No one can believe alone, just as no one can live alone. You have not given yourself faith as you have not given yourself life. The believer has received faith from others and

should hand it on to others. Our love for Jesus and for our neighbor impels us to speak to others about our faith. Each believer is thus a link in the great chain of believers. I cannot believe without being carried by the faith of others, and by my faith I help support others in the faith.

"I believe" (Apostles' Creed) is the faith of the Church professed personally by each believer, principally during baptism. "We believe" (Niceno-Constantinopolitan Creed) is the faith of the Church confessed by the bishops assembled in council or more generally by the liturgical assembly of believers. "I believe" is also the Church, our mother, responding to God by faith as she teaches us to say both "I believe" and "We believe."[43]

To believe, then, implies *sentire cum Ecclesia*. Christian belief presupposes sharing a life in the spirit, a life made up of a communion of thoughts, affection, and intentions. Such communion requires the person to form his answer to God according to this communion, i.e., taking in—when they appear—new dogmatic definitions, moral criteria about problems arising from social progress, pastoral orientations, etc. By acting in this fashion, the believer demonstrates the fidelity of his response to God.[44]

From the theological point of view, we can say that the Church is like a mystical and moral person into whom the believer is incorporated through faith. The act of individual faith, grafted and living in the act of the faith of the whole, is fulfilled in communion with the act of faith of the community. It is the act of an "I" united to a "we," and vice versa. It is a "we" assumed by an "I" in such a way that, without destroying itself, the "I" is enriched, assuming the attitude of the whole Church toward God and the world. "The I of the credal formulas is a collective 'I'; the individual 'I' belongs to the 'I' of the believing Church inasmuch as all of the particulars of the 'I' pertain to the believer. The 'I' of the Creed also includes the step from the private 'I' to the ecclesiastical I."[45]

The Trinity is an object of Christian faith as believed reality, as the motive of belief, and as finality one approaches with the act of faith.[46] Christian faith is to believe that God is Father, Son and Holy Spirit. It is to believe the Father, the Son and the Holy Spirit. It is to direct oneself toward the Father by the Son in the Holy Spirit.

Faith in God implies certain participation in the life of the divine Persons, in their communion of knowledge and love.[47] In other words, the Church and the person participate by faith in intra-trinitarian communion. They have a personal relationship with God; that is, they have a different relation with each one of the divine Persons. In fact, the New Testament sometimes uses the term *koinonia* to expressly indicate the response of Christian faith (cf. 2 Pt 1: 3–4; 1 Jn 1: 3).[48]

The participation in the divine mystery active in Christian faith carries in itself the inter-subjective communion of all participants of the same object with the same act. It means that the theological act of faith unites the faithful in supernatural communion. The key to explaining how it is that community and person are at the same time subjects of faith is as follows: Christian faith is communion with God and, therefore, is in intimate and supernatural communion with those who believe in God.[49]

In summary, God desires the body and—in the body—the members. The body cannot be separated from its members. Nevertheless, if they are compared to each other, the whole is more than the parts. "It is the Church that believes first, and so bears, nourishes, and sustains my faith. Everywhere, it is the Church that first confesses the Lord...with her and in her, we are won over and brought to confess: 'I believe,' 'We believe.'"[50]

CHAPTER 9

FAITH AND WORKS

The Church has always insisted on the intellectual character of super-natural faith. She has always taught that this character is her operative dynamism to shape the life of believers and model their conduct even in particular details. Consequently, the Church has always refuted those propositions attempting to present her witness as a religious or ethical code without a message for the intelligence involving a new comprehension of God, humanity, and the world. These theories tend to restrict the Church's code to a doctrine confined to the realm of abstract ideas unable to affect one's conduct or the real life of human communities.[1]

Biblical teaching presents the faith as a profound attitude that causes one to live and behave in a certain way. We can see the relationship between faith and Divine Revelation in this manner. In fact, faith, as Abraham's witness demonstrates, is knowledge of God and his saving works. Faith extends and manifests itself in actions of obedience and fidelity compatible with such knowledge (cf. Heb 11: 1–40). "Faith working through love" (Gal 5: 6; cf. 5: 22; Eph 2: 8; Rom 2: 13; 8: 5–8; Lk 6: 43–45; Mt 12: 33–35). Faith guides us in our imitation of Jesus (cf. 1 Jn 2: 3–6; 9–11; 3: 10–12; 4: 7–16). The practice of faith leads us to love our neighbors and practice virtues (cf. 1 Pt 1: 3–9,13–23; 2: 11–16). These teachings are formulated most concisely in the Letter of St. James when he explicitly describes a faith without actions as insufficient and dead (cf. Jas 1: 22; 2: 14, 26). The Virgin Mary is the perfect paradigm of a living faith.

I.   The Fullness of Mary's Faith
in Response to Her Vocation

In the fullness of times, the plenitude of revelation deserves a plenitude of the faith response. In human history, only Mary of Nazareth
has given such plenitude. In her response to God's Word, there also
shines the New Testament faith. Mary, in fact, is the Mother of the
incarnate Word and the Mother of the Church.

> The Virgin Mary most perfectly embodies the obedience of
> faith. By faith Mary welcomes the tidings and promise brought
> by the angel Gabriel, believing that "with God nothing will be
> impossible" (Lk 1: 37; cf. Gen 18: 14) and so giving her assent:
> "Behold I am the handmaid of the Lord; let it be [done] unto
> me according to your word" (Lk 1: 38). Elizabeth greeted
> her: "Blessed is she who believed that there would be a fulfillment
> of what was spoken to her from the Lord" (Lk 1: 45). It is for this
> faith that all generations have called Mary blessed (cf. Lk 1: 48).

> Throughout her life and until her last ordeal (cf. Lk 2: 35) when
> Jesus her son died on the cross, Mary's faith never wavered. She
> never ceased to believe in the fulfillment of God's word. And so
> the Church venerates in Mary the purest realization of faith.[2]

A. Obedience, Confidence, and Fidelity to Christ
in Mary's Faith Response

> The plenitude of Mary's faith is united to her plenitude of grace.
> This relates to her vocation as Mother of the Incarnate Word. Her
> faith response belongs to the order of plenitude established by
> Christ, which is the plenitude of times, the height of Revelation.
> "Blessed is she who believed that there would be a fulfillment of
> what was spoken to her from the Lord" (Lk 1: 45). These words
> should be considered alongside the name "full of grace" from
> the angel's salutation. Both texts reveal an essential Mariological
> content. The truth about Mary is really present in the mystery of

Christ precisely "because she has believed." The plenitude of grace, announced by the angel, means the gift of God himself. Mary's faith, proclaimed by Elizabeth in the visitation, constitutes how the Virgin of Nazareth has responded to this gift.[3]

Mary's *fiat* to the angel is her "amen" to revelation, to the invitation that is personally addressed to her and assigns to her a specific role in the plan of salvation. At the same time it is her "amen" to the project God has arranged for the salvation of his people. From this perspective, Mary's response is the summit and plenitude of faith because it is intimately united to the beginning of the new and eternal covenant.[4]

The plenitude of her response corresponds to the plenitude of her free and supernatural participation in the mystery of Christ. "Mary, consenting to the word of God, became the Mother of Jesus. Committing herself wholeheartedly and impeded by no sin to God's saving will, she devoted herself totally, as a handmaid of the Lord, to the person and work of her Son, under and with him, serving the mystery of redemption, by the grace of Almighty God."[5]

Mary's plenitude of faith is manifested in her perfect response to Christ as disciple, servant, and Mother. She is the "the human being who has responded better than any other to God's call. Mary became both the servant and the disciple of the Word to the point of conceiving, in her heart and in her flesh, the Word made man, so as to give him to mankind."[6] "And this son—as the Fathers teach—has been conceived in her mind before conceiving him in her bosom: precisely by means of faith."[7]

Mary's plenitude of faith is manifested in her *permanent and perfect availability to God's works*. Her response of faith was not limited to the moment of the Annunciation. After taking in Jesus, she faithfully accompanied him throughout his life, even at his Crucifixion. Mary always shows herself totally willing to be governed by God's will. She allows the Incarnate Word of God to shape her life, thoughts, and feelings (cf. Lk 2: 19, 51). "The Blessed Virgin advanced in her pilgrimage of faith, and faithfully persevered in her union with her Son unto the cross, where she stood, in keeping with the divine plan, enduring with her only begotten Son the intensity of his suffering, associated herself with his sacrifice in her mother's heart, and lovingly consenting to the immolation of this victim which was born of her."[8]

B. The Efficacy of Mary's Response of Faith for the Good of the Church

Finally, Mary's plenitude of faith is manifested in her most singular efficacy in the order of her own sanctity and the salvation of all mankind. With her *fiat*, Mary transformed her own existence, that of the persons near her, the history of her people, and the history of mankind.

Mary knew how to shape her own existence absolutely according to her vocation as Mother of the Word. This is the way to understand the praise Jesus gives to his Mother, "Blessed rather are those who hear the word of God and keep it!" in response to the praise of the townswoman. "Blessed is the womb that bore you, and the breasts that sucked you!" (Lk 11: 27–28; cf. 8: 20–21). Some have considered these verses of St. Luke and other similar ones (cf. Mt 12: 46–50; Mk 3: 31–35) "against Mary," because they seem to give Mary's role another dimension. On the contrary, Christ's words highlight her faith, which is totally formed by charity.[9] "It was a compliment to his Mother on her *fiat*, her 'be it done.' She lived it sincerely, unstintingly, fulfilling its every consequence, but never amid fanfare, rather in the hidden and silent sacrifice of each day."[10]

The faith of Mary is superior to that of all biblical persons. This point (which is evident from many different perspectives[11]) can be summarized by the objectively verifiable fact of the singular efficacy of her faith response.

> Rightly, therefore, the Fathers see Mary not merely as passively engaged by God, but as freely cooperating in the work of man's salvation through faith and obedience. For, as St. Irenaeus says, she "being obedient, became the cause of salvation for herself and for the whole human race." Hence, not a few of the early Fathers gladly assert with him in their preaching: "the knot of

Eve's disobedience was untied by Mary's obedience: what the virgin Eve bound through her disbelief, Mary loosened by her faith." Comparing Mary with Eve, they call her "Mother of the living," and frequently claim: death through Eve, life through Mary."[12]

The great influence of her faith response can be summarized in St. Thomas's assertion that when Mary pronounced her *fiat* to the angel, she consented in the name of all mankind (*loco totius humanae naturae*) to the union of God's Son with human nature.[13]

II. Works of Faith

In considering the influence and presence of faith in the works and lives of Christians, there are two important questions that are raised: Is it necessary that faith be transformed in works? And in the affirmative case, are there works specifically structured by faith?

A. The Root of the Operative Dynamism of Christian Faith

It is possible to show the supernatural response of faith's intrinsically operative character from diverse standpoints. Three such arguments are now offered, starting from, respectively, the object, act, and finality of supernatural faith.

1. The Relationship between the Operative Capacity of Faith and Adherence to the Creating and Saving Word

The need for works in a living and total faith finds its origin not in an externally imposed need but from its own object, because faith is to take in the creating and saving Word, the Word that love breathes out.

The Word motivates the one who receives it to live and act according to this Word, to transform the world seeking its own salvation and that of others. In fact, the divine Word taken in faith initiates a deep transformation of the person and the human community. Hence, conversion to God and the change of personal conduct are intrinsic and constitutive of the faith response. To truly accept Jesus as Messiah and Lord necessarily implies a change in conduct. It involves a true and proper conversion in the believer (*metanoia*: cf. Mt 4: 17; Mk 1: 15; Acts 2: 38). It always leads to a new life according to the resurrected Christ (cf. Col 3: 1–15; Phil 2: 5–16; Eph 5: 1–20; Rom 6: 8–22). The believer can develop this new life according to diverse intensities and orientations. Still, if this change of conduct, this transformation, were missing, this would signify that the same faith response is missing.

2. The Coherence between Doctrine and Conduct in the Life of Christians

It can also be said that the operative capacity of faith is a necessary consequence of the structure of the supernatural response to divine revelation. In fact, the choice of supernatural faith, the fruit of an intelligence and will elevated by grace, tries to be present—by motives of personal consistency—in other manifestations of the Christian's conduct. The faith response develops similar characteristics to a person's radical option. It must, then, form and qualify the rest of the options, which logically must be submitted to the first and fundamental option.[14] Moreover, supernatural faith takes in the revealed Word as absolute. Therefore, it implies conceding absolute primacy to that Word in the spiritual activity of the person, letting it form and precede all thoughts, words, and actions.

The believer's actions—if he is consistent with himself and with his fundamental decisions—must be moved by faith, because faith is knowledge of the final reality and because it is the radical choice of such reality as final end. This is an important and specific manifestation of all we have seen about the sapient character of biblical faith. Faith, because it is knowledge about the creating, saving, and sanctifying God, lets us know the finality and sense of life and see the path to achieve eternal and true happiness (cf. Jn 14: 6). Because of its nature, faith tends to guide and direct the actions of the believer who—like everyone—wants to be happy forever (cf. Mk 16: 16). "The first truth (that is, the object of faith) is the goal of all our desires and all of our actions: That is why faith acts through charity."[15]

3. The Eschatological Tension of Supernatural Faith

The intrinsically operative character of the faith response proceeds from the finality of the same act of faith. In fact, this is a particular initiation of beatific knowledge; it is the "foundation (*hypostasis*) of expected things," (cf. Heb 11: 1),[16] a veiled initiation of the glorious vision.[17] "Faith inaugurates the vision inasmuch as real participation, although imperfect and dark, in the knowledge with which God knows himself."[18]

Faith tends to act in such a way as to look for the perfect vision of its object. It actively directs itself toward its eschatological plenitude.[19] Faith moves the subject to the actions necessary to reach the vision of God. The operative dimension is intrinsic to faith because the imperfect naturally tends to reach its own perfection and plenitude. Faith follows certain steps toward a goal: We believe in order to reach salvation (cf. 1 Pt 1: 8–9, Mk 16: 16); faith acts to arrive at the perfect knowledge of what it believes without seeing.

Faith necessarily must be transformed into actions. "But some one will say, 'You have faith and I have works.' Show me your faith apart from your works, and I by my works will show you my faith" (Jas 2: 18).

> James, in his letter against those who did not want to do good, presuming that they would be saved with only their faith, praises Abraham's actions, of whose faith Paul praised. The two apostles do not absolutely contradict themselves. In fact, [St. Paul] speaks about an act known by everybody: that Abraham offered his own son in sacrifice to God. It was an admirable act that came from faith. Praise the fulfillment of the work, but reckon the root of faith.... Therefore, let no one consider that his works are good before faith is present: where there was no faith, there was no

good action, either.... Whoever wants to have good hope, I repeat, must have a good conscience; but in order to have a good conscience, he must believe and act.[20]

Because of all of this, the Fathers of the Church have always taught that one who does not manifest faith with actions does not really believe.[21] "Faith. It's a pity to see how frequently many Christians have it on their lips and yet how sparingly they put it into their action. You would think it a virtue to be preached only, and not one to be practiced."[22]

This intrinsically operative dimension of faith—and its tendency to be present in every sphere of human activity—has always been a part of patristic and theological tradition. In spite of that, since the sixteenth century there have been an increasing number of theologians who, in their teachings, tend to ignore this aspect of supernatural faith. For instance, F. Ockam proposed and spread the theory of the two truths, one of supernatural faith and the other, of natural reason. His theory pretended to safeguard the rights of both; however, it actually opened the way to a break between theological thought, which regulates religious life, and the thought originating in human reason without relation to faith, which regulates civil life. This disassociation between faith and reason still exists and has perhaps even worsened: "One of the gravest errors of our time is the dichotomy between the faith which many profess and the practice of their daily lives."[23]

B. Specific Actions of Faith: To Be Personally Shaped in Christ and to Collaborate with Him in the Work of Redemption

We now will examine if the dynamism of faith is spread according to a generic operative capacity or whether it is conveyed by specific acts. In the second case, we need to see if it is about an operating capacity fulfilled according to the discretion of the believer or if it is due to the indications of revelation.

1. Christ, Teacher and Model

The response to this issue can be found at the very heart of the Christian faith. If believing is taking Christ as the absolute Word to whom we grant complete supremacy, then believing in Christ means accepting all of the indications regarding human conduct that are present in Christian revelation. This would include, for instance, the Decalogue, the commandment of love, and the criteria to discern what conduct is to be judged as virtuous and good.[24]

The central point of faith accepts Christ as teacher and model at the same time. A faith response that recognizes him as *rabbi* without adding the idea of life in communion with him with the imitation of his conduct is an imperfect response. Faith requires a radical maturation, an interior change, an absolute availability to the Word. The believer must let the Word form his life, modeling his existence according to the divine wish. In summary, we can consider this prayer of St. Josemaría:"My God, I see that I shall never accept you as my Savior unless I acknowledge you as my Model at the same time."[25]

2. The "Actions of Faith"

This formula can be understood in several interrelated ways. One way to understand it is as an *internal act of faith*. Another way would be as a public or private *oral confession* of what is believed (cf. Rom 10: 8–10). The third way understands it as *all actions fulfilled under the influence of the knowledge of faith*, whether this particular influence organizes them, arranges them to the supernatural end, or affects the manner in which they are in some way fulfilled.

According to the third meaning, faith can inspire the believer's conduct. Consequently, faith motivates Christians to receive the sacraments, especially those that are absolutely necessary for human salvation (baptism and reconciliation). In this fashion, the believer approaches a perfect knowledge of God and Christ. Faith is the basis of all theological work. The *intellectus fidei* is an attempt to better understand, as much as possible, that which is believed.

The operative capacity of faith reaches its maturity in the exercise of theological hope and charity (cf. Gal 5: 6). Nevertheless, even when such perfection is not reached, the operative dynamism of faith is shown in many specific actions related to salvation.[26] For instance, it is demonstrated by prayers, sacrifices, participation in cult, or worship (above all the Mass), attending Christian formation activities, reading texts of the Magisterium or the saints on questions of faith and morals, practicing various acts of Christian testimony, educating Christian children, or making financial contributions to the Church.

The landscape of possible acts of faith is immense and of the utmost variety. It extends to all levels of existence, reaching them in ways suited to the characteristics and dispositions of each person. Clearly, *a total response of theological faith does not leave any sphere of human life out of its influence precisely because it is not a superficial or partial posture, but a total and absolute one.* A personal response of coherent and authentic faith always causes a process of assimilation of the Word that is reflected in the maturation of one's thought, criteria for action, and concrete conduct. It gives birth to a social process aimed at Christianizing civil, legal, and cultural institutions.[27]

3. Faith as Discernment of the Divine Will, and the Willingness to Follow God's Wishes

The practical dimension of faith is not merely a matter of following a set of rules. The operative dimension of faith means *living through faith*. It means surrendering to God and living one's life attentive to his will and to his Word (cf. Hab 2: 4; Rom 1: 17; Gal 3: 11; Heb 10: 38). The deepest root of the spirit gives birth to the fulfillment of precepts. This fulfillment derives from the free and voluntary act of will in identification to the law of the Lord (cf. Ps 119). This has been the example of Abraham's faith and, to a greater degree, Mary's. *Faith implies a personal attitude of intimate surrender to God, which leads the person to confidently take in his projects and to govern one's actions according to the words that manifest the divine will.* It always assumes a profound openness to what God wants. It is not simply a question of obeying orders. This is because, as was said, faith is a response to God's invitation to walk with him (cf. Gen 5: 22, 17: 1; Heb 11: 5, 13–16), to live in communion with him. All of this implies, on the one hand, that the believer will have an attitude of listening and searching toward the Word of God. Additionally, the believer will be disposed to be open to God's will.

We should clarify that this disposition is safe from caprice or error. As faith is a light for the actions of the person, it provides the discernment of what God specifically wants. Moreover, faith offers objective elements to verify the truth of things seen with his light. Just as faith grants the knowledge of God as model and teacher, it also helps the believer see what each person must do in the here and now to shape himself according to God and his mission. As we know, not every manifestation of faith has the same importance. Now we will consider what *specific actions of Christian faith cause the believer to personally identify himself with Christ and to collaborate with him in the work of salvation.*

4. Identification with Christ and Participation in His Mission: The Believer as Disciple and Apostle

Faith is the response to *the God who calls and invites people to communion with him.* It is also the response to *the God who sends* because *all vocations and invitations imply a mission to be fulfilled.* In the cases that we have analyzed in greater detail—Abraham, Moses, the prophets, Mary, the Church, the apostles—the response of faith was an act of obedience to God's Word involving a mission. According to the Bible, faith in God means exactly to accept those words that are related to a specific, precise mission to be fulfilled. The reason for this is that God's Word is creative. It is the beginning of life; it is redemptive and it is the beginning of salvation. To take in faith is to participate in its revitalizing and creating efficacy, in its saving and redeeming mission (cf. Heb 4: 12; Is 55: 10–11).

Disciple and *apostle* are two intimately related expressions even though each one has its own meaning and semantic evolution in the New Testament. While the use of the expression *disciple* becomes generalized into a synonym of "believer in Christ," the use of the term *apostle* applies only to the group of the twelve. We can observe a progressive clarification of the term *disciple* into "to be with him and to accompany him." The term *disciple* means to give testimony with actions and words of his life and doctrine, to witness to his death and Resurrection, to evangelize, and to announce the Good News to everyone.[28]

The actions proper to faith are the effective search for one's holiness and the active promotion of one another's sanctity. In fact, Mary's faith is the paradigm for all believers. She shows us that the response of supernatural faith lies in accepting God's projects and collaborating in them.[29] *Per opposita*, it teaches that faith is harmed in its intimate dynamism when it is not shown in the pursuit of sanctity or in the practice of apostolate.[30] Mary exemplifies discipleship and service of the Word. She is the Mother of the Incarnate Word; that is her specific vocation. In the same way, an authentic response of faith shapes the believer as a disciple and servant of the Word, as an apostle of the Lord Jesus. This is the common vocation of all Christians.[31]

III. Faith and Prayer

"Christian prayer is always determined by the structure of Christian faith where the truth about God and his creatures shines abundantly."[32]

A. The Structure of Faith and the Dialogue of Prayer

Prayer is absolutely necessary in Christian life. This is not only a *practical* issue. It is tied to the very essence of faith and to its fundamental structure. This is because faith is a response to divine revelation, which calls man to a dialogue with God.[33] This dialogue is precisely the center of prayer.

Within the vocation to sanctity and apostolate, God's calling to prayer pertains to the essence of Christian revelation. God calls all Christians to live a *life of prayer*. According to Christ's explicit teaching, this is a universal invitation to pray without ceasing (cf. Lk 18: 1; 21: 36; Rom 12: 12; 1 Thes 5: 17; 1 Tm 2: 8).

There are several ways for this "ascension of the mind to God"[34] to take place. *Within Christian spirituality*, there are diverse manifestations of the inextinguishable richness of faith, hope, and charity. Insofar as prayer responds to the fundamental structure of faith, many consequences arise from praying to God,[35] particularly those related to the character of the dialogue of prayer.

In fact, as we have already considered in relation to cosmic revelation, the same reality of the created world represents an invitation for a dialogue with God: "God has spoken to man manifesting himself in creation: All things were created by his Word (cf. Gen 1: 3; Ps 33: 6, 9) by way of the word and in the word (cf. Jn 1: 3; Col 1: 16), and creation is like words which sing the praises of his 'actions of grace.'"[36] They offer the possibility of positively answering such an invitation. Hence, philosophy and religion, reason and devotion, speculation and prayer have mixed their destiny in the flux of human civilization. Whatever their relationship of alliance or separation, of convergence or divergence and repulsion, they influenced decisively the significance of man, more than any other attitude of the spirit.[37]

Prayer is a *dialogue* with another. It is not simply a speculative meditation or invocation of God. Primarily, this is because it is a human response to God's Word. God's communication is present in the order of creation. It is present in *historical revelation*. It is explicitly directed to each individual in a *personal* way:

> So, our faith must be living—a faith that makes us really believe in God and keep up a continuous conversation with him. A Christian life should be one of constant prayer, trying to live in the presence of God from morning to night and from night to morning. A Christian can never be a lonely man, since he lives in continual contact with God, who is both near us and in heaven.[38]

B. Revelation of the Trinity in Christ and in Prayer

We have studied how divine revelation, which personally reaches everyone in the Church (to whom God has trusted his written and orally transmitted Word), sees its plenitude in Christ. Therefore, the decisive event of the Incarnation determines what is *specifically Christian* in prayer, in human dialogue with God. In fact, "by means of prayer the Christian tries to perceive in the saving actions of God in Christ, Incarnate Word, and in the gift of his spirit, divine depth, what has been revealed in them, always through the human-earthly dimension."[39] For this reason the argument that the Christian does not require Christ's humanity to be united with God in prayer is a vain pretext, if not treasonous.[40] St. Thomas Aquinas dealt with this question in a radical manner, with his famous phrase, "He who had a book where all science were contained, would not pretend to do any other thing but to learn from that book. So, we do not need to search for anything else but Christ."[41]

This does not mean that the mystery of Christ must be explicitly present during every moment of prayer. Meditation will not always be *about* the mystery of the God-Man. Prayer does not necessarily mean that we have to talk *with* him. The radical nature of *Christian* prayer lies in the fact that these realities are always accomplished, in a more or less conscious way, *in Christ*. In fact, prayer expresses "the communion of redeemed creatures with the intimate life of the Trinitarian Persons."[42] Only *in Christ* can mankind obtain access to the intimacy of the Holy Trinity because human *introduction* in the life of God is fulfilled through adoption, in human participation in the sonship of the Word.[43]

As John Paul II has written:

> Creation impatiently expects the *revelation of "sons of God"* (Rom 8: 19). This means that God, having "known them from the beginning," has predestined human beings to be formed to his Son's image (cf. Rom 8: 29). Accordingly, there has been a supernatural "adoption" by means of the Holy Spirit. The Holy Spirit is love and gift; *it is as such that he has been given to humanity*. Further, it is in the *superabundance of the uncreated gift*

that this specific *created gift* has been given life in every human heart, making them "partakers of divine nature" (2 Pt 1: 4). Human life is permeated—in a participated way—by divine life and acquires a divine, supernatural dimension in this *new life*, in which"through him we both have accesss in one Spirit to the Father (Eph 2: 18)."[44]

In other words, "we can really participate in Christ as 'adopted children,' and cry with the Son in the Holy Spirit: 'Abbá, Father.' In this sense, the Fathers are absolutely correct when they write about the deification of men who, once incorporated to Christ, Son of God by nature, become by his grace participants in the divine nature, 'son in the Son.'"[45]

At this time, we will not dwell on the essential question of the reality of this communion with the Father in the Son by the Holy Spirit, which "is founded in baptism and in the Eucharist, the source and highest point in the life of the Church."[46] We need to remember that, precisely because of this fact, prayer—as the whole of Christian existence—finds its summit, center, and root in the Eucharistic sacrifice.[47]

C. The Filial, Personal, and Community Character of Prayer

"Prayer, for a Christian, is, in summary, the fruit or the consequence of being and living in Christ, of the reality of participating in Christ. The Son of God made man, and of man's condition as a child of God. Christian prayer is always—whether one thinks of it or not—an echo of Christ's creation."[48]

The fact that prayer, like any other aspect of Christian life, is carried out in *Christ* means that prayer has an essentially *filial character*. The Holy Spirit shapes and unites us to the only-begotten Son of the Father; so, with Christ and in Christ we can pray "Abbá, Father" (cf. Rom 8: 15; Gal 4: 6). This is undoubtedly an essential part of what is *specifically Christian* in prayer. Filial conduct before Christ in prayer is a sure way for the same prayer to be "permanent prayer."[49] In fact, "the piety that is born of divine filiation is a profound attitude of the soul that eventually permeates one's entire existence. It is there in every thought, every desire, every affection."[50]

Furthermore, to be *in Christ* entails the fact that, in the order of grace and filial adoption, "there is neither Jew nor Greek, there is neither slave nor free, there is neither male nor female; for you are all one in Christ Jesus" (Gal 3: 28). Thereby, the profound assertion according to which Christian prayer "is always and at the same time authentically personal and communal"[51] is understood.

In this manner, in the Our Father, we correctly "pray completely with our hearts, but at the same time we pray with the entire family of God, with the living and with the dead, with people of all social conditions, cultures, and races."[52]

Although communal, prayer is also necessarily personal. It is said in the first person. It involves a deep interior commitment of the person to Christ without any traces of *anonymity*.[53] Prayer is a dialogue; it is essentially an interpersonal reality. To be *one in Christ* does not risk one's individuality but, rather, shapes it according to Christ. This is all quite evident. Another aspect, perhaps less evident, is also very important. When prayer is personal and authentically Christian, it is also communal. In fact, insofar as we pray *in Christ*, we pray *with the Church*. The Church prays in us. This is because "the believer, as such, is never alone: starting to believe means leaving isolation and entering the 'we' of God's sons."[54]

This simultaneously personal and communal dimension of prayer "continually remits love of neighbor."[55] This kind of prayer has nothing to do with solipsistic intimism.[56] It is not possible to be *in Christ* if we do not share in "this mind among yourselves, which was in Christ Jesus" (Phil 2: 5), who, "having loved his own who were in the world, he loved them to the end" (Jn 13: 1). His is a love that "surpasses knowledge" (Eph 3: 19).

D. Prayer, Freedom, and Conversion

Prayer expresses communion with the intimate life of the divine Persons. Hence, it involves "a conduct of conversion and an exodus from the I toward God."[57] For an authentically Christian prayer, the encounter of two freedoms is essential, the infinite freedom of God and the finite freedom of man.[58]

The encounter between these two freedoms is not *exclusive* to Christian prayer. Actually, it belongs to the essence of any true prayer, inasmuch as it can be said that God's freedom and human freedom constitute the *"metaphysical foundation of prayer."*[59] Rather, prayer is specifically Christian because of the way this encounter of freedom occurs. It arises from the way that God offers his love to mankind through the Holy Spirit. This is known only through faith in Christ. This love is not only a creative love. It is also and always a redemptive love that meets the free will of a creature—the human person—who, although reborn in Christ by baptism and faith, remains a sinner (cf. 1 Jn 1: 10).

Hence, authentic prayer always implies an attitude of conversion, an "exodus from the I toward God." This exodus requires the involvement of the whole person. The individual is guided by his free will aided by divine grace. He does not act solely by means of his senses or intellect (much less by his imagination through some simple "psychological game"). This is because the person guides all his faculties and operations by means of his will.[60]

> The purpose of identifying one's will with God's will is, therefore, essential if one's prayer is to be truly *in Christ*, to be an authentically filial *prayer*. In order to find the precise "way" of prayer, Christians will consider…Christ's way; "my food is to do the will of him who sent me, and to accomplish his work" (Jn 4: 34).[61]

> When we make up our minds to tell our Lord, "I put my freedom in your hands," we find ourselves loosed from the many chains that were binding us to insignificant things, ridiculous cares, or petty ambitions. Then our freedom, which is a treasure beyond price, a wonderful pearl that it would be a tragedy to cast before swine (cf. Mt 7: 6), will be used by us entirely to learn how to do good (cf. Is 1: 17).[62]

It is clear at this point that the believer needs to have an attitude of *profound sincerity* in order to recognize what in our existence is not *the life of Christ in us yet* (cf. Gal 2: 20; Phil 1: 21). Consequently, "the search of God through prayer has to be preceded and accompanied by spiritual asceticism and purification of our own sins and errors. This is because, according to Jesus' word, only the 'pure in heart...shall see God' (Mt 5: 8). The Gospel refers mainly to a moral purification of the absence of love and truth and, at a deeper level, to a purification of all egotistical instincts that do not allow man to accept and reckon God's will in its whole purity."[63]

Regarding the encounter of divine freedom with human freedom in prayer, we Christians have the perfect example in *the prayer of Jesus* (cf. Lk 22: 42).[64] We also have the wonderful example of the Mother of God. "She whom the Almighty has made 'full of grace' responds by offering her whole being: 'Behold I am the handmaid of the Lord, let it be [done] to me according to your word.' '*Fiat*': This is Christian prayer: to be wholly God's, because he is wholly ours."[65]

PART TWO

FUNDAMENTALS OF APOLOGETICS

INTRODUCTION

In the second part, we will examine this relationship between Revelation and Faith from the point of view of someone who is questioned by God and called to accept, or assimilate, his Word. We will see how God's Word attracts, convinces and perfects the intelligence, freedom, and heart of man. We will study how and why God's Word is credible.

Credibility is the characteristic of a word or a person being believable, of being accepted as true in what the person says about a reality that is not evident to the person being addressed. Common language distinguishes credible from incredible things, trustworthy people from untrustworthy. Credibility refers, first, to assertions. Undoubtedly, words or statements are always from someone; they *are* somebody's. Thus, credibility always refers to the person asking to be believed concerning what he says, which does not appear evident to his respondent. As has been confirmed, to suppose credibility is to judge that it is prudent and reasonable to believe what someone says.

We make judgments about credibility on a daily basis. It is a continuous activity in human relationships. This is because people continually refer to realities that are not evident in the here and now. Even though one frequently hears things in the streets, on the radio or television, in the workplace, and in gatherings with friends, not all of what is said enjoys the same category of importance. Not all of these things deserve to be heard with the same attention. It is important to distinguish which are the interesting things and which have to be taken seriously. This area comprises an important part of human prudence. Wise people ponder what they hear and from whom they have heard it. They weigh the various reasons to agree, disagree, or simply not take something into account.

This second part of fundamental theology involves whether the issues of credibility in interpersonal relationships also apply to the relationship between people and God, who manifests himself to mankind in history. If it does indeed apply, to what extent does it apply, and what are the criteria and elements that have or can be taken into account when evaluating the credibility of revelation? This is the foundation of apologetics. In fact, apologetics is, specifically, the part of Christian theological discourse that studies the credibility of God's revelation in Christ, evaluating its preservation and transmission to all generations by the Church.

In Chapter 10 we will see how these issues have been explained and solved throughout the history of the Church. We will stress the relevant theological contribution of each epoch regarding the legitimacy, need, and possibility of offering a rational defense of our Christian hope. The historical introduction provided in this chapter will serve to show that we can give reason for our own hope (cf. 1 Pt 3: 15). We can do so in a variety of ways: publicly or privately, in a scientific or common manner. Additionally, arguments of diverse kinds (metaphysical, anthropological, psychological, historical, etc.) can be used to do so.

Many starting points can be taken, including the physical cosmos, human history, and personal experience. For its part, this historical introduction will reveal the scientific aspect of Christian apologetics, which has a character that presents a common core despite its diversity in contents and structure. To show and defend what is reasonable and legitimate of the faith and life in Christ, apologists have always turned to certain actions and words present in revelation. Today as yesterday, one cannot show the reasonableness of belief in Christ without these elements.

In Chapters 11–13 we will study these actions and words regarding credibility. Besides letting something of God's mystery be known, these actions and words perform, in the historical moment that they occur, the role of attracting and guiding those who see them toward faith. Moreover, they manifest God's mystery and his saving will. Further, they act as motives for belief because they inspire a person toward the faith and legitimize one's decision to believe.[1]

These actions and words of Divine Revelation appear to be fundamental and definitive motives of faith. This is because, on the one hand, they proceed from God himself, and, therefore, they grant the individual a certain experience of divine greatness, of God's saving intervention in life and in the history of each person and nation. On the other hand, they are realities that grant one's deepest desire of the heart and constitute an adequate and superabundant response (cf. Rom 5: 15–17) to the human desires for truth, happiness, immortality, triumph, peace, and love. In other words, they direct mankind toward the ultimate goal that makes sense of personal existence, that goal being eternal life with God.

We will begin studying those signs or reasons by considering the great saving prodigies that compelled the Israelites to believe in Yahweh. We will analyze the words and conduct of the prophets, which confirmed and supported the chosen people in their faith (chapter 11). In the next chapter we will see how these great elements of credibility are present in Jesus of Nazareth, manifested as the Lord's Anointed, Son of the Almighty and Lord, who in his glorious Resurrection offers the definitive sign to believe (chapter 12). Then we will see how in her testimony about the crucified and resurrected Jesus, the Church presents herself, her life and teaching, her very structure and all of her activity, as a great reason to believe in the God who intervenes in history and calls all to live with him (chapter 13).

Because these elements are realities with a profound historical core, we must undertake their study in a scientific manner, respecting each one's historical context. Specifically, it is necessary to consider how those elements lead people to faith in the historical moment that they occurred. Respecting these fundamental concerns will enable us to come to a better understanding of these reasons for credibility and how they are useful for contemporary man.

Here, we should make it clear that the present study will show these fundamental elements without proposing a precise apologetic model.[2] We will offer a picture of all of these elements as a body in Chapter 14 so as to deepen our study of the nature and basic structure of credibility. We will concentrate on their intimate relationship with revelation and faith, their progressive and free character, and the limited and dependent efficacy of faith and grace.

CHAPTER 10

THE OBJECT AND HISTORY OF APOLOGETICS

The word *apologetics* comes from the Greek *apología*. It means defense, justification, reasoning, or enlightening discourse.[1] By apologetics, we mean any intellectual and dialectic effort, in the Christian sphere and in a broad sense, carried out to defend the Christian faith from those who challenge it. We also mean those efforts to attract people who are not yet believers to the faith. Consequently, apologists do not only take the defensive. Apologetics mainly consists of the positive attempt to explain and expose the truth in such a way that those who do not know it yet can come to understand and love it.[2]

Strictly speaking, apologetics is the science that deals with the credibility of Christianity from its inception through today. It studies those elements that ground God's message and Christian life in truth. Apologetics is the science of the credibility of God's Word revealed to mankind in history. Because Christ is the plenitude of revelation (due to the fact that he is the Incarnate Word of God), apologetics can be defined as the science of the credibility of the Incarnate Word. That credibility has historical consequences, the most important being the ecclesiastical one, because the Church is the authorized repository and transmitter of the revelation of God in Christ.

This science cannot be separated from theology, not even early in its study, because it is part of theology, concretely belonging to fundamental theology.

Apologetics is a constitutive part of theology because it proceeds from principles received by Revelation and accepted in faith. This necessarily implies a certain need to defend its principles from the erroneous suggestions of those who do not understand or believe in them. Apologetic writers need to engage in the theological attempt to defend these key principles, particularly when they are challenged because theology, much like faith, is a knowledge of wisdom. "Just as it is proper of the wise man to contemplate mainly the truth of the first beginning, and to judge other truths, so it is to reject falsehood."[3] Fundamental theology deals with Revelation and faith using the fundamentals and principles of theological science, and, consequently, it deals with those same principles and examines the credibility of Gods's Revelation.

Historically this was the task carried out by the first Christian writers in the epoch after the apostles and the first disciples. In the second century St. Justin Martyr, St. Quadratus of Athens, Athenagoras of Athens, St. Theophilus, Aristo of Pella, Tatian the Assyrian, St. Apollinaris of Hierapolis, St. Melito of Sardis, Tertullian, and others whose works have not been passed down to us, labored on these topics. Although in later centuries, writers tended to concentrate on dogmatic, ascetic-moral, or scriptural areas, the apologists never disappeared. They were always needed to respond to heretics or those who expressed disbelief.

During the sixteenth century this function, which was part of the presentation of general theology worked out by the Scholastics,[4] was separated from dogmatic and morals textbooks. Subsequently, it was constituted as an independent discipline that proceeded without resorting to the arguments of revealed authority and whose object was proving the credibility of Christian religion. In the nineteenth century, this apologetic function acquired a new facet: the rational justification of theological inquiry.[5]

Doubtlessly, Christian apologetics is a scientific response to St. Peter's invitation in his first letter, which asked Christians to "always be prepared to make a defense to any one who calls you to account for the hope [*logon peri tés en hymin elpidos*] that is in you" (1 Pt 3: 15). The Apostle wanted the recipients of his letter, who were living through difficult times at the hands of unbelievers, not to become paralyzed by these hostilities. Thankfully, these believers faced their challenge with an unwavering spirit. They established open and reasoned dialogue with the unbelievers.[6]

St. Peter very probably had Christ's example in mind when he made the preceding exhortation. Our Lord frequently dealt with people who objected to his preaching and challenged his authority. Jesus refuted those who refused to accept that he had power over demons. He obliged his critics to reconsider their unfounded conclusions (cf. Mt 12: 22–32; Mk 3: 22–30; Lk 11: 14–20). He encouraged his listeners to discern the arrival of God's kingdom in view of the miracles he accomplished, comparing this discernment to that one peasant who forecasts the weather (cf. Lk 12: 54–57; Mt 16: 2–3; Jn 10: 38). Christ's apostles, who never failed to give reasonable explanations about Jesus' messianic mission and its authenticity (cf. Acts 2: 22–24; 3: 14–16; 4: 15–16; 8: 35; 28, 23), also imitated his conduct.

Thus, the Christian apologetic task develops according to the double attitude animating it. First, it is powered by the serene conviction that the defense of the principles of faith is always possible because any assertion against truth is by definition, false.[7] Supernatural reality exceeds the capacity of the human intellect in such a way that it is not possible to know it or prove its truth with arguments from reason alone. Therefore, the opposite is also impossible. Consequently, one can always refute attacks against the faith, or at the very least prove that they are neither conclusive nor based upon truthful information and solid premises.[8]

Second, this task must be inspired by a respectful and humble attitude, which is proper to the one who is aware of possessing the truth. The believer knows that he has received it as an undeserved and free gift. He has not discovered or mastered it through his reading and investigation: "For by grace you have been saved through faith; and this is not your own doing, it is the gift of God—not because of works, lest any man should boast" (Eph 2: 8–9). In fact, St. Peter, in the exhortation that we mentioned earlier, instructs his fellow Christians to remember that Faith is a free gift when giving reason of their hope: "Keep your conscience clear, so that, when you are abused, those who revile your good behavior in Christ may be put to shame" (1 Pt 3: 16).

The objective of this chapter is not historiographical. For this reason we will not go into great detail about authors and texts. We will examine various approaches, concepts, and premises from different epochs. We will study the dialogue among Christians. We will also analyze the dialogue of faith and theology with philosophy and the sciences. In all cases, we intend to review these dialogues in a rational and scientific manner, so as to demonstrate that God's Word is completely credible.

I. The Dialogue of Faith with Non-Christian Culture and Thought in the Second through Fifth Centuries

The Apostolic Fathers and the first Christian writers sought to guide and edify the faithful. For their part, the Greek Apologists directed the Church's literature to the exterior world for the first time by leading it by the hand into new cultural and scientific domains. As a consequence of the aggressive attitude of the paganism of that time, the missionary word, which had been apologetic only on occasion, became predominantly apologetic during the second century. Among vulgar people, coarse rumors were being circulated against the Christian religion. The Roman state considered belief in Christianity a most severe crime against the official cult and the emperor's majesty. The intellectual leaders and more educated classes of society condemned the new religion. They considered it as an ever-increasing menace against the universal empire of Rome.[9]

J. Quasten has observed that, in view of this situation, Christian writers devoted particular time and effort to showing that the Church was no danger to the state as such. Moreover, they expressed how inconsistent and immoral both paganism and its myths were. They went on to show that only Christianity offered a correct and healthy conception of God. In that effort, these writers utilized the philosophy and culture of their interlocutors.[10] This is the framework in which the dialogue of the faithful with their non-Christian contemporaries developed during these early centuries. The dialogue of this general era may be divided into three specific eras. The first era of dialogue was during the second century; the second era was during the period of the Alexandrians in the third century; and the final era we shall term the "existential" period.

A. The Apologists of the Second Century

In this century, from the standpoint of content, apologetics was a rationally articulated response to disbelief and provocation within the social, political, religious, and intellectual dynamic of early Christianity. Apologists sought to explain the Christian message in such a way that people might easily understand it.[11]

We ought to keep in mind that the writers of this era were involved in an intellectual battle with the predominant cultural and religious traditions, either Greek-Latin or Jewish in origin.

When confronting classical culture, the early apologists needed to provide a detailed exposition of everything related to the doctrine. These authors also explained the true nature of religion and differentiated Christianity from polytheism. In their tracts, we can discern the extent of the defamatory attacks against the new religion. They showed that Christianity was not an enemy of man, society, or any political organization. They defended the new religion against the accusations of atheism, infanticide, and cannibalism. The early apologists clarified the essence and truth of Christianity in a scientific manner.[12]

In the confrontation with Judaism, the early apologists wrestled a different set of concerns. They worked to demonstrate that there was both continuity and discontinuity between Judaism and Christianity. This reality grew steadily clearer by the light of the spiritual and doctrinal development of the young Christian communities.[13]

Apologetics in this century was characterized by the discovery and implementation of the following fundamental lines of Christian discourse:

- First of all, the *apologist accepted* his listeners just as they were, with their own ideas, conditioning, and efforts to seek the truth. Apologists of this century worked hard to listen to and understand their audiences, to discover the underlying reasons for their approaches and solutions. They showed a great sensitivity to the circumstances affecting the development of the lives of others.[14]

- Next, the apologist *searched for dialogue,* understood as an authentic exchange and communication of ideas. This process does not deny there are differences between the apologist and the audience while the apologist seeks to communicate the saving gift and truth. Consequently, these apologists understood their dialogue with non-Christians as both intellectual and soteriological. It was never a mere rhetorical or formal exercise; even less so did it take on a sophistic character. In fact, the apologists openly criticized and denounced such sophistry because of the lack of sincerity and truth it involves. Only in this sense can we understand St. Irenaeus's remarks about the attitude of Gnostics, whom he chastises with such irony.[15]

- Finally, *a common ground was created* from which the apologist and his audience might exchange ideas and begin upon a path of dialogue. So, it can be seen that St. Justin Martyr lays down a bridge between pagan and Christian philosophy. He talked about the seeds (*sperma*) of the Word spread throughout mankind, seeds especially present in wise men who have lived according to the Word without knowing it.[16] The bridge between Judaism and Christianity, therefore, can be built only with the full understanding that the old covenant remains within the new covenant. The only changes are found in the particular legal and cultural organization and the recognition that Christ is the Savior in whom the promise is fulfilled and in whom the prophets' forecasts are carried out. He is the fullness of God's communication to humanity.

Ultimately, it can be said that this foundation is rooted in the communion of nature and vocation that unites all mankind. It also involves the various ways, customs, and ideas that define an epoch, culture, or society. Therefore, "we should not be amazed if apologists should purposely enter into the Hellenism of their time."[17] This is a constant characteristic of Christian apologetics.[18] Only some authors of liberal inspiration at the end of the second millennium question the validity of this practice. One of these writers, A. von Harnack, accused the Church of betraying its *kerygma* from the beginning by succumbing to Greek cultural pressure. In truth, the opposite happened. Christianity converted the Greek-Latin world while remaining substantially immutable, despite being slightly influenced by Hellenic forms.[19]

The apologists of this time confronted Greek-Latin thought by making use of common human experience, popular customs, and philosophical reasoning. One should notice the freedom exercised by these apologists when they selected concepts and arguments. They did not feel restricted to specific schools or authors. They weighed everything and then selected what faith taught them as the right criterion. When these apologists dialogued with the Jews, they mainly highlighted prophecy and left accounts of miracles on a secondary plane. The Jewish people appreciated this, and it fitted their sensibilities.

B. The Apologetics of the Alexandrians in the Third Century

During the third century, the confrontation between faith and non-Christian thought and culture matured in the writings of the Alexandrian Apologists. At that moment, the relationship between the wisdom of philosophical origin and the wisdom founded in God's Word was brought to the foreground.[20] In the previous century, some Christian authors (i.e., Tatian the Assyrian and Tertullian) had completely rejected Greek philosophy, considering it corrupt and false. Others appreciated its influence because they perceived in it a glimpse of the Word, writing that the Word is one shining Word. They argued that the *Logos* spoke to the prophets, and it had also spoken to all men of good will (the authentic philosophers). The *Logos* found its full plenitude in Christ. Consequently, Christianity is the only completely true philosophy.[21]

These were the dominant ideas of the Alexandrian School of the third century.[22] St. Clement of Alexandria, for example, wrote that the truth that shines in Greek philosophy, though partial in nature, is still true.

This philosophy served as a way toward Christ for the Greeks, much like the Mosaic law did for the Hebrews.[23] Based on this approach, we can see that all true knowledge comes from the Word, which is the fruit of enlightening action. "He, from the beginning, from the creation of the world has instructed men in many ways and under many forms; to him the perfection of knowing is due (*gnosis*)."[24]

For these authors as well as those of the previous century, the evaluation of philosophical thinking did not force one to indiscriminately accept it. On the contrary, the permanent discernment of the light of the revealed Word—particularly as it is expressed in Scripture—corresponded undoubtedly and forever to Christ.

By acknowledging the enlightening action of the Word and its universal reach—all people who come to this world live in him and by his light (cf. Jn 1: 4–11)—these authors demonstrated, mainly by means of philosophy, an essential understanding of what Christ did and said. They recognized that Greek philosophy would play a part in deepening the knowledge of faith. In this, Alexandrian apologetics clearly transcended the approach of the previous century and laid the groundwork for the theological work to come. Thus, an intellectual work was founded that, without eliminating the apologetic dimension, was not limited to it. The new work essentially sought to understand more fully what was already believed.

In this line of argument, St. Clement and the other Alexandrians offered a vision of philosophy that is characteristic and proper to their school. That vision has been conserved and transmitted in the life of the Church, although not always with the same clarity or with complete unanimity. It can be summarized as follows: True wisdom is always in accordance with faith. Moreover, true wisdom is founded upon faith because it is a participation in the uncreated wisdom. It completely reveals itself in the process of Incarnation. As a result, the true philosopher is the Christian who has reflexively assumed his faith. He matures in the comprehension of what he believes.

C. The Apologetics of Existential Character: The Testimonies of the Martyrs and the Writings of St. Augustine

The development of apologetics in the third century was not limited to the cultural, speculative position of the Alexandrian school. It also developed in another direction, in perfect accordance with St. Peter's instruction (cf. 1 Pt 3: 15). Working from an existential and testimonial perspective, some have considered this direction a "minor" argument. Scholars have devoted little attention to it, even though it has wielded considerable influence. This is because it relates to the application of a tremendously efficacious test, one having to do with one's own life. This apology rarely appears in systematic writings. We also may find it in stories and historical documents.

This apology is characterized by the evaluation of precise and concrete circumstances—existential in character—of the protagonists of the dialogue, Christian and non-Christian, and in the ultimate radicalization of issues. It is always directed to the fundamental fact of the person's life that is, definitively, what is being questioned.

The paradigm of this apology is, doubtlessly, *the dialogue of martyrs with judges and executioners*.[25] Sometimes, the martyr appeared before a judge who unequivocally united civic loyalty and religious practice (the religion of the empire). The believer had to explain that Christians were loyal citizens who fulfilled their civic obligations (taxes, law observance, respect for authorities, etc.). However, these obligations cannot be confused with religion itself. The Christian could say that his religion obliged him to be loyal to the empire and the society in which he lived. (Such was the case, for instance, of the Sicilian martyrs before Pro-consul Vigelio Saturnino, who was particularly rigid in identifying civic loyalty and cult to the emperor.) On other occasions, the martyr stood before a judge who falsified facts and took what in reality was a socially legitimate activity as the center of religious activity (for instance, a school of philosophy). Then, it was necessary to clarify to the judge that Christianity could not be identified with a merely human activity or a specific philosophical doctrine or culture. (This was the case, for instance, of St. Justin Martyr, who had a school of philosophy in Rome.)

This dialogue of the martyrs with their judges has often passed unnoticed. Perhaps this is because the moment has traditionally been presented in an extremely simple way. Or, perhaps it is because these moments sought to explain difficult issues in speculative terms. The value of this apologetic activity lies precisely in its capacity to efficaciously explain an aspect of Christianity that is not open to verbal explanation. It requires deep gestures where one commits one's life to the accepted and believed truth. This was the only way to convince the pagan world that this new religion could not be identified with a social or state organization and that God's truth is above any human reasoning, no matter how humane the reasoning.

St. Augustine's approach (which is proposed in his *Confessions* and in *The City of God*) presents another paradigm of this apologetic approach.[26] He started with arguments from earlier writers, but he developed them by stressing personal experiences and a historical worldview. He was an apologist who responded to real problems arising from the reaction of his conscience to certain events that beg for an explanation. St. Augustine knew the great human problems: the problem of evil, the sense of history, and personal existence. Augustine knew how to face the great issues that concern people of all times. He knew how to read the drama of human existence, to discover the thread of pain that goes through it. According to St. Augustine, God attracts us toward himself with this thread. In fact, St. Augustine had the insight to penetrate the real meaning behind the apparent dissatisfaction brought on by the many troubles throughout our earthly sojourn. He taught that the precariousness of earthly happiness signifies the happiness that knows no end. It is a stimulus toward truth, eternal love, and true eternity.

Still, his genius appears in all its greatness when he extends existential motives of the personal and individual order to the collective and historical order. The precise inspiration came to him upon the sack of Rome by Alaric (AD 410). Some Romans claimed that this catastrophe was a punishment inflicted upon the city by the gods of Rome offended by the defection of the empire, which had accepted the expansion and official establishment of the Christian religion in the Edict of Milan in AD 313. Such interpretation of facts hearkened back to the political-ethical approach of religion that was characteristic of the Greek-Latin world. It valued history as a criterion of truth in religious and moral matters. If wars and businesses were going well, then the gods were happy and the official doctrines regarding economics and politics were true, and *vice versa*.

St. Augustine responded to this interpretation by pointing out a deep inconsistency: Before Christianity appeared, the Romans had suffered many misfortunes of all sorts. Consequently, they could not validly blame the disasters they suffered on this new religion. However, this alone was insufficient, because St. Augustine understood that a denial or criticism was not a complete explanation. Then, he explained his own vision of history, which offered a satisfactory response to his audience. He also added other arguments of a deeper nature, which were psychological, social, moral, and theological.

With a great historical perspective, he divided the history of the world into two cities: two men, two loves, two attitudes. Yet, he did not propose these two principles, good and bad, in the way the Manicheans and dualism had proposed them (as an opposition between two irreconcilable forces). According to St. Augustine, the drama of history lay in the interplay of two loves. St. Augustine presented this drama through the eyes of faith, without separating human knowledge—philosophy, rhetoric, etc.—from theological belief. The intelligibility of history is not accessible to unaided reason. People can glimpse its rationality only if God is seen behind everything that happens. Hence, St. Augustine did not sever the order of faith from the order of reason. He differentiated them while maintaining their unity, and this explains how he dealt with revelation. He defended it with the weapons of reason. In the gigantic drama of history, he distinguished five acts, according to the custom of sectioning the ancient tragedies: creation, fall, law, arrival of the Christ, and final judgment. In each of these moments, he studied the great problems of human history, such as our origins, evil, the fight between good and evil, and the victory of good over evil. Above all of them stood the shining light of divine providence, which is wisdom and love, the guide and ultimate reason for all history.[27]

The Augustinian approach did not alienate its audience (be it pagan culture or Jewish heritage). On the contrary, the apologist sought to save all that was good—and that is a great deal—after weighing its diverse elements by the light of faith. Thus, a new synthesis was created that was formed by God's Word and his provident, fatherly love. This encounter with non-Christian culture did not end when it was overcome. Indeed, the process of incorporation to a new culture enlightened by faith will never die. It will only continue to mature in the celestial Jerusalem.[28]

The Bishop of Hippo succeeded in producing the first great synthesis of philosophy and theology, embracing currents of thought both Greek and Latin. In him too, the great unity of knowledge, grounded in the thought of the Bible, was both confirmed and sustained by a depth of speculative thinking. The synthesis devised by St. Augustine remained for centuries the most exalted form of philosophical and theological speculation known to the West. Reinforced by his personal story and sustained by a wonderful holiness of life, he could also introduce into his works a range of material which, drawing on experience, was a prelude to future developments in different currents of philosophy.[29]

II. The Deepening of the Dialogue between Faith and Reason during the Second Millennium

St. Anselm and other Scholastic doctors initiated the development of Christian discourse about God in the second millennium. To this progress, we need to add another element that affects the historical and critical evaluation of assertions from written sources.

The successful use of the scientific dimension in the discourse about God does not mean that theology ought to be considered solely as a science, even by theologians. Many of them, such as Bl. John Duns Scotus, thought that it was not science since it lacked the evidence of its principles. Other writers, such as St. Thomas Aquinas, responded that theology was a science subordinated to the science of God and the saints. In this view, it is evident that sacred science comes from revelation.[30]

St. Thomas recognized that nature, philosophy's proper concern, could contribute to the understanding of Divine Revelation. Faith therefore has no fear of reason, but seeks it out and has trust in it. Just as grace builds on nature and brings it to fulfilment,[31] so faith builds upon and perfects reason. Illumined by faith, reason is set free from the fragility and limitations deriving from the disobedience of sin and finds the strength required to rise to the knowledge of the Triune God. Although he made much of the supernatural character of faith, the Angelic Doctor did not overlook the importance of its reasonableness; indeed he was able to plumb the depths and explain the meaning of this reasonableness. Faith is in a sense an "exercise of thought;" and human reason is neither annulled nor debased in assenting to the contents of faith, which are in any case attained by way of free and informed choice.[32]

The use of the scientific dimension means that the issues are approached systematically and rigorously. Theologians analyze the need and universality of assertions, always adducing proofs of statements, showing the inter-connection and relations among realities. All these thinkers warn that this project requires approaching the issue of the God-world relation, more specifically God-man. It implies that an effort be undertaken to face the relationship between things that belong to all humanity—the gift of creation, of nature—and those that only some persons have, persons who have believed in the gift of grace and faith.

The relationship between nature and grace that had already attracted the attention of St. Augustine and others because of the teachings of Pelagius was, in this manner, transformed into a continuous reference for all theologians, who all present different solutions to this issue. The fundamental point of the issue lies in the study of the relationship between faith and reason; that comprised the true intellectual challenge of the entire millennium. The study of this relationship constitutes, in a certain way, a true leitmotif in the writings of all of the theologians from St. Anselm to the present. In a very particular way, this has been the case of those involved in fundamental theology.

There have been several interpretations of the relationship between faith and reason. Once the difference between them is recognized, there are basically two solutions: either to understand that faith and

reason are intimately related or to consider them intrinsically uncon-
nected. Both approaches find their paradigm in the response given to
the issue of credibility, which is the standard for any doctrine about
the relationship between faith and reason.

For its part, the solution of credibility is summarized in the answers to
the following questions, which we will consider one at a time:

- Is a reasonable and prudent justification of one's own faith
  legitimate or even necessary?

- Is it possible to find in revelation elements that show its
  credibility?

- Is it possible to know Christian credibility with certainty?

- Is it possible to understand a faith-reason relationship according
  to a model that sees them united and harmoniously fused?

Theologians of the second millennium have neither answered these
questions in the same way, nor have they come to their conclusions in
the same manner. Still, the Church believes—with a conviction that
was reaffirmed and defined by Vatican I—that it is possible to give
reasons for faith in Christ; therefore, faith and reason can maintain a
fertile and harmonious relationship.

A. Reason before Believing: A General Approach to Credibility

Any reflection on credibility cannot be undertaken without first setting forth the valid reasons to believe in a God who manifests himself
in history. One might answer in the negative, claiming faith is purer
without rational support, without motives that respond to aspirations
of happiness and glory. In fact, twentieth-century theologian Rudolf
Bultmann argued that faith must not be supported by historical events
such as miracles or the Resurrection. He claimed that it must be a
leap into a void, a complete gift of one's own existence bereft of any
justification, an unconditional surrender in the sense that it lacks any
human justification. Nevertheless, in the course of the millennium,

many theologians, from the great medieval doctors on, have pointed out the necessity and legitimacy of a prudent and reasoned justification of faith.

We can prove that justification is necessary in different ways. First, the existential-moral order asks for it. Practicing the Christian faith involves a vital compromise: Believing in Christ does not mean accepting only some truths. It involves living in accordance with what is professed. Now, "to renounce egotism, sin, and purely worldly safety is to open oneself to the hope of a new life that transcends the limits of death. Therefore, it means to live like a new man from now on, to give oneself wholeheartedly as the fruit of one's faith in the death and Resurrection of Christ. This effort requires that believers have valid reasons for taking such a demanding option."[33]

There is, furthermore, a psychological-intellectual dimension to this justification. Faith is a deeply human act that uses intelligence and freedom. Clearly, when man believes someone else and accepts his word, he first takes certain precautions. Prudence compels him to make sure that the person can be trusted, that he is knowledgeable and dependable on a subject. Such care can demand more or less rigor, depending on the importance of the issue and the quality of the person proposing it. Yet, nothing is lacking, unless one acts with scant prudence, as Scripture lets us know: "It is not good for a man to be without knowledge, and he who makes haste with his feet misses his way" (Prv 19: 2). St. Augustine commented on this passage: "No one believes something if he does not think beforehand that it can be believed."[34] The grace of faith does not supplant the demands of human psychology. Quite to the contrary, this grace delicately respects human psychology. That is why one must carefully determine if what is proposed to be believed really comes from God. If that inquiry lacked the act of faith, besides being an imprudent action, it would not, according to St. Paul, be a reasonable gift of intelligence to God (cf. Rom 12: 1). It would not even be a truly human act because it would fail to respect the rules of reason. It would, instead, be an act of fanaticism that would serve to lower a person's dignity.[35]

Furthermore, this justification has a social-religious dimension. The human person is related to many others. Since man is a social creature, he cannot do without other people. Consequently, his decisions and choices are influenced by others. These decisions go on to influence others. Above all, religion is not reducible to sentimentality—even though religion certainly involves feelings and affections. It is not a private matter to be kept secretly within one's inner self without external manifestations.[36] Christian faith, precisely because it is lived and communally professed and because it is socially constituted, needs to assert and defend its identity before other religious groups, even before agnostics or declared atheists.

Finally, we need to observe the systematic-scientific dimension to this justification. Theologians feel the need to obtain a place within the scientific world for the science of faith (theology). Any science must justify its own existence, proving that it deals with a specific matter (object) and has a proper methodology. If that were not the case, it could be considered only an aspect of another already-existing science. For theology, it is of paramount importance to show the possibility that faith accords with reason. Otherwise, its existence would be in peril. This is because our ability to show harmony and collaboration between faith and reason is the genesis of Christian belief. It will, therefore, make sense to talk of that same collaboration to deepen and better know what is already believed. That is precisely the object of the science of faith. Were this collaboration not proved, all theological reflection would lack an adequate and safe foundation, and could be interpreted as sophistry.[37]

Accordingly, it is licit to search and study the reasons for our hope, since these are the motives for our belief. Peter's exhortation (cf. 1 Pt 3: 15) implies that the *logos* is truly present in Christian life, that the presence of the *logos* allows Christian existence to be justified, in a credible manner, from the moment of its inception.[38]

The investigation of the credibility of our faith ought not to be viewed as a manifestation of scant devotion or disrespect for grace. It is only a sign that one is acting in a prudent and reasonable manner. Such an investigation would be atheistic or incredulous only when man does not consider the elements offered by God by which he leaves his doubts aside as sufficient.[39] Such was the case when certain Jews requested a sign from Jesus and did not take advantage of or value those he had already offered them (cf. Mt 16: 1–4).

The study of the reasons to believe is not only legitimate; it is necessary to help others grow and to confirm oneself in one's own faith. When St. Peter invited people to be always ready to give reason for their hope, it does not seem that he meant a formal defense before a tribunal or an official interrogation.[40] Rather, he appears to have been referring to the questions and conversations that arise in ordinary life.[41]

Obviously, this obligation for all the faithful to go deeper into their intellectual and scholarly understanding concerns each individual to a different degree.[42] For example, intellectuals have a special responsibility to contribute, with the specific resources of their own scientific field, to the development of apologetics:

> Formerly, when human knowledge—science—was very limited, it seemed quite feasible for a single scholar to defend and vindicate our holy faith. Today, with the extension and the intensity of modern science, the apologists have to divide the work among themselves, if they wish to defend the Church scientifically in all fields. You … cannot shirk this responsibility.[43]

B. Signs and Credibility of Revelation

The second question has to do with whether it is possible and even necessary to search within historical revelation for motives of credibility. One might imagine a negative response, claiming that one must not ask God to prove himself by showing his power, wisdom, and kindness. One must not request those manifestations from God as a condition or requirement to know that in fact he is the one who speaks to and calls each person. Nevertheless, throughout the millennium, many theologians, beginning with the great medieval doctors, have taught that revelation contains many gestures and signs that, besides revealing God and his plans, serve to show his personal intervention in history and make his Word credible.

1. The Medieval Doctors

The Scholastics coincide in distinguishing three levels, or stages, in the movement toward faith: *preambula fidei*, signs, and the specific grace that makes possible the act of faith.

Preambula fidei make up that body of knowledge about God that is humanly attainable by way of contemplation of the world, history, society, and introspection (cf. Rom 1: 18–32). They are preambles because in order to believe in God, it is necessary to already know something about him. "Whoever would draw near to God must believe that he exists and that he rewards those who seek him" (Heb 11: 6). He has to know him in faith, even though faith on earth is not yet supernatural faith, but a human faith, in God. This is human knowledge of God that is obtained by creatures through reason, and it can and must be called faith because it is "to know what is not seen" (*fides est de non visis*). In fact, God remains hidden, since no one has ever seen him.

Signs are miracles and prophesies by which one can know with certitude that God is acting and directing himself through miracle-workers or prophets.[44] The efficacy of these signs is such that, according to Abelard, they relate to "rational faith." This differs from "meritorious and supernatural faith." It undoubtedly shows the presence and action of God in those signs to one's reason. Bl. John Duns Scotus wrote about "acquired faith,"[45] while others would prefer to term it "scientific faith." Everyone agrees that this "faith" based upon signs is not yet saving faith, which is the exclusive effect of grace, which is received after having acquired faith. St. Thomas also considers these signs efficacious, but he does not call the intellectual conclusion that they cause faith. He prefers to designate it "a judgment of credibility." This judgment always and necessarily precedes the act of faith—unless the act is imprudent and foolish—because it definitively shows, based on those signs, that the word that is heard is believable. This judgment does not analyze the content of what the word manifests. However, it examines the origin of that word and discovers, based on the signs, that it comes from God. This is because those signs show a power, wisdom, and kindness that can only be divine.[46]

The medieval doctors agree on two fundamental ideas:

1. The act of faith is possible only by means of supernatural grace; and

2. Historical revelation becomes credible thanks to signs granted by God when he reveals himself. Among those signs are miracles and prophesies.

The doctors differ in the way they serve to explain our supernatural faith.

At the end of this period, various approaches arose that were directed toward a new evaluation of the arguments not strictly based upon signs. So, Girolamo Savonarola wrote about the moral effects and practical value of Christianity; Pedro de la Caballeria highlighted the excellence of Christian faith; Juan Luis Vives showed the relationships of revealed mysteries to human nature.[47]

2. The Protestant Reformers

Calvin and Luther do not explicitly reject apologetics. However, they undermine it indirectly inasmuch as they mistrust reason and present faith only as *fiducia* based on the interior experience of grace.

The Reformers move away from the medieval doctors because they do not take into account the preambles of the faith and do not value the demonstrations of credibility. Still, that does not signify that they completely reject them. For example, Calvin admitted that God is manifested in acts of creation, but he taught that human reason has been so damaged by Adam's sin that the manifestation of God in the world is useless to us. He wrote that creatures are "mute teachers."[48] Alternatively, in opposition to the medieval scholars, the Reformers invoke above all the "taste of the gospel," which man perceives thanks to the interior action of the Holy Spirit in a saving experience that drives one toward Christ. Inasmuch as one cannot understand what the world tells about God, one can learn about God only through the word of Scripture united to "the interior testimony of the Spirit."[49]

This approach to the issue of credibility results from the notion of faith advocated by the Reformers. Luther understands faith only as confidence in our own salvation. He does not deny the aspect of intellectual adherence, but he considers it secondary and accidental. Consequently, only the belief that God will forgive our sins by the love of Christ remains important. He does not deny that other things can be believed, but that is of little significance. Luther's theory of credibility is interrelated with his theory of faith. One's personal experiences drive one's conviction of salvation in Christ. These experiences may have a certain external consistency, but they are substantially internal and spiritual. They are a gift of grace, a gift of the Holy Spirit that guides one toward complete trust and faith in God.

It is possible to find a certain likeness between this explanation and St. Augustine's existential apologetics. Still, we must point out a profound difference: St. Augustine based his argument on elements pertaining to the interior experience of every person. Luther, alternatively, refers to interior experiences that are not had by everybody, at least not unbelievers. St. Augustine builds on the common wish for happiness, the experience of evil and injustice, dissatisfaction of our temporal life, the crying out for wider and long-lasting horizons of beauty, love, and truth. These elements are within everyone's reach and, therefore, are issues that can be dealt with scientifically. On the other hand, the experience that Luther wrote about is indescribable, individual, and subjective. Therefore, it is not possible to put it into objective, scientific terms. Hence, Lutheran apologetics is not properly a science, subject to reason, but a spiritual preparation directed to a dialogue about experiences of a religious character that may lead to Christ.

In any event, we should note that, paradoxically, when the Protestant authors of those centuries defended their religion before unbelievers, they turned to medieval apologetics to support their arguments: prophesies, miracles, and the life of Jesus. For example, Melanchton proposed reason as a preparation for faith. In his work *Loci Communes* in 1536, he relied upon traditional arguments, i.e., the antiquity of biblical revelation, the excellence of Christian doctrine, the continuity of the Church, and the testimony of miracles. Calvin also defended the revealed character of Sacred Scripture using arguments similar to those used by the followers of Bl. John Duns Scotus and William of Ockham from the fourteenth century. Later, many Protestant authors posited the internal or experimental test based on subjective effects produced by a faith that appears as source of peace and spiritual satisfaction. Others argue from the usefulness of Christian dogma for directing life, practicing religion, and understanding the world and humanity.

3. Classical Apologetics

Believers and Catholics found a most demanding intellectual challenge in the ideas born from the Cartesian approach, enriched by Humean critical skepticism, and consolidated by Kantian epistemology. A new and radical response to these ideas was required. In fact, the entire religious worldview was under fire. In addition, Catholics had to respond to Protestant criticism of the validity and necessity of the Church as a means of salvation and everything that that implied, the value of Tradition and the Magisterium, the efficacy of the sacraments, and other issues. Against this background, apologists had to organize themselves according to the structure later called classical: the religious, Christian, and Catholic demonstration of the faith.[50]

This apologetic task was made especially difficult because of trouble initiating a dialogue, caused not only by the great animosity of the opposition, but, above all, by the difference in mentality among the apologists themselves. This mentality arose from a difference in concepts and language that led to mutual misunderstanding and miscommunication.[51]

In view of these circumstances, we cannot help but hold in high regard the apologists of that time, although we should not ignore the limitations of their work. Their efforts were characterized by these three elements:

1. *Discursive and logical rigor,* which was given special attention to insure that the apologetic discourse be presented in a most rational fashion. For instance, C. Wolf started from the theodicy of Leibnitz and, basing his work on the prophets and the apostles, demonstrated that, given the stage of human development in

Christ's time, an immediate divine revelation was required. He presented his apologetics in the form of a mathematical argument: *una methodus rigorem demonstrandi geometricum constanter observat* (a method that consistently observes geometrical rigor in demonstration).[52] With that response, he sought to resolve rationalist criticism by placing Christianity on the same intellectual and human level.

2. *Argumentative objectivity*, so as to make a clear distinction from agnostic subjectivism. To that effect, miracles, prophecy, and the life and Resurrection of Jesus were emphasized since they are external and historically verifiable events.

3. *The extrinsic relationship* between credibility and faith demanded by the two previous elements. As we know, any rigorous and scientific argument requires a demonstration of credibility as a prior, essential condition to the act of faith. They neither showed the relationship between grace and that process toward credibility nor between that process and the act of faith itself. Rather, the whole process of credibility was envisioned as separate from the action of grace. Accordingly, the whole process took place solely under the light of reason. These apologists claimed that credibility did not really require grace because it is in itself attainable by reason. Grace is necessary only to believe. At the same time, they introduced a distinction—almost an axiom—between the fact of revelation (which is positively recognizable by reason from signs or motives of credibility) and the contents of revelation (which can be reached only by the light of faith). They valued the historical events of revelation only slightly.

This extrinsic relationship was partially due to some medieval theological traditions that we have already studied. It was also due in part to the modern philosophical approach that distinguished between pure and practical reason. In this view, science belongs to the former since it is a matter of rational, necessary, and universal argumentation. Faith belongs to the latter since it is a matter of will and affection. Kant proposed this division in his work *Religion within the Limits of Reason Alone*.[53] Kant consigned religion and its justification to the realm of conscience. For faith based upon authority, he substituted belief, which he understood to be a generic assertion postulated for practical reasons. Based upon these premises, any notion of credibility according to the medieval authors and even of the Protestant Reformers is unfounded.[54]

Apologists, therefore, sought to renew their approach so as to face the challenges of the modern era, although their work maintained many of the characteristics we have already indicated. Before the strictly apologetic discourse, they placed a brief treatment of revelation in doctrinal code, that is, in the Magisterium's terms and with the authoritative testimony of God, who demands the adherence of faith once its possibility, utility, necessity, and effective accomplishment are proved. In this vein, G. Perrone (1794–1876), J. Balmes (1810–1848), F. Hettinger (1819–1890), A. Gardeil (1859–1931), L. de Grandmaison (1868–1927) and R. Garrigou-Lagrange (1877–1964) made outstanding contributions.

The evident limits of "classical" apologetics should not make us forget its merits and the difficult circumstances it confronted. Undoubtedly, it helped confirm many Christians in their faith from those centuries well into the twentieth. At the same time, it can be said that its major limitation consists in the lack of demonstrated ability to attract unbelievers to the faith. This inspired a growing effort to radically reorganize apologetics. It seemed to many apologists that the underlying problem was a failure to consider the audience. There needed to be a greater effort to find a common ground that took in the viewpoint of the "other," with the disposition to have a fertile discussion. The ensuing apologetic development took different directions that, nevertheless, coincided in the effort to value the "other inasmuch as other" and at the same time "present in a new way" religion, revelation, and apologetics.

4. The Birth of the Sciences of Religion

A pioneer of presenting religion in a new way was F.D.E. Schleiermacher. He confronted Hegelian idealism, a philosophy that absorbed religion as a transient moment in the evolution of the Spirit, pushing it into the past and reducing it to a concrete aspect of rational and cultural dialectics, forgetting its voluntary and affective dimension. Departing from historical and psychological observation of the inclination toward religion present in every person, Schleiermacher proposed an original path, something that he called "religious feeling." Every person carries that feeling in the unconscious as a blind element that has to receive form from different experiences of God that originate faith. Those experiences find their highest expression in Jesus' redemptive act. In his work *Christian Faith* (1821–1822), he defends Christianity as the highest form of monotheism and monotheism as the highest expression of religion.[55]

Schleiermacher held that God's power to redeem in Christ is in itself enough evidence for all those who experience it. Christianity demonstrates its credibility insofar as it satisfies the person's need for religious feeling in such a way that the elements valued by classical apologetics—miracles, prophesies, Jesus' life, Resurrection—are secondary. In this aspect, Schleiermacher coincides in great measure with F.H. Jacobi, who considered mysticism the only important part of Christianity: The entire justification of faith relates to the fact that it meets a religious and interior necessity of the human person.[56] He also agreed with other contemporary authors, such as J. Butler and J. Erskine, for whom the credibility of revelation was measured by the concurrence between what our conscience tells us about God and our religious needs and duties—and what revelation tell us about it.[57]

In a certain way, Schleiermacher managed to show that religion has an undeniable rational foundation, because of religious feeling, which is present always and in all people. It is a *necessary and universal* reality. In fact, it can be said that thanks to Schleiermacher, the science of religion greatly developed in the nineteenth and twentieth centuries.

The biggest limitation his project faced was its incapacity to adequately defend the specific nature of the Christian faith. This nature was found not to break with the basics of the Enlightenment according to the same conditions of other religions. As a result, Schleiermacher attempted not so much to save Christian doctrine, but the religious act. This allowed for the rise of religious indifference in liberal Protestantism.

5. The Study of Revelation from New Perspectives: Fundamental Theology

Meanwhile, Johann Sebastian von Drey (1777–1853) and other professors of the Tubingen school moved in another direction. Von Drey posited that the intrinsic coherence of the whole history of revelation was an eminent criterion of its credibility. In contrast to Schleiermacher, he attempted to demonstrate that Christianity is the perfect religion in the context of history of all religions and revelation.

Von Drey's project required him to first set forth a philosophical theory of religion and revelation regarding the development of religious conscience.[58] Creation is characterized by the two spheres of nature: spiritual and physical. Divine Revelation also acts through two fundamental forms: miracle and inspiration.

The most representative feature of von Drey's theory is that he considers Jesus Christ the Revelation that surpasses any form of revelation and religion because God is manifest in him not only through words and actions, but also in person. Jesus Christ, therefore, fulfills the religious history of mankind. Von Drey distinguishes three stages of development:

1. Paganism (religion without revelation)

2. Judaism (revealed religion that prepares for the universal revelation)

3. Christianity (the perfect religion of complete and universal revelation)

Von Drey's contribution lies in his presentation of a general theory of revelation in historical-theological terms, not just doctrinal or apologetic ones, in recognizing Christ as the center and pinnacle of salvation history, and in relating Christianity to other religions. His work has served as a starting point for the creation of fundamental theology. Von Drey saw credibility as something not external to revelation, but intimately related to it. This is particularly important because in so doing, he laid down the foundations that allowed classical apologetics to move forward and escape the trap of purely external formalities.

Ehrlich followed this line of thought in his *Fundamentaltheologie*, the first text of this kind in the German language when published in 1859–1862. He also elaborated a theology of revelation in salvation-historical code and conceived of it in terms of a Christocentric human history.

6. The Renewal of Apologetics

As we have pointed out earlier, the great limitation of classical apologetics was its negative attitude toward the "other," the audience of revelation. Once they overcame that defect, Catholic theologians were able to renew the field of apologetics. Consequently, one may observe how these apologists transformed their arguments to respond to the Enlightenment. They sought to investigate the question of persons in dialogue with God and his Word. They made an evaluation of the human being in his entirety, as a person and not only an intelligence that receives God's gift. These areas of renewal cross over and interrelate, even though they are not always equally and explicitly present in each author.

The new apologetic orientation was developed, therefore, according to those basic directions. The apologists rehabilitated arguments that had already been treated by existential apologetics, arguments dormant since the Middle Ages, but not forgotten by Protestant theologians. The new orientation dealt with the correspondence between the Christian message, human aspirations, and the very structure of the human person as subject. It involved elements that were present both in Scholastic tradition and in other streams of thought. The apologists were trying to overcome differences that were causing a separation between various philosophical systems. They were trying to construct a holistic apologetics oriented toward dialogue.

In the last third of the nineteenth century, for example, Ollé-Laprune, without denying the usefulness of returning to traditional arguments, proposed taking into account Christian values. In his opinion, the great apologetic argument is found in the fact that human lives can be perfected by means of the Christian message.

Toward the end of the century, Blondel asked why people must deal with Christianity. As far as he was concerned, it is possible to demonstrate philosophically that man "needs" God's grace. Blondel did not pretend to take grace out of human nature. He only wanted to show the error of those who held that Christ is alien to humanity, an "added one" who had nothing to do with what man is and must be. Blondel argued that between the two possible extremes—that grace proceeds from nature and that grace is completely alien to nature—there is still another way to see the natural-supernatural relationship, in which grace bursts into man's life, calling him to a conversion to which his intimate constitution is directed.

It was to that effect that Blondel analyzed the logic of human action. He considered the different stages of its dynamics, where, clearly, every human endeavor has manifest limitations and, at the same time, has potential for future perfection. Blondel asserted that the issue of the supernatural was an unavoidable and humanly necessary question. Personal experience and philosophical reflection show that nothing in the world is capable of satisfying the fundamental dynamics of the human will. Blondel concluded that it is not possible to find something that extinguishes the need for religion in oneself. He believed that the nature of human action shows that the religious need that is born within man cannot be completely forgotten by man himself.[59] Accordingly, human action, when analyzed in its entirety, carries an inevitable tendency to the transcendent. Indeed, he came to theorize about the "unavoidable transcendence of human action."[60]

It is only on the basis of a transcendent conscience that a person can validly evaluate the prophecies and miracles, words and life of Jesus.[61]

The Church resisted aspects of this philosophical approach at its inception because of certain statements made by anti-Christian authors. As the openness or the immanent capacity toward the supernatural was considered necessary, it led to the differentiation between nature and grace. St. Pius X and Pius XII had to intervene to correct erroneous interpretations.[62] Once these difficulties were resolved, the Church treated this approach with more interest. This began the renewal of apologetics that inspired contemporary Catholic theology to enter into a serious dialogue with other ways of thinking, other sensibilities and religious attitudes, other cultures, and other religions.

In conclusion, barring the differences that have separated *theologians of the second millennium, they agree in maintaining that divine revelation includes a variety of signs that make it credible.* They also have specifically demonstrated that *the same divine proposal appears in the eyes of human reason, to a profound degree, in conformity and in usefulness to what man is and wishes.*

C. Fideism: Denial of the Possibility to Show the Credibility of Christianity

Faced with the question as to whether it is possible to know the credibility of Christianity with certainty, some authors say it is not. The Church has always answered that it is, although she has pointed out the limits of this possibility. She does so to avoid the opposite excess of rationalism, which leaves the faith assertion exclusively in the hands of the human will and human knowledge. Rather, we should say that what is possible is only a "prudent and reasonable justification of faith before reason and the demands of human nature." A prudent and reasonable basis for the decision to believe is important because it excludes precipitous action and allows for reflection. The believer thus avoids fanaticism and consequent irresponsibility.

There have always been a few intellectual positions that have denied human intelligence any capacity to defend revealed truth and delve deeper into it. Sometimes these positions have been born from a misguided sort of reverence before the divine Word. The people advocating these positions have argued that scientific investigation of revelation is offensive to the divine majesty. Taken to extremes, such positions are known as *fideism,* an attitude that denies any root in reason. From an intellectual-psychological standpoint, fideism imagines faith as a jump into emptiness, an absolute risk, and blind adherence without any human guarantees. The fideists hold that faith is the only way to know God in his existence and perfections. Not surprisingly, fideist thinking does not allow for an intimate relationship between faith and reason, between religious and scientific thinking.[63]

The first written manifestations of fideism may be found in the second century. Since then, they have reappeared in an almost uninterrupted pattern. In the sixteenth century, the Protestant Reformers laid the basis for radicalizing and extending the fideist approach. In fact, Lutheran thinking is characterized by its distrust of reason and philosophy. Instead, it grants faith and Sacred Scripture absolute primacy over everything concerning religious knowledge and practice. In that way, it places faith and reason into conflict when they try to deal with common issues. This approach has led many authors, such as Barth and Bultmann, to assume clearly fideist positions.[64]

From the historical point of view, the apogee of fideism occurred in the nineteenth century, mainly in France, where thinkers like Gerbert, Bautain, Bonnetty, and others sought to face the exaggerated Rationalism by moving to the opposite extreme, which utterly humiliated reason. They stressed the weakness of reason, insisting excessively in its errors and contradictions. They ended up denying the capacity of human reason to know God with certitude and to know with certainty that he intervenes in history and reveals himself to mankind.[65] Gregory XVI and Bl. Pius IX in time rejected several assertions made by these theologians.[66]

The First Vatican Council solemnly rejected fideism. It condemned those who assert that "the one, true God, our Creator and Lord, cannot be known with certainty from the things that have been made, by the natural light of human reason."[67] Further, the Council condemned anyone who affirms that "divine revelation cannot be made credible by external signs, and that therefore men and women ought to be moved to faith only by each one's internal experience or private inspiration."[68] The Council taught:

> In order that the submission of our faith should be in accordance with reason (cf. Rom 12: 1), it was God's will that there should be linked to the internal assistance of the Holy Spirit external indications of his revelation, that is to say divine acts, and first and foremost miracles and prophecies, which clearly demonstrating

as they do the omnipotence and infinite knowledge of God, are the most certain signs of revelation and are suited to the understanding of all.[69]

The Council explicitly asserts that "the assent of faith is by no means a blind movement of the mind."[70]

The popes who have served since Vatican I have had occasion to reaffirm these teachings.[71] The Fathers of Vatican II took the opportunity to echo their predecessors on this question: one can assent in faith "with certainty from the created world, by the natural light of human reason,"[72] besides trusting implicitly in him because of the arguments of Divine Revelation.[73] Additionally, the *Catechism of the Catholic Church* promulgated by John Paul II includes the relevant teachings of the two Vatican councils.[74]

However, in actuality, there are also signs of a resurgence of *fideism*, which fails to recognize the importance of rational knowledge and philosophical discourse for the understanding of faith, indeed for the very possibility of belief in God. One currently widespread symptom of this fideistic tendency is a "biblicism" which tends to make the reading and exegesis of Sacred Scripture the sole criterion of truth.... Other modes of latent fideism appear in the scant consideration accorded to speculative theology, and in disdain for the classical philosophy from which the terms of both the understanding of faith and the actual formulation of dogma have been drawn.[75]

D. A Particular Case of Fideism: The Radical Distinction between the Jesus of History and the Christ of Faith

Many Protestant theologians in the nineteenth and twentieth century proposed the fideist approach in the way that they understood and explored the history-faith relationship, which finds its paradigm in the supposed distinction between the Jesus of history and the Christ of faith.

This supposed radical distinction—even opposition—between the Jesus of history and the Christ of faith finds its origin in a strongly anti-dogmatic current. Its development accompanies some Christological frameworks built on the assumption that a specific man called Jesus of Nazareth was God.

M. Kahler appears to have used the expression as such for the first time, putting both terms in conflict, in his work *Der sogennante historische Jesus und der geschichtliche, biblische Christus*, published in 1892.[76] This theologian sought to demonstrate that the only true Jesus is the one who preached, the one believed in faith. Nevertheless, his theory essentially depended on certain previous authors whom we will now analyze.

According to H.S. Reimarus, one must distinguish between Jesus' objective and the objective sought by his disciples. Jesus was nothing other than a political Messiah, inspired by the wish to settle the earthly kingdom of Israel and free his people from the Roman invasion. Despite the "failure" of his activities, his disciples refused to accept the defeat. Instead of returning to their previous work, they stole the corpse of their Teacher and invented the theory of his Resurrection and his return at the end of time. The Christ of faith is nothing more than a cunning invention of his disciples. They tried to legitimize their Messianic hopes in this manner.[77]

By the same token, but with a slightly different approach, D.F. Strauss explicitly denies that the Christ of faith is the Jesus of history. According to Strauss, the disciples placed their Messianic hopes on the Jesus of history and turned him into a myth. They falsified the historical reality.[78] To reach the true historical Jesus, one must rescue him from their mystification. Consequently, any serious historical investigation must keep this in mind. Strauss claimed that Christian myth is characterized by the representation in historical terms of the religious ideal of those first Christians. In this respect, Strauss owes a debt to Hegelian philosophy, wherein the Spirit is neither solely God (infinity) nor solely man but the unity God-man. This unity needs to form over time. Christ has been transformed in a symbolic, therefore mythical, expression of philosophic truth.[79] Strauss's approach considers historical events secondary and unimportant; the only important thing is the idea of Christ. And for Strauss, Christ is nothing but the mythical representation of the Idea.[80]

Following Strauss, but inspired by Heidegger's philosophy, Bultmann held that Scripture is essentially the formulation of possibilities of human existence. The reader must approach it with an open mind and compare his own interpretation of existence with those formulated in the Bible, trying not to make his own vision absolute by being open to other alternatives.[81]

Bultmann argued that Christianity began with the preached Christ, not with the historical Jesus. This is because the preaching of the Church, and the content of her preaching was not the historical Jesus but the Christ of belief. The early Christians mythicized the Jesus of history by making him into the Lord and giving him divine attributes. Therefore, when one reads the Bible, one needs to de-mythicize him, to remove the mythical aspect underlying that preaching. One has to filter out all that conflicts with the cosmo-scientific view of contemporary man. According to Bultmann, the challenge lies in determining what is above the earth as earthly, what is divine as human, and what is supernatural as natural.[82]

The *kerygma* obviously assumes Jesus' historical existence, but we can know practically nothing of the historical aspects.[83] Between the Jesus of history and the Christ of Faith—according to Bultmann—there is no relationship which would allow one to move from one to the other.[84] The only thing that matters is for the existence of Jesus to appear as a part of God's response to the human question about the sense of man's own existence.

In reality, Bultmann's separation of history and faith is, of course, extremely radical in nature. For their part, most historians have not shared Bultmann's low opinion of the New Testament chronicles. However, we need to remember that Bultmann's opinion here is not really driven by the work of historians but by his erroneous vision of faith.[85]

The distinction between the historical Jesus and the Christ of faith depends upon the *a priori* conviction that the Gospels and the other New Testament writings are not trustworthy historical sources because they are the fruit of faith. They are marred by their religious origin. In reality, the opposite is true. Faith does not harm the historical authenticity of the facts of the New Testament but serves as its best guarantee. One must conclude that "the Jesus of the fourth gospel and the Jesus of the synoptics are the same identical person: the true Jesus of history."[86] The identity of the earthly Jesus with the resurrected Christ is fundamental for the community's faith; it prevents any dissociation between the historical Jesus and the *kerygmatic* Jesus.[87]

It was the faith of the early Christians that led them to collect the sayings and actions of Jesus of Nazareth with utmost fidelity. They acted in this fashion, first of all, because piety, reverence and respect for Jesus and everything immediately related to him is proper to the Christian faith. Secondly, they did so because faith itself—in its contents and formulations—cannot lack historical references.[88] Lastly, they did this because they wanted to nourish their reasons to believe with historical data—sayings and facts—which needed to be documented.[89]

One might respond to these objections by saying that believers could always turn to memory to support faith. This is precisely where the problem lies: It is the memory that is conditioned and impregnated with faith from the inside in such a manner that it cannot escape from its influence and perspective. (Memory deforms reality and it is necessary to remove myth from that remembrance to discover the truth.)

For this reason, one must note the link between faith and history, which respects the characteristics and demands of both faith and history. Neither is faith transformed into historical knowledge (certitude founded on data, knowledge derived from facts); nor does history become deformed by faith (transformed in myth and legend).[90]

The relationship between faith and historical authenticity must be classified within the relationships between faith and reason, between faith and science, and, definitively, between nature and grace, grace and freedom.

If faith and reason are considered incompatible, one will need to choose between these two alternatives. One may assert the absolute character of faith and forego any historical foundation (this is

Bultmann's position). Then, the Christ of faith is the only one who counts. Alternatively, one may assert reason's supremacy over faith, in which case the latter loses its importance, and only the historical Jesus is required. Scholars have gone back and forth between these poles of the faith-reason alternatives. Where Reimarus and Strauss denied Christ (faith) and asserted Jesus (history), Bultmann went to the other extreme and denied Jesus (history) to assert Christ (faith) only. Still, the true solution is to say 'yes' to Jesus and Christ at the same time and to confess that Jesus is Christ.[91]

Bultmann's historical skepticism soon met with opposition by those who did not accept his radical fideism or his disregard for the historical value of literature referring to Jesus. For example, Käsemann agreed with Bultmann that historical investigation alone is not enough to unveil the deep dimension of Jesus. He argued that only faith in the Church allows us to recognize him as Christ, the Son of the living God. He disagreed with Bultmann's claim that historical investigation lacked interest in matters of faith, because before we believe, we become aware that God has acted in history.[92]

In the second half of the twentieth century there was significant progress in the historical investigation of Jesus. For example, Schürmann demonstrated that in the Gospel we find not only forms that originated in the living culture of the post-Paschal primitive community, but also of the pre-Paschal apostolic communion. He was able to show the continuity of tradition and profession of faith between the stories after Passover and the community that surrounded Jesus while he was on earth. Schürmann proved that before the last events in the historical life of Jesus, his disciples manifested adherence to his person and that this common adherence united them. They formed a group; they followed the Master. They had faith in him and in his words. They were interested in listening to him and preserving his sayings and actions in their memories.[93]

E. The Phenomenon of Non-belief and Atheism

Apologetics has always been concerned with the very existance of religion. Apologists have approached it in different ways according to diverse cultural contexts. The reason for this is clear: To believe in the God that reveals himself in history, it is necessary to believe beforehand that God is the absolute being, the beginning and end of the world and humanity. Nevertheless, this reality is not always well perceived and it needs to be explained to be understood and accepted. In fact, there have always been people who have given the impression in their external conduct of not taking God into account, of not giving him worship, acting as if God did not exist or had nothing to do with them. If such religious indifference, which has non-religiosity as its extreme manifestation, has long been the path of some people on earth, there exist intentions of theoretical and radical justification of the atheist attitude especially in our time. The last council understood this to be so when it wrote, "Many however of our contemporaries either do not at all perceive, or else explicitly reject, this intimate and vital bond of man to God. Atheism must therefore be regarded as one of the most serious problems of our time, and one that deserves more thorough treatment."[94]

From the theological-fundamental perspective, one must remember that he who declares himself to be without God rejects his conception of God. In fact, the concept of atheism cannot be an intellectual absolute, because God *is*.

No one has proved, or can prove, that God does not exist. Consequently, any form of atheism is merely an interpretation of the world and of man in contradistinction to "religious" interpretations. We say "in contradistinction" because atheism specifically rejects any vision of the world, humanity, and history that demands the presence and intervention of a transcendent being. This is also because that interpretation is concurrently the cause and effect of a non-religious conduct and, sometimes even actions against religion.[95] Accordingly, we can differentiate religious interpretations in several ways in order to separate among them the various formulations of what we call "atheism."[96]

The word *atheism* is used to signify concepts that differ considerably from one another. Some people expressly deny the existence of God. Others maintain that man cannot make any assertion whatsoever about him. Still others admit only such methods of investigation as would make it seem quite meaningless to ask questions about God. Many, trespassing beyond the boundaries of the positive sciences, either contend that everything can be explained by the reasoning process used in such sciences, or, on the contrary, hold that there is no such thing as absolute truth. With others it is their exaggerated idea of man that causes their faith to languish; they are more prone, it would seem, to affirm man than to deny God. Yet others have such a faulty notion of God that when they disown this product of the imagination their denial has no reference to the God of the Gospels. There are also those who never inquire about God; religion never seems to trouble or interest them at all, nor do they see why they should bother about it. Not infrequently, atheism is born from a violent protest against the evil in the world, or from the fact that certain human ideals are wrongfully invested with such an absolute character as to be taken for God. Modern civilization itself, though not of its very nature, but because it is too engrossed in the concerns of this world, can make it harder to approach God.[97]

This atheist interpretation characteristically ignores the existence of God in its explanation of what the world and humanity are, and how individuals and the community are to behave and act. It attempts to explain all as if God did not exist, because it is not necessary to invoke God to explain physical or moral laws. Some theorists go further, positively excluding God, presenting him in various ways as a merely human creation. God is not a transcendent reality but the world itself in its entirety (pantheism). Or, he is the projection of human wishes and needs (Feuerbach). Alternatively, he is the hypothesis of man's social-economic reality (Marx), or the continuity of the child's consciousness that does not want to mature as an adult person (Freud).

The above thinkers held that the "idea" of God as created by man is detrimental to man himself, his freedom, his social life, his psychological maturation, his development, and scientific, and economic growth. (In general, all those authors who present the idea of God as an "enemy" of man and human development have been designated as "teachers of suspicion," because they seem to propose the same insinuation already present in Genesis 3: 4–5.)

The atheist interpretation of the world seems, at its core, to originate from a materialistic vision of humanity and history: that the present *hic et nunc* (here and now), which is within the reach of our senses, is the only thing that one can be sure of, the only thing that can be known with certainty. With that attitude, in fact, it is easy to adopt an agnostic attitude or even to radically deny any kind of transcendence, as the history of non-religious ideas and attitudes proves. This is always related in one way or another to materialism and temporalism,[98] which shows that atheism is not a phenomenon exclusive to our modern age. If the issue is studied from a philosophical—specifically metaphysical—standpoint, we shall discover that pantheism has been proposed repeatedly since olden times. As a matter of fact, theoretically, concerning hermeneutics of the world and mankind at an ontological level, it may be reduced to two possibilities. The first is to admit that neither the world nor man have in themselves the ultimate reason of their being and are, consequently, relative to the Other who causes himself and from whom they have received existence and every perfection that is found in them. Otherwise, one must admit that the world, and man with it, as its center and highest point, is the absolute, the only thing that exists and, therefore, without beginning or end external to himself, without the needed reference to the other being that is transcendent.

Vatican II also refers to the responsibility of people and communities concerning the appearance and spread of atheism:

> Without doubt those who willfully try to drive God from their heart and to avoid all questions about religion, not following the biddings of their conscience, are not free from blame. But believers themselves often share some responsibility for this situation. For atheism, taken as a whole, is not present in the

mind of man from the start (*Atheismus, integre consideratus, non est quid originarium*). It springs from various causes, among which must be included a critical reaction against religions and, in some places, against the Christian religion in particular. Believers can thus have more than a little to do with the rise of atheism. To the extent that they are careless about their instruction in the faith, or present its teaching falsely, or even fail in their religious, moral, or social life, they must be said to conceal rather than to reveal the true nature of God and of religion.[99]

Later, the apostolic constitution *Gaudium et spes* gave some suggestions to help solve this dilemma: "Atheism must be countered both by presenting true teaching in a fitting manner and by the full and complete life of the Church and of her members."[100]

Regarding doctrine, the Council stressed:

> The Church holds that to acknowledge God is in no way to oppose the dignity of man, since such dignity is grounded and brought to perfection in God…. Hope in a life to come does not take away from the importance of the duties of this life on earth but rather adds to it by giving new motives for fulfilling those duties.[101]

Regarding the *apologetic approach*, it is now quite necessary to develop what we have called the immanent happenings of apologetics, i.e., we need to study the anthropological roots of the faith.

> For the Church knows full well that her message is in harmony with the most secret desires of the human heart, since it champions the dignity of man's calling, giving hope once more to those who already despair of their higher destiny. Her message, far from impairing man, helps him to develop himself by bestowing light, life, and freedom.[102]

This anthropology needs to devote special attention to the topics of evil, pain, suffering, and death. These are aspects that oftentimes represent a difficulty and a trial to belief that God exists and governs everything with providence and love. Some, in fact, argue that the existence of evil proves that either God does not exist or he is not omnipotent. The response lies in a detailed analysis; first, we must understand that God manifests his omnipotence by letting evil exist in all its manifestations, precisely because he knows and can bring good out of all of its forms. Second, we should consider Christ's Passion and Death. That is a revelation of the Father's love and the beginning of life for those who believe in Christ as Son of God. It would also do us good to recognize the differences inherent in the various atheist interpretations of mankind. These distinctions have surfaced frequently in history, inflicting serious damage to the followers of those theories and even onto entire countries.[103]

Regarding conduct, the Council observed:

> This is brought about chiefly by the witness of a living and mature faith, namely one that is so well formed that it can see difficulties clearly and overcome them. Many martyrs have borne, and continue to bear, a splendid witness to this faith. This faith should show its fruitfulness by penetrating the whole life, even the worldly activities, of those who believe, and by urging them to be loving and just especially toward those in need. Lastly, what does most to show God's presence clearly is the brotherly love of the faithful who, being all of one mind and spirit, work together for the faith of the gospel and present themselves as a sign of unity.[104]

F. Reason after Believing: A General Vision of its Relation with Faith

What is distinctive in the biblical text is the conviction that there is a profound and indissoluble unity between the knowledge of reason and the knowledge of faith. The world and all that happens within it, including history and the fate of peoples, are realities to be observed, analysed and assessed with all the resources of reason, but without faith ever being foreign to the process. Faith intervenes not to abolish reason's autonomy nor to reduce its scope for action, but solely to bring the human being to understand that in these events it is the

God of Israel who acts. Thus the world and the events of history cannot be understood in depth without professing faith in the God who is at work in them.[105]

The framework of the relationship between Christian faith (understood as *fides qua* and as *fides quae*) and human reason (understood as cognitive potential—not just discursive capacity—and as a body of knowledge acquired according to that innate capacity) is classified within the relationship of nature and grace. It has always been within the unity of the saving plan that it is fulfilled in Christ.

This arrangement may be elucidated by saying that the supernatural gift is shown within the deepest aspirations of the human heart and according to its fundamental structure and innate capacities. These aspirations and capacities are not annulled or infringed upon by grace. Rather, God acts on them through grace, allowing them to reach a most profound level (cf. 1 Cor 2: 9). Christ's mystery, taken in by faith under the guidance of the Holy Spirit, "will satisfy all their inner hopes, or rather infinitely surpass them." It constitutes the beginning of a "spiritual journey by means of which, while already sharing through faith in the mystery of the Death and Resurrection, one passes from the old man to the new man who has been made perfect in Christ (cf. Col 3: 5–10; Eph 4: 20–24)."[106]

On this basis it is possible to outline the fundamental features of the relationship between faith and reason by saying that the former is superior to the latter (*est supra rationem*). Still, this position is in no way anti-reason or contradictory to reason's true achievements (*non tamen est contra rationem*), just as it does not dispense with it (*nec est sine ratione*). Quite to the contrary, it shows how useful and necessary reason is in this endeavor (*est autem conveniens rationi*).[107]

Throughout the life of the Church, most especially during the second millennium, theologians have recognized the distinction between Christian faith and human reason (excepting some authors of pantheist thinking, who have reduced supernatural faith to the sphere of human reason).

Given this distinction, the relationship between both has been presented principally according to five models. The first two relate to fideism, uniquely expressing the lack of relationship between faith and reason. This is either a *parallel model*, which considers them alien to one another, or an *antagonist model*, which sees them in permanent conflict because it considers them incompatible.

Those two models have been rejected by Christian theological tradition. The Church has accepted only the dialogue, spousal, and incarnational models (the last two specially stress the union, communion, and communication between them). The *dialogue* model, which corresponds to the approach of apologists of the second century, presents faith and reason as different but ready to collaborate with each other. This model treats them as if they were different subjects—Christian and non-Christian—whereas the other two models suppose one and the other in the same subject (Christian). The *spousal* model, based on the analogy of the marriage union (two persons in one flesh) explains how it is possible that two intellectual lights, Christian faith and human reason, can simultaneously exist in the same subject. They help each other and jointly contribute—each one according to what is proper to it—to reaching a deep and fertile knowledge of the truth and the love that God is.

The *incarnational* model employs the analogy with the Incarnate Word—two natures in one Person—to explain how faith and reason, while remaining distinct and with their proper operative characteristics, are united and turn at the same time to the same knowledge and activity of the believer.[108]

III. Christian Dialogue with Other Religions at the Beginning of the Third Millennium

Christian theologians have to devote urgent attention to the apologetic challenges inherited from the two preceding millennia. Because of the increasing intercommunications among every nation on earth, contemporary Christians must relate to cultures with which they previously had had little or no contact. In particular, the Church has to dialogue with beliefs and religions with which she has had an only marginal or peripheral relationship up until now.[109] This entirely new situation was noticeable immediately following the Second World War. It was subsequently considered in Vatican II. The Council Fathers explicitly dedicated one of their decrees to the dialogue with non-Christian religions.

While it demands of all who hear it the adherence of faith, the proclamation of the Gospel in different cultures allows people to preserve their own cultural identity. This in no way creates division, because the community of the baptized is marked by a universality which can embrace every culture and help to foster whatever is implicit in them to the point where it will be fully explicit in the light of truth.

This means that no one culture can ever become the criterion of judgment, much less the ultimate criterion of truth with regard to God's Revelation. The Gospel is not opposed to any culture, as if in engaging a culture the Gospel would seek to strip it of its native riches and force it to adopt forms which are alien to it. On the contrary, the message which believers bring to the world and to cultures is a genuine liberation from all the disorders caused by sin and is, at the same time, a call to the fullness of truth. Cultures are not only not diminished by this encounter; rather, they are prompted to open themselves to the newness of the Gospel's truth and to be stirred by this truth to develop in new ways.[110]

A. Religion in the Theological-fundamental Perspective

From the Christian standpoint, this new situation compelled theologians to rethink the theory of religion. In the study of religion, fundamental theology began to displace moral theology, which had been the center of studies in previous centuries. The development of such study initiated under the appearance of a new area, related to fundamental theology, that usually is termed "the theology of religions."

From the theological-fundamental perspective, the Christian theology of religion focuses on the study of the relation of religion, both in general and in the presently existing concrete religions, with the God who manifests himself in creation, who reveals himself in Christ, and with his historical revelation transmitted and guarded in the Church and by the Church.

Given this perspective, one can differentiate among religions according to their relationship to this and those that are not founded on the divine Word. Sometimes these relationships are weak and distant, sometimes intense and deep, as happens in the Israelite religion and even more so in Christianity. This diversity sets out two distinct but inseparable issues: the issue of the relationship of religions among themselves (especially with the Christian religion), and the issue of the value that must be acknowledged in the non-Christian religions. These two issues have important practical implications and consequences in the interfaith dialogue. The following paragraphs will deal with those issues and this dialogue. However, before we do so we should look at some properties common to all religions to better distinguish them from the other similar realities, religious philosophy, and sects.

There are different ways to designate God in human nations and cultures, each with its own nuances, as the being that is Father of everything, Creator, Final Cause, Almighty, and definitive Finality. Scientific language and more properly philosophical language, calls him First Intelligence, Utmost Good, Motionless Force, Supreme or Absolute Being, Transcendent Being, Subsistent Being, Perfect Spirit, etc. Religious language defines God less in himself and more by his relationship to mankind. In fact, in religious language God is named with terms such as the Most High, the Ineffable, the Holy of Holies and similar terms. Distance and transcendence (holiness) are the categories highlighted by religious language. Subsistence and absoluteness (perfection) are the characteristic terms in scientific language.

The scientific approach (mainly the philosophical one) to God is nourished in the contemplation of creation and humanity. It is mainly a cosmological approach developed according to the laws of rational discourse. On the other hand, the religious approach, without denying what we have said and without excluding it, has an anthropological flavor, and it is developed mainly on the basis of the experience of

God in history and in human life. It is influenced and characterized by the living tradition of peoples, for it is perpetuated in their cultures, institutions, and customs.

The religious approach is marked by the inclination—present in every person—toward God. This inclination is summed up in the common human wishes of happiness, immortality, glory, and salvation. Religion, in its concrete forms, appears as the institutionalized response of a people and a society to those deep wishes that are summarized and solved at the same time in the inclination toward God.[111]

> Men look to their different religions for an answer to the unsolved riddles of human existence. The problems that weigh heavily on the hearts of men are the same today as in the ages past. What is man? What is the meaning and purpose of life? What is upright behavior, and what is sinful? Where does suffering originate, and what end does it serve? How can genuine happiness be found? What happens at death? What is judgment? What reward follows death? And finally, what is the ultimate mystery, beyond human explanation, which embraces our entire existence, from which we take our origin and toward which we tend?[112]

Religions are characterized and defined by institutionalizing those answers in a doctrinal, moral, and liturgical structure. The majority of beliefs do this through a personal code, teaching man to relate to God by expressing gratitude and worship of him, by manifesting submission and obedience. Alternatively, some religions (such as Buddhism and other Oriental religions) do not postulate a personal relationship with God, nor do they present him as a personal being. They see religious practice as the person's effort to free himself from his limitation, variation, and imperfection. Religion is how one relates to the Infinite, Immutable and Eternal.

> The religions that are found in more advanced civilizations endeavor by way of well-defined concepts and exact language to answer these questions. Thus, in Hinduism men explore the divine mystery and express it both in the limitless riches of myth and the accurately defined insights of philosophy. They seek

release from the trials of the present life by ascetical practices, profound meditation and recourse to God in confidence and love. Buddhism in its various forms testifies to the essential inadequacy of this changing world. It proposes a way of life by which men can, with confidence and trust, attain a state of perfect liberation and reach supreme illumination either through their own efforts or with the aid of divine help. So, too, other religions that are found throughout the world attempt in their own ways to calm the hearts of men by outlining a program of life covering doctrine, moral precepts, and sacred rites.[113]

Simultaneously and inseparably, the institutionalization of these elements is presented as a consequence and fruit of a revelation or divine enlightenment, even though it may be imprecise and diffuse. In fact, as the sciences of religion have proven, religious doctrines and practices in their diverse manifestations of dogma, morals, and worship always contribute—in a more or less efficacious manner—to our knowledge of God. This knowledge is fulfilled through creatures, by what we know through religious traditions, or through interventions in history.

Throughout history even to the present day, there is found among different peoples an awareness of a hidden power, which lies behind the course of nature and the events of human life. At times there is present even a recognition of a supreme being, or still more of a Father. This awareness and recognition results in a way of life that is imbued with a deep religious sense.[114]

The most structured religions represent themselves as an explicit faith response to a particular revelation of God (in the cosmos, in the origins of mankind, or even in history itself). Faith, in this context, refers not only to an intellectual assent to a reality not visibly evident to the subject, but also a deep attitude of acceptance of the person.

Something similar, yet still distinct, happens with sects and marginal religious groups (sometimes specifically designated with the names "new forms of religiosity" or "new religious movements"). These groups generally present themselves at the margin of socially instituted religions that have a public and defined identity, including doctrine, morals, and worship. Occasionally, these groups do not even want to be considered religious. Still, they look like religions because they credit their origin and contents to a supposed revelation (or experience) of God (or of the sacred) that they think warrants soteriological value. However, it is only a remote similarity.[115]

B. The Value of Religions

Even before Vatican II, the issue arose of whether any religion other than Catholicism is by itself a way of salvation and whether other religions contain useful elements as a "preparation" for receiving salvation: a salvation that only comes from Christ and the Church.[116]

> The Catholic Church rejects nothing of what is true and holy in these religions. She has a high regard for the manner of life and conduct, the precepts and doctrines which, although differing in many ways from her own teaching, may nevertheless reflect a ray of that truth which enlightens all men. Yet she proclaims, and is in duty bound to proclaim without fail, Christ who is the Way, the Truth, and the Life (cf. Jn 14: 6). In him, in whom God reconciled all things to himself (cf. 2 Cor 5: 18–19), men find the fullness of their religious life. The Church, therefore, urges her sons to enter with prudence and charity into discussion and collaboration with members of other religions. Let Christians, while witnessing to their own faith and way of life, acknowledge, preserve, and encourage the spiritual and moral truths found among non-Christians, as well as their social life and culture.[117]

Theologians divided into two lines of thought on this question. The first group was made up of Rahner, Waldenfels, Nys, Schlette, and others. The second group was composed of Danielou, von Balthasar, and de Lubac, to name a few.

K. Rahner based his stance on the veracity of God's universal saving will. He wrote that all history is under the action of God. The same can be said of every individual's life. Consequently, he taught that any person, by the very fact of existing, exists not only with his own nature; but also with the grace of God (a situation that he calls "supernaturally existential"). In this way when he relates—even if not in a completely conscious way—to God, it is sufficient if he has an authentic openness to transcendence. What is important is that one lives according to that relation. In this fashion, it can be said that his religious attitude is truly supernatural, albeit through implicit faith.

According to those premises, Rahner argued that religion must be considered historical objectification of the supernaturally existential. Rahner held that sincere followers of any religion are, in reality, anonymous Christians who already enjoy an implicit faith (although without subject matter and obscure in nature, their faith is sufficient to perceive some features of the mystery of Christ), which prepares them for an explicit faith in Christ.

Rahner taught that religions are truly saving ways because, definitively, in them the mystery of Christ is always present, not always explicitly, but really and effectively. (In the Christian religion this mystery is present in an explicit and reflexive way.)[118]

J. Danielou distinguished between the knowledge of God reached through cosmic revelation and the one God grants through revelation in history. The first one is valid but it is not the final end to which man is called. Therefore, this knowledge is not the most perfect available. In fact, this knowledge is ordered to the other knowledge God grants by revealing himself in history. The fact that the first knowledge is ordered to the second shows that it cannot be identified with it. The continuity of one with the other must be understood at the same time as discontinuity due to passing from one level (natural, of cosmic alliance) to another (supernatural, of historic alliance). Definitely, the natural knowledge of God, particularly the knowledge of God that is found in non-Christian religions, is nothing more than a basic substratum that can prepare one to receive the Word of God, who reveals himself in history. By itself it is not yet saving knowledge. Here, then, is an essential difference between the Judeo-Christian religions and all others.[119]

H.U. von Balthasar grounded his theory of the "concrete universal" along these same, although diversely focused, lines.[120]

The difference between these positions is the way that they conceive the relationship between grace and nature, between the natural and the supernatural. Danielou and von Balthasar distinguished both orders without separating them, and explained that between both, an intimate relation according to the divine plan exists. Rahner did not understand it in this way. In this point he went beyond the patristic and medieval theological interpretation. He proposed his original concept of the "supernaturally existential," which has been the subject of strong criticism, as we have already noted. Von Balthasar also criticized this position. He argued that Rahner's theory of anonymous "Christianity" was akin to the models of evolutionary Christology that see in Jesus Christ "the law of evolution brought to perfection." Such a theory devalues the theology of the cross and at the same time underestimates the seriousness of sin and the need for redemption. Finally, according to von Balthasar, the doctrine of the "supernaturally existential" (and its necessary consequence, "anonymous Christianity,") transforms the supernatural into a function of nature.[121]

Acting before these opinions confused the faithful or led some into error. The Congregation for the Doctrine of the Faith stated[122]:

> Certainly, the various religious traditions contain and offer religious elements which come from God,[123] and which are part of what "the Spirit brings about in human hearts and in the history of peoples, in cultures, and religions".[124] Indeed, some prayers and rituals of the other religions may assume a role of preparation for the Gospel, in that they are occasions or pedagogical helps in which the human heart is prompted to be open to the action of God.[125] One cannot attribute to these, however, a divine origin or an *ex opere operato* salvific efficacy, which is proper to the Christian sacraments.[126] Furthermore, it cannot be overlooked that other rituals, insofar as they depend on superstitions or other errors (cf. 1 Cor 10: 20–21), constitute an obstacle to salvation.[127]

C. The Christocentrism of Revelation and Salvation

He is the Cornerstone (cf. Mt 21: 42; Mk 12: 10; 1 Pt 2: 7; Acts 4: 11), the Door (cf. Jn 10: 7), the High Priest (cf. Heb 7: 26ff.), and the only Mediator (cf. 1 Tm 2: 4). No other name has been given to us in which we can be saved (cf. Acts 4: 12) because without him we can do nothing (cf. Jn 15: 5). Eternal life consists in knowing God and his envoy, Jesus Christ (cf. Jn 17: 3). The Church has always believed and taught that Jesus Christ, the center and culmination of Revelation, is the only Savior. This aspect of Christian dogma is so basic that the Magisterium has not seen fit to solemnly define it.

After Vatican II, theologians developed the issue of the soteriological value of non-Christian religions in order to obtain a greater precision about the ecclesiastical aspect of salvation and Christocentrism.

Regarding the ecclesiastical aspect, it was perfectly clear: explicit and visible membership in the Church is not absolutely indispensable, because sometimes the concrete situation of a person makes this type of membership impossible. Therefore, the axiom *extra Ecclesiam nulla salus* (outside of the Church there is no salvation) does admit an interpretation that recognizes the existence of a spiritual link with the Church without specific, precise social and historical expressions but still exhibits some external manifestations of that interior membership.

> Those who, through no fault of their own, do not know the gospel of Christ or his Church, but who nevertheless seek God with a sincere heart, and, moved by grace, try in their actions to do his will as they know it through the dictates of their conscience—those too may achieve eternal salvation. Nor shall divine providence deny the assistance necessary for salvation to those who, without any fault of theirs, have not yet arrived at an explicit knowledge of God, and who, not without grace, strive to lead a good life.[128]

Christocentrism is also considered indispensable, although it can be implicit.[129] The conciliar constitution *Gaudium et spes* states that Christians receive the fruits of the Spirit, and by him they are incorporated into the Death and Resurrection of Christ. Thus, they live in God and for God.

> All this holds true not for Christians only but also for all men of good will in whose hearts grace is active invisibly. For since Christ died for all, and since all men are in fact called to one and the same destiny, which is divine, we must hold that the Holy Spirit offers to all the possibility of being made partners, in a way known to God, in the Paschal mystery.[130]

Nevertheless some theologians have maintained of late that Christocentrism is not absolutely necessary, not even implicitly. They claim it is not constitutive of salvation, and it is not normative. According to these writers, Christocentrism indicates, at most, a certain perfection. These authors propose theocentrism as the only condition for salvation. For their part, they hold that theocentrism is the action of the Holy Spirit, which blows where it wants. This action can be understood in many ways—sometimes in relation to the Word, sometimes not—but it is always spiritual and leads people to absolute transcendence. The most radical expositors of this approach argue that even at the eschatological level salvation does not have to be Christocentric.[131]

Here, we will attempt to classify these different stances. Amato, following Knitter and Niebuhr, believed that the ways to explain the "theology of religions" can be grouped according to the following five models:

1. "Christ against religions," an exclusive model, which is the approach of Barth and Kraemer;

2. "Christ in religions," an inclusive model that affords certain saving value to religions, but always derived from Christ, who somehow makes himself present in them (Amato claims that this is John Paul II's approach in his encyclical *Redemptoris Missio*.);

3. "Christ above religions," a normative model that claims that salvation can be attained through religions, but perfection and fullness comes only from Christ (Amato thinks that this is the approach of Hans Küng, Schlette, and Camps.);

4. "Christ with religions," a pluralistic model attributed to Hick;

5. "Religions without Christ," a liberation model attributed to Knitter, according to which the last criterion of religions is constituted by the values of the kingdom (promotion of human welfare).[132]

In his encyclical about the missionary activity of the Church, John Paul II asked the following questions: Are missions still valid among Christians? Have missions not perhaps been substituted by interfaith dialogue? Are not good human relations a worthy enough objective? Does the respect of conscience and freedom not exclude every proposal of conversion? Can't one be saved in any religion? What are missions for, then? In his answers, he affirms:

> Going back to the origins of the Church, it is clearly asserted that Christ is the only Savior of mankind, the only one with the possibility of revealing God and guiding to God.... The universality of this salvation in Christ is asserted throughout the New Testament.... Paul reacts against the polytheist religious atmosphere of his time and highlights the characteristic of Christian faith: faith in only one God and in only one Lord, sent by God.... God's revelation is made definitive and complete through his Only-Begotten Son.... In this definitive Word of his revelation, God has made himself known in the most complete manner; he has said to mankind *who he is*. This definitive revelation of God is the fundamental motive by which the Church is missionary by nature. She cannot stop preaching the gospel, which is the fullness of truth that God has given us about himself. Christ is the only mediator between God and men.... Men, therefore, cannot enter into communion with God if it is not by means of Christ and under the action of the Spirit. His mediation, unique and universal, far from being an obstacle on the way toward God, is the way established by God himself, and of that Christ is totally conscious. Even when partial mediations of any type and order are not excluded, these have significance and value only through Christ and cannot be understood as parallel and complementary in nature.[133]

In conclusion, Indeed, the Church, guided by charity and respect for freedom,[134] must be primarily committed to proclaiming to all people the truth definitively revealed by the Lord, and to announcing the necessity of conversion to Jesus Christ and of adherence to the Church through Baptism and the other sacraments, in order to participate fully in communion with God, the Father, Son and Holy Spirit. Thus, the certainty of the universal salvific will of God does not diminish, but rather increases the duty and urgency of the proclamation of salvation and of conversion to the Lord Jesus Christ.[135]

CHAPTER 11

CREDIBILITY OF THE WORD OF GOD IN THE OLD TESTAMENT

We will begin this chapter with the study of the reasons for credibility present in revelation itself. These motives have served believers throughout the ages as well as outside observers who have judged them historically authentic.

In the Old Testament, the journey of the Jewish people toward faith and their sojourn according to that faith was driven and marked by two primary reasons for belief. These were, first, the great saving actions carried out by Yahweh on behalf of his people Israel, and, second, the words and conduct of the prophets. Both reasons were present throughout the entire historical spectrum of the Chosen People. The first stage is prevalent from the Exodus to the institution of the Israelite monarchy, and the second, identified by the word and life of the prophets, lasted during the monarchy until the Babylonian exile.

I. The Great and Admirable Salvific Actions of God in Favor of Israel

The saving events are numerous in the Old Testament. They constitute a truly impressive series of divine interventions that saved the people both from their enemies and other calamities and afflictions, such as their slavery in Egypt and their Babylonian captivity (to cite two of the more serious and significant episodes). This series is presented as *totum* full of meaning integrated by singular episodes that present a similar basic structure, which for its part is summarized in its global whole.

A. The Proper Character of These Events as Reasons to Believe: To Be a Sign

In the Old Testament these events—the Exodus and other events similar to it (cf. Dt 3: 24; Ps 136: 4; Jb 37: 14–16; Is 7: 11; 29: 14; Jl 3: 2)—are indicated with several terms: *ot* (sign; in Greek *sémeion*); *mofet* (prodigy; in Greek *teras*) which, in biblical language, is used only in a religious context; *Pele, nifl'ah* (wonder; in Greek *thaumassion*), which has an ontological value that evokes the notion of "transcendent," "impossible for men" and is a word set aside for the divine action; *Geburah, gedorah* (great event, act of power; in Greek *dynamis*) *ma'sseh, ma'alal, alilah* (actions; in Greek *ergon*), all of which indicate divine actions such as the works of creation (cf. Nm 16: 30; Ex 34: 10); *mora* (actions that provoke terror); and *t'hillot* (tremendous, noteworthy action).[1]

As we can see, these various terms carry significant double meanings. On the one hand, they manifest the spectacular and prodigious character of the events that cause wonder and astonishment. On the other hand, they highlight their noetic value because they allow knowledge (total or in an aspect that is immediately discovered through the event) of a reality unknown until then. Those saving events are simultaneously prodigies and signs. The two orientations are related, but they differ in that the first one points more to the event itself, even if it highlights the reaction aroused in those who witnessed the actions or have heard about them from those who witnessed them. The second, alternatively, stresses the function that the event fulfills.[2]

The function of a sign in the Old Testament is similar to the function of a sign in other cultures. It has a double function: to inform and to allow itself to be recognized. According to the first meaning, the sign shows a person what is not known, what is hidden. Thus, from this standpoint the sign is mainly a word because it reveals what is unknown. According to the second aspect of its function, it is a proof, signal, mark, or identification that allows us to be certain of the origin of something or its ownership.

Nevertheless, the concept of sign in biblical language is richer and deeper than in other languages, as semiotic studies have demonstrated.[3] In this case, what is meant is an event, but, further, the meaning is the saving will of God. God's will shares both his wish for the freedom and good of his people in their earthly life and his wish for their eternal welfare and salvation in the other life that has no end.

Biblical signs always correspond to Yahweh. They are the means that allow the people to get to know him. The great saving events of the Old Testament reveal who Yahweh is, his power, his wisdom, and his kindness to his people, whom he saves. At the same time, his people recognize him in these signs precisely because only he could perform those actions. "The (biblical) notion of sign, broader than our present notion of miracle, involves a double meaning. An event is a sign because it gives testimony of God's Word and leads men to faith; it is also a sign because it encloses a meaning and contains a divine message in itself."[4]

Another unique feature of the biblical sign consists in the fact that it always implies that the subject who receives it experiences a reality and interprets it by the light of his faith. In fact, both actions are necessary for the sign to fulfill its function. For instance, the Exodus, which we will later study in detail, was a sign God preformed so that his people might believe in Yahweh as their only God and Savior. By freeing the Israelites from the power of Egypt, he gave the Chosen People a manifest experience of the divine will and power. Nevertheless, this experience of God's saving will assumed the exercise of faith, on the part of the Hebrews, in the God of their fathers.

Ultimately, the efficacy of a sign in the order of faith is based upon this fact: The reality in which we must believe has already been somehow tested through the concrete historical event that represents it, provided such historical experience is read and interpreted with faith. While the experience of such a reality is, undoubtedly, partial and limited, it remains true and authentic. Thus, it serves as a good foundation for believing what cannot be perceived. In the historical experience of the victory over the Egyptians, the Israelites experienced with faith the power of Yahweh and his will to save Israel. They also understood—again with faith—that their military and political liberation would lead to another greater and long-lasting liberation, of which the earthly victory was merely a sign.

Thus, the saving prodigious action works as a sign of faith in two ways: First, it represents—in a partial and imperfect but real manner—what Yahweh is and wants; second, it inspires the believer to have faith in what he is and wants. It is a representative sign. It proposes a reality that is not seen that, moreover, can be known only through faith. At the same time, it is a confirmatory sign, because it provides a motive to believe. It shows that we can reasonably and prudently believe in a proposed reality.

To believe and to know, therefore, are linked because the sign is by nature propositional and confirmatory at the same time. The event lets us have a certain experience of what has to be believed, and that experimental knowledge—seen with the eyes of faith—inspires us to believe what has not yet been experienced, what has not yet been seen. We would be unable to describe or understand the efficacy and dynamics of these events if we did not recognize how their intrinsic organization meets the fundamental human needs.

These saving events are a special divine response to the universal human need for protection and safety, a need that is closely linked to the common wish for salvation, happiness, and victory. Man permanently experiences his weakness and sickness, both in view of potent and devastating phenomena (earthquakes, epidemics, incurable diseases) and in view of ordinary situations that he is not able to control as he would like (troubles, physical pain, moral preoccupations). Likewise, he continuously faces, to a greater or lesser degree, defeat, failure, and the precariousness of his projects.

This experience is opposed to man's innate desire for happiness and success in every aspect: physical, psychological, economical, familial, social, and moral. The simultaneous experience of this inclination and this anxiety in the human person leads him to search for something to satisfy his wish for happiness and success. So it was, for example, that when God liberated the Israelites from Egyptian slavery, he inspired in them a greater faith in himself by satisfying their wish for salvation, victory, and freedom.

B. The Liberation from Egypt as a Reason for Believing and as a Sign of Faith

In careful detail and as a paradigm of many other similar cases, let us now examine why the liberation from Egypt led the Hebrews from faith in the God of their fathers to faith in Yahweh, the only true God and Savior.[5]

1. Exodus as a Historical Event

The way people understood history and historicity in Greco-Roman culture differed from the way people understood it in Semitic cultures. When speaking of the issue of historicity in Sacred Scripture, exegetes and historians sometimes employ the comparison of a painting and a photograph. A painter's work reflects reality (otherwise, it would not be a portrait). However, the painter acts in an intelligent rather than in a mechanical manner. He communicates aspects of the subject that only the human intelligence can perceive. In contrast, a photograph captures the subject in a mechanical and indifferent way. It is evident that the historicity of a document does not intrinsically depend on its physical or photographic manner of retelling the events. A portrait is no less a historical document than a photograph (which is how we regard many paintings of famous painters), and perhaps it is better than a photograph because it reveals elements that only the intelligence can perceive.

Scholars who deal with this question credit Exodus with historical value that is proper to a genre of literature that recounts facts and matters that were of interest to the scriptural author.[6] Biblical passages that tell events of the Exodus have a certain epochal flavor. Furthermore, we should not exclude the fact that they have been reworked to highlight the character of magnificent achievements. All of this, however, does not confine us to ignorance of what really happened.

> The Bible describes the liberation from Egyptian slavery, involving heaven, earth, sea, heroes, and armies, with a tone of celebration. The panorama looks more like a drawing than a photograph of events. But the historicity of the stories told in these ancient traditions, from the oldest prayer (for example, Ps 77) to the final meditation (Wis 11–19) has been substantially validated by modern investigation. We cannot forget that the Exodus has as a starting point a real and shameful slavery that is in contrast with later nationalistic Hebrew pride. It is hard for the Hebrew to accept the condition of slave, but hard reality forces him to do that.[7]

2. Analysis of the Faith Journey Carried Out by the Israelites in the Exodus

According to the biblical stories repeated in several books, the Exodus from Egypt signified not only the way toward political freedom for the Israelites, but also their journey of faith toward Yahweh. This journey was not a movement from the absence of faith to faith. Rather, it was from faith in the "God of Abraham, Isaac, and Jacob," from faith in "the God of your fathers" to faith in Yahweh as the Savior of Israel and Almighty God (the Shaddai), the one who is (Yahweh). One must understand that the journey across the Red Sea is a process of maturation and growth in faith. We need to understand that the motives for belief relate to this initial faith.

The journey of faith appears in four key moments[8]:

1. *Invitation/initiative of God.* Through Moses, Yahweh presents himself as liberator and asks the Hebrew people to have faith in him and follow him (cf. Ex 3: 16–17).

2. *Acceptance by the Hebrew people of God's invitation, although with some reservations.* The Hebrew people were partially convinced by

the signs Moses made manifest such as the cane transformed into a serpent, the hand covered with leprosy and healed afterwards, and water transformed into blood. They understood that the Lord was visiting them, and they worshipped him (cf. Ex 4: 1–9; 29–31). However, their faith flagged in view of the Pharaoh's obstacles (cf. Ex 5: 21).

3. *Yahweh's saving and prodigious intervention.* God intervened with "a strong hand" (Ex 6: 1), and he multiplied his signs and miracles in Egypt (cf. Ex 7: 3). Such were the different plagues and punishments, which concluded with the death of the firstborn children (cf. Ex 12: 29), the Pharaoh's death and his army's destruction in the Red Sea (cf. Ex 14: 1–28). This abundance of interventions by God was due both to the obstinate attitude of the Pharaoh and the doubts of the Hebrew people. In fact, Pharaoh did not seem to be affected by the onset of the plagues, including the final one when his first-born son died. No, he was absolutely set on subduing the Hebrews. Thus, he pursued them right into the Red Sea. The Hebrew people did not seem convinced by the plagues either, as the faith of which Exodus 4: 31 speaks (ephemeral and fragile) is not the same as the one seen in Exodus 14: 31 (firm and steady).[9]

4. *Acceptance of faith by the Hebrew people.* Moved by the saving miracles worked on their behalf, the Hebrew people finally truly believed (cf. Ex 14: 30–31).

These distinct moments demonstrate that their journey of faith was a real journey because over time the Hebrew people exercised their faith to a greater and greater degree.

3. The Attribution of the Victory over Egypt to Yahweh

To understand according to the sacred books how God's saving intervention guided the Israelites to faith, we need to analyze why they attributed their victory to Yahweh's intervention rather than their own effort and how this attribution opened the path to their faith in Yahweh.

As a matter of fact, the Israelites did not have to attribute their victory to Yahweh. After all, no one had seen him. Other explanations, perhaps less convincing and more complicated, were possible. The attribution of the victory to Yahweh was, undoubtedly, a development of the already possessed faith, but it had to be built on solid elements.

Furthermore, as the texts point out, this victory over the Egyptians, interpreted by the light of their previous faith, definitely opened the Israelites' path toward a deeper and richer faith. The experience of victory—the experience that Yahweh had effectively liberated his people from political slavery as he had promised—inspired the Hebrew people to believe in him as their unique God and liberator from all types of slavery. This new content of faith, which they understood following the Exodus, was included in their basic creed and was henceforward prayed by them every year on the feast of the first fruits (cf. Dt 26: 5–10).[10]

In religions of political-ethnical origin, success or defeat in political or military confrontations against other nations was attributed to the protection or abandonment of the gods. This perspective allows us to understand the attribution of the victory over Egypt and over other nations in later years to Yahweh (cf. Dt 7: 7–10).[11] Nonetheless, there is a peculiar element that we find only in the Israelites' case. They give God credit for *singular and historically very precise events*, and the events are *attributed as accomplished by him personally*. This intense and specific attribution is very different from imputations to other gods we find in the practice of other religions.[12]

Regarding the antiquity of such attribution, we can be sure that history itself has not given the Exodus a salvific-religious interpretation. On the contrary, Exodus alone definitively determined the vision of the history and life of Israel in salvific-religious terms. This conclusion was reached by considering that this attribution was present *throughout the entire history of Israel*, a history that, moreover, the sacred books always interpreted as a continuity of the saving event originating in the Exodus from Egypt. Clearly, a vision of history so unanimous and permanent cannot help but go back to the beginnings of the same people.[13]

If the Hebrews attributed to Yahweh their victory over Egypt, we have to think that they had enough valid and sure motives to believe it was not the result of human action. We can posit at least three motives for credibility:

1. *Knowledge of divine initiative.* The Hebrews knew quite well that the entire episode had been inspired by Yahweh (using Moses as mediator).

   To show the authenticity of this fact, we need only point to how the various biblical traditions come together. That all the sacred books unanimously teach that God takes the initiative in human salvation is of theological importance. That initiative makes salvation a free gift. We cannot ignore this fact without compromising the coherence of the entire biblical message.

2. *Knowledge of the insufficiency of one's own actions.* The Hebrews knew that all their efforts were not enough to free them from the Egyptians. Nevertheless, Moses assured them that Yahweh had assumed the responsibility for accomplishing their liberation and carrying it out successfully.

   The Israelites were sure that only Yahweh could have acted against the Pharaoh and his troops, at least at that precise moment. It was when the Hebrews discovered that the Egyptians were right behind them on the borders of the Red Sea, and there was no possible escape, they became afraid. "And they said to Moses, 'Is it because there are no graves in Egypt that you have taken us away to die in the wilderness? What have you done to us, in bringing us out of Egypt?'... And Moses said to the people, 'Fear not, stand firm, and see the salvation of the LORD, which he will work for you today; for the Egyptians whom you see today, you shall never see again. The LORD will fight for you, and you have only to be still'" (Ex 14: 11, 13–14).

   That was the pivotal experience of the people during the Exodus. Israel overcame Egypt not because of human effort or courage, which was irrelevant, but by the action of Yahweh.[14]

   This element introduces a theological concept that fully belongs to the deepest teachings of the Bible: Man reaches salvation not because of his merits or his worth but because of the dispassionate and most powerful intervention of God.

3. *Perception of the prodigious character of victory and liberation.* This awareness that Yahweh had freed them with his "outstretched arm" (Ex 6: 6), inflicting great punishment on Egyptians, is the third motive that led the Hebrews to attribute their victory over Egypt to him. Their song of victory after passing through the Red Sea expressed this perception extremely well. It covered the different aspects of the confrontation against the Pharaoh, highlighting that God's intervention was "glorious" (Ex 15: 6) and "majestic" (Ex 15: 11). The refrain: "Sing to the LORD, for he has triumphed gloriously" (Ex 15: 21) succinctly summarizes the concept.

It is necessary to stress the importance of this third element, because perceiving the wonderful way in which they were liberated decisively influenced the Israelites, leading them to attribute victory to divine intervention in their favor. The terminology that they used on that occasion and afterwards makes this evident.

When they referred to this event and other similar ones, the Hebrew people expressed a sense of wonder that comes from perceiving a way of acting that is impossible for man, but possible for God alone. Certainly, biblical thinking—especially in the first historical books—is more existential than metaphysical, but this second aspect does not seem to be completely missing.[15]

II. The Predictions of the Prophets and the Congruence of Their Lives and Teachings

Once the Hebrew people had settled in their own homeland with their religious, social, and political institutions well established, the Israelite people were in danger of deviating from the way of faith they had embarked upon when they left Egypt. They risked savoring their temporal prize without appreciating the supernatural and eternal one, thus reducing religious life to external cult without interior conversion and separating daily life from faith in God and the covenant with him. Further, living according to faith in Yahweh proved difficult at times; it required going against the current. It meant not giving way to the idolatry of neighboring peoples. The Chosen People also had to overcome continuous temptations to break the strict commandments of the law.[16]

To help the Israelites overcome these challenges, God sent his prophets. They preached the truth and kindness of the faith of Yahweh and sought to motivate the people to serve their most holy and jealous God, who only desired their good in commanding them to observe the law. The credentials of these holy men were the congruence of their daily lives of sacrifice and the demanding nature of their teachings in conformity with the law. Some of the prophets were also able to prophesize future events.[17]

A. The Vocation and Mission of these Holy Men Sent by God

The Bible designates these men, specially sent by God, with various names that correspond to their different functions. Without denying this diversity, it is possible to discern their common mission. They came to speak for God, to transmit the word of the Almighty (cf. Jer 11: 7; 38: 20; 42: 6), to be the mouthpiece of Yahweh (cf. Ex 4: 16; Ezr 3: 17; Is 5: 9; 22: 14; Jer 23: 16).[18] The mission of these men can be summarized as follows: Their duty was to confirm the Hebrew people in their faith and direct the people to a deeper and more complete understanding of said faith.[19]

Their mission may be located historically by means of three *coordinates* that orient them to the past, present, and future. In fact, their mission is historically located between the covenant and the fulfillment of the promise. Hence, the prophetic message is concurrently the memory and actualization of the promise and the law and the announcement and prophecy of the Emmanuel, the Lord's anointed, the great prophet and king.[20] At the same time, the prophets always taught and acted in the present moment. They sought to direct the life and conduct of their contemporaries according to the covenant and the promise.[21]

1. Biblical Terms Used to Designate the Prophets Sent by Yahweh according to Their Mission

The word *prophet* is a Greek term that the Septuagint substitutes for various Hebrew words. In Greek it means "the one who speaks instead of another." *Pro femi* means "to announce publicly." With the genitive, it means herald, interpreter, translator, and exegete. When *pro* has the temporal value of anticipation, the word means to speak about the future, to prophesy. Even in non-biblical Greek, the term belongs to the religious sphere. It refers to the herald of a god, one who interprets the divine will in an oracle.[22] *Pro* can also have a local meaning, where it indicates the one who speaks to a crowd, the one who proclaims.[23]

The three Hebrew terms to which this Greek word refers are these:

1. *Roeh*, the clairvoyant (cf. 1 Sm 9: 9), later takes on a pejorative sense (cf. Am 7: 12; Mi 3, 7; Is 28: 15; 29: 10). This term can be found linked to others that indicate a fortune teller, which the person sometimes is considered (cf. Is 3: 2), but that, in the end, will be rejected (cf. Dt 13: 2–4; 18: 10–12).[24]

2. Hozeh means the one who has visions, the visionary. It is used, for instance, in the case of Balaam (cf. Nm 24: 4, 16), Amos (cf. Am 1: 1), and Isaiah (cf. Is 1: 1; 2: 1; 13: 1) to indicate their visions.

3. *Nabi'* is the most widely used term, the one that the Septuagint equated with the Greek *prophet*. He is the one who speaks (cf. Jer 14: 18), proclaims (cf. Neh 6: 7), transmits news (cf. Ex 4: 14–17), prophesies (cf. 1 Sm 19: 20), who is even delirious (cf. 1 Sm 10: 5, 10). The term originates from the root *nb'* (to emit noise, to be inwardly agitated). According to this etymology, we could understand the prophet as a man in ecstasy.[25] A. Jepsen qualified the concept and added that ecstasy is followed by vehement talking. *Nabi'* would be the one who forcefully proclaims under the influence of a superior power.[26] Thus understood, it would indicate the speaker, the spokesman. Its origin can be found in the terms *acadico nabbu* that from 3000 BC until to about 500 BC, meant to call. *Nabi'* would be, therefore, the one called by God.[27]

The Old Testament uses also the expression *man of God,* mainly in reference to Elijah and Elisha (cf. 1 Kgs 17: 18, 24; 2 Kgs 4: 7, 9, 16, 21, 25, 27, 40).[28] Nevertheless, the phrase "man of God" is more general and does not seem to have prophet as an exact equivalent. This ancient expression appeared in the first prophetic books of the Hebrews (Joshua, Judges, and the two books of Samuel: cf. 1 Sm 2: 27; 9: 6). It is also found in the New Testament (cf. 2 Pt 1: 21).[29]

2. Past, Present, and Future in the Mission of the Prophets Sent by Yahweh

These three aspects, or coordinates, are interrelated in nature.

1. First of all, in order for us to properly understand the work of the prophets, we must understand how they related themselves to the covenant and the law because their mission was to inspire people to be faithful to God and live according to his precepts.

2. Second, the entire work of the prophets was directed toward the future. They sought to maintain the hope of the promise, to nurture the *eschatology* inherent in the covenant from the announcement of the Savior and Messiah.

3. Finally, these coordinates of the past and the future had an interrelationship with the present arising from the specific conditions in which the people lived. This was because the people looked to the prophets for enlightenment so that the chosen people might be faithful to the covenant and the promise.

B. Criteria for Distinguishing the Prophets Sent by Yahweh

God chose the prophets to guide his people in the faith. They received a special vocation that differed from that of other men who were also named prophets. Because of this diversity of persons acting under the same name—"prophets"—we need to distinguish between the various possible meanings. God himself offers the basic criteria for this task in the Ten Commandments (cf. Dt 13, 18), which warned the Hebrew people against false prophets.[30]

> If a prophet arises among you, or a dreamer of dreams, and gives you a sign or a wonder, and the sign or wonder which he tells you comes to pass, and if he says, "Let us go after other gods," which you have not known, "and let us serve them," you shall not listen to the words of that prophet or to that dreamer of dreams; for the LORD your God is testing you, to know whether you love the LORD your God with all your heart and with all your soul... But that prophet or that dreamer of dreams shall be put to death, because he has taught rebellion against the LORD your God. [To these instructions is added a second:] "But the prophet who presumes to speak a word in my name which I have not commanded him to speak, or who speaks in the name of other gods, that same prophet shall die." And if you say in your heart, "How may we know the word which the LORD has not spoken?"—when a prophet speaks in the name of the LORD, if the word does not come to pass or come true, that is a word which the LORD has not spoken; the prophet has spoken it presumptuously, you need not be afraid of him. (Dt 13: 1–3, 5; 18: 20–22)

In the ancient Orient (Egypt, Mesopotamia, and Canaan) one can easily find mediators—priestly or otherwise—men and women who spoke to the people or to governors (principally to the king) in the temple or outside of it. They announced, spontaneously or in response to questioning, messages that they thought had come from the gods by means of internal inspiration or fortune-telling practices. Their messages might refer to the future—fortuitous or inopportune—and it might refer to the religious or political sphere.[31] We can find testimony of this phenomenon in the Bible itself, not only existent in the cultures of other peoples (cf. Nm 22–24; 1 Kgs 18: 19; 2 Kgs 10: 19; Ez 21: 26; Jer 27: 9) but also within the life of Israel.

How, then, are we to recognize Yahweh's prophets and distinguish them from the seers of Canaan, Egypt, and Babylon? Was there a method for identifying them as heralds of a specific message from Yahweh? The Israelites themselves asked these questions and arrived at the following answers. Distinguishing them from Canaanite seers and diviners was not very difficult because the difference between the latter and God's men was marked (cf. 1 Sm 28: 9–16). It was more difficult to distinguish Yahweh's envoys from prophets who considered themselves as such and belonged to the people of Israel.[32]

We have already cited the fundamental criteria, contained in chapters 13 and 18 of Deuteronomy, used to resolve these doubts. By the light of those indications, which are confirmed in other passages of the Bible, we can say that there are basically three types of criteria for distinguishing true prophets from false ones. They correspond to the three aspects of the prophetic mission.[33]

The first aspect of the prophetic mission is authenticated by the coherence and correspondence between the prophet's teachings and those found in the law.

Some authors presented the prophets as a tension working against the temple and popular cult, based on the denunciations that the prophets made. In reality, the prophets were the great defenders of Yahweh's cult. Many of them lived and carried out their mission in the temple or in its surroundings (i.e., Nahum, Habakkuk, Joel, and Jeremiah).[34]

The second aspect of the prophetic mission was to provide guidance for the life and conduct of their contemporaries. This was authenticated by the correspondence of their personal conduct with the commandments of the law.

The man of God was recognized as such mostly because his life was formed and expressed by the word and will of God. Notice the importance of the biographical references to the prophets found in the Bible—they are seldom missing. These served to show how the past actions and origin of the man of God authenticated his mission.[35]

The third aspect of the prophetic mission (to sustain the people's hope in the coming of the promised Savior) was authenticated by the correspondence between the prophet's words foretelling the future and the reality of the foretold future.

The future that these men, guided by the Spirit, spoke about referred principally to the incarnation of the Word. Yet, it also included—as more immediate signs—other events of human history that, being temporally nearer to them, their contemporaries were able to verify. This was the case, for instance, when Jeremiah announced the future destruction of Jerusalem and foretold the upcoming defeat of Egypt (cf. Jer 44: 29). In his turn, Isaiah foretold the birth of the Savior from a virgin Mother and confirmed this announcement by prophesying the more immediate destruction of the armies that marched against Jerusalem (cf. Is 7: 1–25).

The credibility of the prophet as God's envoy, according to this third aspect, finds its enduring foundation in the *effective accomplishment of the pre-announced event*. In contrast, false prophets and fortune-tellers are moved by a spirit of deception. They mix true and false statements. If true statements attract men, while false prophecies fail to be verified, they are unmasked: "The devil sometimes says true things, but the Holy Spirit never lies."[36] Still, this effective fulfillment, as seen in Deuteronomy 13: 2–4, cannot be isolated as one criterion without the other two aspects.[37]

Historical events foretold by the prophets (excluding the Incarnation) were due to the interrelationship of several factors. Among these elements were free human decisions. Hence, it was not possible to foresee the prophesied events. Moreover, it sometimes seemed that they were not going to happen. Nevertheless, the prophets prophesied that they would occur. Sometimes, as in the case Jonah and the people of Nineveh, the prophet foretold a misfortune that was not fulfilled afterwards. This was because the people, threatened by divine punishment, heeded the warning and converted to God. However, the divine punishment would have been carried out according to the prophet's announcement if the people had not done penance.[38]

Regarding this point, St. Thomas Aquinas proposed a classification by which he considers the prophecy more perfect when it specifies the fact, the time it will happen, its meaning, and its divine origin. This was the case of Jesus' foretelling of St. Peter's triple denial (cf. Mk 14: 30) and Judas's betrayal. The normal prophecy gives an imprecise time when the prophecy event will occur. According to Aquinas, the prophets contemplated the future by the "mirror of eternity," where the present appears as the future and *vice versa*. Hence, a confusion of temporal dimensions is sometimes present in prophetic announcements (the eschatological is mixed with the present, near with far beyond, causing a lack of a temporal point of view, precisely named "the prophetic perspective").[39]

In prophetic utterances, as we saw in the case of the signs, there is an experiential moment in the gestures and words of the prophet. This is not restricted to the moment of the prophecy but also exists when his prophecy is fulfilled. Also, the lives and teachings of these persons and to what extent they themselves were in conformity with the law must be taken into account.

If one is to accept the life, works, and teachings of the prophets as motives for credibility, the observer must have a certain degree of religious background. This includes an understanding of the law and the promise, the saving history of Israel, and definitely requires a certain lived faith in Yahweh.

CHAPTER 12

CREDIBILITY OF JESUS OF NAZARETH AS THE MESSIAH, SON OF GOD

The fullness of credibility of Christ's words and deeds corresponds to the fullness of the Revelation of God in Christ. At the same time, the Revelation in Christ shows us this plenitude and confirms Old Testament Revelation, which was understood as a preparation for God's communication in Christ. So, the elements of credibility in the Old Testament prepared the Israelites to understand credibility born from the gestures and words of Jesus. Thus, they arrive with him to their complete expression.

In this chapter we will see that the Revelation of Jesus of Nazareth as the Messiah, Son of God and Lord was accomplished through a profusion of saving events. Jesus poured forth an abundance of words and discourses that were consistent with God's law, all of which accredited him as God's true envoy and his Son. Later, his glorious Resurrection constituted both the definitive revelation and a sign of his divinity. In this way he definitively showed that he is in everything equal to the Father, the Lord of life and death.

In the past, the historicity of information in the Gospels was universally recognized because of the demonstrable authenticity of its authors.[1] Two of them were eyewitnesses and the other two personally knew and heard the events from direct eyewitnesses. Due to the difficulties and persecution they encountered in preaching the message of Jesus, the historical validity of their writings seemed self-evident. There was never any reason to think that these men wanted to deceive the nascent Christian community.

Nevertheless, there was one problem, as some Fathers of the Church had themselves observed. The diversity among the synoptic Gospels and St. John's Gospel might raise questions. This problem, which D.F. Strauss insistently pointed out, provoked deeper studies about the authors of the Gospels and the nature of their writings, as people sought to discover the reasons for these differences.

The first issue relates to *the role of the Evangelists*, especially Mark and Luke (who did not accompany Jesus in his three years of public life). They are, at the same time, *authors* who have written with a certain creativity and *writers* who have collected information from different sources and, in turn, transmitted it to others.

The second peculiarity has to do with the *religious character* of those writings, a characteristic that pervades them in their deepest sense.

> The New Testament does not have as its objective the presentation of a scientifically historical account about Jesus. The goal of the Evangelists was to transmit the testimony of ecclesiastic faith about Jesus and present him in the total significance of the "Christ" (Messiah) and "Lord" (*Kyrios*, God). This testimony is the expression of faith and was an effort directed to inspire faith. The Evangelists did not intend to produce a "biography" of Jesus in the modern sense of the term. The same thing happened with numerous persons of classical and medieval times.[2]

The third concern refers to the *history of the writing of the Gospels*. By the light of the two previous issues, we should understand that the Gospels are the product of the announcements made by the apostles and the other disciples of Jesus during the first Christian decades. We know that the first Gospel messages were transmitted orally and that considerable time passed before the four Gospels were put on paper. The work of *Formgeschichte* and *Redaktiongeschichte* have highlighted the fact that before this writing, there were other partial writings of some discourses and parables of Jesus and some accounts of miracles. While the oral tradition centered on Christian gatherings and the Eucharistic liturgy, there was a certain crystallization of words and facts about Jesus in the narration of his life. It would not be surprising if the authors of the Gospels collected these elements. Nevertheless, we have to stress that the Evangelists were not simple compilers who gathered texts one by one. This way of portraying the work of the Evangelists, which is characteristic of *Formgeschichte*, has been criticized by post-Bultmannian authors. These critics stress that the Evangelists wrote a valid work, considering that, individually and as a whole, each one shares the unitary characteristics of each Gospel.[3]

In summary, it is necessary to study the history of the writings, *traditions*, and *sources* of the Gospels in order to correctly understand the historical value of the information that they offer and establish the criteria for their historical authenticity. By criteria of authenticity, we understand those "norms applied to evangelical material, that allow us to demonstrate the historical grounds of these narrations and reach a judgment about their authenticity. These norms allow us to establish proof of historical authenticity."[4] Still, we have to understand what these elements are. They are "criteria of historical authenticity of data." They are neither simple clues nor solely proofs that events really happened.

As scholars unanimously pointed out, such criteria vary in efficacy because some are more convincing than others. According to Latourelle, there are four fundamental criteria[5]:

1. *Criterion of multiple testimony.* Evangelical information can be considered authentic if it is found in testimonies from all sources (or the majority of them) of the Gospels and the other writings of the New Testament.

2. *Criterion of discontinuity.* Evangelical information can be considered authentic (if it is about the words and attitudes of Jesus) when it cannot be explained by Judaic or primitive Church conceptions. This criterion has to be applied with care in order to avoid putting Jesus in a non-temporal emptiness, thereby denying his reality as a Jew living in a certain epoch and in a specific situation.

3. *Criterion of conformity.* Sayings or gestures of Jesus can be considered authentic if they are in keeping with his time and environment (linguistic, geographical, social, political, and religious). This is especially true with the fundamental teachings of Jesus, i.e., the coming and settling of the Messianic kingdom in his person. This criterion, obviously, compliments the previous one and must be used in conjunction with it.

4. *Criterion of necessary explanation.* If, in view of a considerable body of facts or information that needs a convincing explanation, we are offered one that illuminates and harmoniously gathers all the necessary elements (which would otherwise continue to be an enigma), we can conclude that the corresponding information to such explanation is historically authentic. Latourelle presents this criterion, which other authors do not value as an addition to the principle of sufficient reason.[6]

Some authors also suggest other criteria. For example, they point to *Jesus' style,* which particularly characterizes and distinguishes him: speaking in parables, symbolic gestures, etc. Others write about the *intelligibility of the narration,* according to which evangelic information can be considered authentic when it is perfectly integrated in its mediate or immediate context and, furthermore, is perfectly coherent with its internal structure.[7]

I. The Presentation and Credibility of Jesus as Someone Sent by God to Save Mankind

Upon closer examination, we can see that although it is true that many believed in Jesus, not everybody believed in him to the same degree. We can specify these differences as well as the various journeys of faith followed by those who were near him and believed in him. This route grows from simple enthusiasm before an extraordinary personage because of his kindness, wisdom, and power, going beyond faith in him as Savior, until they identified him as the eternal Son of the Father who came to free men from sin and slavery of Satan, and from death.

A. The Self-Representation of Jesus of Nazareth as Sent by God to Establish the Kingdom

Jesus revealed himself as sent by God to establish the kingdom and fulfill the promises made by God from Abraham onward. He knew quite well that his contemporaries thought that God would save them in a political manner. Yet, Jesus gave his Messiahship an unexpected meaning and projection that were foretold by the prophets in fulfilling his mission through his suffering and death.[8]

This way to fulfill the promise was even reflected in the way he spoke of himself and his mission. Jesus spoke of the kingdom of heaven and the kingdom of God, but not the kingdom of the Messiah.[9] He called himself "Son of Man," an expression that specifically refers to the mysterious and transcendent dimension, according to Daniel's prophecy, of this personage expected by the Hebrew people. Although certain authors (among them Käsemann and Conzelmann) deny that Jesus applied this title to himself, the majority of scholars concur that on several occasions Jesus called himself "Son of Man."[10] Given these and other similar considerations, Jesus sought to protect his Messiahship from misunderstandings.[11]

Jesus explicitly presented himself as *sent by God and anointed by the Spirit*, and he behaved so that everybody might recognize him as such (cf. Mt 11: 3–6). Luke gives a detailed accounting of the episode at the synagogue of Nazareth (cf. Lk 4: 10–24) because he considers it of great importance.[12] Jesus presents himself as a *prophet*, comparing himself to Elijah and Elisha,[13] although he does not expressly define himself as such. Throughout his life he categorically avoids self-definition.[14]

In the fourth Gospel, St. John honors this wish of Jesus by using the linguistic formula *envoy of the Father*. Meanwhile, in the synoptic Gospels, the Evangelists designate Jesus as envoy, though not as frequently (only in Mt 15: 24 and Lk 4: 43, where the use of the passive voice hints at the action of God as sender). They also speak of the Father as the one who sends (cf. Mt 10: 40; 21: 37; Mk 9: 37; 12: 6; Lk 9: 48; 10: 16; 20: 13). In the fourth Gospel, nevertheless, this terminology appears about forty times, to such an extent that "he who has sent me" frequently substitutes for "Father."[15] The formula is always in the mouth of Jesus, who uses it before every type of audience: the people in general (cf. Jn 6: 29, 38, 39, 44, 57; 7: 28, 29; 8: 16, 18: 26, 29; 11: 42; 12: 44, 45, 49), the Jews (cf. Jn 5: 23, 24, 30, 36, 38; 7: 16, 33; 10: 36), the disciples (cf. Jn 4: 34; 9: 4; 13: 20; 14: 24; 15: 21; 16: 5; 17: 3, 8, 18, 21, 23, 25; 20: 21), and individuals such as Nicodemus (cf. Jn 3: 17).

1. Characteristics of the Expectancy of the Savior by the Jews in the Time of Jesus and Jesus' Desire to Present Himself as the Messiah

Here, we should note Jesus' care to avoid misunderstandings about the true nature of his mission. We will now analyze why that precaution was necessary.

Scholars unanimously recognize that, in Jesus' time, the Israelites were expecting the promised one sent by God. This knowledge is based on Qumran documents, the Sibylline Oracles, the texts of Philo of Alexandria, and other Judaic writings.[16]

The principal source of this popular hope was Sacred Scripture. The Old Testament presented the Messiah as an intermediary and a privileged instrument of divine intervention who would renew the history and condition of Israel.[17] The Bible proposes this concept in an increasingly rich and thorough manner. It gives the *real-Davidic* details of the anointed by Yahweh that decisively characterize the figure of the expected Savior (cf. Ps 2, 20, 21, 45, 72, 89, 110). It also presents him with the characteristics of the prophets that are similar to Moses or Elijah (cf. Dt 18: 15, 18–19; Mal 4: 5), the prerogatives of priests (cf. Hg 1: 1, 14; 2: 2–4, 23; Zec 6: 9–14; 9: 9–10; 11, 12–13; 12: 7–10; Is 61: 1–3), and with *eschatological and apocalyptic perspectives* of those who expected the arrival of the kingdom as a consequence of a decisive heavenly intervention. The Jews hoped that this would take place geographically in Israel and that it would inaugurate the end of times (cf. Dn 7: 14).

Nevertheless, this understanding of the various characteristics of the divine envoy was not unanimous. The people expected that, given the eschatological-apocalyptic character of the Messiah, a prophet would precede him and that an earthly kingdom would introduce the definitive messianic kingdom. Specifically, regarding the expectation of a great prophet (cf. Mt 16: 13–14; Mk 6: 14–15; Lk 7: 16; Jn 6: 14; 7: 40–52), some contemporaries of Jesus thought this prophet and the Messiah were the same (cf. Jn 7: 42). Others considered the prophet his predecessor. In any event, the expectation of a great prophet was united to their expectation of the Messiah.[18]

Based on these elements, the popular expectation was further concretized in different ways by the various interpretations that characterized important political and religious groups in Jesus' time, such as the Sadducees, Pharisees, Essenes, and Zealots.

The *Pharisees* combined a sincere following of the Torah with a religious nationalism that found its highest aspiration in the Messiah. They held a distinct social level, which was above the Sadducees (the Pharisees being of a more popular class). They taught that biblical writings and oral tradition enjoyed the same merit to the extreme of making the latter prevail over the written indications of the law (cf. Mt 15: 1–9). They considered themselves "the pure ones," "the separated ones," because they were preoccupied with avoiding any kind of corruption. Obviously, Jesus' conduct toward sinners directly conflicted with the ideology of the Pharisees. Therefore, they could not possibly view him as a possible Messiah.[19]

The *Sadducees* were representatives of a high priestly class and of the temple in Jerusalem. They had reconciled with Greek civilization, collaborated with Romans, and were theologically conservative. In practice, they accepted only the Pentateuch. They did not afford the same respect to later writings and they rejected oral tradition. When debating with the Sadducees, Jesus based his argument on Exodus 3: 6 (cf. Mk 12: 18–27). They were principally attentive to temporal and political matters. The Sadducees presented themselves as guardians of the law and the temple. They did not preoccupy themselves with messianic aspirations that, according to them, could endanger the normal functioning of Jewish institutions—with revolts, tumult and acts of revenge. Within this context, we can understand the concerns expressed by Caiaphas (cf. Jn 11: 49–50).[20]

The *Essenes* expected, even with a certain degree of impatience, the fulfillment of the prophesies about the liberation of Israel and the establishment of an ideal kingdom. However, they expected two Messiahs, one descended from Aaron and the other descended from Israel. This latter one (the descendant of David) would be subordinate to the former (an eschatological priest) in a nation whose life would be centered around the temple of Jerusalem and its worship. The anointed of Israel had a political, warlike role.[21] Apparently, all Essenes did not share this theory of messianic duplicity; some believed in only one Messiah, who would be a priest and David's son at the same time. We are not certain about this divergence because some critics accept the possibility that some Essenian texts were rewritten afterward. The Essenes were the third most important religious faction in the time of Jesus. Their religious behavior was characterized by a strong union with the Levitical priesthood and by a rigid observance of the law. To cite one example of their practices: "May a babe cry for his mother's milk, if he wish, or may a man drown: Sanctification on Saturdays is what matters above all else."[22]

The *Zealots* were called such because of the zeal that they demonstrated defending the purity of the law. They came from Judea and were united to the priestly class of Israel, with which they shared ideals and spirituality but not strategies. Rather, they were an active political movement that sought to liberate Jerusalem and Judea by force of arms.

The *Sicarii* came from Galilee and shared the spirituality of the Pharisees. Because they fought against the Romans and powerful Jews allied to Rome, they were considered outcasts by the leading Pharisees.

Jesus did not identify himself with any of the important groups of his time, although he did come into contact with them.[23] This separation was historically manifested by Jesus' caution about calling himself the Messiah. As a matter of fact, it is not clear from the Gospels that Jesus called himself the Christ. We find this expression used only once by Jesus in the synoptic Gospels (cf. Mk 9: 41). St. John likewise attributes this term only once to Jesus (cf. Jn 17: 3). Jesus' caution has inspired some authors over the past century to speculate that his disciples recognized his messianic character only after his death.

Others have argued that Jesus' silence had to do with the contemporary political situation. Given the total lack of any political pretensions of Jesus, the disciples resorted to a spiritual and religious messianism.

Most recently, theologians have posited that Jesus' silence was an act of prudence by someone who did not want to be considered a Messiah. Jesus rejected the temporal and political vision of the Messiah as well as the religious vision—spiritual but rigid—that was popular in that period.[24]

Jesus accepted it when people confessed his messianic mission when he thought it right and proper (cf. Mt 16: 16; Jn 11: 27). Besides, Jesus saw it fit to reveal himself at the end of his life in the double judgment before the Sanhedrin and Pilate. Historical criticism reveals that the Sanhedrin set out the issue of the messianism of Jesus in a most direct and explicit manner. Pilate's questioning had to do with the royalty of Jesus, and it was resolved in the affirmative—as the title on the cross points out—with its special significance.[25]

B. Application to Jesus of the Criteria to Recognize the True Envoys of God

The Gospels state on numerous occasions that many people accepted Jesus as the prophet sent by God.

St. Luke says that after the resurrection of the adolescent of Naim, "Fear seized them all; and they glorified God, saying, 'A great prophet has arisen among us!' and 'God has visited his people!'" (Lk 7: 16; cf. 7: 39). The two disciples going to Emmaus, following the death of their Master, talked about him as "a prophet mighty in deed and word before God and all the people" (Lk 24: 19; cf. 24: 21). We find the same conception in St. Peter's discourses on Pentecost day (cf. Acts 2: 22) and at the house of Cornelius (cf. Acts 10: 37–38). St. Matthew recounts this dialogue between Jesus and his apostles at Caesarea of Philippi: "'Who do men say that the Son of man is?' And they said, 'Some say John the Baptist, others say Elijah, and others Jeremiah or one of the pro phets'" (Mt 16: 13–14). Regarding Jesus' triumphal entrance into Jerusalem, this same Evangelist quotes the people as saying, "And when he entered Jerusalem, all the city was stirred, saying, 'Who is this?' And the crowds said, 'This is the prophet Jesus from Nazareth of Galilee'" (Mt 21: 10–11).

St. Mark also refers to similar statements by the people in situations not quoted in the other synoptic Gospels. "King Herod heard of it; for Jesus' name had become known. Some said, 'John the baptizer has been raised from the dead; that is why these powers are at work in him.' But others said, 'It is Elijah.' And others said, 'It is a prophet, like one of the prophets of old'" (Mk 6: 14–15). For his part, St. John described the reactions of several contemporaries of Jesus: Nicodemus (cf. Jn 3: 2), the Samaritan woman at the well of Sichar: "Sir, I perceive that you are a prophet" (Jn 4: 19), the people who witnessed the multiplication of bread: "This is indeed the prophet who is to come into the world!" (Jn 6: 14; cf. 7: 40–41, 46–47, 50–52), and the man who was blind from birth: "He is a prophet" (Jn 9: 17).

We will now analyze how the contemporaries of Jesus identified those three elements in him that, according to the Old Testament, characterize a prophet who is truly sent by God.[26]

1. Conformity and Coherence between the Doctrine of Jesus and the Doctrine of the Law and Prophets

Jesus' contemporaries saw up to what extent *his words were in keeping with the law and how he was motivated to fulfill it conscientiously*, without falsification. Moreover, his message made reference to the perfect and pure fulfillment of the law: "Think not that I have come to abolish the law and the prophets; I have come not to abolish them but to fulfil them. For truly, I say to you, till heaven and earth pass away, not an iota, not a dot, will pass from the law until all is accomplished" (Mt 5

: 17–18; cf. Lk 16: 17). At the same time, they noticed, as Jesus himself acknowledged, that he *taught something entirely new:* "The law and the prophets were until John; since then the good news of the kingdom of God is preached, and every one enters it violently" (Lk 16: 16).

The question that now arises is whether all of his contemporaries equally understood these two aspects of continuity and novelty. The evangelical narration leads us to think that the people, being very simple, had no particular difficulty perceiving the fidelity of Jesus' doctrine to the Mosaic law, as well as the novelty he was introducing. Currently, Hebrew scholars also believe that Jesus' doctrine and attitude toward the law were in conformity with Hebrew thinking and conduct in general.[27]

Nevertheless, the different Hebrew factions were opposed to the teachings of Jesus and how they related to the law.[28] The four Evangelists do not hide the contrast between Jesus and the Pharisees about the correct way to interpret the law. However, these differences, rather than invalidating the mission and prophetic style of Jesus—as if he did not observe the law—definitively confirm them. As Jesus pointed out on several occasions (cf. Mt 23: 29–32, 34), the Pharisees treated him in the same way that they had treated the prophets before him who had proclaimed God's Word and denounced injustices against the law. "Much like the great prophets before him, [Jesus] was challenged by human pride and hypocrisy, by those who follow their own projects of exultation and personal prestige."[29]

Nevertheless, the primary reason for this conflict lay in the authority by which Jesus taught his message, which surpassed differences over how to interpret the law. Everyone was aware of the reach of that authority, as the Evangelists unanimously point out. After the healing of a possessed person, Mark observes, "And they were all amazed, so that they questioned among themselves, saying, 'What is this? A new teaching! With authority he commands even the unclean spirits, and they obey him'" (Mk 1: 27). In this verse, the term *authority* is explicitly joined to Jesus' prodigious actions. Some time before, Mark relates that Jesus entered the synagogue on a Saturday, and as he started to teach, they were amazed by his teachings because he spoke "as one who had authority, and not as the scribes" (Mk 1: 22; cf. Mt 7: 28; Jn 7: 46).

The high priests perceived that their authority was being challenged and displaced because the rabbi of Nazareth spoke as a judge, not as just an interpreter of the law. They attempted to impose their authority on him, indirectly commanding him not to carry out more healing on Saturday and thereby respect the Sabbath (cf. Lk 13: 14). However, Jesus was not intimidated, and he healed every day, even on the Sabbath. He explained the reasons for his singular authority while doing so (cf. Jn 5: 17) and showed his adversaries that one can cure on the Sabbath. He pointed out that his critics did various activities on the day of rest such as taking care of their sheep, carrying domestic animals to water (cf. Mt 12: 9–12; Mk 3: 1–6; Lk 6: 6–11; 13: 15–17) and circumcising children (cf. Jn 7: 23). When the high priests saw that Jesus would not cede on this issue of authority, they decided to eliminate him, as the synoptic Gospels unanimously relate (cf. Mt 12: 14; 21: 23–27; Mk 3: 6; 11: 27–33, Lk 6: 11; 20: 1–8).

2. The Conformity and Coherence of Jesus' Conduct with the Precepts of the Law

Jesus' contemporaries could see that his conduct conformed to the law and was coherent with his own specific message. At the same time, they also understood that he was a man who was truly guided by the Holy Spirit.

This aspect should have been quite evident, because Jesus publicly asked, "Which of you convicts me of sin?" (Jn 8: 46). During the trial before Annas and Caiaphas, after the guard had slapped him, Jesus asked, "If I have spoken wrongly, bear witness to the wrong; but if I have spoken rightly, why do you strike me?" (Jn 18: 23). The synoptic Gospels state that, during this trial, the chief priests could find no reason to condemn him. Finally, they could charge only that he declared himself to be the Christ and the Son of God (cf. Mt 26: 63; Mk 14: 61; Lk 22: 67, 70). "Now the chief priests and the whole council sought false testimony against Jesus that they might put him to death, but they found none, though many false witnesses came forward" (Mt 26: 59–60; cf. Mk 14: 55–56). Luke is less explicit on this point. Yet, he carefully tells that neither Pilate nor Herod found a motive to condemn him (cf. Lk 23: 14–15). Historically, Jesus was not condemned for actions against the morality prescribed by the law or for his teaching about the Torah and the temple. The motive of the sentence—far beyond nuances proper to the four evangelical narrations—lies in his claim to be the Christ, which is a very singular claim because it is intimately united to another fundamental claim: that he is the Son of God.

3. The Prophecies of Jesus

Last of all, some among the people closest to Jesus could verify that his prophecies about future events indeed took place.

Among these prophecies, some were particularly serious and similar in style to those of the prophets of Yahweh found in the Old Testament. Others were formulated in a much simpler way.

Among the first category, some appear in the form of *threat and misfortune* as used by the prophets of Israel. For example, concerning the ruin of Jerusalem: "O Jerusalem, Jerusalem, killing the prophets and stoning those who are sent to you! How often would I have gathered your children together as a hen gathers her brood under her wings, and you would not! Behold, your house is forsaken and desolate" (Mt 23: 37–38; cf. Lk 13: 34–35). In his eschatological discourse, he gives details about the destruction of the city and the ruin of the temple that would take place forty years afterwards. "Do you see these great buildings? There will not be left here one stone upon another, that will not be thrown down" (Mk 13: 2; cf. Mt 24: 1–51; Lk 21: 5–33). He used similar formulas to curse cities that witnessed his saving actions but did not convert (cf. Mt 11: 21–24; Lk 10: 12–15) and to admonish the entire generation of his skeptical countrymen (cf. Lk 11: 29–32).[30]

Other announcements take the Semitic form of the *formulas for blessings* used by the patriarchs and the prophets. Among them, we should note the blessings (cf. Mt 5: 3–12; Lk 6: 20–26) and similar blessings (cf. Mt 11: 6; Lk 7: 23). The historical authenticity of this type of foretelling—validated regarding the historical content of the prophesied event—is attested to by the clearly Semitic style, so frequently found in teachings of this kind. It is also attested to by the concise and easily memorizable writing style in which it has arrived at our day.

Jesus also made prophecies that *simply describe the future without connotation of misfortune or unhappiness*. They are exclusive to Jesus. They cannot be found in the great prophets of the Old Testament, who generally, when they announced events of great importance, tried to do so with certain solemnity because their messages came from God ("Lord's word," "Yahweh's oracle"). They spoke in that way so as to call the attention of their listeners toward the transcendence of the omen. Among Jesus' prophecies of this sort, we find the prophecy that he would be loved or hated, as a sign of contradiction throughout history (cf. Mt 10: 22, 11: 29–30; Jn 7: 7; 12: 32; 14: 17, 27), the prophecy that everywhere his message would be preached, and the prophecy that Mary Magdalen's gesture of pouring ointment upon him would be remembered (cf. Mt 26: 12). All of these effectively happened and still happen even today.

There are also the graces that his apostles received and the persecution they had to suffer. Both prophecies have been confirmed in history (cf. Mt 10: 17–22; Jn 7: 39; 15: 18–20). Other prophecies include the efficacy of his disciples' mission and the spreading of his doctrine all over the world (cf. Mt 8: 10; 24: 14; 28: 18–20; Mk 16: 15–18; Lk 5: 10), and the dispersion of the chosen people until the end of time. "They will fall by the edge of the sword, and be led captive among all nations; and Jerusalem will be trodden down by the Gentiles, until the times of the Gentiles are fulfilled" (Lk 21: 24). The fact that these prophesies have been fulfilled—centuries after he prophesied that they would happen—excludes any interpretation in the sense of there having been a *post-eventum* adaptation on the part of the disciples.

Other prophecies, not so monumental, were verifiable in just a few days or even a few hours. For example, the circumstances the disciples encountered when they were going to Jerusalem to prepare for his triumphal entering and the paschal feast (cf. Mt 21: 2–4; Mk 14: 13). Other examples include St. Peter's triple denial (cf. Mt 26: 34; Mk 14: 30; Lk 22: 34), his disciples' abandonment in Gethsemane (cf. Mt 26: 31; Mk 14: 27;

Lk 22: 31–32), and Judas's treason (cf. Mt 26: 21–25; Mk 14: 18–21; Lk 22: 21–23; Jn 6: 70; 13: 21–30).

Still, *the most important prophecy made by Jesus concerned his Passion, Death, and Resurrection*. On three occasions Jesus explicitly announced his Passion, Death, and Resurrection to his disciples. He spoke to them in a clear-cut manner and described details that could not have been foreseen in any way (slaps, insults, spitting, scourging, a crown of thorns, crucifixion). He made these prophecies despite all the expectations of his disciples, who could not imagine such a gruesome end to his earthly mission given what they had witnessed in the might of his actions and words (cf. Mk 8: 32; 9: 32).[31] Most likely, the references to that bloody ending were generic in his public speeches. He was probably more explicit and detailed only among the restricted group of the apostles.[32]

As the Evangelists recorded Jesus' triple announcement of his Passion, Death, and Resurrection, it cannot be understood solely as an intuition on his part of a possible ending to his proper mission on earth, but should be seen as his prophecy about how his earthly mission would end.

Some authors, for example, Bultmann[33], have questioned the authenticity of this triple prophecy. However, it is possible to establish the historical authenticity of this triple prophecy by applying the criteria we have already reviewed.

The criterion of multiple testimony: The historical authenticity of the threefold prophecy of Jesus is supported in that it was proposed in a specific manner by the three synoptic Gospels in contexts and situations that were not precisely identical (cf. Mt 16: 21–23; 17: 22–23; 20: 17–19; Mk 8: 31–33; 9: 30–32; 10: 32–34; Lk 9: 22; 43–45; 18: 31–34). Therefore, the application of the criterion of multiple testimony validates the prophecy.

The criterion of discontinuity: The prophecy is also valid because Jesus, in referring to his Death and Resurrection, did so *punctum dolens* (suffering having been wounded). This shows how Jesus' vision of his own messianic mission differed from that of his disciples. Some authors reason this another way. In the scandal of the cross, it is assumed that Jesus did not announce his own death in a prophetic manner, or at least he did not do so in a manifest way.[34] This reasoning does not allow for the fact that man can deny a reality that is thoroughly unpleasant to him.

The criterion of conformity: This is met by the coherence between the triple announcement and the entirety of Jesus' life and teachings. In fact, Jesus' evident heroism (particularly, his unconditional and untiring effort to always testify to the truth) and his demands for heroism from his disciples clearly conform to the meaning of his prophecy. On the other hand, it can be reasonably thought that his bloody ending did not catch him unaware, because he had provoked the Pharisees and the chief priests to such a degree that he must have known that his days were numbered. Jesus was well aware of how St. John the Baptist had died, how the Pharisees had reacted in view of Jesus' doctrine and his conduct with sinners, and how the Sadducees felt about his conduct toward the merchants in the temple. Hence, his triple prophecy about his Passion, Death, and Resurrection is perfectly in keeping with the foreknowledge that Jesus had of his proper mission and ending.

The criterion of necessary explanation: Moreover, there is other information in the New Testament that becomes comprehensible once this triple prophecy is accepted as historical. Such is Jesus' determination to go to Jerusalem, a trip characterized in Luke's narration and that needs to be juxtaposed to his words about the destiny of the prophets. "And he said to them, 'Go and tell that fox, "Behold, I cast out demons and perform cures today and tomorrow, and the third day I finish my course." Nevertheless I must go on my way today and tomorrow and the day following; for it cannot be that a prophet should perish away from Jerusalem'" (Lk 13: 32–33).[35] Another example is his frequent references to the banquet in the kingdom of heaven: "Truly, I say to you, I shall not drink again of the fruit of the vine until that day when I drink it new in the kingdom of God" (Mk 14: 25).[36] A third instance is that he tends to use the following formula in these announcements: "The Son of man is to be delivered into the hands of men." This phrase could have hardly been formulated as such after Jesus' Passion and Death, when it was already known that he had been sentenced to death on a cross. Therefore, this evangelical expression is an enigmatic phrase employed by Jesus.

Finally, another confirmation of the historical credibility of this textual tradition is the various times when Jesus speaks about his Passion in a veiled way without explicitly mentioning his Resurrection (cf. Mt 17: 12; Mk 9: 12; Lk 17: 25).[37]

C. The Saving Miracles Worked by Jesus, Signs of His Mission

Jesus' contemporaries came to consider him a great envoy of God and Messiah not only because of his conduct and doctrine, which were proper to a true envoy of Yahweh, but also because of the numerous miracles that he worked before many people.

1. Analysis of the Historicity of the Saving Miracles Performed by Jesus of Nazareth

From the historical standpoint, Jesus of Nazareth must have carried out his healing works in such a manner that they amazed those who witnessed them. Christian and non-Christian sources, both Roman and Hebrew, witnessed Jesus as a miracle worker. He healed diverse illnesses, expelled demons, brought dead people back to life, and performed natural wonders (i.e., calming the winds of the sea, turning water into wine, and multiplying bread and fish).

Some authors may consider the mysteries as later inventions of the early Christian community.[38] For example, in the twentieth century, Bultmann led the strongest opposition to the historical authenticity of these miracles. He distinguished between the maxims and the narrations of miracles. According to Bultmann, the former are more credible, the latter are, in reality, fruits of the mythicizing of the first believers.[39]

W. Trilling pointed out that "the narration of the miracles have such a place in the Gospels that it is impossible that they were made up later on and then attributed to Jesus."[40] A. Richardson argued that, in Mark's Gospel, the narration of miracles takes up thirty-one percent of the entire Gospel. (If the narration of the Passion is excluded, the percentage rises to forty-seven percent.) For this reason, St. Mark's Gospel has been termed "the Gospel of miracles."[41] Something similar is found in the fourth Gospel. C.H. Dodd divided St. John's Gospel into two parts:"the book of signs" and "the book of passion." The first part consists of twelve chapters narrating how Jesus performed seven miracles and then gave explanations and speeches about them.[42] The same pattern may be found in St. Matthew's Gospel. Many authors separate the Gospel of Matthew into seven "books."[43] There is a book for the childhood and a book for the Passion; between these two there are five books, each with its own narrative and discursive parts. The second part follows and explains the first one. There are five speeches: the mountain, the mission, the parables, the ecclesiastical, and the eschatological. The narrative section always narrates miracles performed by Jesus.

The link between miracles and words in the narration of Jesus' life appears in all four Gospels. This link cannot be attributed to a writing project or a concerted group effort, although, of course, the Evangelists shared a common desire to guide their readers to faith in Jesus as Christ and Son of God.[44] Thus, it seems evident that the agreement between the words and miracles of Jesus in the Gospels must reflect the reality of the life of Jesus. Therefore, we must conclude that the miracles in the Gospels are historical facts. The Evangelists use these events in their effort to paint a personal portrait of Jesus. Without these stories, the narration of Jesus' life would be incomplete and deformed, precisely because it would leave out an historical element of fundamental importance for a full understanding of Jesus and his actions.

Besides the miraculous character of these actions of Jesus, their eminently saving character is historically demonstrable. Jesus did not seek his own exultation through magic. He performed miracles with great simplicity, without any desire to call attention to himself. He often instructed the beneficiaries of his favors to keep silent. He did not seek out his own interest. There is no narration of miracles worked on his own behalf. Quite to the contrary, all of the miracles performed by Jesus are characterized by his concern that they serve to benefit one or many persons, either physically or spiritually.

2. The Miracles Performed by Jesus and the Saving Events Performed by Yahweh

All the Evangelists, particularly Luke and John, highlight the fact that those who were present at the miracles praised God upon witnessing his power. This is because they recognized these wonders as manifestations of the might and wisdom of Yahweh.

Thus, after the healing of the paralyzed man in Capernaum we read, "When the crowds saw it, they were afraid, and they glorified God, who had given such authority to men" (Mt 9: 8; cf. Mk 2: 12; Lk 5: 26). After the miraculous catch of fish, St. Peter felt that there was an abyss between his own indignity and the holiness of Jesus: "Depart from me, for I am a sinful man, O Lord" (Lk 5: 8). After the Resurrection at Naim the crowds said, "A great prophet has arisen among us!" (Lk 7: 16) After the healing of the epileptic man, "all were astonished at the majesty of God" (Lk 9: 43). After his healing in Jericho, the blind man "followed him, glorifying God; and all the people, when they saw it, gave praise to God" (Lk 18: 43).

John generally ends his narration of the signs with a remark about their effect on others. For example, after the transformation of water into wine, he remarks, "his disciples believed in him" (Jn 2: 11). After the multiplication of bread, he comments, "When the people saw the sign which he had done, they said, 'This is indeed the prophet who is to come into the world!'" (Jn 6: 14). Following his healing, the man born blind from birth explains to the Pharisees who did not want to believe him, "Never since the world began has it been heard that any one opened the eyes of a man born blind. If this man were not from God, he could do nothing" (Jn 9: 32–33). After Lazarus was brought back to life, many people went to see the resurrected Lazarus and they went away "believing in Jesus" (Jn 12: 11).

Everyone who had immediate experience of these miracles considered them manifestations of the saving action of God. The people recognized the likeness between the historical actions by which Yahweh had manifested himself to Israel (cf. Dt 3: 24; 11: 2–7; Jos 24: 31) and the miracles of Jesus because the people were enlightened by their faith in Yahweh. In fact, the four Evangelists describe these miraculous actions by Jesus with the same words (*teras, sémeia, dynamis, erga*) used by the Septuagint to translate different Hebrew terms that described God's wondrous interventions on behalf of his people. This terminology cannot be solely attributed to the post-paschal period, because it depends upon historically authentic remarks of the crowd.

Therefore, we must conclude that, *from the experience of the miracles performed by Jesus, it was possible to understand that the kingdom of God had arrived and that the promised salvation had been fulfilled.*[45] The multiple testimony of the four Evangelists, each one according to his proper characteristics, leads us to understand that reality. Matthew, for instance, stresses the fact that Jesus' miracles were the proof that the promised kingdom had come. Luke, however, thematically highlights the fulfillment and development of salvation and sees the miracles as pieces in that overall context.

When we study the various arguments in the synoptic Gospels that Jesus had with his critics about his powers and those of Beelzebub (cf. Mt 12: 22–32; Mk 3: 22–30; Lk 11: 14–26), we notice that *Jesus intentionally joined his exorcisms to the coming of God's kingdom.* He attributed them solely to the might of God ("the finger of God" according to Luke, the "spirit of God" according to Matthew and Mark). Jesus held that any claim that his exorcisms were somehow due to Satan was a blasphemy against the Holy Spirit, an explicit resistance of divine grace, and, consequently, led toward a worse spiritual situation. (He had not yet shown through his expulsion of demons that the kingdom of God had come.)[46] According to Jesus, this stubborn incomprehension on the part of his enemies, in the sight of his miracles, that the kingdom of God had come also indicated a great guilt. Hence, he condemned the incredulity of the cities by the lake of Gennesaret (cf. Mt 11: 20–24; Lk 10: 13–15).[47]

D. The Merciful Love of Jesus for Men: A Definite Motive for Believing in Him as Messiah and Savior

The "signs" of divine omnipotence and saving power of the Son of Man and the miracles of Christ as narrated in the Gospels are a revelation of the love of God for man, particularly for those who suffer, who have needs, who beg for healing, forgiveness and respect. They are signs of the merciful love proclaimed in the Old Testament. The reading of the Gospels should lead us to understand and almost "feel" that Jesus' miracles have their source in the loving and merciful heart of the God who lives and whose own human heart pulsates. Jesus accomplishes these wonders to overcome all kinds of evils in the world: physical evil, moral evil, that is to say, sin.... Miracles, therefore, are "for men." They are actions of Jesus that are in harmony with the redeeming finality of his mission. By these works, he reestablishes good where evil exists, it being the cause of disorder and uncertainty.... A careful study of the evangelical texts reveals that Jesus performed his miracles for no other reason than for his love for man. It is in his merciful love that we find the explanation for the "miracles and signs" of the Son of Man.... Jesus worked no miracle to punish anyone, not even those who were guilty.... Yes, certainly, in miracles, we can always find the thundering of divine might that sometimes led the disciples and the people to exclaim that Christ was the "Son of God." Similarly, we discover in the action of Jesus aspects of kindness, sobriety and simplicity, which are the most visible gifts of "the Son of Man." ...If one accepts the evangelical narration of the miracles of Jesus—and there is no reason not to accept them, except for a prejudice against the supernatural—the logic that joins all of these "signs" within the saving economy of God cannot be put in doubt. These are signs of his love for us, of that merciful love that by good overcomes evil, as the presence and action of Jesus Christ demonstrates in the world around us.[48]

There is a close relationship between the miracles performed by Jesus and his love toward mankind. The miracles are the product of his love, of Jesus' will to do good to everyone without distinction. This is because he loved them. Those who dealt closely with Jesus came to understand this relationship.

As we delve into this topic, we are faced with two considerations related to the influence that the lived and preached love of Christ had on his disciples' journey of faith. These are its effects on the dispositions of his beloved and its function as a divine sign.

We can rest assured that the love of Jesus definitively influenced the people who dealt with him. In fact, one must consider that the love that a person has is the key which opens the heart to receive Christ's words in order to believe what he says.

Jesus' merciful love for everyone is a reason to believe, a reason that acts in a singular, unique manner, because it is precisely directed to the heart and will. [49] One might call this a reason "of the heart."[50] This is a motivation to believe that seems only marginally related to intelligence but is still united with it. It combines the intervention of heart and will. The dynamism of the heart and will is as human as the dynamism of the intelligence. On occasion, they appear more important and decisive, without diminishing the value of the intellect.[51] In this way, it is demonstrated that not everything is left to the strictly analytical and rational element when examining the various "reasons" for credibility. There are also motivations and "arguments"—at times more decisive— that proceed based on the heart and the freedom of love without hampering the functioning of reason.

Jesus' merciful love functioned as a divine sign, a sign of faith because it gave testimony and revealed God's love. It motivated people to have an experience of that love that they have not yet perceived or heard announced.

In fact, those who knew the history of Israel could discover that love of Jesus for all *resembled the free love of God toward his people*. This was repeatedly manifested in olden times. It resembled it primarily because it was merciful and saving (cf. Ex 34: 6–7; Nm 23: 19). When remarking upon the miracle Jesus performed at Naim, St. Josemaría has written:

> Jesus crosses paths again with a crowd of people. He could have passed by or waited until they called him. But he didn't. He took the initiative, because he was moved by a widow's sorrow. She had just lost all she had, her son.
>
> The evangelist explains that Jesus was moved. Perhaps he even showed signs of it, as when Lazarus died....
>
> Christ knows he is surrounded by a crowd that will be awed by the miracle and will tell the story all over the countryside. But he does not act artificially, merely to make an effect. Quite simply he is touched by that woman's suffering and cannot keep from consoling her. So he goes up to her and says, "Do not weep." It is like saying: "I don't want to see you crying; I have come on earth to bring joy and peace." And then comes the miracle, the sign of the power of Christ who is God. But first came his compassion, an evident sign of the tenderness of the heart of Christ the man.[52]

More than his words and gestures, Jesus *inspired people to the knowledge of God as love,* to a comprehension of the merciful fidelity of God. Those words and gestures predisposed and helped them to believe and understand that God is love and that Jesus—God's Son—brought and communicated the love that God is.[53]

Finally, the love of Jesus consisted of, and still consists of, *a divine response to the wish and need for love that everyone experiences.* Without love, human existence is empty and meaningless. This is because the human heart has been created to love. Therefore, any happiness unenlightened by a corresponding affection does not deserve such a name. The greatest joy comes from mutual love.

Certainly, the idea of a cold and distant God does not move one either to faith or to a relationship with him. The effect is quite to the contrary. Thus, the love of Jesus has always proved a powerful sign of faith and a mighty motivation for belief.

Many pages of the Gospels testify to the love of Jesus both for those who were close to him and for his enemies. The Evangelists also testify that many of the people responded to his affection. As we review the historical authenticity of this information, we will limit ourselves, for the sake of brevity, to two aspects—the universality and the gratuity of Jesus' love.

In the four Gospels, we find common testimony that Jesus lived and preached love for everyone without exception. The persons who were near to him understood this clearly. He took everyone into his heart. He dined with the rich, shared entertainments with the poor, discoursed with the doctors of the law, addressed those who continually judged the conduct of others according to the law, and healed the sick. He preached to crowds and spoke with individuals. Jesus did not reject anyone who asked him for a favor or an explanation (except those without good intentions or who mistook him for a magician). He discriminated against no one; he harmed no one and respected everyone.

The love that Jesus had for everyone replete with humility and sweetness. Perhaps his most moving expression was his care for little children. The historicity of his interest on behalf of children is beyond doubt. It is considered one of the oldest and most important features of the life and teachings of Jesus.[54]

Among the different manifestations of Jesus' love for humanity, the Evangelists stop to describe his love for sinners: "a friend of tax collectors and sinners" (Mt 11: 19; cf. Lk 7: 34).

> We have to point out that the three marvelous parables of divine mercy (cf. Lk 15: 3–32) all arise from demonstrations of the love of Jesus toward publicans and sinners, especially in response to criticism from the Pharisees and the scribes, "the just ones" (cf. Lk 15: 1–3).[55]

The historicity of this love and its universality is confirmed by the fact that many people responded to it. Jesus attracted a great number of people. He was loved and followed by many men and women who considered themselves his disciples. Among the synoptic Gospels, Mark most stresses this phenomenon (cf. Mk 1: 36–37; 2: 2, 4, 13; 3: 7–8, 20,

32; 4: 1; 5: 21). We also find similar commentaries in the other Gospels (cf. Mt 14: 3–21; 21: 1–11; Lk 9: 10–17; 19: 29–40; Jn 2: 23; 4: 39; 6: 2, 24; 12: 9–12, 19, 21, 29).

Jesus' ability to attract such large numbers of people could have been due to several factors. For instance, it could have been that Jesus performed great miracles that led many to believe he was the Messiah. However, it would be irresponsible not to consider factors such as Jesus' warmth, affability and simplicity, magnanimity, and, above all, his authentic love for and interest in others.

The four Evangelists are in complete agreement that Jesus lived his life on behalf of others, especially in its final consequences (cf. Jn 10: 17–18; 13: 1). It was Jesus' own choice to devote his life to others. He freely elected to give up his life. The following paragraphs examine how well these assertions stand up to historical criticism.

Complying with the rules of historical criticism, H. Schürmann demonstrated Jesus' love for everyone without exception, even for his enemies who led him inevitably to death. This fate he faced without excluding anyone, not even those that procured his death.[56]

Certainly, Jesus' death, which he prophesied as a consequence of testifying to the truth of being God's envoy with supreme authority, indicates that he is the Son of God. The chief priests did not accept his message, and they wanted to get rid of Jesus at all cost. Yet, it is likewise true that his end was also a consequence of his saving love for humanity.

In fact, his brave testimony to the truth when confronted by the chief priests was also moved by his love for men. This is because Jesus knew—as the Evangelists assert on several occasions—that knowledge of the truth is absolutely humanly necessary. Moreover, Jesus taught that human happiness is based upon the knowledge of truth (cf. Jn 8: 32; 17: 17; 18: 37). For him, therefore, loving mankind and testifying to the truth were two inseparably joined aspects of the same reality. Then again, Jesus revealed that God's love contained mercy, the willingness to pardon others without distinction or limitations of any kind.

Furthermore, Christ's boundless love drove him to do good to those in need. All of his behavior could not help but arouse the envy of the powerful, who felt upstaged by a humble carpenter.

One event, among many, can illustrate how this developed. Jesus had retired to "the place where John at first baptized" (Jn 10: 40), to get away from the Jews who had tried to stone him (cf. Jn 10: 32, 39). Once in the desert, he heard the news that Lazarus was ill. The Evangelist writes, "Jesus loved Martha and her sister and Lazarus" (Jn 11: 5). So, he decided go to them, in spite of his disciples' strong advice about the dangers inherent in this situation: "Rabbi, the Jews were but now seeking to stone you, and are you going there again?" (Jn 11: 8). These were not hyperbolic arguments, because when their Master decided to leave, the disciples said to one another: "Let us also go, that we may die with him" (Jn 11: 16). They really believed that his death was imminent. In the light of the resurrection of Lazarus, "the chief priests and the Pharisees gathered the council, and said, 'What are we to do? For this man performs many signs.'… So from that day on they took counsel how to put him to death" (Jn 11: 47, 53). Jesus did not refrain from giving life back to his dead friend, despite the threat to his own life.

II. The Authenticity and Value of Jesus' Testimony about His Filiation to God the Father

Because of the many miracles that Jesus performed, his contemporaries came to consider him more than an ordinary prophet (cf. Mt 16: 13–14; Mk 6: 2–3, 14–15; Jn 7: 40–52). They asked themselves, "Who then is this?" (Mk 4: 41; cf. Mt 8: 27; Lk 8: 25; Jn 8: 25). Simply, his gestures and teachings surpassed those of any other prophet (cf. Lk 11: 31–32).

Jesus interpreted the law with the authority of Lord of the law and salvation. Prophets have always attributed their mission to God and pointed out, each time, that their teachings and prophecies were "the word of God." On the other hand, Jesus always spoke in the first person: "I tell you this.…"[57] We cannot doubt the historical and textual authenticity of Jesus' way of preaching because it is present throughout the

New Testament. Certainly, it impressed the disciples and remained in their memory.

Jesus himself directed listeners to be attentive to the fact that he was "greater than Jonah" (Mt 12: 41) and "greater than Solomon" (Mt 12: 42). He unveiled the mystery of his personal identity when he declared that he spoke with authority, not like the scribes, Pharisees and priests. He assured them he could do so because he was the Son of God.

As to the value and historical authenticity of Jesus' testimony about himself, nineteenth century authors have expressed some reservations and objections. Bultmann and others argued that all statements where Jesus presents himself as Messiah or Son of God were products of editing by the early Christian community. These thinkers afford Jesus only the self-knowledge of having been a prophet.[58] Bultmann's thesis, nevertheless, has been rejected by many other writers, who, after having studied this point further, concluded that from the standpoint of historical and textual criticism, "Jesus' life attests to his own consciousness filial relationship with the Father.... He was conscious of being the only Son of God and, in this sense, of being God himself."[59]

Jesus' testimony about his person is valid from the *legal* point of view, because, as the law demanded, other testimonies coincide with his: Moses, the prophets, and the Baptist (cf. Nm 35: 30; Dt 17: 6; Mt 18: 16; Jn 5: 33–47; 8: 17). It is also valid from the *moral* standpoint because his words are consistent with his actions and conduct: Jesus is the true witness (cf. Jn 14: 6, 18, 37; Rv 1: 5; 3: 14). Finally, it is valid from the *theological* standpoint, because it is in harmony with the mission that God gave him to fulfill (cf. Jn 5: 36–31; 8: 18; 1 Jn 5: 9) and with the testimony of the Spirit of truth (cf. Jn 15: 26; 16: 13). In fact, the miracles that Jesus carried out, besides indicating the arrival of the kingdom, also functioned as signs of his being the Son. This function was inseparably joined to his testimony on his own behalf, as observed in the fourth Gospel.[60]

A. Testimony with Words:
The Presentation of Jesus as Son of God

Jesus never called himself God, nor did he use the expression "Son of God" about himself (this term appears only once in the Gospels, in John 10: 36, although his use was indirect on that occasion). He always called God "Father" when he addressed him directly. He employed the phrase "my Father" when speaking to others and making reference to God. He never used the expression "Our Father," except when teaching his disciples how they should pray. However, he did call himself "the Son."[61] Jesus addressed God as "Father" rather than as "God." This conduct shows his awareness of having a singular and highly familiar relationship with God.

Today, historical criticism allows us to be confident that Jesus himself made these statements and that they were not fabrications of the early Christian community. Jesus used them in a strong, transcendent sense. There are many elements to support these assertions.

The *jubilation hymn* (cf. Mt 11: 25–30) puts the Son on the same level as the Father regarding knowledge and revelation; therefore, his filiation cannot be understood only as adoptive or procreative.

In *the parable of the vineyard workers* (cf. Mt 21: 23–46; Mk 12: 1–2; Lk 20: 9–19; Is 5: 1–7), Jesus spoke overtly about his relationship with the Father. He showed that he was fully aware of his impending end, and referred to himself as the favored Son, the only one, the heir beloved by God.[62]

Jesus used the word *abba* when conversing with God. This was unusual, because the Hebrews normally used this term only in the context of family intimacy.[63] They never used it when referring to God. In the times of the Diaspora, it appears only twice as an invocation to God as Father (cf. Sir 23: 1, 4).[64] Although Jesus has been quoted as using this exact term only one time in the Gospels (cf. Mk 14: 36), scholars have demonstrated that, in all of his prayers, Jesus probably invoked the Father with this word.

As a matter of fact, there are reasons to believe that, on the twenty-one occasions when Jesus addressed God by calling him Father, he used this familiar Hebrew expression, subsequently translated into Greek as "father." J. Jeremias pointed out that in the Greek translation the vocative is sometimes used. On other occasions the nominative is used with the article, which thereby assumes the value of the vocative. This fluctuation led him to believe that in Jesus' day the word *abba* was used as vocative and as an emphatic nominative capable of acting as vocative.[65]

Finally, we may deduce from the *reaction of some of his contemporaries* that Jesus presented himself as Son of God and *equal* to God. If Jesus had spoken about himself as the adopted Son of God, he would have avoided many of his problems with the authorities. The expression "Son of God" was familiar in biblical tradition. In fact, heavenly beings—which in the Greek are called "angels"—were sometimes designated with that term (cf. Jb 1: 6; 2: 1), *people of God* (cf. Ex 4: 22; Dt 14: 1; Hos 11: 1; Jer 31: 9, 20), and *the just person* (cf. Sir 4: 10; Wis 2: 17–18).[66]

However, *Jesus presented himself as Son in a proper and true meaning, in a strong and transcendent sense as equal to God.* When he made this assertion, Jesus challenged monotheism as it was understood by the chief priests. They considered Jesus' claim nothing short of blasphemy. The contradistinction is well documented; John wrote that some people wanted to stone him for blasphemy (cf. Jn 10: 33). The synoptic Gospels point out that he was sentenced to death because he declared that he really was the Son of God (cf. Mt 26: 63–66; Mk 14: 61–64; Lk 22: 70–71). According to Luke, Caiaphas specifically sentenced him to death because he had declared himself Son of God. This was, in Caiaphas's eyes, blasphemy.[67]

According to John, the Jews had exhausted all arguments to sentence Jesus as a political agitator (cf. Jn 18: 28; 19: 6). Further, the procurator openly exposed the true reason for the chief priests' desire to sentence Jesus to death: where they said "We have a law, and by that law he ought to die, because he has made himself the Son of God" (Jn 19: 7). The force of their assertion must have been quite strong, and the Roman procurator surely understood it that way, because "when Pilate heard these words, he was the more afraid" (Jn 19: 8).[68]

B. Testimony with Actions: Jesus' Miracles as Signs of His Person

In the Gospel of St. John, the link between Jesus' claim that he was the Son of God and the miracles he performed is frequently highlighted. It may be considered a *leitmotif* of that Gospel.

> Jesus answered them, "I have shown you many good works from the Father; for which of these do you stone me?" The Jews answered him, "It is not for a good work that we stone you but for blasphemy; because you, being a man, make yourself God." Jesus answered them... "Do you say of him whom the Father consecrated and sent into the world, 'You are blaspheming,' because I said, 'I am the Son of God'? If I am not doing the works of my Father, then do not believe me; but if I do them, even though you do not believe me, believe the works, that you may know and understand that the Father is in me and I am in the Father." (Jn 10: 32–34, 36–38)

This link is the central argument in the polemic speeches of Jesus with his Jewish critics. St. John categorizes the three arguments accordingly:

1. *The assertion of his singular divine filiation*: "This was why the Jews sought all the more to kill him, because he not only broke the Sabbath but also called God his Father, making himself equal with God" (Jn 5: 18).

2. *His deeds*: "For the Father loves the Son, and shows him all that he himself is doing; and greater works than these will he show him, that you may marvel" (Jn 5: 20).

3. *The connection between his assertion and his deeds*: "You sent to John, and he has borne witness to the truth.... But the testimony which I have is greater than that of John; for the works which the Father has granted me to accomplish, these very works which I am doing, bear me witness that the Father has sent me" (Jn 5: 33, 36).

Jesus gave these explanations after he cured a paralyzed man on the Sabbath by the temple pool where the sick waited to be cured. These were miracles performed by Jesus. His greatest deeds were giving life back to the dead and his judgment of all humanity (cf. Jn 5: 21, 26, 27).

On the last day, upon seeing the apostles' hesitation, Jesus reasoned with them in the same way: "Do you not believe that I am in the Father and the Father in me? The words that I say to you I do not speak on my own authority; but the Father who dwells in me does his works. Believe me that I am in the Father and the Father in me; or else believe me for the sake of the works themselves" (Jn 14: 10–11). Based on his deeds, Jesus passed judgment on the incredulity of those who had rejected him: "If I had not come and spoken to them, they would not have sin; but now they have no excuse for their sin. He who hates me hates my Father also. If I had not done among them the works which no one else did, they would not have sin; but now they have seen and hated both me and my Father" (Jn 15: 22–24).

St. John tends to call these deeds of Jesus *signs* (cf. Jn 2: 11, 23; 4: 54; 20: 30–31). He uses the notion of sign in its broadest sense with the aim of showing how the glory of the incarnate Word was revealed (cf. Jn 1: 14).

In the fourth Gospel, besides showing their soteriological and mediating character, St. John takes advantage of the miracles to demonstrate the identity of Jesus. He examines these deeds from different perspectives, which can enlighten different aspects of the person of Jesus. These prodigies are salvific signs related to the sacramental economy and the divine banquet. They are signs of Jesus' divine power and human compassion to such a degree that through them one can discern the mystery of the unity of the divine and the human in Jesus. They are signs of the arrival of God's kingdom in Jesus, and they introduce us to an eschatological perspective, because with Jesus the last and decisive intervention of God in history has arrived.[69]

St. John shows how all of these perspectives merge in the fundamental and primary reality: *Miraculous deeds are signs of the glory of the Son.* "With the expression sign, he wants to indicate what is most essential in those deeds. They are demonstrations of the action of God in person, present in Christ, whereas the word *miracle* serves to point out the 'extraordinary' aspect that those events have compared to those that people have seen or heard others talk about."[70] Therefore, the miracles fulfilled by Jesus were not only signs that proved that he was the promised Messiah or Savior. Specifically, they demonstrated that he was the Son of God.

C. The Testimony of His Filial Obedience until His Death upon the Cross

Jesus' verbal testimony about his filiation was linked to his filial conduct. He also testified to his filiation by obedience to his Father. The filial relationship of Jesus with his Father was an internal union. It was manifested at the level of personal conduct. Jesus said that he was in the Father and the Father in him. Thus, it was impossible for Jesus to ever disobey what his Father wanted, even in the smallest matters. On the contrary, Jesus was constantly guided by the will of his Father in every one of his actions. John recalls hearing this message most clearly from the lips of his Master: "My judgment is just, because I seek not my own will but the will of him who sent me" (Jn 5: 30).

In the fourth Gospel, St. John highlights the importance of filial obedience in the life of Jesus (cf. Jn 4: 34; 5: 30; 8: 28). John's was not an exclusive observation; we also find it in the synoptic Gospels, although there this topic was not so highly developed (cf. Mt 10: 32–33; 11: 25; 15: 24; 18: 14; Mk 14: 36ff.; Lk 2: 49; 10: 21). St. John was, therefore, most attentive to this historical element in his writings.

This link between filiation and obedience has been proven from the historical standpoint. Jesus guided his life by the Father's will, even when this commitment implied pain and suffering. The three synoptic Gospels state that he prayed at Gethsemane, "Abba, Father, all things are possible to thee; remove this cup from me; yet not what I will, but what thou wilt" (Mk 14: 36; cf. Mt 26: 39; Lk 22: 42). In another context, St. John recorded Jesus saying, "Now is my soul troubled. And what shall I say? 'Father, save me from this hour'? No, for this purpose I have come to this hour. Father, glorify thy name" (Jn 12: 27–28).[71]

Jesus suffered in fulfillment of his Father's will, and this suffering has a special merit as a proof of his fidelity and obedience. "When you have lifted up the Son of man, then you will know that I am he, and that I do nothing on my own authority but speak thus as the Father taught me" (Jn 8: 28). "Precisely, this obedience to the Father, freely accepted, this submission to the Father, in contradistinction to the 'disobedience' of the first Adam, continues being the expression of the deepest relationship between the Father and the Son, since it is a reflection of the Trinitarian unity."[72]

By his death on the cross, Jesus faithfully obeyed the Father, giving a most definitive testimony—the highest possible—one of his divine filiation while he was on earth.[73] "Christ, revealer of the Father and revealer of himself as Son of the Father, died because he gave truthful testimony of his divine filiation until the end of his life."[74]

The cross is the ultimate expression of Jesus' testimony about his filiation. At the same time, it is the definitive proof of the truthfulness of his testimony, because he sacrificed his own life in fidelity to this truth. In St. John's writings, one cannot miss this link between the truthful and faithful testimony of Jesus and his death upon the cross.

III. Fullness of the Revelation of the Divinity of Jesus: His Glorious Resurrection

According to Jesus' own words, his Death and Resurrection are the ultimate and definitive reasons that he offered to people for believing in him (cf. Mt 12: 39–40; 16: 1–4; Lk 11: 29–30; Jn 2: 20–22).

Now, we will review how Jesus acted in this manner upon the apostles and the other people who had direct experience with him in his resurrected state (cf. Acts 1: 22; 10: 40–41). This analysis necessarily must be done by means of the testimony of these persons. This is because they are the only ones who can report about these events and about their capacity to lead a person to faith in Jesus.

A. The Resurrection of Jesus according to theTestimony of the Apostles: Historical Fact and Mystery

The center of the apostolic *kerygma* is the announcement of Jesus' Death and Resurrection. He died to redeem mankind from their sins and accomplished his Resurrection so as to lead mankind to a new life. *This announcement is presented as testimony because it is about the experience of a fact that truly happened.* The apostles really saw Jesus risen from the dead. They speak about the Resurrection of Jesus as a reality in which they believed, and, at the same time, they saw it as a reason for believing. On the one hand, they present themselves as *martyres tés anastaseos* (cf. Acts 1: 21–22; 2: 32; 4: 33; 5: 32; 10: 41; 13: 31) sent by Christ to share with all persons his authorized testimony concerning his saving Death and Resurrection and to call them to faith in him. On the other hand, they consider the Resurrection a definitive motive for belief. As St. Paul admonished the Corinthians, "if Christ has not been raised, then our preaching is in vain and your faith is in vain" (1 Cor 15: 14).[75]

In all of the New Testament passages about the Resurrection, one can see in a more or less obvious manner the same tripartite structured proposition:

1. Jesus has been crucified, has died and was buried.

2. God has raised him from the dead.

3. There are immediate eyewitnesses of these events.

When witnesses formulate the second element of this triad, they express themselves according to the nature of the context. They say that Jesus has been "alive in the spirit" (1 Pt 3: 18), he "died and lived again" (Rom 14: 9), is "exalted" (Phil 2: 9; Acts 2: 33; 5: 31), "glorified" (Jn 7: 39; 12: 16; 17: 1), and that he has "enter[ed] into his glory" (Lk 24: 26; cf. Heb 2: 10).

In the New Testament, it is understood that Resurrection cannot be limited to the realm of the holy and transcendent. It cannot be cut off from contact with human history. In New Testament expressions, the language and the sense of the assertions about resurrection allow us to understand that, on the one hand, it deals with a mysterious and transcendent phenomenon, and on the other hand, it is a real event. Regarding this second aspect, note that the verbs *egheiró* and *anistémi* express two common experiences of mankind: to rise (from the horizontal to the vertical position) and to awake (from sleep). These words are frequently used in the New Testament to indicate natural processes in the usual sense.

We read that Jesus "came and took her by the hand and lifted her up [*égheiren*]" (Mk 1: 31) and "she rose [*égherté*] and served him" (Mt 8: 15; cf. 8: 25; Mk 4: 39; 9: 27; Lk 8: 24).[76] The fact that the Evangelists and the apostles also applied such terminology to the Resurrection points to the idea of coming out from the condition of death (being a form of sleep), abandoning the position of death to come back to the position of life. (The idea of abandonment of the tomb is less certain.)[77] This teaching of the Evangelists and the apostles cannot be considered secondary or casual because these passages always speak about the Resurrection, Crucifixion, and Death of Jesus simultaneously. This obliges us to put all of these events on the same level. If the Death of Jesus is historical, his Resurrection must also be historical, despite the fact that his Resurrection includes a-historical aspects. According to the New Testament writers, it is equally true that the Death of Jesus contains a great mystery.

In summary, according to New Testament information, *we need to keep in mind elements of both mystery and history when we speak about Jesus' Resurrection*. These two aspects of the Resurrection are interrelated in the New Testament. The apostles found it quite difficult to express what they had witnessed, knowing that it was real.

B. Critical Discussion about the Historical Authenticity of the Information in the New Testament about the Resurrection

We will now study the historical authenticity of the New Testament information about the Resurrection. According to the proper methodology of this section, we will obey the following reasoning: Given that the apostles speak of the Resurrection as an historical and mysterious event, there should exist some way to verify the historicity of the Resurrection.[78]

The Resurrection, as it is presented by the Apostles, is unlike any other event in human history. For this reason, one must be precise with terms we use about the historicity of an event *that begins in history* (in the sense that the term *a quo* denotes Jesus of Nazareth dead and buried) but ends out of history (because the condition of the Resurrected Jesus does not remain the same). His Resurrection is not like Lazarus's but is eschatological and glorious.

As such, we consider that the *adjective historical may be applied to the Resurrection because it happened in a precise moment and a concrete place in history*. The event has left a trail in human history. This use of this concept implies that we have the potential to verify it; that it was not an invention, but a fact that really happened within space and time. In fact, such confirmation is possible thanks to some elements of the apostolic experience of the Resurrection, which can be analyzed according to the norms of historical criticism of the writings of the New Testament.

Rationalist critics of the nineteenth century considered the Resurrection an invention of the disciples of Jesus of Nazareth. Some authors, ignoring the historical and moral worth of the apostles' testimony, argued that the followers of Jesus stole his corpse and then dreamt up the doctrine of the Resurrection. Other thinkers appealed to psychological reactions. For example, the apparitions were inventions of the emotional agitation of the disciples, who would not resign themselves to the idea of their Messiah's ignominious death. Because of their fanatical love for Jesus, they still considered him alive, suffering a collective hallucination.

Previously, rationalists had abandoned these explanations as ungrounded and ridiculous. Still, they continued to posit that the Resurrection must be understood only as an act of faith, not as an historical act. Thus, Bultmann proposed an explanation for the Resurrection according to which it is not a "marvelous" event that goes outside the natural course of nature. It is, instead, an action of God in our favor that is known by us, or, better yet, believed by us. "The paschal event, if understood as Christ's Resurrection, is not an event that affects history. As an historical event we should consider the paschal faith of the first disciples."[79] According to Bultmann, we should restrict ourselves to the parameters that "Jesus has resurrected in the *kerygma*."[80] Bultmann's explanation depends on his general theological approach, particularly his fideism, and it deserves the same criticism that his philosophical-theological position invokes. "If we do not want to defend the thesis of the justification of faith, we have to admit…that it is likewise certain that faith is mainly founded on the apparitions of the Resurrection and on the testimony of the eyewitnesses."[81]

The difficulty defining the relationship between the Resurrection and history is due not only to the reality itself, but also to the difficulty in defining the relationship between faith and history. Given that this definition is ambiguous, the response about the historicity of Jesus' Resurrection will be so as well.

In recent years, some authors have posited the distinction between reality and history in the following manner: the Resurrection might be real in a certain way, but it still would not be an historical event. For example, C. Kannegiesser asserted faith in the reality of the physical Resurrection of Jesus, but he based this upon an "evangelical realism." He has done so in such a way that faith in the Resurrection would be reduced to simply believing that the disciples believed in it. Consequently, according to Kannegiesser, Jesus and the apostles invented the Resurrection.[82]

Before him, X. Léon-Dufour had denied the "reanimation" of Jesus' dead body because Jesus' Resurrection instead would have involved the assumption by Jesus' soul of the whole transformed universe. His resurrection is certainly real, but it is not an historical event.[83] E. Schillebeeckx joined these authors and denied the historicity of the empty tomb and the apparitions of the Resurrected one. According to Schillebeeckx, it would be more precise to speak about the "manifestation" of Jesus, an experience of grace, rather than about a Resurrection. Using this line of reasoning, the apparitions of the resurrected Christ should then be understood as a process of conversion carried out by the apostles. Therefore, there is no essential difference between the apostles' encounters with the resurrected Christ and the way that the other believers related themselves to him.[84]

1. Analysis of the Historicity of the Empty Tomb

There have been no reasonable doubts about the historical existence of the tomb since one was discovered in 1968. This tomb was made for a man who had been crucified in the surroundings of northern Jerusalem on the way to Nablus. At that time it was possible to bury an executed person in his own tomb and preserve his identity. Likewise, it was possible to ask the Roman authorities for the corpse for the purposes of burial. The Evangelists provide specific and precise references that are consistent with the legal and moral practices of that time. These writings include the name of the owner of the land and the tomb, specific details concerning the petition for the corpse made by St. Joseph of Arimathea to Pilate, the names of people who buried him, and indications of the official measures adopted by the Hebrews and Romans to guard the tomb. Furthermore, it seems unlikely that these writings were a forgery, because when they were written, some of the people who knew these very details were still alive and could have challenged the information contained in the narration, but this did not happen.[85]

The empty tomb is highly significant because it is a decisive element in knowing how the apostles would portray the Resurrection. According to them, it was impossible to speak about the Resurrection if the corpse was still in the tomb. What else did resurrection mean if not re-animation and re-vivification of the body, which, consequently, was not dead in the tomb and resurrected at the same time? Some contemporary authors have claimed that the reality of resurrection would not be compromised if the tomb either had not been empty or had not been found empty.[86] Many other scholars, who consider it incompatible with Hebrew mentality, documented the historical facts, and the mentality of those who lived during the events, have contested this position from the historical standpoint.[87]

The narration of the verification of the empty tomb is more explicit in Luke and John than in the other two Gospels, though in those writings the fact is not missing. It may be found in all of the Gospels precisely because of the need to defend this element of the Resurrection doctrine that some denied. This arose from a certain materialist mentality or because of Gnostic or Docetist deviations. The apostolic teaching compares Christian baptism to the Death and Resurrection of Jesus, as in Romans 6: 3–4. In this baptism, the body, submerged underwater (similar to the burial of a corpse, and so participating in the death of Jesus), emerges (similar to his Resurrection, in which he participates). This parallelism between baptism and the Resurrection allows us to assume that the former is considered as a reality affecting Jesus' historical body.

The discovery of the empty tomb is also important because it permits us to establish the event of the Resurrection in time and space: It was carried out in the tomb. It happened between the first and third day after the Crucifixion. It is not possible to go beyond this information using the tools of historical criticism, because no one saw Jesus at the moment of the Resurrection. All of the attempts to describe that moment have always been understood as literary inventions.[88]

The empty tomb is not a demonstration of the Resurrection. It is only an element that assures its concrete place in history and disposes the mind toward knowledge of it. "The empty tomb is not a 'proof' of Resurrection, but something that leads to it. It is like a sign of the Resurrection."[89] The idea of the Resurrection did not appear first, followed by the idea of the empty tomb. On the contrary, the empty tomb was found first, and then the people sought an explanation. As a matter of fact, the women and the apostles were amazed and disconcerted by the empty tomb. Some Evangelists point out the women's fear (cf. Mk 16: 8) and that of the apostles (cf. Jn 20: 19). They are faced with an enigma. They can think only that the corpse has been stolen (cf. Jn 20: 2, 13, 15).

Other elements prove the historicity of the empty tomb. In the New Testament, there is not the least indication that the disciples venerated the tomb of Jesus. According to the faith and devotion of these people for their Master, some type of veneration and cult would have been organized from which we would have picked up some evidence that the corpse had been in the tomb which had been left intact.[90] Moreover, all references to the organization of the care of the tomb or corpse, as was Jewish custom, are missing. In contrast, the discovery of the empty tomb has always appeared in the evangelic narration of the Resurrection, although not always in an identical manner.

Certain scholars have claimed that the apostles were not emotionally stable enough to protect the tomb. Jesus' adversaries also failed to keep proper watch over the tomb because they considered the case closed after the crucifixion on Calvary. Finally, it has been proposed that the watch set over the tomb was not legitimate according to Hebrew law. From the critical and literary standpoint, some have objected that the whole narration of the empty tomb depends upon Mark—i.e., there is only one source that provides some reason to believe in the historicity to the empty tomb.

In response to these objections, we should mention that the Gospels do not say that the apostles went to the tomb by their own initiative to see if Jesus had risen from the dead, and whether the tomb was empty or not. The women went to the tomb to anoint the corpse. They had no intention of verifying whether or not his corpse was still in the tomb. Rather, it seems that they did not even consider this possibility, as their surprise shows (cf. Jn 20: 11; Mk 16: 1). The women were acting according to well-documented Jewish custom. In the Talmudic treatise about death, burial, and mourning, *Semahot* explains that not only can one go to a person's tomb to mourn for him, but that one must go "until the third day" after his death.[91] John informs us that Martha objects to Jesus when he commands the stone to be removed from Lazarus's tomb: "Lord, by this time there will be an odor, for he has been dead four days" (Jn 11: 39). John himself points out that with the corpse of Jesus everything was done "as is the burial custom of the Jews" (Jn 19: 40).

Regarding sources, it has been proven that all evangelic narration about the empty tomb cannot be traced to a single source. The contents of John 20: 1–3 and older texts are demonstrably independent from Mark.[92] Matthew provides details that are not contained in Mark: He speaks of the sealed tomb that was surveyed by temple guards, as well as their corrupt collaboration with the chief priests of the Jews, and how that corruption affected public opinion (cf. Mt 28: 15).[93]

We should take into account Matthew's apologetic intention. The Evangelist takes issue with the misinformation that the disciples had gone to steal the corpse at night while the guards slept (cf. Mt 28: 11–15). The explanation of the supposed burglary in the general context of the Resurrection obliges us to consider it an historical reality that was organized by the chief priests. To confront this gossip directly and as part of our apologetic work, we need to be able to verify that the tomb was truly empty.

The starting point for this dialogue with the Jews lies in the fact of the empty tomb and the disappearance of the corpse. Should the basis for this dialogue be denied, the whole issue becomes absurd. On the other hand, there are also reasons to believe that the inhabitants of Jerusalem knew of the disappearance of the corpse (the empty tomb). Otherwise, the disciples' enemies would not have spoken so openly about the burglary of the corpse. They would have been able to accuse and unmask the early Christians as shameless braggarts by showing everyone the corpse of the crucified rabbi.

2. Analysis of the Historicity of the Apparitions

Next, we will see that the historicity of apparitions can be reasonably demonstrated by applying the aforementioned criteria.

The references to the Resurrection are presented in very different contexts and in a variety of manners: speeches (cf. Acts 2: 22–36; 3: 12–26; 4: 8–12; 5: 29–32; 10: 34–43; 13: 16–42; 17: 22–32), professions of faith joined to the baptismal liturgy (cf. Acts 2: 38; 8: 12; 10: 48), liturgical hymns (cf. Eph 5: 14; Phil 2: 6–11; 1 Tm 3: 16), and other narrations.[94]

They are in substantial agreement in their statements concerning the Resurrection, particularly in its historical aspect. According to the rules of historical criticism, such variety combined with substantial concordance reasonably excludes the possibility of deception.

The differences among diverse narrations of apparitions, instead of proving their falsehood, confirm their authenticity. In fact, they are not true contradictions, but differences that admit a plausible explanation. These differences prove that the authors / writers have not bothered to elaborate unified texts in agreement with each other but have instead depended directly on the immediate sources who narrated the events to them.[95]

Experts in the psychology of legal testimony have demonstrated the complexity of the processes that a person undergoes when serving as a witness. This process cannot be understood as a photographic reproduction of an objective fact. It is the result of multiple factors derived partially from the objective fact. The entire process is affected by the personality of the one who gives and receives testimony.[96]

If to testify is essentially to refer to a fact directly observed, testimony always and undoubtedly entails a perception. Clearly, such a perception cannot be completely adequate for physical, physiological, and psychological reasons. When there are different witnesses, they often do not completely coincide in what they have seen. Among the several factors for these differences, the one called "distribution of attention" is of great importance. When attention is concentrated on a certain object, many other stimuli pass unnoticed or remain imprecise. Hence, they do not necessarily surface in testimony while the elements that have been most attentively observed and perceived assume the most important and privileged positions. Furthermore, an event that is incidentally observed is not remembered in the same way as a reality voluntarily observed.

In summary, the presence of small differences among the witnesses of the Resurrection does not undermine the factual credibility. Instead of diminishing its credibility, this reality reinforces it. These divergences must necessarily appear in declarations of different persons when they speak about events that happened some time ago. The events surrounding the Resurrection were particularly susceptible—because of their mysterious character—to being seen from different viewpoints.

> Disagreement among these witnesses about the main circumstances, that is, about the time, place, or people who are usually seen would undermine the credibility of the evangelic narrations. If they do not coincide in such basic things, it can be decided only that they are individual testimonies referring to different facts.... On the other hand, if the disagreement refers to things not affecting the substance of the fact, such as the state of the weather, decoration of a house or similar things, then the disagreement does not harm the worth of the testimony. This is because men do not usually pay attention to such details and easily forget them. Furthermore, disagreement in those circumstances makes the testimony more believable, as St. John Chrysostom has observed.[97] Obviously, if the writers agreed in every single detail, one would be suspicious that they had come to agreement before.[98]

Application of the criterion of discontinuity proves that, according to the normal laws of psychology and of human creativity, it is not possible to explain the Resurrection as the fruit of a psychological reaction of the disciples or as a religious invention attributed to them.[99] Three great manifestations of discontinuity, at least, can be determined:

1. As it happened, Jesus' Resurrection did not correspond to the mentality of the Israelites of that time.

2. The Gospels point out the incredulity of the apostles upon being informed about Jesus' Resurrection by the women.

3. The cultural and religious education of the apostles did not allow them to create a religious doctrine like the one that was spread about Jesus and his Resurrection.

First of all, the apostles could not contemplate the Resurrection of only one person before the events that would end history. There was no place for this reality in the disciples' mentality, even though they considered him the Messiah. Given the abject failure of the messianic program as they had imagined it, this prospect would have seemed even more unbelievable to them.

It seems most logical that the apostles would have ideas similar to their contemporaries about the Resurrection. Within this ideology, the believers expected a resurrection at the end of time, as a consequence of messianic intervention, and without individual anticipation. Such an event had all the required characteristics, so they considered it improbable and even impossible that it would take place in the near future. According to their mentality, eschatological resurrection—the one preached by Jesus—was not a simple revivification. It was reserved to the end of times. Thus was pointed out in the few passages of the Old Testament that dealt with this issue. The Pharisees taught this in their debates with the Sadducees (cf. Mk 12: 13–23). Consequently, the eschatological resurrection of an individual, even the Messiah, would have indicated that the end of time had arrived. The apostles saw that, despite everything they witnessed, the world continued existing as before.[100]

One can ask up to what point the apostles could have foreseen the Resurrection, based on Jesus' teaching about the resurrection of the dead (cf. Lk 14: 12–14; 16: 19–31; Jn 5: 1–18) and his prophecies regarding himself. One may observe that the disciples did not understand Jesus' teachings about his Resurrection before the fact, even though they had preached it everywhere. The apostles' incomprehension of the triple prophecy of Jesus about the end of his earthly activities included the reference to the Resurrection that, although misunderstood, was very succinct. It was not easy for them to apply the concept of "resurrection" to their Master Jesus, despite their having seen how he brought back to life the daughter of the widow of Naim and their friend Lazarus.[101]

In his Gospel, Luke occasionally stresses the individual aspect of the Resurrection, according to Jesus' teachings. Still, the impression that one gets of the expectations of the apostles about Jesus' Resurrection is always the same.[102]

The second manifestation of discontinuity may be found in the disciples' difficulty in accepting news of the Resurrection from the women. All four Evangelists recall this circumstance (cf. Mk 16: 9–11, 14;

Lk 24: 10–12, 22–24; Jn 20: 1–10, 24–25). We should consider this information historically accurate because the demonstration of this incredulity in view of the news of the Resurrection directly contradicts the teachings and beliefs of the primitive Church. Such a remarkable confession of incredulity manifested by those who presided over the community of faithful did not do the apostles much credit and could even have caused them some internal authority problems with those who had believed more easily.

The third manifestation is found in the disproportion between the human condition of the apostles and their preaching of the Resurrection. The first people who were conscious of this disproportion seem to be the apostles themselves. In fact, all the details about their shortcomings have arrived to us through their own testimony. The apostles and Evangelists did not hesitate to reveal their defects and, on some occasions, specifically confessed this disproportion (cf. 1 Cor 1: 27–29; 2: 1, 4; 2 Cor 11: 6; 12: 10). Others who knew and saw the disciples were conscious of their limitations. Having said this, we should recognize that several passages of the Acts of the Apostles give testimony to the heroism of these same individuals. For example, in the Sanhedrin: "Now when they saw the boldness of Peter and John, [they] perceived that they were uneducated, common men" (Acts 4: 13). The Greek text uses the term *idiótai*, which indicates persons without qualifications, formation, or culture. The contemporary religious elite, therefore, believed that Jesus' apostles lacked the cultural, intellectual, social, economic, or religious training necessary to create and spread the doctrine of Jesus throughout the world, particularly one that included the teaching concerning his Resurrection from the dead.

The substantial concordance of New Testament information about the Resurrection combined with incidental differences requires an explanation. Contemporary scholars find this explanation in the existence of a *paradosis* (tradition) identically present in all the communities who believed in the Resurrected one.

St. Paul makes explicit reference to the *paradosis* in his initial letters, which, we know, are the first writings of the New Testament.

A critical-literary analysis of 1 Corinthians 15: 3–7 shows that those verses are a formula used long before Paul employed it. It is not strange to find formulas in the Pauline letters that were already part of the evangelization or liturgy (cf. Rom 10: 9–10; 1 Cor 11: 23–25; Eph 5: 14; Phil 2: 6–11; 1 Tm 3: 16). His introductory reference before offering the formula proves it: "I delivered to you…what I also received" (1 Cor 15: 3). Another proof lies in the fact that the words and expressions that are in Pauline writings are found only in formal and traditional texts. They have a concise style with parallel phrases without long explanations. According to the nearly unanimous judgment of exegetes, the text of 1 Corinthians 15: 3–5 represents the oldest tradition, something akin to an original form of the Gospel prior to Paul and the writing of the Gospels.[103]

This antiquity and universality of the *paradosis* excludes the possibility of a progressive creation and elaboration of the fact of the Resurrection by the disciples. The writers of the New Testament made a tremendous effort to express that event, showing respect for its great richness and trying to make it as clear as possible for the mentalities of the different peoples to whom it was announced. They also worked particularly hard to better understand all of the theoretical and practical implications of the mystery of the Resurrected one.[104] Nevertheless, there is no trail of the genesis of this concept. It was always spoken about in the same manner. This synthetic and always substantially identical announcement is precisely what constitutes the *paradosis* of which St. Paul speaks.[105]

Of late, some authors have suggested the hypothesis that the Resurrection initially was nothing more than an image, myth, or interpretative plan with which the importance of Jesus for his disciples was expressed. Only later was the Resurrection formally "historicized" (in other words, presented as a historical event).[106] Others hold that some groups in the primitive Church spoke solely about elevation or exultation.[107] These hypotheses have no support in the relevant documentation, which does not give the slightest indication of any process that can be considered a progressive development of the idea of the Resurrection. The documentation is all to the contrary, as we have demonstrated. In every text—and some of them are very old—the writers always speak about the Resurrection as an event that historically happened.[108]

If the concept of the Resurrection was not progressively created, might we speculate that it was created over a short period of time? Was it due to an almost immediate creation, chronologically speaking? That is not a possibility given what we have seen when the criterion of discontinuity is applied.

> The profession of faith that we make in the Creed when we proclaim that Jesus Christ "was resurrected from the dead on the third day" is based on evangelical texts that, for their part, pass on to us and make known the earliest teachings of the apostles. These sources come from that faith in the Resurrection that is, from the beginning, a conviction based on a fact. It is a real event, and not a myth or "conception." It is not an idea concocted by the apostles and spread about by the early Christian community gathered around the apostles in Jerusalem as a tonic to soothe their disappointment after their defeat on Calvary. The apostles and disciples did not fabricate the Resurrection (and they clearly were totally incapable of doing so). There is no evidence of any personal or group exultation that could have led them to speculate about an expected event and somehow artfully project it onto public opinion as reality.

> There is no clue of any creative process within the psychological-sociological-literary order, even in the primitive community of believers or among the authors of the first centuries. The apostles were the first to believe, and not without strong initial resistance, that Christ had been raised from the dead. Simply, they lived the Resurrection as a real event of which they were to become personally convinced when they encountered Christ living again on various occasions before his Ascension into heaven. Subsequent Christian generations have accepted that testimony, thereby trusting the apostles and the rest of the disciples as credible witnesses. The Christian faith in Christ's Resurrection is linked, therefore, to concrete facts with precise historical dimensions.[109]

C. Resurrection: The Highest Point of Historical Revelation and the Definitive Sign of Faith

From the Gospels one can understand that the apostles did not immediately arrive at complete faith in Jesus. They did so only little by little, as if they were on a journey. The final step seems to have been their encounter with the resurrected Christ. Now, we will look at the characteristics of the pre-Paschal and Paschal faith of the apostles so as to obtain a better understanding of how the Resurrection was and is a reason to believe in Jesus of Nazareth.

1. The Pre-Paschal Faith of the Apostles: Adherence to Jesus as Messiah and Son of God

Schürmann, Jeremias, some members of the school of Uppsala, and other contemporary scholars have demonstrated the reality of the disciples gathering around Jesus, which implies a certain faith in him. Therefore, from that historical viewpoint, the disciples certainly had faith in Jesus even before his Death and Resurrection.

On the other hand, the apostles doubtlessly also returned after the Resurrection to Jesus' words and gestures, so as to better understand them. The question is this: What exactly was the content of disciples' faith before the Death and Resurrection of their Master? From the outset, it must be admitted that the historian cannot hope to reach a completely satisfactory answer to this question. Nevertheless, at least a partial answer may be obtained. Furthermore, it is possible to make some observations about the quality of the pre-Paschal faith.

It is without doubt that many contemporaries of Jesus really considered him a great teacher and a prophet sent by God. The apostles accepted him as Messiah and Savior of Israel. Regarding these two points, we can conclude that they were totally convinced. However, in the other two aspects of utmost importance, things were not so clear: i.e., the manner of his messianism and the divine filiation of Jesus. Regarding the former, the apostles did not understand their Master's stated intention to save mankind and establish the kingdom through his sacrifice upon the cross. They imagined that there would be some politically based messianic intervention. This explains their undeniable discouragement following Jesus' Crucifixion. Regarding the latter, we need to recognize that their faith in Jesus' divine filiation was weak. Here again, they were confused by the events of the Passion and Death of Jesus.

Some authors believe that the expression "Son of God" is exclusively post-Paschal and precisely expresses the faith of the disciples after the Resurrection. Some have accepted a possible use of the title during Jesus' historical life,[110] while others deny such a possibility.[111] Other authors think that this title was applied to Jesus during his lifetime, thus expressing a true and proper faith in his singular divine filiation. This idea would be strengthened and asserted following the Easter events.[112]

From the standpoint of the historical critic, it is clear, as we have seen, that Jesus represented himself as the Son of God and that the chief priests and many others understood the scope of his assertion.

As to what extent the apostles and some disciples recognized Jesus' claims of divine filiation, several pre-Paschal confessions have been preserved in the Gospels (cf. Mt 14: 33; 16: 16; 27: 54; Jn 1: 49; 11: 27). The present development of historical criticism does not allow us to further clarify this issue. On the other hand, specialists continue to search for solutions to this question by investigating the disciples and the attitudes of the apostles.[113] It is hoped that this path of inquiry will eventually shed some light on this point.

As we have previously seen, Jesus presented himself as God's envoy with authority that placed him above all the prophets and even above the law. He declared himself "Lord of the Sabbath" and said that the temple was "his Father's house." It was precisely this claim to a higher authority that precipitated his mortal combat with the chief priests, scribes, and Pharisees. Historical analysis shows that Jesus would not abdicate this authority because it was intimately joined to his deepest understanding of himself. Therefore, to be a true disciple of Jesus implied acceptance of this fundamental claim. It meant believing in him as Son of God and as supreme Master as well.

Matthew and Mark point out the lack of faith of so many people, which led Jesus to sternly reproach the inhabitants in the cities by the lake. John spoke about this phenomenon during the Eucharistic speech at the synagogue in Capernaum (cf. Jn 6: 66–70). Jesus also suffered lack of understanding and abandonment following his ministry in Galilee. Despite all of this, his disciples did not back down and persevered in following him—even though they faced serious risks and tests (cf. Lk 22: 28). They accepted all of his teachings, even the difficult and mysterious ones, and all of his wishes. They considered him the supreme Teacher and believed in him as the Son of the living God.

2. Paschal Faith: Absolute Personal Adherence to Jesus as the Messiah and Son of the Living God

The experience of the Resurrection acted upon the two weak points of the pre-Paschal faith of the apostles. They became aware that the kingdom was to be established through the death of Jesus (cf. Lk 24: 27, 32, 45) and they firmly believed that Jesus received life from God for all eternity. Consequently, we find that their post-Paschal faith is substantially continuous with their pre-Paschal one, while, at the same time, it does have a certain novelty to it.

Contemporary exegetes have highlighted the fact that the confession of Jesus as Lord (*kyrios* in Greek, *mari* in Aramaic) needs to be put in perspective with the experience of the Resurrection. It is possible that even before this happened, the disciples had addressed Jesus with that title. They followed him as their Master, and the title *mari*, besides being applied to gods and kings, had a broader use. It was also used for important personages as an expression of respect.[114] Nevertheless, the use of the title within its entire Christological scope is not solely an evolution or enhancement of the Aramaic rabbi, or *mari*. It is linked to the Paschal experience, the only one that permitted the apostles to know that Jesus was glorified and to recognize him as absolute Lord of life and death, as Judge of the living and dead. Accordingly, they can applaud him with the formula of biblical tradition from the Covenant: "My Lord and my God!" (Jn 20: 28; cf. 1 Kgs 18: 39; Jer 31: 18).[115]

Recently, critics have disregarded W. Bousset's theory that the cult of Jesus developed as a consequence of the disciples' immersion in Hellenistic culture, specifically in Antioch, where they imitated certain Oriental religions.[116] Alternatively, scholars have shown that the application of the title of *Lord* for Jesus is linked to his Resurrection and *parousia*.[117] According to the Hebrew mentality of his time, and therefore his apostles' mentality, overcoming death—as they saw Jesus had done—was equivalent to overcoming everything and everybody. It was the same as being above everything and everyone. Life is the reality that comprehends everything—the ultimate definitive value. To be is to live and to live is to be. Hence, *overcoming death implied possessing the secret of life*, of being "the Author of life" (Acts 3: 15) as St. Peter would say, of being "the Lord of eternal life."[118]

Contemporary exegesis has also highlighted the connection—as evidenced by the apostles—between the Resurrection and the filiation of Jesus.[119] Among the many texts, one example lies in the beginning of the Letter to the Romans: "his Son, who was descended from David according to the flesh and designated Son of God in power according to the Spirit of holiness by his resurrection from the dead, Jesus Christ our Lord" (Rom 1: 3–4).

> This means that, since the first moment of his human conception and birth (from David's descent), Jesus was the eternal Son of God who made himself Son of Man. But, in the Resurrection, that divine filiation was manifested in all its plenitude, with the power of God who, by the work of the Holy Spirit, gave life back to Jesus (cf. Rom 8: 11) and constituted him in the glorious state of *"Kyrios"* (cf. Phil 2: 9–11; Rom 14: 9; Acts 2: 36). Consequently, Jesus deserves a new messianic title, along with due recognition, cult, and glory to the eternal name of Son of God (cf. Acts 13: 33; Heb 1: 1–5; 5: 5).[120]

The faith of the apostles in Jesus as Son of God, equal to the Father, definitely matured after the Resurrection. Jesus manifested his humanity to them, the glory of his divine life eternally received from the Father (cf. Jn 1: 14–18). John Paul II has commented about this concept several times in his teachings in the *Catechism* about the Creed. "By the light of Jesus' deeds and words, it becomes clearer and clearer that he is the true Son of God. Due to the rigid monotheism of the time, this was a truth that was very difficult for his Jewish contemporaries to accept. Our teachings in the *Catechism* about Jesus will now enter precisely into this truth that determines the originality of the Gospel and the whole of Christianity as a religion founded on faith in the Son of God, that made himself man for us."[121] Necessarily, this "faith in the divine filiation of Christ is formed step by step by the revelation of the Father, in the consciousness of the apostles.... After the Resurrection it acquired a much greater strength."[122] He has explained the concept saying, "Jesus of Nazareth is the Messiah announced in the Old Covenant. The Messiah (which means Christ)—real man (the "Son of Man")—is, in his same Person, Son of God, true God. This truth about him emerges from the body of works and words that definitively reach their climax in the Paschal event of Death on a Cross and his Resurrection."[123]

Nevertheless, John Paul II cautions:

> "it is necessary that we take heed that all written testimonies about this issue have come from the period that followed Christ's departure from this earth. Certainly, these documents carry direct knowledge about the actual events that are reflected within them: the Death on the Cross and Resurrection of Christ.... At the same time, nevertheless, these written testimonies also speak about the entire activity of Jesus, about his whole life, beginning from his birth and childhood. We can see that these documents testify to a definite fact of the faith of the apostles and therefore the faith of the very first community of the Church. It had already been formed in the pre-Paschal stage of the life and ministry of Christ, to be subsequently manifested in a powerful manner following Pentecost."[124]

Because of all this, we are obliged to admit that apparitions are a gift of revelation.[125]

> It is in the Resurrection that "in him the whole fullness of deity dwells bodily," *is revealed* (Col 2: 9, cf. Col 1: 19). Thus, the Resurrection "completes" the manifestation of the meaning of

the Incarnation. That is why we can say that the Resurrection is the plenitude of Revelation. Therefore, as we have said, the Resurrection lies within the center of the Christian faith and the preaching of the Church.[126]

In the oldest formulas, Jesus' *Resurrection is always attributed to the Father*: "God raised him up" (Acts 2: 24).[127] If Jesus had provided definitive proof of being Son while obeying the will of his Father even to death, death on a cross, Yahweh now gave proof of really being Jesus' Father by bringing him back to life.[128] Christ's Death on the Cross for love and obedience was the definitive proof of filiation offered by the pre-Paschal Jesus. The Resurrection is the great definitive proof offered by Yahweh of his unique and exclusive paternity toward Jesus.

3. From Pre-Paschal to Paschal Faith: The Resurrection as a Definitive Sign

Having seen how the apostles understood the filiation and divinity of their Master by means of the glorious Resurrection, we will examine how this guided them to believe in Jesus as Lord, Son of God and saving Messiah. We may observe this in two fundamental ways. On the one hand, the Resurrection represented a divine confirmation of Jesus' words. On the other hand, in apparitions, the Resurrected Jesus presented himself as the great and definitive sign of faith in him.

As John Paul II has observed, the classical reasoning of Christian apologetics has maintained the validity of the Resurrection:

> The Resurrection constituted in the first place *a confirmation of everything that Christ himself had "done and taught."* It was the divine seal put upon his words and his life. He himself had pointed out to his disciples and adversaries this definitive sign of his truth. The angel of the tomb recalled this truth to the women the morning of "the first day after the Sabbath": "he has risen, as he said" (Mt 28: 6). If this word and promise of his was revealed as the truth, the rest of his words and promises also possess the power of truths that would not pass, as he himself had

proclaimed. "Heaven and earth will pass away, but my words will not pass away" (Mt 24: 35, Mk 13: 31, Lk 21: 33). Nobody could have imagined or wished for a more authoritative, stronger, more determined proof than his Resurrection from the dead. Every truth, even the most unattainable ones for the human mind, find their justification in the sphere of reason, if the resurrected Christ has given the definitive proof, promised by him, of his divine authority.[129]

Jesus himself pointed out the value of the sign of his Resurrection when he compared himself to Jonah, the prophet who was a sign for the Ninevites.

An evil and adulterous generation seeks for a sign; but no sign shall be given to it except the sign of the prophet Jonah. For as Jonah was three days and three nights in the belly of the whale, so will the Son of man be three days and three nights in the heart of the earth. (Mt 12: 39–40; cf. 16: 1–4)[130]

The Resurrected Jesus was a sign first and foremost for the apostles. The case of the Apostle Thomas is paradigmatic. "Unless I see…I will not believe," he states (Jn 20: 25). After his encounter with the Resurrected Jesus, he recognizes him as "My Lord and my God!" (Jn 20: 28). Then Jesus says to him, "Have you believed because you have seen me? Blessed are those who have not seen and yet believe" (Jn 20: 29). The relation between "seeing" and "believing," appears to express the role of the Paschal experience in the journey toward faith.[131] When commenting on this event, St. Thomas Aquinas, following St. Gregory the Great's lead, observed that the Apostle Thomas *saw one thing and believed another*. But, the thing seen and the thing believed in cannot be two completely different realities, because then the link between both would be missing and there would be no logic or consequences. In fact, doubting Thomas saw the victorious and glorious humanity assumed by the eternal Son and believed in it.[132]

The Paschal faith of the apostles is grounded upon evidence. They saw the glory of the Son of God who overcame death in his humanity. They believed that he is the Lord who made himself man. In the experience of the Resurrection, it is possible to recognize that the apostles knew the fundamental plan of the biblical sign: partial experience of a reality, read by the light of faith that leads us to accept and believe the totality of that reality.

As in other biblical signs, the Paschal experience was a faith experience not only because it led to faith, but also because it required the exercise of faith. That is why it has been said of the apostles, "after the Resurrection, they saw the living Christ with a faith that had eyes (*oculata fides*)."[133]

In the continuity of the Paschal Jesus with the earthly Jesus, the apostles perceived the deep unity linking the Cross and the Resurrection. They saw two sides of the same coin, two actions in a process carried out to the very limits of love.

On three occasions, St. John quotes the Resurrected Jesus as greeting others by saying: "Peace be with you" (Jn 20: 19, 21, 26; cf. Lk 24: 36). He thereby stresses the affection and understanding of the Resurrected one for his apostles (cf. Lk 24: 50–52). The resurrected one's words of reproach to the apostles always refer to their incredulity at his victory, never to their cowardly behavior during the Passion and Crucifixion. The experience of the Resurrection in itself conveys—such as it has been transmitted to us by the main characters—the experience of the complete and radical pardon from God of human infidelities and sins (cf. Jn 20: 22–23; 21: 15–19; 1 Cor 15: 8–10; Gal 1: 13–24).[134]

Furthermore, the Easter experience constitutes a definitively satisfactory response to the desire for eternity and immortality (which is present in every person), a yearning that somehow synthesizes all human wishes. People experience the passing of time that destroys everything: health, beauty, money, fame, intelligence, strength. Time devours happiness itself when it has been reached after no little sacrifice. Despite this experience, people insist on trying to live forever by trying to extend moments of joy and love. Moreover, man vainly seeks to surpass his own limits, to extend his own consciousness to a total perception of the transcendent realities that he can hardly make out with his limited human capacity. This desire or need is sometimes transformed into longing, nostalgia, melancholy, apathy, or nausea.

By means of the experience of the Resurrection, Jesus offered the apostles the opportunity to know in advance what the Resurrection he promised to those who believe in him would be like (cf. Jn 5: 21, 28–29; 6: 48–51, 54–58; 11: 25–26; Col 1: 18). This was a more than satisfactory answer to the final and definitive existential human demand. The experience of the Resurrection was the experience of eternal and eschatological life already present in the Resurrected Jesus. Unlike utopian doctrines that promise a future of happiness without historical antecedents, the apostles' experience of Jesus' Resurrection was an intra-historical perception of the meta-historical glory promised by him to all of his faithful. In the encounter of St. Paul with Jesus on the road to Damascus, "Paul is the beneficiary of a revelation (apocalypse) from the Son of God, from the heavenly Messiah.... His vision brings him, in person, an anticipation of the *parousia* that will enable him to announce it to the pagan world."[135]

CHAPTER 13

THE CREDIBILITY OF THE CHURCH AND HER TESTIMONY ABOUT JESUS OF NAZARETH

The credibility of Christianity presents a double Christological and ec-clesiological aspect that requires analysis in two distinct sections. This is because each one of these aspects has its own proper, interrelated characteristics.[1]

The Christological moment always focuses on the issue of how to justify faith in Christ as the Messiah, the Lord and Son of God. This is certainly the ultimate issue in the credibility of Christianity. Christian apologists have followed different strategies to achieve this common goal. They have attempted to understand Jesus by means of the original testimony because it is not possible to respond to questions about Christ's cred-ibility without evaluating the human testimonies about him. These testimonies are the only intra-historical means for us to reach Jesus.

We have seen how the Incarnate Word made himself credible to his contemporaries. We studied this question mainly using written tes-timony about Jesus in the New Testament. Because of the force of the historical value of the New Testament, the credibility of Jesus is be-lieved to this day. Still, there are other ways to testify about Christ that are worthy of attention because of their quality and efficacy.

We will now study the testimony about Christ in its complete expres-sion. We will not stop with the written testimony of the New Testament;

we will examine the testimony that the Church renders to her Lord throughout the centuries, in many ways and on many occasions (cf. Heb 1: 1). It is a testimony with multiple forms (with his words, deeds, and entire life), which has made Jesus credible for over twenty centuries.

We will pass from this Christological moment of credibility to the ecclesiastical moment. By taking this step, we do not mean to forget or abandon the Christocentrality of the ecclesiastical moment. Quite to the contrary, this moment is rooted in Christocentrism and extends and enriches it.[2] It takes this centrality into account when passing on revelation and faith.

"Christianity as an historical phenomenon has an ecclesiastical form. Men find Christianity in the Church and as the Church. That is why they ask the Church to explain the word that she proclaims, the sacraments that she celebrates, the existential sense of the Gospel that she expresses."[3] Therefore, the credibility of Christianity is inseparably linked to the credibility of the Church as a religious group.

The credibility of the testimony of the Church and her reason for believing in her life, doctrine, structure, and activity depend upon God's action in her and through her. That is to say, *she is a sign and an intra-historical instrument of Christ,* Son of God and Lord.

After studying the Church's testimony about Christ and her character as his sign, we will conclude our study with the intimate connection of those two aspects (she gives testimony because she is a sign, and she is a sign because she testifies) and a consequence of utmost importance from the theoretical and practical point of view. The Church's credibility—her testimony and her status as a sign of Christ—is predicated upon the testimony of all of her members and upon her identification with Christ. Further, the Holy Spirit pays irrefutable testimony to Christ the Lord in the Church and on behalf of the Church.[4]

Testimony and *sign* are functional terms that lead us to the realization that the Church in Christ is a mystery of the communion of people with God, thanks to the presence and action of the Holy Spirit.[5] We may, therefore, understand that the Christological moment and the ecclesiastical movement concerning the credibility of Christianity are inseparable. They are as inseparable as Christ and his Church through the action of the unique and same Spirit in the new and eternal covenant.

I.   The Testimony of the Church about Jesus of Nazareth

In this section we will see that the Church's testimony about Jesus of Nazareth is credible. To this end, we will analyze her testimony according to the rules that establish the authenticity and veracity of human testimony, rules that apply to three aspects of testimony: legal, moral, and theological. From this triple perspective we will study the worth (credibility) of the Church's testimony about Jesus' words and deeds, specifically his Death and Resurrection. This study, moreover, offers an additional benefit. It makes the words and gestures of Christ—particularly his glorious Resurrection—efficacious for people in today's world. This can be considered authentic because the Church, with valid testimony, has said it. For obvious reasons, our study will differentiate between the testimony of the apostles and that of subsequent Christian generations.

A. Moral and Theological Worth of the Testimony of the Apostles

We touched on the testimony of the apostles when we dealt with the Resurrection. Yet, we considered it only from the historical standpoint. We will now consider the moral and theological aspects of their testimony.

1. Moral Worth of the Apostolic Testimony about Jesus

From this view, the apostles' testimony is sincere and convincing because it is personally and socially consistent.

It is *personally* consistent because one can prove that the apostles lived according to what they said and preached about Jesus. The apostles not only spoke about Jesus' Resurrection; they considered all the theoretical and practical consequences of that event and taught others to do the same. That they preached Jesus in the midst of tremendous challenges and troubles without ever waning in their efforts provides eloquent witness. They even gave their lives in this work; they sealed their testimony about the crucified and resurrected Jesus with their own blood (cf. Acts 12: 2).

The apostles' unity in life between doctrine and practice that they carried out—even to the point of accepting pain and death—is a proof of the sincerity and honor of their testimony. Obviously, Jesus had changed their lives. Moreover, it is the best proof and, in a certain way, the only valid one, for in regard to existential conviction and moral conduct, the cornerstone of the truth of one's own theories is acting on them effectively and consistently.[6] Since fanaticism is not observable in the lives or writings of these men, only the experience of the resurrected Jesus can serve to explain, from a moral and psychological standpoint, such a unanimous and coherent testimony on the apostles' part.

It is *socially* consistent because their conduct and doctrine were not in conflict with the common ethical values and assumptions of the people among whom they lived. The texts of the New Testament and some events of the time demonstrate that the apostles were not considered emotionally disturbed by their contemporaries. Rather, people tended to view the highly demanding apostolic doctrine and conduct as something in complete accordance with the dignity of the human person (cf. Acts 16: 32; 24: 24–26; 26: 24, 28).

2. Theological Worth of the Apostolic Testimony

The apostles presented themselves as sent by God to act as intermediaries between the resurrected Jesus, whom they announced as Lord and Son of God, and the rest of mankind (cf. Acts 10: 41–42). Their testimony, then, if it is to be accepted as authentic, should confirm that mediation, showing the same means of identification that God's envoys have always demonstrated. Indeed, the apostles did accompany their preaching with signs, prophecies, and charisma of several kinds (cf. Mk 16: 20; Acts 4: 8–10; 2: 43; 3: 6, 13, 15–16; 4: 30; 5: 12, 15–16; 14: 8–10; 19: 11–12; 1 Cor 2: 3–5).[7]

St. Paul defends the truth of his preaching by invoking signs. "If Christ has not been raised, then our preaching is in vain and your faith is in vain. We are even found to be misrepresenting God, because we testified of God that he raised Christ, whom he did not raise if it is true that the dead are not raised" (1 Cor 15: 14–15). His argument is quite powerful: It is hard to imagine that God would confirm, with his power and deeds, a preaching of which he does not approve (cf. 1 Cor 12–14; Gal 3: 1–2, 4–5).

For his part, St. Luke refers these signs to the resurrected Jesus, saying that he performs them through his apostles. Luke uses the formula "in the name of Jesus," an expression that appears in the Acts of the Apostles in several contexts and during the narration of certain miracles. The formula was used in the narration of the healing of the paralyzed man seated by the temple door (cf. Acts 3: 1–10), the healing of Aeneas (cf. Acts 9: 32–35), and in the episode with the seven exorcists (cf. Acts 19: 13–20).

Besides finding the formula in use here, a fact significant in itself, we have to reflect that this formula, in the three cases, was the core of the entire narration. That is to say that, by the virtue of his name, the paralyzed man was cured.[8] St. Luke highlights the fact that Jesus had really been raised from the dead and that he now continued to heal, much as he did during his earthly life, by means of his apostles.[9] This is particularly evident in the healing of Aeneas, when St. Peter said, "'Aeneas, Jesus Christ heals you; rise and make your bed.' And immediately he rose" (Acts 9: 34).

Regarding the theological worth of the apostolic testimony, we can also say that the apostles *always testified that prophesies about the Savior promised by God were fulfilled in Christ*. References to ancient promises and prophecies are never missing (cf. Acts 2: 14–36; 3: 12–26; 7: 52; 8: 30–35; 10: 43; 13: 27–33; Rom 10: 4; Gal 3: 16) and constitute a powerful proof of the theological worth of their testimony (cf. 2 Pt 1: 19–21). In the same way that their testimony centered upon the Death and Resurrection of Jesus, their references to the Old Testament centered upon the final events in the life of their master. Their reading of the Old Testament, centered in the Resurrection, is manifested in the formula "He rose according to the Scriptures."[10]

The apostles were guided by Jesus' direct teaching and the help of the Holy Spirit. They came to understand how to identify the messianic message of the Old Testament and its references to the humiliation and exultation of the promised Savior. The word *paschal* reflected this penetrating understanding of the Bible. The Exodus—the saving act of God in favor of the Israelite people—was a great saving and eschatological sign in favor of all humanity, carried out by God through his incarnate Son. He who has passed from death to life (*phase, pasqua*: transit, pass) was transformed into the cause of salvation (passing from death to life) for all who will believe in him as Son of God and Savior of mankind.[11]

B. The Value of the Testimony of Christians

The testimony about Jesus given by disciples who were not immediate witnesses of his words and gestures is credible only if it coincides with the apostles' testimony in both content and form. Their testimonies about a real fact, if they are believable, must be consistent. The same holds true about the theological and moral aspect of the testimony. Fundamentally, *the testimony of Christians about Jesus is credible only insofar as it is in keeping with apostolic testimony.*

We need to identify the substantial meaning and essential characteristics of the apostolic testimony about Jesus, particularly about his Death and Resurrection. These elements will define the testimony.[12] Data that fundamentally referred to the Easter event but also included pre-Paschal deeds and words allows for both interpretations. The way to testify was characterized by the triple dimension which we have already seen—with their words, signs, and lives, the early Christians testified to their faith in the Resurrection.[13] They testified to Jesus of Nazareth by fulfilling his every precept and by living as he did, especially fulfilling his precept to love everyone (cf. Jn 13: 34) which constituted the ultimate proof that they were his disciples (cf. Jn 13: 35).

Therefore, the conditions of the credibility of the testimony of the first Christians and the nascent Church are met when the testimony is in accord with what and how the apostles taught (the apostolic content of preaching and the doctrine of the Church). They did so with their words, signs, miracles, and lives (the consistency of their testimony with the testimony of the apostles).

1. The Preaching of the Church's Doctrine Has Always Proposed the Apostles' Teachings about Jesus of Nazareth

St. Luke summarizes the evangelical actions of Sts. Stephen, Phillip, Barnabas, and the other disciples with the same formulas he uses to summarize the preaching of the apostles (cf. Acts 2: 36; 8: 5, 12, 35, 40; 9: 22; 17: 3; 18: 5, 28). Furthermore, that the preaching of Jesus and the preaching of the apostles had the same content becomes clear when one compares the writings of the New Testament—beginning with the Gospels of St. Mark and St. Luke, which do not have an apostle as their immediate author—to those of the other disciples.

The contents of the preaching and doctrine of the Church have remained substantially unchanged through the course of the centuries, with progress in its understanding and formulation.[14] The rifts among Christians that have affected the life of the Church have not affected this essential testimony, which allows all believers to call themselves Christians. Jesus is the Lord, Christ, Son of God, who has come to earth, preached, suffered, and died to save people from their sins. He has been raised from the dead and will come to judge everyone, giving eternal life to those who believe in him.[15]

2. The Preaching and Evangelizing Action of the Church Has Always Been Accompanied by Signs and Miracles

In the Acts of the Apostles, St. Luke teaches that the preaching of the first disciples was accompanied by signs and miracles (cf. Acts 6: 8; 8: 5–40; 1 Cor 12–14; Eph 4: 11; 1 Thes 5: 19–21; 1 Jn 4: 1–3; Rv 2–3), even though it is true that some specific signs, such as resurrecting the dead, were carried out mainly by the apostles.[16]

Miracles have never been absent from the life of Church, occurring with greater or lesser frequency depending on places and times. It is evidence enough to think about such saints as Gregory the Thauma-tourgos, Anthony of Padua, Vincent Ferrer, Joseph of Cupertino and many others, and to think about the many historically documented events that have saved the faithful—collectively and individually— from the calamity of war, epidemics, and hunger. These interventions remind us of God's saving interventions in the Old Testament and Je-sus' miracles during his time on earth.[17] Among Jesus' miracles, freeing people from demons has been a constant practice although, for obvi-ous reasons, the use of exorcism has not been given much publicity.[18]

To all this we have to add the continuous manifestation of the power of prophesy within the Church, according to its diverse and numerous expressions.[19] In the second century, St. Justin Martyr argued with the Jews that Christianity was truly God's because the gift of prophecy that the Jews had once enjoyed was later found among the Christians.[20]

3. The Church Has Always Confirmed Her Preaching of Jesus and His Doctrine with Her Own Life

The Acts of the Apostles and the Pauline letters testify that the first faithful lived and behaved according to Jesus' doctrine and precepts with faith and hope in the Resurrection of the Lord. The same has happened throughout the centuries.

It is well documented that many faithful in the first centuries of Church lost their lives simply because they believed in Christ as Lord and God. They testified to their faith to the point of preferring death to denying Christ because they expected to rise with him. Hence, they were called *martyrs* (witnesses) par excellence. In fact, the Church judged that this word, which the New Testament uses for Jesus and the apostles, could also be applied to those faithful who died confessing their faith and hope in the Resurrection. Martyrs (witnesses) are not so because they die, but rather because they testify. It is precisely their testimony that gets them killed.[21]

Still, many other faithful have heroically given testimony of Jesus. Even if they did not suffer death, they suffered serious injustices solely because they were known as Christians (cf. Acts 8: 3; 9: 1–2; 21: 30–31; 22: 5; 26: 9–11; 2 Cor 11: 24–25; Heb 10: 32–34).

It is important to stress that bloody testimony is specifically related to the Resurrection, not only to faith or religion in general. Martyrs accepted death because they were loyal to their Lord and because they expected the resurrection promised to those who were faithful to the end (cf. Acts 7: 55–56; Heb 3–4; 10: 32–34; 12: 1–3; 13: 7–8; Phil 1: 20–24; 1 Thes 4: 13–14; 2 Tm 4: 6–8; Rv 2: 8–10). Their testimony cannot be questioned because it was written in blood and the words of the Resurrection.[22]

It is now necessary to address a possible objection: What can we say about those faithful who did not give testimony with their own lives, those who did not live according to the faith they supposedly professed? It is a historically demonstrated fact that some Christians were not faithful in the sense that their deeds did not totally correspond to their faith in Christ (cf. Acts 5: 1–11; 1 Cor 5: 1–2; 6: 1–10; 8: 1–13; 10: 27–33; 11: 17–22; 2 Thes 3: 6–15; 1 Tm 5: 11–15; 6: 3–10; Jas 2: 1–13; 4: 1–13; 5: 1–6; Rv 2–3).

St. Luke himself provides the answer: He recognizes the lack of fidelity of some individuals but, nevertheless, asserts that the body of faithful—the Christian community and the Church—paid powerful and efficacious testimony to Jesus Christ. He argues that the infidelity of some believers did not diminish the validity of the group's testimony. Perhaps they were scant and exceptional cases in a group that had quite a lot of fervor and fidelity. Simply, infidelity is a "lack of testimony." It is not"testimony of the opposite position."

C. The Value of a Massive and Persistent Testimony on a Personal and Collective Level

The unity and continuity of the apostles' testimony, the Church's testimony, and Christians throughout history increase the value and credibility of this testimony, because it thus acquires a new dimension as a whole. Since Jesus' life, Death, and Resurrection, a human and social *totum* of testimony has been unanimously given for two thousand years.

Scripture relates this in the primitive Church (cf. Acts 2: 33, 42, 46; 4: 23–24, 27–30, 32; 5: 12; 6: 7; 8: 4, 15–16; 9: 32; 11: 19–20, 22, 29–30; 12: 5, 12; 14: 27; 20: 17–38; 21: 10–17; 28: 14–15). The collective aspect of these testimonies and their unanimity are reinforced with the passing of time in such way that their worth increases with time.

Thus, we confront an *exceptional testimony*, unequalled in human history. It is the testimony of a great multitude of persons linked together and in accordance with the centuries-old testimony about Jesus throughout the length and breadth of the world. This is the testimony of countless men and women who belong to different nations and cultures, different ages and conditions. They agree in their belief in Jesus—despite their deep differences, their moral weaknesses, and cultural deficiencies. They assert with their words and lives that Jesus of Nazareth suffered and was crucified and rose on the third day. This testimony has been given not just once or twice during a particular era, but has been repeated on numerous occasions without retractions or changes.

II. The Church as a Sign of Faith

The question of the credibility of Christianity, in fact, is expressed in question of the credibility of the Church. Some apologists, such as Tertullian, St. Irenaeus, St. Clement of Alexandria, Origen and others, have argued this from the beginning. Nevertheless, this ecclesiastical implication of Christ's credibility reached new prominence in the sixteenth century in response to the Protestant Reformation.

A. Theological Responses to the Issue of the Credibility of the Church

Post-tridentine ecclesiastical apologetics has three forms, which correspond to as many methodologies. The first form is characterized mainly by its *historical approach*. It seeks to show through documents of Christian antiquity that the Catholic Church is the one in complete continuity with the primitive Church. The second form pursues the same objective as the previous one, but defines itself by *resorting to the marks* of unity, sanctity, catholicity, and apostolicity. The third, without neglecting the grounding in antiquity and reference to marks of the Church, is characterized by considering the Church by herself and according to her appearance and development in history as a *moral miracle, a divine sign* that confirms her intrinsic transcendence.[23]

Of these three paths, the second one is the most widely used in theological treatises from the sixteenth century to the first half of the twentieth, though it is always somehow linked to the other two, from which it is hardly separable. The practice of resorting to the marks of the Church is nurtured in Sacred Scripture and the testimony of the Fathers differently according to the author's sensibility and the prevalent thinking of the time.

Vatican I introduced an important development in apologetics. The dogmatic constitution *Dei Filius* reminded man of his obligation to accept his faith and persevere in it. It explained how God helps to fulfill that obligation by granting the gift of interior faith and by his use of the Church, which presents man with what he should believe. The Church in herself also offers man the seal of her divine origin. Here, "in herself" does not mean independent of Christ. It means only that everything that is historically observed in her (expansion, stability, etc.) is already sufficient to transform her into a "great sign and permanent reason of credibility," *veluti signum levatum in nationes* (as an ensign to the peoples, cf. Is 11: 10). The Council did not want to speak about demonstrative proof, only indicative proof, preferring the term *signum* to *argumentum*.[24]

Without ignoring the apologetic importance of miracles and prophesies, the Council wished to stress the Church's very special role as a reason for believing in Christ. The new direction continued its course during the inter-conciliar period. Thus, we arrive at Vatican II with its presentation of the Church as the "universal sacrament of salvation."[25] This assertion includes two aspects that are important for what we are studying now. First, it reminds us that the Church is at the service of Christ's saving mediation; she does not set herself at its periphery. Next, the Council positively develops the axiom *extra Ecclesiam nulla salus* (there is no salvation outside the Church), thereby helping to rediscover that many elements of sanctification and of truth are found outside of its visible structure. "These elements, as gifts belonging to the Church of Christ, are forces impelling toward catholic unity."[26]

B. The Church as a Sign of Faith and Reason to Believe in God and in Christ

To be a faithful Christian and to belong to the Church depends essentially on holding Christ as one's center and foundation. It follows that the Church's credibility depends upon Christ. The Church is credible because, as the sign and sacrament of him that she is, she makes Christ present. In summary, *the Church is credible because she reflects the credibility of Christ.* This credibility in the Incarnate Word is perpetuated in history, particularly and mainly through his Church.

The Church considers herself a sign capable of guiding people to faith in Christ. The Church says of herself that she is "'a sign (or banner) raised in the midst of nations' (cf. Is 11: 12). She invites to herself those who do not yet believe and she insures that the faith they profess is supported by a firm foundation."[27]

Next, we will see how it is possible to recognize in the Church a sign that leads people to faith in God and in Christ. The sign of faith proposes a reality without utterly manifesting it, only doing so partially, in such way that what is perceived and tested in the Church invites us to believe. For, she bases this reality, on what is still unseen.

The Church presents herself to people throughout history as a community of faith whose members do not live in isolation from others, but in the midst of them and as their equals. As a community, the Church considers herself in permanent and close communication with the world and all people. The most recent Council reminded us of this doctrine in a particularly emphatic and solemn manner. The Church knows that she is in the world and has been sent by her Lord (cf. Jn 17: 11, 15–16, 18). At the same time, she knows that she is not of this world because she participates in divine life and fulfills a mission that transcends the horizons of history. She is the communion of humanity with God and she wants to lead all people to communion of life with God (cf. Jn 17: 24; 1 Jn 1: 3). It is precisely in that struggle between the "here" and the "other world," between the temporal and eternal, between the visible and invisible, between the human and divine,[28] where the Church's function as a sign of faith is established and developed.[29]

In fact, what is experiential and perceptible about the Church in history manifests what is still unseen, and this is what directs people to accept the truths of faith. The life and doctrine of the Church, her structure and activity, can be considered a sign of faith in her multiple expressions. This is because:

- they transmit a certain experience of God's saving action in history;
- they allow a certain anticipation of the definitive condition in glory.
- they make the crucified and resurrected Christ present to mankind.[30]

1. The Church as a Sign of God and His Saving Action

Because they intrinsically depend upon faith in God, the life and doctrine of the Church themselves constitute a call to believe in him and behave accordingly, in expectation of the promised afterlife. The Church reminds us that God "exists and that he rewards those who seek him" (Heb 11: 6).

The Church, with her life and doctrine, her structure and activity, depends upon God's action and revelation in history. He invites all to communion with him. The Church offers to those who come to know her the possibility of perceiving and appreciating that divine action in human history. His revelation is directed without exception to all. For this purpose, as Vatican I teaches, it is timely to think about some specific aspects in the life of the Church that are particularly accessible. For example, there is her expansion on earth among people of different cultures and conditions.[31]

The universal spreading of the Church constitutes a sign of intra-historical divine action. The phenomenon of people converting to faith in Jesus—something truly universal in nature—is marvelous because no other religion compares with it.[32] As St. Augustine has written, "Look at what exists now, consider what you see. This is because we neither speak of what has happened nor of what is going to happen. What is present is shown to you. Do you think it is a small thing, do you think it is not a miracle, moreover, a marvelous miracle, that the whole of mankind follows after a crucified man?"[33]

St. Thomas Aquinas deepened his inquiry in the same vein:

> Not by the violence of weapons or by the attraction of promised pleasures, but quite to the contrary, in the midst of persecution by tyrants, a countless mass, not only of poorly educated people but also of the wisest of men, has embraced the Christian faith. This is quite astonishing. This religion preaches ideas above any human intellect. It inhibits the lustfulness of the flesh. It teaches people to disdain the things of this world. The fact that mortal

spirits give their assertion to these things is the greatest of miracles. Nevertheless, we have to attribute to divine inspiration the fact that, leaving aside things that are seen, these believers wish to attain unseen objectives alone.[34]

And, he concluded:

Such an admirable conversion of the entire world to the Christian faith is a true indication of signs already carried out, up to the point that it is unnecessary that they be repeated, because they are evident in their effects. In fact, it would be a miracle superior to all signs, that the world, without them, would have been induced to believe such demanding teachings, carry out such difficult undertakings and have such high expectations. Furthermore, God does not stop, even in our own times, to act through miracles performed by his saints to inspire faith in his people.[35]

2. The Church as a Sign of Definitive Salvation

The Church offers herself as a spiritual communion to all, as a universal community where all noble human aspirations can concur, bringing forward in history when the heavenly Jerusalem will be linked forever to God in Christ by the Holy Spirit. "[T]he Church is in Christ like a sacrament or as a sign and instrument both of a very closely knit union with God and of the unity of the whole human race."[36] This self-consciousness can already be seen, although not perfectly or totally, as a reality.

In fact, men and women, without distinction of language, race, culture, condition, health, wealth, or any other characteristic that differentiates persons, form a part of the Church and have done so throughout the centuries from her very beginning. This highly diverse multitude believes the same Creed, prays in the same way (the Lord's Prayer), and shares the same hope (the glorious resurrection). This unity in the precise acts of faith and hope of a truly universal group is certainly a sign of that perfect concord, harmony, and unity to which all mankind aspires and which it hopes to attain someday.

The Church is aware that *this Catholic unity constitutes a particularly worthy argument for credibility*, as Jesus himself had already announced, "that they also may be in us, so that the world may believe that thou hast sent me" (Jn 17: 21). The unity of all Christians in faith, hope, and love is a sign of faith in Jesus as Son of God and faith in God, who is one and trinitarian.

If we value the singularity of the Church, we can come to understand its function as a sign. In fact—and in this she is different from other religions—the Church presents herself as a *people*, as an intimately organized community. On the one hand, she has an internal hierarchy and a well-defined structure (dogma, morals, and worship), a public law, a common discipline, and well-clarified institutions. On the other hand—and in this she is different from peoples and human communities of socio-political character—she brings together people of different languages, races, cultures, lands, and epochs. The Church presents herself as a permanent and universal communion without spatial or temporal limitations in true communion with the Holy Spirit.

Likewise, *the Church's stability through the centuries makes her a sign of that condition of permanency proper to the eschatological and definitive situation.* Human reasons are insufficient to explain the permanency of the Church, because she has had to face very serious external and internal difficulties, among them the weakness of her members. This permanency is in contradistinction with what is proper to human things: ideas, cultures, enterprises and human institutions, and earthly kingdoms and powers. Experience shows that what is proper to God does not perish because he is eternal.

Additionally, the stability of the Church has not been overly rigid in character. Quite to the contrary, it has been alive and dynamic. We have seen this in the case of her living tradition. She has led people to formulate their faith with greater understanding in the most suitable way in every era, in every epoch and in each human situation, without changing, diminishing, or adding to her message. "Thus, as the centuries go by, the Church is always advancing toward the plenitude of divine truth, until eventually the words of God are fulfilled in her."[37]

If we are to explain the stability of the Church, we need to turn to God's saving action. Gamaliel understood the question thus when he warned the Sanhedrin who intended to persecute the apostles:

> Men of Israel, take care what you do with these men. For before these days Theudas arose, giving himself out to be somebody, and a number of men, about four hundred, joined him; but he was slain and all who followed him were dispersed and came to nothing. After him Judas the Galilean arose in the days of the census and drew away some of the people after him; he also perished, and all who followed him were scattered. So in the present case I tell you, keep away from these men and let them alone; for if this plan or this undertaking is of men, it will fail; but if it is of God, you will not be able to overthrow them. You might even be found opposing God! (Acts 5: 35–39)

3. The Church as a Sign of the Crucified and Resurrected Christ

The Church manifests a deep and permanent inter-dependency at a historical and institutional level in her doctrine, morals, and worship regarding Jesus of Nazareth. She confesses him in her faith, speaks about him in her dogma, celebrates him in her worship, imitates him in her morals, invokes him in her prayers, obeys him in her organization, desires him in her hope, and loves him in the hearts of her children. Because of that dependency, she can already be considered a sign of him, as she permanently revolves around him—to borrow an expression of the Fathers—as the moon revolves around the earth.[38]

Moreover, the Church represents Christ because she does not speak about him as an historical personage who has already died, but as someone alive and well. She considers herself his instrument on earth, an instrument that makes the saving action of her Lord present to humanity with her preaching and permanent activity. As St. Augustine has written:

> The disciples saw the Lord accomplishing miracles and then suffering and dying and then, after his Resurrection, living full of strength and activity. It was then that his disciples believed in the Church and his Mystical Body, which should be extended to all peoples and last until the end of time. We, when we see the Church who shows herself to us as extended to all persons, blessed with all perfection and riches, should believe that Christ is her head. Divine virtue and power are not manifested to our eyes in the life of Christ. That we have not seen. But we do see these in present things, in his Church that lives now. The first disciples that saw Jesus did not see the Church. They saw the head and believed in the Body. For our part, what do we see? The Church. What is it that we don't see that they saw? We don't see Jesus in his human shape. Therefore, as they, seeing the head, believed in the Body, so we, seeing the Body, should believe in the head.[39]

The Church cannot be understood without an explicit reference to Christ, as a sign cannot be perfectly understood without understanding its relationship to the signified. This is valid to the extent that she reflects upon her proper being, her activity, and intra-historical structure, the presence of her human and divine elements that are proper to the Incarnate Word. The Church is the bride of Christ and reflects the features of her husband. The gestures that reveal God in Christ continue to be manifested in the Church. The glory shining from Christ's face shines today on the face of the Church.[40]

It is important to see the Church as a sign of Christ so as not to consider her at the periphery of her Lord. In her function as sign, she depends on him. All signs of faith come from Christ; they direct us to him and they are recapitulated in him.

4. The Church as a Sign of Christ that also Refers to His Passion and Resurrection

In fact, the various trials and tribulations during her historical journey echo those Jesus himself suffered during his passage on earth, culminating with his Crucifixion and Death upon Golgotha. To this end, we should remember St. Paul's words to the Corinthians: "For while we live we are always being given up to death for Jesus' sake, so that the life of Jesus may be manifested in our mortal flesh" (2 Cor 4: 11). At the same time, the Church's stability and continuity in history, despite so many difficulties, also reflect the Resurrection of the Lord, who lives in her and does not die. The Church participates, mysteriously, but really and efficaciously, in her spouse's new and eternal life.[41]

Summarizing these concepts, Vatican II taught:

> The Church "like a stranger in a foreign land, presses forward amid the persecutions of the world and the consolations of God," announcing the Cross and Death of the Lord until he comes (cf. 1 Cor 11: 26). But by the power of the risen Lord she is given strength to overcome, in patience and in love, her sorrows and her difficulties, both those that are from within and those that are from without, so that she may reveal in the world, faithfully, however darkly, the mystery of her Lord until, in the consummation, it shall be manifested in full light.[42]

C. Efficacy and Perceptibility of the Church as a Sign of Faith

The Church's credibility faces specific difficulties. Undoubtedly, the two most important are the following: First, in the Church, as history shows, there are limits and defects that seem to taint her credibility as an instrument of salvation. Second, the Church lives in a continuous *fieri* (state of development), which hampers the definition of her goodness as an object of study.

The Church announces a spiritual message of salvation that calls everyone to holiness, to human perfection in all spheres, and, especially, to the love of God. The Church makes this call to all people indiscriminately. Furthermore, the Church shows the quality and viability of her doctrine mainly through the life of her faithful. The lack of sanctity and virtue of some of her members does seem to stain the Church's sanctity and, consequently, diminish the credibility of a community that explicitly proclaims sanctity and salvation. How can we believe in a group that proposes an ideal but does not pursue it?

Without denying historical fact, the lack of virtue of some members of the Church may darken her sanctity in the eyes of some observers. Nevertheless, her sanctity is not diminished either in substance or appearance, for there are so many saintly and virtuous realities in her dogma and morals, her worship and institutions, and the lives of many of her faithful children.

The lack of sanctity of some Christians may even serve to reinforce the credibility of the Church by showing that she is authentically divine and human. It demonstrates that she is human because she reflects the present condition of our nature, which is weak. It demonstrates that she is divine in everything that is of virtue and heroism because beyond human miseries and limitations shines the power of God's grace (cf. 1 Cor 1: 26–29).

The Church, appearing as the portent of the presence of God and his grace, is already definitively victorious and acts as such in history. At the same time, she remains in the condition of a wayfarer, still on the way to total and perfect actuation of victory.[43]

> This Church, composed of weak men, produces incontestable fruits of sanctity in spite of everything. It is therefore legitimate to conclude with a spirit of faith: The finger of God is here. Through the darkness one perceives the light from above.[44]

All of these explanations are summarized in the *evaluation of the character as a sign of the Church*. That means, as we have mentioned before, that the Church "may reveal in the world, faithfully, however darkly, the mystery of her Lord until, in the consummation, it shall be manifested in full light."[45] The sanctity of the Church is a sign because it is immediately verifiable in history, but only in anticipation because her sanctity is not yet perfect as it will be at the end of time.

III. The Contribution of Each Christian to Ecclesiastical Credibility

The Church's credibility depends on her being a sign of Jesus of Nazareth. The credibility of her testimony and her identification with the testimony of the apostles depends upon Jesus' testimony about himself. This double subordination arises from an even more radical dependency of being. Ecclesiastical credibility exists insofar as the Christian community as a whole, and each Christian individually, acts in his own life and respective activities as other Christs. "The Church is a sign insofar as she tends to identify herself with the reality that she signifies."[46]

We can now address the difficulty born from the fact that ecclesiastical credibility is found in a constant *fieri*. The Church is a historical reality, a living community that really exists in space and time; she evolves and progresses. Hence, her credibility also depends—at least to a certain extent—on her actions at each place and historical moment. In other words, the credibility of Christianity depends upon Christ and his Church and, to a certain extent, on Christian behavior. Every Christian has the responsibility to give reason for his hope. Every believer is obliged to make the Church and the faith credible to his contemporaries by leading a life that is in keeping with Christian teachings (cf. 1 Pt 3: 15).

This consists in nothing more than the fulfillment of one's baptismal and confirmation promises. In fact, as we have already seen, we make the faith more attractive and credible to the extent that our words and deeds reflect Christ himself. The credibility of a Christian and a Christian community, inasmuch as it depends on a particular place and time, stands in direct relation to the authenticity of their Christian practice.[47]

Vatican II exhorts all the faithful: "In keeping with the state of life and condition proper to each of us, we will be able to arrive at perfect union with Christ, that is, holiness."[48] Ecclesiastical credibility, then, requires

all Christians to make an intellectual effort to study the possible implications that can be understood and accepted by different participants. It also requires an individual effort to reproduce in themselves
the features of Jesus.[49] So, each Christian—and, consequently, specific
and particular Christian communities as well—will be transformed
into an efficacious sign and credible witness of Christ, the Savior of all
mankind.

> Our responsibility is great, because to be Christ's witness im-
> plies first of all that we should try to behave according to his
> doctrine; that we should struggle to make our actions remind
> others of Jesus and his most lovable personality. We have to act
> in such a way that others will be able to say, when they meet
> us: This man is a Christian, because he does not hate, because
> he is willing to understand, because he is not a fanatic, because
> he is willing to make sacrifices, because he shows that he is a
> man of peace, because he knows how to love.[50]

Building ecclesiastical credibility is not limited to solely intellectual
and cultural endeavors. It also involves how people behave, because
their deeds should reflect the life and teachings of Jesus. "But some
one will say,'You have faith and I have works.' Show me your faith apart
from your works, and I by my works will show you my faith" (Jas 2: 18).
Only the disciples, whose deeds are consistent with their faith, are
signs of Jesus and render him true testimony because they act as Jesus
did, who "began to do and teach" (Acts 1: 1).[51]

The demand to look like Jesus must be extended to the whole of life. A
response of total and true faith begins an assimilation process with the
Incarnate Word that extends to all spheres of our own existence, both
individually and collectively. In a way, this process frustrates any and
all attempts at reductionism. St. Josemaría explained this phenomenon in a graphic manner: "Nonsectarianism. Neutrality. Old myths
that always try to seem new. Have you ever stopped to think how absurd it is to leave one's Catholicism aside on entering a university, or
a professional association, a cultural society, or Parliament, like a man
leaving his hat at the door?"[52]

If Christians are to build ecclesiastical credibility, they must lead lives that are completely in keeping with their faith. This conduct excludes, for example, attitudes of indifference in view of frequent and uninhibited infringement of the law of God or acts of injustice, arrogance, and oppression of some people over others.[53] Therefore, we can understand the apologetic importance of the Magisterium's teachings about society, culture, economics, property,[54] the family, the right and duty to care for and promote human life,[55] ecumenism, and the need for unity among all Christians.[56]

CHAPTER 14

A REFLECTION ABOUT THE RELATIONSHIP OF REVELATION, FAITH, AND CREDIBILITY

The study of credibility is composed of two mutually compatible elements. In the first, credibility presents its own proper features in each epoch, because signs offered by God have sometimes differed in type or quantity. Qualitatively as well as quantitatively, they reach their fullness in Christ, who shows himself as the Sign par excellence. One can speak, therefore, about a certain historicity of credibility that is reflected, as we noted, in the historicity of apologetics. It utilized different perspectives and approaches according to various social, cultural, and religious contexts.

Alternatively and simultaneously, it is possible to observe the permanency of some types of signs offered by God in his communication to humanity as elements that characterize the credibility of historical revelation. We can thus recognize it as a fundamental structure of credibility constituted by that body of signs always present throughout the centuries which responds to the precise and unquestionable human needs.[1]

We will now see how all the signs offered by God to make his revelation humanly credible are articulated and converge. Then we will see how the process of credibility develops with the intervention of intelligence and freedom and when credibility is interrelated with faith in God. Next, we will review the limits of this process in order to reach a deeper understanding of the act of faith. We will conclude by considering, once again, the faith-reason relationship to show how it exists in harmony with believers and how it contributes to the development of persons.

I. Credibility as a Gift of Revelation: Its Fundamental Structure

The credibility that allows one to have faith in words or persons depends upon the being and characteristics of those words or persons. One does not require the same intensity and quality of previous judgment to believe the results of a football game as one needs to believe a witness in a court of law. God's testimony is similar to human testimony. The divine Word is eternal and co-substantial with the Father. Theological faith is a much greater thing than human faith, although it shares some similarities with it. Similarly, God's credibility is not like human credibility. God is more credible than people are because he is always truthful, being Truth itself. The same cannot be said about human beings (cf. Ps 115: 11; Rom 3: 4).

Faith is related to revelation, and credibility is relative to both. For credibility to exist, it must be coherent with the already established notions of revelation and faith. On the one hand, it must be proportional to supernatural faith, which involves absolute devotion to a person and complete devotion of the person. Only God in Revelation itself can offer the necessary elements to sustain a credibility that is sensible and reasonable for both aspects of such a relationship.

Nevertheless, it must respond to the reality of revelation: an invitation to communion of life with God (holiness), to the manifestation of divine intimacy, and to an encounter of God and people within history. From this viewpoint, only God's self-revelation can offer elements that satisfy demands derived from this threefold aspect. All this allows us to say that credibility is a gift of revelation in the sense that the elements that establish it come from God and are part of the same process of divine communication with humanity.

Beyond individuating among people arising from different factors and conditioning, we have to consider elementary what is always present in any judgment of credibility about revelation. It can be summarized in the satisfaction of the demands of credibility required by the threefold fact that God invites people to eternal life with him. God announces the news to humanity about his being and his plans. He uses human beings as intermediaries in his communication. These three aspects of divine manifestation present humanity with a proper challenge and require a reasonable and wise justification. The judgment of the credibility of revelation can be considered reasonably concluded with a threefold judgment about the credibility of the invitation to live with God, the credibility of the news of what God is and wants, and the credibility of God's mediators in his dialogue with humanity.

All elements provided by God for credibility of his Revelation support all three aspects. Yet, some elements are particularly suited to one of those three judgments. For instance, credibility of the invitation can be mainly recognized by considering its conformity with what man is and wishes to be. The credibility of words that relate the news about God and his plans can be evaluated by the miraculous deeds that accompanied them. Mediators may be judged by their conduct and prophecies. So, in this section we will study the apologetics of immanence, the theology of miracles, and the theology of prophesies, in that order. We will need to remember that maturity of credibility judgments comes precisely from the integration and convergence of those three judgments. In this way we overcome the insufficiency of each of them when it is considered independently from the other two.

A. The Anthropological Roots of Faith: The Apologetics of Immanence

We have seen that credibility is, before anything else, a gift of revelation. Now we must reconcile this with its constitutive anthropological dimension.

In fact, the same judgment of credibility is demanded by man, and man must elaborate that judgment and formulate it according to his needs, ways of thinking, and desires. However, the elements offered by God for that judgment present characteristics that correspond to the inherent demands of human nature, and adapt themselves—in their particular historical moment—to circumstances of individual persons and human communities. Finally and most importantly, credibility has a deep and radical anthropological dimension because revelation it-self is a gift of God to mankind that is perfectly coherent with human-ity. It is a divine donation that respects the person in his whole natural being. It projects one toward a plenitude that surpasses any thought and aspiration of the human heart. This, fundamentally, is the issue of the anthropological roots of faith and of the invitation that God makes to humanity when he reveals himself.

Historical revelation appears as an unveiling of the God who invites, as an anticipatory communication that calls humanity to a fuller communion. This invitation involves, for those who receive it, some uncertainty because of its mysterious character. It requires some clarification before it is accepted.

Christianity's proposal to mankind may be summarized as follows: a steady and complete alliance with God; a life alongside of him, know-ing him as Father, Brother, and Love; and a participation in what God thinks, wants, loves, and does. Christianity offers people the opportu-nity to participate in God's life and work: his omnipotence, eternity, and glory and his beneficent and providential action. Christianity chal-lenges humanity—"You are gods" (Jn 10: 34)—but not in the way the serpent suggested, which induced our first parents to distrust God and disobey him. On the contrary, the Church invites mankind to trust in God and believe in him, obey him, and fulfill his will in a filial manner, imitating him in everything, following the example of Jesus of Naza-reth, Son of the Father. He was incarnated to be Teacher and Model to all humanity. The Holy Spirit will give them the strength, grace, and virtue to live that vocation.

Clearly, this constitutes an invitation of life and love. There are two possible responses to this proposition: One either accepts it or renounces it. There is no third solution. Within the second solution one can distinguish what might be called a third consideration. This would be to think that the invitation is real, good, and feasible but that it is a deceitful and even harmful ideal. It would hamper one's pursuit of other objectives that may be considered feasible in the human context. The first option leads us to accept the invitation while the latter two involve a refusal of the divine invitation.[2] We will now analyze these approaches.

1. Christ and the Search for the Sense of Our Own Existence

The first one of these considerations is based upon proper knowledge of God's being and man's being. It requires, nevertheless, a certain grasp of the authenticity of the invitation born from a reasonable doubt of its feasibility due to human weakness in the present situation and the serious demands of the invitation itself.

These conditions of total self-giving are precisely the essential sign of the authenticity of the invitation. Any kind of happiness that would consist in the possession of and communion with the Absolute must include an absolute dedication from the persons who wish to reach it. As in human affairs, "no ideal becomes a reality without sacrifice."[3] Regarding the question of human weakness, Scripture states that this lofty goal is attainable: "You shall receive power when the Holy Spirit has come upon you" (Acts 1: 8), with the help of grace that God grants to all.

In any event, the above answers may seem somewhat inadequate because people frequently deceive themselves about the value of ideals that require great sacrifice. Thus, the people cried out about that "which we have looked upon and touched with our hands, concerning the word of life" (1 Jn 1: 1). It is necessary to turn to personal experience and the testimony of others' experience. Therefore, the question is set in specific, personal terms: It is the basic question about the ideal of our own life, about the meaning of our existence.

As we understand it at this juncture of our study, this question about the meaning of life is not the metaphysical question about the origin of being and its finality. Rather, it concerns an existential and specific question: the question of personal fulfillment, an authentic self-fulfillment of our own being and possibilities. This question involves vital and personal elements regarding our own capacities, freedom, and direction as well as the context and human environment in which we are to develop them. It is, most definitely, the search of the ego that each one of us is and the "you" with whom each one of us must relate in order to really be "somebody." Otherwise, one is lost in oneself, in one's selfishness, in the emptiness of one's personal immaturity because one does not know how to give oneself to God and to others: "Whoever would save his life will lose it, and whoever loses his life for my sake will find it" (Mt 16: 25).

The question about the meaning of life leads us to the issue of the definitive and ultimate You, the transcendent and absolute You who is the One who eternally remains, the You who questions each one and to whom an answer must be given. This is the You who attracts everyone much like a magnet, yet whose face no one has seen, even though many things and events speak about him. This is the You who uses various things and events to attract everyone to himself. Thus, *the question about the sense of life is the search for the personal Being that is over everything and everyone.* When one senses and perceives—one stops to think, sometimes compelled by the hardship of certain situations—that only by making reference to this personal Being can one find a satisfactory response to what he is and what he is worth. Only by making reference to that Being can one understand the meaning of his personal existence.

The modern science of religion speaks about the human need and desire—present in many religious experiences and rooted in human psychology—for an understanding of the omnipotent figure who solves all uncertainties affecting human life. It speaks about the desire for God, identified by some as "a religious nostalgia for a paternal God."[4] We can say, then, that the fundamental and primary inclination repeatedly highlighted from different perspectives by these sciences is precisely the common inclination toward God.[5] They have not identified other human inclinations with religious yearnings, which appear to be the fundamental ones. Experts have found that these desires are at the root of the rest. They explain, unify, and define what is most transcendent and absolute in our lives.[6]

Therefore, the search for meaning in our own existence entails, at some point, the search for God.[7] Christianity responds to this pursuit in two ways. First, the Church presents Christ to mankind. To those who ask who God is (besides other questions common to other religions), Christianity proclaims that Jesus of Nazareth is the Messiah, the Son of God and Lord. Then, she sets forth the lives of Christians, which serve as an experiential verification about the life and doctrine of Christ for believers. This double presentation constitutes an adequate response—because it is presented in existential and experimental terms—to the question that was originally formulated precisely in those terms.

St. Philip spoke to St. Nathaniel about Jesus as Christ, and Nathaniel did not believe him: "Come and see" (Jn 1: 46). Another example lies in Jesus' asking the apostles whether they wanted to leave him after his announcement of the Eucharist in the synagogue of Capernaum. St. Peter replied at once, "To whom shall we go? You have the words of eternal life" (Jn 6: 68). We can also turn to the famous introductory words from the *Confessions* of St. Augustine: "Lord, you have made us for yourself, and our heart is restless until it rests in you."[8] St. Josemaría commented upon the encounter of the resurrected Lord with the disciples going to Emmaus:

> The journey ends when they reach the village. The two disciples who, without realizing it, have been deeply stirred by the words and love shown by God made Man, are sorry to see him leaving. For Jesus "appeared to be going further" (Lk 24: 28). This Lord of ours never forces himself on us. He wants us to turn to him freely, when we begin to grasp the purity of his Love, which he has placed in our souls. We have to hold him back ("they pressed him") and beg him: "Stay with us, for it is toward evening and the day is now far spent" (Lk 24: 29); night is coming on.
>
> That's just like us. Always short on daring, perhaps because we are insincere, or because we feel embarrassed. Deep down, what we are really thinking is: "Stay with us, because our souls are shrouded in darkness, and you alone are the light. You alone can satisfy this longing that consumes us." For "we know full

well which among all things fair and honorable is the best: to possess God forever."[9]

Without a doubt, this double presentation offers the possibility to aspire to the model that the Church proclaims—Christ—a model that responds to the deepest yearnings of the human heart. One, thus, discovers the essential unity between what man is and what he comes to know.[10] We will now study the second one of these approaches.

2. Christ, and What Man Is and What He Aspires to Be

The second class of reasoning considers the Christian ideal deceitful, being harmful to humanity and to its possibilities of personal and collective development. This argument has been developed mainly in the modern age, during which a scientific and philosophical vision that willingly excludes God has been formulated and popularized. In this conception, culture has no room for religious notions. They have become insignificant and irrelevant. The mature, cultivated, and progressive person has no interest in these topics. This line of thinking has had enormous cultural repercussions to which we have already made reference.

During this period, theologians have tried to foster a vision of God and his plans in such a manner that the modern man might understand that things religious and Christian do not imply a threat to existence or rationality.

These various attempts seek to demonstrate the immanence of the human vocation to its final end. This focuses on the natural inclination of the human person toward the divine Word.

This reasoning always refers to the fact that each person, from creation, is intimately constituted as *an image of God*. Hence, for man to grow in such likeness to the utmost perfection that God grants is the most worthy undertaking imaginable. In other words, theologians have sought to show that *authentic anthropology must be intrinsically open to what God has revealed*. This is a great discovery for mankind. People have been created to know, love, and serve God in this life and enjoy him in the next. Mankind has been created to be in Christ and like Christ— God's Son in Christ by the Holy Spirit. Man has been created to know God, taking in his Word, thanks to the Holy Spirit. Man has been created so that, by faith, he may direct himself toward the vision of the Father through his Word and in the Holy Spirit.

Along this line of thinking, G. Colombo and others believe that human psychological dynamism perfectly corresponds to the structure of faith. Therefore, we can discover that the first has been created in accord with the latter.

> The Holy Trinity creates man "in Christ" not to abandon him to himself, but precisely to "call him," by creating him from nothing, inviting him to communion with the Trinity through Jesus Christ. According to this perspective, man has been created for faith. He has the characteristics of originality, universality and necessity. It can be said that the invitation to believe is proposed as a transcendental issue with which each man must inevitably decide in his personal history. This he must decide with the exercise of his own freedom, toward his salvation or ruin…. As a consequence, given that man is created for faith, faith is what logically imposes the original structure of man. In other words, man's constitution is explained and understood in function of faith: not faith in general, but faith that recognizes the revelation of God in Christ.[11]

H.U. von Balthasar argues from an anthropological perspective. He is particularly attentive to the needs of contemporary man, someone who is intent upon verifying the validity of the Christian message. To that purpose, von Balthasar centers his approach upon the person of Christ, in whom God reveals himself as love. According to von Balthasar, this love is manifested in the Incarnation, the life of Jesus, and the Church. These are the criterion of authenticity of revelation that can now be better understood because they manifest a God who gives himself to us, who gives us the freedom to enter into communion with him through a free act. (We refer here not to mere human love, but divine love.)[12]

3. Saving Gestures of God and the Human Hope of Attaining True Happiness

The final approach considers the Christian invitation real and good but not feasible. According to this critique, the Christian ideal is attractive and might give sense to our own existence, but it is beyond human reach. This approach is characterized by warnings of the risks involved—known as the sad experience—that a soteriological doctrine implies when it involves a beautiful but unobtainable goal. We can conquer this pessimism once we allow for the tangible elements that prove the validity of the saving proposal presented in revelation. Here, we need to consider the signs that we have seen in previous chapters.

As a matter of fact, God has performed many miracles in favor of Israel, throughout the history of the Church and by means of Christ. People have experienced God's saving will and his saving power through these actions. By means of these interventions, God has taught his people that his promise of eternal salvation and life in himself is as genuine as his miracles. Thus, God himself saves if one allows God to save him—if one accepts God's invitation to believe and act in accordance with that faith, thanks to the strength that comes from above.

We are not here talking about miracles insofar as they manifest the divine reality or confirm revelation by reliably showing the power, wisdom, and kindness of God. We are talking about those acts that respond to profound aspirations of the human person and are etched deeply and permanently in his spirit. For example, we refer to the human desire for salvation and happiness, victory and triumph, eternity and immortality, life, glory, love, and, above all, the desire to live his life without fault.

These signs are presented with a deep human meaning. This is because they are based on the human relationship as the recipient of the divine message, a message that involves the person from all levels and all standpoints (socially and personally, bodily and spiritually, intellectually and willingly, affectively and psychologically, theoretically and practically). This profound relationship may be seen in the observable correspondence between these signs and human aspirations.

God's great saving gestures always satisfy the irrepressible wish for life, immortality, glory, and triumph that motivate the human spirit.

Inasmuch as those signs are understood as divine, they enclose something divine that is perceptible and attracts the person. This is because they come from God according to an extremely singular providence that manifests his power, wisdom, and kindness. At the same time, they appear in a most human fashion. Consequently, they demonstrate both the divine and the human. They grant us *an experience of the union of the divine with the human.* These signs prove the consistency and strength of the Christian ideal, of the life in Christ, which is God and Man, of a human living next to God, in God, and with God.

It is by showing the saving signs in this perspective that we give—quite properly—the "defense to any one who calls you to account for the hope that is in you" (1 Pt 3: 15) that St. Peter called for.

B. The Theology of Miracles

In divine revelation, the mysterious character of the revealed reality makes it inherently difficult to judge the truth or falsehood of the Christian message. An internal analysis alone will not certify the worth or invalidity from an intellectual, verifiable viewpoint. Hence, "it is necessary that the word have some confirmation for it to be believed."[13]

We reach the same conclusion when we seek to define supernatural faith. This is the adherence by a believer to an unseen Truth, and it needs to be discerned in another way if we do not want the believer's act to be a blind, careless, or insensible act. As a matter of fact, *when the divine Word enters history, it carries in itself the elements necessary to be utterly and reasonably accepted* (cf. Nm 14: 11; Mk 16: 20; Jn 15: 24; Heb 2: 4).

1. The Need for Facts that Confirm the Truth of Words

"Love consists of deeds, and not good reasons." This phrase was born from the human experience of many false promises, of so many nice words that were not backed up in daily conduct. This saying conveys an understanding of many negative experiences that support its validity, some perhaps quite bitter.

We need to confirm the truth of words using the conduct and capacities of the speaker. This becomes even more important when those words refer to realities unknown by the listener. If such an inquiry is impossible, we should seek a generic appraisal of the verisimilitude of what we have been told, trying to compare it to what we already know about related matters. If we discover a conflict between what we hear and what we already know, then we will have grounds to doubt the truth of those words. Alternatively, if we do not find any important disagreement, we should consider these words true until such time as we can be better informed about the capability and truthfulness of our sources.

St. Thomas Aquinas taught that we cannot expect a merely intellectual analysis of the contents of the Christian message to lead us to a definitive conclusion about its truthfulness. This is because the First Truth completely transcends the judgment and scope of human reason. While it is possible to affirm the coherence of the Christian message, its lack of contradictions, and its conformity with the human sciences (philosophical, anthropological, historical, biological), this is still insufficient to reasonably conclude that the Christian proposal is true or to assert that it comes from God. By means of an internal analysis of Christianity, people can, certainly, become convinced from the standpoint of the inclination to happiness, from the instinct toward transcendence.

Still, this is not enough:

> Any reasoning, if it is not evident in itself, needs to be confirmed before being accepted. Things that pertain to faith are not manifested to reason; hence, it was necessary to confirm the word of faith. As it is not possible to confirm it through demonstrations based upon principles of reason, because things that must be believed exceed reason, the Word had to be confirmed by signs that accompanied it and that only God could perform.[14]

St. Thomas explains this possibility by comparing the access to God who reveals himself in history to the access to God who creates all things.

> It is natural for man to arrive at the intelligible truth through sensible realities. Therefore man, when guided by natural reason, can get to know something about God through creatures. In the same way, by means of some supernatural effects that we call miracles, man is led to the recognition of some supernatural realities.[15]

Based on these elements, which are an inherent part of the activity of the Incarnate Word,[16] man can reasonably overcome reservations that are due to the pretensions of mediators who speak in God's name (cf. 2 Cor 5: 20; 1 Thes 2: 13). One can take part in a message and an invitation that surpasses the aspirations of the human mind and heart without contradicting them (cf. Is 64: 1–3; 65: 17–18; 1 Cor 2: 9).

Divine speech characteristically expresses reality with words and deeds that surpass human gestures. Human deeds are certainly expressive and revealing, but they do not create or substantially communicate what the person really means. In Divine Revelation, words and deeds intermingle, enlighten, and complete one other. From the standpoint in which we are interested, divine deeds fulfill what words promise and explain; they communicate what words mean. On the one hand, they reveal because they grant experience from what the words teach. On the other hand, they confirm the truth of those words and prove that they are not expressed in vain.[17]

2. Historical Development of the Theology of Miracles

During the course of history, the theology of miracles has focused primarily on the *theological* character of miracles, mainly as it refers to their origin from God as gifts from him. In their finality they manifest God and inspire faith in him. They also serve to confirm communion with him. They have an important relationship to the saving economy established by God, an economy that is recapitulated in Christ and continues in his Church.

Consequently, miracles have a *Christological* character. Jesus of Nazareth recapitulates in himself all signs of faith. He himself is the miracle par excellence. By their very structure, miracles reproduce the human-divine binomial present in Christ. Further, they have an ecclesiastical character, because:

> To the Catholic Church alone belong all those things, so many and so marvelous, which have been divinely ordained to make for the manifest credibility of the Christian faith. What is more, the Church herself by reason of her astonishing propagation, her outstanding holiness and her inexhaustible fertility in every kind of goodness, by her Catholic unity and her unconquerable stability, is a kind of great and perpetual motive of credibility and an incontrovertible evidence of her own divine mission.[18]

Theologians did not undertake a systematic reflection on miracles until rather late in Christianity. This did not appear to be one of their first priorities. We should remember that in the Israelite religion, specifically, in Jewish tradition, miracles play a somewhat secondary role. The Hebrews gave greater emphasis to the words and deeds of the prophets. The early Christians seem to have followed their approach. Only as a consequence of their increasing involvement with Greco-Roman culture did they come to pay more attention to miracles.[19]

The first studies of miracles examined the term and its place in biblical language. The Latin word *miraculum* is used to indicate prodigies and wonderful deeds. The variety of terms used to express the word "miracle" allows for a richly nuanced and complex concept of miracles with opportunities for precision. Theologians have emphasized two aspects of these words—the wonderful character and significant worth—without neglecting their transcendent and ontological dimension, which is also present in the biblical vocabulary.[20]

Along that line, St. Augustine said, "I name as a miracle everything that, being difficult and unusual, surpasses the expectations and power of the spectator. That is why the spectator is amazed."[21] In this brief definition, St. Augustine balanced the various elements that will later be broadly developed. He stressed the aspect of surprise, which attracts people's attention. That is why surprise can initiate a path toward faith. Consequently, Christ performed miracles so that "through those temporal wonders that could be seen, faith might be built on things not seen."[22]

While St. Augustine recognizes the special relationship that exists between the miracle and creative power, he does not center his inquiry on that question. Moreover, he warns that people run the risk of seeing God only in great miracles. "A dead person is brought back to life, and men are astonished. Many people are born every day and no one is amazed. Nevertheless, if we consider things wisely, we will reckon that the beginning of a life that did not exist is certainly a greater miracle than reviving a life that had already existed."[23] St. Augustine is trying to point out that the recognition of a divine action requires that one have a minimum of religious sensibility. When one's religious sensibility is weakened, his sense of divinity is also weakened and he perceives with greater difficulty—or simply does not perceive—God's wisdom and power in everyday life. Then he needs special and outstanding interventions in order to be shaken out of blindness so that he might recognize the actions and presence of God.[24]

Without leaving aside the definitions of miracles present in biblical vocabulary and in the writings of the Church Fathers,[25] St. Thomas Aquinas offered his own strict definition of miracle in its proper sense, distinguishing it from other more or less wondrous deeds.

Aquinas begins by looking at how miracles relate to the psychological element of surprise and wonder. He decides that this element alone is insufficient to consider an event miraculous. It is not enough for the cause of an event to be unknown to the observer. That is enough to raise admiration, but it does not mean that a miracle has really taken place. Miracles are marvelous in the absolute sense, not in a relative sense (regarding us). "Miracles, strictly speaking (rigorously, *proprie*), are deeds accomplished outside of the order generally observed in creation."[26] In order for an event to be miraculous in this strict sense, the intervention of the first cause is necessary without utilizing second causes according to the dynamic that is proper to them. This, as is the case with biblical signs, is the reason miracles appear and are signs of faith.[27]

St. Thomas Aquinas elaborates three categories of miracles according to the differences between an act of divine intervention and the possibilities for any second causes:

1. Miracles in which God does something that never could be accomplished by nature (for instance, causing the sun to go backwards or stop)

2. Miracles in which God performs some action possible in nature but according to another order (for example, creatures can give life naturally but cannot bestow life upon a dead person)

3. Miracles in which God does some deed that creatures also do, but God does it without complying with the normal requirements of nature (for instance, giving health immediately without a healing process or without the use of medicines).[28]

If we are to attribute to God an effect that seems to contradict the dynamics proper to second causes, we are faced with the following problem: How is it possible that God does not respect the order that he himself established on earth? St. Thomas resolves this difficulty by referring to God's absolute divine dominion. Since God is creator and first cause of everything that is, he exists in a completely free manner, without any restrictions. Therefore, in nature, he can fulfill whatever he desires, even when this involves surpassing the natural limitations of his creation.[29]

Later, his response clarifies this matter. God does everything with order, wisdom, and kindness. Therefore, his miracles necessarily involve the supremely wise order established by his divine kindness. Any vision that presents miracles as a correction to the order of creation must be rejected. *Miracles are facts that must be categorized within the plan of salvation.*

St. Thomas Aquinas concludes by saying that *the meaning of miracles consists in their bringing to mankind the knowledge of Christ as Incarnate Word for human salvation.* "The finality of Christ's miracles was to allow us to know his divine power to save men."[30] Also, St. Thomas has written, "The Incarnation of the Word is the miracle of miracles, as the saints have said, because it is greater than any miracle, and the rest of miracles are ordered to it. That is why [the Incarnation] not only leads us to believe in other things, but the rest of miracles contribute so that we might believe in the Incarnation."[31]

Since the seventeenth century, important thinkers have raised several objections to miracles that center on the supposition that the acceptance of miracles is based on a misstep of reason: The cause of a physical fact is ignored due to the insufficient development of the sciences of nature. Thus, primitive people attribute a certain action to God's intervention.[32] For many, miracles are a conclusion without a foundation.

This criticism led to others of a more *historical and textual* character. Certain experts argued that the passages of Scripture that dealt with miracles were fabrications that were explicable in several ways. These critics, who deny the existence of the supernatural and the preternatural, are starting with false premises.

The First Vatican Council dealt with the question of miracles, but mostly from the biblical-patristic conception of *miracles as signs*. The Council highlighted their efficacy;[33] hence, it considers them both as *argument* and as reasons for faith in that they are divine deeds that manifest the might and wisdom of God.[34] This is obvious in the Council's texts:

> In order that the submission of our faith should be in accordance with reason (cf. Rom 12: 1), it was God's will that there should be linked to the internal assistance of the Holy Spirit external indications of his revelation, that is to say divine acts, and first and foremost miracles and prophecies, which, clearly demonstrating as they do the omnipotence and infinite knowledge of God, are the most certain signs of revelation and are suited to the understanding of all. Hence, Moses and the prophets, and especially Christ our Lord himself, worked many absolutely clear miracles and delivered prophecies.[35]

If anyone says that all miracles are impossible, and that therefore all reports of them, even those contained in Sacred Scripture, are to be set aside as fables or myths; or that miracles can never be known with certainty, nor can the divine origin of the Christian religion be proved from them: let him be anathema.[36]

Contemporary theology[37] has understood the need to abandon the overly rigid and schematic approach to miracles that was previously posited by "classical apologetics." Accordingly, they have sought to develop a richer and broader response to face modern-day criticisms. Their efforts have sought to:

1. recover the richness of the biblical and patristic notion of prodigious and saving signs; and

2. perfect the appreciation of the relationship between miracles and the laws of nature, avoiding simplistic formulas.[38]

By proceeding in this way, they highlight the idea that miracles served to point out that the world is not a closed system. It has not yet reached its end and perfection. It is not completely finished; moreover, it is not isolated in itself and independent of its Creator. Miracles are signs that the world still enjoys a divine providence that embraces it in a free manner, assuming it in a great and transcendent project.[39]

Miracles show that there is an invisible beyond what is visible. They demonstrate that beyond the second cause, there is an existing first cause. They show that there are not only physical, biological, psychological, and social laws, but also a divine law, which is over and above all other laws of nature. God's freedom transcends the exigencies of his creation. Immanent and temporal objectives and goals are not the be-all and end-all.

The greatest achievement of this theological renovation lies in the identification of the *intimate link between miracles and mysteries*, one founded on the relationship that both of them have with the Absolute. *Miracles*, in the strict sense, are phenomena that allow persons to see the action proper to the Creator. Hence, they are prodigious, wonderful, and superb. *Mysteries*, for their part, are an exclusive property of reality. They transcend the world and humanity, precisely by being truly transcendent—a reality beyond human comprehension, in the proper sense of comprehension (embracing). In the intellectual sense, they cannot be perfectly explained.

This intimate link is manifested in many ways. For instance:

- Miracles are physical realities, but their being is not exhausted in the physical—in either their origin or their finality, because in both ways they belong to the order of mysteries.[40]

- Miracles are presented as an intervention in history and the physical world by the absolutely transcendent reality.[41]

- Miracles, in many ways, enclose great mysteries within them.[42] Their sensory existence is inseparable from their mysterious existence, so much so that they remind us of the great mystery of the Incarnation because they also present a historical and mysterious event.[43]

- Miracles are proposed as a participation and derivation of the mystery of the Incarnation and, at the same time, as an anticipation of that great mystery and its total revelation in the Resurrection and *parousia*.[44]

- Miracles fulfill a significant function of all mysteries. They point out the existence of the order of mysteries, and they specifically reveal some aspects of that order.[45]

From this mystery-miracle link, the two great functions of miracles acquire their meaning in the biblical sense. Here, we find their *theological function* (to propose and make known some aspects of the mysteries, of the absolutely transcendent reality) and their *apologetic function* (to confirm and induce people to accept the mysteries of the faith).

The main achievements of this theological progress were discussed by the Second Vatican Council, which was characterized by Christocentrism in a propositional-manifestational as well as a confirmatory-probative dimension.[46] *Christ is the sign par excellence* because he reveals the Father and confirms this revelation:

After God had spoken many times and in various ways through the prophets, "in these last days he has spoken to us by a Son" (Heb 1: 1–2). For he sent his Son, the eternal Word who enlightens all men, to dwell among men and to tell them about the inner life of God. Hence, Jesus Christ... "speaks the words of God" (Jn 3: 34), and accomplishes the saving work which the

Father gave him to do (cf. Jn 5: 36; 17: 4). As a result, he himself—to see whom is to see the Father (cf. Jn 14: 9)—completed and perfected Revelation and confirmed it with divine guarantees. He did this by the total fact of his presence and self-manifestation—by words and works, signs and miracles, but above all by his death and glorious Resurrection from the dead, and finally by sending the Spirit of truth. He revealed that God was with us, to deliver us from the darkness of sin and death, and to raise us up to eternal life.[47]

In summary, all signs are concentrated in Jesus of Nazareth. They lead us to him and come from him because they participate in him. The Church is also a sign that cannot be understood apart from Christ. She also subsists in him regarding her function as a sign. Every one of the miracles must be contained in the unique and decisive miracle that is Christ himself, the true witness of God.[48]

3. The Discernment of Miracles

The discernment of miracles assumes a double dimension: before anything else, corroborating the *extraordinary character* of the fact that distinguishes it from ordinary manifestations of divine providence. Afterwards, the control of its *religious nature* distinguishes the miraculous fact from natural phenomena unrecognized as such by people (in general, or, in particular, to "that" person who sees the miraculous fact).[49]

The first moment of discernment is developed in three phases: historical verification of the fact, analysis of the laws of nature (according to the relevant sciences), and metaphysical study. In the first phase we try to find out *if the studied fact that appears miraculous really has a transcendent cause.* It is possible to assert this about a fact if its effect is possible only for God because it requires an infinite power. According to that hypothesis, a possible ignorance of the laws of creation does not handicap the judgment about the miraculous character of the fact. The need for the intervention of a Cause of infinite power in each case is positively established by a metaphysical study grounded in a historical and scientific analysis. For example, the multiplication of bread carried out by Jesus required an infinite power because it assumes an increase of matter. Lazarus' resurrection from the dead clearly necessitated the intervention of the Lord of life and death. The instantaneous healing of a sick man without any medicines or process entailed an immediate transmutation without any mediation proper to the action of second causes.

Events in which it is not possible to identify a transcendence present in the effect (because the occurrence does not necessarily seem to require an infinite power) cannot be recognized as miracles in the strict sense (some authors prefer the term *major miracles*), but as minor miracles or wonderful facts.[50]

Next, we analyze the *human context* of the fact that seems miraculous. Here, the study is directed mainly and specifically to find the necessary link between miracles and mysteries, the presence of which is absolutely essential to be able to speak about miracles in the proper sense. The religious-saving context can be manifested in a variety of ways. In any event, the miracle-mystery link must appear in the miraculous fact so as to *somehow show the omnipotence, wisdom, and kindness of God.*

These criteria permit us to *differentiate between miracles and diabolic prodigies.* The first are saving prodigies that carry light and happiness, that benefit persons bodily or spiritually. Diabolic prodigies provoke astonishment but are basically vain and useless, at least for the soul and almost always for the body. Normally, they involve objects flying about or moving without apparent cause, actions that require disproportionate strength on the part of a person, voices, or words in strange and unintelligible languages. Furthermore, diabolic prodigies, when submitted to a metaphysical study, show no requirement of an infinite power although they are due to a power that is certainly superior to human capacity.[51]

C. The Theology of Prophecies

The presence of mediators in revelation requires accepting the words of these intermediaries as the Word of God. It requires a careful, rigorous verification of their condition as envoys of God and the divine origin of what they say on God's behalf.

The Bible explicitly teaches the need to monitor the quality of mediation. It is dealt with in the case of Moses. When Yahweh gives him the mission to go to the Pharaoh to ask that Israel be released from Egypt (cf. Ex 3: 10), Moses gives God the objections of the Hebrews: "They will not believe me or listen to my voice, for they will say, 'The LORD did not appear to you'" (Ex 4: 1). Yahweh's response leads to a series of miraculous events; the first one of them is small but amazing: "'What is that in your hand?' He said, 'A rod.' And he said, 'Cast it on the ground.' So he cast it on the ground, and it became a serpent; and Moses fled from it.... [Yahweh concludes:] 'that they may believe that the LORD, the God of their fathers...has appeared to you'" (Ex 4: 2–3, 5).

St. Thomas Aquinas reminds us that, in a similar way, human ambassadors show their credentials to those to whom they are sent. "God himself testifies that the teachings of faith are true. If a king sent a letter with his seal, no one would dare to say that that letter did not come from the king. Thus, everything that the saints have believed and have transmitted to us is also marked with the seal of God. This seal is that which no creature can do."[52] He also has written: "All mediators, through whom faith comes to us, are wholly credible. In fact, we believe the prophets and apostles because the Lord has testified in their favor, performing miracles, as it was written in Mark 16: 20: 'confirmed the message by the signs that attended it.' And we believe their successors only insofar as they have announced things that have been written before."[53]

Saving and prodigious acts are, effectively, a way God accredits his envoys, but he also uses the very conduct of the prophets and their prophecies for this purpose.

In a certain sense, the second way is more effective. In any event, in the history of salvation the second way is more frequent than the first. Further, the Israelite people and the first Christians gave it more merit.

From a theological standpoint, prophecies have a singular and specific importance. Prophecies are necessary because they give reason to an aspect that mystery does not clarify: the mystery of how the divine Word uses and expresses himself through human words. We will now deal with this issue from the apologetic perspective, because *prophecies are the precise reasons for believing specifically that the divine Word is expressed through human words.*

In his manifestation to prophets, God on some occasions infused images and new concepts. At other times, he used knowledge they already possessed, perhaps better disposing the prophet for what he wanted to tell them. Many times God used the knowledge they used in their normal dealings and conversation with the rest of humanity.[54] Although God used the elements of the prophet's memory or knowledge to manifest what he wanted,[55] the prophet's capacity to express the divine did not come from within, but from God, who used his mediator to shine forth his prophetic light in a new way.[56]

All these explanations of the divine work in the prophets have an apologetic purpose. The knowledge of the intimacy of God and his plans is not made known according to a dynamism that is different from the one causing the knowledge of the future or the secrets of the heart. In both cases, infused light and species are combined. Prophets are defined by a way of knowing that reaches *different* realities. By means of the revelation communicated to them—through signs and light—they come to share in divine and human secrets as well as the divine and human decisions. Prophetic knowledge is not diversified because of its object. It is characterized by its structure, which has both immediate and eternal value. Hence, it is important that we immediately accredit mediators and their messages so that their words, although human, might properly express to mankind what God is and wants.[57]

II. The Perception of Credibility: An Intelligent and Free Process

Faith is said first to be an obedient response to God. This implies that God be acknowledged in his divinity, transcendence and supreme freedom. By the authority of his absolute transcendence, God who makes himself known is also the source of the credibility of what he reveals. By faith, men and women give their *assent* to this divine testimony. This means that they acknowledge fully and integrally the truth of what is revealed because it is God himself who is the guarantor of that truth. They can make no claim upon this truth which comes to them as gift and which, set within the context of interpersonal communication, urges reason to be open to it and to embrace its profound meaning. This is why the Church has always considered the act of entrusting oneself to God to be a moment of fundamental decision which engages the whole person. In that act, the intellect and the will display their spiritual nature, enabling the subject to act in a way which realizes personal freedom to the full.[58]

The historical experience proves that not all who have witnessed the signs of revelation have arrived at faith. Such was the case, for example, of Pharaoh, or those who convicted Jesus.

It is by no means sufficient to simply witness a divine sign or hear a message coming from God. It is necessary to recognize it as such, which demands an attentive analysis involving the use of the intelligence and the will.

One must intelligently employ knowledge and experience in these affairs so as to make a wise judgment. Given the importance of the issue, it would be very unwise to immediately believe that a certain preaching heard or miracle seen was of divine origin without serious and careful corroboration. It would also be imprudent to disregard the possibility that preaching or a miracle came from God without proper study. The judgment of the intellect, certainly, must be serious and responsible, but it can be enacted in different dimensions, according to the capacities of the person's culture and his present situation.

It is normal to differentiate between a common or spontaneous dimension, a scientific-philosophic one, and, finally, a theological one.

The human will is also involved in this analysis because the discernment under consideration affects the identification of the last end.[59] We will not now analyze how the will acts and specifically resolves the decision about the final end. That issue is dealt with in moral theology. However, we will stop to analyze how freedom has influenced the perception of miracles. From this viewpoint, it is possible to speak about the perception of credibility based upon signs as a process containing three stages, phases, or moments. These are the moment of experience, the assimilation of different experiences of religious and transcendental character, and the stage of significant convergence of those experiences, i.e., the integration among them with the other elements of our own spiritual experience.

This analysis shows that the subject of God's miracles needs to be disposed to believe, to convert, and to do whatever God wishes. Once a person recognizes God's action, he must be ready to accept the implications of that discovery. This is because that discovery requires following wherever the path toward happiness leads. It is our final end, which gives meaning and perfection to our existence. This disposition of openness to the divine designs of human paths toward God finds its maximum expression in the act of faith. It should already be partially present in the way opened by *miracles* and the preaching of the prophets sent by God.

A. The Role of Freedom in the Experience of Miracles

All miracles are phenomenological and historical realities. People have experienced them, although in different ways.

All people, therefore, share this capacity of experiencing miracles, although it presents some individualized characteristics. It involves the experience of the historical and phenomenological reality that miracles represent. It also requires the experience—through signs and faith—of the spiritual reality signified by miracles. Further, it implies the experience—also in faith and linked to the experience of signs—of the link between miracles and realities and what they mean. (This last experience is the recognition of the meaning of the miracle as such.[60])

As is well known, various theories have been used to explain the *notion of experience*.[61] Beyond these differences and setting the extreme positions aside, different schools agree that experience is a modality of human knowledge, mainly, as *knowledge of what is unique*. Experience is mainly knowledge about things and deeds present to the senses. It refers, therefore, to the existential horizon and allows us to judge if particular things truly exist, and if they really have the properties and characteristics attributed to them. It can be defined as *existential knowledge of specific, singular, and historical realities and events*.

Regarding the experience in which we are now interested, one aspect requires clarification: How is it possible to perceive realities that are not only spiritual but also transcendent? Within the realm of religious experience, we consider the possibility of an experience of God. This has been the subject of numerous studies in the twentieth century.[62] The answer is positive: It is possible to speak about an experience of God as long as such experience is understood as spiritual, not immediate and direct (cf. Jn 1: 18). One can experience God in a mediate and indirect way through certain effects of his actions in history and in the world, which can be perceived and recognized as signs of the divine reality.[63]

The positive character of this response is based upon a fundamental principle of human gnosiology: People can perceive intelligible and spiritual truth through certain sensible effects.[64] This principle is necessary if we are to adequately understand the relationship of mankind with God without falling into fideism or atheism.

This capacity of perception is conditioned by the subject, or more precisely, it depends on him. This is because the subject is the one who knows. As we have already pointed out, recognition and belief in the truth involves the exercise of the intellect and the will.

Strictly speaking, the moral and religious interior attitudes and, above all, the sense and practice of justice are those that radically predispose a person to experiencing God. For instance, the Pharaoh, though he witnessed the miracles carried out by Yahweh in favor of Israel, did not want to see the hand of God in them, and in this, he was encouraged by his own wise men and counselors (cf. Ex 8: 15). He said about Yahweh, "I do not know the LORD" (Ex 5: 2). He did not want to know him, being too obstinate to be *humbled*. In order to speak about Pharaoh's attitude, Yahweh's narration uses the term *kabed*. It denotes immobility of a heart besmirched in the avarice and pleasures of this world and of political power (cf. Ex 7: 14; 8: 11, 28; 9: 7, 34; 10: 1). In priestly narration the word *hzq lb* is preferred. It means the immobility proper to the callused or hardened heart (cf. Ex 7: 13, 22; 8: 15; 9: 12, 35; 10: 27).[65]

Personal dispositions and attitudes can, nevertheless, change. Biblical history proves this often and in many ways. The Bible also shows that God's action in history goes precisely in that direction. God seeks to change people's attitudes towards him. He *forms* persons and whole nations in an attitude of faith and openness and allows them to recognize him in his works in such a way that his people somehow attest to his power, wisdom, kindness, promises, plans, and saving actions.

B. The Role of Freedom in the Personal and Progressive Assimilation of Miracles

The dynamics of miracles are fundamentally interpersonal: the interpersonal character proper to human communication implies intentionality in the one who offers a miracle and availability in the one who accepts the miracle. The one who offers certainly has an idea that he wants to communicate, and his pursuit of that goal moves him to communicate that idea through an action: He wants or expects something from the other. For his part, the one who accepts the action is questioned by the one who offers it so—through it, moving toward its meaning—as to discover the intention of the one who gives and communicates with him. The beneficiary of the miracle is called to share something with the one who offered it. The communicator, at the same time, looks for and seeks communion.

It is necessary for the recipient to want to enter the mental and intentional world of the giver. It is equally important for the giver to want the recipient to participate in his ideas and projects, in his understanding of existence and its representative code.[66]

In these considerations, we can see that the efficacy of miracles depends upon the governance and domain of freedom. People decide how they will lead their own lives and view the world. A person can maintain and develop interior conditions that allow him to understand divine language, or he can neglect and even lose them to a major or minor extent. Samuel's call and his correspondence to God's voice and wishes exemplify a positive response in this situation (cf. 1 Sm 3: 1–21).

Some miracles or signs seem to mean little or nothing to some, whereas others see them as highly eloquent. Consider, for example, Zachariah's experience. The angel's word was not proof enough for him and he requested another sign. In marked contrast, Mary needed nothing else. She only asked how the project manifested by the angel—in which she believed—was to be fulfilled. St. John saw the wrappings and sheets in the tomb and believed. St. Thomas heard from the women and the other apostles that the Lord had risen from the dead, but still demanded to touch the wounds of Jesus with his own hands.

C. The Role of Freedom in the Convergent and Unitary Integration of Miracles and other Spiritual Elements of Persons

Human knowledge is composed of an integration of many different controlled, interrelated experiences.

As we have seen, the dynamic of miracles is substantially based upon experience, and it develops as a convergent integration of various experiences from God: our own and those of others, in the world and in ourselves, in collective and personal history. Spiritual experiences do not remain isolated in themselves. They tend toward unity and build an explanation that makes a spiritual reality understandable. Miracles are not isolated from each other in persons who see or hear about them.

They constitute a unitary body that makes mysteries present—even if they do not make them evident—which inspires us to accept them in faith.

This dynamism of the signs of faith was studied by Cardinal Newman, who set out the motivation and justification of faith as a *convergent accumulation of arguments.* Some have also written of this motivating faith in a cumulative structure of justification, that is to say, in a series of arguments, that are related but do not correspond to the habitual model of deductive or inductive reasoning.[67] These arguments permit a uniting of rational and discreet judgment and give consistency to the election of faith. Such a cumulative structure is necessary because the idea of God and the message of the kingdom refers to a whole reality and includes facts, values, and ways of behavior. Consequently, this represents Christian faith as a cumulative understanding of the last and omni-comprehending reality. Basically, the cumulative argument tries to justify that wish by offering interlocutors many and very different, if convergent, reasons.[68]

This stage of cumulative convergence requires the intervention of the subject's freedom. This is because the result of such integration is not exposed with complete evidence to the intellect. It always needs the acquiescence of the will to be considered true. It is precisely in that convergence, which does not give total, clear perception of reality, that we find the characterization of biblical miracles. They are incompletely evidenced mysteries.

Mankind is introduced to mysteries by miracles, which grant a certain anticipation, a certain perception of what will be eschatologically attained. Every miracle manifests a certain experience and perception (not necessarily immediate or direct) of the transcendent and mysterious reality. The integration of several miracles reinforces, confirms, and enriches what each one of them has already granted. The experience of miracles is an anticipated experience of the mystery of God, who is infinite power, wisdom, and kindness. For the apostles, the experience of the Resurrection meant—among other things—an anticipated experience of the glorious condition of Christ and humanity at the end of history. *The convergence of all of these integrated and related experiences builds the experience of the miracle that is the faith in the reality that he signifies and reveals.*

III. The Genesis of the Act of Faith

As we have seen, this process involves *preaching* (proposition of the revealed word) performed by *prophets* (or mediators in general) and *miracles* (which confirm the truth of preaching and inspiring us to embrace it). The interior gift of the *grace of faith* makes the *personal response* to divine revelation both intelligent and free. St. Thomas summarized how these elements intervene in the genesis of faith as follows:

> For faith, two things are necessary. First, there is a proposition of things in which to believe. This is necessary for someone to believe something in an explicit manner. Second, the action of he who believes in what is proposed to him. Regarding the first aspect, it is necessary that faith come from God, because the truths of faith exceed human reason. They do not fit within man's contemplation, if God does not reveal them. God reveals himself to some in a direct manner, as was the case of the apostles and the prophets. To others, on the contrary, God works through preachers of faith, according to the Apostle's words: "How can men preach unless they are sent?" (Rom 10: 15).
>
> Regarding the second aspect, that is, referring to the action of the one who believes, a double cause can be distinguished. One, which induces the external action, as an observed miracle or the persuasive powers of a man, attracts us to the faith. None of these reasons is sufficient motive, because among those who see the same miracle, and hear the same preaching, some believe and others do not. That is why it is necessary to assign an internal cause that motivates man to accept the truth of faith. According to the Pelagians, that cause would be man's free will alone. That is why they said that the beginning of faith is within us, as long we are willing to believe. They admit that the consummation comes from God, who proposes to us what we should believe. But this is not true, because, to consent to the truth of faith, man

is elevated above his own nature and that is why it is necessary that there is in him a supernatural principle that moves him from inside, and that principle is God. Therefore, faith, regarding the assertion, that is its main act, comes from God who, from inside man, inspires him by grace.[69]

We now examine the function and value that should be recognized as the confirming works of miracles. There are three solutions to this question: first, to deny that they are important for belief; second, to recognize their efficacy in obtaining "acquired faith" as an extrinsic requirement of the act of faith (the apologetic orientation of Bl. John Duns Scotus); or third, to admit that they intrinsically belong to the process of the genesis of faith but that they are not the proper or definitive cause of the act of supernatural faith (the apologetic orientation of St. Thomas Aquinas). The solution to this issue, fundamentally, is linked to the formal foundation of faith. Further, it assumes that we can explain how the convergence of reason, grace, and freedom in the genesis of faith is developed and structured.

A. The Theological Issue of *Analysis Fidei*

In the genesis of faith, we can distinguish several movements of the act of faith as an interior response to historical revelation from God in which the intelligence, the will, grace, and freedom all participate. Since the sixteenth century, theology has analyzed the logical and psychological structure of the act of faith. The issue of the knowledge of the formal reason for the act of faith—the issue of its formal epistemological foundation—has been called the *analysis fidei*. It has given birth to many studies without offering a universally accepted theological interpretation.[70] Perhaps that is why this issue is considered a *crux theologorum*.[71]

If we leave aside details that separate the various authors and focus our attention on those points that seem decisive, we can assert that, before anything else, man can, without the need of supernatural assistance, judge that the Christian message *can be believed* as divine.[72] God can give supernatural help at any moment and, particularly, as normally happens, can help one carry out the judgment of credibility.

The Church admits that motives of credibility have an efficacy of their own independent from the help of grace.[73] Nevertheless, she also affirms that God permanently helps people on the path toward him, in the pilgrimage in faith and toward faith.[74]

Nonetheless, to affirm that the revealed message *must be believed* as divine seems to demand that the human mind be made "con-natural" with supernatural truth through the *habitus fidei.* According to this way of thinking, the intellect "sees" its own co-naturality with the revealed truth (otherwise, it would not judge that it "must" assent).

Finally, the grace of faith is undoubtedly necessary for the will to *command the act of faith* ("to believe"), thereby inspiring the intelligence to assert "I believe." In fact, within the act of faith there is a double dependence on God because he produces the act of faith. He *enlightens* the intelligence and *disposes* the will. The grace of faith influences both powers, each according to its nature. Grace acts as light in the intelligence and as impulse and inclination in the will. St. Thomas summarized this, saying, "the light of faith...does not move by way of the intelligence, but rather by way of the will. That is why it does not make us see things that are believed, or compel us to agree, but makes us consent in a voluntary manner."[75]

Clearly, the issue of *analysis fidei* particularly highlights the fact that faith is a mysterious reality we cannot completely explain. Nevertheless, as Aquinas has written, we can pretend to an approximate understanding, since light perceived by the senses is the beginning of vision and sensory knowledge. It not only manifests things enlightened by it but manifests itself as well. Similarly, it is possible to say that people participate in divine light through faith. One knows (in faith, not yet in vision) both things manifested by that light and the light itself, which is the beginning of supernatural knowledge. (Recall that faith is knowledge, a participation of the knowledge that God has of himself.) The Psalmist says, "in thy light do we see light" (Ps 36: 9). These words can be understood to refer to the glorious situation when man, with *lumen gloriae*, will see the light that God is. That light can be understood from the present situation of the faithful because faith is a certain anticipated knowledge of the glorious vision.[76]

In other words, believers accept the Word that is announced to them. They know—by the light of faith—that the Word comes from God. The act of supernatural faith, in its proper and final form, is to accept the Word because, aided by grace from the Holy Spirit, we know it is God's (cf. 1 Thes 2: 13; Jn 6: 66–69). B. Duroux has suggested that this recognition has an experimental core that is spiritual in character, that is to say, an interior experience—which is already the effect of grace—of supernatural affection for the announced Word. This is the effect that Tradition terms *pius credulitatis affectus* (pious feelings of belief), and that is the first effect that grace imprints upon the will.[77]

Finally and most importantly, the reasons to believe, or the motives of credibility, are not the formal reason of faith: We do not believe for reasons of credibility. *We formally believe because of God's authority, because of his divine testimony.*[78]

Reasons are not sufficient motive to fulfill the act of faith. For that action, the grace of faith is always necessary. Therein, it enjoys an absolute and formal priority. Signs of faith may induce, direct, inspire, and can even constitute a sure proof of the presence and intervention of God, but they are not a sufficient reason to accept the divine Word as such.

For example, Christ's Resurrection is a demonstrable historical fact, but historical demonstration of an unexplainable natural fact is not sufficient for people to believe in supernatural mysteries. In fact, as Jesus said to St. Thomas, "Have you believed because you have seen me?" (Jn 20: 29). St. Gregory the Great commented on this passage: "He saw one thing and believed another." St. Thomas saw the resurrected Jesus, and he believed he was God. Certainly, seeing was believing. This motive was based on the continuity between the seen and believed reality. Still, as what was believed was not exactly what was seen, there remained a certain discontinuity between seeing and believing. That distance might be bridged only with the help of grace.

All this allows us to understand that the efficacy of the reasons of credibility cannot be understood through mathematical or logical arguments or by proofs offered by the experimental sciences. The Magisterium of the Church has answered these questions in various ways (*rite probari*,[79] *recta ratio fidei fundamenta demonstret*,[80] *revelationis argumenta...quae Dei omnipotentiam et infinitam scientiam luculenter commonstrant*,[81] *evidentem fidei christianae credibilitatem*[82]). These formulas need to be understood in the sense that the consent of faith is supported by a solid rational foundation that may even be formulated scientifically. However, the act of faith must not be conceived of as if it were the result of apodictic proofs giving evidence for a formal motive of faith or for believed truths.

B. The Concurrence of Reason, Freedom, and Grace in the Genesis of Faith

The genesis of supernatural faith cannot be conceived as a deductive-rational, psychological-existential, or cultural-sociological process that concludes with the act of faith in a divine message. The act of faith is not an opinion reinforced by good arguments, nor the fruit of scientific investigation. It is, always and simply, the fruit of grace freely chosen by one who, thanks to that assistance, can believe in the Word of God who reveals himself. Nevertheless, along the journey toward faith, there are certainly intellectual, affective, and sociological elements, personal and familiar circumstances, educational factors, and existential experiences that can either make it easier and help along the way, or, make it more difficult and retard it.

The reasons to believe reveal a structure, the dynamics of which require a permanent intervention of the intelligence. The Church considers these dynamics the "external indications of his revelation."[83] They involve repeated decisions on the part of the person to believe. At the same time, we have seen the indispensable need for grace in this process.

The human will, in its intertwining of reason and grace, is not the first thing that takes part in the journey of faith, nor is it the most important element. Nevertheless, it has a continuous and important presence, for freedom takes part in at least three ways: first, to impose the assertion of an unseen truth; second, to believe in a radically mysterious Word; and third, to accept the grace of faith—light and motion—which is an unmerited gift of God granted to humanity without making any demand (cf. Eph 2: 9). People recognize God by signs of faith and allow themselves to be guided and educated by testimonies of the Word until they arrive at the miracle and believe in God's testimony about himself.

This presence of freedom is a fundamental and constitutive element of this process. It is intrinsically decisive for personal growth and fulfillment, which is according to divine design. In fact, the economy of revelation corresponds to the nature and finality of the communication of God to mankind. God is love, and his revelation is an invitation to live in his love and from his love, transformed by his love. One needs to be free to love: Freedom and its exercise are a constitutive part of love.

The deep defect is the denial that one may know through reason that God exists and that he takes part in human life and history. Another form of fideism denies the human freedom to receive or refuse the grace of God. J. Quasten offers some enlightening words on this case with which he concluded his study of the Apologists of the second century. "Perhaps apologists reach their highest point of greatness when they proclaim themselves champions of the freedom of conscience, as root and source of any true religion, as an indispensable element so that religion may survive."[84]

We should, therefore, understand that liberty is not just a condition for believing and loving. It is also an impulse toward faith and love. Freedom allows one to accept the Word of God and give proper thanks for his gift.[85]

> The kingdom of Christ is a kingdom of freedom. In it the only slaves are those who freely bind themselves, out of love of God. What a blessed slavery of love, that sets us free! Without freedom, we cannot respond to grace. Without freedom, we cannot give ourselves freely to our Lord, for the most supernatural of reasons, because we want to.[86]

IV. Harmony of Reason and Faith in the Life of the Believer

"Gifts of grace are added to nature in a way that they do not destroy it, but perfect it."[87] This also happens with "the light of faith, that is infused in us with grace: It does not destroy the natural light of reason put in us by God."[88]

Faith does not contradict reason. It does not infringe upon or eliminate it. Faith simply surpasses it. Faith perfects mankind because it brings a knowledge of a superior order. It allows man to know God, what is related to his last happiness, and the way of reaching it more fully. That is why God helps people know themselves better and know the world and its meaning in a more profound way.

> Faith and reason are like two wings on which the human spirit rises to the contemplation of truth; and God has placed in the human heart a desire to know the truth—in a word, to know himself—so that, by knowing and loving God, men and women may also come to the fullness of truth about themselves (cf. Ex 33: 18; Ps 27: 8–9; 63: 2–3; Jn 14: 8; 1 Jn 3: 2).[89]

Clearly, all of this knowledge is most useful for human beings because human nature tends to the knowledge of God as the source of his most intimate joy and last happiness. It is also clear that, since faith comes from God, it is impossible for *faith to contradict what natural reason might discover by itself* in the world and in history. Hence, the knowledge that is the fruit of faith is put in continuity and, at the same time in discontinuity—because it surpasses and transcends man's mere human knowledge.

The knowledge of God, man, history and the world, reached by faith, is presented as wisdom beyond any merely human horizon and opens unthinkable and unsuspected perspectives to man (cf. 1 Cor 2: 6–9). Such transcendence is manifested in the deeply mysterious character of the revealed realities and, therefore, in the impossibility of its resolution by the principles of reason and simply natural knowledge.[90] *Salvation—and faith, which is its beginning—is out of human reach* because the knowledge of God in his intimacy falls outside the possibilities of human intelligence. This is St. Paul's deep meaning when he teaches about justification by faith: "For we hold that a man is justified by faith apart from works of law" (Rom 3: 28); "by works of the law shall no one be justified" (Gal 2: 16). If the grace of God is lacking, no human, cultural, or religious work or activity leads to a knowledge of God as he is or to communion with him (cf. Gal 5: 6, 22; Eph 2: 8, 10; 1 Thes 1: 3; 2: 12, 14; 4: 1–12).[91]

Still, this superiority of the knowledge of faith over the mere knowledge of reason does not mean that between them there are no points of intersection. Theologians who have denied this relationship have placed the knowledge of God in a fideism that does not recognize the importance of human intelligence. Avoiding that position, some authors have thought of the faith-reason relationship as a co-habitation that, without seeing them in conflict, has enclosed each one in its own sphere, independent, without interference or mutual influence. This is the late Scholastic teaching of the "double truth." The Church Fathers, for their part, took another direction. The Apologists of the second century—following the instruction of 1 Peter 3: 15—worked hard to create a dialogue between Christian doctrine and the different expressions of Greco-Roman culture.

In subsequent centuries, St. Clement of Alexandria, Origen, St. Augustine, and others promoted a harmonious view of reason and faith that permitted an integrated vision of the world, mankind, and history that brought together the culture of that society and epoch with Christian teachings. This is the orientation that best reflects the spirit of the Church in Vatican I when she called for a greater collaboration between reason and faith, between theology and the human sciences. In Vatican II, the Council Fathers emphasized the need for an increased dialogue between the Church and the world, between faith and culture, between theology and philosophy, that might lead individuals and human communities to a greater development and a greater knowledge and love of God.[92]

Faith is not against reason. Rather, it is "a gift that conforms to reason" (cf. Rom 12: 1).[93] The mysterious superiority of revealed knowledge neither humiliates reason nor forces itself on reason's proper sphere of activity. On the contrary, revealed knowledge serves to perfect, complete, and correct reason in whatever is deficient or wrong.[94] In reality, *there can be no conflict in the proper and true sense between reason and faith* because both have the same origin: the Father of lights from whom every perfect gift comes (cf. Jas 1: 17). They are directed to the same end—knowledge of the truth. So, there is no formal contradiction between what one and the other know when they see reality according to their proper light.[95] "Things of faith are above reason, not against reason."[96]

Whenever an apparent conflict has presented itself in history, it has sprung from a misunderstanding born out of an erroneous presentation of what faith teaches or what science has proved in such a way that something was falsely attributed to one or the other.[97] Since the sixteenth century, these misunderstandings have unfortunately been repeated, in part because faith was conceived—according to Protestant thinking—only as a subjective feeling or practical attitude before life and the human community. Neither faith as supernatural knowledge nor its participation—by the Word and gift—in the knowledge that God has of himself was properly valued. A certain undue exaltation of the capacity of reason that arose in this period may be joined to that error. Here, reason was thought to be the only cause and only judge of all true knowledge.

Faith and reason are related to such an extent that the former cannot do without the latter and reason itself does not attain to its full potential without faith.

> Faith implies reason and perfects it, and reason, illuminated by faith, finds the strength to rise to knowledge of God and of spiritual realities. Human reason loses nothing when it is open to the contents of faith; what is more, the latter calls for its free and conscious adherence.[98]

We have insisted that faith is knowledge in a formal sense—it implies the action of the intellect and necessarily acts in reference to a horizon of human understanding.[99] Also, we have shown that the process toward faith is permanently marked by intellectual exercise.

So, then, we can disprove any accusation that the Christian faith may be considered fanaticism. Fanaticism is based on people believing an idea that contradicts rational evidence. Fanaticism is solely supported by personal decisions and an incapacity for dialogue and critical study. Christianity has very high standards of self-criticism. Christ asks his faithful to be resolved to lose their lives before denying him (cf. Mt 10: 16–40)—as has happened often in history—but at the same time he is reasonable with others (cf. 1 Pt 3: 15–16).[100]

Supernatural faith collaborates with reason and shares its acquisitions after discerning what is right and wrong. From this process comes a mutual collaboration that benefits the work of intelligence when it tries to unravel accessible truths, and that also benefits faith by making it better understood. In the words of Vatican I, reason, rightly cultivated, "establishes the foundations of the faith"[101] and, illuminated by its light, "develops the science of divine things."[102]

Finally, faith shows itself in accordance with reason. In fact, nothing is more humanly natural than to accept the Word of God and receive his gift (cf. Jn 4: 10).[103] For man, it is immensely good to know the truth. When man believes in God who reveals himself, he does not abdicate his desire to find the truth and good. On the contrary, he accomplishes his mission by finding God who is infinite truth and supreme good (cf. Jn 14: 6).

Therefore, the communication of God to humanity, offered in Christ and taken in faith, responds in a surpassing way to the deepest human aspirations. It fills his capacity for life, happiness, and beauty beyond measure.

In conclusion, the relationship between Christian faith and human reason must be seen as the relationship of two different realities. They are harmoniously linked and intermingled such that *each is ordered to the other and perfects and elevates the other*. It is necessary to recognize their radical difference and assert their convergence and collaboration in the development of the human person and human communities. The distinction must recognize the primacy of faith. Their collaboration cannot make us forget that both have their own dynamics and function, and they should be mutually respected. In that way, they contribute to the complete growth of individuals and nations along their way toward God, who is perfect light and life.

At this point we would do well to consider the following words of John Paul II concerning this relationship at the beginning of his encyclical on the inviolable value and character of human life:

> Man is called to a fullness of life that goes beyond the dimension of his earthly existence. This is because it consists in the participation in the same life of God. The sublime aspect of this supernatural vocation manifests the greatness and worth of human life even in its temporal phase. In fact, life in time is a basic condition, initial moment, and integral part of the whole unitary process of human life. This process is enlightened by the promise and renewed by the gift of divine life in an unexpected and undeserved way that will reach its utter fulfillment in eternity (cf. 1 Jn 3: 1–2). At the same time, this supernatural call stresses the relative character of the earthly life of men and women. In fact, our life here on earth is not the "last" reality, but the "second to last." It is a sacred reality that is entrusted to us so that we might guard it with responsibility and take it to perfection, in the love and gift of ourselves to God and to our brothers and sisters.[104]

ENDNOTES

FOREWORD

1. Cf. H. Stirnimann, in "Freiburger Zeitschrift f. Philosophie und Theologie"
    24 (1977) 291-301. G. Ebeling, in a study dated prior to that of Stirnimann,
    claimed that the first to use the term was J.N. Ehrlich, Leitfaden...
    Fundamentaltheologie I, Prague 1859: cf. "Zeitschrift f. Theologie und
    Kirche" (1970) 479–524.

2. A view of the principal models can be seen in J. Schmitz, Fundamental
    Theology in the twentieth century, in R. Vander Gucht, H. Vorgrimler,
    Theology in the 20th Century, Madrid 1978, II, pp. 171–212. For a statement
    of the historical evolution of this discipline, you may also consult
    R. Fisichella, Revelation: event and credibility, Sigueme, Salamanca,
    1989, pp. 14–41; S. Pie-Ninot, Treatise on Fundamental Theology, Ed.
    Secr. Trinitario, Salamanca 1991 (2nd ed.), pp. 18–54; G. Ruggieri (ed.)
    Enciclopedia di Teologia Fondamentale, Marietti, Genova 1987, vol. 1,
    passim, sp. pp. XVII–XXVI and 33–58.

3. John Paul II, Exhort. Apost. *Pastores dabo vobis*, March 25, 1992, n. 54.

4. Commentaries on that interrelation, as they appear in those council
    documents, can be found in H. de Lubac, La Revelation divine, Cerf, Paris
    1980; R. Latourelle, Theology of the revelation, Sigueme, Salamanca 1982
    (5th ed.), pp. 289–304 and 351–398; G. Colombo, La ragione teologica,
    Glossa, Milan 1995, pp. 73–90; A. González Montes, *Dei Verbum* sullo sfondo
    di *Dei Filius*, in R. Fisichella (ed.), La Teologia Fondamentale. Convergenze
    per il terzo millennio, Piemme. Casale Monferrato 1997, pp. 83–104.

5. Second Vatican Council, Past Const. *Gaudium et spes*. December 7, 1965,
    n. 22.

6. John Paul II, *Discurso*, September 30, 1995, Cf. R. Fisichella (ed.) *La Teologia
    Fondamentale, Convergenze per il terzo millenio*, cit. pp. 281–284.

7. Paul VI, Enc. *Ecclesiam suam*, August 6, 1964: in AAS 56 (1964) 641–643.

8. There are many who today maintain the need for this distinction that we
    have just proposed; cf., for example, M. Seckler, *Teologia Fondamentale;
    compiti e structurazione, concetto e nomi*, in W. Kern, H.J. Pottmeyer,
    M. Seckler (ed.) *Corso di Teologia Fondamentale*, vol. IV; *Tratato di
    Gnoseologia teologica*, Queriniana Brescia 1990, pp. 565–599; idem., *Teologia
    fondamentale e Dogmatica*, in R. Fisichella (ed.) *La Teologia Fondamentale,
    Convergenze per il terzo millennio*, cit. pp. 126–148. This distinction, as
    admitted by the author himself, is one of the reasons that led R. Latourelle
    to write his *Theology of Revelation*; cit. p. 11.

9.   F. Ocáriz has written chapters I–V and VII, and epigraph IX, 3; A. Blanco, chapters VI, VIII, and X–XIV and epigraphs IX, 1–2.

10.   Cf. R. Latourelle, *Apologetique Fondamentale, Problemes de nature et de methode*, in "Salesianum" 28 (1965) 256–273; H. Bouillard, *Le sens de l'apologetique*, in "Bulletin du Comite des etudes," no. 35, Paris 1961, 311–327; N. Dunas, *Les problems et le statut de l'apologetique*, in "Revue des Sciences Philosophiques et Theologiques 43 (1959) 643–680.

11.   For an understanding of the positioning of apologetics together with Christian theology, see A. Blanco, *What is Theology*, Palabra, Madrid 1990, pp. 119–122.

12.   The teachings of the authors cited are considered valid in that which is explicitly accepted in these pages; therefore, other ideas of these writers not proposed as explicitly accepted in this book are not necessarily shared.

PART ONE — INTRODUCTION

1.   John Paul II, Ap. Letter *Tertio millennio adveniente*, 6.

2.   Second Vatican Council, Dogm. Const. *Dei Verbum*, 15.

3.   Ibid., 2.

4.   Cf. ibid., 7–10.

5.   This explains, for example, the reference to Pontius Pilate that we find in the Creed.

6.   *Dei Verbum*, 2.

7.   Cf. ibid., 5.

8.   Cf. *Catechism of the Catholic Church*, 142–143.

9.   For an extensive review of the historical panorama, cf. R. Latourelle, *Teología de la Revelación*, 169–398; G. Ruggieri, *Sapienza e Storia*; H. Fries, *La Revelación, en Mysterium Salutis*, t. I, 210–227; M. Seybold, H. Waldenfels, L. Scheffczyk, P.R. Cren, U. Horst, A. Sand and P. Stockmeier, *La Revelación, en Historia de los Dogmas*, t. I: *La Existencia en la Fe*, 1st quarter: "La Revelación;" B. Sesboué, C. Theobald, ed., *La Parola della Sapienza*, IV; R. Fisichella, *La Revelación*, 11–42; A. Kolping, *Fundamentaltheologie*, I, 21–87, 132–261; S. Pié-Ninot, *Tratado de Teología Fundamental*, 55–109; P.A. Sequeri, *Il Dio Affidabile*, 21–118.

10.   John Paul II, *Fides et ratio*, 7.

11.   St. Thomas Aquinas, *Summa Theologiae*, I, q. 1, a. 1.

12.   First Vatican Council, Dogm. Const. *Dei Filius*, 2: DS 3005.

13.   Ibid.: DS 3027.

14.   Ibid.: DS 3028.

15.   Cf. A. Gardeil, *Le Donné Révélé et la Théologie*; J.V. Bainvel, *De Vera Religione et Apologetica*; R. Garrigou-Lagrange, *De Revelatione per Ecclesiam Catholicam Proposita*; H. Dieckmann, *De Revelatione Christiana*; C. Pesch, *Compendium Theologiae Dogmaticae*; L. Lercher, *Institutiones Theologiae Dogmaticae*; S. Tromp, *De Revelatione Christiana*; J. Brinktrine, *Offenbarung und Kirche*.

16. See, for instance, these definitions: *Revelatio divina stricte dicta est locutio Dei, qua Deus ex iis quae cognoscit, quaedam cum hominibus communicat, ita ut homines ea propter auctoritatem Dei loquentis credant*: C. Pesch, *Compendium Theologiae Dogmaticae* I, 29. *Revelatio est actio divina libera et essentialiter supernaturalis qua Deus, ad perducendum humanum genus ad finem supernaturalem qui in visione essentiae divinae consistit, nobis loquens per prophetas et novissime per Christum, sub quadam obscuritate manifestavit mysteria supernaturalia naturalesque religionis veritates, ita ut deinceps infallibiliter proponi possint ab Ecclesia sine ulla significationis mutatione, usque ad finem mundi*: R. Garrigou-Lagrange, *De Revelatione per Ecclesiam Catholicam Proposita*, I, 132.

17. Cf. R. Guardini, *Die Offenbarung, ihr Wesen und ihre Formen*; J. Mouroux, *Creo en Ti; L'Expérience Chrétienne*; G. Söhngen, *Die Einheit in der Theologie*; L. Charlier, *Essai sur le Problème Théologique*; J. Danielou, *Méssage Evangelique et Culture Hellénistique*; M.D. Chenu, *Une École de Théologie*; R. Aubert, *Le Problème de l'Acte de Foi*; H. Bouillard, *Lógica de la Fe*; H. de Lubac, *De la Connaissance de Dieu*.

18. Cf. J. Dupont, *Gnosis*; C. Spicq, *Les Epitres Pastorales*, 116–125; H. Schlier, *Wort Gottes*; R. Schnackenburg, *La Théologie du Nouveau Testament*; H. Schulte, *Der Begriff der Offenbarung im Neuen Testament*; G. Kittel, *aokoyo*, in *TWNT* I, 217–225; *lelò, logos*, in *TWNT* IV, 100–140; G. Friedrich, *euaggelion*, in *TWNT* II, 714–718, 724–733; *kéryssò*, in *TWNT* III, 701–717; A. Oepke, *apocalyptò*, in *TWNT* III, 565–597; A. Althaus, *Die christliche Wahrheit*; H. Strathmann, *martys*, in *TWNT* IV, 492–520; K.H. Rengstorf, *didaskò*, in *TWNT* II, 138–168.

19. Cf. *Dei Verbum*, 5, 6. For analysis of this document, cf. U. Betti, *La Rivelazione Divina nella Chiesa*; R. Latourelle, *Teología de la Revelación*, 351–389; AA.VV., *Commento alla Costituzione Dogmatica Sulla Divina Rivelazione; Concilio Vaticano II: Comentarios a la Constituciòn sobre la Divina Revelación; Vatican II: La Révélation Divine*; H. de Lubac, *La Révélation Divine*; G.H. Tavard, *The Dogmatic Constitution on Divine Revelation of Vatican Council II*.

20. Cf. *Dei Verbum*, 2.

21. Detailed theological criticisms of these approaches are taken up in later chapters.

22. *Dei Verbum*, 2.

23. Ibid., 4.

CHAPTER 1

1. Cf. R. Latourelle, *Teología de la Revelación*, 18.

2. Cf. ibid., 25–26.

3. Cf. G. Ziener, "Palabra," 744.

4. Cf. R. Latourelle, *Teología de la Revelación*, 18, 29–30.

5. Cf. C. Westermann, *Teologia dell'Antico Testamento*, 22–32.

6. Cf. J. Ratzinger, *Teoría de los Principios Teológicos*, 174.
7. Cf. R. Latourelle, *Teología de la Revelación*, 33–35; C. Westermann, *Teologia dell'Antico Testamento*, 36–40.
8. Second Vatican Council, Dogm. Const. *Dei Verbum*, 9.
9. E. Jacob, *Théologie de l'Ancien Testament*, 104.
10. Due to important differences of structure and content between historical (supernatural) revelation and cosmic (natural) revelation, some authors prefer to speak of cosmic revelation as *manifestation* instead of *revelation*. Cf., for example, R. Latourelle, "Revelación," 1286; S. Pie-Ninot, *Tratado*, 163.
11. John Paul II, *Fides et ratio*, 19.
12. J. Danielou, *Dieu et Nous*, 44.
13. Cf. St. Thomas Aquinas, *Summa Theologiae*, I, q. 1, a. 1; *Summa contra Gentiles*, I, c. 4; First Vatican Council, Dogm. Const. *Dei Filius*, 2: DS 3005.
14. Benedict XVI, Meetings with the Representatives of Science, 12/09/2006.
15. Cf. *Dei Filius*: DS 3004, 3026; *Dei Verbum*, 1, 3.
16. See especially K. Barth, *Die kirchliche Dogmatik*, II, 1, sez. 27, 224–229.
17. Cf. E. Brunner, "Zur Lehre von der *analogia entis*," 50ff. C. Fabro makes a brief but profound analysis of Barth's thesis regarding this issue, with particular reference to the influence that the philosophy of Kant, Hegel, and Kierkegaard had on Barth. Cf. C. Fabro, *L'Uomo e il Rischio di Dio*, 383–393; S.A. Matzak, *Karl Barth on God*.
18. *Inter Creatorem et creaturam non potest similitudo notari, quin inter eos maior sit dissimilitudo notanda* (Fourth Lateran Council, *De Fide Catholica*, 2: DS 806).
19. Cf. C. Fabro, *Partecipazione e Causalità*, 499–526.
20. *Dei Verbum*, 3.
21. Cf. Second Vatican Council, Past. Const. *Gaudium et spes*, 13.
22. Cf. *Dei Verbum*, 3.
23. Cf. J. Coppens, "Le Protoévangile: Un Nouvel Essai d'Exégèse," 5–36; L. Arnaldich, "Protoevangelio," 300–302.
24. R. Lavatori, *Dio e l'Uomo: Un Incontro di Salvezza*, 45.
25. Cf. J. Galot, *La Rédemption*, 31–37; J. Schildenberger, "Alianza," 32–34.
26. Cf. L. Bouyer, *La Biblia y el Evangelio*, 19–86.
27. Cf. M. Serentha, *Gesù Cristo Ieri, Oggi e Sempre*, 64.
28. Cf. J. Danielou, *Dieu et Nous*, 107–130.
29. Cf. C. Westermann, *Teologia dell'Antico Testamento*, 49–61. Westermann does not give sufficient importance to the concept of the covenant.
30. Cf. J. Schildenberger, "Profeta," 851–852.
31. J. Danielou, *Cristo e Noi*, 92.
32. STh, II–II, q. 173, a. 2.
33. Cf. ibid., a. 4.
34. Cf. L. Bouyer, *La Biblia y el Evangelio*, 139–175, 293–297.

CHAPTER 2

1. Second Vatican Council, Dogm. Const. *Dei Verbum*, 4.
2. R. Lavatori, *Dio e l'Uomo*, 68.
3. Cf. J. Schmitz, *La Revelación*, 114–115.
4. *Filius ex hoc ipso quod est Verbum perfecte exprimens Patrem, exprimit omnem creaturam* (St. Thomas Aquinas, *De veritate*, q. 4, a. 5.
    He had written a little before: *Quantum ad modum significandi non est eadem ratio nominum trium praedictorum (Filius, Imago, Verbum): Verbum enim non solum importat rationem originis et imitationis, sed etiam manifestationis; et hoc modo est aliquo modo creaturae, inquantum scilicet, per Verbum creatura manifestatur* (ibid., a. 4 ad 6).
5. The Word is *ratio factiva eorum quae Deus facit* (St. Thomas Aquinas, *Summa Theologiae*, I, q. 34, a. 3). Cf. E. Bailleux, "La Création, oeuvre de la Trinité, selon Saint Thomas," 27–50.
6. Cf. J. Ratzinger, *Creazione e Peccato*, 18–20.
7. Cf. R. Latourelle, *Teología de la Revelación*, 94–98, 103–113.
8. For this exegesis, cf. AA.VV., *La Sagrada Escritura*, II, 825–828.
9. Cf. J.H. Nicolas, *Synthèse Dogmatique: De la Trinité à la Trinité*, 459–460.
10. Cf. Second Vatican Council, Past. Const. *Gaudium et spes*, 22.
11. Ibid.
12. F. Ocáriz, "Naturaleza, gracia y gloria," EUNSA, Pamplona, 2nd edition 2001, 324.
13. St. Josemaría Escrivá, *Christ is Passing By*, 109.
14. Cf. D. Mollat, "Nous Avons vu sa Gloire," 310–327.
15. Cf. M. Meinertz, *Teología del Nuevo Testamento*, 556.
16. Cf. L. Cerfaux, *La Théologie de l'Eglise suivant Saint Paul*, 258.
17. About the glorification of the body as deification of matter, cf. M. J. Scheeben, *Los Misterios del Cristianismo*, 772–779; F. Ocáriz, "Naturaleza, gracia y gloria," 329–333.
18. Cf. St. Irenaeus, *Adversus haereses*, 1, 10, 1: PG 7, 549.
19. Cf. St. John Chrysostom, *In Epist. ad Ephesios homiliae*, I, 4: PG 62, 16.
20. Cf. ibid.
21. Cf. St. Theodoret of Cyrrhus, *Interpretatio Epist. ad Ephesios*, I, 10: PG 82, 511.
22. Cf. St. John Damascene, *In Epist. ad Ephesios*, I, 9–10: PG 95, 823–826.
23. Cf. St. Augustine, *Enchiridion*, 61: PL 40, 261.
24. Cf. St. Jerome, *In Epist. ad Ephesios commentarii*, I, I, 10: PL 26, 483–484.
25. *Instaurare omnia: nam inquantum facta sunt propter hominem, omnia instaurari dicuntur* (St. Thomas Aquinas, *In Epist. ad Ephesios*, c. I, lect. 3).
26. *Sicut enim humanum corpus induetur quaedam forma gloriae supernaturali, ita tota creatura sensibilis, in illa gloria filiorum Dei, quandam novitatem gloriae consequetur, secundum illud Ap 21, 1: 'Vidi caelum novum et terram novam.'*

Et per hunc modum creatura sensibilis expectat revelationem gloriae filiorum Dei (St. Thomas Aquinas, *In Epist. ad Romanos*, c. VIII, lect. 4).

27. For an exposition and assessment of the history of the exegesis of Ephesians 1: 10, cf. J.M. Casciaro, *Estudios sobre Cristología del Nuevo Testamento*, 308–324.

28. Ibid., 324; cf. also D. Spada, *L'Uomo in Faccia a Dio*, 104–106.

29. *Ad hanc visionem essentiae (Dei) oculus carnis attingere non poterit; et ideo, ut ei solatium congruens sibi de visione Divinitatis praebeatur, inspiciet Divinitatem in suis effectibus corporalibus, in quibus manifeste indicia divinae maiestatis apparebunt, et praecipue in carne Christi; et post hoc in corporibus beatorum; et deinceps in omnibus aliis corporibus; et ideo oportebit ut etiam alia corpora maiorem influentiam a divina bonitate suscipiant; non tamen speciem variantem, sed addentem cuiusdam gloriae perfectionem; et haec erit mundi innovatio* (St. Thomas Aquinas, *In IV Sent.*, d. 48, q. 2, a. 1 c).

30. John Paul II, Enc. *Dominum et vivificantem*, 50.

31. Cf. Council of Calcedon, *Definitio*: DS 301–302.

32. Christ, as man, is not an adopted son of God, because sonship is a person-to-person relationship, and in him there is not a human person but only a divine Person. That is why, Christ, in his whole reality of God-Man, is the consubstantial Son of the Father: cf. F. Ocáriz, L.F. Mateo Seco, J.A. Riestra, *El Misterio de Jesucristo*, 3rd edition, 2004, 246–249.

33. Cf. John Paul II, Enc. *Redemptor hominis*, 9.

34. Cf. R. Latourelle, *Teología de la Revelación*, 1235–1241; O. Ruiz Arenas, *Teología de la Revelación*, 109–124.

35. R. Lavatori, *Dio e l'Uomo*, 4575. Cf. *Dei Verbum*, 2.

36. *Gaudium et spes*, 22.

37. Second Vatican Council, Dogm. Const. *Lumen gentium*, 9.

38. Cf. P. Bläser, "La Ley en el Nuevo Testamento," 572–587. About the issue in St. Paul, cf. M. Meinertz, *Teología del Nuevo Testamento*, 323–332.

39. Cf. STh, I–II, q. 107, a. 2 c.

40. *Lex nova est ipsa gratia Spiritus Sancti, quae datur fidelibus* (ibid., q. 106, a. 1 c.).

41. Cf. ibid. The specifically ceremonial precepts of the Old Testament lost their binding power, precisely because their function was only to preannounce or prefigure future goods that became present in Christ. They were, consequently, abolished because they were "fulfilled," because the promise had become a present reality (cf. ibid., ad 1). On the contrary, considering judicial precepts, St. Thomas taught that their reason was preserved and is still being perfected because they belong to the love of justice (cf. ibid., ad 4).

42. Cf. F. Prat, *La Théologie de Saint Paul*, II, 525–529.

43. Benedict XVI, *Jesus of Nazareth*, (New York: Doubleday, 2007), 100.

44. *Dilige, et quod vis fac* (St. Augustine, *In Epist. Ioannis ad parthos*, VII, 8: PL 35, 2033).

45. *Nullum est vinculum necessitatis, quia libertas est caritatis* (St. Augustine, *De natura et gratia*, 65, 78: PL 44, 286).

46. *Quanto aliquis plus habet de caritate, plus habet de libertate* (St. Thomas Aquinas, *In III Sent.*, d. 29, q. un., a. 8, qla. 3 s.c.).

47. Cf. F. Ocáriz, "Naturaleza, gracia y gloria," 111.

48. *Obligatio praecepti non opponitur libertati nisi in eo cuius mens aversa est ab eo quod praecipitur: sicut patet in his qui ex solo timore praecepta custodiunt. Sed praeceptum dilectionis non potest impleri nisi ex propria voluntate. Et ideo libertati non repugnat* (STh, II–II, q. 44, a. 1 ad 2).

49. Cf. R. Latourelle, *Teología de la Revelación*, 50.

50. St. Thomas Aquinas, *In Epist. ad Gal.*, c. I, lect. 2.

51. J. Ratzinger, *Teoría de los Principios Teológicos*, 328.

52. Cf. *Dei Verbum*, 4.

53. J. Ratzinger, Commentary on Chapter I of *Dei Verbum*, in LThK, Suppl. II, 510.

54. *Dei Verbum*, 4.

55. Cf. J.M. Casciaro, "Tiempo (en la Sagrada Escritura)," 436–440.

56. Cf. F. Prat, *La Théologie de Saint Paul*, II, 129–130.

57. Cf. John Paul II, *Creo en Jesucristo* (II), 34.

58. Ibid.

59. Cf. O. Cullmann, *Cristo y el Tiempo*, 98–101.

60. Ibid., 69–70.

Chapter 3

1. Second Vatican Council, Dogm. Const. *Dei Verbum*, 4.

2. Ibid., 8.

3. Cf. M. Zerwick, *Analysis Philologica Novi Testamenti Graeci*, 564.

4. Cf. ibid., 478.

5. Cf., i.e., St. Irenaeus, *Adversus haereses*, III, 1 and 15: PG 7, 844 and 917.

6. *Quid est depositum? Id est quod tibi creditum est, non quod a te inventum; quod accepisti, non quod excogitasti; rem non ingenii sed doctrinae, non usurpationis privatae sed publicae traditionis; rem ad te perductam, non a te prolatam; in qua non auctor debes esse sed custos, non institutor sed sectator, non ducens sed sequens. Depositum, inquit, custodi; catholicae fidei talentum inviolatum illibatumque conserva* (St. Vincent of Lerins, *Commonitorium*, 22: PL 50, 667).

7. Cf. especially, Second Council of Nicea, *Actio VII*: DS 602–603; Council of Trent, Decr. *Sacrosancta*: DS 1501; First Vatican Council, Dogm. Const. *Pastor aeternus*, 3: DS 3061; *Dei Verbum*, 8.

8. Cf. S.C.S. Oficio, Decr. *Lamentabili*, 21: DS 3421.

9. St. Cyprian, *De oratione Dominica*, 23: PL 4, 553; cf. Second Vatican Council, Dogm. Const. *Lumen gentium*, 2–4.

10. About this issue, cf. J. Ratzinger, *La Chiesa*, 9–31. About the criticism of the thesis that denies that Christ wished to found the Church, cf. M. Schmaus, *Teología Dogmática*, IV, 101–116.

11. *Lumen gentium*, 5.

12. R. Latourelle, *Teología de la Revelación*, 467.

13. Cf. W. Warnach, "Iglesia," 477–479.

14. To affirm that the Word of God engendered the Church is not necessarily to agree with Luther, who stressed that *tota vita et substantia Ecclesiae est in verbo Dei*. Cf. Weimar (ed.), *D. Martin Luthers Werke*, VII, 721.

15. *Dei Verbum*, 7.

16. Ibid., 8.

17. Cf. P. Rodríguez, "La Salvación en la Vida de la Iglesia," 9–29.

18. Concerning the inspiration and formation of the books of the Holy Bible, read the prefaces of Bibles regarding the history of Sacred Scripture.

19. About the concept of Tradition, cf. J. Ratzinger, "Un Tentativo circa il Problema del Concetto di Tradizione," 27–73. For a brief synthesis, cf., V. Proaño Gil, "Tradición," 661–670.

20. U. Betti, *La Rivelazione Divina nella Chiesa*, 224–225.

21. *Dei Verbum*, 11.

22. Cf. Y. M. Congar, "La Tradition et les traditions," 70–73. Nevertheless, this terminology is not uniformly used by authors. Look, for instance, at the different uses of the terms *inhesive*, *declarative*, and *interpretative* in A. Franzini, *Tradizione e Scrittura*, 24.

23. *Dei Verbum*, 8.

24. J. Ratzinger, *Iglesia, Ecumenismo y Politica*, 93.

25. U. Betti, *La Rivelazione Divina nella Chiesa*, 228–229.

26. First Vatican Council, Dogm. Const. *Dei Filius*, 4: DS 3020.

27. *Dei Verbum*, 10.

28. Cf. St. Vincent of Lerins, *Commonitorim*, 2: PL 50, 639.

29. For a brief exposition of the criteria for the discernment of traditions, cf. O. Ruiz Arenas, *Jesús: Epifanía del Amor del Padre*, 228–231.

30. Cf. J. Quasten, *Patrología*, I, 11–15.

31. *Dei Verbum*, 8. About the significance of the popes in the structure of our faith, cf. J. Ratzinger, *Teoría de los Principios Teológicos*, 157–180.

32. Cf. V. Proaño Gil, "Tradición," 668.

33. *In rebus fidei et morum ad aedificationem doctrinae christianae pertinentium is pro vero sensu sacrae Scripturae habendus sit, quem tenuit ac tenet sancta mater Ecclesia, cuius est iudicare de vero sensu et interpretatione Scripturarum sanctarum; atque ideo nemini licere contra hunc sensum aut etiam contra unanimem consensum Patrum ipsam Scripturam sacram interpretari* (*Dei Filius*, 2: DS 3007).

34. About the primacy of both Peter and the Magisterium, refer to the corresponding chapters of "Eclesiologia," in J. Ratzinger, *La Chiesa*, 33–53.
35. *Lumen gentium*, 20.
36. Cf. ibid., 21, 24.
37. *Dei Verbum*, 10.
38. Cf. St. Thomas Aquinas, *In IV Sent.*, d. 19, q. 2, a. 2, qla. 2 ad 4; *Quodlib.*, III, a. 9 ad 3.
39. Cf. U. Betti, *La Rivelazione Divina nella Chiesa*, 250.
40. Cf. *Lumen gentium*, 25. On this theme, cf. I. Schinella, "Il Magistero Autentico: Genesi Semantica e Significato Teologico di 'Autentico,'" 253–263.
41. Cf. R. Latourelle, *Teologia della Rivelazione*, 511.
42. *Dei Verbum*, 10.
43. Cf. ibid., 8.
44. Cf. St. Augustine, *Epist.* 54, 6: PL 33, 203; *Sacrosancta*: DS 1501; *Lumen gentium*, 25.
45. John Paul II, *Fides et ratio*, 50.
46. Cf. V. Proaño Gil, "Magisterio Eclesiástico," 732–733.
47. *Dei Verbum*, 8.
48. Cf. *Pastor aeternus*, 3: DS 3050–3058; *Lumen gentium*, 18.
49. Cf. J. Ratzinger, *Teoría de los Principios Teológicos*, 354 and 357.
50. *Dei Verbum*, 10.
51. For a criticism of Protestant theology about this issue, cf. O. Karrer, "Successione Apostolica e Primato," 251–298; M. Schmaus, *Teología Dogmática*, IV, 142–156.
52. O. Cullmann, *La Tradition: Problème Exégétique, Historique et Théologique*, 44; cf. "Il Mistero della Redenzione nella Storia," 414.
53. Cf. A. Franzini, *Tradizione e Scrittura*, 282–283.
54. Ibid., 283.
55. *Lumen gentium*, 1.
56. Pius XII, Enc. *Mystici Corporis*, 93.
57. *Lumen gentium*, 9.
58. Cf. *Dei Verbum*, 7.
59. *Certum est quod iudicium Ecclesiae universalis errare in his quae ad fidem, pertinent, impossibile est* (St. Thomas Aquinas, *Quodlib.*, 9, q. 8, a. 1).
60. Congregation for the Doctrine of the Faith, Decl. *Mysterium Ecclesiae*, 2.
61. Cf. ibid., 4.
62. *Ipsa est Ecclesia sancta, Ecclesia una, Ecclesia vera, Ecclesia catholica, contra omnes haereses pugnans: pugnare potest, expugnari tamen non potest. Haereses omnes de illa exierunt, tamquam sarmenta inutilia de vite praecisa: ipsa autem manet in radice sua, in vita sua, in caritate sua. Portae inferorum non vincent eam* (cf. Mt 16: 18) (St. Augustine, *De Symb. ad Cathec.*, 6: PL 40, 635).

63. *Intellectus circa proprium obiectum semper verus est. Unde ex se ipso numquam decipitur* (STh, I, q. 94, a. 4).

64. Cf. ibid., q. 85, a. 6; I–II, q. 17, a. 6; II–II, q. 1, a. 4.

65. *Lumen gentium*, 25; cf. *Pastor aeternus*, 4: DS 3074.

66. John Paul II, Discourse of October 15, 1988, 4; cf. J. Ratzinger, *Le Nouveau Peuple de Dieu*, 94–95; H. de Lubac, *Les Églises Particulières dans l'Eglise Universelle*, 80–81.

67. *Mysterium Ecclesiae*, 2.

68. *Lumen gentium*, 12; cf. St. Augustine, *De praedestinatione sanctorum*, 14, 27: PL 44, 980. For the history of the writing of this text, cf. J. Sancho Bielsa, *Infalibilidad del Pueblo de Dios*, 104–136. *Sensus fidei* is also quoted by the Council in other places: *Lumen gentium*, 35; Decr. *Presbyterorum ordinis*, 9; *Gaudium et spes*, 52.

69. It seems that St. Vincent of Lerins used the expression for the first time (cf. *Commonitorium*, 23: PL 50, 669), but with a different meaning. St. Thomas Aquinas used the expression *sensus fidei* only once (cf. *In III Sent.*, d. 13, q. 2, a. 1 sol.).

70. Cf. St. Augustine, *De Baptismo contra Donat.*, 2, 9, 14: PL 43, 135; *De dono perseverantiae*, 23, 63: PL 45, 1031; *Sermo* 294, 17: PL 38, 1346.

71. Cf. DS 1635, 1726, 1820.

72. Cf. Pius IX, Ap. Const. *Ineffabilis Deus*; Pius XII, Ap. Const. *Munificentissimus Deus*. For patristic testimonies and the history of theology regarding *sensus fidei* until the Second Vatican Council, cf. C. Dillenschneider, *Le Sens de la Foi et le Progrès Dogmatique du Mystère Marial* (Rome: Accademia Mariana Internationalis, 1954), 266–277; J. Sancho Bielsa, *Infalibilidad del Pueblo de Dios*, 191–235.

73. Cf. M. Seckler, "Glaubenssinn," 945. This was said by St. Thomas: *rectitudo iudicii potest contingere dupliciter: uno modo secundum perfectum usum rationis; alio modo propter connaturalitatem quamdam ad ea de quibus est iudicandum* (STh, II–II, q. 45, a. 3; cf. q. 97, a. 2 ad 2).

74. That is why St. Thomas assured us that *habitus scientiae inclinat ad scibilia per modum rationis…; sed habitus fidei, cum non rationi innitatur, per modum naturae, sicut et habitus moralium virtutum, et sicut habitus principiorum* (St. Thomas Aquinas, *In III Sent.*, d. 23, q. 3, a. 3, sol. 2 ad 2).

75. Cf. J. Sancho Bielsa, *Infalibilidad del Pueblo de Dios*, 254; P. Rodríguez, "Infallibilis? La Respuesta de Santo Tomás de Aquino," 68.

76. Cf. A. del Portillo, *Fieles y Laicos en la Iglesia*, 33–45.

77. *Ex ratione ipsius fidei est quod intellectus semper feratur in verum, quia fidei non potest subesse falsum* (STh, II–II, q. 4, a. 5).

78. *Discretionem credendorum habet homo per lumen fidei, sicut discretionem spirituum per aliquam gratiam datam. Unde homo lumen fidei habens non consentit his quae contra fidem sunt, nisi inclinationem fidei derelinquat ex sua culpa* (St. Thomas Aquinas, *In III Sent.*, d. 24, a. 3, sol. ad 3). Cf. J. de Guibert,

"A Propos des Textes de S. Thomas sur la Foi qui Discerne," *Recherches de Science Religieuse*, 30–44.

79. For this reason, Pius VI condemned as heresy the proposition of the Synod of Pistoia with the words *postremis hisce saeculis sparsam esse generalem obscurationem super veritates gravioris momenti, spectantes ad religionem, et quae sunt basis fidei et moralis doctrinae Iesu Christi* (Pius VI, Bull *Auctorem Fidei*: DS 2601).

80. J.B. Franzelin, *Tractatus de Divina Traditione et Scriptura*, 96.

81. Cf. *Dei Verbum*, 10.

82. Cf. *Lumen gentium*, 12.

83. Cf. J. Sancho Bielsa, *Infalibilidad del Pueblo de Dios*, 282–284. On the organic character of the infallibility of the Church, cf. M.J. Scheeben, *Handbuch der katholischen Dogmatik*, 11.151, 12.159, 13.181–182, 14.194.

84. Naturally, we are referring to the exact matter about which the Magisterium is able to issue an authoritative teaching that obliges the faithful in conscience and not to the many other aspects to which the Magisterium makes or can make reference in its teachings (i.e., statements on the characteristics of the prevailing culture, elements of general history, or suggestions regarding essentially contingent questions).

85. Cf. *Pastor aeternus*, 4: DS 3074.

86. Cf. ibid., 3074–3075.

87. U. Betti, *La Costituzione Dommatica* Pastor aeternus *del Concilio Vaticano I*, 641. Some authors interpret the replacement of the word *credendam* from the first draft with the word *tenendam*, which appears in the definitive text, as indicative that the Council also wished to include among the matters that can be defined *ex cathedra* by the pope those non-revealed truths that have less connection with revelation, that is, a connection that is not essential and necessary. In reality, an analysis of the acts of the Council merely demonstrates that the definitive text, though it does not declare it openly, does not exclude the possibility of this type of infallibility (cf. ibid., 643).

88. One should especially compare the words in italics:
Magisterium non supra verbum Dei est, sed eidem., ministrat, docens nonnisi *quod traditum est*, quatenus illud, ex divino mandato et Spiritu Santo assistente, pie audit, *sancte custodit et fideliter exponit* (*Dei Verbum*, 10). Haec autem infallibilitas…tantum patet quantum divinae *Revelationis depositum, sancte custodiendum et fideliter exponendum* (*Lumen gentium*, 25).

89. *Lumen gentium*, 25.

90. "According to Catholic doctrine, the infallibility of the Church is extended not only to the deposit of the faith, but also to all that is necessary in order to guard and expound it as it should. The extension of the infallibility to the same deposit of faith is a truth that the Church from its beginning has considered as certainly revealed in the promises of Christ" (*Mysterium Ecclesiae*, 3).

91. A revealed truth that is infallibly taught as such is *de fide divina et catholica*, while a truth that is not revealed but infallibly taught by the Magisterium is *de fide catholica*. Nevertheless, this terminology is not universally accepted because it is related to the question of the so-called *fides ecclesiastica*. Regarding this issue, cf. Y.M. Congar, "Fait Dogmatique et Foi Ecclésiastique," 1059–1067. In any case, as far as the full, definitive, and unconditional assent to be given to a doctrine, there is no difference; the difference refers only to the role of the supernatural virtue of faith in that assent.

92. Cf. *Lumen gentium*, 25; *Dei Verbum*, 10.

93. Cf. Idem, *Lumen gentium*, explanatory note, n. 2.

94. Cf. F. Sullivan, *Magisterium: Teaching Authority in the Catholic Church*, 137–152. This thesis is presented as "the more common opinion: particular norms of natural law are not object of infallible teaching" (148). More recently, Sullivan clarified the sense in which he considers this opinion acceptable: If one of those norms is revealed or rather its definitive proposition is necessary for the defense and exposition of the revealed truth, then it is possible to have an infallible Magisterium in that regard. Nevertheless, he believes that complex ethical problems exist that apparently do not meet the conditions necessary to be declared infallible. Cf. F. Sullivan, "Magistero," 848–849.

95. Cf. *Mysterium Ecclesiae*, 3. For a detailed analysis of how the infallible Magisterium can be extended to include specific norms of natural morality, cf. F. Ocáriz, "La Competenza del Magistero della Chiesa 'in Moribus,'" 125–138.

96. Cf. J.R. Geiselmann, "Dogma," 502–506; G.F. Mansini, "Dogma," 345–346.

97. *Dei Filius*, 3: DS 3011. In this text the word *dogma* is not used, but then the Council calls the truths so taught by the Church "dogmas": Cf. *Dei Filius*, 4: DS 3020.

98. Cf. G.F. Mansini, "Dogma," 346–347.

99. This is the modernist proposition that was condemned: *Dogmata, quae Ecclesia perhibet tamquam revelata, non sunt veritates e caelo delapsae, sed sunt interpretatio quaedam factorum religiosorum, quam humana mens laborioso conatu sibi comparavit* (*Lamentabili*, 22: DS 3422). For a theological analysis of modernism, cf. R. Garcia de Haro, *Historia Teológica del Modernismo*.

100. Cf. E. Le Roy, *Dogme et Critique*, 25, 33, 47.

101. Cf. ibid., 51.

102. The following thesis was condemned: *Dogmata fidei retinenda sunt tantummodo iuxta sensum practicum, id est tamquam norma praeceptiva agendi, non vero tamquam norma credendi* (*Lamentabili*, 26: DS 3426). Regarding this issue, cf. G.F. Mansini, *What is a Dogma? The Meaning and Truth of Dogma in Edouard Le Roy and his Scholastic Opponents*, 216–229.

103. This has been, for example, the case of Hans Kung, according to whom, it would not only be necessary to deny the very possibility of an infallibility that is not of God (cf. H. Kung, *Infallibile? Una domanda*, Queriniana,

Brescia 1970, pp. 195 et seq.), but it would also be necessary to deny the existence of a magisterial office in the Church that is an absolutely normative authority for the faith (cf. ibid., pp. 257–275). For a summary of Kung's theories and of the main criticisms he has received, cf. G. Pozzo, *Magisterio e Teologia in H. Kung e P. Schoonenberg,* Citta Nuova Editrice, Rome 1983, pp. 110–229.

104. *Mysterium Ecclesiae,* 5.

105. *Dei Filius,* 4: DS 3020; cf. canon 3, *de fide et ratione: Si quis dixerit, fieri posse, ut dogmatibus ab Ecclesia propositis aliquando secundum progressum scientiae sensus tribuendus sit alius ab eo, quem intellexit et intelligit Ecclesia: anathema sit.*

106. *Crescat igitur… et multum vehementerque proficiat, tam singulorum quam omnium, tam unius hominis quam totius Ecclesiae, aetatum ac saeculorum gradibus, intelligentia, scientia, sapientia: sed in suo dumtaxat genere, in eodem scilicet dogmate, eodem sensu eademque sententia* (St. Vincent of Lerins, *Commonitorium,* I, c. 23: PL 50, 668, cited in *Dei Filius,* 4: DS 3020).

107. *Mysterium Ecclesiae,* 5.

108. Cf. First Vatican Council, Dogmatic Constitution on the Catholic Faith, Chap. 4, *On Faith and Reason: Denzinger 1800* (3020)

109. *Dei Verbum,* 8.

110. Cf. O. Ruiz Arenas, *Jesús,* 276–283.

111. Cf. J.H. Newman, *An Essay on the Development of Christian Doctrine.*

112. Cf. F. Marín-Sola, *La Evolución Homogénea del Dogma Católico.*

113. In general, regarding the relation between faith and culture, cf. P. Rossano, *Vangelo e Cultura.*

114. *Mysterium Ecclesiae,* 5.

115. John Paul II, *Fides et ratio,* 96.; Note: "As for the meaning of dogmatic formulas, this remains ever true and constant in the Church, even when it is expressed with greater clarity or more developed. The faithful therefore must shun the opinion, first, that dogmatic formulas (or some category of them) cannot signify the truth in a determinate way, but can only offer changeable approximations to it, which to a certain extent distort or alter it": Sacred Congregation for the Doctrine of the Faith, Declaration in Defence of the Catholic Doctrine on the Church *Mysterium Ecclesiae* (June 24, 1973), 5: AAS 65 (1973), 403.

116. For the traditional theological explanation of these points, cf. R. Garrigou-Lagrange, *Le Sens Commun: La Philosophie de l'être et les Formules Dogmatiques;* "Natura e Valore delle Formule Dogmatiche," 387–408; A. Gardeil, *Le Donné Révélé et la Théologie;* C. Journet, *Le Dogme: Chemin de la Foi.*

117. Pope Bl. John XXIII, Address opening the Second Vatican Council, October 11, 1962.

118. *Gaudium et spes,* 62; cf. 58.

119. Cf. Second Vatican Council, Decr. *Unitatis redintegratio,* 6.

120. The thesis of A. von Harnack, according to which "dogma is the result of the action of the Greek spirit upon the field of the Gospel" (*Lehrbuch der Dogmengeschichte*, 19), has been shown as false from the strictly historical point of view as well. A profound synthesis of the diverse stages of the encounter between Christianity and Philosophy can be seen in John Paul II, *Fides et ratio*, 36–48.

121. J. Ratzinger, "Sobre la Cuestión de la Validez Permanente de las Fórmulas Dogmáticas," 65–66.

122. *Nemo sane est qui non videat huiusmodi notionum vocabula cum in scholis tum ab ipsius Ecclesiae Magisterio adhibita, perfici et perpoliri posse; ac notum praeterea est Ecclesiam non cuilibet systemati philosophico, brevi temporis spatio vigenti, devinciri posse: sed ea quae communi consensu a catholicis doctoribus composita per plura saecula fuere ad aliquam dogmatis intelligentiam attingendam, tam caduco fundamento procul dubio non nituntur. Nituntur enim principiis ac notionibus ex vera rerum creatarum cognitione deductis; in quibus quidem, deducendis cognitionibus humanae menti veritas divinitus revelata, quasi stella, per Ecclesiam illuxit. Quare mirum non est aliquas huiusmodi notiones a Conciliis Oecumenici non solum adhibita, sed etiam sancitas esse, ita ut ab eis discedere nefas sit* (Pius XII, Enc. *Humani generis*, 16: DS 3883).

123. Paul VI, Enc. *Mysterium Fidei*, 24.

124. Congregation for the Doctrine of the Faith, Decl. *Mysterium Filii Dei*, 6.

125. Vatican Council I: Dogmatic Constitution *Dei Filius*, ch. 4; Conc. Oec. Decr. (3), p. 808 (DS 3016).

126. *Mysterium Ecclesiae*, 5.

127. Cf. G. Bardy, "Paul de Samosate," 50.

128. Cf. First Council of Nicea, *Symbolum*: DS 125.

129. Cf. F. Ocáriz, "Sulla Libertà Religiosa: Continuità del Vaticano II con il Magistero precedente," 71–97.

CHAPTER 4

1. In the New Testament, the *apokalypsis* (revelation) and the corresponding verb *apokalyptò* can refer to, for example, preaching, making manifest, witnessing to the truth, teaching, etc.: cf. R. Latourelle, *Teología de la Revelación*, 46.

2. First Vatican Council, Dogm. Const. *Dei Filius*, 2: DS 3004.

3. Second Vatican Council, Dogm. Const. *Dei Verbum*, 2.

4. Ibid.

5. Ibid.

6. M. Seckler, "Il Concetto di Rivelazione," 74; cf. J. Schmitz, *La Revelación*, 100–103.

7. Cf. *Dei Verbum*, 2.

8. Cf. AA.VV., *La Sagrada Escritura*, I, 1059–1060; H. Zimmermann, "Conocer," 201–209.

9. Cf. A. Blanco, "La Revelación como 'Locutio Dei' en las Obras de Santo Tomás de Aquino," 9–61.

10. Cf. E. Jacob, *Théologie de l'Ancien Testament*, 163–164.

11. Paul VI, Enc. *Ecclesiam suam*, 75. Regarding these characteristics of revelation, coming from its being locutio Dei, cf. A. Blanco, "La Revelación como 'Locutio Dei' en las Obras de Santo Tomás de Aquino," 24–33.

12. *Dei Verbum*, 2.

13. "Dans le vocabulaire du IVè évangile et des épîtres, il semble bien que ce soit le mot *alétheia* qui exprime avec le plus de plénitude le thème johannique fondamental de la *révélation*" (I. de la Potterie, *La Vérité dans St. Jean*, 3).

14. Cf. J.B. Bauer, "Verdad," 1039–1048; W. Kasper, *Il Dogma sotto la Parola di Dio*, 78–98. However, I think that Kasper exaggerates the consequences of the diversity among the biblical concepts of truth and Western cultural tradition when he states that, based on the biblical concept, "one must be able to determine in a new way what the truth of the dogma consists of and what the word *infallibility* means" (ibid., 98).

15. P. Althaus, *Die christliche Wahrheit*, 239.

16. R. Bultmann, "Der Begriff der Offenbarung im Neuen Testament," in *Glauben und Verstehen: Gesammelte Aufsätze*, III, 27. For a brief critical exposition of the thought of R. Bultmann, cf., for example, A. Vögtle, "Rivelazione e Mito," 827–960; R. Latourelle, "Bultmann," 164–169 .

17. R. Bultmann, *Creer y Comprender*, III, 21.

18. *Visio profetica non est visio ipsius divinae essentiae: nec in ipsa divina essentia vident ea quae vident, sed in quibusdam similitudinibus, secundum illustrationem divini luminis* (STh, II–II, q. 173, a. 1; cf. *De veritate*, q. 18, a. 3).

19. St. Thomas Aquinas, *In Ioan. Evang.*, c. XIV, lect. 2.

20. *Dei Verbum*, 2. We will not detain ourselves here to consider the mystery of the human knowledge of Jesus, which is studied in Christology: cf., for example, F. Ocáriz, L.F. Mateo Seco, J.A. Riestra, *El Misterio de Jesucristo*, 214–235.

21. Cf. St. Thomas Aquinas, *Compendium Theologiae*, I, c. 27; C. Cardona, *Metafísica de la Opción Intelectual*, 281–282.

22. R. Latourelle, *Teología de la Revelación*, 461.

23. As St. Thomas explains, among the capacities and powers of creatures, there is one produced by God that goes beyond the creature's nature; it is the *potentia obedientiae* (cf. STh, III, q. 11, a. 1; cf. *De Potentia*, q. 1, a. 3 ad 1; q. 3, a. 8 ad 3; q. 6, a. 1 ad 18). It deals with the passive potential of creatures that only God can set in motion.

24. *Naturaliter anima est gratiae capax; eo enim ipso quod facta est ad imaginem Dei, capax est Dei per gratiam* (STh, I–II, q. 113, a. 10; cf. II–II, q. 18, a. 1 s.c.).

25. "Non ci occupiamo della potentia oboedientialis nei confronti della *grazia* soprannaturale, in quanto eleva ontologicamente l'uomo per renderlo partecipe della vita di Dio, ma solo della potentia oboedientialis rispetto

all'ascolto di una possibile *locuzione* di Dio" (K. Rahner, *Uditori della Parola*, 49).

26. Ibid., 51.
27. Cf. ibid., 49, note 6.
28. For a brief critical synthesis, taking into account the philosophical presuppositions, cf. C. Cardona, "Rilievi critici a due fondamentazioni metafisiche per una costruzione teologica," in *Divus Thomas*, 172–175.
29. For an analysis of Rahner's thinking, cf. F. Gaboriau; *Le Tournant Théologique Aujourd'hui Selon K. Rahner*; C. Fabro, *La Svolta Antropologica di K. Rahner*.
30. Apostolic Letter *Tertio millennio adveniente* (November 10, 1994), 10: AAS 87 (1995), 11.
31. John Paul II, *Fides et ratio*, 11.
32. R. Latourelle, *Teología de la Revelación*, 360–361.
33. Cf. W. Pannenberg, *La Revelación como Historia*, 169ff.
34. Cf. ibid.
35. Cf. ibid., 39–45.
36. For a brief but incisive critique of the concept of revelation in Pannenberg, cf. A. Bandera, *La Iglesia ante el Proceso de Liberación*, 286–307; B. Forte, *Teología de la Historia*; A. Torres, "La Teoría de la Revelación," 139–178.
37. Cf. Congregation for the Doctrine of the Faith, Instr. *Libertatis nuntius*, 9.
38. Cf. A. Millán Puelles, *Ontología de la Existencia Histórica*, 194.
39. Cf. R. Latourelle, *Teología de la Revelación*, 448–449.
40. Cf. M. Meinertz, *Teología del Nuevo Testamento*, 572–573.
41. Cf. AA.VV., *La Sagrada Escritura*, I, 924.
42. Council of Trent, Decr. *De iustificatione*, 8: DS 1532.
43. Cf. A. Feuillet, "Le Plan Salvifique de Dieu dans l'épître aux Romains," 338–340.
44. *Dei Verbum*, 2.
45. Cf. *Gaudium et spes*, 19.
46. Cf. L. Scheffczyk, "La Santidad de Dios: Fin y Forma de la Vida Cristiana," 1021–1036.
47. J. Morales, "La Vocación en el Antiguo Testamento," in *Scripta Theologica*, 61.
48. Cf. A. Pigna, *La Vocación: Teología y Dicernimiento*, 15.
49. Cf. F. Ocáriz, "La Filiación Divina: Realidad Central en la Vida y en la Enseñanza de Mons. Escrivá de Balaguer," 173–214; ibid., "Naturaleza, gracia y gloria," 175–221.
50. STh, II–II, q. 24, a. 7 c. Regarding sanctity as the perfection of charity, cf. q. 184, a. 3.
51. John Paul II, Ap. Ex. *Christifideles laici*, 12. The dynamics of the Christian life can be synthesized thus: "To the Father, in the Son, by the Holy Spirit" (Enc. *Dominum et vivificantem*, 32). For a deeper understanding of these

themes, cf. F. Ocáriz, *Hijos de Dios en Cristo*; ibid., "Naturaleza, gracia y gloria," 69–104.

52. Tertullian, *De Baptismo*, 16: PL 1, 1217; cf. J. Morales, "La Vocación Cristiana en la Primera Patrística," 837–889.

53. *Lumen gentium*, 40.

54. Cf. Second Vatican Council, Decr. *Apostolicam actuositatem*, 2.

55. Cf. Congregation for the Doctrine of the Faith, Ltr. *Communionis notio*, 4.

56. Cf. a solid historical summary in J.L. Illanes, "Dos de Octubre de 1928: Alcance y Significado de una Fecha," 96–101.

57. Cf. a partial but significant summary in J. Daujat, *La Vita Soprannaturale*, 561–573.

58. St. Josemaría Escrivá, *Conversaciones con Mons. Escrivá de Balaguer*, 26.

59. Cf. *Lumen gentium*, 11, 39–41.

60. J. Ratzinger, Homily of May 19, 1992, 113.

61. Cf. P. Rodríguez, *Vocación, Trabajo, Contemplación*, 37–42.

62. St. Josemaría Escrivá, *Conversaciones*, 59.

63. Cf. *Lumen gentium*, 31, 33, 36; *Apostolicam actuositatem*, 2, 5; John Paul II, *Christifideles laici*, 15; A. del Portillo, *Fieles y Laicos en la Iglesia*, 191–197.

64. On the Eucharistic character of the Church as *Corpus Christi*, cf. J. Ratzinger, *Le Nouveau Peuple de Dieu*, 87–102.; Cf. F. Ocáriz, La Iglesia, "Sacramentam salutis," segun Ratzinger, en path le (2007), 161–181.

65. St. Josemaría Escrivá, *Christ Is Passing By*, 87.

66. Cf. *Communionis notio*, 5.

67. Cf. *Lumen gentium*, 1.

CHAPTER 5

1. Cf. A. Feuillet, "De munere doctrinali a Paraclito in Ecclesia expleto iuxta evangelium Sancti Ioannis," 132.

2. For example, the books of Sacred Scripture were not collected into one volume before 381: cf. R. Bandas, "Biblia et Traditio iuxta Scripturam," 180.

3. Cf. L. Cerfaux, "Tradition selon St. Paul," 253–263; P. Lengsfeld, "La Tradició n en le Periodo Constitutivo de la Revelación," 330–331.

4. Cf. M. Zerwick, *Analysis Philologica Novi Testamenti Graeci*, 466. *Krateite* can also mean *kratos* (power, authority) over something, but the second meaning should be understood only in the sense of "making appropriate," not in the sense, which context excludes, of being above those "traditions" given by the Apostle, or having power to change these traditions.

5. Cf. C. Spicq, *Les Épîtres Pastorales*, 158–159.

6. Although the original Greek itself is ambiguous apart from the text, the translation cited here corresponds to a careful exegesis: cf. for example, Facultad de Teología de la Universidad de Navarra, "Sagrada Biblia," vol.5

(Nuevo Testamento), EUNSA (2004) 1447–1448; J.T. Curran, "The Teaching of 2 Peter 1: 20," 350ff.; AA.VV., *La Sagrada Escritura*, III, 313.

7. Cf. J.B. Franzelin, *Tractatus de Divina Traditione et Scriptura*, 201–202; M. Meinertz, *Teología del Nuevo Testamento*, 548–549.

8. Cf. B. Rigaux, "De Traditione apud S. Paulum," 169.

9. Regarding this period, cf. A. Michel, "Tradition," 1256–1262; H. Holstein, *La Tradition dans l'Église*, 61–70.

10. Regarding the doctrine of St. Irenaeus on Tradition, as well as the respective pages of the books cited in the preceding footnote, cf. R. Forni *Problemi della Tradizione: Ireneo di Lione*; H. Holstein, "La Tradition des apôtres chez S. Irénée," in *Revue des Sciences Religieuses*, 229–270.

11. *Non enim per alios dispositionem salutis nostrae cognovimus, quam per eos, per quos Evangelium pervenit ad nos; quod quidem tunc praeconaverunt, postea vero per Dei voluntatem in scripturis nobis tradiderunt* (St. Irenaeus, *Adversus haereses*, III, 1, 1: PG 7, 844).

12. *Traditionem itaque apostolorum in toto mundo manifestatam, in omni Ecclesia adest respicere omnibus qui vera velint videre; et habemus annumerare eos, qui ab Apostolis instituti sunt episcopi, et successores eorum usque ad nos* (ibid., 3, 1: PG 7, 848).

13. *Agnitio vera est apostolorum doctrina, et antiquus Ecclesiae status, in universo mundo, et character Corporis Christi secundum successiones episcoporum, quibus illi eam quae in unoquoque loco est Ecclesiam tradiderunt; quae pervenit usque ad nos custoditione sine fictione scripturarum tractatio plenissima, neque additamentum neque ablationem recipiens; et lectio sine falsatione, et secundum scripturas expositio legitima, et sine periculo et sine blasphemia* (ibid., IV, 33, 8: PG 7, 1077).

14. Cf. H. Holstein, *La Tradition dans l'Église*, 86; A. Benoit, "Ecriture et Tradition chez St. Irénée," 32–43.

15. *Ubi enim Ecclesia, ibi et Spiritus Dei; et ubi Spiritus Dei, illic Ecclesia et omnis gratia; Spiritus autem veritas* (St. Irenaeus, *Adversus haereses*, III, 24, 1: PG 7, 966; cf. IV, 38, 2: PG 7, 1105–1106).

16. Cf. A. Michel, "Tradition," 1265–1276; Y.M. Congar, "La Tradition et les traditions," 41–52.

17. For the substantial identity between St. Irenaeus and Tertullian on these points, in particular, Tertullian, cf. *De praescriptione haereticorum*, cc. 19–21, 28; PL 2, 31–33, 40, comparing them with those of St. Irenaeus cited above. For a brief statement of the principle of the *Praescriptio* in Tertullian, cf. J. Quasten, *Patrologia*, cir. Vol. 1. pp. 552–555.

18. Cf. the corresponding pages of the cited notes in the preceeding notes.

19. *In eis enim quae aperte in Scripturis posita sunt inveniuntur illa omnia, quae continent fidem, moresque vivendi, spem scilicet atque caritatem* (St. Augustine, *De doctrina christiana*, II, 9, 14: PL 34, 42).

20. Cf. A. Michel, "Tradition," 1277–1278; Y.M. Congar, "La Tradition et les traditions," 139–143; J.B. Franzelin, *Tractatus de Divina Traditione et Scriptura*, 211–223.

21. *Ex asservatis in Ecclesia dogmatibus et praedicationibus alia quidem. Habemus e doctrina scripto prodita, alia vero nobis in mysterio tradita recepimus ex traditione apostolorum, quorum utraque vim eamdem habent ad pietatem* (St. Basil the Great, *De Spiritu Sancto*, 27, 66: PG 32, 188).

22. Cf. St. John Chrysostom, *In Epist. II ad Thessal.*, hom. 4, 2: PG 62, 488; St. Augustine, *De Baptismo contra Donat.*, II, 7, 12: PL 43, 133; St.Vincent of Lerins, *Commonitorium*, 2: PL 50, 639; St. John Damascene, *De Fide Orthodoxa*, IV, 12, 16: PG 94, 1136.

23. Cf.Y.M. Congar, "La Tradition et les traditions," 64–69, which contains references to specific passages from the works of the Fathers. Cf. also A. Michel,"Tradition," 1275–1276.

24. Cf. W. Kasper, "Schrift und Tradition," 165.

25. For a complete picture, cf. J. Beumer, "Das katholische Schriftprinzip in der theologischen Literatur der Scholastik bis zur Reformation," 24–52; Y.M. Congar,"La Tradition et les traditions," 123–182; A. Ibañez-Arana, "La Relación Escritura-Tradición en la Teologia Pre-Tridentina," 147–180.

26. Only God is the author of Revelation, but he wanted to make himself known through a variety of intermediaries: above all the humanity of Christ, with the prophets, the apostles, and the Church. For that reason, the *auctoritates* are just as valid as *auctoritas*, which, as far as the originator of this teaching, is the only true *auctor*, God. Cf. A. Franzini, *Tradizione e Scrittura*, 77–78.

27. Regarding the doctrine of St. Thomas on this subject, cf. G. Geenen, "The place of Tradition in the Theology of St. Thomas Aquinas," 110–135; B. D ecker, "Schriftprinzip und Ergänzungstradition in der Theologie des hl. Thomas von Aquin," 191–221; E. Ménard, *La Tradition: Révélation, Écriture, Église, selon St. Thomas d'Aquin*, 137–154; F. Ocáriz, "Il Primato Teologico della Sacra Scrittura, secondo San Tommaso," 7–12.

28. St. Thomas Aquinas, *In Ioan. Evang.*, c. XXI, lect. 6. Note that the context for this affirmation is the commentary on John 21: 25: "But there are also many other things which Jesus did; were every one of them to be written, I suppose that the world itself could not contain the books that would be written."
Cf. *De veritate*, q. 14, a. 10 ad 11: *successoribus eorum* (of the apostles) *non credimus nisi in quantum nobis annuntiant ea quae illi* (the prophets and apostles) *in scriptis reliquerunt.*

29. *Ea enim quae ex sola Dei voluntate proveniunt, supra omne debitum creaturae, nobis innotescere non possunt nisi quatenus in sacra Scriptura traduntur, per quam divina voluntas innotescit* (STh, III, q. 1, a. 3). It is interesting to note that this affirmation of St. Thomas represents a radicalization of what had been written years before about the same question: cf. *In III Sent.*, d. 1, q. 1, a. 3; STh, I, q 1, a. 8 ad 2.

30. *Formale autem obiectum fidei est veritas prima secundum quod manifestatur in Scripturis sacris et doctrina Ecclesiae* (STh, II–II, q. 5, a. 3).

31. *Omnibus articulis fidei inhaeret fides propter unum medium, scilicet propter veritatem primam propositam nobis in Scripturis secundum doctrinam Ecclesiae intellectis sane* (ibid., ad 2). In many other texts, St. Thomas affirms that the doctrine of the Church is precisely the contents of Scripture rightly interpreted, such as when he refers to the symbol of faith as being taken from Scripture (cf. STh, II–II, q. 1, a. 9 ad 1; *In III Sent.*, d. 25, q. 1, a. 1, qla. 3, sol. 3).

32. Cf. St. Thomas Aquinas, *Quodlib.* IX, q. 8, a. 1; XII, q. 17, a. 1; *De potentia*, q. 9, a. 3 s.c.; STh, II–II, q. 1, a. 9 s.c.; III, q. 72, a. 12 s.c.

33. Cf. E. Ménard, *La Tradition*, 186–203.

34. *Unde patet, quod multa in Ecclesia non scripta, sunt ab Apostolis docta, et ideo servanda* (St. Thomas Aquinas, *In Epist. II ad Thessal.*, c. II, lect. 3).

35. *Multa Dominus fecit et dixit quae in Evangeliis non continentur. Illa enim praecipue curaverunt Evangelistae tradere quae ad necessitatem salutis et ecclesiasticae dispositionis pertinent* (St. Thomas Aquinas, *In IV Sent.*, d. 23, q. 1, a. 1, qla. 3, sol. 3 ad 1); cf. STh, Suppl., q. 29, a. 3 ad 1.

36. *Ea vero quae sunt de necessitate sacramenti, sunt ab ipso Christo instituta, qui est Deus et homo. Et licet non omnia sint tradita in Scripturis, habet tamen ea Ecclesia ex familiari Apostolorum traditione* (STh, III, q. 64, a. 2 ad 1).

37. Cf. St. Thomas Aquinas, *In IV Sent.*, d. 23, q. 1, a. 1, qla. 3, sol. 3 ad 1.

38. STh, III, q. 27, a. 1. Here St. Thomas cites as an authority a sermon of St. Augustine (cf. PL 40, 1140–1141) the authenticity of which is generally denied.

39. Cf. St. Thomas Aquinas, *Exposit. salutationis angelicae.*

40. Cf. L. Ciappi, "De mente S. Thomae quoad Traditionem divinam," 229–231.

41. Cf. L. Cristiani, "Réforme," 2039–2047; Y.M. Congar, "La Tradition et les traditions," 183–205.

42. Cf. Council of Trent, Decr. *Sacrosancta*: DS 1501. Regarding the contents of this decree and its elaboration, cf. H. Jedin, *Storia del Concilio di Trento*, II, 67–118; A. Michel, "Tradition," 1311–1317; AA.VV., *De Scriptura et Traditione*, 96–98.

43. *Puritas ipsa Evangelii in Ecclesia conservetur, quod promissum ante per Prophetas in Scripturis sanctis Dominus noster Iesus Christus Dei Filius proprio ore primum promulgavit, deinde per suos Apostolos tamquam fontem omnis et salutaris veritatis et morum disciplinae 'omni creaturae praedicari' (Mc 16: 15) iussit; perspiciensque hanc veritatem et disciplinam contineri in libris scriptis et sine scripto traditionibus, quae ab ipsius Christi ore ab Apostolis acceptae, aut ab ipsis Apostolis Spiritu Sancto dictante quasi per manus traditae ad nos usque pervenerunt, orthodoxorum Patrum exempla secuta, omnes libros tam Veteris quam Novi Testamenti, cum utriusque unus Deus sit auctor, necnon traditiones ipsas, tum ad fidem tum ad mores pertinentes, tamquam vel oratenus a Christo, vel a Spiritu Sancto dictatas et continua successione in Ecclesia*

catholica conservatas, pari pietatis affectu ac reverentia suscipit et veneratur
(*Sacrosancta*: DS 1501).

44. Initially, in the schema, it was stated that revelation was transmitted
through the Church *partim ex Scripturis et partim ex traditione*. In the
final wording, however, the expression *partim…partim* was replaced
by a more general one: Revelation is contained *in libris scriptis et sine
scripto traditionibus*. The acts of the Council did not give a reason for this
change, so the interpretation of the text of the Council regarding this point
remained open.

45. For a detailed analysis of the Tridentine decree and its later interpretations,
cf. J. Saraiva Martins, *Escritura e Tradição Segundo o Concílio de Trento*.

46. For a descriptive vision of this period, cf. A. Michel, "Tradition," 1321–1331.

47. Among those with this opinion are, for example, Y.M. Congar, "La Tradition
et les traditions," vol. I, 215; H. Holstein, *La Tradition dans l'Église*, 103–109;
J. Dupont, "Écriture et Tradition," 449ff.

48. Particularly significant is the case of G.H. Tavard, "Tradition in Early
Post-Tridentine Theology," 377–405, since years before he had maintained
in his work *Holy Writ or Holy Church* the idea that attributed to the
post-Tridentine theology the interpretation of Trent in the sense of two
sources that were also materially different.

49. For a critical exposition and assessment of the thought of Pérez de Ayala,
cf. A. Miralles, *El Concepto de Tradición en Martín Pérez de Ayala*.

50. Cf. Y.M. Congar, "La Tradition et les traditions," vol. I, 237–238.

51. For a overall view of this period, cf. A. Michel, "Tradition," 1331–1339;
Y.M. Congar, "La Tradition et les traditions," vol. I, 244–263; A. Franzini,
Tradizione e Scrittura, 103–110.

52. Cf. J.A. Möhler, *L'Unità nella Chiesa: Il Principio del Cattolicesimo nello
Spirito dei Padri della Chiesa dei Primi tre Secoli*, 51.

53. Cf. P. Rodríguez, "Möhler, Johann Adam," 156–157. In his great work
Symbolik, of 1832, above all in the fifth edition (1838), Möhler gave a clearly
Christological focus to his ecclesiology, which allowed him to better
emphasize the living and organic character of the Church as an expression
of the economy of the Incarnation.

54. J.A. Möhler, *L'Unità nella Chiesa*, 67, 69.

55. Ibid., 34.

56. Ibid., 52.

57. Cf. ibid., 69–71. Also see J.R. Geiselmann, *Simbolica*, 294–316.

58. Cf. J.B. Franzelin, *Tractatus de Divina Traditione et Scriptura*, 211–222.

59. Cf. ibid., 223–232.

60. *Controversia princeps revocari debet ad ipsum principium formale Traditionis*
(ibid., 234).

61. The text of *Munificentissimus Deus*, with which Pius XII defined the dogma,
did not give an unequivocal response to this question (cf. DS 3900–3904).

62. Cf. J.R. Geiselmann, "Das Missverständnis über das Verhätnis von Schrift und seine Überwindung in der katholischen Theologie," 131–150.
63. For example, E. Ortigues, "Écritures et Traditions Apostoliques au Concile de Trente," 271–299; C. Moeller, "Tradition et Oecuménisme," 337–370.
64. Cf. H. Lennerz, "Scriptura Sola?" 39–53; "Sine Scripto Traditiones," 624–635;"Scriptura et Traditio in Decreto Sessionis Quartae Concilii Tridentini,"517–522.
65. H. Lennerz, "Sine Scripto Traditiones," 633.
66. Cf. *Dei Filius*, 2: DS 3006. Regarding the interpretation, cf. D. Iturrioz, "Tradición y Revelación en el Concilio Vaticano y su época," 171–217, 343–377; A. Kerrigan, "Doctrina Concilii Vaticani I de 'Sine Scripto Traditionibus,'" 475–502.
67. Cf. J.R. Geiselmann, *Die Heilige Schrift und die Tradition*, 282; "Tradition," 346.
68. For a brief overview of the reasoning of Geiselmann, cf. A. Franzini, *Tradizione e Scrittura*, 32–36.
69. J. Beumer, "De statu actuali controversiae circa relationem inter Traditionem et Scripturam," 23–28.
70. Regarding the elaboration of this constitution, cf. U. Betti, *La Rivelazione Divina nella Chiesa*; "Cronistoria della Costituzione Dogmatica sulla Divina Rivelazione," 33–67; L. Pacomio, *Dei Verbum: Genesi della Costituzione sulla Divina Rivelazione*; F. Gil Hellín, *Concilii Vaticani II Synopsis: Constitutio dogmatica de divina revelatione Dei Verbum*.
71. *Dei Verbum*, 9. However, the first version said: *sancta mater Ecclesia semper credidit et credit integram revelationem, non in sola Scriptura, sed in Scriptura et Traditione, tamquam in duplice fonte contineri, alio tamen ac alio modo* (Second Vatican Council, *Schemata Constitutionum et Decretorum de quibus disceptabitur in Concilii sessionibus, series prima*, 10).
72. Cf. *Dei Verbum*, 9.
73. Ibid., 10.
74. Ibid., 9.
75. Regarding the relation between Scripture and Tradition in Vatican Council II, cf. F. Castro, *Relaciones entre Sagrada Escritura y Tradición según la Constitución "Dei Verbum,"* 310–322.
76. In this manner we follow a simple yet essential method which has been utilized by many others (for example, P. Lengsfeld, *Tradicion y Sagrada Escritura: Su Relación*, 522–555), although the content of the various points of this method is not always conceived by everyone in the same way.
77. Cf. *Dei Verbum*, 8, and the commentary of J. Ratzinger on this section in *LThK*, Suppl. II, 518–523. Also cf. J. Sanz Rubiales, *La Tradición y su Crecimiento en el Número 8 de "Dei Verbum,"* 243–277.
78. Regarding the history of this examination, cf. H. Lesetre, "Canon des Écritures," 134–184; H. Höpfl, "Canonicité," 1022–1045.
79. St. Hilary, *Ad constantium*, II, 9: PL 10, 570.

80. Regarding these aspects of the apostolic, patristic, and traditional reading of Scripture, cf. Y.M. Congar, "La Tradition et les traditions," vol. I, 76–91.

81. Cf. DS 3066, 3070, 3901.

82. *Dei Verbum*, 10.

CHAPTER 6

1. This is the patristic tradition: cf. St. Ambrose, *Exposit. Ev. sec. Lucam*, II, 26: PL 15, 1561–1562; St. Thomas Aquinas, *In Ioan. Evang.*, c. I, lect. 5–6; *In Heb.*, c. XI.

2. Cf. Council of Orange (AD 529): DS: 376–378; First Vatican Council, Dogm. Const. *Dei Filius*, 3: DS 3008–3014, 3031–3036; Second Vatican Council, Dogm. Const. *Dei Verbum*, 5–6.

3. Cf. P. Antoine, "Foi," 276–310; O. Becker and O. Michel, "Fe," 170–187; A. Weiser, "Pisteuo," in TWNT, X; B. Marconcini, "Fe," 652–671.

4. *Catechism of the Catholic Church*, 145–146.

5. Cf. J.P. Fammatter, "La Fe según la Escritura," 883–884; E.H. Maly, "Génesis," 86–105. For an extensive commentary on the faith of Abraham, cf. the monograph of A. Gonzàlez, *Abraham: Padre de los Creyentes*.

6. Cf. G. Kittel, "*Akouó*," in TWNT, I, 220.

7. CCC 144.

8. St. Thomas Aquinas, *Summa Theologiae*, II–II, q. 1, a. 4; *De veritate*, q. 14, a. 9.

9. *Initium bonae vitae, cui vita etiam aeterna debetur, recta fides est. Est autem fides credere quod nondum vides; cuius fides merces est videre quod credis* (St. Augustine, *Sermo* 43, 1, 1: PL 38, 254; cf. *De fide rerum quae non videntur*, I, 1: PL 40, 171). *Creduntur absentia* (St. Augustine, *Epist.* 147: PL 33, 599).

10. *Dei Filius*, 4: DS 3015.

11. Ibid., 3: DS 3008.

12. Cf. J. Imbach, *Breve Corso Fondamentale sulla Fede*, 52–54, 57–60.

13. Council of Trent, Decr. *De iustificatione*, 12: DS 1562; cf. 19–21: DS 1569–1571; Leo X, Bull *Exsurge Domine*, 27: DS 1477.

14. Cf. St. John Chrysostom, *In Ep. ad Hebr.*, hom. 25, 1: MG 63, 171ff.

15. Cf. A. Weiser, "*Pisteuo*," 399–400; O. Michel, "Fe," 177–179.

16. Cf. B. Marconcini, "Fe," 653–654.

17. P. Antoine, "Foi," 277.

18. Cf. O. Becker, "Fe," 170.

19. Cf. H. Zimmermann, "Fe," 392.

20. Cf. B. Marconcini, "Fe," 664–665.

21. Cf. ibid., 656–657. See also J.A. Fitzmyer, "Teología de San Pablo," 816–818; B. Vawter, "Teología de San Juan," 849–851.

22. Cf. St. Thomas Aquinas, STh, II–II, q. 4, a.1; *De veritate*, q. 14, a. 2; *In Boeth. de Trin.*, q. 3, a. 1 sedc 2. On this point, Aquinas is inspired by Pseudo-Dionysius, *De divin. nomin.*, VII, lect. 5.

23. Cf. *Dei Filius*, 3: DS 3014; *De iustificatione*, 9: DS 1534; St. Augustine, *De peccatorum meritis et remissione*, 2, 7–8: PL 44, 155; *De gratia Christi et de pecc. orig.*, 21: PL 44, 370–371; STh, II–II, q. 1, a. 3.

24. "Now faith is the assurance of things hoped for, the conviction of things not seen" (Heb 11: 1); "For now we see in a miror dimly, but then face to face. Now I know in part; then I shall understand fully, even as I have been fully understood" (1 Cor 13: 12); "Beloved, we are God's children now; it does not yet appear what we shall be, but we know that when he appears we shall be like him, for we shall see him as he is" (1 Jn 3: 2). Keep in mind that in biblical language, the interpersonal relations of participation and communion, as well as that of conjugal relations, is at times expressed with the verb *to know* (*ghinóskò*) (cf. Mt 1: 25; Lk 1: 34).

25. John Paul II, Enc. *Redemptor hominis*, 19.

26. Cf. STh, II–II, q. 1, a. 1.

27. St. Thomas Aquinas, *In Boeth. de Trin.*, q. 1, a. 1 ad 4.

28. Cf. DS 75–76.

29. *Duo nobis credenda proponuntur, scil. occultum divinitatis…et mysterium humanitatis Christi* (STh, II–II, q. 1, a. 8). *Fides nostra in duobus principaliter consistit: primo quidem. in vera Dei cognitione….secundo in mysterio incarnationis Christi* (ibid., q. 174, a. 6).

30. *Dei Filius*, 3: DS 3010.

31. Cf. *De iustificatione*, 6: DS 1526; *Dei Filius*, 3: DS 3008; 4: DS 3015; St. Pius X, Mot. Pr. *Sacrorum antistitum*: DS 3537–3550; *Dei Verbum*, 5.

32. Cf. P. Neuner, "La Fede Principio Soggettivo della Conoscenza Teologica," 46–58. For an extensive analysis of Kantian faith, see J.M. Odero, *La Fe en Kant.*

33. Cf. R. Schnackenburg, *Il Vangelo di Giovanni*, I, 707.

34. Regarding the character of wisdom of the Faith, cf. John Paul II, *Fides et ratio*, 16–23.

35. Cf. R.E. Murphy, "Introducción a la Literatura Sapiencial," 391–408; M. Gilbert, "Sapienza," 1712–1713. For a more complete study, cf. M. Gilbert, *La Sagesse de l'Ancien Testament.*

36. Cf. G. Fohrer, "Sophia," in *TWNT*, VII, 483–489.

37. Ibid., 489–494.

38. Cf. U. Wilckens, "Sophia," in *TWNT*, VII, 518–525.

39. STh, I, q. 1, a. 6.

40. Ibid., II–II, q. 4, a. 8 ad 2.

41. Cf. St. Thomas Aquinas, *In Symb.*, prol.

42. Cf. R. Guardini, *Cristianismo y Sociedad.*

43. St. Josemaría Escrivá, *The Way*, 582.

CHAPTER 7

1. First Vatican Council, Dogm. Const. *Dei Filius*, 3: DS 3008.
2. Second Vatican Council, Dogm. Const. *Dei Verbum*, 5; cf. *Dei Filius*, 3: DS 3008.
3. Cf. M. Meinertz, *Teología del Nuevo Testamento*, 94; R. Latourelle, *Teología de la Revelación*, 473.
4. Cf. M. Meinertz, *Teología del Nuevo Testamento*, 295. Regarding the meaning of the endings *elampsen* and *phótismon*, also cf. M. Zerwick, *Analysis philologica Novi Testamenti Graeci*, 397–398.
5. St. Thomas Aquinas, *Summa Theologiae*, II–II, q. 2, a. 9 ad 3; cf. *In Ioan. Evang.*, c. VI, lect. 5.
6. St. Thomas Aquinas, *In Epist. ad Romanos*, c. VIII, lect. 6.
7. STh, II–II, q. 1, a. 4 ad 3.
8. Cf. St. Thomas Aquinas, *In IV Sent.*, d. 4, q. 2, a. 2, qla. 3 ad 1.
9. Cf. St. Augustine, *De gratia Christi et de pecc. orig.*, c. 25, no. 26–c. 26, no. 27: PL 44, 373 ss.
10. Second Council of Orange, *De Gratia*, 7: DS 377.
11. Cf. B. Duroux, *La Psychologie de la Foi chez S. Thomas d'Aquin*, 165–178.
12. St. Thomas Aquinas, *In III Sent.*, d. 23, q. 2, a. 1 ad 4.
13. STh, I–II, q. 100, a. 4 ad 1.
14. *Fideles habent eorum (quae sunt fidei) notitiam, non quasi demonstrative, sed inquantum per lumen fidei videntur esse credenda* (STh, II–II, q. 1, a. 5 ad 1).
15. Ibid., q. 5, a. 3 ad 1.
16. Regarding the faith of the demons, which is not supernatural, cf. ibid., q. 5, a. 2.
17. St. Augustine *De praedest. sanct.*, c. 2, 5: PL 44, 963.
18. Peter of Poitiers, *Sententiarum libri quinque*, III, 2: PL 211, 1045.
19. St. Thomas Aquinas, *In Epist. ad Romanos*, c. I, lect. 4; cf. *Summa contra Gentiles*, III, c. 40. Regarding the Augustinian definition of faith and influence on Scholasticism, cf. B. Duroux, *La Psychologie de la Foi chez S. Thomas d'Aquin*, 61–88.
20. St. Thomas Aquinas, *De malo*, q. 6 a. Regarding this topic, cf. C. Fabro, "La Dialettica d'Intelligenza e Volontà nella Costituzione Esistenziale dell'Atto Libero," 57–85.
21. John Paul II, *Fides et ratio*, 31.
22. Cf. the reflections of St. Augustine in *De utilitate credendi* and *De vera fide*.
23. Cf. F. Conesa, "La Fe y la Lógica del Testimonio," 483–511.
24. *De Gratia*, 7: DS 377.
25. Cf. *Dei Filius*, 3: DS 3008; *Dei Verbum*, 5.
26. *Catechism of the Catholic Church*, 155; cf. STh, II–II, q. 2, a. 9; *Dei Filius*, 3: DS 3010.
27. STh, II–II, q. 6, a. 1.

28. Ibid., ad 3.

29. Cf. DS 3008; *Dei Verbum*, 5.

30. Cf. STh, II–II, q. 11, a. 1.

31. We will examine these implications further in Chapters VIII and IX.

32. Cf. *Dei Verbum*, 5.

33. Cf. H. Zimmermann, "Fe," 396.

34. St. Josemaría Escrivá, *Friends of God*, 27.

35. Cf. STh, II–II, q. 4, a. 8.

36. Cf. H.J. Pottmeyer, "Segni e Criteri della Credibilità del Cristianesimo," 470.

37. STh, II–II, q. 4, a. 8 ad 1.

38. Cf. St. Augustine, *Sermo de symbolo*, c. 1: PL 40, 1190; *Enarrationes in Psalmos*, 77, 8: PL 36, 988; *In Epist. Ioannis ad parthos*, 29, 6: PL 35, 1630. St. Thomas Aquinas frequently uses this Augustinian expression: cf. STh, II–II, q. 2, a. 2 and par; Cf. C. Izquierdo, *Teologia Fundamental*, 274–276.

39. Cf. St. Thomas Aquinas, *In Epist. ad Romanos*, c. IV, lect. 1.

40. For an extensive study of these three aspects according to St. Thomas, cf. B. Duroux, *La Psychologie de la Foi chez S. Thomas d'Aquin*, 89–214.

41. *Illa voluntas (credendi) nec est actus caritatis, nec spei, sed quidam appetitus boni repromissi (De veritate*, q. 14, a. 2 ad 10).

42. *Fides non praesupponit voluntatem iam amantem, sed amare intendentem* (St. Thomas Aquinas, *In III Sent.*, d. 23, q. 2, a. 5 ad 6).

43. Cf. H. Zimmermann, "Fe," 392–394.

44. Cf. AA.VV., *La Sagrada Escritura: Texto y Comentario*, 1011–1012.

45. Cf. St. Thomas Aquinas, *Expositio primae decretalis*, 1.

46. Cf. DS 40ff.

47. Cf. H. Zimmermann, "Fe," 398–399.

48. Cf. AA.VV., *La Sagrada Escritura*, II, 751, 843.

49. F. Prat, *La Théologie de Saint Paul*, II, 286.

50. St. Cyprian, *De Catholicae Ecclesiae unitate*, 6: PL 4, 503; cf. CCC 167, 169, 171.

CHAPTER 8

1. Second Vatican Council, Dogm. Const. *Lumen gentium*, 9.

2. Cf. for example, M. Polanyi, *La Conoscenza Personale*.

3. John Paul II, Homily of September 4, 1983, 919.

4. *Catechism of the Catholic Church*, 150.

5. Cf. J. Mouroux, *Creo en Tí*, 8–9.

6. Cf. W. Kasper, *Il Dio di Gesù Cristo*, 118.

7. On the mystical dimension present in all knowledge of God, cf. G. Tanzella-Nitti, "La Teologia, Discorso su Dio e Annuncio del Mistero," 505–520.

8. Cf. G. Colombo, *La Ragione Teologica*, 150.

9. The word *Christocentrism*, used in various theological contexts and arrangements, indicates that Christ is at the center of that arrangement and that such centrality is not understood in an external or peripheral way, but rather in an internal and constitutive sense of such an order. So, the other elements of this order receive from Christ meaning and consistency (cf. Col 1: 15–18). In the context of supernatural faith, Christocentrism in theological faith means that everything makes reference to Christ and depends on him. The Christocentrism of the New Testament faith is related to the Christocentrism of revelation and, ultimately, the Christocentrism of salvation, which has in him its fulcrum and foundation (cf. 1 Cor 3: 10–11). For a synthetic and precise view of this topic, cf. G. Biffi, *Approccio al Cristocentrismo*.

10. B. Wauter, "Epìstolas de San Juan," 393.

11. Cf. ibid., 291–294; J. Ratzinger, *Introduzione al Cristianesimo*, 19–20.

12. Cf. P. Antoine, *Foi*, 296–302.

13. J. Pieper, *La Fe*, 74.

14. Cf. W. Kasper, *Il Dio di Gesù Cristo*, 118.

15. Cf. A. Pitta, *Disposizione e Messaggio della Lettera ai Galati*, 212–213. This author writes, "La nuova creazione, cominciata con l'Incarnazione del Figlio di Dio (cf. Gal 1: 4; 4: 4), rappresenta il contenuto centrale del Vangelo in Galati" (213). Cf. S. Zedda, "Cristo e lo Spirito Santo nell'Adozione a Figli Secondo il Commento di S. Tommaso alla Lettera ai Romani," 105–112; F. Prat, *La Théologie de Saint Paul*, 279–300.

16. *Motus fidei non est perfectus nisi sit charitate informatus, unde simul in iustificatione impii cum motu fidei est motus charitatis* (St. Thomas Aquinas, *In Epist. ad Gal.*, c. III, lect. 4; cf. STh, II–II, q. 4, a. 5).

17. Cf. J.M. Yanguas, "La Vida Moral como Expresión de la Fe," 445–454; T.W. Guzie, "The Act of Faith according to St. Thomas," 239–280.

18. For a specific study of this theme: E. Sanz, "La Estructura de la Acción Inmanente." For a study from the point of view of the person, see L. Polo, *La Persona Humana y su Crecimiento*; A. Millán Puelles, *La Libertad: Afirmación de nuestro Ser*, 170–222; M.J. Franquet Casas, *Persona, Acción y Libertad: Las Claves de la Antropología de K. Wojtyla*, 198–286.

19. Cf. A. Aranda, "L'Intelligenza del Cristiano come Questione Teologica," 417–448.

20. For a brief biblical commentary regarding the incorporation into Christ according to St. Paul, cf. J.A. Fitzmyer, "Teología de San Pablo," 820–824.

21. Cf. G. Colombo, *La Ragione Teologica*, 152.

22. On the relation between belief and the liberation of the self from isolation and egoism, cf. J. Ratzinger, *Dogma e Predicazione*, 19ff; R. Fisichella, *Ecclesialità dell'atto di fede*, en id.: *Noi crediamo*, 73–83.

23. Cf. B. Marconcini, *Profeti e Apocalittici*, 50–52, 81–82, 96–98.

24. Cf. J. Ratzinger, *Introduzione al Cristianesimo*, 61–64.

25. The theme complements that which was examined in Chapter IV: We looked at the role of the Church in transmitting the Word; now we will study how the Church receives the Word. These are different perspectives although intimately related: The Church transfers the Word because it welcomes and conserves it faithfully. Regarding the Church as subject of the act of faith,
cf. J. Ratzinger, "Teologia e Chiesa," 87–96; H. de Lubac, "La Fede della Chiesa," 127–152.

26. Cf. Pius XII, Enc. *Mystici Corporis*.

27. STh, II–II, q. 1, a. 9 ad 3.

28. St. Augustine, *In Ioannis Evang. tract.*, 110, 2: PL 35, 1920.

29. Cf. Second Vatican Council, Dogm. Const. *Dei Verbum*, 8. Regarding the invariability of the faith acknowledged and taught by the Church throughout history, cf. J.A. Möhler, *Simbolica*; J.N.D. Kelly, *Early Christian Creeds*; C. Schönborn, *Unità nella Fede*. The thesis of O. Cullmann (*La Foi et le Culte dans l'Eglise Primitive*), which posits a reversal in the structure of the Creed from a Christological model to a Trinitarian one, has not been demonstrated convincingly. In that respect, cf. P. Benoit, "Le Origini del Simbolo degli Apostoli," 461–487.

30. St. Irenaeus, *Adversus haereses*, 1, 10, 1–2: PG 7, 549. For a study of this Irenaen thought, cf. A. Aranda, *Estudios de Pneumatologia*, 76–119.

31. The Church as a subject of faith is understood only in its historical dimension, since in the Church in heaven there is not faith but only vision.

32. Cf. International Theological Commission, *De unitate Fidei et theologico pluralismo*, 4.

33. *Lumen gentium*, 4.

34. Ibid., 64.

35. Cf. First Vatican Council, Dogm. Const. *Pastor aeternus*, 4: DS 3074; *Lumen gentium*, 25.

36. Cf. STh, II–II, q. 1, a. 9 ad 3.

37. *Dei Verbum*, 8.

38. Cf. *Lumen gentium*, 15–16.

39. Cf. ibid., 17.

40. CCC 687–688.

41. Regarding the link between the mystery of the Church and the mystery of the Holy Spirit; cf. H.U. von Balthasar, *Wahrheit III: Der Geist der Wahrheit*.

42. An act of faith in God, one and Trinitarian, is possible for those who are not fully incorporated into the Church but benefit from its teachings and testimonies.

43. CCC 166–167.

44. Cf. *Dei Verbum*, 8.

45. J. Ratzinger, *Teoría de los principios teológicos*, 24; cf. H.U. von Balthasar, *Teología de la Historia*, 121–125. For the nineteenth century, cf. J.A. Möhler, *L'Unità nella Chiesa*, 38ff.

46. For a study of the Trinitarian structure of revelation, see A. Blanco, "Parola, Persona e Storia nella Rivelazione Divina," 263–282.

47. This participation, when charity is lacking, is likened to death but not completely nullified, since the believer also holds a certain relation with the three Persons, that is, he believes that the Father, Son, and Holy Spirit are distinct Persons. Understood like this, as St. Thomas explains, unformed faith has the same nature as faith that is formed (cf. STh, II–II, q. 4, a. 4).

48. F. Zorell translates and explains *koinonia* as community, communion, society, and relation with another person (*Lexikon Graecum Novi Testamenti*, 85). Cf. J. M. Faux, *La Foi du Nouveau Testament*, 269–286. The notion of participation that also is expressed with the term *koinonia* indicates having or receiving a part, of taking part in something. The notion of communion is partially identified with participation, but with the idea of an interpersonal union, since communion exists only among people who make themselves participants in some good; communion relates and unites them.

49. J. Ratzinger, *Teoria de los principios teologias*, 24.

50. CCC 168.

CHAPTER 9

1. The Church, for example, has rejected Luther's doctrine regarding justification by faith without works: cf. Council of Trent, Decr. *De iustificatione*, 8–13, 16, 19–20, 24–27, 32: DS 1532–1541, 1545–1550, 1569–1570, 1574–1577, 1582. For a deeper understanding of the differences between Catholic and Lutheran thought on this point, cf. P. O'Callaghan, *Fides Christi: The Justification Debate*; A. Blanco, "Fede e Giustificazione: Il Loro Riflesso sull'Attività Sociale e Politica del Cristiano Secondo il Pensiero Luterano e Cattolico," 233–242.

2. *Catechism of the Catholic Church*, 148–149.

3. John Paul II, Enc. *Redemptoris Mater*, 12 (emphasis in original).

4. Cf. Ibid., 14.

5. Second Vatican Council, Dogm. Const. *Lumen gentium*, 56.

6. John Paul II, Ap. Ex. *Pastores dabo vobis*, 82.

7. John Paul II, *Redemptoris Mater*, 13; cf. St. Thomas Aquinas, *Summa Theologiae*, III, q. 30, a. 1; *Lumen gentium*, 53; St. Augustine, *De sancta virginitate*, III, 3: PL 40, 398; *Sermo* 215, 4: PL 38, 1074; *Sermo* 196, 1: PL 38, 1019; *De peccatorum meritis et remissione*, I, 29, 57: PL 44, 142; *Sermo* 25, 7: PL 46, 937ff; St. Leo the Great, *Tractatus 21 de natale Domini*, 1: CCL 138, 86.

8. *Lumen gentium*, 58.

9. Cf. C. Pozo, *María en la Obra de la Salvación*, 236, 361.

10. St. Josemaría Escrivá, *Christ Is Passing By*, 172.

11. Cf. G. Roschini, *La Madonna Secondo la Fede e la Teologia*, III, 138.

12. *Lumen gentium*, 56; cf. St. Irenaeus, *Adversus haereses*, III, 22, 4: PG 7, 959; St. Epiphanius, *Haer.*, 78, 18: PG 422, 728–729; St. Jerome, *Epist.* 22, 21: PL 22, 408; St. Augustine, *Sermo* 51, 2, 3: PL 38, 335; St. Cyril of Alexandria, *Cateches.* 12, 15: PG 33, 741; St. John Chrysostom, *In Ps.*, 44, 7: PG 55, 193; St. John Damascene, *Hom. 2 in dorm. B.M.V.*, 3: PG 96, 728.

13. Cf. STh, III, q. 30, a. 1.

14. Cf. John Paul II, Enc. *Veritatis splendor*, 66.

15. STh, II–II, q. 4, a. 2 ad 3.

16. There are many interpretations regarding the meaning that the original Greek term *hypostasis* ought to be given in this passage. However, understanding it as foundation seems to be the best interpretation: cf. J. Ratzinger, *Caminos de Jesucristo*, Ed. Cristiandad, Madrid (2004), 139. For a brief summary of the various positions, cf. M.M. Bourke, "Epistola a los Hebreos," 368.

17. *Prima inchoatio rerum sperandarum in nobis est per assensum fidei* (STh, II–II, q. 4, a. 1). Cf. St. Thomas Aquinas, *De veritate*, q. 14, a. 2; *In III Sent.*, d. 23, q. 2, a. 1–4.

18. R. Latourelle, *Teología de la Revelación*, 526.

19. Cf. St. Thomas Aquinas, *Contra gentes*, III, cc. 47, 152.

20. St. Augustine, *Enarrationes in Psalmos*, 31: 2, 4–5: PL 36, 259, 261. For a comparison between the vision of faith according to St. James and St. Paul, cf. R. Penna, *L'Apostolo Paolo*, 470–495.

21. *Ille etenim vere credit qui exercet operando quod credit* (St. Gregory the Great, *Hom. in Ev.* 26, 9: PL 76, 1202; cf. 14, 3–6: PL 76, 1129–1130). Cf. St. Clement of Rome, *Ad Corinth.*, 32–34: PG 1, 272–277; St. Irenaeus, *Adversus haereses*, 4, 6, 3. 5–7: PG 7, 988–989; St. Augustine, *In Ioannis Evang. tract.*, 124, 5–7: PL 35, 1972–6; St. Aphraates the Persian Sage, *Demonstrationes*: PS 1, 43–44; 370–371.

22. St. Josemaría Escrivá, *The Way*, 579.

23. Second Vatican Council, Past. Const. *Gaudium et spes*, 43; cf. John Paul II, *Veritatis splendor*, 26, 88; Enc. *Evangelium vitae*, 95.

24. Cf. John Paul II, *Veritatis splendor*, 12–20.

25. St. Josemaría Escrivá, *The Forge*, 46.

26. Cf. First Vatican Council, Dogm. Const. *Dei Filius*, 3: DS 3010.

27. Cf. *Gaudium et spes*, 57–62; John Paul II, Enc. *Redemptoris missio*, 52–54.

28. Cf. J. Gnilka, *Gesú di Nazaret: Annuncio e Storia*, 234–246; M. Hengel, *Sequela e Carisma*.

29. Cf. John Paul II, *Redemptoris Mater*, 13.

30. Cf. ibid., 14–18.

31. Cf. *Lumen gentium*, 40–42.

32. Congregation for the Doctrine of the Faith, Ltr. *Orationis formas*, 3.

33. Cf. Second Vatican Council, Dogm. Const. *Dei Verbum*, 2, 25.

34. St. John Damascene, *De Fide Orthodoxa*, lib. III, c. 24: PG 94, 1089. It is about "ascension" that it is not only intellectual, but also affective: *pius affectus mentis in Deum* (St. Bonaventure, *In III Sent.*, d. 17, q. 3, arg. 2).

35. Cf. *Orationis formas*, 3.

36. J. Lopez Diaz, *Oración*, en AAW, *Diccionario* de Teología, EUNSA (2006), 750.

37. Cf. C. Fabro, *La Preghiera nel Pensiero Moderno*, 2.

38. St. Josemaría Escrivá, *Christ Is Passing By*, 116.

39. *Orationis formas*, 11.

40. Cf. St. Teresa of Jesus, *Vida*, 12, 5; 22, 1–5; St. John of the Cross, *Subida al Monte Carmelo*, l. II, c. 22.

41. *Sicut qui haberet librum ubi esset tota scientia, non quaereret nisi ut sciret illum librum, sic et nos non oportet amplius quaerere nisi Christum* (St. Thomas Aquinas, *In Epist. ad Colos.*, c. II, lect. 1). Cf. St. Ambrose, *Expositio in Psalmum CXVIII*, sermon 19, 16: PL 15, 1471; St. John of the Cross, *Cántico Espiritual*, canc. 36, 3.

42. *Orationis formas*, 3.

43. Cf. STh, III, q. 23, a. 4; q. 24, a. 3; *In Ioan. Evang.*, c. I, lect. 8; F. Ocáriz, *Hijos de Dios en Cristo: Introducción a una Teología de la Participación Sobrenatural*; idem, *Naturaleza, gracia y gloria*, 69–106.

44. John Paul II, Enc. *Dominum et vivificantem*, 52.

45. *Orationis formas*, 15. Being and acting in Christ (or in Jesus Christ, in the Lord) synthetically expresses—mainly in Pauline texts, where it is to be found 164 times—the mystery of being Christian (cf. M. Meinertz, *Teologìa del Nuevo Testamento*, 414).

46. *Orationis formas*, 3.

47. Cf. St. Josemaría Escrivá, *Christ is Passing By*, 87; Second Vatican Council, Decr. *Presbyterorum ordinis*, 14.

48. J.L. Illanes, *Tratado de Teología Espiritual*, EUNSA (2007), 440.

49. Cf. *Orationis formas*, 28.

50. St. Josemaría Escrivá, *Friends of God*, 146.

51. *Orationis formas*, 3.

52. J. Ratzinger-Benedict XVI, *Gesù di Nazaret*, 171.

53. Cf. St. Josemaría Escrivá, *Friends of God*, 64.

54. J. Ratzinger, *Iglesia, Ecumenismo y Política*, 36. The Creeds are stated in the plural: "We believe," or in the singular, "I believe," when we have the Church as subject: In saying "we," the Church says "I believe."

55. *Orationis formas*, 13.

56. Cf. ibid., 3.

57. Ibid.

58. Ibid.

59. C. Fabro, *La Preghiera nel Pensiero Moderno*, 19; cf. 21–32.

60. Cf. St. Thomas Aquinas, *De virtutibus in communi*, a. 9 ad 15.

61. *Orationis formas*, 13.
62. St. Josemaría Escrivá, *Friends of God*, 38.
63. *Orationis formas*, 18.
64. About Jesus' prayer, cf. CCC 2599–2606; J.L. Illanes, *Tratado de Teología Espiritual*, 434–438.
65. Ibid., 2617.

PART TWO — INTRODUCTION

1. Cf. St. Thomas Aquinas, *In III Sent.*, d. 23, q. 2, a. 2 sol. 1; q. 3, a. 2 ad 2; q. 3, a. 3 sol. 1; *In Epist. ad Romanos*, c. X, lect. 2.
2. A detailed and well-documented presentation of these models can be found in *Enciclopedia di Teologia Fondamentale*, I; and in *Curso de Teologia Fundamental*, IV, 375–444.

CHAPTER 10

1. Cf. E. Bossetti, "Apologia," 118–121.
2. There has been a great deal of discussion about the object and methodology of apologetics, without any agreement to date. Nevertheless, apologetics and credibility are two intimately related realities. We will present them in this context. Cf. R. Latourelle, *Apologetique Fondamentale: Problèmes de Nature et de Méthode*; H. Bouillard, *Le Sens de l'Apologetique*; R. Latourelle, "Apologética," 114–118.
3. St. Thomas Aquinas, *Summa contra Gentiles*, I, c. 1.
4. Therefore, the first chapters of the first book of the *Summa contra Gentiles* (cc. 1–9) contain the core of St. Thomas's apologetics.
5. Cf. Y.M. Congar, "Theologie," 430–431.
6. For the translation of *logon* for "reason" and the resulting noetic implications, cf. J. Ratzinger, "Teologia e Chiesa," 101. Normally, Peter's commendation is considered to refer strictly to the task of apologetics, but in fact "to give reason of one's own hope" could also be applied to the entire task of theology.
7. Cf. *Summa contra Gentiles*, I, c. 7.
8. Cf. ibid., c. 9; St. Thomas Aquinas, *Summa Theologiae*, I, q. 1, a. ; q. 32, a. 1.
9. J. Quasten, *Patrologia*, I, 187.
10. Cf. ibid., 187–189.
11. For these writers, besides the already-quoted bibliography, cf. R.M. Grant, *Greek Apologists of the Second Century*; E.R. Goodenough, *The Theology of Justin Martyr*; W. Leslie Barnard, *Athenagoras*; R. Joly, *Christianisme et philosophie*; P.H. Donahue, *Jewish-Christian Controversy in the Second Century*; D. Bourgeois, *La Sagesse des Anciens dans la Mystère du Verbe: Evangile et Philosophie chez St. Justin, Philosophe et Martyr*; V. Peri, "Caratter i dell'Apologetica Greca dagli Inizi al Concilio di Nicea," 17–30.

12. Cf. M. Seckler, "Teologia Fondamentale: Compiti e Strutturazione, Concetto e Nomi," 543; J.C.M. van Winden, "Le Christianisme et la Philosophie: Le Commencement du Dialogue entre la Foi et la Raison," 205–213.

13. Cf. G. Bosio, E. dal Covolo, M. Maritano, *Introduzione ai Padri della Chiesa*, I, 156.

14. Cf. W.L. Barnard, *Apologetik I*, in TRE 3, 371–381.

15. Cf. St. Irenaeus, *Adversus haereses*, II, cc. 12–19: PG 7, 737–776.

16. Cf. St. Justin, *Apologia I*, 46, 2–3; II, 2–8: PG 6, 398–399, 444–458; R. Holte, "Logos Spermatikòs," 109–168.

17. Cf. L. Dattrino, *Patrologia*, 39; G. Madec, "La Christianisation de l'Hellenisme,"399–406.

18. Cf. STh, I, q. 1, a. 8.

19. As previously mentioned, Harnack's accusation demonstrably lacks a solid intellectual foundation: cf. M. Guerra, *Antropologìas y Teologìa*; Cf. J. Quasten, *Patrologia*, I, 188.

20. For these authors, cf. V. Peri, "Caratteri dell'Apologetica Greca dagli Inizi al Concilio di Nicea," 30–58; S.R.C. Lilla, *Clement of Alexandria: A Study of Christian Platonism and Gnosticism*; R. Mortley, *Connaissance Religieuse et Hermenéutique chez Clément d'Alexandrie*; J. Danielou, *Origène*; H. Crouzel, *Origene*; M. Harl, *Origène et la Fonction Révélatrice du Verbe Incarné*.

21. Cf. St. Justin, *Apologia II*, 10, 2–3: PG 6, 460–462.

22. Nevertheless, there are some significant differences among them. Cf. M. Rizzi, *Ideologia e Retorica negli Exordia Apologetici*, 171–202.

23. Cf. Clement of Alexandria, *St. Rometa*, VI, 10, 82, 2: PG 9, 299–304; I, 5, 28, 3: PG 8, 713–728.

24. Cf. ibid., VI, 7, 57: PG 9, 282.

25. Cf. L.F. Pizzolato, "L'Apologia nelle Chiese d'Occidente Fino all'età Carolingia," 154–155; F. Halkin, "L' 'Apologie' du Martyr Philéas de Thmuis (Papyrus Bodmer XX) et les Actes Latins de Philéas et Philoromus," 5–27.

26. Cf. L.F. Pizzolato, "L'Apologia nelle Chiese d'Occidente Fino all'età Carolingia," 182–203; A. Trapé, "S. Agostino," 325–434; E. Gilson, *Introduction a l'étude de St. Agustin*; P. Courcelle, *Recherches sur les Confessions de St. Augustin*.

27. Cf. G. Lettieri, *Il Senso della Storia in Agostino d'Ippona*; "Note sulla Dottrina Agostiniana delle due Civitates: A Proposito di Jerusalem and Babylon di J. van Oort," 257–306; R.A. Markus, *Saeculum: History and Society in the Theology of St. Augustine*.

28. Cf. H.I. Marrou, *St. Augustin et la Fin de la Culture Antique*.

29. John Paul II, *Fides et ratio*, 40.

30. Cf. A. Blanco, *Qué es la Teología*, 45–66.

31. Cf. *Summa Theologiae*, I, 1, 8 ad 2: "*cum enim gratia non tollat naturam sed perficiat.*"

32. John Paul II, *Fides et ratio*, 43; Cf. John Paul II, Address to the Participants at the IX International Thomistic Congress (September 29, 1990): *Insegnamenti*, XIII, 2 (1990), 770–771.

33. O. Ruiz Arenas, *Jesús: Epifanía del Amor del Padre*, 349–350.

34. *Nullus quippe credit aliquid, nisi prius cogitaverit esse credendum* (St. Augustine, *De praedestinatione sanctorum*, 5: PL 44, 962). Cf. *De vera religione*, 5, 4: PL 34, 141.

35. The *Catechism of the Catholic Church* highlights that believing is a human, conscious, and free act in conformity with the dignity of the human person (cf. CCC 180, 154).

36. Scholars recognize the social dimension of religion: cf. A. Marchesi, *Linee di uno Sviluppo Storico della Filosofia della Religione*.

37. Cf. A. Blanco, *Qué es la Teología*, 21–27. For more than a century, theologians have been concerned about the issue of the scientific foundation of theology. They have arrived at a solution by developing fundamental theology, an area that gives scientific reason for the foundations of theological science. At the same time, they have provided a new concept of science itself by criticizing the excessively reductive approach of positivism. Cf. M. Seckler, "Teologia Fondamentale," 559–56; H. Bouillard, "De l'Apologétique à la Théologie Fondamentale," 23–31; G. Ruggieri, "L'Apologia Cattolica in Epoca Moderna," 275–348.

38. Cf. M. Seckler, "Teologia Fondamentale," 560.

39. Cf. STh, II–II, q. 2, a. 10.

40. Cf. C. Spicq, *Les Epitres de St. Pierre*, 131.

41. Cf. D. Balch, *Let Wives be Submissive: The Domestic Code in I Peter*, 90–93; R. Fabris, "L'Apologia nel Nuovo Testamento," 3–14.

42. Cf. Second Vatican Council, Decr. *Apostolicam actuositatem*, 6.

43. St. Josemaría Escrivá, *The Way*, 338.

44. *Domine, si error est, teipso decepti sumus; nam ista in nobis tantis signis et prodigiis confirmata sunt et talibus, quae nonnisi per te fieri possunt* (Richard of St. Victor, *De Trinit.*, I, 2: PL 196, 891).

45. For a deeper treatment of the thinking of Duns Scotus on this issue, cf. E. Gilson, *Jean Duns Scoto: Introduction a se Positions Fondamentales*, 177–215.

46. For a more in-depth analysis of St. Thomas's thinking on this question, cf. B. Duroux, *La Psychologie de la Foi chez S. Thomas d'Aquin*, 198–206.

47. Cf. X.M. Le Bachelet, "Apologétique: Apologie," 202–205; A. Lang, *Die Entfaltung des apologetischen Problems in der Scholastik des Mittelalters*.

48. J. Calvin, *Institutes of Christian Religion*, I, c. 5, no. 2.

49. Ibid., I, c. 2, no. 1; II, c. 6, no. 1.

50. It would appear that Pierre Charron was the first writer to carry out apologetics according to this structure in 1514 in his work *Les Trois Vérités*, where he proposed a progressive approach to the fullness of truth. H. Grotius recovered that division in his *De veritate Religionis Christianae*,

1627, as did L.J. Hooke in his work *Religionis naturalis et revelatae principia*, in 1754. Since that time his structure has become increasingly popular in writings and handbooks and has influenced Catholic thought well into the twentieth century, despite repeated attempts at renovation.

51. Cf. F. de B. Vizmanos, "La Apologética de los Escolásticos Postridentinos," 418–446.

52. See X.M. Le Bachelet, "Apologétique," 209.

53. For a critical study of the other work, cf. A. Rodríguez, *I. Kant: La Religión Dentro de los Límites de la Razón*.

54. Cf. J.M. Odero, *La Fe in Kant*, 99–109, 305–378.

55. Cf. A. González Montes, *Fundamentación de la Fe*, 165–175; R. Latourelle, *Teología de la Revelación*, 306–307; W. Pannenberg, *Teología Sistemática I*, 1–64; L. Cristiani, "Schleiermacher," 1500.

56. See. X.M. Le Bachelet, "Apologétique," 215–218.

57. Cf. T. Erskine, *Remarks on the Internal Evidence for the Truth of Revealed Religion*.

58. Cf. J.S. von Drey, *Apologetik als Wissenchaftliche Nachweisung der Göttlichkeit der Christentums*. For a specific study about this author, see A.P.M. Kustermann, *Die Apologetik J.S. Dreys*; W.L. Fehr, *The Birth of the Catholic Tübingen School: The Dogmatics of Johan Sebastian Drey*; A. González Montes, *Fundamentación de la Fe*, 259–262.

59. Cf. M. Blondel, *La Acción: Ensayo de una Crítica de la Vida y de una Ciencia de la Práctica*, 373–436, 521–546.

60. Cf. ibid., 386.

61. Cf. ibid., 445–519. For this aspect of the Blondelian thinking, see C. Izquierdo, *Blondel y la Crisis Modernista*, 277–340.

62. For a listing of these errors, see St. Pius X, Enc. *Pascendi*: DS 3475–3500; Pius XII, Enc. *Humani generis*: DS 3875–3899.

63. For an exposition of fideism, its history, foundation, and theoretical development, cf. S. Harent, "Fideisme," 174–236; G. Rotureau, "Fideisme," 1260–1261.

64. For these implications of Lutheran thinking, cf. G. Ebeling, *The Study of Theology*, 153–165.

65. Cf. P. Poupard, *L'Abbé Louis Bautain: Un Essai de Philosophie Chrétienne au XIX Siècle*.

66. Cf. Gregory XVI, *Theses a Ludovico Eugenio Bautain iussu sui Episcopi Subscriptae*, 1, 3, 6: DS 2751, 2753, 2756; Pius IX, Enc. *Qui Pluribus*: DS 2778, 2779, 2780.

67. First Vatican Council, Dogm. Const. *Dei Filius*, 2: DS 3026; cf. DS 3004.

68. Ibid., 3: DS 3033.

69. Ibid.: DS 3009.

70. Ibid.: DS 3010.
71. Cf. Leo XIII, Enc. *Aeterni Patris*: DS 3135–3138; St. Pius X, *Pascendi*: DS 3499–3500; Mot. Pr. *Sacrorum antistitum*: DS 3538–3539; Pius XII, *Humani generis*: DS 3875.
72. Second Vatican Council, Dogm. Const. *Dei Verbum*, 6; cf. Decr. *Ad gentes*, 12.
73. Cf. Second Vatican Council, Decl. *Dignitatis humanae*, 11.
74. Cf. CCC 31–36, 156, 286, 447, 589–591, 651, 670, 812.
75. John Paul II, *Fides et ratio*, 55.
76. Cf. R. Latourelle, "Jesús de la Historia y Cristo de la Fe," 744–745.
77. Before his death in 1768, Reimarus wrote a work entitled *Apologie, oder Schutzschrift f. die vernunftigen Verehrer Gottes* (*Apology, or Writing in Defense of the Rational Worshipers of God*). It was published several years after his death by G.E. Lessing.
78. Cf. D.F. Strauss, *Das Leben Jesu kritisch hearheitet*, I, vii; II, 686, 736; W.G. Kummel, *Il Nuovo Testamento: Storia dell'Indagine Scientifica sul Problema Neotestamentario*, 173.
79. For a detailed study of Strauss's thinking, cf. M.A. Tabet, *David F. Strauss*.
80. Cf. R. Bultmann, *La Teología del Nuevo Testamento*. For a study of these aspects of Bultmann's thinking and his use of Heidegger, see D. Fergusson, *Bultmann*, 50–71.
81. Cf. P. Grech, "Hermenéutica," 753.
82. Cf. D. Fergusson, *Bultmann*, 108–113.
83. Cf. R. Bultmann, *Creer y Comprender*, I.
84. Cf. R. Bultmann, "Theologie als Wissenchafts," 447–469, which refers to a lecture he gave in 1941, published posthumously on the occasion of the centenary of his birth.
85. Cf. J.M. Casciaro, *Exégesis Bíblica: Hermenéutica y Teología*, 58–73; P. Grech, "Il Problema Cristologico e l'Ermeneutica," 147.
86. J. Ratzinger-Benedict XVI, *Gesù di Nazaret*, 138.
87. Cf. J. Ratzinger, *Dogma e Predicazione*, 115.
88. Cf. G. Bornkamm, "The Significance of the Historical Jesus for Faith," 84.
89. Cf. H.R. Niebuhr, *The Meaning of Revelation*, 59.
90. Cf. J.D. Gosey, "Christian Faith's Partnership with History," 261–278.
91. Cf. J. Ratzinger, *Introduzione al Cristianesimo*, 153–154.
92. Cf. E. Käsemann, "Das problem des historischen Jesus," in *Zeitschrift f. Theologie und Kirche*, 125–153. About Käsemann's criticism of Bultmann, cf. J.M. Casciaro, "El Acceso a Jesús y la Historicidad de los Evangelios," 907–941. Bultmann responded to Käsemann by redesigning his thesis: cf. *Das Verhaltnis des urchristlichen Christusbotschaft zum historischen Jesus*. H. Conzelmann, W. Marxen, Jeremias, G. Bornkamm, G. Ebeling, E. Fuchs, H. Schürmann and others have shown that it is possible to identify facts and words of Jesus using historical-critical methods.

93. See H. Schürmann, "Die vorösterlichen Anfänge der Logientradition."

94. *Gaudium et spes*, 19.

95. Cf. John Paul II, Ap. Ex. *Reconciliatio et Paenitentia*, 14.

96. For an analysis of atheism, its appearance, formulation and development in recent centuries, cf. C. Fabro, *El Problema de Dios; Introduzione all'Ateismo Moderno*; P. Hazard, *El Pensamiento Europeo in el Siglo XVIII*; E. Gilson, *L'etre et Dieu*; J. Maritain, *Il Significato dell'Ateismo Contemporáneo*; J. Lacroix, *El Ateìsmo Contemporàneo*; A. Kolping, *Fundamentaltheologie*, I, 262–281.

97. *Gaudium et spes*, 19.

98. Cf. ibid. To learn what results from this proposition, cf. H. Ley, *Geschichte der Aufklärung und des Atheismus*. St. Thomas Aquinas deals with this in speculative terms in the STh, II–II, q. 15 (*de caecitate mentis et hebetudine sensus*).

99. *Gaudium et spes*, 19.

100. Ibid., 21.

101. Ibid.

102. Ibid.

103. Cf. for example, ibid., 4–10, 21–22, 36–39, 43–44; John Paul II, Enc. *Redemptor hominis*, 15–17; Enc. *Dives in misericordia*, 10–12; Enc. *Dominum et vivificantem*, 33–38; Enc. *Sollicitudo rei socialis*, 11–26; Enc. *Centessimus annus*, 12–21; H. de Lubac, *El Drama del Humanismo Ateo*; C. Tresmontant, *Los Problemas del Ateìsmo*.

104. *Gaudium et spes*, 21; cf. 43, 62; *Apostolicam actuositatem*, 28–29; *Ad gentes*, 10.

105. John Paul II, *Fides et ratio*, 16.

106. *Ad gentes*, 13.

107. For a more complete study and very extensive bibliography, M. Artigas, *Ciencia, Razón y Fe*; E. Agazzi, *Scienza e Fede: Nuove Prospettive su un Vecchio Problema*; cf. P. Poupard, ed., *Scienza e Fede*.

108. Cf. M.J. Scheeben, *Los Misterios del Cristianismo*, 7841–7860.

109. For a description and analysis of this new situation, cf. H. Fitte (ed.), *Fermenti nella Teologia alle Soglie del Terzo Millennio*, 37–75.

110. John Paul II, *Fides et ratio*, 71.

111. Etymologically, religion can come from *re-legere* (to repeatedly consider God's works), *re-eligere* (to choose God again), *or re-ligare* (to tie oneself again to God). This is how St. Thomas considers the question in STh, II–II, q. 81, a. 1. By religion, we can understand the moral disposition that inclines one to worship God, the human response to the inclination to the Absolute, and the need to relate to the Transcendent Being. We can also view religion as the body of doctrines, life norms, and sacred rites that express and specify the human worship given to the Creator. The several meanings of this term are interrelated, because the worship paid to God is founded in the human knowledge of him. The natural inclination toward God is,

of course, inseparable from the conduct with which the person subjects himself to God's plan and law, inasmuch as he knows them.

112. Second Vatican Council, Decl. *Nostra aetate*, 1.

113. Ibid., 2.

114. Ibid.

115. Cf. M. Guerra, *Los Nuevos Movimientos Religiosos: Sectas*, 41–70; M. Introvigne, J.F. Mayer, and E. Zucchini, *I Nuovi Movimenti Religiosi: Sette Cristiane e Nuovi Culti*; J. Garcia Hernando, ed., *Pluralismo Religioso*, vol. II: *Sectas y Religiones no Cristianas*.

116. Cf. *Nostra aetate*, 2; *Lumen gentium*, 16; *Gaudium et spes*, 22; *Ad gentes*, 3, 9, 11; John Paul II, Enc. *Redemptoris missio*, 4–11; Ap. Letter *Tertio millennio adveniente*, 1.

117. *Nostra aetate*, 2.

118. K. Rahner deals with these issues in *Curso Fundamental de la Fe*, and in the various essays of his *Schriften zur Theologie*. On this supposition, see that of H.R. Schlette, *Die Religion als Thema der Theologie*. Similarly, but with its proper nuances, there is the "sacramental" proposal of E. Schillebeeckx, *Le Christ: Sacrament de la Rencontre de Dieu*; "L'Eglise et l'Humanité," 57–78.

119. J. Danielou dealt with these issues in several of his works, for example, *Les Saints Païens de l'Ancien Testament*; *Le Mystère du Salut des Nations*; *Essai sur le Mystère de l'Histoire*.

120. H.U. von Balthasar frequently dealt with these issues, but mainly in *Teología de la Historia*; *Die Gottesfrage des heutigen Menschen*; "El Misterio Pascual," 9; *Das Christentum und die Weltreligionem*.

121. For this criticism, see H.U. von Balthasar, *Cordula, oder der Ernstfall*.

122. Congregation for the Doctrine of the Faith, *Dominus Iesus*, 21.

123. These are the seeds of the divine Word (*semina Verbi*), which the Church recognizes with joy and respect (cf. Second Vatican Council, Decree *Ad gentes*, 11; Declaration *Nostra aetate*, 2)

124. John Paul II, Encyclical Letter *Redemptoris missio*, 29.

125. Cf. ibid.; *Catechism of the Catholic Church*, 843.

126. Cf. Council of Trent, *Decretum de sacramentis*, can. 8, *de sacramentis in genere*: DS 1608.

127. Cf. John Paul II, Encyclical Letter *Redemptoris missio*, 55.

128. *Lumen gentium*, n. 16; About the need to belong to the Church and how it must be understood, cf. G. Philips, *La Iglesia y su Misterio in el Concilio Vaticano II: Historia, Texto y Comentario de la Constituciòn "Lumen gentium,"* I, 260–275; AA.VV., *L'Appartenenza alla Chiesa*; G. Canobbio, "Extra Ecclesiam nulla Salus: Storia e Senso di un Principio Teologico," 428–446; A. Cattaneo, "Salvezza e Appartenenza alla Chiesa," 236–247.

129. Catholic theologians did not accept K. Barth's explanation. He held that the explicit confession of faith in Jesus Christ is absolutely necessary for salvation: *Die kirchliche Dogmatik*, I, 2; IV. 3. On a second occasion, he

slightly qualified his original position: cf. C.E. Braaten, *No other Gospel! Christianity among the World Religions*. Barth's theory has been widely developed and applied to non-Christian religions, H. Kraemer, *The Christian Message in a Non-Christian World*; *World Cultures and World Religions*.

130. *Gaudium et spes*, 22. Note that the conciliar document does not identify the situation of the Christian with one who is not, although it recognizes that grace is present in those persons who profess Christianity and have "good will." In fact, the Church teaches that God already knows who will participate in the mystery of Christ. Therefore, it would seem that there is a step from "knowing" God to "associating oneself to the paschal mystery," a step that demands an explicit conversion of the person, even though it is not always accomplished according to an external link to Christ's Church: cf. *Lumen gentium*, 16.

131. The authors who do not see Christocentrism as absolutely necessary for salvation do not justify that opinion, nor do they explain what are the indispensable elements for building up a truly salvific religious path. Several representatives of this approach are J. Hick, *God and the Universe of Faiths: Essays in the Philosophy of Religion; The Centre of Christianity; The Second Christianity; An Interpretation of Religion: Human Responses to the Transcendent; The Metaphor of God Incarnate; The Rainbow of Faiths*; P. Knitter, *No other Name? A Critical Survey of Christian Attitudes towards the World Religions; One Earth Many Religions: Multifaith Dialogue and Global Responsability*; S.J. Samartha, *One Christ, Many Religions: Towards a Revised Christology; Between Two Cultures: Ecumenical Ministry in a Pluralistic World*; A. Race, *Christians and Religious Pluralism: Patterns in the Christian Theology of Religions*; A. Pieris, *Love Meets Wisdom: A Christian Experience of Buddhism; Une Théologie Asiatique de la Libération; Fire and Water: Basic Issues in Asian Buddhism and Christianity*.

132. Cf. A. Amato, "Gesù e le Religioni non Cristiane: Una Sfida all'Assolutezza del Cristianesimo," 46–79; *The Unique Mediation of Christ as Lord and Saviour*, en Pontificum Consilium Pro Dialogo Inter Religiones, "Pro Diologo Bulletin," 85 / 86 (1994), 15–39; also cf. G. Tanzella-Nitti, "Cristocentrismo e Dialogo Interreligioso," 113–129.

133. John Paul II, *Redemptoris missio*, 5.

134. Cf. Second Vatican Council, Declaration *Dignitatis humanae*, 1.

135. Congregation for the Doctrine of the Faith, *Dominus Iesus*, 22.

CHAPTER 11

1. For an extensive study of this terminology, cf. F.E. Wilms, *I Miracoli nell'Antico Testamento*, 29–147; M. Lefevre, *Miracles*, 1300–1301; W. Grudmann, "Dynamai-Dynamis," in *TWNT*, II, 286–319; G. Bertram, "Thauma," in *TWNT* III, 27–42; "Ergon," in *TWNT* II, 632–649.

2. Cf. O. Hofius, "Milagro," 85–94.

3. Cf. P. Ricoeur, *La Metafora Viva*.

4. P. Grelot, *Sens Chrétien de l'Ancien Testament*, 266.

5. For a brief overview, among other commentaries, cf. J.E. Huesman, "Exodo," 163–175.

6. Cf. J.J. Durham, "Exodus," *World Biblical Commentary*, xxv–xxvi; H. Cazelles, *Autour de l'Exode*, 245–268; E.W. Nicholson, *Exodus and Sinai in History and Tradition*.

7. G.F. Ravasi, *Introduzione all'Antico Testamento*, 75–76. Also, cf. H. Cazelles, *Alla ricerca di Mosé*. That there may have been other flights from Egypt not led by Moses in no way detracts from the historicity of the Mosaic exodus.

8. For that which refers only to the events after the flight from Egypt and the crossing of the Red Sea, one can see the framework offered by B.S. Childs, *Exodus*, 47–239; and F.E. Wilms, *I Miracoli nell'Antico Testamento*, 155–160.

9. Regarding this difference, cf. J.L. Ska, *Le Passage de la Mer*, 143–145.

10. Regarding the historical value of this creed, cf. G. von Rad, *Deuteronomy*, 158–159.

11. Cf. M. Guerra, *Storia delle Religioni*, 40–46; J. Delorme, "Les Livres Prophétiques Anterieures," 462–464.

12. Cf. M. Guerra, *Storia delle Religioni*, 146; G.F. Ravasi, *Introduzione all'Antico Testamento*, 81.

13. Cf. A. Gelin, *Les Idées Maitrises de l'Ancien Testament*, 25; Y.M. Congar, *Le Mystère du Temple*, 21–72.

14. Cf. J.L. Ska, *Le Passage de la Mer*, 144–145.

15. Cf. C. Tresmontant, *Etudes de Métaphysique Biblique*, 13–38, 223–228; L. Scheffczyk, "Creación y Providencia," 2–12.

16. Cf. M. Guerra, *Storia delle Religioni*, 33–40, 51–62; G. von Rad, *Theologie des Altes Testament*, I, 23–127; L. Monloubou, F.M. du Buit, *Dizionario Biblico: Storico-Critico*, 796.

17. Cf. B. Vawter, *Introducción a la Literatura Profética*, 608–618.

18. Cf. E. Testa, B. Marconcini, *Profetismo, Profeti, Apocalittica*, 19.

19. Cf. P. Antoine, "Foi," 289.

20. Cf. S. Pié-Ninot, *Tratado de Teologia Fundamental*, 192.

21. Cf. R. Lavatori, *Dio e l'Uomo: Un Incontro di Salvezza*, 56.

22. Cf. C.H. Peisker, "Profeta," 413–416; J.C. Holman, "Profeta," 211.

23. Cf. A. Condamin, "Prophetisme," 386ff; E. Fascher, *Prophète: Eine Sprach uns religionsgeschichtliche UnterSuchung*.

24. Cf. C. Conroy, "Profetas," 1086.

25. Cf. G. von Rad, *Theologie des Altes Testament*, II, 24; L. Ramlot, "Prophetisme, "921.

26. Cf. A. Jepsen, *Nabi: Soziologische Studien zur altertestamentische Literatur und Religionsgeschichte*.

27. Cf. W.F. Albright, *From the Stone Age to Christianity*, 231–232.

28. Cf. L. Monloubou, F.M. du Buit, *Dizionario Biblico*, 793.

29. Cf. J.C. Holman, "Profeta," 212.

30. G. Savoca, "Profecía," 1524–1525.

31. This has happened, among other peoples, among the American Indians, in the Arctic, Africa, India, etc. See T.W. Overholt, *Prophecy in Cross-Cultural Perspective.*

32. Regarding the problem in its entirety, cf. W. Vogels, *Les Profètes*, 9–31, 137–155.

33. Cf. St. Thomas Aquinas, *Summa Theologiae*, II–II, q. 172, a. 6.

34. Cf. S. Mowinckel, *Psalmenstudien III. Die Kultprophetie und prophetische Psalmen; The Psalms in Israel's Worship*, II, 53–73; A. Haldar, *Associations of Cult Prophets Among the Ancient Semites*; A.R. Johnson, *The Cultic Prophet in Ancient Israel; The Cultic Prophet and Israel's Psalmody.*

35. Cf. C. Conroy, "Profetas," 1085–1086.

36. Attributed to St. John Chrysostom, *Opus imperf. in Matthaeum*, hom. 19: PG 56, 742; cf. STh, II–II, q.172, a. 5 ad 3.

37. Cf. STh, II–II, q.172, a. 6.

38. Cf. ibid., a. 1.

39. Cf. ibid., q. 171, a. 5; q. 173, a. 4.

CHAPTER 12

1. For an extensive treatment of these testimonies, cf. H. Felder's masterpiece, *Jesus Christus.*

2. International Theological Commission, "Quaestiones selectae de Christologia," (1979), I.A.1.1.

3. Many authors joined in this reaction against the *Formgeschighte* and Bultmann's interpretations, among them H. Conselmann, W. Marxen and W. Trilling. Their commentaries focus on the Gospels of Luke, Mark, and Matthew, respectively.

4. R. Latourelle, *L'Accès à Jésus par les Evangiles*, 220.

5. Cf. ibid., 248–252. Latourelle argues that by applying all these of criteria one can determine the historical authenticity of most of the teachings and actions of Jesus. Such is the case with the key themes of his ministry, his beginnings in Galilee, the enthusiasm of the people in view of the miracles he performed, their progressive lack of understanding, his ministry in Jerusalem, and the political and religious trials. This also applies to his teaching on baptism, the temptations he endured, his transfiguration, his preaching about the coming of the kingdom, his exhortations to penance and conversion, the Beatitudes, the Lord's Prayer, the miracles and exorcisms as signs of the kingdom, Judas' treason, his agony, crucifixion, burial, and Resurrection. Non-Christian sources have confirmed significant information about Jesus and his life on earth. For instance, Tacitus, *Annales*, XV, 44; Suetonius, *Nero*, XVI; Pliny, *Epist.*, X, 96; Flavius Josephus, *Antichitates Judaicae*, XVIII, 3, 3; XX, 9, 1; We can also find references to Jesus in the Talmud as analyzed by H.L. Strack, *Jesus, die Heretiker und die Christen*, 37. The activity of Jesus was observed by St. Justin Martyr in

Dialogo con Trifón, 8, 4; 32, 1; 49, 1–7. Cf. C. Martini, "Introduzione Generale ai Vangeli Sinottici," 101–107.

6. Cf. R. Latourelle, *L'Accès à Jésus par les Evangiles,* 220–252.

7. Cf. F. Lambiasi, *L'Autenticità Storica dei Vangeli: Studio di Criteriologia.*

8. Cf. J.B. Freuy, "Le Conflit entre le Messianisme de Jesus et le Messianisme des Juifs de Son Temps," 133–149, 269–293.

9. From the broad bibliography about the issue, cf. J. Schlösser, *Le Règne de Dieu dans les dits de Jésus;* About the discussion of whether or not Jesus thought the kingdom's arrival was imminent, and whether it was historical or meta-historical, cf. R. Schnackenburg, *Signoria e Regno di Dio.*

10. Cf. the conclusions of the study of D.R.A. Hare, *The Son of Man Tradition,* 280–282. Hare notes that these differences refer to the meaning of the expression and the reasons for its use and about how the Israelites understood the meaning of Daniel's prophecy. Cf. J. Coppens, "Fils de l'Homme Danielique et les Relectures de Dan 7,13 dans les Apocriphes et les Écrites du Nouveau Testament," 5–51; "Le Chapitre VII de Daniel," 87–94; "Les Origines du Symbole du Fils de l'Homme en Dan VII," 497–502; *Où en est le problème de Jesus Fils de l'homme,* 283–287; cf. J. Jeremias, *Teologia del Nuovo Testamento,* 293–314; L. Sabourin, *Les Noms et les Titres de Jésus,* 233ff.

11. Regarding the title "Son of Man," see also J. Ratzinger-Benedict XVI, *Jesus of Nazareth,* 321–335.

12. To this event others may be added, particularly Jesus' statement to Herod (recounted only by Luke) that he would continue working miracles up to the third day. "It cannot be that a prophet should perish away from Jerusalem"(Lk 13: 33). Cf. C.J. Schreck, "The Nazareth Pericope: Luke 4: 16–30," 399–471. Matthew also relates the event at the synagogue (cf. Mt 13: 53–58), as does Mark (cf. Mk 6: 1–6). The presentation of Jesus as a prophet has been verified from a historical standpoint. Differences among some authors refer to nuances. Cf. R. Meyer, *Der Prophet aus Galiläa;* F. Schnider, *Jesus der Prophet.* On Luke's emphasis in presenting Jesus as a prophet, cf. G.W.H. Lampe, "The Lucan Portrait of Christ," 160–175.

13. About the explicit comparison during Jesus' life, between him and Moses, Elijah, Solomon, and the Baptist, cf. J. Caba, *El Jesús de los Evangelios,* 69–79; A. George, "Le Parallele entre Jean-Baptiste et Jesus en Luc 1–2," 147–171; M.E. Boismard, *Moses or Jesus: An Essay in Johannine Christology.*

14. Note that it is one thing to *define oneself* as prophet or to *call oneself* a prophet and another to *present oneself* as prophet. Once this has been taken into account, it is possible to conjugate these verb forms according to the observations of other contemporary authors, as F. Gils did in his *Jesus Prophète d'Après les Évangiles Synoptiques,* 44–47.

15. Cf. E. Haenchen, *Der Vater, der mich gesandt hat,* in "New Testament Studies" 9 (1962–63) 208–216.

16. Cf. E. Schürer, *Geschichte des jüdischen Volkes im Zeitalter Jesu Christ;* J. Bonsirven, *Le Judaïsme Palestinien au Temps de Jesus-Christ;* J. Jeremias,

"Jerusalén en tiempos de Jesús," *Cristiandad*; P. Grelot, *La Speranza Ebraica al Tempo di Gesù*; S. Cavalletti, *Il Giudaismo Intertestamentario*.

17. Cf. A. Gelin, DBS, V, 1165–1212; L. Dennefeld, DTC, X, 1404–1568; S. Mowinckel, *He that Cometh: The Messiah Concept in the Old Testament and Later Judaism*, B. Blackwell; J. Coppens, *Le Messianisme Royal*; H. Cazelles, *Il Messia della Bibbia*.

18. Cf. J. Giblet, "Prophetisme et Attente d'un Messie Prophète dans l'Ancien Judaisme," 117–128; J. Coppens, *Le Messianisme et sa Relève Prophetique*.

19. Cf. R. Meyer, "Farisaios," 858–921; H.F. Weiss, "Farisaios," 921–956; A. Salda rini, "Pharisées," 289–303.

20. Cf. G. Stemberger, *Farisei, Saducei, Esseni*, 94–112.

21. Cf. R.E. Brown, "The Messianisme of Qumran," *Catholic Biblical Quarterly*, 533–582.

22. Cf. J. Jeremias, *Il Significato Teologico dei Reperti del Mare Morto* (Brescia: Paideia, 1964), 15. Jesus must have had this severity in mind when he healed the man with the withered hand on the Sabbath (cf. Lk 6: 6–11).

23. Cf. J.M. Casciaro, *Jesucristo y la Sociedad Política*.

24. This long-standing interpretation has been suggested by some Fathers of the Church. Among Protestants, the expert discussion of the historical-textual issues may be found in O. Cullmann, *Cristologia del Nuovo Testamento*, 103, 192–194, 201–205.

25. About this issue, see R. Feuillet, "Le Triomphe du Fils de l'Homme d'Après la Déclaration du Christ aux Sanhedrites," 164–168.

26. It is possible to establish other criteria substantially in accordance with the one we have just sketched. For example, in his *Jesus der Prophet*, 69–88, F. Schnider proposes five "reference models" that allow us to evaluate whether or not Jesus was a true prophet sent by God: He interpreted the Scriptures, prophesied, performed prophetic gestures, predicted his passion, and had visions. Cf. F. Schnider, "La Profezia come Segno di Credibilità della Rivelazione," R. Fisichella (ed.), *Gesù Rivelatore*, 217–218; R. Fisichella, *Profecía*, 1072–1074.

27. Cf. M. Buber, *Zwei Glaubensweisen, in Werke*, I, 658, 728–735.

28. Cf. H. Waldenfels, *Teologia Fondamentale nel Contesto del Mondo Contemporaneo*, 322.

29. G. Savoca, *Profecía*, 1533.

30. About the historical authenticity of these menacing predictions, cf. J. Jeremias, *Jesu Verheissung für die Völker*, 42ff; W. Trilling, *Jesus davant l'Histoire*, 139–140.

31. Cf. A. Feuillet, "Les Trois Grandes Prophéties de la Passion et de la Résurrection des Évangiles Synoptiques," 533–560, 68 (1968): 41–74.

32. Cf. H. Schurmann, *Gesù di Fronte alla Propria Morte*, 65–68.

33. R. Bultmann, *Exegetica*, 169, 170.

34. Cf. H. Conzelmann, *Grundriss der Theologie des Neuen Testaments*, 153.

35. From the point of view of historical science, we must consider as authentic the words in Luke 13: 32–33. Cf. H. Schürmann, *Gottes Reich—Jesus Geschick*, 226–229; G. Bornkamm, *Gesù di Nazaret*, 150.

36. There is a general consensus that this verse is also authentic.

37. Cf. R. Fabris, *Gesù di Nazareth: Storia e Interpretazione*, 251.

38. A specific study about this issue may be found in R. Latourelle, *Miracles de Jésus et Théologie du Miracle*, 93–268; F. Mussner, *I Miracoli di Gesù*; J.A. Sayés, *Cristologia Fundamental*, 195–239.

39. Cf. R. Bultmann, *Die Geschichte der Synopthischen Tradition*, 236–253; M. Dibelius, *Die Formgeschichte des Evangeliums*, 34, 66.

40. W. Trilling, *Jesus davant l'Histoire*, 138.

41. Cf. A. Richardson, *Las Narraciones Evangélicas sobre Milagros*, 48–49.

42. Cf. C.H. Dodd, *L'Interpretazione del Quarto Vangelo*, 359–361.

43. Among these authors are Nestle, Bacon, Findlay, Vaganay, and others. Cf. J. Quinlan, "Matthew," 497–498. Although other explanations are possible, the structure we are now discussing is undeniable.

44. Cf. J.B. Colon, "Marc," 850–851; C.H. Dodd, *L'Interpretazione del Quarto Vangelo*, 542–553.

45. Cf. L. Cerfaux, J. Cambier, "Luc," 582–583.

46. About the historicity and sense of that debate, cf. A. George, "Paroles de Jesus sur ses Miracles," 218, 223, 230; J. Jeremias, *Teologia del Nuovo Testamento*, 114.

47. Matthew and Luke agree in his reason for this reproach. It was the people's lack of conversion after having witnessed so many miracles. Cf. J. Jeremias, *Teologia del Nuovo Testamento*, 9–29; A. George, "Paroles de Jesus sur ses Miracles," 294–295.

48. John Paul II, Discourse of December 9, 1987, 195–198.

49. About this concept, cf. H.U. von Balthasar, *L'Amour seul est Digne de Foi*, 93–103.

50. B. Pascal has become famous, among other things, because he explicitly posited these arguments, which were considered worthless by the rationalists of his age: "The heart has arguments that reason does not understand." Cf. *Pensées*, IV, 277.

51. Cf. A. Orozco, *La Libertad en el Pensamiento*.

52. St. Josemaría Escrivá, *Christ is Passing By*, 166.

53. The Catholic Church has developed this theological concept by saying that the Son is the Word that emanates love. *Verbum spirans Amorem*, because the Son—with the Father—is the sole principle of the breath of the Holy Spirit. Cf. STh, I, q. 36, a. 2–4.

54. Cf. J. Jeremias, *Teologia del Nuovo Testamento*, 133.

55. S.A. Panimolle, "Amor," 91.

56. H. Schürmann, *Gesù di Fronte alla Propria Morte*, 52.

57. Cf. J. Jeremias, *Teologia del Nuovo Testamento*, 474–478.

58. For an analysis of the different positions, cf. P. Grech, "Il Problema Cristologico e l'Ermeneutica," 142–145.

59. International Theological Commission, "De Jesu autoconscientia quam scilicet Ipse de se Ipso et de sua missione habuit," 571–575.

60. The concept of sign and testimony are characteristic of the fourth Gospel and constitute an important key for interpreting it.

61. For a complete enumeration of the times that the terms "Son of God," "Son" and "Father" appear in the Gospels, cf. J. Caba, *El Jesús de los Evangelios*, 202ff.; L. Sabourin, *Les Noms et les Titres de Jésus*, 233ff.

62. Cf. J. Jeremias, *Le Parabole di Gesú*, 83–93.

63. Cf. ibid., 85–87.

64. Cf. J. Jeremias, *Teologia del Nuovo Testamento*, 27–30, 80ff.

65. Cf. ibid., 82–87; For a more extensive analysis of this issue, cf. J. Jeremias, *Abba*.

66. R. Fabris, *Gesù di Nazareth*, 227–228.

67. Cf. J. Blinzer, *Der Prozess Jesu: das jüdische und das römische gerichsverfahren gegen Jesus Christus auf Grund der ältesten Zeugnisse*; D.R. Catchpole, *The Trial of Jesus: A Study in the Gospels and Jewish Historiography from 1770 to the Present Day*, 72–152.

68. Regarding the title "Son" and "Son of God," cf. J. Ratzinger-Benedict XVI, *Gesu di Nazaret*, 384–395.

69. Contemporary Catholic theology has rediscovered the richness of this specific issue in the writings of St. John. For a summary cf. R. Latourelle, *Miracles de Jésus et Théologie du Miracle*, 326–340.

70. John Paul II, Discourse of November 11, 1987, 180.

71. The centrality of divine filiation in the life and testimony of Jesus and the identification of obedience to the Father as its characteristic and proper expression is also followed in the idea of divine filiation by adoption as the center of the Christian life (cf. St. Josemaría Escrivá, *The Way of the Cross*, 1.1). For a more extensive study of the relationship between divine filiation, obedience, and fidelity, cf. F. Ocáriz, "La Filiación Divina," 173–214.

72. John Paul II, Discourse of June 24, 1987, *Creo en Jesucristo*, 96. The Church Fathers unanimously taught the connection—in Jesus—between divine filiation, obedience, and fidelity. Cf. St. Thomas Aquinas, *In Ioan. Evang.*, c. VIII, lect. 3. The most recent theological reflections have echoed this connection and have begun to value it more explicitly. Cf. H.U. von Balthasar, *El Misterio Pascual*; V. Battaglia, *Gesù Crocifisso: Figlio di Dio*, 25–34; P. Martinelli, *La Morte di Cristo come Rivelazione dell'Amore Trinitario*, 119–196, 279–314, 367–396.

73. Cf. John Paul II, Discourse of July 8, 1987, 100–108, 117–121, 277–282, 383–387.

74. John Paul II, Discourse of October 30, 1985, XXX.

75. Cf. L. Cerfaux, *Témoins de Christ d'Après le Livre des Actes*, II, 157–174.

76. Cf. A. Rodríguez Carmona, "Origen de las Fórmulas Neotestamentarias de Resurrección con Anistémi y Egheiró," 25–58.

77. Cf. G. Ghiberti, "Testimonianze sulla Risurrezione di Gesù," 405.

78. The apostles themselves seem to lead their listeners toward a verification of this kind: cf. Mt 27: 62–66; 28: 11–15; 1 Cor 15: 6–11.

79. R. Bultmann, *Nuovo Testamento e Mitologia: Il Manifesto della Demitizzazione,* 170.

80. R. Bultmann, *Exegetica,* 188.

81. H. Waldenfels, *Teologia Fondamentale,* 343; the author refers to G. Bornkamm, *Gesù di Nazaret,* 180.

82. Cf. C. Kannegiesser, *Foi en la Résurrection: Résurrection de la Foi,* 128ff., 150.

83. Cf. X. Léon-Dufour, *Résurrection de Jesus et Message Pascal,* 252, 305.

84. Cf. E. Schillebeeckx, *Jesus, het verhaal van een levende,* 271–273, 291–293; *Die Auferstehung Jesu als Grund des Erlösung,* where he attempts to clarify his thinking, maintaining, nevertheless, the approach that has already been described.

85. About the historical authenticity of the tomb, cf. J. Blinzer, "Die Grabñegung Jesu in historicher Sicht," 56–107.

86. Cf. F. Brandle, "Musste das Grab Jesu leer sein?" *Orientierung,* 109: "An authentic faith in Jesus' Resurrection is possible without faith in the empty tomb."

87. Among them, cf. F. Mussner, *I Miracoli di Gesù,* 134.

88. For example, J. Gnilka, *Il Vangelo Secondo Matteo,* 726–727.

89. H. Schlier, *La Risurrezione di Gesù Cristo,* 28.

90. Cf. J. Gnilka, *Il Vangelo Secondo Matteo,* 723.

91. Cf. R. Fabris, *Matteo,* 563; J. Gnilka, *Marco,* 909–910. To verify their dates, the authors refer to S. Kravis, *Talmudische Archäologie,* II, 54–82; P. Billerbeeck, H. Strack, *Kommentar zum NT aus Talmud und Midrash,* I, 1047–1051.

92. Cf. R. Fabris, *Giovanni,* 1018.

93. An echo of that popular tradition is found in the following century. Cf. St. Justin Martyr, *Dialogue with Trypho the Jew,* 108, 2: PG 6, 725–728.

94. Textual criticism today tends to expose this diversity, distinguishing three great groups: kerygmatic texts, those from tradition (mainly of cultic, narrative, dogmatic, and apologetic), and those meant for catechesis. Cf. J. Schmitt, *Résurrection de Jesus dans le Kerygme, la Tradition et la Catechèse,* 490–582. B. Rigaux distinguishes the forms as kerygmatic, confessional, hymnal, and narrative: *Dio l'ha Risuscitato,* 83–384.

95. Cf. R. Marlé, "Resurrección de Jesús," 100.

96. Cf. C.L. Musatti, *Elementi di Psicologia della Testimonianza,* 9–10.

97. St. John Chrysostom, *In Matth. hom.,* 1, 2: PG 57, 16.

98. STh, II–II, q. 70, a. 2 ad 2.

99. Cf. F. Ocáriz, "La Resurrección de Jesucristo," 755; P. Grelot, "L'Historien davant la Résurrection de Christ," 233.

100. Cf. M. González Gil, *Cristo: El Misterio de Dios*, II, 316; R. Martin-Achard, "Résurrection dans l'Ancien Testament et le Judaisme," 437–458.

101. Cf. A. Feuillet, "Les Trois Grandes Prophéties de la Passion et de la Résurrection des Évangiles Synoptiques," 533–560; J. Guillet, *Gesù di Fronte alla sua Vita e alla sua Morte*, 146–167.

102. Cf. B. Rigaux, *Dio l'ha Risuscitato*, 72–73; J. Dupont, "L'Après Mort dans l'Oeuvre de Luc," 3–21.

103. Cf. K. Lehmann, *Auferweckt am dritten Tag nach der Schrift. Früheste Christologie, Bekenntnisbildung und Schriftauslegung im Lichte von 1 Cor 15: 3–5, 17–157*; J. Kremer, *Das älteste Zeugnis von der Auferstehung Christi*.

104. For a concise presentation of the indications in the New Testament about this effort, cf. Schmitt, *Résurrection de Jesus dans le Kerygme, la Tradition et la Catechèse*, 487–532.

105. About the worth of *paradosis* and, specifically, how it was received in the early Church, cf. M.A. Tabet, "I Testi Paolini sulla Paradosis nei Commenti Patristici (secoli I–III)," 39–53.

106. Besides Bultmann and Marxsen, another author who supports this thesis is J. Becker, *Auferstehung der Toten im Urchristentum*.

107. In this sense, besides Becker, one should also consider P. Hoffmann, "Auferstehung II / 1, Neues Testament," 478–513.

108. Cf. J. Kremer, "La Risurrezione di Gesù Cristo," 210–211.

109. John Paul II, Discourse of February 1, 1989, 405–406.

110. Cf. E. Kasemann, *Das problem des storischen Jesu*; P.E. Davies, "Experience and Memory: The Role of the Exalted Christ in the Life and the Experience of the Primitive Church," 181–192; C.H. Dodd, *The Founder of Christianity*. W. Kasper includes this title within the Christology implicit in the New Testament: *Gesù il Cristo*, 132–151.

111. This is the opinion of the majority of the followers of the Formgeschichte, for example, R. Bultmann, *La Teología del Nuevo Testamento*, 46; H. Conzelmann, "Jesus Christus," 650–653; G. Bornkamm, *Gesù di Nazaret*; W. Trilling, "Vom historischen Jesus zum Christus des Glaubens," 48–52.

112. Cf. P. van den Berghe, "Gij zijt de Zoon van de levende God," 448–472; H. Anderson, *Jesus and Christian Origins: A Commentary on Modern Viewpoints*; A. Amato, in *Gesù il Signore*, 105–106, prefers to speak about "open" (rather than "implicit") Christology, because it better expresses the opening of the pre-Paschal faith of the disciples to the certitude and firmness of the post-Paschal faith.

113. The interest in studying Jesus' disciples is growing among scholars because it is considered critical for resolving important historical-textual issues. Among the first to pursue this line of investigation is H. Schurmann, *Die*

vorösterlichen Anfänge der Logientradition, and more recently, J. Gnilka, *Gesù di Nazaret,* 211–245.

114. Cf. B. Rigaux, *Dio l'ha Risuscitato,* 106–107.

115. Cf. ibid., 100, 106–107, 122, 125, 127–128; 138, 166, 168; L. Cerfaux, "Kyrios," 200–228; R. Fabris, *Giovanni,* 1042–1043. There is general scholarly agreement that the primitive formula was *Kyrios Iesus,* not *Kyrios Christos,* as asserted by Bousset, Lohmeyer, and afterwards O. Cullmann in *Cristo y el Tiempo,* 13–134. Cf. W. Foerster, "Kyrios," 1342–1391, 1450–1488, especially 1468–1481; B.F. Meyer, "Jesus Christ," 794.

116. Cf. W. Bousset, *Kyrios Christos;* E. Lohmeyer, *Christuskult und Kaiserkult.*

117. Cf. L. Cerfaux, *Le Christ dans la Théologie de St. Paul,* 348.

118. Cf. John Paul II, Discourse of April 19, 1989, 449.

119. For an analysis of faith in Jesus as Son of God based upon their experience of the Resurrection; J. Schmitt, *Jesus Resuscité dans la Prédication Apostolique,* 213–216; G. Schneider, *Gli Atti degli Apostoli,* II, 179.

120. John Paul II, Discourse of March 8, 1989.

121. John Paul II, Discourse of May 20, 1987.

122. John Paul II, Discourse of June 3, 1987.

123. John Paul II, Discourse of March 2, 1988.

124. Ibid., 230.

125. Cf. John Paul II, Discourse of March 8, 1989, in ibid., 426–427; STh, III, q. 55, aa. 1–4.

126. John Paul II, Discourse of March 8, 1989, in *Creo en Jesucristo,* 427.

127. Cf. the careful and detailed analysis of B. Rigaux, *Dio l'ha Risuscitato,* 429–443.

128. Cf. J.H. Nicolas, *Synthèse Dogmatique,* I, 521–522.

129. John Paul II, Discourse of March 8, 1989, in *Creo en Jesucristo,* 422.

130. Cf. J. Jeremias, "Ionas," in *TWNT,* III, 413. Cf. G.D. Cova, "Il Profeta e la Grande Città: Prolegomi a una Lettura Biblica dall'Annuncio a Ninive al Segno di Giona," 72–80; V. Mora, *Le Signe de Jonas.*

131. Cf. R. Fabris, *Giovanni,* 1015–1018; R. Brown, L. Dupont, G. Segalla, I. de la Potterie, R. Schnackenburg, and D. Mollat.

132. Cf. St. Thomas Aquinas, *In Ioan. Evang.,* c. XX, lect. 6.

133. Ibid., a. 2 ad 1. Some authors have translated *oculata fides* as "with the eyes of faith." What seems more precise, from the grammatical and contextual standpoint, is the one used here, taken from F. Ocáriz, J.A. Riestra, and F.L. Mateo Seco, 464.

134. Cf. J.A. Sayés, *Razones para Creer,* 167–173.

135. L. Cerfaux, *Le Christ dans la Théologie de St. Paul,* 59.

CHAPTER 13

1. Cf. J.L. Illanes, "La Dimensione Cristologica della Teologia Fondamentale," 97–111; S. Pié-Ninot, "La Dimensione Ecclesiale della Teologia Fondamentale," 113–129.

2. About the ecclesiological worth of Christocentrality, cf. J. A. Domínguez, "Las Interpretaciones Posteriores al Concilio," 63–87.

3. T. Citrini, "La Chiesa e i Sacramenti," 557. In this article, the author offers a presentation of the credibility of the Church in its entirety, different from the one that will be elaborated on here. It is an interesting presentation as an example of a possible apologetic ecclesiastical model inspired by the search for the meaning of modern man.

4. Cf. S. Pié-Ninot, "La Dimensione Ecclesiale della Teologia Fondamentale," 125–126.

5. Cf. J. Leuba, "La Notion Chrétienne de Temoignage," 309–312.

6. Cf. C. Geffré, "Le Témoignage comme Expèrience et come Langage," 291–307.

7. Regarding the historicity of the various miracles to be found in the Acts of the Apostles, cf. L. O'Reilly, *Word and Sign in the Acts of the Apostles*; B. Prete, *L'Opera di Luca: Contenuti e Prospetive* (Turin, Leumann, LDC, 1986), 426–452.

8. Cf. B. Prete, A. Scaglioni, *I Miracoli degli Apostoli*, 82.

9. Cf. G. Schneider, *Gli Atti degli Apostoli*, II, 64.

10. G. Savoca, "Profecía," 1533–1534.

11. For an overall view of the fulfillment of the messianic prophesies of Jesus, cf. A. Feuillet, *L'Accomplissement des Prophéties*. For what specifically refers to the Resurrection, cf. B. Rigaux, *Dio l'ha Risuscitato*, 179–183.

12. About the different kinds of testimony, cf. P. Ricoeur, "L'Herméneutique du Témoignage," 35–61; Z. Trenti, *Invocazione*, 63–70.

13. Cf. R. Koch, "Testimonianza," 908.

14. Regarding the first post-apostolic generation, cf. St. Clement of Rome, *Ad Corinth.*, 16. 21. 23–26: PG 1, 239–242, 255–260; St. Ignatius of Antioch, *Epist. ad Smyr.*, 1–4; PG 5, 839–846; St. Polycarp of Smyrna, *Epist. ad Phil.*, 2: PG 5, 1017–1018.

15. About the validity of this judgment, cf. J.N.D. Kelly, *Early Christian Creeds*; J.H. Walgrave, *Newman: Le Dévelopment du Dogme*; A. Grillmeier, *Gesù il Cristo nella Fede della Chiesa*; C. Schönborn, *Unità nella Fede*.

16. About predictions in those first Christian communities, cf. C. Perrot, "Prophètes et Prophetisme dans le Nouveau Testament," 25–40.

17. Cf. A. Läpple, *I Miracoli: Documenti e Verità dagli Archivi della Chiesa*; L. Monden, *El Milagro: Signo de Salud*, 176–287.

18. For a contemporary exposition about exorcisms, cf. G. Amorth, *Un Esorcista Racconta*.

19. Cf. P. Vallin, "Prophetisme," 2434–2446.

20. Cf. St. Justin Martyr, *Dialogue with Trypho the Jew*, 82: PG 6, 6690670.
    Cf. St. Irenaeus, *Adversus haereses*, II, 32, 4; III, 11, 9: PG 7, 828–830, 890–892.

21. Cf. Y.M. Congar, *Credo nello Spirito Santo*, II, 50; H. Strathmann, *Martyrs*, 1325–1329.

22. Cf. St. Ignatius of Antioch, *Epist. ad Rom.*, 6, 2: PG 5, 813–814.

23. Cf. S. Pié-Ninot, "La Chiesa come Tema Teologico Fondamentale," 142–144.

24. Cf. ibid., 146.

25. Second Vatican Council, Dogm. Const. *Lumen gentium*, 48; *Gaudium et spes*, n. 45, Decr. *Ad gentes*, n. 1.

26. Second Vatican Council, Dogm. Const. *Lumen gentium*, 8.

27. First Vatican Council, Dogm. Const. *Dei Filius*, 3: DS 3014.

28. Cf. *Lumen gentium*, 8.

29. Cf. J. Ratzinger, *Le Nouveau Peuple de Dieu*, 83–85.

30. For an exposition of the issue, cf. R. Latourelle, *Cristo y la Iglesia: Signos de Salvaciòn*.

31. Cf. *Dei Filius*, 3: DS 3012–3013. For a study of the origin of these texts and the influence of the Fathers and Catholic theologians, cf. S. Pesce, *La Chiesa Cattolica Perenne Motivo di Credibilità*.

32. Cf. St. Thomas Aquinas, *Summa contra Gentiles*, I, c. 6.

33. St. Augustine, *De fide rerum quae non videntur*, IV, 7: PL 40, 176.

34. *Summa contra Gentiles*, I, c. 6.

35. Ibid. He explicitly relates this wonderful conversion to the Incarnation of the Son of God in IV, c. 54.

36. *Lumen gentium*, 1.

37. Second Vatican Council, Dogm. Const. *Dei Verbum*, 8; cf. *Dei Filius*, 4: DS 3019–3020.

38. Cf. *Catechism of the Catholic Church*, 748.

39. St. Augustine, *Sermo* 116: PL 38, 659–660.

40. Cf. N. Cottugno, "La Testimonianza della Vita del Popolo di Dio, segno di Rivelazione alla Luce del Concilio Vaticano II," 232.

41. Cf. Second Vatican Council, Const. *Sacrosanctum concilium*, 6.

42. *Lumen gentium*, 8. Cf. St. Augustine, *De civitate Dei*, XVIII, 51, 2: PL 41, 614.

43. Cf. T. Citrini, "La Chiesa e i Sacramenti," 558–559.

44. G. Philips, *La Iglesia y su Misterio in el Concilio Vaticano II*, 159.

45. *Lumen gentium*, 8.

46. N. Cottugno, "La Testimonianza della Vita del Popolo di Dio," 238.

47. Here, we understand authenticity as the correspondence between what a thing is and its appearance. Therefore, what is authentic reveals its nature—its being—under forms or activities that belong to it. For a deeper treatment of this issue, cf. R. Yepes Stork, "La Persona como Fuente de Autenticidad," 83–100.

48. *Lumen gentium*, 50.

49. Cf. Second Vatican Council, Past. Const. *Gaudium et spes*, 19.

50. St. Josemaría Escrivá, *Christ Is Passing By*, 122.

51. Cf. J. Ratzinger, Commentary to Chapter I of *Dei Verbum*, LThK, Suppl. II, col. 511; St. Ignatius of Antioch, *Epist. ad Eph.*, X, 1–3: PG 5, 653–654.

52. St. Josemaría Escrivá, *The Way*, 353.

53. Cf. G. Baum, *The Credibility of Church Today*.

54. Cf, John Paul II, Enc. *Centesimus annus*.

55. Cf. *Gaudium et spes*, 27; John Paul II, Enc. *Evangelium vitae*, 10–11.

56. Cf. John Paul II, Enc. *Ut unum sint*.

CHAPTER 14

1. For a panorama of the various ways to understand the nature and structure of the credibility of Divine Revelation, cf. H. Bouillard, *Le Sens de l'Apologetique*; P.J. Cahill, "Apologetics," 669–674; N. Dunas, *Les Problèmes et le Statut de l'Apologétique*; R. Fisichella, "Credibilidad," 205–225; A. Gardeil, "Credibilité,"
2001–2310; A. Lais, "Apologetik," 723–731; R. Latourelle, *Apologetique Fondamentale: Problèmes de Nature et de Méthode*; "Apologética," 114–118; X.M. Le Bachelet, "Apologétique: Apologie," 189–251; H. de Lubac, "Apologetique et Théologie," 361–378; L. Maisonneuve, "Apologetique," 1511–1580.

2. There are three possible approaches regarding this proof. The last two relate to the causes of the sin of man and the angels as seen by St. Thomas Aquinas. The first one leads us to accept; the other two, to reject God's invitation in Christ, although one may be searching for the goodness of God through ways other than obedience and imitation of Jesus. The question is whether one is really struggling to live for God and seeking perfection according to the strength of one's own nature. Cf. St. Thomas Aquinas, *Summa Theologiae*, I, q. 63, a. 3; II–II, q. 163, a. 2. For a study of the issue as a whole and in detail, cf. A. Rodríguez, *La Scelta Etica*.

3. St. Josemaría Escrivá, *The Way*, 175.

4. Cf. G. Mensching, "Vatername Gottes, religiongeschichtlich," 1232ff; M. Meslin, *L'Experience Humain du Divin*, 297–320.

5. This relationship is accepted even by authors who call themselves atheists or non-believers; Cf. M. Horkheimer, *La Nostalgia del Totalmente Altro*, 69–78.

6. Cf. J. Imbach, *Nostalgia di Dio*, 73–77; L. Kolakowski, *Le Religioni*, 184.

7. Cf. Second Vatican Council, Past. Const. *Gaudium et spes*, 19.

8. St. Augustine, *Confessions*, I, 1, 1: PL 32, 661.

9. St. Josemaría Escrivá, *Friends of God*, 314; cf. St. Gregory of Nycene, *Epistulae*, 212: PG 37, 349.

10. It is about a judgment that does not follow the rational-discursive process but instead progresses by comparing the object presented with the object to which affection or instincts tend. About this question, cf. STh, I, q. 64,

a. 1; I–II, q. 26, a. 1 ad 3; II–II, q. 45, a. 2; q. 97, a. 2 ad 2; q. 162, a. 3 ad 1. For a study of the issue, cf. R.T. Caldera, *Le Jugement par Inclination chez saint Thomas d'Aquin*; M. d'Avenia, *La Conoscenza per Connaturalità in S. Tommaso d'Aquino*.

11. G. Colombo, *La Ragione Teologica*, 149–150. Cf. J.M. Galvan, "Fede Debole, Amore Debole: A Proposito del 'Credere di credere' di G.Vattimo," 537–548.

12. Cf. H.U. von Balthasar, *La Percepción de la Forma; Seul l'Amour est Credibile.*

13. STh, II–II, q. 178, a. 1: *Necesse est quod sermo prolatus confirmetur, ad hoc quod sit credibilis.* Cf. *Summa contra Gentiles*, III, c. 154.

14. *Summa contra Gentiles*, IV, c. 154.

15. STh, II–II, q. 178, a. 1.

16. Cf. R. Lavatori, *Dio e l'Uomo: Un Incontro di Salvezza*, 165; A. Léonard, *Razones para Creer*, 30–34.

17. Cf. Second Vatican Council, Dogm. Const. *Dei Verbum*, 2.

18. First Vatican Council, Dogm. Const. *Dei Filius*, 3: DS 3012.

19. Cf. K. Gatzweiler, "La Conception Paulinienne du Miracle," 813–846; B. Lindars, "Elijah, Elisha and the Gospel Miracles: Miracles in their Philosophy and History," 63–79.

20. Cf. A. Lefevre, "Miracle," 1299–1308.

21. St. Augustine, *De utilitate credendi*, 16, 34: PL 42, 90.

22. St. Augustine, *Sermo* 88, 1: PL 38, 539.

23. St. Augustine, *In Ioannis Evang. tract.*, 8,1: PL 35, 1450.

24. Cf. ibid., 24, 1: PL 35, 1593; Cf. D.P. de Vooght,"La Notion Philosophique de Miracle selon St. Augustin," 342; "La Theologie du Miracle selon St. Augustin," 197–222; F.M. Brazzale, *La Dottrina del Miracolo in S. Agostino.*

25. About the doctrine of miracles in St.Thomas, cf.V. Boublik, *L'Azione Divina 'Praeter Ordinem Naturae' secondo S. Tommaso d'Aquino.*

26. *Summa contra Gentiles*, III, q. 100. Cf. St.Thomas Aquinas, *De potentia*, q. 6, a. 2. "*Ex hoc ergo aliquid dicitur esse miraculum, quod fit praeter ordinem naturae creatae. Hoc autem non potest facere nisi Deus*" (STh, I, q. 110, a. 4).

27. It seems certain that in this regard the Angelic Doctor owes more to St. Anselm than to St. Augustine; Cf. F.Taymans,"Le Miracle: Signe du Surnaturel," 225–245.

28. Cf. *Summa contra Gentiles*, III, c. 100.

29. Cf. St.Thomas Aquinas, *De potentia*, q. 6, a. 1.

30. Idem., *Summa Theologiae*, III, q. 44, a. 4.

31. St.Thomas Aquinas, *De potentia*, q. 6, a. 2 ad 9.1

32. Cf. R. Latourelle, *Miracles de Jésus et Théologie du Miracle*, 312–313.

33. Cf. *Dei Filius*: DS 3009, 3033–3034. External to persons, not to revealed religion. The Reformers had denied the possibility of arriving at faith by objective elements, not by subjective elements. The Council taught the exteriority of miracles, not related to revelation, but to persons who received the revealed Word.

34. Cf. ibid., DS 3009.

35. Ibid.

36. Ibid., 3, 4: DS 3034. The influence of post-Tridentine theology and classical apologetics is undeniable in this text. It is not evident, however, that the text should be read exclusively by the light of that theology or that its reach should be limited by it. Rather, it seems clear that the Council was able to offer a vision of miracles that was not reductive or trapped in the theological perspectives of the time. For a somewhat different thinking on this issue, cf. H.J. Pottmeyer, "Segni e Criteri della Credibilità del Cristianesimo," 456–460.

37. For precedents, see J.H. Newman, *Two Essays on Miracles*; M. Blondel, "La Notion et le Role du Miracle," 337–361; J. de Tonquedec, *Introduction a l'Etude du Merveilleux et du Miracle*; L. de Grandmaison, *Jesus Christ: Sa Personne, Son Message, Ses Preuves*, II, 225–255; A. van Hove, *Het Mirakel*.

38. Cf. J. Morales, "El Milagro en la Teología Contemporánea," 196; E. Dhanis, "Q'est-ce qu'un miracle?" 201–241; M. Bordoni, *Teologia del Miracolo*, Pont. Univ. Lateranense, Roma 1964; M.J. le Guillou, *Le Christ et l'Eglise*.

39. Cf. H. Fries, Wunder. *Wegbereiter und Wege*, 115–120.

40. G. Sohngen insists that miracles are not a reality epistemically different from revelation: *Die Einheit in der Theologie*, 264–265.

41. L. de Grandmaison wrote that miracles are the sensitive material coming forth from Christ's spiritual work. They carry out the spiritual work of liberation that Jesus fulfills in the physical order: *Jesus Christ*, II, 366.

42. P. Ternant concluded, "The Old Testament presents miracles as revelations from God and efficacious signs of his salvation": "Miracle," X.L. Dufour, *Vocabulaire de Theologie Biblique*.

43. J. Mouroux wrote that miracles are prodigies that are signs: cf. "Discernément et discernibilité du miracle," 538.

44. Cf. L. Monden, *El Milagro: Signo de Salud*, 28–38.

45. R. Latourelle summarized his own considerations and those of other authors by enumerating the following significant functions of miracles: They are signs of God's power, the love feast, the kingdom, the divine mission, Christ's glory, the Trinitarian mystery, the sacramental economy, and the world's eschatological transformation: *Miracles de Jésus et Théologie du Miracle*, 326–340.

46. Cf. J.P. Torrell, "Chronique de Théologie Fondamentale," 65–67; R. Latourelle, *Assenza e Presenza della Fondamentale al Concilio Vaticano II*, 1404–1407.

47. *Dei Verbum*, 4.

48. Cf. J. Ratzinger, Commentary on Chapter I of *Dei Verbum*, in LThK, Suppl. II, 511.

49. Cf. A. Locatelli, *Teologia Fondamentale*, 184–185.

50. Cf. L. Monden, *El Milagro*, 155–316.

51. Cf. ibid., 126–152. True prophecies are also distinct from diabolic predictions: These do not refer to future events that depend on free

decisions, but to natural phenomena that are cosmic, psychological, and social in character and that the devils know better because of their natural intellectual keenness: cf. STh, II–II, q. 172, a. 5.

52. St. Thomas Aquinas, *In symbolum*, prol.

53. St. Thomas Aquinas, *De veritate*, q. 14, a. 10 ad 11.

54. Cf. St. Thomas Aquinas, *De veritate*, q. 12, a. 7 in c. and ad 7.

55. Cf. STh, II–II, q. 173, a. 2 ad 1.

56. Cf. ibid., ad 3.

57. Cf. A. Blanco, "La Revelación como 'Locutio Dei' en las Obras de Santo Tomás de Aquino," 19–24, 34–45.

58. John Paul II, *Fides et ratio*, 13; The First Vatican Council, to which the quotation above refers, teaches that the obedience of faith requires the engagement of the intellect and the will: "Since human beings are totally dependent on God as their creator and Lord, and created reason is completely subject to uncreated truth, we are obliged to yield through faith to God the revealer full submission of intellect and will": Dogmatic Constitution on the Catholic Faith *Dei Filius*, III: DS 3008.

59. Cf. STh, I–II, q. 1, a. 7. For a deeper study of these concepts, cf. A. Rodríguez, *La Scelta Etica*.

60. J.E. Smith has studied the unity of the experiential act, keeping the differences between its diverse contents—about miracles and the signified reality and the connection between both of them. Cf. J.E. Smith, *Experience and God*; L. Scheffczyk, "Christology in the Context of Experience," 383–408; H.J. Pottmeyer, "Segni e Criteri della Credibilità del Cristianesimo," 475.

61. Cf. A. Cazzullo, *Il Concetto e l'Esperienza*; G. Bontadini, *Saggio di una Metafisica dell'Esperienza*; "Esperienza e Metafisica," *Rivista di Filosofia Neoscolastica*, 64; C. Fabro, *Dall'Essere all'Esistente*, 45–48; J.B. Lotz, *Esperienza Trascendentale*, 163–253.

62. Cf. J. Mouroux, *L'Expérience Chrétienne*; R. Guardini, *Fede, Religione, Esperienza*; H. de Lubac, *Mistica e Mistero Cristiano*; G. Crinella, "Religione come Esperienza," 157–193; J. Schmitz, *La Revelación*, 19–56.

63. About the dimensions of human experience that cannot be limited to the physical and biological sphere but must be recognized as possible in other orders, cf. J.B. Lotz, *Esperienza Trascendentale*. For what refers specifically to the experience of God, cf. J.E. Smith, *Experience and God*, 90.

64. Cf. STh, II–II, q. 178, a. 1.

65. Cf. R.R. Wilson, "The Hardening of Pharaoh's Heart," 18–36.

66. Cf. H.J. Pottmeyer, "Segni e Criteri della Credibilità del Cristianesimo," 473–474.

67. Cf. J. Meyer zu Schlöchtern, *Glaube-Sprache-Erfahrung*, 333.

68. Cf. H.J. Pottmeyer, "Segni e Criteri della Credibilità del Cristianesimo," 470–471.

69. St. Thomas Aquinas, STh, II–II, q. 6, a. 1c.

70. Cf. R. Aubert, "Questioni Attuali Intorno all'Atto di Fede," 655.

71. Cf. E. Kunz, "Conoscenza della Credibilità e Fede (*Analysis fidei*)," 506.

72. Cf. *Dei Filius*, 3: DS 3009; 3: DS 3033; Pius XII, Enc. *Humani generis*, 12: DS 3876.

73. This was explicitly taught by Pius XII: cf. *Humani generis*: DS 3875; Pius IX, Enc. *Qui pluribus*.

74. Cf. Pius XII, *Humani generis*: DS 3875.

75. St. Thomas Aquinas, *In Boeth. de Trin.*, lect. 1, q. 1, a. 1 ad 4: "*Lumen autem fidei… non movet per viam intellectus, sed magis per viam voluntatis; unde non facit videre illa quae creduntur, nec cogit assensum, sed facit voluntarie assentiri.*" Cf. *De veritate*, q. 27, a. 3 ad 12.

76. Cf. St. Thomas Aquinas, *Summa Theologiae*, STh, II–II, q. 175, a. 3 ad 2; *De veritate*, q. 14, a. 1 ad 8.

77. Cf. B. Duroux, *La Psychologie de la Foi chez S. Thomas d'Aquin*, 103–105.

78. Cf. *Dei Filius*, 2: DS 3008.

79. Cf. ibid., 3: DS 3034.

80. Cf. ibid., 4: DS 3019.

81. Cf. ibid.: DS 3009.

82. Cf. ibid.: DS 3013.

83. Ibid., 3: DS 3009.

84. J. Quasten, *Patrología*, I, 189.

85. For a development of these concepts, cf. John Paul II, Enc. *Veritatis splendor*, 38–45; St. Josemaría Escrivá, *Friends of God*, 23–38.

86. St. Josemaría Escrivá, *Christ Is Passing By*, 184.

87. St. Thomas Aquinas, *In Boeth. de Trin.*, q. 2, a. 3.

88. Ibid.

89. John Paul II, *Fides et ratio*, Introduction.

90. Cf. *Dei Filius*, 2: DS 3005; 4: DS 3015–3020, 3041–3043. For a study of the historical context of these teachings, cf. J.M. Gonzalez-Heras, "Ciencia y Fe: Doctrina del Magisterio sobre las Relaciones entre la Razon y la Fe durante la Década 1850–1860," 109–166; P. Rodríguez (ed.), *Fe, Razón y Teologia*.

91. Cf. St. Augustine, *Enarrationes in Psalmos*, 31, 6: PL 36, 261–262.

92. Cf. *Dei Filius*, 2–4; *Gaudium et spes*, 53–62; Second Vatican Council, Decr. *Gravissimum educationis*. Among John Paul II's frequent references to this issue, see specifically "Discurso a los Intelectuales y los Hombres de Ciencia," 49–58.

93. *Dei Filius*, 3: DS 3009; 4: DS 3017.

94. Cf. St. Augustine, *Contra Faustum*, 26, 3: PL 42, 480–481; STh, I, q. 2, a. 1.

95. Cf. Fifth Lateran Council, Bull *Apostolici regiminis*: DS 1441; *Dei Filius*, 4: DS 3017.

96. St. Thomas Aquinas, *In III Sent.*, d. 24, a. 3, sol 2 ad 2; cf. *Summa contra Gentiles*, I, c. 7; *In Rom.*, c. X, lect. 1.

97. Cf. *Dei Filius*, 4: DS 3017.

98. Benedict XVI, General Audience, 28 / 01 / 2007.

99. Cf. H. Verweyen, "Razón y Fe," 1101.

100. The Christian faith is not *opinio iuvata virtutibus*. Cf. also C. Cardona, *Metafísica de la Opción Intelectual*, 7–23, 261–283.

101. *Dei Filius*, 4: DS 3019. The conciliar expression seems to have been inspired by the formula used by Pius IX in his encyclical *Qui pluribus*. But Pius IX stated that reason, when correctly employed, "demonstrates the *truth* of faith." The Council preferred to say that "it demonstrates the *fundamentals* of the faith."

102. We have already pointed out that, "when a person has his reason enlightened by faith and searches with effort, love, and sobriety, that person reaches, with God's help, a certain intelligence about the mysteries in a very fruitful manner." Ibid., 4: DS 3016.

103. Cf. St. Augustine, *In Ioannis Evang. tract.*, 15, 12–17: PL 35, 1514–1516; *Summa contra Gentiles*, III, 100.

104. John Paul II, Enc. *Evangelium vitae*, 2; cf. 38.

BIBLIOGRAPHY

AA.VV., *Commento alla Costituzione Dogmatica sulla Divina Rivelazione*. Milan: Massimo, 1966.

——, *Concilio Vaticano II: Comentarios a la Constituciòn sobre la Divina Revelación*. Madrid: Ed. Católica, BAC, 1968.

——, *De Scriptura et Traditione*, Pontificia Accademia Mariana Internationalis, Roma, 1963.

——, *Fe, razón y teología*, EUNSA, Pamplona, 1979.

——, *La foi agisant par l'amour (Galates 4: 12—6: 16)*, "Benedictine," Abbaye de S. Paul, Rome, 1996.

——, *La osadía de creer*, Palabra, Madrid, 1969.

——, *L'Appartenenza alla Chiesa*. Brescia, 1991.

——, *La Sagrada Escritura: Texto y Comentario*, vol. II. Madrid: Ed. Católica, BAC, 1962.

——, *Storia della teologia*, Ed. Dehoniane, Bologna: vol. I: *Dalle origini a Bernardo da Chiaravalle*, por E. del Couolo (ed.), 1995.

——, *Vatican II: La Révélation Divine*. Paris: Cerf, 1968.

——, vol. III: *Da Victus Pichler a Henri de Lubac*, by R. Fisichella (ed.).

Adam, K., *Jesucristo*, Herder, Barcelona, 1970.

Agazzi, E., *Scienza e Fede: Nuove Prospettive su un Vecchio Problema*. Milan: Massimo, 1984.

Albright, W.F., *From the Stone Age to Christianity*. Baltimore 1946.

Althaus, P., *Die christliche Wahrheit* (Gütersloh, 1947).

Amato, A., "Gesù e le Religioni non Cristiane: Una Sfida all'Assolutezza del Cristianesimo," in M. Farina, M.L. Mazzarella (ed.), *Gesù è il Signore: La Specificità di Gesù Cristo in un Tempo di Pluralismo Religioso* (Rome: LAS, 1992).

——, *Gesù il Signore* (Bologna: EDB, 1988.

Ambrose, St., *Exposit. Ev. sec. Lucam*.

——, *Expositio in Psalmum CXVIII*.

Amorth, G., *Un Esorcista Racconta*, 2nd ed. Rome: Dehoniane, 1991.

Anderson, H., *Jesus and Christian Origins: A Commentary on Modern Viewpoints*. New York: Oxford University Press, 1964.

Antiseri, D., *Dal Non-Senso all'Invocazione*. Brescia: Queriniana, 1976.

Antoine, P., "Foi," in *DBS*, III, 276–310.

Aphraates the Persian Sage, *Demonstrationes.*

Aquinas, St. Thomas, *Compendium Theologiae.*

———, *Contra gentes.*

———, *De anima.*

———, *De malo.*

———, *De potentia.*

———, *De veritate.*

———, *De virtutibus in communi.*

———, *Expositio primae decretalis.*

———, *In Boeth. de Trin.*

———, *In Epist. ad Colos.*

———, *In Epist. ad Ephesios.*

———, *In Epist. ad Gal.*

———, *In Epist. ad Romanos.*

———, *In Epist. II ad Thessal.*

———, *In Heb.*

———, *In II Sent.*

———, *In III Sent.*

———, *In Ioan. Evang.*

———, *In IV Sent.*

———, *In Rom.*

———, *In symbolum.*

———, *In Timon.*

———, *Quodlib.*

———, *Summa contra Gentiles.*

———, *Summa Theologiae.*

Aranda, A., *Estudios de Pneumatologia* (Pamplona: EUNSA, 1985).

———, "L'Intelligenza del Cristiano come Questione Teologica," in *Annales Theologici* 10 (1996): 417–448.

Arnaldich, L., "Protoevangelio," in *GER*, XIX, pp. 300–302.

Artigas, M., *Ciencia, Razón y Fe*, Palabra, Madrid, 1984.

Aubert, R., *El acto de fe*, Barcelona, 1965.

———, *Le Problème de l'Acte de Foi*. Louvain, 1945.

———, "Questioni Attuali Intorno all'Atto di Fede," in AA.VV., *Problemi e Orientamenti di Teologia Dommatica*, II, 655.

Auer, J., Ratzinger, J., *Curso de Teología Dogmática*, t. II: *Dios, uno y Trino*, Herder, Barcelona, 1982, pp. 17–134.

Augustine, St., *Confessions.*

———, *Contra Faustum.*

———, *De Baptismo contra Donat.*

———, *De civitate Dei.*

———, *De doctrina Christiana.*

———, *De dono perseverantiae.*

———, *De fide rerum quae non videntur.*

———, *De gratia Christi et de pecc. orig.*

———, *De natura et gratia.*

———, *De peccatorum meritis et remissione.*

———, *De praedestinatione sanctorum.*

———, *De sancta virginitate.*

———, *De symb. ad Cathec.*

———, *De utilitate credendi.*

———, *De vera religione.*

———, *Enarrationes in Psalmos.*

———, *Enchiridion.*

———, *Epist.* 54.

———, *In Epist. Ioannis ad Parthos.*

———, *In Ioannis Evang. tract.*

———, *Sermo* 294.

———, *Sermo de symbolo.*

Bailleux, E., "La Création, oeuvre de la Trinité, selon Saint Thomas," in *Revue Thomiste* 62 (1962), 27–50.

Bainvel, J.V., *De vera religione et apologetica.* Paris, 1914.

Balch, D., *Let Wives Be Submissive: The Domestic Code in I Peter.* Chico, 1981.

Bandas, R., "Biblia et Traditio iuxta Scripturam," in AA.VV., *De Scriptura et Traditione*, 180.

Bandera, A., *La Iglesia ante el Proceso de Liberación* (Madrid: Ed. Catolica, BAC, 1975).

Bardy, G., "Paul de Samosate," in DTC, XII, 50.

Barnard, W.L., *Apologetik I.*

———, *Athenagoras: A Study in Second Century Christian Apologetics.* Paris, 1972.

Barth, K., *Das Wort Gottes und die Theologie.* Munich: Kaiser, 1924.

———, *Der Römerbrief*, 2nd ed. Munich: Kaiser, 1922.

———, *Die kirchliche Dogmatik.* Zollikon, Zurich Evangelischer, 1932.

———, *Fides quaerens intellectum: Anselms Beweis der Existenz Gottes.* Munich: Kaiser, 1931.

Basil the Great, St., *De Spiritu Sancto.*

Battaglia, V., *Gesù Crocifisso: Figlio di Dio.* Rome: P. A. Antonianum,1991.

Bauer, J.B., "Verdad," in *Diccionario de Teología Bíblica*, col. 1039–1048.

Baum, G., *The Credibility of Church Today*, Burns and Oates, London, 1968.

Beaucamp, E., *La Bible et le sens religieux de l'univers*, Paris, 1959.

Becker, J., *Auferstehung der Toten im Urchristentum*. Stuttgart, 1976.

Becker, O., O. Michel, "Fe," in L. Coenen, E. Beyreuther, H. Bietenhard, *Diccionario Teológico del Nuevo Testamento*, II (Salamanca: Sígueme, 1980), 170–187.

Beni, A., *Teologia Fondamentale*, Lib. Ed. Fiorentina, Florencia, 1980.

Benoit, A., "Ecriture et Tradition chez St. Irenée," in *Revue d'Histoire et Philosophie Religieuses* 40 (1960) 32–43.

Benoit, P., "Le Origini del Simbolo degli Apostoli," in AA.VV., *Esegesi e Teologia* (Rome 1964), 461–487.

———, *Rivelazione e inspirazione secondo la Bibbia, in S. Tommaso e nelle discussioni moderne*, Brescia 1965.

Bertram, G., "Ergon," in *TWNT* II, 632–649.

———, "Thauma," in *TWNT* III, 27–42.

Betti, U., "Cronistoria della Costituzione Dogmatica sulla Divina Rivelazione," in AA.VV., *Commento alla Costituzione Dogmatica sulla Divina Rivelazione* (Milan: Ed. Massimo, 1966), 33–67.

———, *La Costituzione Dommatica* Pastor aeternus del *Concilio Vaticano I*, Pont. Ateneo Antonianum, Roma, 1961.

———, *La Rivelazione Divina nella Chiesa*, Città Nuova, Roma, 1980.

Beumer, J., "Das katholische Schriftprinzip in der theologischen Literatur der Scholastik bis zur Reformation," in *Scholastik* 16 (1941) 24–52.

———, "De Statu Actuali Controversiae circa Relationem inter Traditionem et Scripturam," in *De Scriptura et Traditione*, 23–28.

Biffi, G., *Approccio al Cristocentrismo*. Milan: Jaca Book, 1993.

Billerbeeck, P., H. Strack, *Kommentar zum NT aus Talmud und Midrash*, I, 3rd ed. Munich, 1961.

Blanco, A., "Fede e Giustificazione: Il Loro Riflesso sull'Attività Sociale e Politica del Cristiano Secondo il Pensiero Luterano e Cattolico," in J. Galvan, *La Giustificazione in Cristo* (Vatican City: Lib. Ed. Vaticana, 1997), 233–242.

———, "La Revelación como 'Locutio Dei' en las Obras de Santo Tomás de Aquino," *Scripta Theologica* 13 (1981).

———, "Parola, Persona e Storia nella Rivelazione Divina," in *Annales Theologici* 4 (1990): 263–282.

———, *Qué es la Teología*.

Bläser, P., "La Ley en el Nuevo Testamento," in *Diccionario de Teología Bíblica*, 572–587.

Blenkinsopp, J., *Une Histoire de la Prohétie en Israël*, Cerf, Paris, 1993.

Blinzer, J., *Der Prozess Jesu: das jüdische und das römische gerichsverfahren gegen Jesus Christus auf Grund der ältesten Zeugnisse*. Regensburg: F. Pustet, 1960.

———, "Die Grabñegung Jesu in historicher Sicht," E. Dhanis, ed., *Resurrexit: Actes du Symposium International sur la Résurrection de Jesus*, 56–107.

Bloch, E., *Das Prinzip höffnung*. Frankfurt: Suhrkamp, 1959.

———, *Religione in Eredità*. Brescia: Queriniana, 1979.

Blondel, M., *La Acción: Ensayo de una Crítica de la Vida y de una Ciencia de la Práctica*. Madrid: Ed. Católica, BAC, 1996.

———, "La Notion et le Role du Miracle," *Annales de Philosophie Chretienne*, 1907, 337–361.

Boismard, M.E., *Moses or Jesus: An Essay in Johannine Christology*. Louvain: Leuven University Press, Uitgeverij Peeters, 1993.

Bonaventure, St., *In III Sent.*

———, *Itinerarium mentis in Deum: in Opera omnia.*

Bonsirven, J., *Le Judaïsme Palestinien au Temps de Jesus-Christ*, 2 vols. Paris, 1935.

Bontadini, G., "Esperienza e Metafisica," *Rivista di Filosofia Neoscolastica*, 1949, 64.

———, *Saggio di una Metafisica dell'Esperienza*. Milan, 1938.

Bordoni, M., *Teologia del Miracolo*, Pont. Univ. Lateranense, Rome 1964.

Bornkamm, G., *Gesù di Nazaret*. Turin: Claudiana, 1968.

———, "The Significance of the Historical Jesus for Faith," in F. Hann, W. Lohff, and G. Bornkamm, *What Can We Know about Jesus* (Philadelphia: Fortress, 1969), 84.

Bosio, G., E. dal Covolo, M. Maritano, *Introduzione ai Padri della Chiesa*, SEI, Torino, 1990.

Bossetti, E., "Apologia," in *Diccionario de Teologia Fundamental*, 118–121.

Boublik, V., *Incontro con Cristo, Credibilitá della religione cristiana*, P.u. Lateranense, Roma, 1968.

———, *L'Azione Divina 'Praeter Ordinem Naturae' secondo S. Tommaso d'Aquino*. Rome: P. U. Lateranense, 1968.

———, *Los signos de la credibilidad de la Revelación cristiana*, Andorra, 1965.

———, *Teologia dell religioni*, Studium Roma, 1973.

Bouillard, H., "De l'Apologétique à la Théologie Fondamentale," in *Les Quatre Fleuves* 1 (1973): 23–31.

———, *Karl Barth*, 3rd vol. Paris: Aubier, 1957.

———, *Le Sens de l'Apologetique.*

———, *Lógica de la Fe*. Madrid, 1964.

Bourgeois, D., *La Sagesse des Anciens dans la Mystère du Verbe: Evangile et Philosophie chez St. Justin Martyr, Philosophe et Martyr*. Paris, 1981.

Bourke, M.M., "Epistola a los Hebreos," in *Comentario Biblico "San Jerónimo,"* IV, 368.

Bousset, *Kyrios Christos*. Göttingen, 1913.

Bouyer, L., Gnosis, *La conoscenza di Dio nella Scrittura*, Lib. Ed. Vaticana, 1991.

———, *La Biblia y el Evangelio*, Rialp, Madrid, 1977.

Braaten, C.E., *No other Gospel! Christianity among the World Religions*. Minneapolis: Fortress Press, 1992.

Brandle, F., "Musste das Grab Jesu leer sein?" *Orientierung* 31 (1967): 109.

Brazzale, F.M., *La Dottrina del Miracolo in S. Agostino*. Rome: Marianum, 1964.

Brinktrine, J., *Offenbarung und Kirche*. Paderborn, 1947.

Brown, R.E., "The Messianisme of Qumran," *Catholic Biblical Quarterly* (1957): 533–582.

Brunner, A., "Das Kriterium der Konvergenz," in AA.VV., *Erkenntnistheorie*, Köln 1946, 77.

———, *Offenbarung und Glaube*, München, 1985.

Brunner, E., *Natur und Gnade*. Basilea, 1934.

———, "Zur Lehre von der *analogia entis*," in *Dogmatik*, II, (Zürich, 1950).

Buber, M., *Zwei Glaubensweisen, in Werke*, vol. I. Munich, Heidelberg, 1962.

Bultmann, R., *Creer y Comprender*, 2 vols. Madrid, 1975–76.

———, *Das Verhaltnis des urchristlichen Christusbotschaft zum historischen Jesus*. Heidelberg: Carl Winter, 1960.

———, "Der Begriff der Offenbarung im Neuen Testament," in *Glauben und Verstehen: Gesammelte Aufsätze*, vol. III, 27.

———, *Die Geschichte der Synopthischen Tradition*. Göttingen: Vandenhoeck and Ruprecht, 1961.

———, *Exegetica*. Turin: Borla, 1971.

———, *Jesucristo y Mitología*. Madrid, 1970.

———, *La Teología del Nuevo Testamento*. Salamanca, 1981.

———, *Nuovo Testamento e Mitologia: Il Manifesto della Demitizzazione*. Brescia: Queriniana, 1970.

———, "Theologie als Wissenchafts," in *Zeitschrift f. Theologie und Kirche* 81 (1984): 447–469.

Caba, J., *El Jesús de los Evangelios*, BAC, Madrid, 1977.

Cahill, P.J., "Apologetics," in *NCE* I, 669–674.

Caldera, R.T., *Le Jugement par Inclination chez saint Thomas d'Aquin*. Paris: Vrin, 1980.

Calleja, J., *Jesus: Resurrection and Life for All His Believers*, Diss. ad Laur. Rome: P.A. Seraphicum, 1989.

Calvin, J., *Institutes of the Christian Religion*. Geneva, 1618.

Canobbio, G., "Extra Ecclesiam nulla Salus: Storia e Senso di un Principio Teologico," in *Rivista del Clero Italiano* 71 (1990): 428–446.

Cardona, C., *Metafísica de la Opción Intelectual*, 2nd ed. Madrid: Rialp, 1973.

———, "Rilievi critici a due fondamentazioni metafisiche per una costruzione teologica," in *Divus Thomas* 75 (1972): 172–175.

Cartonaro, E., "Testimonianza," *Enciclopedia Filosofica*, IV, ed. Sansoni (Florence: Centro di Studi Filosofici di Gallarate,1957), 1179.

Casciaro, J.M., "El Acceso a Jesús y la Historicidad de los Evangelios: Balance de Veinticinco Años de Investigación," in *Scripta Theologica* 12 (1980): 907–941.

———, *Estudios sobre Cristología del Nuevo Testamento*, EUNSA, Pamplona, 1982.

———, *Exégesis Bíblica: Hermenéutica y Teología*. Pamplona: EUNSA, 1983.

———, *Jesucristo y la Sociedad Política*. Madrid: Palabra, 1973.

———, *Las palabras de Jesus: transmission y hermenéutica*, EUNSA, Pamplona, 1992.

———, "Tiempo (en la Sagrada Escritura)," in *GER*, XXII, pp. 436–440.

Castelli, E. (ed.), *La testimonianza, Istitutu di Studi Filosofici*, Roma, 1972.

Castro, F., *Relaciones entre Sagrada Escritura y Tradición según la Constitución "Dei Verbum,"* doctoral thesis. Pamplona: University of Navarre, 1984.

Catchpole, D.R., *The Trial of Jesus: A Study in the Gospels and Jewish Historiography from 1770 to the Present Day*. Leiden: E.J. Brill, 1971.

Cf. *Catechism of the Catholic Church.*

Cattaneo, A., "Salvezza e Appartenenza alla Chiesa," in J.M. Galvan, ed., *La Giustificazione in Cristo*, 236–247.

Cavalletti, S., *Il Giudaismo Intertestamentario*. Brescia: Queriniana, 1991.

Caviglia, G., Le ragioni della speranza (1 Pt 3: 15), *Teologia Fondamentale*, LDC, Turín, 1981.

Cazelles, H., *Alla ricerca di Mosé*. Brescia: Queriniana, 1982.

———, *Autour de l'Exode*. Paris: Gabalda, 1987.

———, *Il Messia della Bibbia*. Rome: Borla, 1981.

Cazzullo, A., *Il Concetto e l'Esperienza*. Milan: Jaca Book, 1988.

Cerfaux, L., "Kyrios," in *DBS*, V, 200–228.

———, *La Théologie de l'Eglise suivant Saint Paul*. Paris, 1942.

———, *Le Christ dans la Théologie de St. Paul*. Paris: Cerf, 1951.

———, *Témoins de Christ d'Après le Livre des Actes*, II. Gembloux: Duculot, 1954.

———, "Tradition selon St. Paul," in *Recueil L. Cerfaux*, vol. II, (Gembloux 1954), 253–263.

Cerfaux, L., J. Cambier, "Luc," in *DBS*, V, 582–583.

Cessario, R., *Christian Faith and the Theological Life*, The Catholic University of American Press, Washington, DC, 1996.

Charlier, L., *Essai sur le Problème Théologique*. Thuillies, 1938.

Chenu, M.D., *Une École de Théologie: le Saulchoir*. Le Saulchoir, Kain-les-Tournai, and Etiolles, 1937.

Childs, B.S., *Exodus, OTL*, 6th ed. London: SCM Press, 1987.

Chmiel, J., "Semantics on the Resurrection," in *Journal for the Study of the Old Testament*, Supplement series 11 (1978): 59–64.

Ciappi, L., "De mente S. Thomae quoad Traditionem divinam," in *De Scriptura et Traditione*, 229–231.

Citrini, T., "La Chiesa e i Sacramenti," *Enciclopedia di Teologia Fondamentale*, 557.

Clement of Alexandria, *St. Rometa.*

Clement of Rome, St., *Ad Corinth.*

Colombo, G., *La Ragione Teologica*, Glossa, Milano, 1995.

——— (ed.), *L'evidenza e la fede*, Glossa, Milano, 1988.

Colon, J.B., "Marc," in *DBS*, V, 850–851.

Condamin, A., "Prophetisme," in *DAFC*, IV.

Conesa, F., *Creer y conocer*, EUNSA, Pamplona, 1994.

———, "La Fe y la Lógica del Testimonio," in *Scripta Theologica* 26 (1994), 483–511.

Congar, Y.M., *Credo nello Spirito Santo*, II. Brescia: Queriniana, 1982.

———, "Fait Dogmatique et Foi Ecclésiastique," *CATH*, IV, 1059–1067.

———, *La fe y la teologia*, Herder, Barcelona, 1981 (3 ed.).

———, "La Tradition et les traditions," *Essai Théologique*, vol. II (Paris: Fayard, 1963), 70–73.

———, *Le Mystère du Temple*, Cerf, Paris, 1958.

———, "Theologie," in *DTC*, XV, 430–431.

———, *Vera e Falsa Riforma nella Chiesa*. Milan: Jaca Book, 1972.

Congregation for the Doctrine of the Faith, Decl. *Mysterium Ecclesiae*.

———, Decl. *Mysterium Filii Dei*.

———, Instr. *Libertatis nuntius*.

———, Ltr. *Communionis notio*.

———, Ltr. *Orationis formas*.

Conroy, C., "Profetas," in *Diccionario de Teología Fundamental*, 1086.

Conzelmann, H., *Grundriss der Theologie des Neuen Testaments*. Munich: Kaiser, 1968.

———, "Jesus Christus," in K. Galling, ed., *Die Religion in Geschichte und Gegenwart*, III, (Tübingen, 1957), 650–653.

Coppens, J., "Fils de l'Homme Danielique et les Relectures de Dan 7,13 dans les Apocriphes et les Écrites du Nouveau Testament," in *Ephemerides Theologicae Lovanienses* 37 (1961): 5–51.

———, "Le Chapitre VII de Daniel," in *Ephemerides Theologicae Lovanienses*, 39 (1963): 87–94.

———, *Le Messianisme et sa Relève Prophetique*. Gembloux: Duculot, 1974.

———, *Le Messianisme Royal*. Paris: Cerf, 1968.

———, "Le Protoévangile: Un Nouvel Essai d'Exégèse," in *Ephemerides Theologicae Lovanienses* 26 (1950) 5–36.

———, "Les Origines du Symbole du Fils de l'Homme en Dan VII," in *Ephemerides Theologicae Lovanienses*, 44 (1968): 497–502.

———, "Oú en est le problème de Jesus Fils de l'homme," in *Ephemerides Theologicae Lovanienses*, 66 (1980): 283–287.

Cottugno, N., "La Testimonianza della Vita del Popolo di Dio, segno di Rivelazione alla Luce del Concilio Vaticano II," in R. Fisichella, *Gesù Rivelatore*, 232.

Council of Chalcedon, *Definitio*.

Council of Trent, Decr. *De iustificatione*.

———, Decr. *Sacrosancta*.

Courcelle, P., *Recherches sur les Confessions de St. Augustin*, 2nd ed. Paris, 1968.

Cova, G.D., "Il Profeta e la Grande Città: Prolegomi a una Lettura Biblica dall'Annuncio a Ninive al Segno di Giona," *EDB*, (Bologna 1993), 72–80.

Coventry, J., *The Theology of Faith*, Cork, 1968.

Crinella, G., "Religione come Esperienza," in P. Grassi, *Filosofia della Religione: Storia e Problemi*, Queriniana, Brescia 1988, 157–193.

Cristiani, L., "Réforme," in *DTC*, XIII, 2039–2047.

———, "Schleiermacher," in *DTC*, XIV, 1500.

Crouzel, H., *Origene*. Rome, 1986.

Cuervo, M., "El Deseo Natural de Ver a Dios y los Fundamentos de la Apologética Inmanentista," *Ciencia Tomista* 37 (1928): 310–340.

Cullmann, O., *Cristo y el Tiempo*. Barcelona: Estela, 1968.

———, *Cristologia del Nuovo Testamento*. Bologna 1971.

———, "Il Mistero della Redenzione nella Storia," *Il Mulino*, (Bologna, 1966), p. 414.

———, *La Foi et le Culte dans l'Eglise Primitive*, Neuchatel, 1963.

———, *La Tradition: Problème Exégétique, Historique et Théologique*, Cahiers théologiques de l'actualité protestante.

Curran, J.T., "The Teaching of 2 Peter 1: 20," in *Theological Studies* 4 (1943): 350ff.

Cyprian, St., *De Catholicae Ecclesiae unitate*.

———, *De oratione Dominica*.

Cyril of Alexandria, St., *Cateches*.

d'Avenia, M., *La Conoscenza per Connaturalità in S. Tommaso d'Aquino*. Bologna: EDB, 1992.

Danielou, J., *Cristo e Noi*, 3rd ed. Alba: Ed. Paoline, 1968.

———, *Dieu et Nous*. Paris: Grasset, 1956.

———, *Dios y Nosotros*.

———, *Essai sur le Mystère de l'Histoire*. Paris: du Seuil, 1953.

———, *Le Mystère du Salut des Nations*. Paris: du Seuil, 1948.

———, *Les saints païens de l'Ancien Testament*, Paris, 1956.

———, *Méssage Evangelique et Culture Hellénistique*. Paris, Tournai, Rome: Desclée, 1961.

———, *Origène*. Paris, 1948.

Dattrino, L., *Patrologia*. Rome, 1987.

Daujat, J., *La Vita Soprannaturale* (Rome: Ares, 1958), 561–573.

Dautzenberg, G., *La fe en el kerygma apostólico*, in AA.VV., *La osadìa de creer*.

Davies, P.E., "Experience and Memory: The Role of the Exalted Christ in the Life and the Experience of the Primitive Church," *Interpretation* 16 (1962): 181–192.

de B.Vizmanos, F., "La Apologética de los Escolásticos Postridentinos," in *Estudios Eclesiásticos* 143 (1934): 418–446.

de Grandmaison, L., *Jesus Christ: Sa Personne, Son Message, Ses Preuves.* Beauchesne, Paris, 1928.

de Guibert, J., "A Propos des Textes de S.Thomas sur la Foi qui Discerne," *Recherches de Science Religieuse* 9 (1919): 30–44.

de Haro, R. Garcia, *Historia Teológica del Modernismo*. Pamplona: EUNSA, 1972.

de la Potterie, I., *La Vérité dans St. Jean*, 2 vol., Roma, 1977.

de Lubac, H., "Apologetique et Théologie," *Nouvelle Revue Théologique* 57 (1930): 361–378.

———, *Catholicisme, Les Aspectes sociaux du Dogme*, Lyonne, 1938.

———, *De la Connaissance de Dieu*. Paris, 1948.

———, *El Drama del Humanismo Ateo*. Madrid: Epesa, 1966.

———, *La fe cristiana, Ensayo sobre la estructura del Simbolo de los Apóstoles*, Sígueme, Salamanca, 1988.

———, "La Fede della Chiesa," in AA.VV., *La Fede in Gesù Cristo* (Rome, 1968), 127–152.

———, *La Révélation Divine*, Cerf, Paris, 1966.

———, *Les Églises Particulières dans l'Eglise Universelle*. Paris: Aubier, 1971.

———, *Mistica e Mistero Cristiano*. Milan: Jaca Book, 1979.

de Margerie, B., "La Foi, Mystère de Foi, Rèvélé par Dieu," *Divinitas* 28 (1984): 276–282.

de Sanctis, A.S., *Psicologia Sperimentale*. Rome, 1930.

de Tonquedec, J., *Introduction a l'Etude du Merveilleux et du Miracle*, Paris 1916.

de Vooght, D.P., "La Notion Philosophique de Miracle selon St. Augustin," *Revue de Théologie Ancien et Medieval* 10 (1938): 342.

———, "La Theologie du Miracle selon St. Augustin," *Revue de Théologie Ancien et Medieval*, 11 (1939): 197–222.

Decker, B., "Schriftprinzip und Ergänzungstradition in der Theologie des hl. Thomas von Aquin," in AA.VV., *Schrift und Tradition, Deutsche Arbeitsgemeinschaft für Mariologie*, Essen 1962, pp. 191–221.

del Portillo, A., *Fieles y Laicos en la Iglesia*, EUNSA, Pamplona, 1981 (2 ed.).

Delorme, J., "Les Livres Prophétiques Anterieures," in A. Robert, A. Feuillet, *Introduction a la Bible* I (Tournai: Desclée, 1962), 462–464.

Deneken, M., *La foi pascale, Rendre compte de la Résurrection de Jésus aujourd-hui*, Cerf, Paris, 1997.

Dhanis, E., "Q'est-ce qu'un miracle?" in *Gregorianum* 40 (1959) 201–241.

——— (ed.), *Resurrexit. Actes du symposium international sur la Résurrection de Jésus*, Lib. Ed. Vaticana, Ciudad del Vaticano, 1974.

Dibelius, M., *Die Formgeschichte des Evangeliums*. Tübingen, 1933.

Diccionario Teológico Interdisciplinar, 4 vol., Sígueme, Salamanca 1985–87.

Dieckmann, H., *De Revelatione Christiana*. Fribourg, 1930.

Dillenschneider, C., *Le Sens de la Foi et le Progrès Dogmatique du Mystère Marial*. Rome: Accademia Mariana Internationalis, 1954.

Dodd, C.H., *L'Interpretazione del Quarto Vangelo*. Brescia: Paideia, 1974.

———, *The Founder of Christianity*. London, New York: Collier, MacMillan, 1970.

Domínguez, J.A., "Las Interpretaciones Posteriores al Concilio," P. Rodríguez (ed.), *Eclesiología: 30 años después de Lumen gentium* (Madrid: Rialp, 1994), 63–87.

Donahue, P.H., *Jewish-Christian Controversy in the Second Century: A Study in the Dialogus of Justin Martyr*, Dissertation of Yale University. New Haven,) 1973.

Dondeyne, A., *Fe cristiana y pensamiento contemporáneo*, Madrid, 1963 (2 ed.).

Doré, J., *Éthique, religion et foi*, Paris, 1985.

———, *Theologie Fondamentale, Regards sur la théologie contemporaine*, en "Revue des Sciences Religieuses" 83 (1995) 73–94, 305–324, and 447–490.

Ducocq, C., *Christologie*, II. Paris: Cerf, 1973.

Dulles, A., *History of Apologetics*, London-Philadelphia-New York, 1971.

———, *The Assurance of Things Hoped For*, Oxford University Press, 1994.

Dunas, N., *Conocimiento de la fe*, Barcelona, 1965.

———, *Les Problèmes et le Statut de l'Apologétique*.

Duponcheele, J., *L'Etre de l'Alliance*. Paris: Cerf, 1992.

Dupont, J., "Écriture et Tradition," in *Nouvelle Revue Théologique* 85 (1963) 449ff.

———, *Gnosis: La Connaissance Religieuse dans les Epitres de Saint Paul*. Louvain, Paris, 1949.

———, "L'Ambassade de Jean Baptiste," *Nouvelle Revue Théologique* 83 (1961): 805–821.

———, "L'Après Mort dans l'Oeuvre de Luc," *Revue Thomiste* 3 (1972): 3–21.

Dupuis, J., *Vers une Théologie Chrétienne du Pluralisme Religieux*. Paris: Cerf, 1997.

Durham, J.J., "Exodus," *World Biblical Commentary*. Waco: Word Books, 1987.

Duroux, B., *La Psychologie de la Foi chez S. Thomas d'Aquin*, Tequi, Paris, 1977.

Durrwell, F.X., *La Résurrection de Jesus*.

Ebeling, G., *The Study of Theology*. London, 1979.

Epiphanius, St., *Haer*.

Erskine, T., *Remarks on the Internal Evidence for the Truth of Revealed Religion*, 5th ed. Edinburgh, 1821.

Escrivá, St. Josemaría, *Christ Is Passing By* (Manilla: Sinag-Tala, 1974).

———, *Conversaciones con Mons. Escrivá de Balaguer*, 17th ed., Madrid: Rialp, 1989.

———, *Friends of God*, Manila: Sinag-tala, 1994.

———, *The Forge*, Scepter Press, New Rochelle, NY, 1988.

———, *The Way*, Quezon City: Aletheia Foundation, 1991.

———, *The Way of the Cross.*

Fabris, R., *Gesù di Nazareth: Storia e Interpretazione.* Assisi: Cittadella, 1983.

———, *Giovanni.*

———, "L'Apologia nel Nuovo Testamento," in *Enciclopedia di Teologia Fondamentale,* I, 3–14.

———, *Matteo.* Borla, 1982.

Fabro, C., *Dall'Essere all'Esistente.* Morcelliana, Brescia, 1957.

———, Dios, *Introducción al problema teológico,* Madrid, 1961.

———, *El Problema de Dios.* Barcelona, 1963.

———, in *L'Uomo e il Rischio di Dio.* Rome: Studium, 1967.

———, *Introduzione all'Ateismo Moderno,* 2nd ed., 2 vol. Rome: Studium, 1969.

———, "La Dialettica d'Intelligenza e Volontà nella Costituzione Esistenziale dell'Atto Libero," in *Riflessioni sulla Libertà* (Rimini: Univ. di Perugia-Maggioli Editore, 1983), 57–85.

———, *La Preghiera nel Pensiero Moderno.* Rome: Edizioni di Storia e Letteratura, 1979.

———, *La Svolta Antropologica di K. Rahner.* Milan: Rusconi, 1974.

———, *Partecipazione e Causalità,.* Turin: SEI, 1960.

Fammatter, J.P., "La Fe según la Escritura," in *Mysterium Salutis,* II, 883–884.

Fascher, E., *Prophète: Eine Sprach uns religionsgeschichtliche UnterSuchung.* Giessen, 1927.

Faux, J.M., *La Foi du Nouveau Testament.* Brussels: Inst. d'Etudes Theologiques, 1977.

Fehr, W.L., *The Birth of the Catholic Tübingen School: The Dogmatics of Johan Sebastian Drey.* Michigan: Scholars Press, 1981.

Feiner, J., and Lohrer, M., ed., *Mysterium salutis* (Manual de Teología como Historia de la salvación), Ed. Cristianidad, Madrid, 1969, vol. I en 2 tomos: *Teología Fundamental como Historia de la salvación.*

Felder, H., *Jesus Christus.* Paderborn, 1911–1912.

Fergusson, D., *Bultmann.* New York: Chopmann, 1962.

Feuillet, A., *L'Accomplissement des Prophéties.* Paris: Desclée, 1991.

———, "De Munere Doctrinali a Paraclito in Ecclesia Expleto iuxta Evangelium Sancti Ioannis," in AA.VV. *De Scriptura et Traditione,* 132.

———, "Le Plan Salvifique de Dieu dans l'épître aux Romains," in *Revue Biblique* 57 (1950): 338–340.

———, "Les Trois Grandes Prophéties de la Passion et de la Résurrection des Évangiles Synoptiques," *Revue Thomiste* 67 (1967): 533–560, 68 (1968): 41–74.

Feuillet, R., "Le Triomphe du Fils de l'Homme d'Après la Déclaration du Christ aux Sanhedrites," in AA.VV., *La Venue du Messie* (Paris, 1972), 164–168.

Fifth Lateran Council, Bull *Apostolici regiminis.*

First Council of Nicea, *Symbolum.*

First Vatican Council, Dogm. Const. *Dei Filius.*

———, Dogm. Const. *Pastor aeternus.*

Fisichella, R., "Credibilidad," in *Diccionario de Teología Fundamental,* 205–225.

———, *La Revelación: Evento y Credibilidad,* Sígueme, Salamanca, 1989.

——— (ed.), *La Teologia Fondamentale,* Convergenze per il terzo millennio, Piemme, Casale Monferrato, 1997.

——— (ed.), *Noi crediamo,* Dehoniane, Roma, 1993.

———, *Profecía.*

Fitte, H., ed., *Fermenti nella Teologia alle Soglie del Terzo Millennio.* Vatican City: Lib. Ed. Vaticana, 1998.

Fitzmyer, J.A., "Teología de San Pablo," in *Comentario Bíblico "San Jerónimo,"* V, 816–818.

Foerster, W., "Kyrios," in *GLNT,* V, 1342–1391.

Fohrer, G., "Sophia," in *TWNT,* VII, 483–489.

———, *Storia d'Israele,* Paideia, Brescia, 1980.

Forni, R., *Problemi della Tradizione: Ireneo di Lione.* Milan: Ed. Vita e Pensiero, 1939.

Forte, B., *Teología de la Historia.* Salamanca: Sígueme, 1985.

Fourth Lateran Council, *De Fide Catholica.*

Fraijo, M., *El Sentido de la Historia: Introducción al Pensamiento de W. Pannenberg.* Madrid: Cristiandad, 1986.

Franquet Casas, M.J., *Persona, Acción y Libertad: Las Claves de la Antropología de K. Wojtyla.* Pamplona: EUNSA 1996.

Franzelin, J.B., *Tractatus de Divina Traditione et Scriptura,* 4th ed. Rome: Typ. Polygl. Sacred Congregation of the Propagation of the Faith, 1896.

Franzini, A., *Tradizione e Scrittura.* Brescia: Morcelliana, 1978.

Freuy, J.B., "Le Conflit entre le Messianisme de Jesus et le Messianisme des Juifs de Son Temps," in *Biblica* 14 (1933): 133–149, 269–293.

Fries, H., *La Revelación,* in *Mysterium salutis.*

———, *Wunder. Wegbereiter und Wege,* Fribourg: im Br., 1968.

Gaboriau, F., *Le Tournant Théologique Aujourd'hui Selon K. Rahner.* Paris: Desclée, 1968.

Galot, J., *La Rédemption: Mystère d'Alliance.* Rome-Bruges, 1965.

Galvan, J.M., "Fede Debole, Amore Debole: A Proposito del 'Credere di credere' di G.Vattimo," *Annales Theologici* 10 (1996): 537–548.

Garcia Hernando, J., ed., *Pluralismo Religioso,* vol. II: *Sectas y Religiones no Cristianas.* Salamanca, 1983.

Gardeil, A., "Credibilité," in *DTC,* III, 2001–2310.

———, *Le Donné Révélé et la Théologie,* 2nd ed. Juvisy: Ed. du Cerf, 1932.

———, *Le Donné Révélé et la Théologie.* Paris, 1909.

Garrigou-Lagrange, R., *De revelatione per Ecclesiam Catholicam proposita*, 5th ed. Rome: Desclée y Brouwer, 1950.

———, *Le Sens Commun: La Philosophie de l'être et les Formules Dogmatiques*, 4th ed. Paris: Beauchesne, 1936.

———, "Natura e Valore delle Formule Dogmatiche," in AA.VV., *Problemi e Orientamenti di Teologia Dommatica*, vol. I, 387–408.

Gatzweiler, K., "La Conception Paulinienne du Miracle," *Ephemerides Theologicae Lovanienses* 37 (1961): 813–846.

Geenen, G., "The Place of Tradition in the Theology of St. Thomas Aquinas," in *The Thomist* 15 (1952) 110–135.

Geffré, C., "Le Témoignage comme Expèrience et come Langage," E. Castelli (ed.), *La Testimonianza*, 291–307.

Geiselmann, J.R., "Das Missverständnis über das Verhätnis von Schrift und seine Überwindung in der katholischen Theologie," in *Una sancta* 11 (1956): 131–150.

———, *Die Heilige Schrift und die Tradition*, Fribourg, 1962.

———, "Dogma," in AA.VV., *Dizionario Teologico* (Brescia: Ed. Queriniana, 1967), 502–506.

———, *Simbolica,*. Milan: Jaca Book, 1984.

———, "Tradition," in *Encyclopédie de la Foi*, vol. IV (Paris, 1967), col. 346.

Gelin, A., *Les Idées Maîtrises de l'Ancien Testament*, Cerf, Paris, 1959.

George, A., "Le Parallele entre Jean-Baptiste et Jesus en Luc 1–2," in *Melanges Bibliques en Hommage au R.P.B. Rigaux* (Gembloux: Duculot, 1970), 147–171.

———, "Paroles de Jesus sur ses Miracles," in J. Dupont, *Jesus aux Origines de la Christologie* (Louvain: Leuven Univ. Press, Peeters, 1989), 218, 223, 230.

Ghiberti, G., "Testimonianze sulla Risurrezione di Gesù," *Il Messaggio della Salvezza*, VI, 405.

Giblet, J., "Prophetisme et Attente d'un Messie Prophète dans l'Ancien Judaisme," in AA.VV., *L'Atteinte du Messie* (Bruges, 1954), 85–130.

Gil Hellín, F., *Concilii Vaticani II Synopsis: Constitutio Dogmatica de Divina Revelatione Dei Verbum*. Vatican: Lib. Ed. Vatican City, 1993.

Gilbert, M., *La Sagesse de l'Ancien Testament*. Leuven, 1990.

———, "Sapienza," in *Nuevo Diccionario de Teología Bíblica*, 1712–1713.

Gils, F., *Jesus Prophète d'Après les Évangiles Synoptiques*. Louvain: Publ. Universitaires, 1957.

Gilson, E., *Introduction a l'étude de St. Agustin*. Paris, 1943.

———, *Jean Duns Scoto: Introduction a se Positions Fondamentales*. Paris: Vrin, 1952.

———, *L'etre et Dieu*. Paris, 1983.

Gnilka, J., *Gesú di Nazaret: Annuncio e Storia*. Brescia: Paideia, 1993.

———, *Il Vangelo Secondo Matteo*. Brescia: Paideia, 1991.

———, *Marco*. Assisi: Cittadella, 1987.

González Gil, M., *Cristo: El Misterio de Dios*, II. Madrid: Ed. Católica, BAC., 1976.

González Montes, A., *Fundamentación de la Fe*, Ed. Secr. Trinitario, Salamanca, 1994.

Gonzàlez, A., *Abraham: Padre de los Creyentes*. Madrid, 1963.

Gonzalez-Heras, J.M., "Ciencia y Fe: Doctrina del Magisterio sobre las Relaciones entre la Razon y la Fe durante la Década 1850–1860," in *Scripta Theologica* 3 (1971): 109–166.

Goodenough, E.R., *The Theology of Justin Martyr*. Leiden, 1923.

Gosey, J.D., "Christian Faith's Partnership with History," in J.T. Carroll, C.H. Cosgrove, and E.E. Johnson, *Faith and History* (Atlanta, Georgia: Scholars Press, 1991), 261–278.

Gossman, E., *Storia delle dottrine cristiane*, Augustinas, Palermo, 1991.

Grandmaison, M., *L'Eglise pour elle même, motif de crédibilité. Histoire de l'argument*, P.U.G., Roma, 1961.

Grant, R.M., *Greek Apologists of the Second Century*. London, 1988.

Grech, P., "Hermenéutica," in *Nuevo Diccionario de Teología Bíblica*, 753.

———, "Il Problema Cristologico e l'Ermeneutica," in R. Latourelle, G. O'Collins, *Problemi e Prospettive di Teologia Fondamentale* (Brescia: Queriniana, 1982), 147.

Gregory the Great, St., *Hom. in Ev.*

Gregory XVI, *Theses a Ludovico Eugenio Bautain iussu sui Episcopi Subscriptae*.

Grelot, P., "L'Historien davant la Résurrection de Christ," in *Revue d'Histoire de la Spiritualité* 48 (1972): 233.

———, *La Biblia, Palabra de Dios*, Barcelona, 1968.

———, *La Speranza Ebraica al Tempo di Gesù*. Rome: Borla, 1981.

———, *Sens Chrétien de l'Ancien Testament*, Desclée, Tournai, 1962.

Grillmeier, A., *Gesù il Cristo nella Fede della Chiesa*. Brescia: Paideia, 1982.

Grudmann, W., "Dynamai-Dynamis," in *TWNT*, II, 286–319.

Guardini, R., *Cristianismo y Sociedad*. Salamanca: Sígueme 1982.

———, *Die Offenbarung, ihr Wesen und ihre Formen*. Würzburg, 1940.

———, *Fede, Religione, Esperienza*, Morcelliana, Brescia 1984.

———, *La esencia del cristianismo*, Cristiandad (3 ed.), Madrid, 1984.

———, *La fe en nuestro tiempo*, Madrid, 1965.

———, *Libertad, gracia, destino*, Dinor, San Sebastian, 1960.

———, *Mundo y persona*, Guadarrama, Madrid, 1964.

———, *Sobre la vida de fe*, Madrid, 1958.

———, *Verdad y orden*, Guadarrama, Madrid, 1960.

Guerra, M., *Antropologìas y Teologìa*. Pamplona: EUNSA, 1976.

———, *Los Nuevos Movimientos Religiosos: Sectas*. Pamplona: EUNSA, 1993.

———, *Storia delle Religioni*. La Scuola: Brescia, 1989.

Guillet, J., *Gesù di Fronte alla sua Vita e alla sua Morte*. Assisi: Cittadella, 1972.

Guzie, T.W., "The Act of Faith according to St. Thomas," in *The Thomist* 29 (1965): 239–280.

Haldar, A., *Associations of Cult Prophets among the Ancient Semites*. Uppsala: Almqvist and Wiksell, 1945.

Halkin, F., "L''Apologie' du Martyr Philéas de Thmuis (Papyrus Bodmer XX) et les Actes Latins de Philéas et Philoromus," in *Analecta Bollandiana* 81 (1963): 5–27.

Hare, D.R.A., *The Son of Man Tradition*. Minneapolis: Fortress Press, 1990.

Harent, S., "Fideisme," in *DTC*, VI/1, 174–236.

Harl, M., *Origène et la Fonction Révélatrice du Verbe Incarné*. Paris, 1958.

Hazard, P., *El Pensamiento Europeo in el Siglo XVIII*. Barcelona: Alianza, 1985.

Hengel, M., *Sequela e Carisma*. Brescia: Paideia, 1990.

Hick, J., *An Interpretation of Religion: Human Responses to the Transcendent*. New Haven, London: Yale University Press, 1989.

———, *God and the Universe of Faiths: Essays in the Philosophy of Religion*. London: Macmillan, 1973.

———, *The Centre of Christianity*. London: SCM Press, 1977.

———, *The Metaphor of God Incarnate*. London: SCM Press, 1993.

———, *The Rainbow of Faiths*. London: SCM Press, 1995.

———, *The Second Christianity*. London: SCM Press, 1983.

Hilary, St., *Ad constantium*.

Hoffmann, P., "Auferstehung II/1, Neues Testament," in G. Krause, G. Muller, *Theologische Realenzyklopädie*, IV (Berlin: W. der Gruyten, 1976), 478–513.

Hofius, O., "Milagro," in *Diccionario Teológico del Nuevo Testamento*, vol. III, 85–94.

Holman, J.C., "Profeta," in *GER*, XIX, 211.

Holstein, H., *La Tradition dans l'Église*, Grasset, Paris, 1960.

———, "La Tradition des apôtres chez S. Irénée," in *Revue des Sciences Religieuses* 36 (1949): 229–270.

Holte, R., "Logos Spermatikòs," in *Studia Theologica* 12 (1958): 109–168.

Höpfl, H., "Canonicité," in *DBS*, I, 1022–1045.

Horkheimer, M., *La Nostalgia del Totalmente Altro*. Brescia: Queriniana, 1972.

Huesman, J.E., "Exodo," in *Comentario Bíblico "San Jerónimo,"* 163–175.

Hume, D., "Essay on Miracles," *An Enquiry Concerning Human Understanding* (1758).

Ibañez-Arana, A., "La Relación Escritura-Tradición en la Teologia Pre-Tridentina," in *Victoriense* 5 (1958) 147–180.

Ignatius of Antioch, St., *Epist. ad Eph.*

———, *Epist. ad Rom.*

———, *Epist. ad Smyr.*

Illanes, J.L., "Dos de Octubre de 1928: Alcance y Significado de una Fecha," in *Mons. Josemaría Escrivá de Balaguer y el Opus Dei*, 96–101.

————, *Historia y sentido: estudios de teología de la historia*, Rialp, Madrid, 1997.

————, "La Dimensione Cristologica della Teologia Fondamentale," G. Tanzella-Nitti, ed., *La Teologia, Annuncio e Dialogo* (Rome: Armando, 1996), 97–111.

Illanes, J.L., Saranyana, J.I., *Historia de la teología*, BAC, Madrid, 1997 (2 ed.).

Imbach, J., *Breve Corso Fondamentale sulla Fede*. Brescia: Queriniana, 1993.

————, *Nostalgia di Dio*. Rome: Studium, 1992.

International Theological Commission, "De Jesu Autoconscientia quam Scilicet Ipse de se Ipso et de sua Missione Habuit," in *Documenta-Documenti*.

————, *De unitate Fidei et theologico pluralismo*.

————, "Quaestiones selectae de Christologia," (1979), I.A.1.1, in *Documenta-Documenti* (1969–1985) (Ciudad del Vaticano: Lib. Ed. Vaticana, 1988).

Introvigne, M., J.F. Mayer, E. Zucchini, *I Nuovi Movimenti Religiosi: Sette Cristiane e Nuovi Culti*, LDC, Turìn 1990.

Irenaeus, St., *Adversus haereses*.

Iturrioz, D., "Tradición y Revelación en el Concilio Vaticano y su época," in *Estudios Eclesiásticos* 37 (1962): 171–217, 343–377.

Izquierdo, C., *Blondel y la Crisis Modernista*, EUNSA, Pamplona, 1990.

————, *Teologia Fundamental*, EUNSA, Pamplona, 2002 (2nd Ed.).

Jacob, E., *Théologie de l'Ancien Testament*. Neuchâtel-Paris, 1968.

Jacquier, E., *Les Actes des Apotres*. Paris, 1926.

Jedin, H., *Storia del Concilio di Trento*, II, Morcelliana, Brescia, 1962.

Jepsen, A., *Nabi: Soziologische Studien zur altertestamentische Literatur und Religionsgeschichte*. Munich, 1934.

Jeremias, J., Abba: *Jésus et son Père*, Seuil, Paris, 1972.

————, *Il Significato Teologico dei Reperti del Mare Morto*. Brescia: Paideia, 1964.

————, "Ionas," in *TWNT*, III, 413.

————, "Jerusalén en tiempos de Jesús," *Cristiandad* (Madrid, 1980).

————, *Jesu Verheissung für die Völker*. Stuttgart, 1956.

————, J., *Le Parabole di Gesú*, Paideia, Brescia, 1973.

————, *Paroles di Jésus*, Cerf, Paris, 1969.

————, *Teologia del Nuovo Testamento*. Brescia: Paideia, 1976.

Jerome, St., *Epist.*

————, *In Epist. ad Ephesios commentarii*.

John Chrysostom, St., *In Ep. ad Hebr.*

————, *In Epist. ad Ephesios homiliae*.

————, *In Epist. II ad Thessal.*

————, *In Ps.*

————, *Opus imperf. in Matthaeum*.

John Damascene, St., *De Fide Orthodoxa*.

———, *Hom. 2 in dorm. B.M.V.*

———, *In Epist. ad Ephesios.*

John of the Cross, St., *Cántico Espiritual.*

———, *Subida al Monte Carmelo.*

John Paul II, Ap. Ex. *Christifideles laici.*

———, Ap. Ex. *Pastores dabo vobis.*

———, Ap. Ex. *Reconciliatio et paenitentia.*

———, Ap. Letter *Tertio millennio adveniente.*

———, *Creo en Jesucristo: Catequesis sobre el Credo* (II) (Madrid: Palabra, 1996).

———, Discourse of October 15, 1988, 4, in *Insegnamenti di Giovanni Paolo II.*

———, Discourse of October 30, 1985, in *Creo en Dios: Catequesis sobre el Credo*, I (Madrid: Palabra, 1996).

———, "Discurso a los Intelectuales y los Hombres de Ciencia," *Colonia*, AAS 73 (1981): 49–58.

———, Enc. *Dominum et vivificantem.*

———, Enc. *Evangelium vitae.*

———, Enc. *Redemptor hominis.*

———, Enc. *Redemptoris Mater.*

———, Enc. *Redemptoris missio.*

———, Enc. *Veritatis splendor.*

———, Homily of September 4, 1983, in *Insegnamenti di Giovanni Paolo II.*

John XXIII, Address opening the Second Vatican Council, October 11, 1962.

Johnson, A.R., *The Cultic Prophet and Israel's Psalmody*, Cardiff: University of Wales Press, 1979.

———, *The Cultic Prophet in Ancient Israel*, 2nd ed., Cardiff: University of Wales Press, 1962.

Joly, R., *Christianisme et Philosophie: Etudes sur Justin et les Apologistes grecs du II Siècle*, Fac. Phil. et Lettres, Univ. Libre de Brussels. Brussels 1973.

Journet, C., *Le Dogme: Chemin de la Foi*, Fayard, Paris, 1963.

Justin, St., *Apologia I.*

———, *Dialogue with Trypho the Jew.*

Kannegiesser, C., *Foi en la Résurrection: Résurrection de la Foi*. Paris: Beauchesne, 1974.

Karrer, O., "Successione Apostolica e Primato," in AA.VV., *Problemi e Orientamenti di Teologia Dommatica*, vol. I, 251–298.

Käsemann, E., "Das problem des historischen Jesus," in *Zeitschrift f. Theologie und Kirche* 51 (1954): 125–153.

Kasper, W., *Gesù il Cristo*, 7th ed., Brescia: Queriniana, 1992.

———, *Il Dio di Gesù Cristo*, 2nd ed., Brescia: Queriniana, 1985.

————, *Il Dogma sotto la Parola di Dio*. Brescia: Queriniana, 1968.

————, "Schrift und Tradition," in *Theologische Quartalschrift*, 170 (1990) 165.

Kay, J.A., *Theological Aestetics*. Berna, Frankfurt: Lang, 1975.

Kelly, J.N.D., *Early Christian Creeds*, Oxford 1950.

Kern, W., Pottmeyer, H.J., Seckler (ed.), *Corso di Teologia Fondamentale*, vol. IV: *Trattado di Gnoseologia teologica*.

Kerrigan, A., "Doctrina Concilii Vaticani I de 'Sine Scripto Traditionibus'" in AA.VV., *De Scriptura et Traditione*, 475–502.

Kittel, G., "*Akouó*," in *TWNT*, I, 220.

Knitter, P., *No other Name? A Critical Survey of Christian Attitudes towards the World Religions*. Maryknoll, New York: Orbis Books, 1985.

————, *One Earth Many Religions: Multifaith Dialogue and Global Responsability*. Maryknoll, New York: Orbis Books, 1995.

Koch, R., "Testimonianza," in AA.VV., *Enciclopedia della Bibbia*, VI (Leumann: LDC, 1972), 908.

Kolakowski, L., *Le Religioni*. Milan, 1983.

Kolping, A., *Fundamentaltheologie*, 3 vol. Regensberg, Münster, 1968–1981.

Kraemer, H., *The Christian Message in a Non-Christian World*. London: Edinburgh House Press, 1938.

————, *World Cultures and World Religions*. London: Lutterworth Press, 1960.

Kravis, S., *Talmudische Archäologie*, II,. Leipzig, 1911.

Kremer, J., *Das älteste Zeugnis von der Auferstehung Christi*.

————, *Die Osterevangelien. Geschickten um Geschichte*. Stuttgart: KBW, 1977.

————, "La Risurrezione di Gesù Cristo," *Corso di Teologia Fondamentale*, II, 209–210.

Kummel, W.G., *Il Nuovo Testamento: Storia dell'Indagine Scientifica sul Problema Neotestamentario*. Bologna: Il Mulino, 1976.

Kunz, E., "Conoscenza della Credibilità e Fede (Analysis Fidei)," in *Corso di Teologia Fondamentale*, IV, 506.

Kustermann, A.P.M., *Die Apologetik J.S. Dreys*. Tübingen, 1988.

Lacroix, J., *El Ateìsmo Contemporàneo*. Barcelona: Herder, 1968.

Lais, A., "Apologetik," in *LThK*, I, 723–731.

Lambiasi, F., *L'Autenticità Storica dei Vangeli: Studio di Criteriologia*, Dehoniane, Bologna, 1976.

Lampe, G.W.H., "The Lucan Portrait of Christ," *New Testament Studies* 2 (1955–56): 160–175.

Lang, A., *Die Entfaltung des apologetischen Problems in der Scholastik des Mittelalters*. Frieburg, Basilea, Vienna, 1962.

Lapide, P., *Auferstehung: ein jüdisches Glaubenserlebnis*. Munich, Stuttgart: Calwer-Kössel, 1977.

Läpple, A., *I Miracoli: Documenti e Verità dagli Archivi della Chiesa.* Verona: Mondadori, 1993.

Latourelle, R., *A Jesús el cristo por los evangelios,* Sígueme, Salamanca, 1982.

———, "Apologética," in *Diccionario de Teologia Fundamental,* 114–118.

———, *Apologetique Fondamentale: Problèmes de Nature et de Méthode.*

———, *Assenza e Presenza della Fondamentale al Concilio Vaticano II*

———, *Assenza e presenza della Teologia Fondamentale al Concilio Vaticano II,* Sígueme, Salamanca, 1982; *Vaticano II, Bilancio e Prospettive venticinque anni dopo,* Cittadella, Assisi 1987, pp. 1381–1411.

———, "Bultmann," in *Diccionario de Teología Fundamental,* 164–169.

———, *Cristo y la Iglesia: Signos de Salvaciòn,* Sígueme, Salamanca, 1971.

———, *El hombre y sus problemas a la luz de Cristo,* Sígueme, Salamanca, 1984.

———, "Iglesia: Motivo de Credibilidad," Diccionario de Teología Fundamental, 659.

———, "Jesús de la Historia y Cristo de la Fe," in *Diccionario de Teología Fundamental,* 744–745, Ed. Paulinas, Madrid, 1992.

———, *L'Accès à Jésus par les Evangiles.* Paris, Montréal: Desclée, Bellarmin, 1978.

———, *Miracles de Jésus et Théologie du Miracle,* Bellarmin-Cerf, Montréal-Paris, 1986.

———, "Revelación," in *Diccionario de Teología Fundamental,* Ed. Paulinas, Madrid, 1992.

———, *Teología de la Revelación,* Sígueme, Salamanca, 1982 (5 ed.).

Latourelle, R., O'Collins, G., *Problemas y perspectivas de Teología Fundamental,* Sígueme, Salamanca, 1982.

Lavatori, R., *Dio e l'Uomo: Un Incontro di Salvezza,* Ed. Dehoniane, Bononia, 1985.

Le Bachelet, X.M., "Apologétique: Apologie," in *DAFC* I, 202–205.

le Guillou, M.J., *Le Christ et l'Eglise,* Centurion, Paris 1965.

Le Roy, E., *Dogme et Critique.* Paris, 1907.

Lefevre, A., "Miracle," in *DBS* V, 1299–1308.

Lefevre, M., *Miracles.*

Lehmann, K., *Auferweckt am dritten Tag nach der Schrift. Früheste Christologie, Bekenntnisbildung und Schriftauslegung im Lichte von 1 Cor 15: 3–5.* Fribourg: Herder, 1968.

Lengsfeld, P., "La Tradición en le Periodo Constitutivo de la Revelación," in *Mysterium salutis,* I, t. I, 330–331.

———, *Tradición y Sagrada Escritura: su relación,* in *Mysterium Salutis.*

Lennerz, H., "Scriptura et Traditio in decreto sessionis quartae Concilii Tridentini," in *Gregorianum* 42 (1961): 517–522.

———, "Scriptura sola?" in *Gregorianum* 40 (1959): 39–53.

———, "Sine scripto Traditiones," in *Gregorianum* 40 (1959): 624–635.

Leo the Great, St., *Tractatus 21 de Natale Domini.*

Leo X, Bull *Exsurge Domine.*

Leo XIII, Enc. *Aeterni Patris.*

Léonard, A., *Coherence de la foi*, Desclée, Paris, 1989.

———, *Foi et philosophies*, Ed. Culture et verité, Paris, 1991.

———, *Razones para Creer*, Herder, Barcelona, 1990.

Léon-Dufour, X., *Résurrection de Jesus et Message Pascal*, 2nd ed., Paris: du Seuil, 1971.

Lercher, L., *Institutiones Theologiae Dogmaticae*, 4th ed., Barcelona, 1945.

Lesetre, H., "Canon des Écritures," in *DB*, II, 134–184.

Lessing, G.E., "Sopra la Prova dello Spirito e della Forza," *Grande Antologia Filosofica* XV (Milan: Marzorati, 1968): 1556ff.

———, *Il Senso della Storia in Agostino d'Ippona*. Rome: Borla, 1988.

Lettieri, G., "Note sulla Dottrina Agostiniana delle due Civitates: A Proposito di Jerusalem and Babylon di J. van Oort," in *Augustinianum* 33 (1993): 257–306.

Leuba, J., "La Notion Chrétienne de Temoignage," E. Castelli (ed.), *La Testimonianza*, 309–312.

Lewis, I.M., *Ecstatic Religion*. Harmondsworth: Penguin Books, 1971.

Ley, H., *Geschichte der Aufklärung und des Atheismus*, 3 vol. Berlin, 1966–1971.

Lilla, S.R.C., *Clement of Alexandria: A Study of Christian Platonism and Gnosticism*. London, 1976.

Lindars, B., "Elijah, Elisha and the Gospel Miracles: Miracles in their Philosophy and History," *Cambridge Studies* (London: Mowbray, 1966), 63–79.

Locatelli, A., *Teologia Fondamentale*, Centro "Ut Unum Sint," Rome 1969.

Lohmeyer, E., *Christuskult und Kaiserkult*. Tübingen, 1919.

Lotz, J.B., *Esperienza Trascendentale*. Milan: Vita e Pensiero, 1993.

Madec, G., "La Christianisation de l'Hellenisme," in *Humanisme et Foi Chrétienne: Mélanges Scientifiques du Centenaire de l'Institut Catholique de Paris* (Paris 1976), 399–406.

Maisonneuve, L., "Apologetique," *DTC* I / 2, 1511–1580.

Malevez, L., *Histoire de Salut et Philosophie: Barth, Bultmann, Cullmann*. Paris: Cerf, 1971.

Maly, E.H., "Génesis," in R.E. Brown, J.A. Fitzmyer, R.E. Murphy, *Comentario Bíblico "San Jerónimo,"* Cristiandad, Madrid 1971, I, 86–105.

Manaranche, A., *Les raisons de l'esperance, Théolgie Fondamentale*, Fayard, Paris, 1978.

Mancini, I., *Barth, Bultmann, Bonhöhher: Novecento Teologico*. Milan: Celuc, 1971.

Mansini, G.F., "Dogma," in *Diccionario de Teología Fundamental*, 345–346.

———, *What is a Dogma? The Meaning and Truth of Dogma in Edouard Le Roy and His Scholastic Opponents*. Rome: Ed. Pont. Univ. Gregoriana, 1985.

Marcel, G., *Le Mystère de l'être. II. Foi et réalité*, Paris, 1951.

Marchesi, A., *Linee di uno Sviluppo Storico della Filosofia della Religione*. Parma: Ed. Univ. Zara, 1988.

Marchesi, G., *La Cristologia di H.U. von Balthasar*. Rome: Gregoriana, 1977.

Marconcini, B., "Fe," in P. Rossano, G.F. Ravasi, A. Girlanda, *Nuevo Diccionario de Teología Bíblica*, Paulinas, Madrid 1990, 652–671.

———, *Profeti e Apocalittici, LDC.* Turin: Leumann, 1995.

Marín-Sola, F., *La Evolución Homogénea del Dogma Católico*, BAC, Madrid, 1952.

Maritain, J., *Il Significato dell'Ateismo Contemporáneo*. Brescia, 1973.

Markus, R.A., *Saeculum: History and Society in the Theology of St. Augustine*. Cambridge, 1970.

Marlé, R., "Resurrección de Jesús," *Conceptos Fundamentales de Teologia*, IV (Madrid, 1967): 100.

Marrou, H.I., *St. Augustin et la Fin de la Culture Antique*. Paris: Boccard, 1949.

Martin-Achard, R., "Résurrection dans l'Ancien Testament et le Judaisme," in *DBS*, X, 437–458.

Martinelli, P., *La Morte di Cristo come Rivelazione dell'Amore Trinitario*. Milan: Jaca Book, 1995.

Martini, C., "Introduzione Generale ai Vangeli Sinottici," in *Il Messaggio della Salvezza*, IV (Turin, Leumann: LDC, 1988), 101–107.

Martini, M., *La Civiltà Cattolica*. 1971.

Marxsen, W., *La Risurrezione di Gesù di Nazareth*. Bologna: EDB, 1970.

Matzak, S.A., *Karl Barth on God: The Knowledge of the Divine Existence*. New York, 1962.

Meinertz, M., *Teología del Nuevo Testamento*, Fax, Madrid, 1966 (2 ed.).

Ménard, E., *La Tradition: Révélation, Écriture, Église, selon St. Thomas d'Aquin*, Desclée, Bruges-Paris, 1964.

Mensching, G., "Vatername Gottes, religiongeschichtlich," *Religion in Geschichte und Gegenwart*, VI, 1232ff.

Merlé, R., *Bultmann y la Fe Cristiana*. Bilbao: Mensajero, 1968.

Mertens, H., *L'Hymne de Jubilation chez les Synoptiques*. Gembloux: Duculot, 1957.

Meslin, M., *L'Experience Humain du Divin*. Paris: Cerf, 1988.

Metelli, F., "Prova di Testimonianza," Florian, Niceforo, and Pende, *Dizionario di Criminologia* (Milan, 1943), 788–792.

Meyer zu Schlöchtern, J., *Glaube-Sprache-Erfahrung*. Frankfurt 1978.

Meyer, B.F., "Jesus Christ," in *The Anchor Bible Dictionary*, III (New York: Doubleday, 1992), 794.

Meyer, R., *Der Prophet aus Galiläa*. Leipzig, 1940; reprint: Darmstadt, 1970.

———, "Farisaios," *GLNT*, XIV, 858–921.

Michel, A., "Tradition," in *DTC*, XV, 1256–1262.

Millán Puelles, A., *La Libertad: Afirmación de nuestro Ser*. Madrid: Rialp, 1994.

———, *Ontología de la Existencia Histórica*, 2nd ed. Madrid: Rialp, 1955.

Minette de Tillesse, G., *Le Secret Messianique dans l'Évangile de Marc*. Paris: Cerf, 1968.

Miralles, A., *El Concepto de Tradición en Martín Pérez de Ayala*, EUNSA, Pamplona, 1980.

Moeller, C., "Tradition et Oecuménisme," in *Irénikon* 25 (1952): 337–370.

Möhler, J.A., *L'Unità nella Chiesa: Il Principio del Cattolicesimo nello Spirito dei Padri della Chiesa dei Primi tre Secoli*. Rome: Città Nuova Editrice, 1969.

———, *Simbolica*.

Mollat, D., "Nous Avons vu sa Gloire," in *Christus* 11 (1956): 310–327.

Monden, L., *El Milagro: Signo de Salud*, Herder Barcelona, 1963.

Monloubou, L., F.M. du Buit, *Dizionario Biblico: Storico-Critico*. Rome: Borla, 1987.

———, *Prophète, qui est-tu? Le Prophetisme avant les Prophètes*. Paris: Cerf, 1968.

Mora, V., *Le Signe de Jonas*. Paris: Cerf, 1983.

Morales, J., "El Milagro en la Teología Contemporánea," in *Scripta Theologica* 2 (1970): 196.

———, "La Vocación Cristiana en la Primera Patrística," in *Scripta Theologica* 23 (1991): 837–889.

———, "La Vocación en el Antiguo Testamento," in *Scripta Theologica* 19 (1987): 61.

Mortley, R., *Connaissance Religieuse et Hermenéutique chez Clément d'Alexandrie*. Leiden, 1973.

Morujao, G., "A 'imanencia mutua' do Pai e do Filho em alguns sintagmas verbais grecos do IV Evangelo," *Theologica* 22 / 23 (1987 / 1988): 13–25.

———, "A unidade de Jesus com o Pai em Jo 10: 30," *Estudios Biblicos* 47 (1989): 47–64.

———, *Relaçoes Pai-Filho em S. Joao*. Ist. Pol. Viseu, 1989.

Mouroux, J., *Creo en Ti, Estructura personal de la fe*, Flors, Barcelona, 1960.

———, "Discernément et discernibilité du miracle," in *Revue Apologetique* 60 (1937) 538.

———, *L'Expérience Chrétienne*. Paris: Aubier, 1952.

———, *Sens Chrétien de l'Homme*. Paris: Aubier, 1945.

Mowinckel, S., *He that Cometh: The Messiah Concept in the Old Testament and Later Judaism*, B. Blackwell. Oxford, 1957.

———, *Psalmenstudien III. Die Kultprophetie und prophetische Psalmen*. Kristinia: Ddywad, 1923.

———, *The Psalms in Israel's Worship*. Nashville: Abingdon Press, 1957.

Murphy, R.E., "Introducción a la Literatura Sapiencial," in *Comentario Bíblico "San Jerónimo,"* II, 391–408.

Musatti, C.L., *Elementi di Psicologia della Testimonianza*. Padova, 1931.

Mussner, F., *I Miracoli di Gesù*, Queriniana, Brescia, 1969.

Neher, A., *L'Essence du Prophetisme*. Paris: PUF, 1955.

Neuner, P., "La Fede Principio Soggettivo della Conoscenza Teologica," in *Corso di Teologia Fondamentale*, IV, 46–58.

Newman, J.H., *An Essay on the Development of Christian Dogma*, Longmans, London, 1914, (edition 1878).

——, *El asentimiento religioso*, Herder, Barcelona, 1960.

——, *Two Essays on Miracles*. London, 1987.

Neyrinck, F., "Marc 16: 1–8. Tradition et Rédaction," *Ephemerides Theologicae Lovanienses* 36 (1980): 56–88.

Nicholson, E.W., *Exodus and Sinai in History and Tradition*. Richmond: John Knox Press, 1973.

Nickelsburg, G.W., *Resurrection, Immortality, and Eternal Life in Intertestamental Judaism*. Cambridge, Mass.: Harvard Univ. Press, 1972.

Nicolas, J.H., *Dieu connu comme inconnu*, Desclée, Paris, 1966.

——, *Synthèse Dogmatique: De la Trinité à la Trinité*. Fribourg: Ed. Universitaires, Paris: Ed. Beauchesne, 1985.

Niebuhr, H.R., *The Meaning of Revelation*. New York: Macmillan, 1946.

Nuvoli, F., *Il Mistero della Persona e l'Esperienza Cristiana*. Milan: Jaca Book, 1989.

O'Callaghan, P., *Fides Christi: The Justification Debate*. Dublin: Four Courts, 1997.

O'Reilly, L., *Word and Sign in the Acts of the Apostles: A Study in Lucan Theology*. Rome: Pont. Univ. Gregoriana, 1987.

Ocáriz, F., *Hijos de Dios en Cristo: Introducción a una Teología de la Participación Sobrenatural*. Pamplona: EUNSA, 1972.

——, "Il Primato Teologico della Sacra Scrittura, secondo San Tommaso," in *Atti del IX Congresso Tomistico Internazionale*, Lib. Ed. Vaticana, Vatican City 1992, vol. VI, 7–12.

——, "La Competenza del Magistero della Chiesa 'in Moribus,'" in *Atti del II Congresso Internazionale di Teologia Morale* (Milan: Ares, 1989), 125–138.

——, "La Filiación Divina: Realidad Central en la Vida y en la Enseñanza de Mons. Escrivá de Balaguer," in P. Rodríguez, P.G. Alves de Sousa, J.M. Zumaquero, *Mons. Josemaría Escrivá de Balaguer y el Opus Dei*, 2nd ed. (Pamplona: EUNSA, 1985), 173–214.

——, "La Resurrección de Jesucristo," in AA.VV., *Cristo: Hijo de Dios y Redentor del Hombre* (Pamplona: EUNSA, 1982), 751.

——, "Lo Spirito Santo e la Libertà dei Figli di Dio," in *Atti del Congresso Teologico Internazionale di Pneumatologia* (Vatican City: Lib. Ed. Vaticana, 1982), 1242.

Ocáriz, F., L.F. Mateo Seco, J.A. Riestra, *El Misterio de Jesucristo*. Pamplona: EUNSA, 1991.

Odero, J.M., *La Fe en Kant*. Pamplona: EUNSA, 1992.

——, *Propuestas sobre la teología fundamental y su lugar en los estudios teológicos*, in "Ciencia Tomista" 124 (1997) pp. 319–346.

——, *Teología de la fe*, Eunate, Pamplona, 1997.

Orozco, A., *La Libertad en el Pensamiento*. Madrid: Rialp, 1977.

Ortigues, E., "Écritures et Traditions Apostoliques au Concile de Trente," in *Recherches de Science Religieuse* 36 (1949): 271–299.

Overholt, T.W., *Prophecy in Cross-Cultural Perspective*. Atlanta: Scholar Press, 1986.

Pacomio, L., *Dei Verbum: Genesi della Costituzione sulla Divina Rivelazione*. Rome: Marietti, 1971.

Panimolle, S.A., "Amor," *Nuevo Diccionario de Teología Bíblica*, 91.

Pannenberg, W., *Cuestiones Fundamentales de Teología Sistemática*. Salamanca: Sígueme, 1976.

———, *El Destino del Hombre*. Salamanca: Sígueme, 1981.

———, *La Revelación como Historia*. Salamanca: Sígueme, 1977.

———, *Teología Sistemática* I. Madrid, 1992.

———, *Teología y Reino de Dios*, Sígueme, Salamanca 1974

Parente, P., "Il Primato dell'Amore e S. Tommaso d'Aquino," *Acta Pontificia Accademia Romana di San Tommaso d'Aquino* 10 (1945): 197–229.

Pascal, B., *Pensées*.

Paul VI, Enc. *Mysterium Fidei*.

Peelman, A., *H.U. Balthasar et la Théologie de l'Histoire*. Berna-Frankfurt: Lang, 1978.

Peisker, C.H., "Profeta," in *Diccionario Teológico del Nuevo Testamento*, 413–416.

Penna, R., *L'Apostolo Paolo: Studi di Esegesi e Teologia*, Paoline, Cinisello B., 1991.

Peri, V., "Caratteri dell'Apologetica Greca dagli Inizi al Concilio di Nicea," in G. Ruggieri (ed.), *Enciclopedia di Teologia Fondamentale*, I, 17–30.

Perrot, C., "Prophètes et Prophetisme dans le Nouveau Testament," *Lumière et Vie*, 22 (1973): 25–40.

Pesce, S., *La Chiesa Cattolica Perenne Motivo di Credibilità*. Turin: SEI, 1960.

Pesch, C., *Compendium Theologiae Dogmaticae*, 5th ed., Fribourg: 1935.

Peter of Poitiers, *Sententiarum libri quinque*.

Petersen, D.L., "The Roles of Israel's Prophets," *JSOT Supp. Series* 17 (Sheffield, 1981).

Pfammater, J., *La fe según la Sagrada Escritura*, in *Mysterium Salutis*.

Philips, G., *La Iglesia y su Misterio in el Concilio Vaticano II: Historia, Texto y Comentario de la Constituciòn "Lumen gentium."* Barcelona: Herder, 1968–69.

Pié-Ninot, S., "La Chiesa come Tema Teologico Fondamentale," R. Fisichella, *Gesù Rivelatore* (Casale Monferrato: Piemme, 1988), 142–144.

———, "La Dimensione Ecclesiale della Teologia Fondamentale," G. Tanzella-Nitti (ed.), *La Teologia, Annuncio e Dialogo* (Rome: Armando, 1996), 113–129.

———, "La Teologia Fonamental Avui," in *Revista Catalana di Teologia* 5 (1980): 479–502.

———, *Tratado de Teología Fundamental*, Ed. Serr. Trinitario, Salamanca, 1991 (2 ed.).

———, *Treinta años de Teología Fundamental: un balance desde el Concilio Vaticano II (1965–1995)*, en "Revista Española de Teología" 56 (1996) pp. 293–315.

Pieper, J., *La fe*, Rialp, Madrid, 1976.

Pieris, A., *Fire and Water: Basic Issues in Asian Buddhism and Christianity*. Maryknoll, New York: Orbis Books, 1996.

———, *Love Meets Wisdom: A Christian Experience of Buddhism*. Maryknoll, New York: Orbis Books, 1988.

———, *Une Théologie Asiatique de la Libération*. Paris: Centurion, 1990.

Pigna, A., *La Vocación: Teología y Dicernimiento*, 2nd ed., Madrid: Ed. Atenas, 1988.

Pinard de la Boullaye, *Estudio comparado de las religiones*, 2 vol., Barcelona, 1964 (2 ed.).

Pitta, A., *Disposizione e Messaggio della Lettera ai Galati: Analisi Retorica e Letteraria*. Rome: Pontifical Biblical Institute, 1992.

Pius IX, Bl. Ap. Const. *Ineffabilis Deus*.

———, Enc. *Qui pluribus*.

Pius VI, Bull *Auctorem fidei*.

Pius X, St., Enc. *Pascendi*.

———, Mot. Pr. *Sacrorum antistitum*.

Pius XII, Ap. Const. *Munificentissimus Deus*.

———, Enc. *Humani generis*.

———, Enc. *Mystici Corporis*.

Pizzolato, L.F., "L'Apologia nelle Chiese d'Occidente Fino all'età Carolingia," in *Enciclopedia di Teologia Fondamentale*, I, 154–155.

Polanyi, M., *La Conoscenza Personale*. Milan: Rusconi, 1990.

Polo, L., *La Persona Humana y su Crecimiento*. Pamplona: EUNSA 1996.

Polycarp of Smyrna, St., *Epist. ad Phil.*

Pottmeyer, H.J., "Segni e Criteri della Credibilità del Cristianesimo," in *Corso di Teologia Fondamentale*, IV, 470.

Poupard, P., *L'Abbé Louis Bautain: Un Essai de Philosophie Chrétienne au XIX Siècle*. Paris, Tournai, Rome, New York: Desclée, 1961.

——— (ed.), *Scienza e Fede*. Casale Monferrato: Piemme, 1986.

Pozo, C., *María en la Obra de la Salvación*, 2nd ed., Madrid: Ed. Católica, BAC, 1990.

———, *Valor religioso del acto de fe*, Granada, 1961.

Prat, F., *La Théologie de Saint Paul*, 12th ed., vol. II. Paris: Beauchesne, 1925.

Prete, B., *L'Opera di Luca: Contenuti e Prospetive*. Turin: Leumann, LDC, 1986.

———, Scaglioni, A. *I Miracoli degli Apostoli*, LDC, Leumann, 1989.

Proaño Gil, V., "*Magisterio Eclesiástico*," in *GER*, XIV, 732–733.

———, "Tradición," in *GER*, XXII, 661–670.

Pseudo-Dionysius, *De divin. nomin.*

Quasten, J., *Patrología*, vol. I. Madrid: Ed. Católica, BAC, 1961.

Quinlan, J., "Matthew," in *NCE*, IX, 497–498.

Race, A., *Christians and Religious Pluralism: Patterns in the Christian Theology of Religions*. London: SCM Press, 1983.

Rahner, K., *Curso Fundamental de la Fe: Introducción al Concepto de Cristianismo*. Barcelona: Herder, 1989.

———, *Uditori della Parola*. Turin: Borla, 1967.

Ramlot, L., "Prophetisme," in *DBS*, VIII, 921.

Ramos Lissón, D., Merino, M., Viciano, A., *El diálogo fe-cultura en la antigüedad cristiana*, Eunate, Pamplona, 1966.

Randellini, R., "L'Inno di Giubilo: Mt 11: 25–30; Lc 10: 24–24," *Rivista Biblica Italiana* 22 (1974): 183–235.

Ratzinger, J., *Creazione e Peccato*. Rome: Ed. Paoline, 1986.

———, *Dogma e Predicazione*. Brescia: Queriniana, 1973.

———, *El Nuevo Pueblo de Dios*, Barcelona, 1972.

———, Homily of May 19, 1992, in AA.VV., *La Beatificazione di Josemaría Escrivá, Fondatore dell'Opus Dei* (Milan: Ares, 1992), 113.

———, *Iglesia, Ecumenismo y Politica*. Madrid: Ed. Católica, BAC, 1987.

———, *Introducción al cristianismo*, Sígueme, Salamanca, 1971; Id., *La via della fede*, Ares, Milano, 1996.

———, *Introduzione al Cristianesimo*, 9th ed., Brescia: Queriniana, 1990.

———, *La Chiesa*, Paoline, Roma, 1991.

———, *Le Nouveau Peuple de Dieu*.

———, *LThK*.

———, "Sobre la Cuestión de la Validez Permanente de las Fórmulas Dogmáticas," in AA.VV., *El Pluralismo Teológico* (Madrid: Ed. Católica, BAC, 1976), 65–66.

———, "Teologia e Chiesa," in *Communio* (1986): 87–96.

———, *Teoría de los Principios Teológicos: Materiales para una Teología Fundamental*, Herder, Barcelona, 1985.

———, *Theologische Prinzipienlehre*. Munich: Erich Wewel, 1982.

———, "Un Tentativo circa il Problema del Concetto di Tradizione," in K. Rahner, J. Ratzinger, *Rivelazione e Tradizione* (Brescia: Morcelliana, 1970), 27–73.

Ravasi, G.F., *Introduzione all'Antico Testamento*. Casale Monferrato: Piemme, 1991.

Richard of St. Victor, *De Trinit*.

Richardson, A., *Las Narraciones Evangélicas sobre Milagros*. Madrid, 1974.

Ricoeur, P., "L'Herméneutique du Témoignage," in E. Castelli, ed., *La Testimonianza*, 35–61.

———, *La Metafora Viva*. Milan: Jaca Book, 1981.

Rigaux, B., "De Traditione apud S. Paulum," in AA.VV., *De Scriptura et Traditione*, 169.

———, *Dieu l'ha ressucité*, Duculot, Gembloux, 1973.

———, *Dio l'ha Risuscitato*. Milan: Paoline, 1976.

Rizzi, M., *Ideologia e Retorica negli Exordia Apologetici: Il Problema dell'Altro*. Milan, 1993.

Rodríguez Carmona, A., "Origen de las Fórmulas Neotestamentarias de Resurrección con Anistémi y Egheiró," *Studia Ecclesiastica* 55 (1980): 25–58.

Rodríguez, A., *I. Kant: La Religión Dentro de los Límites de la Razón*. Madrid: Emesa, 1979.

———, *La Scelta Etica*, Ares, Milano, 1985.

Rodríguez, P. (ed.), *Fe, Razón y Teologia*. Pamplona: EUNSA, 1979.

———, "Infallibilis? La Respuesta de Santo Tomás de Aquino," *Scripta Theologica* 7 (1975): 68.

———, "La Salvación en la Vida de la Iglesia," in *Salvezza Cristiana e Culture Odierne: Atti del II Congresso Internazionale*, LDC, Leumann 1985, vol. II, 9–29.

———, "Möhler, Johann Adam," in *GER*, XVI, 156–157.

———, *Vocación, Trabajo, Contemplación*, 2nd ed., Pamplona: EUNSA, 1987.

Roschini, G., *La Madonna Secondo la Fede e la Teologia*. Rome: Ferrari, 1953.

Rossano, P., *Il problema teologica delle religioni*, Paoline, Catania, 1975.

———, *Vangelo e Cultura*. Rome: Ed. Paoline, 1985.

Rotureau, G., "Fideisme," in *CATH*, IV, 1260–1261.

Rousseau, J.J., *Letteres Écrites de la Montagne*, 1765.

Ruggieri, G., ed., *Enciclopedia de Teologia Fondamentale*, Marietti, vol. I, Genova, 1987.

———, "L'Apologia Cattolica in Epoca Moderna," in *Enciclopedia di Teologia Fondamentale*, Marietti, vol. I, 275–348, Genova, 1987.

———, *Sapienza e Storia*. Milan: Jaca Book, 1971.

Ruiz Arenas, O., *Jesús: Epifanía del Amor del Padre*, Celam, Bogotá, 1987.

———, O., *Teología de la Revelación*.

Sabourin, L., *Les Noms et les Titres de Jésus*. Bruges, Paris: Desclée.

Sabugal, S., *Anástasis*, BAC, Madrid, 1993.

———, *La Embajada Mesiánica de Juan Bautista: Mt 11: 2–6; Lk 7: 1–23: Historia, Exégesis Teológica, Hermenéutica*. Barcelona: Herder, 1978.

Saldarini, A., "Pharisées," *The Anchor Bible Dictionary*, V (New York: Doubleday, 1992), 289–303.

Samartha, S.J., *Between Two Cultures: Ecumenical Ministry in a Pluralistic World*. Ginebra: WCC Publications, 1996.

———, *One Christ, Many Religions: Towards a Revised Christology*. Maryknoll, New York: Orbis Books, 1991).

Sancho Bielsa, J., *Infalibilidad del Pueblo de Dios*, EUNSA, Pamplona, 1979.

Sanz, E., "La Estructura de la Acción Inmanente," Pontifical Academy of the Holy Cross, Doctoral thesis edit., Rome, 1997.

Sanz Rubiales, J., *La Tradición y su Crecimiento en el Número 8 de "Dei Verbum,"* doctoral thesis. Pamplona: University of Navarre, 1985.

Saraiva Martins, J., *Escritura e Tradição Segundo o Concílio de Trento*, in "Divus Thomas" 67 (1964) pp. 183–277.

Savoca, G., *I profeti di Israele: voce del Dio vivente*, EDB, Bologna, 1985.

———, "Profecía," in *Nuovo Diccionario de Teologia Bíblica*, 1524–1525, 1533.

Sawyer, J.F.A., "Hebrew Words for the Resurrection of the Dead," *Vetus Testamentum* 23 (1973): 218–234.

Sayés, J.A., *Cristologia Fundamental*, CETE, Madrid, 1985.

———, *Razones para Creer*, Paulinas, Madrid, 1992.

———, *Señor y Cristo*.

Scheeben, M.J., *Handbuch der katholischen Dogmatik*. Freiburg in Br.: 1874.

———, *Los Misterios del Cristianismo*, 2nd ed., Barcelona: Herder, 1957.

Scheffczyk, L., "Christology in the Context of Experience," *The Thomist* 48 (1988) 383–408.

———, *Comprensión de la fe hoy*, in AA.VV., *La osadía de creer*.

———, "Creación y Providencia," in M. Schmauss, A. Grillmaier, ed., *Historia de los Dogmas* (Madrid: Ed. Católica, BAC., 1974), 2–12.

———, *Glauben in der Bewährung*, Eos, S. Ottilien, 1991.

———, "La Santidad de Dios: Fin y Forma de la Vida Cristiana," in *Scripta Theologica* 11 (1979): 1021–1036.

———, *Schwespunkte des Glaubens*, Johannes, Einsiedeln, 1973; *Glauben als Lebens-Inspiration*, Johannes, Einsiedeln, 1980.

Scheffczyk, L., Ziegenaus, A., *Katholische Dogmatik*, Band II: *Der Gott der Offenbarung*, Aachen 1996, pp. 13–192.

Schenke, L., *Auferstehungsverkündigung und leeres Grab*. Stuttgart, 1969.

Schillebeeckx, E., *Die Auferstehung Jesu als Grund des Erlösung*. Freiburg: Herder, 1979.

———, *Jesus, het verhaal van een levende*. Bloernendaal: Nelissen, 1974.

———, "L'Eglise et l'Humanité," in *Concilium* 1 (1965): 57–78.

———, *Le Christ: Sacrament de la Rencontre de Dieu*. Paris: Cerf, 1960.

Schinella, I., "Il Magistero Autentico: Genesi Semantica e Significato Teologico di 'Autentico,'" *La Scuola Cattolica* 118 (1990), 253–263.

Schlette, H.R., *Die Religion als Thema der Theologie*. Fribourg: Herder, 1963.

Schlier, H., *La Risurrezione di Gesù Cristo*. Brescia: Morcelliana, 1971.

———, *Uber die Auferstehung Jesu Christi*, Johannes, Einsiedeln, 1968.

———, *Wort Gottes*. Würzburg, 1958.

Schlösser, J., *Le Règne de Dieu dans les dits de Jésus*, 2 vols. Paris: Gabalda, 1980.

Schmaus, M., *Teología Dogmática*, vol. IV. Madrid: Rialp, 1960.

Schmitt, J., *Jesus Resuscité dans la Prédication Apostolique*, Paris, 1949.

———, *La Revelación*, Herder, Barcelona, 1990.

————, *La teología fundamental en el siglo xx*.

————, *Résurrection de Jesus dans le Kerygme, la Tradition et la Catechèse*.

Schnackenburg, R., *Il Vangelo di Giovanni*, I. Brescia: Paideia 1973.

————, *La Théologie du Nouveau Testament*. Bruges, 1961.

————, *Signoria e Regno di Dio*. Bologna: Il Mulino, 1971.

Schneider, G., *Gli Atti degli Apostoli*. Brescia: Paideia, 1986.

Schnider, F., *Jesus der Prophet*. Göttingen: Vandenhoeck and Ruprecht, 1973.

————, "La Profezia come Segno di Credibilità della Rivelazione," R. Fisichella (ed.), *Gesù Rivelatore* (Casale Monferrato: Piemme, 1988), 217–218.

Schönborn, C., *Unità nella Fede*. Casale Monferrato: Piemme, 1990.

Schreck, C.J., "The Nazareth Pericope: Luke 4: 16–30," in F. Neirynck (ed.), *L'Evangile de Luc—The Gospel of Luke* (Louvain: Leuven Univ. Press, Uitgeverij Peeters, 1989), 399–471.

Schulte, H., *Der Begriff der Offenbarung im Neuen Testament*. Munich, 1949.

Schürer, E., *Geschichte des jüdischen Volkes im Zeitalter Jesu Christ*, 3 vols. Leipzig, 1901–1909.

Schürmann, H., "Die vorösterlichen Anfänge der Logientradition," in H. Ristow, K. Mathiae (ed.), *Der historische Jesus und der kerygmatische Christus*, 2nd ed. (Berlin: Evangelische Verlagsanstalt, 1961).

————, *Gesù di Fronte alla Propria Morte*. Brescia: Morcelliana, 1983.

————, *Gottes Reich—Jesu Geschick*. Fribourg: Herder, 1983.

S.C.S. Oficio, Decr. *Lamentabili*.

Seckler, M., "Glaubenssinn," in *LThK*, IV, col. 945.

————, "Il Concetto di Rivelazione," in *Corso di Teologia Fondamentale*, vol. II, 74.

————, "Teologia Fondamentale: Compiti e Strutturazione, Concetto e Nomi," in *Corso di Teologia Fondamentale*, vol. IV, 543.

Second Council of Nicea, *Actio VII*.

Second Council Orange, *De gratia*.

Second Vatican Council, Const. *Sacrosanctum concilium*.

————, Decl. *Dignitatis humanae*.

————, Decl. *Nostra aetate*.

————, Decr. *Ad gentes*.

————, Decr. *Apostolicam actuositatem*.

————, Decr. *Gravissimum educationis*.

————, Decr. *Presbyterorum Ordinis*.

————, Decr. *Unitatis redintegratio*.

————, Dogm. Const. *Dei Verbum*.

————, Dogm. Const. *Lumen gentium*.

————, Past. Const. *Gaudium et spes*.

Sequeri, P.A., *Il Dio Affidabile, saggio di teologia fondamentale*, Queriniana, Brescia, 1996.

Serentha, M., *Gesù Cristo Ieri, Oggi e Sempre*. Leumann-Turin: LDC, 1982.

Sesboué, B., Theobald, C. (ed.), *La Parola della Sapienza*, IV. Casale Monferrato: Piemme, 1998.

Seybold, M., Waldenfels, H., Scheffczyk, L., Cren, P.R., Horst, U., Sand, A., and Stockmeier, D., *La Revelación*, en Schmauss, M., Grillmeier, A., Scheffcyk, L. (ed.), *Historia de los dogmas*, t. I: *La existencia en la fe*, BAC, Madrid 1972ss.

Simmons, E., *Philosophie der Offenbarung: Auseinandersetzung mit K. Rahner*. Stoccarda: Kolhammer, 1966.

Ska, J.L., *Le Passage de la Mer*, Biblical Institute Press, Rome, 1986.

Smith, J.E., *Experience and God*. New York, 1968.

Söhngen, G., *Die Einheit in der Theologie*. Munich, 1952.

Spada, D., *L'Uomo in Faccia a Dio*. Imola: Ed. Galeati, 1983.

Spicq, C., *Les Epitres de St. Pierre*. Paris: Gabalda, 1966.

———, *Les Epitres Pastorales*. Paris, 1947.

———, *Lexique Théologique du Nouveau Testament*. Fribourg: Cerf, Ed. Univ. Fribourg, 1991.

———, *Teología moral del Nuevo Testamento*, EUNSA, Pamplona, 1970.

Spinoza, B., *Tractatus Theologicus-Politicus*. Hamburg, 1670.

Stemberger, G., *Farisei, Saducei, Esseni*. Brescia: Paideia, 1993.

Strack, H.L., *Jesus, die Heretiker und die Christen*. Leipzig: Schrifsten des Institutum Judaicum in Berlin, 1910.

Strathmann, H., *Martyrs*, 1325–1329.

Strauss, D.F., *Das Leben Jesu kritisch hearheitet*.

Sullivan, F., *Magisterium: Teaching Authority in the Catholic Church*. New York / Ramsey: Paulist Press 1983.

———, "Magistero," in *Diccionario de Teología Fundamental*, 848–849.

Tabet, M.A., *David F. Strauss: La Vida de Jesús*. Madrid: Emesa, 1977.

———, "I Testi Paolini sulla Paradosis nei Commenti Patristici (secoli I–III)," in AA.VV., *La Tradizione: Forme e Modi* (Rome: P. I. Augustinianum, 1990), 39–53.

Tanzella-Nitti, G., "Cristocentrismo e Dialogo Interreligioso," in *Annales Theologici* 12 (1998): 113–129.

———, "La Teologia, Discorso su Dio e Annuncio del Mistero," in *Annales Theologici* 10 (1996): 505–520.

Tavard, G.H., *Holy Writ or Holy Church*. London, New York, 1959.

———, *The Dogmatic Constitution on Divine Revelation of Vatican Council II*. London, 1966.

———, "Tradition in Early Post-Tridentine Theology," in *Theological Studies* 23 (1962) 377–405.

Taymans, F., "Le Miracle: Signe du Surnaturel," *Nouvelle Revue Theologique* 77 (1955): 225–245.

Teresa of Jesus, St., *Vida.*

Ternant, P., "Miracle," X.L. Dufour, *Vocabulaire de Theologie Biblique*, Cerf, Paris 1961.

Tertullian, *De Baptismo.*

———, *De praescriptione haereticorum.*

Testa, E., B. Marconcini, "Profetismo, Profeti, Apocalittica," *LDC*, Torino-Leumann, 1990.

Theodoret of Cyrrhus, *Interpretatio Epist. ad Ephesios.*

Torrell, J.P., "Chronique de Théologie Fondamentale," *Revue Thomiste* 66 (1966) 65–67.

Torres, A., "La Teoría de la Revelación," in *Estudios Eclesiásticos* 59 (1984): 139–178.

Trapé, A., "S. Agostino," in A. Di Berardino (ed.), *Patrologia* (Casale Monferrato: Piemme, 1978).

Trenti, Z., *Invocazione.* Rome: LAS, 1993.

Tresmontant, C., *Etudes de Métaphysique Biblique.* Paris: Gabalda, 1955.

———, *Los Problemas del Ateìsmo.* Barcelona: Herder, 1974.

Trilling, W., *Jesus davant l'Histoire.* Paris: Cerf, 1971.

———, "Vom historischen Jesus zum Christus des Glaubens," in *Bible und Kirche* 24 (1969): 48–52.

Tromp, S., *De Revelatione Christiana*, 6th ed., Rome: P. Univ. Gregoriana, 1950.

Vacant, A., *Etudes Théologiques sur les Constitutions du Concile du Vatican.* Paris, Lyons, 1885.

Valentini, D., *La Rivelazione*, Mesaggero, Padova, 1996.

Vallin, P., "Prophetisme," DSp, XII, 2434–2446.

van den Berghe, P., "Gij zijt de Zoon van de levende God," in *Collationes* 21 (1975): 448–472.

Van Den Eynde, D., *Les Normes de l'enseignement chrétien dans la littérature patristique des trois premiers siécles*, Gembloux-Paris, 1933.

van Hove, A., *Het Mirakel.* Brussels, 1932.

van Winden, J.C.M., "Le Christianisme et la Philosophie: Le Commencement du Dialogue entre la Foi et la Raison," in *Kyriakon: Festschrift Johannes Quasten*, I, Münster 1970, 205–213.

Vanhoye, A., "L'oeuvre du Christ, don du Père (Jn 5: 36 et 17: 4)," *Revue des Sciences Religieuses* 48 (1960): 377–419.

Vawter, B., *Introducción a la Literatura Profética.*

———, "Teología de San Juan," in *Comentario Bíblico "San Jerónimo,"* V, 849–851.

Vergotte, A., *Psychologie Religieuse.* Brussels: Dessart, 1966.

Verweyen, H., "Razón y Fe," in *Diccionario de Teología Fundamental*, 1101.

Vincent of Lerins, St., *Commonitorium.*

Vogels, W., *Les Profètes*. Quebec: Novalis, 1990.

Vögtle, A., Pesch, R. *Wie kam es zum Osterglauben?* Düsseldorf: 1975.

———, "Rivelazione e Mito," in AA.VV., *Problemi e Orientamenti di Teologia Dommatica*, vol. I (Milan: Ed. Marzorati, 1957), 827–960.

Voltaire, F., *Dictionnaire Philosophique ou la Raison par Alphabet*. 1770.

von Balthasar, H.U., *Cordula oder der Ernsfall*. Einsiedeln: Johannes, 1966.

———, *Das Christentum und die Weltreligionem*. Fribourg: Informationszentrum Berufe der Kirche, 1979.

———, *Das Ganze im fragment*. Einsiedeln: Benziger, 1963.

———, *Die Gottesfrage des heutigen Menschen*. Vienna, 1956.

———, *El Misterio Pascual*, en la obra colectiva, *Mysterium salutis*, cit. vol. III, c. 9.

———, "El Misterio Pascual," in *Mysterium Salutis*, vol. III, 9.

———, *Ensayos Teológicos I: Verbum Caro*. Madrid: Guadarrama, 1964.

———, *Ensayos Teológicos II: Sponsa Verbi*. Madrid: Guadarrama, 1964.

———, *Gloria: Una Estética Teológica*. Madrid, 1985–1989.

———, *Karl Barth: Durstellung und Deutung seiner Theologie*. Cologne: Hegner, 1951.

———, *L'Amour seul est Digne de Foi*.

———, *La gloire et la croix*, I, Paris, 1965.

———, *La Percepción de la Forma*.

———, *Seul l'Amour est Credibile*. Paris: Aubier-Montaigne, 1966.

———, *Teodramática*. Madrid, 1990.

———, *Teología de la Historia*. Madrid: Guadarrama, 1959.

———, *Wahrheit III: Der Geist der Wahrheit*. Einsiedeln: Johannes, 1987.

von Campenhausen, H., *Der Ablauf der Ostereignisse und das leere Grab*, Heidelberg: Sitzungsberichte der Heidelberger Akademie, 1958.

von Drey, J.S., *Apologetik als Wissenchaftliche Nachweisung der Göttlichkeit der Christentums*, 3 vol., Tübingen.

von Harnack, A., *Lehrbuch der Dogmengeschichte*, 4th ed., Darmstadt: 1964.

von Rad, G., *Deuteronomy, OTL*, 6th ed., London: SCM Press, 1984.

———, *Theologie des Altes Testament* I. Munich: Kaiser, 1957.

Vorgrimler, H., C. Muller, *Karl Rahner*. Paris: Fleurs, 1965.

Walgrave, J.H., *Newman: Le Dévelopment du Dogme*. Tournai, Paris: Casterman, 1957.

Warnach, W., "Iglesia," in *Diccionario de Teología Bíblica*, 477–479.

Wauter, B., "Epìstolas de San Juan," in *Comentario Bìblico "San Jerònimo,"* cit., IV, p. 393.

Weger, K.H., *Karl Rahner: Eine Einführung in sein theologisches Denken*. Fribourg: Herder, 1978.

Weimar (ed.), *D. Martin Luthers Werke*.

Weiser, A., *"Pisteuo,"* in *TWNT*, X.

Weiss, H.F., "Farisaios," *GLNT*, XIV, 921–956.

Westermann, C., *Teologia dell'Antico Testamento*, Paideia, Brescia, 1983.

Wilckens, U., "Sophia," in *TWNT*, VII, 518–525.

Wilms, F.E., *I Miracoli nell'Antico Testamento*, EDB, Bologna, 1985.

Wilson, R.R., "The Hardening of Pharaoh's Heart," in *Catholic Biblical Quarterly*, 41 (1979) 18–36.

Wojtyla, K., *La fe según San Juan de la Cruz*, BAC, Madrid, 1980.

Yanguas, J.M., "La Vida Moral como Expresión de la Fe," in *Scripta Theologica* 19 (1987): 445–454.

Yepes Stork, R., "La Persona como Fuente de Autenticidad," in *Acta Philosophica* 6 (1997): 83–100.

Zedda, S., "Cristo e lo Spirito Santo nell'Adozione a Figli Secondo il Commento di S. Tommaso alla Lettera ai Romani," in *Atti del Congresso Internazinale "Tommaso d'Aquino nel suo Settimo Centenario,"* (Naples: Ed. Domenicane Italiane, 1974), 105–112.

Zerwick, M., *Analysis Philologica Novi Testamenti Graeci*, 4th ed. (Rome: Pont. Inst. Biblicum, 1984), 564.

Ziener, G., "Palabra," in J.B. Bauer (ed.), *Diccionario de Teología Bíblica* (Herder: Barcelona 1967) col. 744.

Ziesler, A., "The Name of Jesus in the Acts of the Apostles," Journal Studies, New Testament 4 (1979): 28–41.

Zimmermann, H., "Conocer," in *Diccionario de Teología Bíblica*, 201–209.

———, "Fe," in J. Bauer, *Diccionario de Teologia Biblica*, Herder, Barcelona 1985, col. 392.

Zorell, F., *Lexikon Graecum Novi Testamenti*.

INDEX

INDEX OF AUTHORS